Export Practice and Management

To

David and Daniela

Books by the same author:

Elements of Shipping
Maritime Economics Management and Marketing
Shipping and Air Freight Documentation for Importers and Exporters
International Purchasing and Management
Elements of Port Operation and Management
Dictionary of Shipping International Business Trade Terms and Abbreviations
Dictionary of Commercial Terms and Abbreviations
Dictionary of English-Arabic Shipping/International Trade/Commercial Terms and Abbreviations
Dictionary of Multilingual Commercial/International Trade/Shipping Terms in English French German Spanish
Global Supply Chain Management and International Logistics

Export Practice and Management

Fifth Edition

Professor Alan E. Branch
FCIT, FIEx, FILT

International Business/Shipping Consultant

Examiner in Export Practice/Shipping/International Marketing; Visiting Lecturer Cardiff University/Reading University/Plymouth University/Leicester University/London City College/Rennes International School of Business, France

Fellow Chartered Institute of Transport and Fellow Institute of Export

CENGAGE
Learning™

Australia • Brazil • Japan • Korea • Mexico • Singapore • Spain • United Kingdom • United States

**Export Practice and Management,
Fifth Edition**

Alan Branch

© 2011, Cengage Learning EMEA

For product information and technology assistance, contact **emea.info@cengage.com**.

For permission to use material from this text or product, and for permission queries, email **emea.permissions@cengage.com**.

British Library Cataloguing-in-Publication Data
A catalogue record for this book is available from the British Library.

ISBN: 9781844800810

Cengage Learning EMEA
Cheriton House, North Way, Andover, Hampshire, SP10 5BE United Kingdom

Cengage Learning products are represented in Canada by Nelson Education Ltd.

For your lifelong learning solutions, visit
www.cengage.co.uk

Purchase your next print book, e-book or e-chapter at
www.cengagebrain.com

Printed by Lightning Source, UK

Contents

Preface to the fifth edition

It is appropriate that the fifth edition of this book, which today is firmly established as the standard work on the subject and market leader in its field, should be published on its 27th anniversary. The title is read in over 200 countries by both students and undergraduates studying the subject and international entrepreneurs, who use it as an *aide memoir*. A Chinese edition is also available.

Moreover it reflects the International Trade experience of Alan Branch spanning 50 years in terms of consultancy, lecturing and formulating courses in over 25 countries, reflecting different cultures, embracing Governments, Business Schools, Chambers of Commerce and Export Councils.

The fifth edition has been completely up-dated, including 40 per cent of new material and reflects the many changes that have emerged in the past five years in this fast changing global market. Moreover, it takes full account of the likely future trends in the conduct of international trade, its environment and its undoubtedly increasing complexity. Emphasis remains on management and control techniques and strategy in the computer literate e-commerce logistically focused globalization of today's international trade.

The book falls into three parts: the export office and transport modes at the commencement; constituents of the export contract including finance, rates, customs and insurance; and finally a strategic input embracing execution of the export order, documentation, market entry options, international trade law, EU, and international trade strategy and management. The text will contain, throughout, case studies, further recommended reading and focus on e-commerce.

The opportunity has been taken to introduce a chapter on International Trade Law embracing law of contract, product specification, compliance, intellectual property, litigation and arbitration.

Many individual chapters have been restructured to reflect the wide range of changes since the previous edition. This includes e-commerce, the conduct/negotiation of international trade including culture aspects, the globalization development, expansion of logistics, the B2B and B2C development, paperless trading including Bolero, and European Union, including enlargement. The text contains case studies and further reference to recommended reading.

The book continues to focus on risk/problem areas and their solutions, the importance of developing a continuous dialogue with the importer, the need to have regard to the international environment in which the exporter and ultimately the global entrepreneur, strives to operate on a profitable basis. Emphasis is again placed on the constituents of the export price including Incoterm 2000 selection criteria. Full cognizance has been taken of the e-commerce environment throughout. Stress has been given to adopting strategies which respond to situations and are capable of being executed and finally 'add value' at all times to the B2B and B2C transaction.

Such enrichment of the fifth edition will further its popularity in colleges of higher education and universities throughout the world. It reflects current and future trends/best practice. This includes degree level undergraduates studying International Business and International Marketing, International Physical Distribution, Maritime Transport and International logistics, and students taking professional examinations sponsored by one of the numerous institutes such as the Chartered Institute of Marketing, Chartered Institute of Purchasing and Supply, the Institute of Export, the Institute of Chartered Shipbrokers, Institute of Commercial Management, the Chartered Institute of Logistics and Transport, the British Institute of Management, and the British International Freight Association and Chartered Institute of Bankers. It is a very popular title for Chambers of Commerce, Trade Associations and Training Agencies located across the world conducting short courses and seminars on International Trade, Export Practice, International Marketing and Developing Overseas Markets.

Additionally, the title is very popular among 60 universities across the world expanding their International Trade degree portfolios and requiring publications written in a lucid style and providing a pragmatic yet professional approach to the subject. This includes Diploma in Management Studies and BTEC Higher National Certificate and Diploma courses.

The fifth edition contains a much enlarged input from International Agencies and Export driven companies around the world reflecting good practices, new strategies and current and future developments. This not only enriches the book, but also enables the reader to have a better understanding of world cultures and strategies as emphasized in the numerous examples and case studies found in this publication. The extent and breadth of such input is exemplified in the increasing number of organizations who have helped me so enthusiastically with each new edition as recorded in the Acknowledgements and for whose assistance I am most grateful. Also, I very much appreciate the interest shown by many colleges and universities.

Finally, I would particularly like to acknowledge with grateful thanks the generous secretarial help from Mr and Mrs Splarn and Mrs Jane Salter, and as always my dear wife Kathleen in proof reading. This quartet has provided encouragement, forbearance, and above all complete professionalism in enabling this much enriched fifth edition to be completed, for which I am greatly indebted.

Professor Alan Branch
19 The Ridings
Emmer Green
Reading
Berkshire
England RG4 8XL
Tel. (0044) 01189476291
Email: *kathleenbranch@hotmail.com*   August 2005

Acknowledgements

Alex Lawrie Factors Ltd
Alstom
AT&T Istel
Atlantic Container Line Agencies Ltd
Baltic Exchange
Belo-o-Pak (UK) Ltd
Bibby Factors International Ltd
Bowring Credit
British Airways
British International Freight Association
British Standards Institution
Chamber of Shipping (UK)
Chartered Institute of Marketing
Confederation of British Industry
Cotechna International Ltd
Credit Insurance Association
Danzas UK
Department of Trade and Industry
Euler Hermes
European Central Bank
Euro Tunnel
Export Credit Guarantee Department
Export Master Systems Ltd
Felixstowe Dock and Railway Company
Foreign and Commonwealth Office
Freight Network Ltd
Freight Transport Association
GE SeaCo
Hamriyah Free Zone Sharjah UAE
HM Customs and Excise
HSBC Trade Services (Midland Bank)

International Air Transport Association
International Chamber of Commerce
International Maritime Organisation
International Software Marketing Ltd
Kay O'Neill
KPMG Peat Marwick
London Chamber of Commerce and Industry
London Fox
Lloyd's Bank (International)
Lufthansa Airline
Norman Shipping
Maersk Line
MAT Transport Ltd
OPEC
P&O Nedlloyd
Pira International
Port Klang
Port of London
Port of Rotterdam
Port of Singapore Authority
Price Waterhouse
Royal Mail International
Sea-Land
Simpler Trade Procedures Board
Staple Inn Actuarial Society
Syn quest
Thai Cargo
Trade Indemnity
United Nations Conference on Trade and Development
World Customs Organisation
World Trade Organisation

International trade

1.1 Scope of book

Since this book was first published 27 years ago, it has become an established standard work on the subject and the market leader in its field. Moreover, the pattern and complexity of world trade has changed enormously. Today it is a very high profile international business which is driven by many elements including technology, logistics, marketing, politics, finance, E-commerce, innovative strategies, social/economic well-being, wealth creation and the economic development of markets/regions. Overall, trade means wealth and political power and influence worldwide. It encourages investment and develops high professional standards. The fifth edition is the vehicle for knowledge and good practice to realise this objective.

Furthermore, trade has become increasingly complex and this is best exemplified by citing the exporter who hitherto designed, manufactured and assembled the product in the exporter's country. Today, more and more exporters are out-sourcing most of their components to take advantage of high-tech and lower cost and assembling the product in the importer's or third world country. Additionally, we are experiencing an enormous increase in Business to Business (B2B) and Business to Consumer (B2C) trade. Much of this is driven by E-commerce and logistics.

Hence, there is a paramount need for all involved in the conduct of international trade to be completely professional and focused on developing a competitive global product/service.

The book is structured in three parts: the export office and transport modes at the commencement; constituents of the export contract including finance, rates, customs and cargo/credit insurance; and finally a strategic input embracing execution of the export order, documentation, trade law, market entry options, E-commerce, EU, international physical distribution management and planning. The text contains, throughout, case studies and further recommended reading.

The book is written primarily for the student or business person (export/import/shipping executive) who has limited knowledge of export practice involving the development of a viable export business with a strategic focus. The fifth edition has been completely updated throughout. It features in depth an overview of major trading areas of the world, additional chapters on EU and trade law, enlarged chapters on market entry options featuring additional culture, numerous case studies, and enlarged focus on E-commerce, globalization and logistics. The book will identify risk/problem areas and their solutions; the importance of developing a continuous dialogue with the importer/buyer; the need to have regard to the international environment in which the global entrepreneur strives to operate on a profitable basis and also a focus on third world country assembly/out-sourcing and the re-export markets.

Overall, the book is written in a simple but lucid style and reflects the author's experience in the export industry spanning 50 years embracing not only work and consultancy on a worldwide scale in the industry itself, but also as a lecturer/examiner at home and overseas. This has involved governments overseas, trade associations, shipper councils, business schools/universities and multinational industries. This book treats the subject on the basis that international trade must be developed on a profitable basis and it is only realized through complete professionalism at all levels.

Basically, there are three major trading areas of the world: Europe incorporating the expanded European Union (25 countries and possibly 28 by 2007/08) and single market (Chapter 18), North America featuring NAFTA (p. 17) and the Far East/Sub Continent featuring ASEAN, Japan, China and India.

An analysis of the growth in world merchandise trade by region 1995–2002 (Table 1.1) and by commercial services 1995–2002 (Table 1.2) is given below and merits close study. There is a particular focus on China and the EU.

The main driving force in the world economy remains trade and investment. Service trade will continue to grow faster than goods trade, and goods trade and investment will continue to grow faster than trade.

Overall, exporters worldwide are focusing their attention on developing a global strategy in their search for new markets and lower production costs. This embraces all the elements of export strategy which this text seeks to realise. Overall, it requires constant review in a changing market and the development of an export-led strategy. Basically, it requires complete professionalism at all levels of management – a feature extolled in this book.

TABLE 1.1 Growth in the value of world merchandise trade by region, 2002 (Billion dollars and percentage)

Exports					Imports			
Value	Annual percentage change				Value	Annual percentage change		
2002	1995–00	2001	2002		2002	1995–00	2001	2002
6272	5	−4	4	World	6510	5	−4	4
946	6	−6	−4	North America[a]	1431	10	−6	2
350	10	−3	0	Latin America	350	9	−2	−7
2657	2	0	6	Western Europe	2659	3	−2	4
2449	2	0	6	European Union (15)	2447	3	−2	4
314	7	5	10	C./E. Europe/Baltic States/CIS	299	4	11	11
148	8	12	14	Central and Eastern Europe	177	9	9	11
107	5	−2	4	Russian Federation	61	−6	20	13
140	6	−6	2	Africa	135	0	2	2
244	12	−8	0	Middle East	178	4	6	7
1620	5	−9	8	Asia	1458	3	−7	6
417	2	−16	3	Japan	337	2	−8	−3
326	11	7	22	China	295	11	8	21
603	5	−12	6	Six East Asian traders	550	2	−13	4

[a] Excluding Mexico throughout this report.

Note: It should be mentioned at the outset that there are breaks in the continuity of the figures at the country and regional levels.

Reproduced by kind permission of WTO.

1.2 Function of International Trade

International Trade is the process of exchanging goods or services between two or more countries, involving the use of the Euro or more currencies. Overall, it produces a more efficient employment of the productive forces of the world. Hence, it embraces two basic elements. First, it is carried out between two or more nations. Thus, when trade is executed beyond national frontiers, it is invariably subject to political, social, economic, and environmental policies introduced by nations from time to time. To a large extent, such policies (though desirable from a national or trading bloc point of view) have either encouraged or hampered the free flow of merchandise in international trade. The second factor is the use of different currencies with their inherent exchange rate differentials – this is eliminated in the Euro-zone countries (p. 551); the terms of trade (p. 8); or alternatively the balance of trade. This produces a favourable result in some countries but unfavourable in others.

TABLE 1.2 Growth in the value of world trade in commercial services by region, 2002 (Billion dollars and percentage)

	Exports				Imports			
Value	Annual percentage change				Value	Annual percentage change		
2002	1995–00	2001	2002		2002	1995–00	2001	2002
1570	4	0	6	World	1545	4	1	5
309	7	−3	1	North America[a]	248	9	−1	1
56	6	−2	−4	Latin America	65	5	1	−9
763	4	2	9	Western Europe	716	4	3	9
686	4	3	10	European Union (15)	669	4	3	9
60	2	7	10	C./E. Europe/ Baltic States/CIS	65	2	12	16
31	3	0	2	Africa	40	2	2	2
29	10	−10	−1	Middle East	45	5	−6	1
322	3	−1	7	Asia	367	2	−2	3
65	1	−7	2	Japan	107	−1	−7	0
39	10	9	20	China	46	8	9	18
150	3	−2	6	Six East Asian traders	137	3	−4	4

[a] Excluding Mexico throughout this report.

Note: It should be mentioned at the outset that there are numerous breaks in the continuity of the figures at the country and regional levels due to frequent revisions to the trade in services data. See the Technical Notes.

Reproduced by kind permission of WTO.

Study Table 1.1 featuring the growth in the value of world merchandise trade by region 1995–2002 and Table 1.2 detailing the growth in the value of world trade in commercial services by region 1995–2002. Factors contributing to Tables 1.1 and 1.2 include exchange rates and price developments; the depreciation of the United States dollar against the currencies of major traders in Asia and Western Europe; sluggish import demand in Western Europe; a short contraction of Latin America's imports constituted a drop on global trade expansion; China's trade expansion (both imports and exports) was three times faster than global trade and between 2000 and 2002 its exports and imports rose by 30 per cent – China has become the fourth largest merchandise trader (if one counts the EU as a single trader) in 2002; and chemicals emerged as the strongest trade growth during period 2000–2002. It must be emphasized that the aforementioned Chinese level of trade growth is not sustainable.

The foregoing demonstrates the range of factors contributing to why Nations trade with one another and these can be further exemplified in differences in taste, preferences and consumption patterns.

This applies to consumer goods, clothing and foodstuffs. It manifests itself through culture (p. 499), and it is stimulated by travel and education. Production costs differ by country and this is influenced by labour costs, technology, volume of production, transportation and product costs. Lack of mobility is a major factor. Products/resources can only be utilized where they are located or found (tourist attractions or minerals for example). Economies of scale vary by product/service both internally and externally within an economy. Finally, differences arise in factor endowments, which extend to differences both in qualities and quantities and variations in climatic conditions.

The benefits derived from the development of international trade are numerous, including a wider range of goods/services becoming available. This permits a wider consumer choice and higher levels of consumer satisfaction. Lower production costs, through economies of scale, result in lower prices to the consumer. Enlargement of the market is achieved through increased production, lower production costs, increased investment and expansion of the economy. The electronics market is an example of an area where research and development is continuous and high cost. Moreover, such investment is worldwide; likewise, production plants and consumers which become ubiquitous through competitive pricing.

International trade increases competition and prevents the monopolistic control of the home market by local exporters. It also provides a stimulus to economic growth, developing technology and raising living standards. Overall, it provides wealth to the economy and extends opportunities to exchange ideas and develop the infrastructure of a country or region and its resources. Trade develops beneficial links between countries and encourages tourism and education. This brings both political and economic stability to a country or region.

The rapid growth in international trade and specialization raises the question of the economic reasons for trade. Why does Japan export mainly manufactured goods and import principally raw materials? Why is the agricultural sector in the USA so different to that of the Netherlands? But most important of all, do countries gain or lose from opening up their boundaries to international trade?

The key to such questions lies in the theory of comparative advantage. This principle holds that a nation can raise its standard of living and real income by specializing in the production of those commodities or services in which it has the highest productivity or comparative advantage. The benefits of specialization may also be affected by transport costs: goods and raw materials have to be transported around the world and the cost of the transport will narrow the limits between which it will prove profitable to trade.

Extending the principle of comparative advantages a little further, where a country has 'absolute advantage' in the production of two or more products, it is still beneficial to trade. For example, the USA may have a higher output per worker (or per unit output) than the rest of the world both in steel and computers. However, it might still benefit the USA to engage in trade – exporting computers (in which it is relatively more productive) and importing steel (in which it is relatively less productive). Similarly, a country will gain by trading with the USA, even if it is absolutely less efficient in the production of a range of goods. It is unrealistic to believe a country has no comparative advantage in anything. It may be the least efficient at everything, but it will still have a comparative advantage in the industry in which it is relatively least bad. Even if a country were the most efficient in every industry, giving it an absolute advantage in everything, it could not have a comparative advantage in everything. In some industries, its margin would be more impressive than in others.

Further examples of comparative and absolute advantage are as follows: country A is better than country B in manufacturing washing machines, and country B is better than country A at producing oranges. Hence, both would benefit if B specialized in oranges and A specialized in washing machines and they traded their products, thereby extolling the law of absolute advantage.

Comparative advantages arise if countries A and B trade with each other even if A is better than B at making everything. If A is superior at making washing machines but only slightly better at producing oranges, then A should still invest resources in what it does best – producing washing machines and export the product to country B.

However, country B should still invest in what it does best – producing oranges, and export that product to country A, even if it is not as efficient as country A. Both would still benefit from the trade. A country does not have to be best at everything to gain from trade. The theory goes back to classical economist David Ricardo. Every country has a comparative advantage.

To conclude our review of absolute advantage, a country with no absolute advantage should concentrate on the products and/or services which bring the greatest comparative advantage; and for a country having an absolute advantage in all lines of production, then it would still be worthwhile to enter into trade provided there are comparative advantages in certain commodities. In such circumstances, the country should concentrate on the products which bring the greatest comparative advantage. Trade will not take place, however, if there is no comparative advantage.

In examining the theory of comparative advantage it should be remembered that it assumes free trade which limits the benefits from specialization. Additionally, the theory ignores foreign exchange difficulties; fails to take account of transportation and logistics costs, where increasing costs can wipe out gains from trade; assumes constant cost of production and free mobility of factors of production; and finally, it assumes full employment and flexibility in the economy. A rigid state-controlled economy allows partial specialization. Such constraints must be considered when examining the theory of comparative advantage in any trade strategy.

International trade can disadvantage some countries. For example, it lowers the standard of living in a poor country as the specialized industries, such as those with high technology, may not generate enough jobs, and unemployment results. Countries specializing in agriculture may face

TABLE 1.3 World trade in agricultural products, 2002 (Billion dollars and percentage)

Value	583
Annual percentage change	
1980–85	−2
1985–90	9
1990–95	7
1995–00	−1
2000	1
2001	0
2002	5
Share in world merchandise trade	9.3
Share in world exports of primary products	42.5

Reproduced by kind permission of WTO

TABLE 1.4 Major regional flows in world exports of agricultural products, 2002 (Billion dollars and percentage)

	Value	Annual percentage change		
	2002	1995–00	2001	2002
Intra-Western Europe	189.3	−2	0	7
Intra-Asia	64.6	−2	−2	6
Intra-North America	34.0	5	1	1
North America to Asia	32.8	−5	−6	−4
Latin America to Western Europe	19.2	−1	0	6
Latin America to North America	18.4	5	−2	2

Reproduced by kind permission of WTO

persistent adverse terms of trade which will result in an adverse balance-of-payments situation.

This can be corrected by adopting modern agricultural husbandry techniques which may involve inwards investment and joint ventures (p. 490). Study Table 1.3 World Trade in agricultural products 2002, Table 1.4 Major regional flows in world exports of agricultural products 2002 and Table 1.5 Share of agricultural products in trade in total merchandise and in primary products by region 2002. Moreover, backward countries may become dumping grounds for obsolete products. International trade increases monopoly and this can be abused. Finally, international trade transmits slumps and booms between countries, and this is particularly serious in economic terms when a slump hits a poor country with limited resources. The strategies of WTO and ILO have endeavoured to lessen such disadvantages and practices.

TABLE 1.5 Share of agricultural products in trade in total merchandise and in primary products by region, 2002 (Percentage)

	Exports	Imports
Share of agricultural products in total merchandise		
World	9.3	9.3
North America	10.7	6.2
Latin America	19.3	9.8
Western Europe	9.4	10.2
C./E. Europe/Baltic States/CIS	8.9	10.2
Africa	15.8	15.9
Middle East	3.5	13.4
Asia	6.6	9.5
Share of agricultural products in primary products		
World	42.5	42.5
North America	59.9	35.1
Latin America	48.7	47.4
Western Europe	57.6	48.5
C./E. Europe/Baltic States/CIS	22.1	43.0
Africa	22.3	59.5
Middle East	4.7	69.0
Asia	48.1	36.0

Note: Import shares are derived from the Secretariat's network of world merchandise trade by product and region.

Reproduced by kind permission of WTO

Finally, it is appropriate to examine the relationship between the balance of trade and terms of trade. It will be recalled that the balance of trade is the relationship between the total volume of exports and imports of a country for a certain period of time. Examples are given below.

Balance of trade
   Country A exports 1000 units of x at $3.00 each
   Country A imports 700 units of y at $4.00 each
   The value of exports is 1000 × $3.00 = $3000
   The value of imports is 700 × $4.00 = $2800
   The Balance of Trade = Total exports − Total imports
                     = $3000 − $2800
                     = $200 surplus

Hence the balance of trade is favourable.

The terms of trade (TOT) are defined as the quantity of domestic goods that must be given up to get a unit of imported goods. They refer to the opportunity cost of obtaining goods through international trade rather than producing them directly.

Measurement of terms of trade

$$\text{TOT index} = \frac{\text{Index of export prices}}{\text{Index of import prices}} \times 100$$

Base year = 2001 (100)

Year	Export price index	Import price index	TOT
2002	100	110	$\frac{100}{110} \times 100\% = 91\%$
2003	80	100	$\frac{80}{100} \times 100\% = 80\%$
2004	120	100	$\frac{120}{100} \times 100\% = 120\%$

Comparing 2002 and 2003 TOT worsened by 11 per cent for the year 2003; in 2004 TOT improved by 40 per cent.

Favourable terms of trade do not necessarily lead to a favourable balance of trade. This is because as the prices of exports rise, importers will substitute with cheaper goods. This results in the loss of foreign exchange earnings. Hence the balance of trade will be less favourable or even adverse.

Unfavourable terms of trade do not lead to unfavourable balance of trade. As the prices of exports fall, demand for them rises. With an increase in the volume of exports, foreign exchange earnings will also increase, resulting in a favourable balance of trade.

In regard to the relationship between the terms of trade and balance of trade, an improvement in the former will lead to a favourable result of the latter only if the demand for imports and exports is relatively inelastic. If the demand is elastic, then the balance of trade will be less favourable or even worse.

A decline in the terms of trade does not imply an unfavourable balance of trade. If the demand for imports and exports is relatively elastic, then a decline in the terms of trade will cause demand to rise. Hence foreign exchange earnings will be increased, resulting in a favourable balance of trade.

To sum up, the terms of trade and balance of trade are not directly connected. The relationship between these two depends on the elasticity of the demand for imports and exports. The foregoing analysis does not take account of any government intervention policy to stimulate favourable results.

1.3 Survey of international trade

In our brief examination of a survey of international trade we will focus on the international agencies of the International Chamber of Commerce (ICC), the Organisation for Economic Co-operation and Development (OECD) and the World Trade Organisation (WTO); a number of the regional trading areas of the world (the EU is examined separately in Chapter 18) and a selection of countries which provide both short- and long-term favourable opportunities to the exporter.

A study of Table 1.6 Intra-regional trade of major regional trade agreements (RTA) 1995 and 2002 concludes that by the end of 2002, 176 regional trade agreements were operational, 17 more than at the end of the preceding year. Recent regional trade agreements are often spread across geographical regions and are increasingly of a bilateral nature. Reviewing RTA trade agreements one should bear in mind that many RTAs are only a fraction of intra-regional trade and are conducted at preferential and duty free level. Exporters should monitor RTA development for trade opportunities. Four key points arise in the analysis of Table 1.6.

(a) Intra-trade developments in the six RTAs were very much affected by the overall trade developments of their region. Hence, the value of intra-trade decreased in the three RTAs located in South and North America with poor trade growth in 2002 (ANDEAN, MERCOSUR and NAFTA) but increased in the three RTAs in Europe and Asia (EU, CEFTA, and AFTA) where trade expanded faster than global average.

(b) In 2002 there was no clear trend in respect of the relative development of intra-RTA trade. The shape of intra-trade increased in a majority of RTAs on the import side but not on the export side. AFTA is the only RTA which reported a recovery of the intra-regional trade share for both exports and imports of 2002.

(c) The relative weight of intra-regional trade of the major plurilateral RTAs has not increased in 2002. Intra-regional trade of the six RTAs combined, expanded as fast as world trade leaving the share of these trade flows in world merchandise trade (exports plus imports) unchanged at 35 per cent.

(d) Neither the short- nor the medium-term developments (1995–2002) point to a general increase of the share of intra-RTA trade. For the EU and CEFTA, the share of intra-regional trade decreased in the medium, partly due to the dynamic bilateral trade generated by the EU enlargement process. MERCOSUR's relative decline in intra-regional trade is particularly pronounced on the export side and reflected the impact of the regional financial crisis. On the import side, the share of intra-regional trade started to decline with the sharp devaluation of the Brazilian currency in 1999. The share of AFTA's intra-regional trade increased steadily on the import side since

TABLE 1.6 Intra-regional trade of major RTAs, 1995 and 2002 (Billion dollars, percentage)

RTA	Intra-trade		Share of intra-trade in:			
	Value	Share in world exports	Exports		Imports	
			1995	2002	1995	2002
EU (15)	1509	24.1	64.0	61.6	65.2	61.9
NAFTA (3)	626	10.0	46.0	56.5	37.7	38.1
AFTA (10)	97	1.6	25.5	24.0	18.8	23.6
CEFTA (7)	19	0.3	14.6	12.2	11.3	10.2
MERCOSUR (4)	10	0.2	20.5	11.5	18.1	17.0
ANDEAN (5)	5	0.1	12.3	10.2	12.9	13.9
Total	2266	36.3	–	–	–	–

Reproduced by kind permission of WTO

1995. However, for exports, the corresponding share has not yet regained the level prevailing before the Asian financial crisis. NAFTA is the only RTA which recorded a significant increase in the share of intra-trade between 1995 and 2002.

To provide exporters with a correct perspective of individual countries market share two tables are reproduced: Table 1.7 features leading exporters and importers in world merchandise trade 2002 and Table 1.8 identifies leading exporters and importers in world trade in commercial services 2002. The opportunity will now be taken to analyse the trade developments in the first half of 2003 with a brief analysis of the 2002 results.

In the first half of 2003 world merchandise exports rose by 15 per cent in dollar terms over the corresponding period in 2002, a strong acceleration compared to the average 4 per cent annual growth in 2002. This was due to the depreciation of the US dollar against the currencies of major traders in Europe and Asia in the first six months of 2003. Higher oil and non-fuel commodity prices also contributed to the dollar price increase in international trade.

The exports and imports of Western Europe and the transition economies expanded by more than 20 per cent in dollar terms, largely due to price and exchange rate developments. In Asia where currency changes against the dollar were more limited, exports rose by 15 per cent and imports by nearly 20 per cent. China's trade remained the strongest component of Asia's trade. China's imports growth rose by 45 per cent and exceeded in value that of Japans.

Partly due to higher oil prices, Japan's import growth (17 per cent) was stronger than that of exports (13 per cent). The six newly industrialized

TABLE 1.7 Leading exporters and importers in world merchandise trade, 2002 (Billion dollars and percentage)

Rank	Exporters	Value	Share	Annual percentage change	Rank	Importers	Value	Share	Annual percentage change
1	United States	693.9	10.7	−5	1	United States	1202.4	18.0	2
2	Germany	613.1	9.5	7	2	Germany	493.7	7.4	2
3	Japan	416.7	6.5	3	3	United Kingdom	345.3	5.2	4
4	France	331.8	5.1	3	4	Japan	337.2	5.0	−3
5	China	325.6	5.0	22	5	France	329.3	4.9	0
6	United Kingdom	279.6	4.3	3	6	China	295.2	4.4	21
7	Canada	252.4	3.9	−3	7	Italy	243.0	3.6	4
8	Italy	251.0	3.9	4	8	Canada	227.5	3.4	0
9	Netherlands	244.3	3.8	6	9	Netherlands	219.8	3.3	5
10	Belgium	214.0	3.3	12	10	Hong Kong, China	207.2	3.1	3
						retained imports[a]	24.3	0.4	−22
11	Hong Kong, China	201.2	3.1	5	11	Belgium	197.4	2.9	10
	domestic exports	18.3	0.3	−10	12	Mexico	173.1	2.6	0
	re-exports	182.9	2.8	7	13	Spain	154.7	2.3	0
12	Korea, Republic of	162.5	2.5	8	14	Korea, Republic of	152.1	2.3	8
13	Mexico	160.7	2.5	1					
14	Taipei, Chinese	135.1	2.1	7	15	Singapore	116.4	1.7	0
15	Singapore	125.2	1.9	3		retained imports[a]	58.1	0.9	−4
	domestic exports	66.8	1.0	1					
	re-exports	58.3	0.9	5	16	Taipei, Chinese	112.6	1.7	5
					17	Switzerland	83.7	1.3	−1
16	Spain	119.1	1.8	2	18	Malaysia	79.9	1.2	8
17	Russian Federation	106.9	1.7	4	19	Austria	78.0	1.2	4
18	Malaysia	93.3	1.4	6	20	Australia	72.7	1.1	14
19	Ireland	88.2	1.4	7					
20	Switzerland	87.9	1.4	7					
21	Sweden	81.1	1.3	7	21	Sweden	66.2	1.0	5
22	Austria	78.7	1.2	11	22	Thailand	64.7	1.0	4
23	Saudi Arabia[b]	73.9	1.1	1	23	Russian Federation	60.5	0.9	13
24	Thailand	68.9	1.1	6	24	India	56.6	0.8	12
25	Australia	65.0	1.0	3	25	Poland	55.1	0.8	10
26	Norway	61.0	0.9	3	26	Ireland	51.9	0.8	3
27	Brazil	60.4	0.9	4	27	Brazil[b]	49.7	0.7	−15
28	Indonesia[b]	57.1	0.9	1	28	Turkey	49.7	0.7	20

TABLE 1.7 *(continued)*

Rank	Exporters	Value	Share	Annual percentage change	Rank	Importers	Value	Share	Annual percentage change
29	Denmark	57.0	0.9	10	29	Denmark	49.4	0.7	9
30	India	49.3	0.8	14	30	Czech Republic[c]	40.8	0.6	12
31	United Arab Emirates[b]	47.3	0.7	−1	31	Portugal	38.5	0.6	−3
32	Finland	44.8	0.7	4	32	Hungary	37.6	0.6	12
33	Poland	41.0	0.6	14	33	Israel	35.5	0.5	0
34	Czech Republic	38.4	0.6	15	34	Philippines	35.2	0.5	12
35	Philippines	36.3	0.6	11	35	Norway	34.8	0.5	6
36	Turkey	34.6	0.5	10	36	Finland	33.6	0.5	3
37	Hungary	34.3	0.5	13	37	Saudi Arabia[b]	32.3	0.5	3
38	South Africa	29.7	0.5	2	38	United Arab Emirates[b]	32.2	0.5	7
39	Israel	29.5	0.5	2	39	Indonesia[b]	31.3	0.5	1
40	Venezuela[b]	26.9	0.4	−2	40	Greece	31.3	0.5	11
41	Portugal	25.6	0.4	5	41	South Africa	29.3	0.4	4
42	Argentina	25.4	0.4	−5	42	Iran, Islamic Rep. of	22.2	0.3	24
43	Iran, Islamic Rep. of	24.4	0.4	3	43	Vietnam	19.0	0.3	19
44	Algeria[b]	19.1	0.3	−1	44	Romania	17.9	0.3	15
45	Chile	18.3	0.3	−1	45	Chile	17.1	0.3	−4
46	Ukraine	18.0	0.3	10	46	Ukraine	17.0	0.3	8
47	Vietnam	16.5	0.3	9	47	Slovak Republic[c]	16.5	0.2	12
48	Kuwait	15.4	0.2	−5	48	New Zealand	15.1	0.2	13
49	Nigeria	15.1	0.2	−12	49	Luxembourg	13.2	0.2	7
50	Slovak Republic	14.4	0.2	14	50	Colombia	12.7	0.2	−1
	Total of above[d]	6109.7	94.6	–		Total of above[d]	6187.8	92.5	–
	World[d]	6455.0	100.0	4		World[d]	6693.0	100.0	4

[a] Retained imports are defined as imports less re-exports. See the Technical Notes.
[b] Secretariat estimates.
[c] Imports are valued f.o.b.
[d] Includes significant re-exports or imports for re-export.

Note: For annual data 1992–02, see Appendix Tables A4 and A5.

Reproduced by kind permission of WTO

TABLE 1.8 Leading exporters and importers in world trade in commercial services, 2002 (Billion dollars and percentage)

Rank	Exporters	Value	Share	Annual percentage change	Rank	Importers	Value	Share	Annual percentage change
1	United States	272.6	17.4	1	1	United States	205.6	13.3	2
2	United Kingdom	123.1	7.8	12	2	Germany	149.1	9.6	9
3	Germany	99.6	6.3	20	3	Japan	106.6	6.9	0
4	France	85.9	5.5	7	4	United Kingdom	101.4	6.6	9
5	Japan	64.9	4.1	2	5	France	68.2	4.4	10
6	Spain	62.1	4.0	7	6	Italy	61.5	4.0	10
7	Italy	59.4	3.8	4	7	Netherlands	55.7	3.6	7
8	Netherlands	54.1	3.4	8	8	China	46.1	3.0	18
9	Hong Kong, China	45.2	2.9	9	9	Canada	41.9	2.7	−2
10	China	39.4	2.5	20	10	Ireland	40.4	2.6	14
11	Canada	36.3	2.3	−2	11	Spain	37.6	2.4	12
12	Austria	34.9	2.2	6	12	Korea, Republic of	35.1	2.3	8
13	Belgium	34.9	2.2	–	13	Belgium	34.9	2.3	–
14	Ireland	28.1	1.8	21	14	Austria	34.4	2.2	10
15	Switzerland	27.9	1.8	7	15	Taipei, Chinese	24.3	1.6	3
16	Korea, Republic of	27.1	1.7	−4	16	Hong Kong, China	24.2	1.6	0
17	Singapore	26.9	1.7	3	17	Denmark	23.6	1.5	0
18	Denmark	25.5	1.6	−6	18	Sweden	23.1	1.5	1
19	India	23.5	1.5	12	19	India	21.8	1.4	−5
20	Sweden	22.5	1.4	3	20	Russian Federation	21.5	1.4	16
21	Taipei, Chinese	21.1	1.3	9	21	Singapore	20.6	1.3	1
22	Luxembourg	20.1	1.3	–	22	Australia	17.5	1.1	7
23	Greece	20.1	1.3	4	23	Mexico	17.0	1.1	3
24	Norway	19.1	1.2	8	24	Thailand	16.6	1.1	14
25	Australia	16.7	1.1	5	25	Norway	16.5	1.1	10
26	Thailand	15.2	1.0	18	26	Malaysia	16.2	1.1	−2
27	Malaysia	14.8	0.9	3	27	Indonesia	16.0	1.0	2
28	Turkey	14.7	0.9	−7	28	Switzerland	15.3	1.0	1
29	Russian Federation	12.9	0.8	22	29	Brazil	13.6	0.9	−14
30	Mexico	12.5	0.8	−1	30	Luxembourg	13.6	0.9	–
31	Israel	10.4	0.7	−13	31	United Arab Emirates[a]	11.4	0.7	–
32	Poland	10.1	0.6	4	32	Israel	11.2	0.7	−9
33	Portugal	9.7	0.6	12	33	Greece	10.3	0.7	−8
34	Egypt	9.0	0.6	2	34	Poland	8.9	0.6	0

TABLE 1.8 (continued)

Rank	Exporters	Value	Share	Annual percentage change	Rank	Importers	Value	Share	Annual percentage change
35	Brazil	8.8	0.6	1	35	Finland	8.3	0.5	4
36	Hungary	7.7	0.5	1	36	Saudi Arabia	7.2	0.5	0
37	Czech Republic	7.0	0.4	0	37	Hungary	7.1	0.5	30
38	Finland	6.1	0.4	5	38	Portugal	6.6	0.4	7
39	Croatia	5.5	0.4	14	39	Czech Republic	6.3	0.4	16
40	Indonesia	5.4	0.3	0	40	Turkey	6.3	0.4	−3
	Total of above	1440.0	91.8	–		Total of above	1405.0	90.8	–
	World	1570.0	100.0	6		World	1545.0	100.0	5

[a] Secretariat estimate.

Note: Figures for a number of countries and territories have been estimated by the Secretariat. Annual percentage changes and rankings are affected by continuity breaks in the series for a large number of economies, and by limitations in cross-country comparability. See the Technical Notes. For annual data 1992–02, see Appendix Tables A6 and A7.

Reproduced by kind permission of WTO

economies expanded both exports and imports by 13 per cent. Latin American imports remained unchanged from the preceding year's level while exports rose by 8 per cent thereby strengthening the region's trade surplus. In contrast to the Latin American trade balance, the North American trade deficit continued to widen in the first half of 2003, as imports rose by 10 per cent, or twice as fast as exports.

Adjusted for price and exchange rate changes, a different and less bright trade picture emerges. OECD countries' real trade in goods and services (exporters plus imports) expanded by 4 per cent in the first half of 2003.

Finally, developments in the first half of 2003 and improvements of the leading indicators in the third quarter suggest a world merchandise growth projection of 3 per cent, basically unchanged from the preceding year's rate.

International Chamber of Commerce (ICC)

The International Chamber of Commerce (ICC) was founded in 1919 with the objective to serve world business by promoting trade and investment, open markets for goods and services and the free flow of capital. Today, it has become a world business organization with thousands of member companies and associations representing every major industrial and service sector in over 130 countries. It is based in Paris and in 1945 was granted consultative status with the UN and its specialized agencies.

The ICC has 16 specialized committees/commissions representing experts from the private sector which drive the ICC in formulating new strategies. Subjects include anti-corruption; arbitration; banking technique and practice; bio-society; business in society; commercial law and practice; competition; customs and trade regulations; e-business; IT and telecoms; environment and energy; financial services and insurance; intellectual property; marketing and advertising; taxation; trade and investment policy; and transport and logistics. Overall, the ICC has national committees in 75 countries.

The ICC is dedicated to business self-regulation and to enforcing the rule of law when incorporated in contracts. They feature primarily in four areas:

(a) Rules – the most widely used are Incoterms 2000 (pp. 395–402) and Uniform Customs and Practice for Documentary Credits (UCP) which banks use to finance trade. The UCP500 will be superseded by UCP600 with a revised set of rules (p. 296), probably in 2007.

(b) Contracts – ICC model contracts and clauses which provide guidelines to executives and lawyers in drafting contracts.

(c) ICC codes and guidelines covering every aspect of marketing and advertising.

(d) Guidelines – outlining business principles for efficient customs administrations. For e-business ICC offers guidance on digital signatures and provides best practices for customer redress in settling B2C and C2C disputes.

The ICC International Court of Arbitration is the world's leading body for resolving international commercial disputes by arbitration. A further area of ICC activity is the role of the Commercial Crime Services (CCS) which confronts increasing criminal threats to business on every front, especially on financial fraud, cybercrime, piracy and counterfeiting. The CSS International Maritime Bureau (IMB) deals with crime affecting shipping and trade. This includes trade finance, fraud and piracy, whether by crude robbery or carefully co-ordinated attacks masterminded by crime syndicates. Organized gangs seize ships and run them as 'phantoms' under false identities, ready to abscond with cargoes at enormous gain. The IMB broadcasts daily from Kuala Lumpur bulletins via satellite to ships at sea detailing the location of piracy attacks.

The CSS has launched the Financial Investigation Bureau (FIB) to offer anti-fraud services to banks and other financial institutions. It puts out frequent e-mail alerts to its members in the following areas: suspected frauds and fake financial instruments in circulation; reports on piracy incidents throughout the world; information on shipping and container frauds and alerts on counterfeit pharmaceuticals.

Overall, the ICC continues to take a leading role in the development of world trade facilitating a sound business infrastructure of confidence, essential for the exchange of goods in a competitive global market.

Organisation for Economic Co-operation and Development (OECD)

The Organisation for Economic Co-operation and Development (OECD) is based in Paris, France. It has 25 member countries plus 33 countries classified as partners in a transition programme – a forum permitting the governments of the industrialized democracies to study and formulate the best possible policies in all economic and social spheres.

Areas examined by the OECD in recent years include the creation of employment, economic growth and raising living standards through fiscal, monetary and structural economic policies, managing competition among nations in an era of globalization of production and of the continuing opening of borders to trade and investment; trade facilitation such as thorough certification of agricultural seeds; consolidating and advancing reform in agricultural policies; and improving the efficiency of government and quality of public sector spending and taxation.

The OECD has neither supranational legal powers nor financial resources for loans or subsidies; its sole function is to direct co-operation among the governments of its member countries, the principal industrialized countries of the world. It focuses on specific issues through the expertise of the various OECD Directorates. Additionally, it encourages co-operation among nations in domestic policies where these interact with other countries – in particular trade and investment. The reports produced by the OECD are useful to the exporter in the market evaluation and selection process.

European Free Trade Agreement (EFTA)

The European Free Trade Agreement is a trading and economic bloc involving seven countries: Austria, Finland, Iceland, Liechtenstein, Norway, Sweden and Switzerland. The Agreement covers the free movement of goods, services, capital and people. In 1991 political agreement was reached in the creation of the European Economic Area (EEA) by the European Community (EC) and EFTA. The aim is to extend most of the single market principles to the EFTA countries.

North American Free Trade Agreement (NAFTA)

In August 1992, 14 months of negotiations involving Mexico, Canada and the USA were completed to establish the world's largest and richest trading bloc. It ratified the North American Free Trade Agreement (NAFTA) which over a period of 15 years will abolish almost all tariffs and trade barriers. This involves 360 million consumers with a $6000 billion gross domestic product. In 2002 NAFTA exports totalled 107 billion US$ and imports 1603 billion US$.

Association of South East Asian Nations (ASEAN)

The Association of South East Asian Nations (ASEAN) was formed in 1967. Today it has ten members including Brunei Darussalam, Cambodia, Indonesia, Lao PDR, Malaysia, Myanmar, Philippines, Singapore, Thailand and Vietnam. As a trading group it is very active and has certain economic and free trading links designed to develop the resources in the region and increase wealth. An area of significance is the recent formation of the ASEAN Investment Area (AIA). Its objective is the promotion of inter-ASEAN investment and investment from countries outside the group. This involves the provision of three segments which will become fully operational by 2010 and include investment facilitation and co-operation; investment promotion and investment liberalization. The facilitation segment involves the free flow of capital, technology and skilled labour within the region.

Operative from 1993, the ASEAN nations agreed to accelerate tariff cutting of key product sectors from 15 to 10 years. The 10-year timeframe provides for the reduction of tariffs over 20 per cent. For products with a tariff of less than 20 per cent there is a timeframe of seven years. Overall, the objective is to have a tariff level below 5 per cent within the ASEAN group by the year 2008. ASEAN identified 15 product sectors comprising 4000 items for tariff cutting, including chemicals, pharmaceuticals, plastics, ceramics and vegetable oils. Emerging from the currency crisis ASEAN decided in 1998 to accelerate tariff liberalization and further open up foreign direct investment. The ASEAN region is attracting much inward investment, technology transfer, indigenous capital and is developing a low-cost fast-improving technical workforce with assiduous and very competitive attitudes. Emerging from the Far East currency crisis in 1997, the ASEAN nations continue to refocus their economic and fiscal strategies with a view to the development of a more stable economic region to attract, as hitherto, global trade and investment.

In 2002 total exports was 405 billion US$ and imports 353 billion US$.

Andean Common Market (ANDEAN)

A trading block embracing Bolivia, Colombia, Ecuador, Peru and Venezuela. In 1990 its exports totalled 1325 million US$ which by 2002 totalled 5414 million. Imports in 1990 totalled 1351 million US$ and in 2002, 5447 million US$.

MERCOSUR

Mercosur currently unites Brazil, Argentina, Uruguay and Paraguay with Chile and Bolivia as associate members. It was formed in 1995. It is one of the world's largest integrated markets and has a population of 200 million and represents half the gross domestic product (GDP) of Latin America as a whole. Mercosur is a free trading region which became operative from 1995 with the aim of removing internal tariffs in all but 25 products – a policy which accelerated in 1998.

The customs union was introduced in 1995. Work continues to reduce bureaucracy, streamline customs procedures and encourage regional trade – but the Mercosur message of low inflation, strong and sustainable economic growth and stable democratic structures is clear.

As Brazil, Argentina, Uruguay and Paraguay liberalize their domestic economies, they are becoming increasingly attractive markets. As regional trade barriers come down, the potential of Mercosur remains favourable. Enormous investment, both financial and technical, has gone into gas distribution, oil and petrochemicals. The need remains paramount to improve all aspects of infrastructure, from ports and airports to roads and telecommunications.

Mercosur has proved to be successful. The original forecast for regional trade in 2000 was achieved in 1997. Chile and Bolivia have joined as associate members, and negotiations are underway with Mexico, Canada and the Andean Community (Peru, Venezuela, Colombia, Ecuador). A free trade area covering the whole of South America, with Mercosur at its heart, is now a real long-term possibility. In 2002, total exports were 89 billion US$ and imports 62 billion US$.

Asia Pacific Economic Co-operation (APEC)

The Asia Pacific Economic Co-operation forum objective is to create a grand goal of free trade in the Pacific by 2020, but no trade agreement exists at the moment. It was formed in 1993 and has a membership of 21 countries including Australia; Brunei Darussalam; Canada; Chile; China; Hong Kong China; Indonesia; Japan; Republic of Korea; Malaysia; Mexico; New Zealand; Papua New Guinea; Peru; Philippines; Russian Federation; Singapore; Taipei Chinese; Thailand; USA; and Vietnam.

CEFTA

A trading bloc embracing Bulgaria, Czech Republic, Hungary, Poland, Romania, Slovenia and the Slovak Republic. In 2002 total exports were 157 billion US$ and imports 187 billion US$ compared with 68 billion US$ exports and 80 billion US$ imports in 1994.

SAFTA

A trading bloc embracing Bangladesh, Bhutan, India, Maldives, Nepal, Pakistan, and Sri Lanka. In 2002 total exports were 71 billion US$ and imports 83.3 billion US$. This represented a world trade share in 2002 of

4.4 per cent exports and 5.7 per cent imports, compared with 3.6 per cent exports and 4.7 per cent imports in 1995.

COMESA (Common Market for Eastern and Southern Africa)

COMESA is a trading bloc embracing a common market for Eastern and Southern Africa territories.

CARICOM

The Caribbean Community and Common Market is the Caribbean trade bloc and a regional community whose principal objective is economic integration. It has 14 members and in 1998 it reached an agreement with the Dominican Republic to help prepare their economies for a hemisphere free trade area to be created in 2005. The pact took effect from January 1999 and covers trade in goods and services, the reciprocal promotion, and protection of investment, government procurement, sanitary measures and standards, and technical barriers to trade.

Free Trade Area of the Americas (FTAA)

In 1998 an agreement was signed between 34 countries to create the Free Trade Area of the Americas by 2005.

Africa

In 1998 the new Economic and Monetary Union embracing Francophone countries, based in West Africa, including the Ivory Coast, Guinea, Senegal, Central African Republic, Gabon, etc. laid plans, among other objectives, to bring into effect a common external tariff. In Southern Africa negotiations to create a free trade area among the members of the Southern African Development Community (SADC) continue. This includes the South Africa Customs Union embracing Botswana, Lesotho, Namibia, South Africa and Swaziland who are also renegotiating their customs unions relations.

1.3.1 Asia-Pacific Region

The region offers a diversified industrial and commercial base with massive natural resources and large areas still to be developed, together with substantial populations. To the exporter it offers good prospects with growth as the region recovers from its currency crisis of 1997.

Being far less homogeneous than the other two large regional markets of Western Europe and North America, the Asia-Pacific markets have quite distinct characteristics. They are at widely different states of development, diverse in their trade and investment demand profiles, and with differing industrial, commercial and social priorities. Prior to the financial crisis the region had been fuelled in the main from Japan. The Chinese economy has been less affected by the Far East currency crisis and remains an excellent market for a large range of goods and services. In particular major projects are continuously available for infrastructure development.

Overall, the region has a full spectrum of goods and services including high technology, industrialization, basic infrastructure (water, transport and power) and consumer goods, and a range of services including health care, education, technical and professional training.

The Asia-Pacific region remains an excellent cost effective import source of finished and intermediate goods and an internationally competitive manufacturing base for labour-intensive to high tech finished products and services. It is an ideal area for out-sourcing component manufacture (see p. 507). It is important that the exporter develops a viable market entry strategy as fully explained in Chapter 17.

A brief commentary on some of the countries in the Asia-Pacific region is given below while the more important territories of China, Japan, Malaysia, South Korea and India are examined in Chapter 17, p. 512 together with their culture.

Brunei – area 5765 km^2, population 260 000. A rich small nation anxious to diversify away from the oil and gas sector which currently dominates the economy, together with petrochemicals. Brunei plans investment in infrastructure to support its aim of becoming a trade and tourism hub for the region. Opportunities lie in hotel and medical projects, infrastructure development and defence.

Cambodia – area 181 035 km^2, population 10.2 million. An underdeveloped market with limited economic growth.

China – area 9 579 000 km^2, population 1250 million. China is an important export market and provides good opportunities for services and investment. (See p. 505).

Hong Kong – area 1067 km^2, population 5.0 million, per capita GNP US$23 260. Hong Kong was absorbed into China in 1997. China, however, has undertaken to maintain a 'one country' 'two systems' policy for the first 50 years. It is now a special administrative region of China. Overall, it remains a regional trade centre. It is a new industrialized economy. Hong Kong offers good opportunities for the discerning exporter.

Indonesia – area 1904 559 km^2, population 205 million, per capita GNP US$680. Indonesia is a country addressing significant currency depreciation, private sector debt and a range of austerity measures. It is a country with opportunities for joint ventures, consulting and investment.

Japan – area 370 000 km^2, population 127 million, per capita GNP US$32 520. Japan has the third largest economy in the world. (See p. 509.)

Laos – area 236 800 km^2, population 5.2 million. An underdeveloped country, but one rich in resources. In 1997 its currency was devalued by 90 per cent.

Malaysia – area 329 293 km^2, population 22.6 million, per capita GNP US$3890. (See p. 511.)

North Korea – area 121 200 km^2, population 24.8 million. An underdeveloped market, but one rich in resources. Ultimately, North Korea could merge with South Korea.

The Philippines – area 300 000 km^2, population 77 million, per capita GNP US$930. Generally a low growth market, but there is an opportunistic market for particular types of investment, goods and services. The Philippine economy suffered less from the financial crisis and export opportunities include agri-business, infrastructure developments including power, ports, marine transport, water, oil, gas, environmental technology and consumer goods featuring retail and health care.

Singapore – area 639 km^2, population 4 million, per capita GNP US$20 850. A wealthy city state moving into the higher-value industrial and commercial sectors for trade and investment. Singapore is also a regional centre for trade and investment with many multi-national businesses; it is a newly industrialized economy. Overall, Singapore economic strength has helped to insulate it against the region's economic problems. Export opportunities include aerospace, financial services, environmental technology, ports and marine, education and training, energy, information technology, telecommunications and railway infrastructure.

Taiwan – area 36 179 km^2, population 22 million, per capita GNP US$12 660. A newly industrialized economy – a regional power in both trade and investment; resources are poor, but industrially and economically it is wealthy and with significant domestic markets for all types of goods and services.

Thailand – area 513 115 km^2, population 63.6 million, per capita GNP US$1805. Thailand has experienced an economic downturn, currency depreciation and other problems in its financial sector, in common with South Korea. An IMF recovery package has been formulated. Export opportunities include education, environment, food processing, health care, power, transportation and consultancy. It is a major location for foreign investors and has a large industrial base.

Vietnam – area 331 688 km^2, population 79.2 million, per capita GNP US$410. An underdeveloped market. The country faces serious economic problems but has been largely insulated from the worse effects of the crisis. Direct foreign investment and aid are driving the economy forward. Export opportunities include agriculture, airports, construction, oil, gas, power and road transport. Participation in joint ventures also exists.

1.3.2 Central and Eastern Europe

Albania – population 3.18 million. A country endeavouring to become Westernized in its economic international strategies and encouraging inwards investment, business and joint ventures. The privatization programme of small- and medium-sized companies is scheduled for completion in the next two years together with the larger strategic sector state companies featuring banks, telecommunications, ports, mines and utilities.

Bulgaria – population 7.9 million, per capita GNP US$1720. A country eager to pursue market-related reforms and development of an enterprise economy. An attractive country for inward investors with a well-developed industrial base, a highly skilled and educated workforce and a work ethic which has survived the communist rule. Ideal for inwards investment and joint ventures.

Poland – population 38.6 million, per capita GNP US$4570. (See p. 549.)

Romania – population 22.4 million, per capita GNP US$1730. Romania has a fragile economy and experiences a relatively slow pace of economic reform. Its political future is rather uncertain. It has a serious foreign debt repayments situation.

Russia, Poland and Hungary – Poland and Hungary are both EU members and their economies are examined in Chapter 18, p. 547. Likewise, Russia is evaluated on page 512 with a culture focus.

1.3.3 Other trade associations

Gulf Markets

The Gulf market of Saudi Arabia, United Arab Emirates, Kuwait, Oman, Bahrain, Qatar and Yemen are developed markets with generally sophisticated and well-off consumers who seek good quality and well designed products. It is a market which is steady within the local cultural bounds becoming increasingly westernized and therefore broadening the range of products which can be marketed.

There is a wide range of potential sectors including oil and gas, construction, leisure and tourism, education (the large youth population generates a large demand for education services and equipment), health care and the youth market. Most people are under 30 and Western influence such as computers, video games and the Internet are all contributing to broadening the buying habits of these young people.

An analysis of export opportunities in each market in the Gulf region is given below.

Saudi Arabia – The key opportunities for exporters include: food products, consumer goods, electrical equipment and machinery, building materials, medical equipment and supplies, computer hardware and software and telecommunications equipment, oil, gas and petrochemical equipment and supplies, and desalination equipment. Emerging sectors include leisure, home entertainment, education and training and electronic publishing.

United Arab Emirates (UAE) – Abu Dhabi holds vast oil reserves and accounts for two-thirds of the UAE's GDP, with Dubai claiming a quarter. Abu Dhabi offers opportunities in the oil, gas and petrochemical sectors, water and power, construction and sport, tourism and leisure. It is considering privatization in the power sector.

Dubai's oil resources are running out and over recent years it has developed a strong base as the commercial and tourism centre of the UAE. It has very good transport infrastructure in roads, seaports and airports, as well as hotels and leisure facilities. Opportunities are in sport and leisure, power generation, medical supplies and construction including building materials.

The northern emirates are in various states of development. Sharjah is bidding to become the manufacturing base, concentrating on light and medium industry.

Bahrain – The first centre in the Gulf to develop oil, Bahrain is now striving to develop various niches which other parts of the Gulf are not undertaking. Education, training and human resources are areas of specialization. Opportunities exist in oil and gas, water and sewerage, telecommunications, financial services, construction, health care and tourism.

Kuwait – In Kuwait the main emphasis is on developing the oil and gas resources further. These, along with consumer goods and other sections, provide scope for companies to do business.

Oman – Oil resources are declining but gas is being developed in Oman. Tourism is another area to explore because of the country's natural beauty. Other growth sectors include power generation, water, agriculture, ports and fisheries.

Qatar – Development of what is believed to be the largest gas field in the world will bring Qatar huge wealth in the future. The main opportunities for exporters are in food products, consumer goods, building materials, oil, gas and petrochemical equipment and supplies.

Yemen – The Yemeni economy is now in good shape following some IMF treatment and it is the one country in the region which does not have large oil or gas reserves. It is developing a manufacturing base centred on light industrial products to complement its expanding oil sector and the agricultural and fisheries industries.

Commonwealth of Independent States (CIS)

In December 1991 the Commonwealth of Independent States (CIS) was formed as a successor to the Soviet Union. This involves the states of Armenia, Turkmenistan, Tajikistan, Kyrgystan, Georgia, Russian Federation, Uzbekistan, Azerbaijan, Ukraine, Belarus, Moldova and Kazakhstan.

Listed below are other major international organizations concerned with economies and trade development:

Asociación Latinoamericana de Integración (ALADI)

(Latin American Integration Association, LAIA). Members: Argentina, Bolivia, Brazil, Chile, Colombia, Ecuador, Mexico, Paraguay, Peru, Uruguay, Venezuela.

Central American Common Market (CACM)

Members: Costa Rica, Guatemala, El Salvador, Honduras, Nicaragua.

Colombo Plan for Co-operative Economic and Social Development in Asia and the Pacific

Members: Afghanistan, Australia, Bangladesh, Bhutan, Burma, Canada, Fiji, India, Indonesia, Iran, Japan, Kampuchea, Korean Republic, Laos, Malaysia, Maldives, Nepal, New Zealand, Pakistan, Papua New Guinea, Philippines, Singapore, Sri Lanka, Thailand, UK and USA.

The Commonwealth

Members: Antigua and Barbuda, Australia, Bahamas, Bangladesh, Barbados, Belize, Botswana, Brunei, Canada, Cyprus, Dominica, Gambia, Ghana, Grenada, Guyana, India, Jamaica, Kenya, Kiribati, Lesotho, Malawi, Malaysia, Maldives, Malta, Mauritius, Naura, New Zealand, Nigeria, Pakistan, Papua New Guinea, St Kitts and Nevis, St Lucia, St Vincent and Grenadines, Seychelles, Sierra Leone, Singapore, Solomon Islands, South Africa, Sri Lanka, Swaziland, Tanzania, Tonga, Trinidad and Tobago, Tuvalu, Uganda, United Kingdom, Vanuatu, Western Samoa, Zambia and Zimbabwe.

South Africa – population 43.8 million, per capita GNP US$2590. South Africa is the most recent re-entry to the Commonwealth. International confidence in the country's economic management and in its policy implementation had been growing in the mid-1990s. The government's medium term economic strategy stresses the importance of privatization, fiscal prudence and the overall direction of economic policy is acknowledged. By mid-1999 the tentative first steps in the privatization process, action reducing the remaining exchange controls has been phased in and trade policy formulated within the WTO guidelines. Major exports to

South Africa include machinery and transport equipment, chemicals, food and a wide range of consumer and manufactured goods. Inward investment, particularly in joint ventures, is strong.

Communauté Française Africaine (CFA) (The Franc Zone)

Members: Benin, Burkina Faso, Cameroon, Central African Republic, Chad, Comoro Islands, Congo, Côte d'Ivoire, Equatorial Guinea, Gabon, Mali, Niger, Togo and Senegal.

Co-operation Council for the Arab States of the Gulf

Members: Bahrain, Kuwait, Oman, Qatar, Saudi Arabia and United Arab Emirates.

Council of Arab Economic Unity

Members: Egypt, Iraq, Jordan, Kuwait, Libya, Mauritania, Palestine Liberation Organization, Somalia, Sudan, Syria, United Arab Emirates, Yemen Arab Republic and Yemen People's Democratic Republic.

Economic Community of West African States (ECOWAS)

Members: Benin, Burkina Faso, Cape Verde, Gambia, Ghana, Guinea, Guinea-Bissau, Côte d'Ivoire, Liberia, Mali, Mauritania, Niger, Nigeria, Senegal, Sierra Leone and Togo.

League of Arab States

Members: Algeria, Bahrain, Djibouti, Egypt, Iraq, Jordan, Kuwait, Lebanon, Libya, Mauritania, Morocco, Oman, Palestine, Qatar, Saudi Arabia, Somalia, Sudan, Syria, Tunisia, United Arab Emirates, Yemen Arab Republic and Yemen People's Democratic Republic.

Nordic Council

Members: Denmark (with the autonomous territories of the Faroe Islands and Greenland), Finland (with the autonomous territory of the Aland Islands), Iceland, Norway and Sweden.

Organization of African Unity (OAU)

Members: Algeria, Angola, Benin, Botswana, Burkina Faso, Burundi, Cameroon, Cape Verde, Central African Republic, Chad, Comoro Islands, Congo, Côte d'Ivoire, Djibouti, Egypt, Equatorial Guinea, Ethiopia, Gabon, The Gambia, Ghana, Guinea, Guinea-Bissau, Kenya, Lesotho, Liberia, Libya, Madagascar, Malawi, Mali, Mauritania, Mauritius, Mozambique, Niger, Nigeria, Rwanda, São Tomé and Príncipe, Seychelles, Sierra Leone,

Somalia, Sudan, Swaziland, Tanzania, Togo, Tunisia, Uganda, Zaire, Zambia and Zimbabwe.

Organization of American States (OAS)

Members: Antigua and Barbuda, Argentina, Bahamas, Barbados, Bolivia, Brazil, Chile, Colombia, Costa Rica, Dominica (Commonwealth of), Dominican Republic, Ecuador, El Salvador, Grenada, Guatemala, Haiti, Honduras, Jamaica, Mexico, Nicaragua, Panama, Paraguay, Peru, St Kitts and Nevis, St Lucia, St Vincent and the Grenadines, Suriname, Trinidad and Tobago, USA, Uruguay and Venezuela.

The activities of the various trading groups have to conform to the principles laid down in the General Agreement on Tariffs and Trade (GATT), which requires its signatories to conform to the following:

1. To concert together, to achieve a mutual reduction of tariff barriers and preferences.
2. To avoid discrimination by means of tariffs against foreign products which compete with home products.
3. To abolish quantitative controls.
4. To remove existing restrictions imposed by exchange control.

Although several of these objectives have been given practical application as trade has been liberalized, it is unlikely that the general requirements of GATT, and now WTO, will be implemented in the present state of world trade.

It is important that the exporter takes a close look at the foregoing preferential trading groups and identifies those which best suit his/her needs, having regard to product quality, competitive pricing, on-going commitment and relationships between buyer/seller, market profile, political situation and so on. Full use should be made of the National Chambers of Commerce (Appendix A) commercial attachés to obtain more data. At the same time, advice should be sought from the trade associations and Department of Trade and Industry (DTI).

1.4 World Trade Organisation

The World Trade Organisation (WTO) is the legal and institutional foundation of the multilateral trading system. It provides the principal contractual obligations determining how governments frame and implement domestic trade legislation and regulations. And it is the platform on which trade relations between countries evolve through collective debate, negotiation and adjudication. The WTO was established on 1 January 1995. Governments had concluded the Uruguay Round of negotiations on 15 December 1993 and ministers had given their political backing to the results by signing the Final Act at a meeting in Marrakesh, Morocco, in April 1994. The 'Marrakesh Declaration' of 15 April 1994 affirmed that the results of the Uruguay Round would 'strengthen the world economy and lead to more trade, investment, employment and income growth throughout the World'. The WTO is the embodiment of the Uruguay Round results and the successor to the General Agreement on Tariffs and Trade (GATT): see p. 34.

Out of a potential membership of 152 countries and territories, 76 governments became members of the WTO on its first day, with some 50 other governments at various stages of completing their domestic ratification procedures, and the remainder engaged in negotiating their terms of entry.

Not only does the WTO have a potentially larger membership than GATT (147 by the end of 2004 with a further 26 countries negotiating accession), it also has a much broader scope in terms of the commercial activity and trade policies to which it applies. The GATT applied only to trade in merchandise goods; the WTO covers trade in goods, services and 'trade in ideas' or intellectual property. In 1998 it started to focus attention on potential international trade gains from electronic commerce.

The WTO is based in Geneva, Switzerland. Its essential functions are: administering and implementing the multilateral and plurilateral trade agreements which together make up the WTO; acting as a forum for multilateral trade negotiations; seeking to resolve trade disputes; overseeing national trade policies; and cooperating with other international institutions involved in global economic policy making.

1.4.1 The principles of the trading system

The WTO Agreement contains some 29 individual legal texts – covering everything from agriculture to textiles and clothing, and from services to government procurement, rules of origin and intellectual property. Added to these are more than 25 additional ministerial declarations, decisions and understandings which spell out further obligations and commitments for WTO members. However, a number of simple and fundamental principles run throughout all of these instruments which, together, make up the multilateral trading system.

1.4.2 Trade without discrimination

For almost 50 years, key provisions of GATT outlawed discrimination among members and between imported and domestically produced merchandise. According to Article 1, the famous 'most-favoured-nation'

(MFN) clause, members are bound to grant to the products of other members treatment no less favourable than that accorded to the products of any other country. Thus, no country is to give special trading advantages to another or to discriminate against it: all are on an equal basis and all share the benefits of any moves towards lower trade barriers.

There are a number of exceptions to Article 1 – notably that covering customs unions and free trade areas. However, most-favoured-nation treatment generally ensures that developing countries and others with little economic leverage are able to benefit freely from the best trading conditions wherever and whenever they are negotiated. A second form of non-discrimination, known as 'national treatment', requires that once goods have entered a market, they must be treated no less favourably than the equivalent domestically produced goods. This is Article III of the GATT.

Apart from the revised GATT (known as 'GATT 1994'), there are several other WTO agreements which contain important provisions relating to MFN and national treatment. Those on Trade-Related Aspects of Intellectual Property Rights (TRIPS) contains, with some exceptions, MFN and national treatment requirements relating to the provision of intellectual property protection by WTO members. The General Agreement on Trade in Services (GATS) requires members to offer MFN treatment to services and service suppliers of other members. However, it permits listed exemptions to the MFN obligation, covering specific measures for which WTO members are unable to offer such treatment initially. Where such exemptions are taken, they are to be reviewed after five years and should not be maintained for more than ten years. On the other hand, national treatment is only an obligation in GATS where members explicitly undertake to accord it for particular services or service activities. This means that national treatment is often the result of negotiations among members.

Other WTO agreements with non-discrimination provisions include those on rules of origin; pre-shipment inspection; trade-related investment measures and the application of sanitary and phytosanitary measures.

1.4.3 Predictable and growing access to markets

The multilateral trading system is an attempt by governments to provide investors, employers, employees and consumers with a business environment which encourages trade, investment and job creation as well as choice and low prices in the market place. Such an environment needs to be stable and predictable, particularly if businesses are to invest and thrive.

The existence of secure and predictable market access is largely determined by the use of tariffs or customs duties. While quotas are generally outlawed, tariffs are legal in the WTO and are commonly used by governments to protect domestic industries and to raise revenues. However, they are subject to disciplines – for instance, that they are not discriminatory among imports – and are largely 'bound'. Binding means that a tariff level for a particular product becomes a commitment by a WTO member and cannot be increased without compensation negotiations with its main trading partners (Article XXVIII of GATT 1994). Thus it can be the case that the extension of a customs union can lead to higher tariffs in some areas for which compensation negotiations are necessary.

Following the establishment of the GATT in 1948, average tariff levels fell progressively and dramatically (see below) through a series of seven trade rounds. The Uruguay Round added to that success, cutting tariffs substantially, sometimes to zero, while raising the overall level of bound tariffs significantly. The commitments on market access through tariff reductions made by over 120 countries in the Uruguay Round are contained in some 22 500 pages of national tariff schedules.

Tariff reductions, for the most part phased in over five years, will result in a 40 per cent cut in developed countries' tariffs on industrial products, from an average of 6.3 per cent to 3.8 per cent, and a jump from 20 to 44 per cent in the value of imported industrial products that receive duty-free treatment in developed countries. At the higher end of the tariff structure, the proportion of imports into developed countries from all sources that encounter tariffs above 15 per cent will decline from 7 to 5 per cent and from 9 to 15 per cent for imports from developing countries.

The Uruguay Round increased the percentage of bound product lines from 78 to 99 per cent for developed countries, 21 to 73 per cent for developing economies and from 73 to 98 per cent for economies in transition – results which are providing a substantially higher degree of market security for traders and investors.

The 'tariffication' of all non-tariff import restrictions for agricultural products provided a substantial increase in the level of market predictability for agricultural products. More than 30 per cent of agricultural produce had been subject to quotas or import restrictions. Virtually all such measures have now been converted to tariffs which, while initially providing substantially the same level of protection as previous non-tariff measures, are being reduced during the six years of implementation of the Uruguay Round agricultural agreement. The market access commitments on agriculture will also eliminate previous import bans on certain products.

While tariffs at the border do not exist for trade in services, there is no less of a need for predictable conditions. To meet that need, governments undertook an initial set of commitments covering national regulations affecting various service activities. These commitments are, like those for tariffs, contained in binding national schedules and will be extended through further rounds of services negotiations in the future.

Many other WTO agreements seek to ensure conditions of investment and trade are more predictable by making it very difficult for member governments to change the rules of the game at whim. In almost every policy area which impinges on trading conditions, the scope of members to pursue capricious, discriminatory and protectionist policies is constrained by WTO commitments.

The key to predictable trading conditions is often the transparency of domestic laws, regulations and practices. Many WTO agreements contain transparency provisions which require disclosure at the national level – for instance, through publication in official journals or through enquiry points – or at the multilateral level through formal notifications to the WTO. Much of the work of WTO bodies is concerned with reviewing such notifications. The regular surveillance of national trade policies through the Trade Policy Review Mechanism provides a further means of encouraging transparency both domestically and at the multilateral level.

1.4.4 Promoting fair competition

The WTO is not the 'free trade' institution it is sometimes described as – if only because it permits tariffs and, in limited circumstances, other forms of protection. It is more accurate to say it is a system of rules dedicated to open, fair and undistorted competition.

Rules on non-discrimination are designed to secure fair conditions of trade and so too are those on dumping and subsidies. Previous GATT rules, which laid down the basis on which governments could impose compensating duties on these forms of 'unfair' competition, were extended and clarified in WTO agreements.

The WTO agreement on agriculture is designed to provide increased fairness in farm trade. That on intellectual property will improve conditions of competition where ideas and inventions are involved, and the GATS will do the same thing for trade in services. The plurilateral agreement on government procurement will extend competition rules to purchases by thousands of 'government' entities in many countries. There are plenty of other examples of WTO provisions which are designed to promote fair and undistorted competition.

1.4.5 Encouraging development and economic reform

Over three-quarters of WTO members are developing countries and countries in the process of economic reform from non-market systems. During the seven-year course of the Uruguay Round – between 1986 and 1993 – over 60 such countries implemented trade liberalization programmes. Some did so as part of their accession negotiations to GATT, while others acted on an autonomous basis. At the same time, developing countries and transition economies took a much more active and influential role in the Uruguay Round negotiations than in any previous round.

This trend effectively killed the notion that the trading system existed only for industrialized countries. It also changed the previous emphasis on exempting developing countries from certain GATT provisions and agreements. With the end of the Uruguay Round, developing countries showed themselves prepared to take on most of the obligations that are required of developed countries. They were, however, given transition periods to adjust to the more unfamiliar and, perhaps, difficult WTO provisions – particularly so for the poorest, 'least-developed' countries. In addition, a ministerial decision on measures in favour of least-developed countries gives extra flexibility to those countries in implementing WTO agreements; calls for an acceleration in the implementation of market access concessions affecting goods of export interest to those countries; and seeks increased technical assistance for them. Thus, the value to development of pursuing, as far as is reasonable, open market-orientated policies based on WTO principles is widely recognized. But so is the need for some flexibility with respect to the speed at which those policies are pursued.

Nevertheless, the provisions of the GATT which were intended to favour developing countries remain in place in the WTO. In particular, Part IV of GATT 1994 contains three articles, introduced in 1965, encouraging industrial countries to assist developing nation members 'as a matter of conscious and purposeful effort' in their trading conditions and not to expect reciprocity for concessions made to developing countries in negotiations. A second measure, agreed at the end of the Tokyo Round in 1979 and normally referred to as the 'enabling clause', provides a permanent legal basis for the market access concessions made by developed to developing countries under the generalized system of preferences (GSP).

Open Trade

The economic case for an open trading system based on multilaterally agreed rules manifests itself in the data which shows a definite statistical link between freer trade and economic growth. All countries, including the poorest, have assets – human, industrial, natural, financial – which they can employ to produce goods and services for their domestic markets or to compete overseas. It is the law of comparative advantage (p. 9). Hence liberal trade policies – policies that allow the unrestricted flow of goods and services – sharpen competition, motivate innovation and breed success. They multiply the rewards that result from producing the best products, with the best design at the best price.

But success in trade is not static. The ability to compete well in particular products can shift from company to company when the market changes or new technologies make cheaper and better products possible. Producers are encouraged to adapt gradually. They can focus on new products, find a new 'niche' in the market place or expand into new areas.

Experience confirms that competitiveness can also shift between whole countries. A country that may have enjoyed an advantage because of lower labour costs or because it had good supplies of some natural resources, could also become uncompetitive in some goods or services as its economy develops. However, with the stimulus of an open economy, the country can move on to become competitive in some other goods or services. This is normally a gradual process. Nevertheless, the temptation to resist the challenge of competitive imports is always present. Moreover, richer governments are more likely to yield to protectionism – for short term political gain – through subsidies, complicated red tape, and hiding behind legitimate policy objectives such as environmental preservation or consumer protection as an excuse to protect producers.

Protectionism ultimately leads to inefficient producers supplying consumers with outdated, unattractive products. In the end, factories close and jobs are lost despite the protection and subsidies. If other governments around the world pursue the same policies, markets contract and world economic activity is reduced. One of the objectives that governments bring to WTO negotiations is to prevent such a self defeating and destructive drift into protectionism.

1.4.6 A brief history of GATT

The WTO's predecessor, the GATT, was established on a provisional basis after the Second World War in the wake of other new multilateral institutions dedicated to international economic cooperation – notably the 'Bretton Woods' institutions now known as the World Bank and the International Monetary Fund (IMF). The original 23 GATT countries were among over 50 which agreed a draft Charter for an International Trade Organisation (ITO) – a new specialized agency of the United Nations. The Charter was intended to provide not only world trade disciplines but also contained rules relating to employment, commodity agreements, restrictive business practices, international investment and services.

In an effort to give an early boost to trade liberalization after the Second World War – and to begin to correct the large overhang of protectionist measures which remained in place from the early 1930s – tariff negotiations were opened among the 23 founding GATT 'contracting parties' in 1946. This first round of negotiations resulted in 45 000 tariff concessions affecting US$10 billion – or about one-fifth – of world trade. It was also agreed that the value of these concessions should be protected by early – and largely 'provisional' – acceptance of some of the trade rules in the draft ITO Charter. The tariff concessions and rules together became known as the General Agreement on Tariffs and Trade and entered into force in January 1948.

Although the ITO Charter was finally agreed at a UN Conference on Trade and Employment in Havana in March 1948, ratification in national legislatures proved impossible in some cases. When the US government announced, in 1950, that it would not seek Congressional ratification of the Havana Charter, the ITO was effectively dead. Despite its provisional nature, the GATT remained the only multilateral instrument governing international trade from 1948 until the establishment of the WTO.

1.4.7 International trade and shipping scene

Although, throughout its 55 years the basic legal text of the GATT remained much as it was in 1948, there were additions in the form of 'plurilateral' – voluntary membership – agreements and continual efforts to reduce tariffs. Much of this was achieved through a series of 'trade rounds' as detailed in Table 1.9.

TABLE 1.9 GATT trade rounds

No.	Year	Subjects covered	Participating countries
1	1947	Geneva Tariffs	23
2	1949	Annecy Tariffs	13
3	1951	Torquay Tariffs	38
4	1956	Geneva Tariffs	26
5	1960–61	Geneva (Dillon Road) Tariffs	26
6	1964–67	Geneva (Kennedy Round) Tariffs and anti-measures	62
7	1973–79	Geneva (Tokyo Round) Tariffs, non-tariff measures, 'framework' agreements	102
8	1986–94	Geneva (Uruguay Round) Tariffs, non-tariff measures rules, service, intellectual property rights, dispute settlement, textiles and clothing, agriculture, establishment of the WTO, etc.	123
9	2001–2003	Doha Development Agenda embracing 21 subjects covering agriculture, anti-dumping, cross-cutting issues, TRIPS, trade facilitation, dispute settlement, public health, transparency in government procurement and integration of LDCs in the multilateral trading system.	

The ninth trade round – the Doha Development Agenda has presented enormous challenges throughout WTO membership in terms of its implementation. Undoubtedly it will prove to be a further stimulant to world trade development in both merchandise and commercial services.

As we progress through the twenty-first century the influence of the WTO in trade development and facilitation will grow immensely. It has already become the driving force of trade development and business confidence on a global scale.

1.4.8 Lomé Conventions

The fourth Lomé Convention, signed in 1989 between the EC and the 69-strong ACP (African-Caribbean-Pacific) group of countries provides for an increase in EC aid, duty and quota-free access for almost all ACP exports, guaranteed sugar purchases and funds for trade promotion and development. Moreover, they will receive aid in both absolute and per capita terms.

Recommended reading

Annual Report – WTO.
International Trade Statistics – WTO.
The World Business Organisation – ICC – www.iccwbo.org
Understanding the WTO – www.wto.org
WTO Focus – latest issues available from the Media Division of the WTO.

CHAPTER 2

Advantages of trading overseas and the role of the export and shipping office

2.1 Export benefits and risk

The responsibility of moving from a domestic market to an export market and ultimately to a global market (see p. 146) is a management task at Director level. It involves new management culture internationally focused; multi-lingually equipped at all management levels; computer and logistical equipment; empathy with the buyer; a good knowledge of international regulations and the international environment; creative innovative thinking; and complete commitment to developing and serving the export market. Two key factors emerge, namely innovation and adaptation flexibility to the needs of the importer coupled with continuing commitment to the buyer. Moreover, one must, at all times, be professional.

Successful exporting emerges from the following strategies:

1. The development of ideas and techniques should be seen as being as important as physical goods and services.
2. A belief that growing world competition drives companies growth strategies.
3. Recognizing the importance of technology.
4. An increasing blurring of the distinction between low tech and high tech.
5. Developing long-term strategies on a growth market basis – this encourages a proactive rather than a reactive strategy.
6. Striving to find new markets opening up new sales opportunities.
7. Continuously reviewing and implementing internal company changes such as new manufacturing and disciplines dedicated to improving product specification.
8. Exploiting new technology and new technological processes such as E-commerce, the Internet and websites.
9. Developing a strong service philosophy.
10. Developing empathy with the buyer.

11. Undertaking continuous market research.
12. Logistically focused.
13. Employ personnel who are experienced/educated in the products/services and have forward thinking international trade ideologies.
14. Continuously review the range of market entry options (pp. 475–98).
15. Review/adopt a strategy of procurement with a view to re-exporting on a componentized basis maybe in a third country to lower cost and become closer to the market place (p. 470 and International Purchasing and Management text).

We will now briefly consider the benefits and risks involved in the export business.

2.1.1 Export benefits

1. There is the potential for greatly increased company turnover.
2. Higher calibre staff of a professional managerial status can be attracted to the business due to the potential for greater challenges, improved confidence/self-esteem and more job satisfaction. Personnel working in an export environment must be culturally focused at all times which develops more *esprit de corps*.
3. The company becomes more competitive in all areas of the business: product specification, management skills, and value added benefit transmitted to the buyer in both price and non-price areas – the latter featuring servicing warranty.
4. Economies of scale are achieved through a larger order book and better utilization of company resources, especially in the areas of production, design, administration and procurement.
5. Company exposure is greatly increased on an international scale through publicity and product/service analysis and market penetration.
6. The product or service offered is more competitive. It reflects overseas market needs and conforms to a wider legal environment.
7. Company risk and business is not confined to one market as is found at the domestic level, but is spread throughout ten or more markets depending on the nature of the business. The number of markets served, their location, and the culture presented in each market is closely related to company resources, level of profitability, degree of risk and market forecast. An analysis of market entry options is found in Chapter 17. Hence, by operating in a range of markets the company should experience peaks and troughs at differing times in each market, thereby spreading the risk and opportunities.
8. Companies become more integrated with the market they serve and this encourages higher standards and the use of more high technology,

which they would not obtain when serving only the domestic market, an environment which may be shielded through high import tariffs imposed to protect local manufacturers.

9. Potential levels of profitability are much increased. This provides more income for investment and research and development – ingredients which all work to ensure a company remains competitive.

It is stressed that the benefits outlined will vary by company and product/service and it is unlikely that all the benefits will apply to any one individual company or product/service. Similar remarks apply to the risks inherent in exporting.

2.1.2 Export risks

1. The export market involves a longer time scale of payment. This may be 90 or 180 days, or several years. In the domestic market it is usually 30 days. This may pose a serious cash flow problem for a smaller company. Possible solutions include factoring (see p. 313); cash in advance; or operating an open account.

2. Problems are inherent in the increased range of interest rates, exchange rates and economic and trade cycles. Forward planning can counter such problems, particularly in the short-term with strategies such as hedging the market on exchange rate variation, keeping in contact with the International Bank and focusing continuously on the political, legal and economic environment in the buyer's market.

3. Export risk can be divided into economic/political risk involving a country (see item (2)); financial risk such as foreign exchange, interest rates and working capital (see item (1)); or commercial risk such as buyer default or contractual dispute. Such risks can be reduced by having a buyer status audit conducted by a bank, and employing a solicitor to formulate an agency–distributor agreement or an export sales contract featuring an arbitration mechanism. Debt defaults can be difficult to resolve, particularly those with a political content.

4. Trade barriers (see p. 498) are politically and economically manipulated. This includes both customs tariff and non-tariff barriers.

5. Corruption, crime, expropriation and fraud are regretfully on the increase despite government's and international agencies' efforts to counter them. Such bodies include the London based International Maritime Bureau and the Paris-based Commercial Crime Services all under the auspices of the International Chamber of Commerce (see p. 15).

6. New skills are required which emerge from the foregoing items including methods of financing and how to cope with cash management; and issues such as the collection of receivables, repatriation of

funds and foreign exchange, and interest rate exposure and Forex risk. Adding value to enhance competitive advantage can make a difference: exporters should make it easy for customers to buy; credit should be part of the product proposition; and foreign exchange risk should be managed and not passed on. Exporters should develop a strategy to ensure they receive payment where the key risks are identified and then managed. Realistic financial plans should be identified and much of the aforementioned risk can be minimized by consulting the company's bank.

7.   A product launch in an overseas market is more costly and complex in comparison with a domestic launch. The product specification must comply with all the overseas market legislation and the legal environment of the market in which it is to be sold. Good research and visits to the intended market can serve to reduce such risk.

The way to reduce the risks outlined above is to employ experienced, professionally qualified and internationally focused personnel. The export company must have a company business plan with an international focus and put the necessary resources into finance, production, technology and personnel to ensure the plan's execution. Comprehensive control systems are essential to monitor performance and to adapt it when necessary as a remedial measure. Empathy with the buyer is vital on an on-going basis. Distribution, logistics and the outsourcing of components and assembly in a third country play a decisive role in competitive exporting today. Overall, the exporter must have complete commitment to the buyer, the market and the product they are selling overseas. An area of increasing opportunity for the exporter is the development of the regional trade agreements which are conducted at preferential and duty-free terms (p. 10).

2.2 The export office role

Exporting today is exceptionally complex and functions in a rapidly changing market. Moreover, the international entrepreneur is taking full advantage of the development of the regional trade agreements offering preferential and duty-free terms (p. 11) and sourcing and assembly in such markets. It is highly competitive and manufacturers now frequently outsource their products to keep up with technology and competitiveness in the market. It is driven by logistics (see p. 124) and high technology, making it essential for the company to employ computer literate, multilingual, professionally trained personnel. An example of a product which embodies these attributes is NIKE footwear: it is designed in the USA; prototypes are adopted in Taiwan; the soles are manufactured in South Korea; the leather is bought from Spain; the cloth is produced in Bangladesh; the footwear is assembled in the Peoples Republic of China using Chinese labour; and the distribution is logistically handled from Hong Kong to serve a global market.

A key factor is to manufacture the consumer or industrial product to the required standard. Such standards vary by market with the USA and Japanese markets out of step with those found in the European Union (see p. 533).

With a growing level of privatization in many countries bringing about a move away from state owned enterprises, export manufacturers are having to adapt to the changing needs of their customers. The increasing emphasis is on reduced product lifecycle costs, improved efficiency and greater equipment availability. There has been an enormous change in the customer-supplier relationship. The traditional concept of carrying out corrective maintenance and unscheduled repairs has been expanded to include preventive inspections, maintenance partnerships, plant upgrading, training and joint production.

The growth of B2B and B2C (p. 450) is developing a new dimension in international trade eliminating the intermediary and thereby developing a stronger empathy between the exporter and importer. The Internet has greatly contributed to this expansion.

A further factor is the globalization of markets with the buyers sourcing a range of products from different markets and conducting the assembly and distribution in a third country. This is possible through an increasingly sophisticated, logistically-driven global container network offering combined transport services with complete reliability and cost efficiency. An increasing number of the mega-container operators now have logistic organizations dedicated to their shippers, offering a transparent transport system in a high tech communication network (see Chapter 6).

It is in the light of the foregoing factors that the role of the export/shipping office must be considered. Many companies call it the logistics office. One other vital factor is the structure of the organization itself, which must be capable of achieving its objectives as found in the business plan.

Exporting today is a highly skilled and professional operation. To be successful in this field requires an adequate and cost effective organization designed to enlarge the company product market share overseas. Above all, the results of exporting must be profitable and, accordingly, it is most desirable that the export personnel are of a high calibre, with language proficiency, adequately qualified and rewarded, to attain this objective.

To be successful the Company must have an export culture management strategy with all personnel totally focused to an international business entrepreneur environment. This requires continuous training, and total commitment to work with the global markets they serve and their buyers. It must embrace the total product. This includes not only the product delivered on time in accordance with the export sales contract, but also involves continuous communication with the buyer to sustain and develop existing business opportunities. Moreover, the exporter must be fully informed of the environment in which the product will be used and identify how best to reduce the product lifecycle cost (see p. 289).

The size of the company, its products, and scale of export business will largely influence the form of export organization. Moreover, cognizance must be taken of company structure and organization, and how the export role can best be injected into it. In broad terms, the industrial company has three functions – production, finance and sales. Additionally, there are various other subsidiary activities which significantly contribute to the running of the company, which include personnel, administration, research/development, training, purchasing, etc.

If the company is rather small with only an element of export business, it is likely that an export manager with a secretary and a clerk would be adequate but, as the export trade grows, it will soon become necessary to have a properly structured export organization with qualified specialist staff designed to exploit the export trade potential. One can no longer rely on inexperienced unqualified personnel in the export field (whether it be marketing, sales, or shipping), as standards will tend to be low, overseas product reputation poor and the overall financial results probably very indifferent. Exporting is a highly professional activity which is increasing annually in terms of its overseas market competition.

The export department has two main functions: marketing and shipping/logistics. The former is responsible for sales, pricing enquiries, quotations, recording and checking orders, and other marketing functions such as promotion, research, after sales service, product servicing and development, etc., while the latter is responsible for transportation/distribution and the relevant documents involved, packaging, costings for distribution, etc. There must be at all times close liaison with the accounts department particularly on credit audit and control, costings and financial documentation/information. Overall, the export department objective is to ensure that the export order proceeds smoothly from start to finish to obtain complete customer satisfaction and produce a modest profit for the company. Unless the profit motive is present throughout the export activities of the company, it will produce indifferent results with little discipline or technique. Hence, all the aspects of an export operation are interlinked with clearly defined functions and responsibilities. The export office may be horizontally or vertically organized, but it must have efficient and well-trained specialist and professional staff. Moreover, the export organization must have a strong interface and be fully integrated with other departments, nowadays the computer facilitates this communication. Finally, the exporter must have a sound financial strategy conducting international trade and evaluate the option most ideal (pp. 469–75).

2.3 The export office organization and structure

The smallest export department may consist of an export manager, shipping/logistics executive and accounts executive. All would conduct much of their business over the Internet and communicate through e-mail. At first, the department may be engaged merely in shipping orders secured by the sales organization, but as the export trade develops the department will enlarge and have its own sales organization, attend to their shipment and collect payment. Hence, it will become a self-contained export-focused unit fully integrated within the company structure.

In such circumstances, the overall aim of the export department is to collect sufficient data to enable them to quote promptly and accurately a competitive CPT, FCA (p. 401), or other delivery term price for any consignment to the important centres of the world. This involves an evaluation of the most suitable method of despatch and requires knowledge of rates, services, routes, terminal charges, insurance, packaging, documentation and so on. It is likely the exporter will be responding to a logistically driven order and be in contact with the logistics division of a mega-container operator such as P&O Nedlloyd.

The department must study the needs of different markets, their trends and likely future developments together with possible methods of increasing overseas sales. A full understanding of the global logistic mechanism is essential (see p. 124). This extends to keeping up-to-date with the changing infrastructure and opportunities to speed up transit times, as well as regional trade agreements developments (pp. 10–12). It involves the scrutiny of overseas agents and branch reports and the provision of adequate publicity by overseas journals/publications. Additionally, close liaison must be maintained with trade associations and relevant government departments on overseas market development opportunities. Moreover, a continuing dialogue must be maintained with overseas representatives on all developments at home. This involves manufacturing and technical aspects of the commodity, distribution methods and future developments (e.g. a new product range). Such an exchange of information is vital to the future well-being of the company, and any reports indicating shortcomings in product, distribution, inadequate packing, faulty products, etc. should be acted on quickly and remedial measures taken.

The export department has the task not only of obtaining and executing the export orders, but also of ensuring payment is received without undue delay in accord with the terms of sale as prescribed in the export contract. Enforcement of rights in foreign courts of law is often a troublesome business and tends to create a bad public image for the company. The exporter must have a good knowledge of export trade law (p. 559). It is prudent to liaise closely with and/or use the export services provided by banks and the credit insurance companies on financial matters.

FIGURE 2.1 Structure of shipping manager logistic organization

In the larger export-oriented company a greater degree of specialization is essential which usually involves the appointment of an export marketing manager, an export sales manager, and a shipping manager, each with defined responsibilities (Figures 2.1 and 2.2). In the small- to medium-sized firm an export manager is usually found dealing alone with all sections of his company's export business. In the larger firm, on the other hand, the work is split between the three appointments in the following manner:

1. The export marketing manager has overall executive control usually under an export marketing director. He controls and coordinates the activities of the other two functions, deals with policy, and usually represents the export department at internal sales conferences.

2. An export sales manager is generally responsible to the export marketing manager and in a limited way is involved with sales inasmuch as he controls the agents and representatives and promotes actual sales to customers everywhere. His job is done when the export order is obtained and passed on to the export office for issuing to the factory or, in the case of a merchant, to the manufacturer. This involves the following stages:

    (a) receiving the enquiry, ascertaining its feasibility, ensuring that the price is calculated and preparing the quotation, in particular to confirm the product specification complies with the national standards applicable in the buyers/consumers' country (p. 417);

Export director
Overall policy-strategy and export development

Export marketing manager
Advertising (sales promotion) Agency appointments Brochure production Budget formulation/monitoring Economic statistics and analysis Electronic data interchange – E-commerce Export planning/strategy formulation Export sales contract Export trade law compliance Liaison with trade associations/chambers of commerce etc. Marketing and sales plan Market analysis and development/selection Market research Product research/development Regional trade agreements Trade exhibitions, trade weeks, store promotions.

Shipping manager	Export marketing manager
Accounting Claims Conditions of carriage and customs/transport regulations Costing/computerization of order/transit analysis and execution Credit control – audit and liaison Documentation – completion and control Electronic data interchange Filing and order analysis Insurance finance and invoicing Management data on freight rates, schedules, transit times, currency rates etc. in computerized form Market research on transport distribution strategy Liaison with airlines, shipowners, port, airports, customs, freight forwarders, underwriters, liner conferences Liaison with production and technical departments Regarding execution of the order Liaison with consuls, embassies, commercial attaches, diplomatic corps relative documentation attestation Order processing Packing Planning – resources/distribution Production/assembly Strategy formulation on distribution policy Supervision, appointment of personnel – traffic assistant, clerical personnel Training Transportation to airport/Seaport/ICD	After-sales Agents' reports Budgets – execution/accountability Claims Costing – all elements in quotation Customer audit/monitoring with credit control Export sales contract Liaison with Production Department etc. Licensing – overseas/monitoring Management information Market intelligence Market trends Monitoring of sales records Product specification Quotations Sales conferences/seminars Sales reports Selling – direct or via agents Supervision of overseas sales personnel Training

FIGURE 2.2 Export office job description of senior managerial personnel. Overall it will have a strong logistic and computerized E-commerce throughout

(b) ascertaining the despatch date by the specified mode of transport;

(c) obtaining the sanction of the credit controller and approval of a quotation before it is sent to the customer;

(d) ensuring the quotation is sent to the customer and following it up, initiating investigations into orders presumed to be lost;

(e) receiving the order from the customer and checking it against the quotation (where the order is received without earlier quotation much of (a)–(c) has to be done at this time);

(f) obtaining production controller's sanction, priority rating and credit controller's permission (if applicable);

(g) acknowledging the order and informing the local agent (if necessary) of the order or the Business (buyer) or consumer under the B2B or B2C;

(h) arranging for the preparation and issue of the works order;

(i) informing records or statistics department of the details of the order;

(j) confirming date of despatch to clients, agents or distributors and notifying any unavoidable changes;

(k) progress chasing;

(l) handing over the order to the shipping department to arrange the delivery procedure (overall one can conclude by saying the export sales office function is to deal with enquiries and orders up to the point of despatch).

3. The export shipping manager is informed of any orders booked, usually by a copy order and later receives definite notice from works/ manufacturer when the goods are nearing completion. This involves the following stages:

(a) linking with export sales, checking that the order complies with import/export controls and establishing from letters of credit relevant details of items which have to be reconciled with the ultimate forwarding arrangements (see also Chapter 15);

(b) deciding on the method of transportation (if not already specified);

(c) issuing instructions for packing and marking (if not already given);

(d) chartering or booking shipping (or air) space;

(e) pre-entering at customs (if necessary);

(f) issuing instructions to works, transport office, and freight forwarders;

(g) drawing up all the necessary documents and later collecting, collating and cross-checking all documents after shipment;

(h) passing documents to accounts department for collection of payment.

The export shipping function normally commences when the works order is issued and takes over fully when the goods ordered have been produced and are ready for despatch. It is a section where a sense of urgency is essential. The Shipping Manager is responsible for obtaining shipping or air freight space, arranging despatch, documentation, insurance, possibly packing and customs clearance (Figure 2.2).

The export salesman involved in direct selling overseas in the field has a very demanding job requiring many aptitudes. He must be multilingual, ideally have good product knowledge, with good managerial potential and knowledge of export practice. Moreover, the person must be tenacious, have good judgement and be sufficiently diplomatic to secure the most favourable export sales contract.

The foregoing sequential stages are fully computerized involving an adequate software package. This develops cost efficiency relative to the processing of an export order. This embraces all aspects of the order processing task and enables the exporter to reduce costs and improve efficiency throughout (see Figure 15.3, p. 435).

It cannot be stressed too strongly that the ultimate organization structure will depend on the size of the company and the nature/volume of export business. Likewise, the precise relationship and division of responsibilities between the foregoing three functions will vary from firm to firm. In many companies the departments are fully integrated to avoid duplication, promote co-ordination and encourage transparency. The managers would head up the functions while encouraging dialogue among their executives.

The organization structure of the export department is very much geared to the overseas markets served and the complexities involved. Software packages are available to process the orders and 'online' access is available to customs and transport/logistics operators to provide guidance and identify the options available. Executives handling export orders tend to specialize on a region/trading-bloc/country basis to develop the necessary skills in documentation, packaging, customs, trade finance, insurance, culture, terms of trade etc. Alternatively, it may be on a product basis.

Basically there are three types of sales office as detailed below and in Figure 2.3.

1. Products orientated. This type tends to be warranted where the products are technically complex, or the number of products in the range is vast, or where the products are completely unrelated. It is ideal for the company which feels that product knowledge is paramount in the interests of giving good customer service. For example, it is suitable for a company selling overseas medical equipment, cycles, bathroom fittings, etc. Conversely, it can inflate cost as various representatives will call on the same customer which could cause customer irritation.

2. Customer orientated. Under this system each representative specializes in a class of customer thereby gaining expert knowledge of the industry concerned, its technology, its decision patterns and so on. Thus the

FIGURE 2.3 Sales office organization

salesman will get to know the specific customer needs and will be able to satisfy them more efficiently. Conversely, it does encourage duplication of journeys involving increased costs of the export product when more than one representative visits the same area to see different types of companies. It tends to be used by the larger companies.

3. Market group or area-based organization. This involves allocating the salesman a specific world area to service. It results in a clear definition of responsibility and interest in that area which will tend to lead to the cultivation of local business and personal ties. Travelling expenses will be kept to a reasonable level. This system works satisfactorily when the area is not too large, where the products and customers are homogeneous, but once the situation arises where the company's products become diversified to the extent that the representative is physically incapable of learning everything about the products, then this method becomes less effective.

For the export department to function efficiently close cooperation and complete transparency with other sections of the business is imperative.

There must be a zero failure rate to despatch the specified product on schedule otherwise orders will be cancelled and heavy financial penalties and loss of subsequent orders incurred. Moreover, it may jeopardize future business culture relations. For the export business to operate efficiently a computerized tracking system must be operative. Hence, from the time the order is received until the period when the goods are despatched, it is closely monitored and remedial measures are taken on any deviation. This involves complete transparency in all sectors within the company to execute the order: design; procurement; production; assembly; traffic/logistics embracing customs; packaging; documentation; trade finance; transport operations; and trade law.

Finally it must be recognized (see p. 525) that in many multinational companies the technical division is internationally focused with a very large part of their order book being overseas. This embraces not only supplying the product as specified, but also providing technical commitment in terms of servicing, technical training, contractual maintenance and product development. It may be a turnkey project and could apply to power stations, railway rolling stock, a mass transit system, hydro-electric power plant, etc.

2.4 Export policy and records

As we progress through the twenty-first century, manufacturing based companies which rely on international markets will be the norm and companies relying almost exclusively on their domestic market the exception. The latter usually will be very vulnerable to home market recession as they cannot rely on the multi-country, broadly based overseas markets inherent in the export focused company.

The chief concern of a company will be to combine stability with the highest financial return obtainable. In many industries this is achieved by a balance or mixture between home and overseas markets, but much depends on the product. This is important where:

1. exports may rely on the continued existence of one or two foreign markets, which may be cut off by changes in import licensing laws, etc. in the countries concerned;
2. demand abroad may be seasonal for goods which require a constant market to make them pay;
3. overseas enthusiasm for a product may depend on the fact that it is in use in the home market;
4. regional trade agreements and large trading blocs such as the EU change the economics of selling in a particular market.

Some businesses virtually exist solely for export with no significant home market. In such a situation, it is prudent, where possible, to have the export markets broadly based and extending to several countries, thereby lessening the impact of a change of export demand in any one of the countries.

Cluster market strategy can prove very beneficial. This involves servicing a collection of countries contiguous to each other with similar cultures and market needs. One country can be the distribution centre thereby encouraging volume shipments and reducing distribution costs. It is particularly effective in trading blocs. Serving the market is more efficient. Overall, it encourages development of the market through lower cost and extols the economies of scale and a more effective logistically-driven organization within the markets served.

The distribution centre country may feature FTZs, Distriports, Economics Zones, or ICDs (p. 100).

Export marketing research is an important function and involves fact-finding enquiry on which marketing policy is then based. Overall there are four basic areas to focus on continuously.

1. *Statistical.* This involves the determination of the total existing market insofar as the quantity bought, the price range and their locations. Additionally, it should indicate, where relevant, a comparison with the company's own sales in the area, and whether the total market is expanding or otherwise.
2. *Economic.* This involves evaluation of the product market potential and its acceptable market price bearing in mind competition.
3. *Social.* This indicates the public attitude towards the products and their adequacy in terms of design, durability, and so on.
4. *Psychological.* This involves what motivates the consumer to buy the product; an evaluation of measures which could be devised to further its market growth; and in what ways it is adversely influenced by competition/substitutes.

The results of research in the export market can be correlated with parallel activities on (a) the home market and (b) the international marketing plan projections so that an overall marketing policy may be formulated. However, the divergence of treatment called for by home and overseas markets makes a fusion of the export department with the home marketing organization under a general marketing manager most unwise.

Today much statistical and economic data is available as countries worldwide develop their information resources. Moreover, market research database companies are available providing 'online access' to export orientated company subscribers. Such companies specialize in commodities, products or markets and provide up-to-date information to help the export strategist's decision-making process.

With regard to accounting, there is no fundamental difference between the accounting methods adopted in an export company and those in any other concern. In a manufacturing or wholesaling business which maintains an export department certain accounts will be subdivided with the export department having separate sales, cash, etc. returns budgets.

There does arise however, the need to have a strategic focus on how to deal with funds generated from the overseas markets. The multinational enterprise could form an overseas subsidiary which may generate tax advantages in transfer pricing and display total commitment to the market. Also all the sales revenue would not be repatriated to the parent company but would remain *in situ*. The smaller company may decide to set up an offshore account in the buyer's country to which all monies on overseas sales in that territory would be remitted and thereby avoid bank transfer charges. The account could also be used for local expenses and monies could be transferred to the parent company when exchange rates are most favourable. Advice from an international bank should be sought (see also pp. 287–330).

A trading firm engaged solely in the export business does so either (a) as an export merchant on its own account exporting its own goods to buyers overseas; (b) as a commission agent for foreign importers; or (c) as export agents undertaking the export business of manufacturers in a variety of industries. This may involve B2B or B2C. Freight forwarders do not engage in a trade of goods, but undertake the transportation arrangements on a logistic basis, sometimes including a packaging service.

In the case of a manufacturer, it is usual for the export department to keep separate accounts. Hence, when an order is received from an overseas buyer, the goods will be subsequently invoiced giving details of the sale price. Where appropriate, further records will be maintained of such other charges as insurance, freight, packaging, etc. The usual method of charging export orders is to use serially numbered invoice sets. These give instructions to finished stores department, and advise and charge the customer. An alternative method is to issue warehouse instructions and process it through the various offices. The former is the most modern and is often computerized.

If the exporter does not manufacture their own products, the business either buys the goods for export on their own account or exports on behalf of a manufacturer. An exporter using their own account may concentrate solely on the overseas trade which may be a general wholesaler maintaining an export department. In the latter case, the accountancy of the export department will be similar to that in a manufacturing concern, the sole difference being that instead of producing merchandise for home and overseas markets, the business merely purchases the goods, bulking or breaking bulk as the case may be. The organization of the export department is thus much the same in either type of concern.

There is no doubt today that the export and shipping office structure should be well thought-out and adequate to exploit the company products overseas. It should be able to market successfully and to develop the export market profitably, particularly in terms of identifying, processing and executing the export order. Full use should be made of computers to improve cost efficiency. Ideally the organization should be reviewed every two or three years to reflect and take advantage of new market opportunities and changes in market structure, including threats. Moreover, close liaison should be maintained with all the various organizations, particularly trade associations and government departments, available to facilitate overseas market development. These additionally include identifying new markets and taking up opportunities to exhibit at overseas trade fairs and exhibitions.

Today, more and more small companies are entering the export business. Usually this involves the appointment of an export manager with a small staff. Transportation arrangements are normally undertaken by the freight forwarder, leaving the export management department to concentrate on sales, pricing enquiries, quotations, receiving the checking orders, together with other marketing functions. As the business prospers, the export department expands and the shipping office emerges.

One must stress in conclusion that export companies today are usually fully computerized in all activities of their business and thereby rely on Internet and E-commerce for communication, including research. The processing of the export order is fully computerized with very limited manual input. Moreover, the distribution is logistically driven with a high tech communication and an international documentation transmission network. Logistics and supply chain management feature strongly in the export strategy. Many companies have a merged export and shipping office (Chapter 20).

CHAPTER 3

Characteristics of international transport modes: 1

3.1 The role and essentials of a transport system

Transport is an essential facility for the exploitation or development of economic resources on a national or international scale. It allows articles or materials to be conveyed from areas of low utility to areas of high utility and thereby adds value to the product.

Transport's provision arises for economic, social or political reasons. In a society where transport costs are relatively high, the need for a balanced social policy is paramount, otherwise isolated communities may cease to exist.

The political influence on transport is often considerable, to the extent that many large transport operators are state-owned. Moreover, such policies extend to the provision of uneconomical services for political reasons, such as an international air service retained for reasons of national prestige in the face of competition from other national airlines. Another example of the political influence on transport is flag discrimination practised in shipping whereby countries insist on certain imported cargoes being moved in ships of their own flag, so sustaining their fleet.

Transport permits the development of economic resources to the full. It makes possible specialization in economic development whether it be mining, car manufacturing or farming. Without a low-cost reliable and well-managed transport system, goods or services would not be exchanged, to the serious detriment of living standards worldwide. It embraces the supply chain in a logistic-driven international trade environment. Today we have an efficient professionally managed global transport network which is the prime stimulant to the continuous expansion of world trade. Goods will not be moved unless a good transport infrastructure exists. Moreover, the global transport network must keep ahead of market needs through continuous investment and strive to reduce transit times and offer realistic rates. Overall, it is driven by logistics (see Chapter 6) in a high tech environment.

Transport is a product which is consumed immediately it is produced. Hence it cannot be stored. Its intensive economic deployment is, therefore, paramount to help ensure its viability.

The essentials of a transport system embrace three elements: the way route, the vehicle (including motive power unit), and the terminal. The way route may be naturally occurring such as the seas or river, or artificially made by man such as the railway, canal or motorway. One can have a combination of these two circumstances embracing the inland waterway system where new canals have been built into an established river or lake network such as the St Lawrence Seaway thereby offering a through inland waterway network. The way route may be for general public use administered in user terms by the state as, for example, the vehicle registration licensing system in the UK and most other countries. Alternatively, the exclusive use system is found in the railway network. The latter has the distinct advantage of operating under a disciplined timetable to obtain maximum use of the network but conversely, unlike the road operator, is responsible for financing all the initial, maintenance and replacement cost of the railway system. Moreover, the railway company provides a policing system through a signalling complex, but the road user relies on traffic control which is financed by the state.

The transport unit may either be of the integral type embracing the carrying and motive power unit, such as an aircraft or ship, or have an independent motive power unit, such as a railway locomotive. Examples of the carrying unit are found in the road trailer and barge. A further refinement exists whereby the integral or separate motive power unit either carries its own energy fuel, such as cars, ships or aircraft, or relies on remotely situated generated energy such as electric rail traction. The advantage of separate carrying and motive power units is their independence and flexibility in operation. Moreover, while the carrying unit contents are being transhipped, the motive power unit can be operational elsewhere. A further factor is that the failure of the motive power unit does not immobilize the carrying unit, as one merely obtains a standby unit.

The terminal must be artificially made by man, and be well designed to ensure the most efficient operation/utilization of the transport unit using it. This is particularly important today when more and more emphasis is on more intensive unit operation. Basically, the terminal is the link in the transport chain and merges at an interchange point involving one or more forms of transport, to offer through transit such as airport or seaport. Terminals require adequate area for expansion and a good layout to permit an unimpeded flow of traffic passing through it.

As we proceed through the early years of the twenty-first century, it is paramount that efficiency plays a major role in the transport infrastructure. Each decade provides a new generation of transport technology. More emphasis is on the overall performance of transport unit aligned to the value added benefit to the user/shipper and logistically focused. International distribution is the partnership between the transport operator and the user. Moreover, it is the efficiency of the supply chain from the supplier to the consumer which is a key factor in driving international trade development on a global basis. Each transport mode must have a strong transparent interface with the other transport mode(s) with no impediments to overall efficiency to develop a free flowing logistics chain. Efficient transport networks drive trade, open up new markets and substantially contribute to the globalization of trade. A notable example is the growth of the Far East trade, whereby a substantial volume of industrial production has been relocated from Europe and North America to this region.

To conclude, the essential elements of a transport system embrace the way route, the vehicle, its motive power and the terminal. Each must have a strong interface with the other to generate efficiency and facilitate trade development. To produce an efficient system, it must preferably be capital intensive, with low labour content, but very skilled technically. Overall, it should be high-tech and attract economic volume levels to encourage low tariffs. This will facilitate traffic development to contribute to economic and social development. A study of the individual forms of transport now follows.

3.2 Canals and inland waterways

Canals and inland waterways throughout the world are developing at a time of intermodal development driven by a logistics environment. In many countries, especially Europe, increased road congestion and the introduction of tolls on major highways, coupled with the need for a cleaner environment, is encouraging the pro-canal and inland waterway political lobby. The growth of containerization is also making a contribution with its ease of intermodal transfer.

In continental Europe we have the most modern and extensive inland waterway networks serving many major seaports, especially in the northern seaboard. It is continuously being modernized together with the vessels/barges embracing both bulk cargo and containerized transhipments.

Rotterdam is a key hub in the barge network and is served by 25 000 kilometres of navigable inland waterways (see pp. 107–10 – seaports). Additionally, Rotterdam is served by over 30 inland waterway operators, run over 120 scheduled container services to 70 industrial centres spread over the entire heartland of Europe (see Table 3.1 European Inland Container Terminals). Moreover, the growth of inland container shipping is a notable modal shift as demonstrated in Table 3.2 Development of the Modal Split.

TABLE 3.1 European Inland Container Terminals 2003

Country	Number of inland container terminals
Germany	29
Netherlands	26
Hungary	1
Slovakia	1
Austria	4
Switzerland	2
France	5
Belgium	8

TABLE 3.2 Development of the Modal Split – Port of Rotterdam 1993–2001

Marine terminals, Port of Rotterdam
Sea–sea transhipment is 20–25 per cent.
The number of containers transported by land is considered as 100 per cent again and divided as follows:

	Barge	Rail	Road
1993	26	8	66
1994	27	9	64
1995	30	10	60
1996	31	11	58
1997	34	13	53
1998	35	13	52
1999	36	14	50
2000	39	13	48
2001	39	12	49

An analysis of the traffic volume between Northern Germany and Rotterdam reveals about 25 million tons of cargo travel by barge annually. This compares with 90 million tons over the north-south axis: the Netherlands (including Rotterdam), Belgium, including Antwerp and France. Some 80 per cent of this volume is connected with Belgium. Traffic volume between Netherlands and France totals eight million tons compared with 17 million tons on the Mosel and Saar. Heavy industry around Thionville, Metz and Nancy in the French district of Lorraine accounts for a lot of this volume. But there is also cargo that goes through to destinations further to the south, past Nancy. Navigating the canals everywhere in navigable France, ships sail into what could be called 'capillaries' or smaller canals, which constitute one of the most important forms of waterway in this part of the world. Of the 20 million tons of inland cargo transported on the north-south axis (Rhine–Schelde–Gent–Lille) about ten million tons are connected with Rotterdam. A similar volume applies to transport over the Maas. Together with the Schelde, this river constitutes an equally important connection which draws cargo to Liege. From this river a great deal of cargo finds its way through to the capillaries of northern, eastern and even southern France. The estimated 17 million tons of inland cargo mentioned above in the area to the south of the German city of Trier, is seen as the 'roundabout category' in the north-south navigation because this volume first travels around the Rhine. Ships travel up the Mosel past the city of Koblenz, towering at the confluence of three rivers. Overall, 95 per cent of inland navigation in Saarland and Lorraine is connected with Rotterdam.

The Netherlands share of the north-south traffic totals 45 per cent on the Rotterdam Antwerp line, of which 80 per cent is containerized totalling 850 000 TEUs in 2002. The remaining 55 per cent is conveyed in Belgian and French vessels. The most important varieties of cargo for the north-south trade are coal and building materials – especially sand and gravel; petroleum; chemicals; fertilizers; grain (import and export); rolled steel and iron ore. Additionally, there exists mixed cargo to bulk liquids by small tanker tonnage.

All of industrial Belgium is accessible at least by Kempenaar inland barges with a length of 63 metres, a seven metre beam and capacity of 550 tons. However, vessels of 110 metre length with 2000 tons capacity operate to Brussels, Gent and Liege on the Maas. The largest vessel between Netherlands and France on the Canal du Nord has a maximum capacity of 800 tons. The Kempenaar vessels have a 32 TEUs capacity or 48 TEUs when stacked three high. A recent development to counter overland competition has been the provision of the pallet ship. Similar in size to the Kempenaar tonnage, the pallet ship has automatic self loading and unloading with a capacity of 650 euro pallets. Overall, between France and the Netherlands (Rotterdam) one million tons of cargo travel on the east-west route.

As has already been demonstrated, the Rhine waterway between Rotterdam, Antwerp and on to Germany and France remains Europe's busiest network.

The push barge sector is a major feature of the barge industry in the Port of Rotterdam. In 2001 41 million tons of ore and 22 million tons of coal were transhipped, representing 20 per cent of the total cargo handled at the port. A leading German operator – Veerhaven – has a fleet of five big push tugs and 53 tug-pushed dumb barges. Six fully loaded barges lashed together with a pusher behind can move 16 500 tons of bulk cargoes in a single transport movement.

A container movement which has grown considerably in the lower region of the Rhine is operated by Haeger & Schmidt, Haniel Reederei and Rhine-container. Each vessel has a capacity of 156 TEUs and the consortium operate 19 sailings per week between Rotterdam and Duisburg.

The sailings run from Rotterdam and Antwerp to Nijmegen, Emmerich, Duisburg, Neuss, Stuizeberg, Düsseldorf, Cologne and Leverkusen. Duisburg is Europe's largest inland port handling 37 million tons annually. It represents a major hinterland hub. In 2003 a modern intermodal terminal was opened, with direct access to Antwerp and Rotterdam, and a new Rhine/Ruhr Shuttle which connects with Dortmund and the eastern part of the Ruhr region and North Seaports.

An example of the most recent new waterway completion emerged in 1992 when the Rhine and Danube were finally joined by the new Rhine Main–Danube (RMD) link canal. It will open up a 3500 km cheap inland waterways route between the North Sea and the Black Sea, and will serve nine east and west European countries. The RMD route runs through Holland and Germany to Mainz, and up the Main to Bamberg, the northern canal entrance. On the other side of the Franconian Jura, the canal joins the Danube at Kelheim. That river flows through Austria, clips the former Czechoslovakia and continues south through Hungary and Yugoslavia. Turning east again, it forms the border between Bulgaria and Romania before turning north to touch in Romania the southern tip of the CIS and finally empties itself into the Black Sea.

Inland waterways barge distribution acting as port feeder services operates in many developing and less developed countries. Such services are long established and examples are found in the markets of Africa, the subcontinent and the Far East. Examples are found too in the ports of Bangkok and Klang which permit overside loading thereby speeding up the turnround of vessels. They tend to be in the bulk and consumer unitized markets, and such business is tending to be transferred to the containerized network as the infrastructure is modernized and markets expand with modern methods of handling and distribution.

To conclude our brief analysis of the canal and inland waterways networks, the developed economies of the world, particularly Europe, are now focusing more emphasis and investment on providing a transport infrastructure in which inland waterways play a more significant role in their economic development. Overall, it remains a low-cost form of distribution for volume cargoes often of low value with modern transhipment facilities and high economic utilization of modern tonnage. The development of containerization with inland hub distribution centres, as found in Duisburg, is an example of intermodal transport logistically driven networks.

3.3 International air transport

Air transport is one of the youngest forms of transport and undoubtedly continues to make a major contribution to the exploitation of world resources. At the moment air freight constitutes 1 per cent in volume and about 20–30 per cent in value terms of total world trade. The global air freight market could be divided into three broad sectors: express, special commodities and traditional air cargo.

To examine the express market first, this is now dominated by integrators such as Fedex, TNT, United Parcels Service (UPS) and DHL. Hence the main role for most international air express markets is as carriers acting for the integrators or wholesalers. British Airways provides a courier service for shipments less than 32 kg (1000 kg per consignment) – no pre-notification in required. 'Check in' is 60 minutes before scheduled time of departure. It guarantees the shipment arrives at its destination within 24 hours of the original scheduled time of arrival.

British Airways also provides an express service with a fast priority service with freight and documents available for collection 90 minutes prior to departure. Collection times are 90 minutes after arrival. Again, shipments are 32 kg per piece (1000 kg per consignment). Overall, British Airways world cargo services operate to nearly 200 destinations in 80 countries.

A further division is found in the international air freight services. This involves special commodities such as perishable products, live animals, project outsized cargoes and hazardous goods. This business is primarily orientated towards the traditional carriers, the airlines and freight forwarders.

The third sector is the traditional air cargo. This embraces the transportation of normal industrial and commercial shipments moving in parcel, container or pallet form. The integrators are already making substantial inroads into that market, forcing the airlines and forwarders to look at ways of improving their services. A large volume of this trade is represented by the consolidation market under agents' sponsorship. Attention will be directed to improve product quality. In particular, it must strive to develop an unmistakable performance profile through product enhancement of which improved information systems will be an integral part and logistically focused.

As we progress through the early part of the twenty-first century, the growth of airfreight is manifest in the development of logistics. More Airline operators are merging or forming an operating alliance to increase capacity, develop flight frequency and lower cost especially at airports by having common facilities and resources. This extends to computerized systems and despatch of air waybills electronically. More international and regional hubs are being developed to improve transit times and provide more 'value added' services to the shipper. Airlines have become more customer focused and Governments have become more aware of the need to develop modern airports to enhance their economy. This is especially so in the Asian markets where the topography of the region favours air transport for quick transits.

3.3.1 Advantages of air freight

1. High speed and quick transits.
2. Low risk of damage/pilferage with very competitive insurance rates.
3. Simplified documentation system – one document, an air waybill, is used for throughout air freight transit and is interchangeable between IATA accredited airlines. The IATA air waybill is, therefore, acceptable on any IATA airline permitting flexibility of through routeing with no transshipment documentation problems at airports en route.
4. Common code of liability conditions to all IATA accredited airlines.
5. Virtually eliminates packing cost. This is an important cost saving attributed to air freight and the shipper may find it worthwhile to engage professional packaging services to ensure the merchandise has the correct packing specification for this mode of transport. Significant packaging cost savings can be realized to offset the higher air freight rate compared with surface transport.
6. Ideal for palletized consignments. A substantial volume of merchandise is now moving on pallets which aids handling, reduces packing needs, facilitates stowage and lessens the risk of damage/pilferage. Again for the shipper new to the export business, it may prove worthwhile to establish whether it would be advantageous to have the merchandise palletized. Many such palletized consignments are using the shrink-wrap packaging technique (p. 190).
7. Quick transit reduces the amount of capital tied up in transit. This facilitates prompt financial settlement of individual consignments thereby aiding the exporter's cash flow situation. On this point much depends, of course, on the export sale contract terms of delivery.
8. Quick, reliable transit eliminates the need for extensive warehouse storage accommodation provided by the importer, reduces the risks of stockpiling, that is, obsolescence, deterioration, and the capital cost tied up in warehouse/stock provision. Moreover, it enables the importer to replenish his stock quickly, such as when demand for a commodity has become exhausted more rapidly than forecast.
9. Ideal for a wide variety of consumer-type cargoes, particularly consignments up to 1500–2000 kg. In addition, the average consignment size is increasing as larger air freighters are introduced (p. 62).
10. The existing very extensive international air freight network continues to expand which aids its development and increases its share of the international trade market. This in turn encourages new markets to the air freight sector thereby aiding international trade development. For example, in some large countries major car manufacturers guarantee a replacement spares service through the medium of air freight, which in itself has a status symbol and thereby aids the exporter's sales. Likewise air freight services generate new markets to

the exporter such as day-old chicks being transported 3000 miles which obviously would not be possible or practicable by sea transport.

11. Parity obtains on rates on IATA scheduled international services and competition exists only on service quality. This, in the long-term, benefits the shipper as no rate wars, which would be detrimental to the service and trade, arise.

12. Services are reliable and to a high quality.

13. Major airports worldwide – compared with major seaports – tend to be situated in the centre of commercial/industrial areas. In consequence the airport is, in many situations, more closely situated to the industrial/commercial market, giving it a competitive advantage in terms of lower collection/distribution cost.

14. Air freight facilitates the 'just-in-time' concept logistically focused, with the air freight distributor forming the link between the central warehouse or manufacturing plant and the 'point of sale'. Goods are simply replenished as they are sold at the importer's premises. Examples are fashionable goods and perishable products such as flowers and food products.

15. The air freight network worldwide is more extensive and offers more frequent flights than the maritime services.

16. The 'value added benefit' found in fast transits and service frequency is profound. For example, the spares replacement market serving factory plant or the computer software and hardware industries are good examples. The sooner the goods arrive, the greater is the financial benefit to the importer.

17. Services are continuously being improved and new ones developed through the 'combined transport operation' concept. An example is the sea–air hubs which are slowly being developed on a global basis. A comparison of sea–air services in various hubs is found in Table 3.3. The transfer hub is totally reliant on whether the operation can offer a relatively faster transit time and lower transportation cost. In marketing the sea–air product via multi-modal services, a comprehensive sailing programme covering all possible origins and destinations on a monthly basis is required. A 'hot box' arrangement is essential in which sea–air containers on transfer hubs have priority of discharge otherwise containers are delayed. Overall, it is a multi-modal logistics operation.

18. Air freight capacity is continuously increasing as the latest generation of aircraft emerge. Air freighters are now becoming more common. Overall, airline operation costs are being reduced.

19. New airports continue to be introduced globally. Hong Kong, Malaysia, Kuala Lumpur and Japan, for example. All are hub airports which offer feeder air freight services within the region.

20. Globally the role of air freight continues to expand and this is extolled as major airports continue to expand their air freight terminals in a

TABLE 3.3 Comparison of sea–air services in various major transfer hubs

Transfer hub	Cargo origin	Destination	Total transit time
UAE	Hong Kong	Europe	15–16 days
Dubai/Sharjah	Taipei	Europe	14–15 days
Abu Dhabi	Singapore	Europe	8–9 days
	India	Europe	7–8 days
Khor Fakkan			2 days less
West Coast (Seattle/Vancouver)	Hong Kong	Europe	15–16 days
	Taipei	Europe	14–15 days
	Japan	Europe	11–12 days
	Korea	Europe	14–15 days
	China (North)	Europe	17–18 days
Korea (Seoul)	China (North)	Europe/USA	6–7 days
West Coast (Los Angeles)	Taipei	America	15–17 days
	Korea		14–16 days
	Japan		13–15 days
Russia (Vostochny)	China (Shanghai)	Europe	14–15 days

logistic driven market environment. This is particularly evident in the Far East, USA and major European countries. It focuses primarily on the hub concept.

3.3.2 Disadvantages of air freight

1. Limited capacity of air freighter and overall dimensions of acceptable cargo together with weight restrictions.
2. Very high operating expenses and initial cost of aircraft when related to overall capacity – average capacity is in the region of 20 000–25 000 kg. It is for the latter reason that many air freighters are converted passenger aircraft. Moreover, some 80 per cent of air freight is conveyed on passenger scheduled services.
3. The service is vulnerable to disruption by the weather, for example fog and ice, particularly at airports with less modern traffic control equipment.
4. Airline operation today is very sophisticated in all areas including air freight. It is vulnerable to rates and transit time competition in short hauls by surface transport, due to the high airport cost and landing fees which inflate terminal costs. Consequently, most major operators with air freight from London for Paris and Brussels rely on surface distribution which is more economical in cost and also because the smaller aircraft operating the short hauls do not have capacity to carry the larger, more economical, pallet loads.

It must be recognized that an increasing volume of cargo is now conveyed on air freight charter flights and integrators (p. 58). Air freight is a growing market and the trend towards developing larger capacity air freighters will continue to meet such demand and facilitate optimum performance and operation. It is particularly ideal for the small exporter and this form of international distribution should be continuously borne in mind by the discerning shipper.

Moreover the role of the freight forwarder IATA agent in air freight development has now become extremely important. It involves the provision of a consolidated consignment. Under such arrangements, the freight forwarder markets the service and embraces in the tariff structure not only the air freight tariff, but also the collection and delivery charges and other ancillary rates such as documentation, customs clearance and so on. The freight forwarder would have a contract with the airline guaranteeing a specified cube space on a specified flight on a regular basis for which an overall freight rate is charged by the airline to the freight forwarders. In such circumstances, the freight forwarder is able to quote very competitive composite rates, while the airline operator no longer becomes involved in direct marketing and selling the service. The latter development has enabled many airline operators to achieve substantial labour cost savings. It has resulted in a market expansion on some airline routes through the freight forwarder offering more competitive composite rates coupled with a guaranteed service.

The growth of the international air freight market has been spectacular in recent years with an 8 per cent rise in 1996 followed by 11 per cent in 1997. This trend is likely to continue and is being driven by a more logistic internationally focused market. Many other factors contribute to this continuing growth, including the expansion of the integrator market and courier service, the development of Cargo Website and the new EDIFACT message to replicate the Cargo IMP FSA and FWB messages which pass information between airlines and freight forwarders and form an integral part of the EDI implementation programme.

An example of a modern air freight terminal is located in Frankfurt. It is the largest air freight transhipment site in Europe and is operated by Lufthansa. It has a $25\,780\,\text{m}^2$ freight transhipment hall which is linked to various warehouses of modular design. It handles 700 000 tonnes annually and processes 1900 tonnes daily, involving 6000 shipments. The heart of the cargo centre is the central monitoring station, where various computer systems control and monitor the flow of freight within the terminal. A conveyor system transports the pallets and stores them in the highbay warehouse while a box system transports medium-sized shipments to the box warehouse in special boxes. A mini-shipment system controls the storing of the small shipments. From the central control station, the storing and removal of freight from storage is controlled and monitored via computer-controlled conveyor tracks and automatically operated stacker cranes. The physical flow of freight is accompanied by the electronic flow of information. The systems communicate with one another and exchange data, enabling the retrieval of warehouse and air waybill data at any time. A computer controlled warehouse check is conducted daily. Furthermore, the direct link to the customs computer system guarantees that shipments cross borders quickly and without hitch.

A central master data processing system handles the processing of all freight data 24 hours a day. The structural centre of the Lufthansa Cargo Centre is the enormous freight transhipment hall. Here the containers and pallets are stacked and removed and the mixed cargo processed; the freight shipments are sorted into large, medium-sized and small shipments and then forwarded to the appropriate warehouses via automatically controlled conveyor systems. Large shipments are taken to the highbay warehouse, the capacity of which was more than doubled in the second stage of construction. In the six aisles of the five- or nine-storey highbay warehouse, special stacker cranes store items in and remove items from over 2000 storing places. Medium-sized shipments are placed in boxes and stored in the two-storey box highbay warehouse with its over 4800 storing places. In the mini-shipment system, small shipments are conveyed and distributed by computer control, then stored manually by destination in the handracking warehouse which holds more than 10 000 small shipments.

The reliable 'warehouse system' is employed in the box and pallet highbay warehouse, i.e. the individual storing places in use are merely placed in the computer memory as they are unimportant for the actual processing of the shipments; a computer-controlled warehouse check is conducted for added security. The rapid loading and unloading of aircraft, the transshipment from one Lufthansa jet to another, is achieved by using the latest loading devices such as standardized pallets and containers. Work alongside and in the aircraft is monitored using the Lufthansa ramp agent's precise loading diagram. Loading and unloading is conducted with time-saving mechanical loading systems, including highloaders and electrically driven conveyors.

Transit freight passes through Frankfurt in six to ten hours; direct transshipment of complete load units at the freight yard is handled in two hours, and the high-performance satellite near the passenger terminal can be handled in one to six hours. Here scheduled 'quick transfers', the transshipment of very urgent shipments, takes one hour. Not only are the direct transshipment of entire load units and quick transfers handled here, but also all airmail transhipments.

Today the air freight operator tends to formulate a global approach to the market using high tech means, involving the most advanced satellite and computer links available. An example of such a strategy is Thai Airlines: its operation is based on direct flights or via a worldwide system of cargo hubs covering different regions and customer priorities. Bangkok is the hub for Asia serving 46 destinations; Paris is the European hub which is linked to direct onward transfer by road to key industrial centres – it also serves 12 European destinations on direct flights; and finally Seattle is the North American hub with three direct destinations. Australasia has no hub, but relies on seven direct destinations. Onward connections with the hubs in Paris and Seattle are quick and may involve either air or surface transport. Additionally, to supplement the Thai network, it has inter-line service and cooperation agreement with over 100 airlines. Computerized cargo control is exercised through ORCHIDS, the online Revenue Cargo Handling and Information Distribution System.

3.4 International road transport

The road vehicle is a low capacity but very versatile unit of transport which is most flexible in its operation. Since the early 1970s, the international road haulier has become increasingly dominant in the UK/ Continental trade with some services extending to Asia and the Middle East. Road haulage has the following features.

1. One of its most significant advantages is the road vehicle distributive ability. Overall it can offer a door-to-door service without intermediate handling.
2. No customs examination arises in transit countries provided the haulier is affiliated to TIR as the cargo passes under bond when the unit is passing through one of their countries. Insofar as transit countries within EU are concerned, no customs examination arises.
3. It is very flexible in operation which is particularly useful when circumstances demand a change in routeing through road works, a blockage or disrupted shipping services.
4. It is very competitive within certain distance bands compared with air freight, both in terms of transit times and rates.
5. Documentation is simple as, under CMR, a through consignment note is operative with a common code of liability conditions.
6. The service tends to be reliable and to a high standard. Delays usually only occur when bad weather prevails or due to some other exceptional circumstances.
7. The TIR vehicle may be 12.20 m (trailer) or 15.50 m (articulated vehicle) with an overall gross weight capacity of 42 tonnes (44 tonnes in Continental Europe). Hence, initial cost is low when compared to an air freighter. However, limited capacity imposes certain weight and dimensional restrictions on the traffic which can be carried.
8. It is ideal for general merchandise and selective cargo in bulk in small quantities conveyed in a specialized road vehicle. The service is

renowned for its groupage flow under a freight forwarder's sponsorship and, therefore, ideal for the small exporter. An increasing number of shippers are now using their own vehicles to distribute their own goods.

9. Packing costs are less when compared with conventional shipping (break-bulk cargo) services.

10. The driver accompanies the vehicle throughout the road transit thereby exercising personal supervision and reducing the risk of damage and pilfering. Accordingly, the operator can control his vehicle at all times as the driver usually 'reports in' to his company control office at staged points en route.

11. A wide range of routes and types of service exist between the UK and the Continent. Services are frequent and many operators have a European operation which is highly sophisticated. An example is DANZAS, a global freight forwarder which has daily trailer scheduled services between 13 countries in Western Europe; the range is between 24–48 hours door-to-door, consignor and consignee or factory-to-factory schedules. Warehouse distribution centres in key industrial and commercial areas are located in each of the countries.

    A wide-range of trailer units are used in the European road distribution network, usually operating warehouse-to-warehouse or factory-to-factory schedules; details are given in Table 3.4.

12. The trailer service is very flexible and this helps to develop business. In many situations, it can be customized to meet the shipper's needs aiding cost efficiency and substantially improving the quality of service.

13. Major highways continue to be developed globally as trans-continental trade routes. An example is the St Petersburg to Vladivostok highway – a distance of 6620 miles completed in early 2004. It travels through seven time zones and provides a trade route to the Far East. In comparison the Trans Canada highway is 4860 miles long linking overland the Pacific and Atlantic oceans as a trade route. The longest continuous road route in the world is the Pan-American highway which runs 16000 miles from Argentina to Alaska, but is broken by a boat journey in Central America.

14. Most new major highway routes being developed today are funded by tolls contributed by the road user.

During the past 20 years, roll on-roll off traffic between the UK and the Continent has developed very substantially under CMR/TIR conditions conveyed on vehicular ferries. The freight forwarder has featured greatly in this development offering groupage services to many countries under scheduled services usually working in correspondence with a Continental-based freight forwarder. Such services have developed much faster than

TABLE 3.4 Trailer units in use in European road haulage

Name	Description
Refrigerated semi-trailer	Triaxle 38–40 tonne operation – multi-compartment/ dual temperature
Tail lift refrigerated semi-trailer	Triaxle 38–40 tonne operation – standard refrigeration fitted with roller shutter doors and 1500 kg tail lift
Dry freight van	Triaxle 38–40 tonne 24 or 26 pallet capacity
Step frame van	Triaxle 38–40 tonne – racking for garment carrying
Curtainsider	Triaxle 38–40 tonne – 24 or 26 pallet capacity, high-tension load restraining curtains and variety of optional cargo control systems
Insulated curtainsider	Triaxle 38–40 tonne – 24 or 26 pallet capacity, designed to carry chilled produce at maximum thermal efficiency
Tilt semi-trailer	Triaxle 38–40 tonne – 24 or 26 pallet capacity, four or five dropsides per side, sliding roof
Step frame tilt semi-trailer	Triaxle 38–40 tonne – 24 or 26 pallet capacity, three dropsides on lower deck and two on upper deck
Bulk tipping semi-trailer	Triaxle 38 tonne with 42–55 cubic yard capacity – hinged rear tailgate and grain hatch
Bulk liquid tanker	Triaxle 38–40 tonnes – foodstuffs, chemicals, spirits
Platform skeletal	Triaxle 38–40 tonnes – detachable headboard
Platform semi-trailer	Triaxle 38–40 tonnes – option for brick crane
Extendable flat platform	Triaxle 38–40 tonnes – designed to convey overlength indivisible loads. Extends between 40 ft (12.20 m) and 60 ft (18.30 m)
24 ft (7.20 m) skeletal	Two axle 32 tonne, conveyance 1 TEU
Step frame skeletal	Triaxle 38–40 tonnes – designed to convey 1 TEU tank container
40 ft (12.19 m) skeletal	Triaxle 38–40 tonnes, conveyance 2 TEUs
Extendable semi-low loader	Broshuis semi-low loader – 27 ft (8.50 m) well extends to 45 ft (13.50 m) – overall 45 tonne gross combination weight, option rear steer
Dual-purpose coil carrier	Triaxle 38–40 tonne – conveyance steel coils, option curtainsided

originally envisaged and in some cases to the detriment of air freight, and container services in the UK/Continental trade. In some countries, the environmental lobby has slowed down the expansion of the European trailer network and some Continental countries restrict the times/periods/ routes over which such traffic may be conveyed. A problem for the road operator is to obtain balanced working, that is, a full profitable load in each direction.

The trailer operation is ideal for a small exporter and it is worth making an enquiry to a freight forwarder for a particular stream of international consumer type traffic, insofar as rates, transit times, routeing, schedules, etc. are concerned (p. 609).

As we progress into the twenty-first century, the pattern of the European truck network will change to meet market conditions. The Euro Tunnel (pp. 3–5) has resulted in many hauliers centralizing their services in the two portals. Many of the larger hauliers tend to dispatch their trailers unaccompanied on the EuroTunnel freight trains and thereby improve the productivity of the drivers who work to and from the portals.

The EU Single Market will further stimulate trade and greater competition will result. Undoubtedly, more emphasis will be placed on cost efficiency in the European distribution strategy, with quicker schedules and development of the 'just-in-time' concept by the larger shippers. An increasing number of the larger industrial companies will be reviewing their European distribution strategy and relocating their distribution and warehouse centres closer to their markets, thereby reducing haulage and distribution costs. Key distribution centre areas could be northern France near Dunkerque, the Iberian peninsula, southern Germany and northern Italy. This is being stimulated by the EU enlargement to 25 countries which opens up new markets and permits a customs-free examination movement of goods on an Intra-EU basis. Hauliers are developing logistically driven services in line with their customers in all 25 states. The EU strategy towards road haulage market is not favourable as it is not an environmentally friendly mode of transport. This would favour rail, especially volume business, on an Intra-EU basis (p. 541). Road remains the most dominant mode, with over 70 per cent.

Our evaluation of international road transport would not be complete without stressing that the European trailer network model strategy could be developed in other parts of the world. Trucking between Canada–USA and USA–Mexico is firmly established and will grow under NAFTA (p. 17). It could also be developed more extensively in the area of South East Asia in the next decade. This would depend on the scale and pace of infrastructure development and the provision of adequate Ro-Ro services. Rail services in this region are gradually being improved and developed but primarily on the basis of existing routes, with no new routes being built. The tendency is to develop motorway networks between major industrial and commercial centres involving major ports and places of tourism. The topographical features of the region present problems in developing the transport infrastructure. A major factor will be the development of trade among South East Asian countries.

The twenty-first century continues to witness the expansion of the international road transport service as its flexibility and cost factors remain dominant factors among the selection criteria of transport modes. This will be evident in all developed and developing markets.

3.5 International rail transport

The growth of the railways as an international link with seaports offering quick reliable low cost transport movement in a volume focused trade environment is likely to continue unabated in the foreseeable future. It is driven by the shipper who is demanding quicker transits in a multi-modal transport environment embracing dedicated services with no delays at transhipment points logistically driven. The strategy is ideally to have the railway network connected to an inland clearance depot (see p. 100) which is close to the importer's/exporter's premises to facilitate quick customs clearance. Additionally, many volume shippers are opting for local customs clearance on the shippers' premises (p. 239) which is road serviced to/from the railway network. The result of this new strategy at Government, Trading Blocs and International Agencies level is that economic planning now focuses more on the railways as a reliable distributor.

International rail distribution in Europe has been stimulated by the EuroTunnel. It has highlighted the social and economic benefits of offering trans-European rail freight services in three sectors: the wagon or train load movement; the inter-modal system relying on rail for the main leg, and road for the feeder units; and finally maritime containers. The question posed is whether rail freight and combined rail/road transport will be viable for a wide range of goods in addition to the former traditional bulk traffics. Crucial factors will include the development of efficient trans-shipment operations and good consignment control capabilities. In fact, good information technology systems – increasingly including EDI – are already playing an important role in general distribution service development. The EU has become increasingly conscious of the need to develop a trans-European rail network to aid economic development.

Historically, most European road and rail infrastructure was built to serve mainly, if not solely, national interest. Formation of the EU and its subsequent growth from six to 25 Member States increased the importance of the international transport network dimension. Moreover, most transport infrastructure was financed from taxation on a nationally focused basis with little regard to the need to provide a fully integrated trans-European transport network.

The growth of intra-EU trade was accompanied by an increase in congestion on major international routes resulting in bottlenecks. Subsequently, the Single European Act 1986 and the emergence of the Single Market in 1992 throughout 15 states presented new opportunities and also new problems. Ultimately, the Maastricht Treaty accepted the earlier published guidelines produced by the European Commission. This was on the basis of EU governments calling for the development and inter-connection of trans-European networks (TENS) including 'the most efficient surface communications links'. In late 1994 the EU summit in

TABLE 3.5 TENS (Trans-European Network): Priority Projects

Project	Distance	Cost
Oresund Denmark–Sweden fixed road/rail link	52.5 km	ecu4.148bn (£2.75bn)
Nordic triangle	1800 km	ecu10.070bn (£6.7bn)
Ireland–United Kingdom–Benelux road link	1530 km	ecu3.629bn (£2.4bn)
United Kingdom West Coast main railway line	850 km	ecu3bn (£1.99bn)
Rail link Cork–Dublin–Belfast–Larne–Stranraer	502 km	ecu357m (£235m)
Rail freight/combined transport Betuwe line Rotterdam–Dutch/German border	160 km	ecu4.094bn (£2.7bn)
High speed/combined transport rail line Lyon–Turin–Milan–Venice–Trieste	734 km	ecu18.260bn (£12bn)
High speed/combined transport rail line Berlin–Munich–Brenner–Verona	958 km	ecu15.102bn (£10bn)
Pathe and Via Egnatia motorways in Greece to Bulgarian/Turkish borders	1580 km	ecu9.242bn (£6.1bn)
LisbonValladolid (Portugal–Spain) motorway	details not yet finalized	
High speed rail line London/Paris–Brussels–Cologne/Amsterdam	1176 km	ecu17.232bn (£11.5bn)
High speed rail line Madrid–Barcelona–Perpignan–Montpellier	1601 km	ecu14.072bn (£9.3bn)
High speed rail line Paris–Metz–Strasbourg–Karlsruhe	551 km	ecu4.777bn (£3.1bn)
Malpensa airport Milan		ecu1.047bn (£700m)

List approved by EU Essen Summit, December 1994

Essen adopted 14 priority projects, spread both geographically and across all transport modes (see Table 3.5).

This programme demonstrates the EU commitment to an integrated transport network so essential in the economic development of a Single Market. A further ten projects to feature in the next phase have been formulated including new airports at Athens and Berlin; 37 combined transport projects in Germany, Italy, Belgium and Portugal; a high speed rail/combined transport Danube Axis Munich/Nuremberg–Vienna-Budapest; a high speed rail in Denmark; a Trans-Appenine Bologna–Florence highway and two motorway projects in France and Portugal–Spain. Today, many of these projects are in the process of construction and some are complete, such as the Oresund Denmark–Sweden fixed road/rail link (pp. 72–3).

Details of the general cargo and steel rail wagons operating on the Anglo-Continental network are given in Table 3.6.

An example of the use of purpose-built wagons operating in train load formation is the movement of cars from factory to destination rail-head. This includes Amsterdam, Cologne, Brussels, Lille, Paris, Basle, Munich, Turin, Port Bout and Hendaye. STVA is the leading European rail transporter.

TABLE 3.6 Wagons operating on the European rail network

Wagon type	Description
Covered freight/wagon – general cargo	Two axles – capacity 28 000 kg, two sliding doors per wagon side, capacity 34 Euro-pallets; ideal for high-volume palletized or break bulk goods
Covered freight wagon – general cargo	Bogie – capacity 33 000 kg, three sliding doors per wagon side, capacity 48 Euro or 38 industrial pallets; ideal for heavy or high-volume palletized or break bulk goods, each door gains access to one-third of area
Covered freight wagon – general cargo	Bogie – capacity 52 000 kg, two sliding doors per wagon side; provides wider access to the load area, capacity 51 Euro or 40 industrial pallets; ideal for heavy or high-volume palletized or break bulk goods
Covered freight wagon	Bogie – capacity 60 500 kg, five wells set into wagon floor can accommodate steel coils; for transport of steel sheets, plates and other heavy goods, wells covered by integral drop flaps to give completely flat loading surface
Covered freight wagon	Bogie – capacity 6500 kg, five wells set into wagon floor for transport of steel coils

The second division is the inter-modal system involving rail and road. This embraces the swap-body concept and the development of the inter-modal system providing a door-to-door service; it involves road, rail and sea. Overall, this is a growth market as more dedicated services and facilities are introduced. A description of a number of swap-bodies is given in Table 3.7. All are suitable for road/rail/sea movement and transshipment by lift truck and top loading crane. The swap-bodies can also be mounted/demounted on/off draw bars and semi-trailers giving a quick turnaround time; most swap-bodies can be stacked up to three high.

Swap-bodies provide complete flexibility for distribution by rail, road and inland waterway. In 2001 GE SeaCo introduced a range of swap bodies embracing Class A (13.6 m) and Class C (7.15 m and 7.45 m) featuring both box and curtainside designs, tailored to meet specific operational requirements for carriage of palletized cargo in Europe. The swap bodies can be easily transferred between rail wagon and truck and between truck and barge to complete an overland journey. The increased capacity of the 13.6 m units which carry the same number of pallets as standard European road vehicles allows pallets to be carried more economically than in standard marine pallets (see p. 107). The units can be utilized in lift on/lift off short sea and barge operations, and may be stacked in terminals and yards saving valuable storage space. Design features such as the demountable legs on 7.15 m and 7.45 m units allow the transport to be driven away with the container left in place for loading or unloading. Features of the swapbody include steel construction for strength and ease

TABLE 3.7 Swap-bodies

Swap-body type	Distribution
Steel swap-body (DTY van)	Corrugated steel with grappler pockets with roller rear door and/or side door and mounted on four adjustable legs. It has a payload of 13 680 kg, length 7.15 m, width 2.5 m and height 2.67–2.75 m. Also available in lengths of 7.45 m and 7.82 m and 3 m high
Full-side access swap-body	Corrugated steel with grappler pockets with full width or 2.50 m side doors and mounted on four adjustable legs. It has a payload of 12 620 kg, length 7.15 m, width 2.5 m and height of 2.67–2.75 m. Also available in lengths of 7.45 m and 7.82 m and 3 m high
Refrigerated swap-body	Pallet wide ATP/FRC insulated with grappler protection plates – refrigeration unit and mounted on four adjustable legs. It has a payload of 12 930 kg, length 7.15 m and width 2.6 m. Also available in lengths of 7.45 m, 7.82 m and 13.6 m
Curtainsiders access swap-body	Steel construction with end door of ply metal construction and one piece aluminium roof and curtains running each side throughout its length. It is mounted on four adjustable legs. It has a payload of 16 000 kg, length 7.15 m, width 2.480 m, height 2.36/2.44/2.69 m and side opening length 6.86 m. Also available in 7.45 m and 7.820 m length. Ideal for automotive and drinks industries

of repair; all designs both top and bottom lifted; 7.15 m and 7.45 m laden units can be stacked three high (two high for 13.6 m units); more pallets than standard marine containers; internal lashing points and more efficient cargo handling.

A further example of combined transport operation is the piggyback system. This involves rail conveying the road trailer throughout the major part of the transit and the road vehicle collecting and delivering the goods. The trailer is either driven on and off the rail wagon or may be loaded/unloaded by a lift on/lift off crane operation.

In the longer term, it is envisaged that the European market will grow in such a way that international road haulier/freight forwarders will service 'block train movements' of hauliers' vehicles including dismountable bodies in purpose-built wagons. Hence rail will convey the trailers over the greater part of the total journey. Such services will operate between key centres in Europe (p. 541).

The final category is the movement of maritime ISO containers to and from the seaports. This may involve an international movement between the major ports such as Felixstowe, Liverpool, London, Southampton and the 40 purpose-built terminals including eight situated at ports. The trains are run in fixed formation between terminals to a prescribed timetable in the same way as a passenger train. The wagons are tailor-made to carry only containers. The transfer from road to rail (or ship) is carried out at specially built terminals and it is smooth, safe and fast. The method of transfer is by means of 'portal'-type cranes which can operate over the whole length of the specially laid rail sidings. Each of the rail-served container bases has a direct distribution facility which eliminates intermediate warehousing. This rail operation has been established for over 25 years and is very reliable and cost effective. Individual major container/shipowners have contracts with Freight Liner Ltd for the charter of complete trains on a regular basis. This is completely integrated with the sailing schedules and container base operation – the latter managed by an international consortium of international trade interested parties.

The opening of the EuroTunnel railway has provided a potential market for the international containerized rail movement between major container ports such as Rotterdam, Antwerp, Hamburg, Dunkerque, Cherbourg, Zeebrugge and the UK container bases; Rotterdam could become a major distribution point.

The movement of containers by train is very much a growth movement in all parts of the world. Overall, it is quicker and cheaper compared to road, subject to movement being in complete train formation on a regular scheduled basis and thereby attaining good infrastructure utilization.

In Malaysia, Port Klang is served by an inland container base at Ipoh. It is called a 'dry port' and has played a major role in developing the Malaysian economy and Port Klang (p. 101).

Another example is the movement of rail-borne containers from the west to east coasts of North America, plus of course the hinterland market distribution. An example is the Port of Seattle. Today the port now occupies 78 hectares, double its original size with on-dock facilities for handling up to four double stack container trains in 'low loader' railway wagons with a capacity of 280 TEUs. This investment has been undertaken to cope with the growth of the West-coast container trade and the North America interior markets. This embraces the sea-rail-sea bridge from the Far East to Europe. Transit time to Chicago is 62 hours, and to New York five days. Similar services operate from the ports of Oakland, Los Angeles and Long Beach, including direct to the east coast and New York. Such a container movement is called a 'land-bridge' with much of the traffic originating in Japan, Singapore and Hong Kong. It has resulted in a decline of the North American east coast ports and a speeding up of container transits, from the Far East and Europe, with lower freight rates. An example of two new recent rail links is found in Southern Scandinavia and Australia. In 2000 a permanent link between two land masses linking Denmark and Sweden was created between Öresund and Malmo. It reduced the journey time between the two countries to ten minutes and created a region of 3.2 million people embracing the unification of Copenhagen and Malmo. Overall, it has the 8th largest gross national product in Europe. The project involved an artificial island – Pepper Island – linked to Copenhagen by a 4 km tunnel with a four lane motorway and twin-track high-speed railway, and a 7.8 km bridge to Malmo. The bridge is a two-level steel structure with the motorway placed above the railway. Overall, the multi-modal project has opened up the economy and demonstrates the role that rail/road transport plays in international trade and tourism markets in developed economies.

Likewise, the completion in 2004 of the Australian north/south railway link between Adelaide and the deep water port of Darwin, spanning 3000 km with a transit time of 43 hours will further stimulate the Australian economy and provide easier access to Asian markets. Moreover, Northern Hemisphere trades will benefit from shorter voyage times to Darwin deep water port rather than the longer voyage to South Eastern Australia seaports. It will favour not only containerized traffic, but also dry bulk cargo such as iron ore. Overall, the transit time to/from Singapore to/from Adelaide/Melbourne via Darwin will be four days quicker. Darwin has become the regional deep seaport as a gateway to/from SE Asia in Australia.

3.6 EuroTunnel

In 1994 the EuroTunnel was opened linking the British Rail network with the European rail system which extends to over 150 000 route miles. It continues to have a profound impact on the pattern and development of freight distribution between the UK and Europe. Currently, the bulk of the business is through passenger trains London/Paris/Brussels, and portal to portal services on the shuttle train service carrying accompanied cars, coaches and road haulage vehicles. A growing volume of through freight trains conveying containers and a range of commodities is being developed. The freight trains convey cars, steel, and a wide range of consumer goods. Ultimately, major container operators will adopt a strategy of having fewer European ports of call and centralize their services in one or two major ports, relying more on rail as the distributor/feeder. The ports of Rotterdam, Antwerp, Hamburg, Dunkerque, and Cherbourg could feature in this hub and spoke strategy. It is unlikely to take place in high volume terms until the dedicated rail track for EuroTunnel service between Folkestone and North London (Kings Cross) is completed in 2008 thereby enabling high speed freight trains to operate to Birmingham/ Manchester/Liverpool/Scotland/Wales/West of England. In 2003 rail freight projects were underway from UK, especially Manchester, Leeds and Daventry to Dourges (Lille – France), Italy, Spain, Belgium, Germany and the Netherlands.

The EuroTunnel is a 31-mile subterranean rail tunnel between Folkestone (UK) and Fréthun near Calais (France). It is built below the seabed in the English Channel and comprises of three tunnels – two of which are 7.6 m diameter to convey trains, and one of 3.3 m which is a service tunnel. Terminals with road and rail access are provided at both portals (Ashford and Calais).

Two types of trains use the tunnel. Cars and coaches at the portals drive onto a special shuttle train service. Cars use double-decker wagons and coaches single-deckers. Passengers stay with their vehicles or stroll around the train. Road haulage vehicles drive on to a separate single-decker shuttle train service. The other type of train is the through international service involving passengers, freight wagons and maritime containers. Such services are operated by the BR/SNCF rail personnel linking key UK and Continental destinations situated in industrial and commercial centres.

Other significant railway developments focused on developing and accessing international trade markets embrace the electrification completion of the Trans-Siberian railway with a length of 9213 km. It is the world's longest track and carries 30 per cent of Russian exports. Plans have been devised to link the line with the railway being built between North and South Korea to provide a fast freight route to Europe.

A further development is the Kazakhstan State-owned railway which plans to build a Trans-Kazakhstan railway link of 3943 km. It will operate between Urumqi (China), going west through Kazakhstan, Turkmenistan and Iran, all the way to Germany. It will reduce the transit time from seven to three days and open up the markets between China, Iran and Turkey. It will take seven years to construct. Currently (2005) investors are being sought.

ASEAN transport leaders are planning a new railway link between Singapore and Kunming called the Trans Asia Rail Link to cater for the trade growth following the liberalization of trade measures to take effect in 2005 under the Asean Free Trade Area agreements. In South Korea a new high speed cargo railway system has been built between Uiwang in the Gyeonggi Province – the country's largest inland container depot – to Busan South Korea's largest port city. In 2003 the government of Thailand announced an ambitious railway modernization plan focused particularly on freight traffic and increased line capacity through double tracks to cater for container growth through the ports.

Many landlocked countries in sub Saharan Africa rely primarily on road between the ports and inland destinations. Limited rail traffic in these countries is due to the lack of maintenance and investment as found on the Abidjan-Ouagodougou line and Cameroonian railways that are operated by Delmas. However, it is planned shortly to have privatized railway networks in Kenya, Uganda and Tanzania. In contrast the European railway network is in continuous process to develop new high speed lines and increase capacity especially in France, Germany, Netherlands, Belgium, Switzerland and the Iberian peninsula. For example, the first rail link in Europe, the Betuwe route, designed exclusively for freight traffic will be operational in 2005 between Rotterdam, Duisburg, Basel and Copenhagen. It involves the provision of a 160 km-long rail network in the Netherlands connected to the German railway system. This will enable the port of

Rotterdam to operate container rail services to the ports of Duisburg (p. 57) Basel and Copenhagen. Likewise, in North America the railway network is increasing its capacity on its West/East coast tracks to cater for the growth of double stack container train services (p. 72).

To conclude, today's modern railway system is capable of providing a high capacity form of transport operating on a disciplined, controlled, reliable and exclusive artificial way. Economically, it provides the most efficient land use of a transport network and is environmentally friendly.

Recommended reading

Annual report of EuroTunnel.
Annual report of Port of Rotterdam.

Characteristics of international transport modes: 2

4.1 Containerization

Containerization is a method of distributing merchandise in a unitized form thereby permitting an inter-modal transport system to be evolved providing a possible combination of rail, road, canal and maritime transport. The system is long established and was in being at the turn of the century, albeit in a somewhat modified form to that which exists today. It became particularly evident in the North American coastal trade in the 1930s when the vessels were called 'Van ships'.

By 2005 we had five 8100 TEU capacity ships operated by the China Shipping Container Lines. The deployment of such tonnage is restricted to the main east–west mainline routes owing to the volumes required to fill such vessels. An alternative would be to use these very large vessels to call exclusively at a few very large transhipment hubs at both ends of the route. Alternatively on the basis of diminishing economies of scale above the 2500 to 3500 TEU size would be direct services with smaller vessels calling at multiple ports at both ends of the route. Large carriers operating along main line routes espouse the former view and are progressively relying on dedicated transhipment terminals and feeder services provided by their subsidiaries. In South East Asia a number of regional carriers such as Samudera Shipping Line, Regional Shipping Line, and Pacific International Lines favour the second view. These lines, which provide feeder services notably from Singapore to a number of countries with relatively undeveloped land-based transport networks, have also started to provide direct services at multiple ports scattered in the region. A significant initiative relating to container operators serving the US ports is the logistic culture being developed (p. 72).

The growth of containerization will continue throughout the next decade, emerging from three sectors: (a) the transfer from the bulk cargo division, particularly the reefer, dry bulk, and fruit carriers; (b) organically as the benefits of containerization through multi-modalism and logistic focus accelerate trade development; and (c) the outsourcing/relocation of industrial production from high labour cost, highly regulated developed economies in Europe and North America to lower cost, less regulated developing economies in the Far East and China/India.

The massive growth in the world container trade during the past decade has been manifest in three areas:

(a)   the remodelling of container schedules embracing the hub and spoke concept – this often involved the formation of operating alliances among carriers;

(b)   the investment in ports and terminals exceeding US$30 billion during the past five years providing an extra 100 million TEU handling capacity and an extra 200 terminals involving the continued expansion of the hub and spoke system; and

(c)   the growth in world container fleet. In 1970 it represented 0.9 per cent of the world tonnage which rose to 9.8 per cent in 2002. By 2003 there were 2890 ships with a total capacity of 5 896 154 TEUs, an increase of 4.9 per cent in the number of ships and 10.1 per cent in TEU capacity over the previous year. Ship sizes also continued to increase, with average carrying capacity per ship growing from 1824 TEUs in 2001 to 2040 TEUs in 2003 reflecting the building of larger vessels to achieve economies of scale. Vessels over 3000 TEUs capacity made up 67 per cent of total deliveries of cellular tonnage for 2002, and 79.8 per cent of the order book.

The concentration process of recent years is resulting in increased carrying capacity being deployed by the largest liner operators. Table 4.1 indicates over a one year period, ended 30th September 2002, that the top ten liner operators increased their carrying capacity by 14 per cent to 3.4 million TEUs – 43.9 per cent of the world total container carrying capacity. Similarly, the share of the top 20 liner operators increased by 12.1 per cent to 4.8 million TEUs – 61.8 per cent of the world total carrying capacity. A clear indication of industry consolidation is the single new entry into the list of the top 20 carriers.

The growth of containerization is further stimulated by the accelerating expansion of the integration of containerized shipping movement with either air freight or a rail land-bridge. An example of the land-bridge is the North American double-stack container trains between the west and east coast ports (p. 72), and Dubai and Singapore (p. 110) offer an example of the air freight bridge to Europe involving cargoes from the Far East. Furthermore, the development of the high-cube container market continues to expand to meet the growing business needs of the high-cube low-weight ratio cargoes such as garments, foodstuffs and light machinery, especially those goods originating from the Far East. This involves containers of 13.75 m (45 ft), 14.65 m (48 ft) and 16.20 m (53 ft) length and 2.9 m (9 ft 6 in) in height (p. 112).

TABLE 4.1 Leading 20 container service operators as of 30 September 2002 on the basis of number of ships and total shipboard capacity (TEUs)[a]

Ranking	Operator	Country/territory	No. of ships in 2002	TEU capacity in 2002	TEU capacity in 2001[b]
1	A.P. Moller Group	Denmark	312	773 931	693 237
2	MSC	Switzerland	183	413 814	296 064
3	P&O Nedlloyd	UK/Netherlands	160	406 654	380 009
4	Evergreen Group	Taiwan Province of China	143	403 932	348 650
5	Hanjin/DSR-Senator	Republic of Korea/ Germany	81	304 409	299 490
6	COSCO	China	140	255 937	228 060
7	NOL/APL	Singapore	71	227 749	244 848
8	CMA-CGM Group	France	107	225 436	176 278
9	MOL	Japan	68	188 326	144 014
10	CP Ships Group	Canada	92	187 890	160 206
Total 1–10			1357	3 388 078	2 970 856
11	NYK	Japan	73	177 700	169 921
12	K Line	Japan	56	168 413	151 945
13	Zim	Israel	77	164 350	117 293
14	OOCL	Hong Kong (China)	50	157 493	144 450
15	China Shipping	China	88	148 212	128 387
16	Hapag Lloyd	Germany	38	135 953	114 827
17	Hyundai	Republic of Korea	32	122 713	140 979
18	Yang Ming	Taiwan Province of China	40	120 319	125 207
19	PIL Group	Singapore	83	97 827	90 000[c]
20	CSAV	Chile	39	90 625	91 803
Total 1–20			1933	4 763 013	4 245 668
World fleet	estimated at 1 July 2002			7 713 000	7 067 000

[a] All subsidiaries are consolidated.
[b] As of September 2001.
[c] Estimated.

Source: UNCTAD secretariat, compiled on the basis of data from *Containerization International*, issues November 2002 page 45 and January 2003 page 12; and ISL issue August/September 2002 page 26.

Reproduced by kind permission of UNCTAD

Details of the leading 20 ports of the world handling containers are featured in Table 4.2. There were ten ports of developing countries and territories and socialist countries of Asia with the remaining ten located in market-economy countries. Of the latter, there were six in Europe, three in the United States and one in Japan. Overall, traffic in these top-twenty ports

TABLE 4.2 Top 20 container terminals and their throughput, 2002 and 2001 (Millions of TEUs and percentage change)

Port	TEUs 2002	TEUs 2001	TEUs 2000	2002/2001	2001/2000
Hong Kong, China	18.61	17.90	18.10	3.97	−1.10
Singapore	16.94	15.52	17.04	9.15	−8.92
Busan	9.33	8.07	7.54	15.61	7.03
Shanghai	8.62	6.34	5.61	35.96	13.01
Kaoshiung	8.49	7.54	7.43	12.60	1.48
Shenzhen	7.61	5.08	3.99	49.80	27.32
Rotterdam	6.52	6.10	6.28	6.89	−2.87
Los Angeles	6.11	5.18	4.88	17.95	6.15
Hamburg	5.37	4.69	4.25	14.50	10.35
Antwerp	4.78	4.22	4.01	13.27	5.24
Long Beach	4.52	4.46	4.60	1.35	−3.04
Port Klang	4.53	3.76	3.21	20.48	17.13
Dubai	4.19	3.50	3.06	19.71	14.38
New York	3.75	3.32	3.00	12.95	10.67
Quingdao	3.10	2.64	2.12	17.42	24.53
Bremenhaven	3.03	2.90	2.71	4.48	7.01
Gioia Tauro	2.99	2.49	2.65	20.08	−6.04
Manila	2.87	2.80	2.87	2.50	−2.44
Tokyo	2.83	2.77	2.96	2.17	−6.42
Felixstowe	2.80	2.80	2.80	0.00	0.00
Total top 20	126.99	112.08	109.11	13.30	2.72

Source: *Containerization International*, March 2003, and *Port Development International*, April 2003.
Reproduced by kind permission of UNCTAD

increased by 13.3 per cent, much higher than the 2.2 per cent recorded for all world ports and confirmed the trend towards traffic concentration. The top 20 ports for 2002 recorded a total of 127 million TEUs, which is equivalent to 53.6 per cent of the world throughput (48.4 per cent in 2001).

During 2002 China's top ten container ports recorded a 35 per cent increase in traffic to 30.3 million TEUs. Shanghai recorded 8.62 million TEUs, overtaking for the first time Kaoshiung (Taiwan Province of China) which recorded 8.49 million TEUs. Hong Kong (China) again took the top place among container ports worldwide, reaching 18.6 million TEUs. The second Chinese container port, Shenzhen, located close to Hong Kong (China), recorded 7.6 million TEUs in 2002, a 50 per cent increase from the previous year's traffic. The foregoing demonstrates the growth in Chinese trade as recorded in Table 1.7 (p. 12).

A further development in container tonnage arises with the post Panamax vessel. Hitherto, due to the limitation on canal width, vessels were restricted to a 4600 TEU capacity. Today, new builds exceed 5800 TEUs which has enhanced the productivity of the Panama Canal trade route.

Undoubtedly, long-term containerization will be virtually the only method of general merchandise distribution in major deep-sea trades, and already some 90 per cent of such trades are containerized. These developments have heralded a new era in international trade distribution to both the small and large exporter. The exporter may use a complete ISO (International Standards Organisation) container (full container load – FCL) or despatch his merchandise to a container base or an inland clearance depots (ICD) for it to be consolidated with other compatible cargo en route to a similar destination country or area for despatch as a less than container load (LCL).

Features of containerization can conveniently be summarized as follows:

1.   It permits a door-to-door service which may be from the factory production site to the retail distributor's store – an overall distance of some 6000 km. Or it may be an FCL or LCL movement.
2.   No intermediate handling at terminal transhipment points, namely rail/road terminals or seaport.
3.   Low risk of cargo damage and pilferage enables more favourable cargo premiums to be obtained compared with break-bulk cargo shipments and individual airfreight consignments.
4.   The absence en route of intermediate handling plus quicker sea transits compared with break-bulk cargo shipments permits less risk of damage and pilferage.
5.   Elimination of intermediate handling at maritime terminal transfer points, that is, seaports, enables substantial dock labour savings to be made. In industrial countries, where there is a high income *per capita,* this can realize considerable financial savings.
6.   Less packing needs for containerized consignments. In some cases, particularly with specialized ISO containers such as refrigerated ones or tanks (liquid or powder), no packing is required. This produces substantial cost savings and raises service quality.
7.   The elimination of intermediate handling coupled with the other inherent advantages of containerized shipments tends to permit the cargo to arrive in a better condition thereby enhancing the quality of service.
8.   Emerging from the inherent advantages of containerization, rates are likely to remain more competitive. A significant reason is that containerization is, in the main, a capital-intensive transport network, compared with the individual consignment distribution system which tends to be more labour intensive. This is particularly so with maritime container distribution which has produced substantial labour cost savings.

9. Maritime container transits are much quicker compared with break-bulk cargo. This is usually achieved through a combination of circumstances, namely faster vessels, a rationalization of ports of call and substantially quicker transshipments. For example, the Europe to Tokyo sailing time is 24 days.

10. As a result of faster transits and the advantages under items (7) and (8), containerization encourages trade development and permits quicker payment of export invoices.

11. Maritime containerization has permitted maritime fleet rationalization producing substantial capital cost replacement savings as fewer ships are needed. However, these ships must be more intensely operated and of an overall larger capacity. On average, one container ship – usually of much increased capacity and faster speed – has displaced up to ten break-bulk cargo vessels on deep-sea services. This development has been facilitated by the rationalization of ports of call. Overall, a container vessel spends less than 10 per cent of her time in port.

12. Container vessels attain much improved utilization and generally are very much more productive than the break-bulk tonnage.

13. Faster transits, usually coupled with more reliable maritime schedules and ultimately increased service frequency, is tending to encourage many importers in selective shipping trades to hold reduced stocks and spares. This produces savings in warehouse accommodation needs, lessens the risks of obsolescent stock and reduces importers' working capital. It exploits the benefits of the 'just-in-time' concept and improves inventory stock control and warehouse management results. These are good selling points to be borne in mind by the shipper when deciding on the mode of transport to be used.

14. Containerization produces quicker transits and encourages the rationalization of ports of call. This, in many trades, is tending to stimulate trade expansion through much improved service standards. This is resulting in increased service frequency which will aid trade development.

15. Provision of through documentation or combined transport bill of lading, involving a common code of liability for the through transit.

16. Provision of a through rate. For example, this embraces both the maritime and surface transport cost of the ISO container. Again, this aids the marketing of the container concept.

17. More reliable transits – particularly disciplined controlled transit arrangements in maritime schedules. Most major container ship operators have computer equipment to facilitate the booking, stowage, and control of containers throughout the transit.

18. New markets have emerged through container development and its inherent advantages.

19. Maritime containerization is a capital-intensive project and as such is beyond the financial limit of many shipowners.

20. Not all merchandise can be conveniently containerized. However, the percentage of such traffic falls annually as new types of maritime containers are introduced.
21. Maritime containerization has greatly facilitated the development of consolidated or break-bulk consignments. This particularly favours the small exporter unable to originate a full container load which is consolidated through a container base.
22. Containerization facilitates the maximum use of computerization in many areas, especially container control, customer billing, container stowage in the vessel, documentation processing, and so on.
23. The international maritime container network expands annually as ports/berths are modernized, together with their infrastructure. This involves the development of the dry port such as Ipoh (p. 10); the development of new container berths; the relocation of container berths to accommodate larger vessels such as in the ports of Bangkok and Klang; the development of air freight and land-bridges (p. 114); electronic data interchange (p. 446); the development of feeder services to serve the major ports; and the new generation of high-capacity containers (p. 76). All these factors improve the 'value added benefit' which the shippers obtain from the use of the container network.

There is no doubt multi-modalism (Chapter 5) and logistics (Chapter 6) are driving the accelerated growth of containerization together with the fast expanding hub and spoke system. Countries which are not part of the global container network will be severely disadvantaged in terms of their growth and development.

4.2 Container distribution

The world container fleet in 2003 has a capacity of 5 896 154 TEUs which is served by a ratio of 2.5 for every TEU tonnage slot. Production annually varies and in 2002 reached 1.6 million TEUs of which the largest share, 50 per cent, was for lessors. China was the predominant manufacturer responsible for 87 per cent with Europe totalling 6 per cent. The annual level of production depends on many factors with new build and replacement containers as major factors. For example, demand for new slots in the container fleet in 2002 was 0.1 million TEUs. Lessors and carriers contributed to the demand as they replaced obsolete boxes and this totalled 0.7 million TEUs or 46 per cent of production.

Most production was for the standard dry freight container which represented 1.3 million TEUs in 2002. The balance is made up of integral reefer containers, dry freight specials, tank containers and non-ISO containers adapted to the special needs of the European (i.e. wide bodies) and North American markets.

In 2002 the fleet of leased dry freight containers was seven million TEUs. For other types of leased boxes – such as tanks, reefers, open tops and open side boxes – the variation of fleet sizes/specification reflected different market demands. In recent years lessors tend to expand their supply of high cube reefers while reducing their fleets of regular reefers, tanks and open top and open sided boxes. This trend was consistent with the annual production of the respective special boxes. Lessors acquire about a quarter of the total of the special boxes annually. The carriers' strategy varies and in 2002 shipowners preferred to lease rather than purchase new boxes as freight rates improved only marginally during most of the year (p. 5). The lease price is determined by the container type, the length of lease – one or more years – and the route it will ply. Some routes generate a high intensive user while others are less intensive.

A key factor is the control systems in place to marshal and monitor the container as found in the electronic tracking of the system (p. 342). The need is to reduce to a minimum the period/transits of empty container movement. It is a major problem and embraces the repositioning of empty containers. It is very costly and arises through economic and political developments. The Far East currency crisis has exacerbated the situation. It is a long-term problem and varies with trade route and container type. In the Europe-Far East trade – heavy cargo – raw materials and semi finished goods are imported in 6.10 m (20 ft) containers, while Asia exports light cargo – consumer goods in 12.20 m (40 ft) containers. Repositioning the containers or transporting them to the right place is costly and reduces profit margins both on shipping lines and leasing companies.

A number of possible solutions exist:

1. The container owner shifts the boxes to where they are most needed at the lowest possible cost. This may involve despatching them by a circuitous route, adopting a policy of cabotage, or renting them out at a reduced rate or even lending them free of charge.
2. The lease company prefers the container to be returned to a strategic location, so the return location is written into the contract, even if it is a five-year contract. This strategy also influences the lease price.
3. In situations where a serious imbalance arises as in the Far East trade, the best option is to charter shipping space to reposition the boxes.

A case study of the Port of Rotterdam manifests the problem. An analysis of the data below focuses on the situation in 1997 which was worsened by the Far East currency crisis.

To:	Rotterdam empty containers		
From:	Europe	24.4 per cent	(270 250)
	Africa	55.9 per cent	(31 000)
	North America	7 per cent	(29 500)

	Central and South America	25.5 per cent	(38 250)
	Middle East	30.8 per cent	(14 750)
	Asia	7.8 per cent	(84 750)
From:	Rotterdam empty containers		
To:	Europe	9.2 per cent	(106 000)
	Africa	6.2 per cent	(4 500)
	North America	9.5 per cent	(36 750)
	Central and South America	12.9 per cent	(11 000)
	Middle East	5.2 per cent	(6 250)
	Asia	8.7 per cent	(72 000)

Because Europe has always exported more containers than it imports, Rotterdam has acted as both supply source and store port for empty containers; thus fulfilling a balancing function in empty container logistics. The position is worsened as over 50 per cent of the container movements are empty within Europe. Rotterdam has 15 depôts which can store about 25 000 containers to meet the increasing demand in the European hinterland. Rotterdam also stores feeder containers for smaller ports that have no depôts themselves such as Norway. Empty containers are consigned to a port as without these empties there would be no full ones.

A number of areas are being examined to reduce box repositioning. The Internet provides the opportunity to match supply with demand in a revolution in the method of working in transport and logistics. The interchange of containers between shipowners and leasing companies does offer flexibility and optimizes use of containers and equipment. Central planning units and collaborative agreements among carriers and owners present a further solution. All the foregoing concepts are in the process of operation and development, often based on a localized port or trade. Overall, it improves profit margins and ship productivity, as is evidenced in the Port of Rotterdam which is applying these strategies.

Finally, it is important to stress that containers represent a huge capital investment globally. Prices fluctuate significantly. Table 4.3 focuses on container prices in China. Average prices for new built containers in China bottomed in the first quarter of 2002, after declining during 2001. The drop between the first quarter of 2001 and that of 2002 was around 22 per cent across all the regions. During 2002 prices increased and by the third quarter they were up 17 per cent from the levels that had prevailed at the beginning of the year. There were several reasons for the price increases. Manufacturers operating at reduced capacity since 2001 were reluctant to raise production to full capacity in view of the evolution of the shipping market. The delay in increasing production resulted in declines in inventory, which partially explains the increase. The cost of container manufacturing also increased as prices of intermediate and raw materials which were at their lowest level as a result of a fall in box production in 2001, increased owing to their limited availability (i.e. corten Steel and plywood).

TABLE 4.3 Container prices in China *(in $)*

Period	China – Central			China – South			China – North		
	20ft	*40ft*	*40ft HC*	*20ft*	*40ft*	*40ft HC*	*20ft*	*40ft*	*40ft HC*
1Q-2001	1 480	2 370	2 485	1 520	2 430	2 555	1 540	2 465	2 585
4Q-2001	1 350	2 160	2 270	1 380	2 210	2 320	1 400	2 240	2 350
1Q-2002	1 150	1 840	1 930	1 180	1 890	1 980	1 180	1 890	1 980
3Q-2002	1 350	2 160	2 270	1 380	2 210	2 320	1 400	2 240	2 350

Source: *Containerization International*, August 2002, and *Containerization International Yearbook 2002*. Reproduced by kind permission of UNCTAD

Container lease rates also bottomed in the first quarter of 2002 in conjunction with the low level of container leases – only 303 302 TEUs, as compared with 680 932 TEUs the previous year. In the following months of 2002, lease rates improved owing to carrier demand, with carriers preferring to lease rather than purchase new boxes as freight rates improved (p. 10) only marginally during most of the year. In fact, re-hiring aged boxes and idle boxes accumulated in low demand areas was preferred by many carriers. As demand and prices for new boxes increased, lease rates and the number of leases improved slightly. By the start of 2002, the fleet of leased dry freight containers stood at little more than seven million TEUs. For other types of leased boxes – such as tanks, reefers, open top and open sided boxes – the variation of fleet sizes reflected different market demands. For the period 2000–2003 lessors chose to expand their supply of high-cube reefers, while reducing their fleets of regular reefers, tanks, and open top and open-sided boxes. This trend was consistent with the annual production of the respective special boxes. Lessors acquire about a quarter of the total of the special boxes produced every year.

4.3 Container types

It would be appropriate to examine the size and types of both ISO and International Air Transport Association (IATA) containers, which now follows.

The range of ISO container types tends to expand annually to meet the increasing market demands on this fast-growing primarily deep-sea international method of distributing merchandise. Basically, the majority of containers used are built to ISO specification thereby permitting their ease of ubiquitous use on an international scale. Many of the containers are built to a standard outlined by one of the major ship classification societies such as Lloyd's Register of Shipping. The basic container most commonly built of steel or aluminium modual size is 2.45 m (8 ft) × 2.45 m (8 ft) but there exist some of 2.45 m (8 ft) × 2.60 m (8 ft 6 in) which tend to be applicable to the North American trade. Their length is 3.05 m (10 ft), 6.10 m (20 ft), 9.15 m (30 ft), 10.70 m (35 ft), or 12.20 m (40 ft). The 3.05 m (10 ft) and 10.70 m (35 ft) are not very common and the former is usually found in the short sea trades.

The most popular size is the 6.10 m (20 ft) or 12.20 m (40 ft) length with a module of either 2.45 m (8 ft) × 2.60 m (8 ft 6 in) or 2.45 m (8 ft) × 2.45 m (8 ft). More recently, containers of a module of 2.45 m (8 ft) × 2.75 m (9 ft) or 2.45 m (8 ft) × 2.90 m (9 ft 6 in) have emerged but their use is limited due to the extra height clearance, particularly by rail. The 6.10 m (20 ft) and 12.20 m (40 ft) length containers with a module of 2.45 m (8 ft) × 2.45 m (8 ft) have a cubic capacity of 30 m^3 and 66.5 m^3 and a maximum load weight of 18 000 kg and 27 070 kg respectively. The 2.45 m^3 (8 ft) × 2.60 m (8 ft 6 in) module have a cubic capacity of 31 m^3 and 68.1 m^3, with a maximum load capacity of 18 720 kg and 27 580 kg. In some countries, the 12.20 m (40 ft) container cannot be used to the full capacity due to road weight restrictions. An increasing number of the 6.10 m (20 ft) containers currently built have a maximum load weight of 21 600 kg, and the 12.20 m (40 ft) have a maximum 32 210 kg load weight (see Figure 4.1).

Cargo is usually stowed in the air freighter under a unit load device (ULD). This may involve a pallet, container or igloo. Details of the range of ULD used on the Boeing 737F (cargo capacity, 16 tonnes) and 747F (cargo capacity, 102 tonnes) are given in Table 4.6. These containers are used by Lufthansa Boeings 737F and 747F, and similar pallets and containers are used by other major air freight carriers. The 6.10 m (20 ft) and 3.05 m (10 ft) containers may be used for combined transport schedules which is a growth market in air freight consolidation.

The Shipping Companies and Container Leasing Companies are very conscious of the need to keep ahead of the market requirement. An example is the high-cube container (HCC) which has a height in excess of 2.59 m, a length over 12.19 m and width over 2.44 m. The increased cube has been designed to meet strong market needs to despatch more economically worldwide the expanding range of commodities which have a high volume and low weight ratio. These include light machinery, foodstuffs, furniture and so on. Such markets are very strong in the Orient where low-cost labour, aggressive marketing and high technology have facilitated a major export region for such products.

The container specifications tend to fall into the following categories:

Height (m)	Width (m)	Length (m)
2.90	2.59	12.19
2.90	2.59	14.93
2.90	2.59	16.15

The cost benefits of the high-cube and oversize containers include a reduction in the number of boxes handled, attained through higher load

FIGURE 4.1 Container types

(a) 20 ft platform flat (bolster) – 40 ft size available – for building materials, vehicles, indivisible loads, lumber, etc.

(b) 20 ft half height with ramp end door – tarpaulin roof – for heavy loads, building materials.

(c) 20 ft open top – 40 ft size available – for large awkward items such as machinery – tarpaulin roof for water tight integrity – door header swings to assist loading of high items.

(d) 40 ft refrigerated container with integral refrigeration machinery for chilled and frozen cargoes.

(e) 20 ft spring assisted folding end flat rack – 40 ft size available – can be provided with built in interlocking mechanism for multiple empty transportation.

(f) 20 ft covered container – 8 ft 6 in high – 40 ft available.

FIGURE 4.1 *continued*

(g) 20 ft bulk container for grain, powders, etc.

(h) 7.15 m swap body with demountable legs – 2.5 m width for two pallet wide European operation.

(i) 40 ft high cube 9 ft 6 in high – 45 ft also available – for cargoes that cube out.

(j) 20 ft ventilated container for cargoes such as coffee and cocoa that experience condensation damage.

(k) 40 ft sea deck style combination flat rack and platform flat – 20 ft size available for large items of machinery, construction equipment, etc.

(l) 20 ft tank container for bulk hazardous and non-hazardous liquids.

Reproduced by kind permission of Sea Containers

factor. Also under certain tariff conditions, the port handling charges per unit of product may be reduced. There is reduction in the number of container movements in the port area, which reduces road congestion in the area; and fewer boxes will reduce the level of documentation and administration, and overall distribution costs will fall, thereby permitting a lower market price.

The development of the high-cube and oversize container will have a profound effect on the international distribution infrastructure. This involves container ship specification, including lifting apparatus, port equipment and straddle carriers, fork lift trucks, gantry cranes, road transport trailers, railway wagons and the relative regulations.

The trade in which they feature strongly is primarily based in the Orient, especially the ports of Hong Kong, Japan and Singapore and the feeder ports they serve, and it involves the seaboards of North America and Europe.

A wide range of ISO containers exists today and the more common ones are detailed in Figure 4.1. A brief description of container types is given below:

1. The dry freight container and (formerly called) general purpose container, is ideal for both the FCL and LCL markets. It is designed for all types of general merchandise and, with suitable modification, for the carriage of bulk cargoes both solid and liquid. It is available in 20 ft, 40 ft, and 40 ft hi-cube sizes. Additionally, there is the 45 ft hi-cube container designed to carry similar products as the 40 ft, but with much greater cargo volume. It is the world's most widely used container for the movement of general cargo.

2. Insulated containers protect against heat loss or gain and are used in conjunction with a blown-air refrigeration system to convey perishable or other cargo which needs to be carried under temperature control. An ideal container for the movement of foodstuffs which is a rapidly expanding international market.

3. The fruit container has been developed to carry fresh deciduous and citrus fruit, the internal dimensions being slightly larger than the standard insulated container to accommodate the packing of standard fruit pallets and cases.

4. Refrigerated containers are designed to operate independently of a blown-air refrigerated system and are fitted with their own refrigeration units which require an electrical power supply for operation. Each container is capable of being set at its own individual carriage temperature. Ideal for meat, dairy products and fruit. GE SeaCo are container market leaders and have a refrigerated lessor fleet of over 100 000 available in 20 ft, 40 ft, and 40 ft hi-cube for shipment of perishable and frozen cargoes. The containers embrace the latest design and construction methods; hi-grade stainless steel on exterior panels;

TABLE 4.4 Range of ULD on Boeing 737F and 747F

Container type	Loading capacity			Tare weight (max.) (kg)	Cubic capacity	Max. load	Description
	Length (cm)	Height (cm)	Width (cm)				
6.10 m (20 ft) container with ISO fittings	594	230	228	1000	33.0	10 340	The container is loaded through a double-wing door located on its front panel. Customs seals may be obtained. Surface transport is possible. Built-in garment racks are provided
3.05 m (10 ft) container	293	237	220	255	16.5	6 549	The container is made entirely of light-weight metal. The container is loaded through a double-folded door or an opening (closed by a net and tarpaulin). Customs seals may be obtained for international cargo. Built-in garment racks are provided
LD 7 container-igloo shell	294	153	200	225	9.6	5 808	The igloo shell is affixed to the pallet. The load opening is closed with a net and tarpaulin. Surface transport is possible. Built-in garment racks are provided. It is also available as a refrigerated container
LD 3 container	146	160	144	80	4.0	1 508	The container consists of a box-type construction of light metal. The opening is closed by a flexible door of coated fabric plastic. Built-in garment racks are provided. It is also available as a refrigerated container
Pallet	592	230	–	–	–	–	The pallet consists of an aluminium case (the loading surface) and surrounding sectional frame

Type					Description
Car transport	485	—	230	—	—	The pallet consists of an aluminium case (the loading surface) and surrounding sectional frame. Additionally, it features special tie-down tracks for securing car transport racks and wheel lashing belts
Pallet	304	—	230	—	—	The pallet consists of an aluminium case (the loading surface) and surrounding sectional frame
Pallet	304	—	210	—	—	The pallet consists of an aluminium case (the loading surface) and surrounding sectional frame. Installed in the frame is a tie-down track on which pallet nets, tension belts and lashing rings are secured. For better utilization of lower-deck capacity the pallets in the standard 304 cm length can be equipped with side extensions
Pallet	304	—	139	—	—	The pallet consists of an aluminium case (the loading surface) and surrounding sectional frame. Installed in the frame is a tie-down track on which pallet nets, tension belts and lashing rings are secured. For better utilization of lower-deck capacity the pallets in the standard 304 cm length can be equipped with side extensions
Container – for 3 horses – open with front doors	208	208	228	510	3 horses	An aluminium assembly on a 304 cm × 210 cm pallet. The watertight floor pan and ramp are equipped with slip-proof, noise clamping floor covering. The horses' head area features bite-guards and tarpaulins; inner walls are padded

corrosive resistant hot-zinc-sprayed Corten steel frame, and for added resistance all exterior surfaces are primed and coated with thick gloss topcoat.

5. Bulk containers are designed for the carriage of dry powders and granular substances in bulk. To facilitate top loading three circular hatches (500 mm diameter) are fitted in some containers in the roof structure. For discharge a hatch is fitted in the right-hand door of the container.

6. Ventilated containers are broadly similar to the dry freight container specification except for the inclusion of full length ventilation galleries sited along the top and bottom side rails, allowing the passive ventilation of the cargo. Ideal for products such as coffee.

7. Flat rack containers are designed to facilitate the carriage of cargo in excess of the dimensions available in either dry freight or open top containers. Such containers have a collapsible end. A combination of two or more flat rack containers can be used to form a temporary break-bulk space for uncontainerable cargo moved on a port to port basis provided the total weight and point loading of the cargo does not exceed the static capabilities of the flat racks. Overall a container ideal for the carriages of oversized, awkward and heavy cargoes. Also described as platform flats. They are available in 20 ft and 40 ft sizes. Flat rack containers are ideal for trades where there is cargo in one direction and nothing in the other. The end walls are folded down and five units can be returned in one stack back to the point where the cargo is loaded.

8. Open top containers with their top loading facility are designed for the carriage of heavy and awkward shaped cargoes and those cargoes whose height is in excess of that which can be stowed in a dry freight container. It may also be described as an open sided/open top container. Tarpaulin tilts are available to protect the cargo. The container is ideal for sheet glass, timber and machinery. They are available in 20 ft and 40 ft sizes. The open top containers offer increased versatility over standard boxes and are designed for loading through both the top of the container and the doors.

9. The half height open top container is designed for the conveyance of heavy, dense cargoes such as steel, pipes, tubes, metal waste, ingots, copper bar, marble, stone and heavy drums. It is ideal for shippers whose premises have a restricted height for loading or discharge.

10. One of the most important developments in container technology in recent years came with the tank container. GE SeaCo remains the market leader and offers five types:

(a) The IMO type 1 for chemicals involving hazardous cargo and a capacity ranging from 12 000 litres to 35 000 litres.

(b) Lightweight tanks offering reduced tareweight for increased payload. Designed for a range of chemical and bulk liquids with a capacity of 21 000 litres.

(c) Food grade tanks for edible cargo with a gross weight of 34 000 kgs and tareweight of 3300 kgs.

(d) New insulated tanks for liquids which are non-heat sensitive with a gross weight of 34 000 kgs and tareweight of 3345 kgs.

(e) Special tanks for highly hazardous liquids and gases with a capacity ranging from 12 000 litres to 35 000 litres.

Overall, the tank container offers a safe and simple method of controlling cost while using a recyclable resource. On arrival the tank discharges directly into the production process, saving both valuable time and costly handling and heating charges. Shippers not only save time and money, but the tank unit provides up to 35 per cent additional cargo over drums in each ISO shipment, with wastage from drums through spillage or damage at an estimated 5 per cent per journey; annual savings are significant. Also other cost savings include the drum provision and its disposal in an environmentally conscious global society. The range of specialist tanks designed for particular applications also includes units for the transport of food-grade cargo intended for human consumption and for the safe carriage and storage of toxic and hazardous products.

11. Artificial between-deck containers are without end walls, side walls, or a roof and are also known as platform carriers. These units are used for oversize and overweight cargo which cannot otherwise be containerized. They are 6.10 m long and 2.4 m wide or 12.20 m long and 2.4 m wide.

12. The larger cube containers were introduced in the late 1980s and are used for dry cargo and equipped with removable beams in the upper part. They are used especially for garments on hangers and are very popular in some trades. The container is 12.20 m long, 2.4 m wide and 3.0 m high, or 6.10 m long, 2.4 m wide and 3.0 m high.

13. Bin containers have a cargo capacity of 21 600 kg and a tare weight of 2400 kg and a length of 6.06 m, a width of 2.44 m and a height of 1.30 m. They are ideal for heavy dense cargoes such as steel pipes.

14. Bolster flat containers have a capacity of 23 000 kg and a tare weight of 1040 kg, a length of 6.06 m, width 2.44 m and height 0.23 m. They are ideal for heavy cargoes.

15. The Stak bed container is a piece of equipment that offers the three-in-one capability of being a cargo platform (or flat), a fixed-end flatrack and a folding-end flatrack. It has vertical corner posts with horizontal bracing pieces. Recesses in the cargo platform permit the end-frame to stow when folded, flush with the deck, to provide an unrestricted surface area for cargo loading.

16. Sea Cell container has been recently developed by Sea Containers to meet the growth market needs of palletized cargo. The 6.10 m (20 ft) Sea Cell has 1.5 m^3 and the 12.20 m (40 ft) box 3 m^3 extra capacity and both carry 27 per cent more pallets than a standard box container. Overall, it is an intermodal extra-width container within a standard ISO frame. With corner castings at the usual locations, it can be lifted by any type of standard container-handling equipment and loaded into both cellular and non-cellular container ships providing complete intermodal capability. Unlike conventional dry freight boxes, Sea Cell container's unique side-wall corrugations extend beyond the frame width and are designed to allow Sea Cell pallets to be located side by side with other Sea Cell pallets or standard ISO boxes, even on the tightest 25 mm deck locations. This permits in a 20 ft Sea Cell container 14 (11), 40 ft 30 (25) and 45 ft 33 (27) pallets. Figures in parenthesis represent the conventional dry freight box. Each pallet is 1200 mm × 800 mm.

    To summarize, the Sea Cell is fully intermodal suitable for use on deep sea as well as short sea and overland; compatible with ISO container types from boxes to flat racks; cellular friendly for use in cellular and non-cellular ships, barges, and Ro-Ro vessels; easier to load and unload pallets than standard ISO container; increased cubic capacity; less damage to cargo and elimination of dunnage and lower operating costs.

17. Overseas military forces and peace keeping missions are much on the increase and are successfully meeting the challenges of out-of-area rapid deployment by supplying equipment from an extensive range of specialized containers. These include conventional units such as tanks, dry freight and refrigerated containers. These also feature side door containers and Quadcon and Tricon mini containers used by the US Military.

As we progress through the next decade, it is likely more container types will be introduced.

An example of a modern third-generation Ro-Ro container ship is operated by the Atlantic Container Line. It has a capacity of 2911 TEUs, and trailer lane capacity of 3839 m. Such a vessel is highly versatile in terms of the cargo mix, and conveys containers, road trailers, 20 ft (6.10 m) and 40 ft (12.20 m) dry vans, special heavy lift equipment for abnormal loads, extendable road trailers, railway rolling stock on road bogies, 12.20 m (40 ft) full high open-top trailers, 'U' beam frames on pier-to-pier trailers for steel products, block-stowed cargo such as logs, neo-bulk cargo on 6.10 m (20 ft) bolsters such as woodpulp and paper rolls, 6.10 m (20 ft) and 12.20 m (40 ft) flats and so on. Such a vessel exploits the advantages of combined transport. The vessel has a 52 000 dwt. and speed of 20 knots.

4.4 Container bases

The container base forms an important part of an integrated international transport system designed to link container terminals where ships are handled, with inland centres, using a rail system or road haulage distribution network. In some countries they are called container freight stations (CFSs). Usually they are under the management of a consortia of ship operators; a consortia of container operators engaged in the freight forwarding business; or a consortia comprising freight forwarders, road hauliers, etc. and others engaged in such businesses, e.g. a local port authority. It can be situated in the port itself, or the seaport or airport environs, or an industrial area which can support the facility in generating adequate quantities of containerized import/export traffic through it, involving both LCL and FCL. A summary of the services offered is given below:

1. Container handling and storage. A range of comprehensive container handling and storage facilities which cover all types, both loaded and empty, together with purpose-built stacking areas and on-site repair and maintenance resources for containers and related equipment.
2. Specialist cargo resources to handle dangerous cargo; consignments 'over height', 'over width' and 'out of gauge'; and container stowage of all types of cargo.
3. Export and import LCL. Container bases are used by consolidators NVOCCs particularly for the following needs or reasons: cargo handling; professional container packers; efficient de-vanning checking and customs clearance of imports; and quick vehicle turn-round when collecting or delivering cargo.
4. On-site customs clearance. Full customs and port health facilities including the CP system (p. 239) for computerized preparation and handling of customs entries. Such a customs facility enables any problem to be resolved quickly and locally, not at a seaport or airport distant from the importer's or exporter's premises.
5. Adequate security of the goods through on-site guards, CCTV, perimeter alarms and cargo systems and procedures.
6. FCL cargo handling. An increasing number of exporters and importers use the container base for the full container load.
7. Customs warehousing. This yields savings to the importer on VAT payment and import duty as the payment is only made when goods are withdrawn from the bonded warehouse.
8. Office accommodation for tenants using the container base on a regular basis.
9. Workshops for vehicle maintenance and repair, washing and steam-cleaning services for the containers.

10. A fully computerized system of services embracing customs, inwards/outward cargo 'check in'/'checkout'; accountancy; 'online' booking; electronic documentation transmission; interface with road/rail/airline/port operators; and a whole range of ancillary activities (Chapter 9).

The major advantages of container bases are to provide a service to the importer/exporter situated in the container base hinterland and relieve the port authority of local customs clearance of import/export cargoes. This latter advantage tends to reduce the problems of port congestion, that is, containers awaiting clearance due to non-availability of documents, and enables the throughput of the container berth to be maximized. Ultimately, it speeds up the transit, as no inordinate delay is usually experienced at the port, and thereby the development of international trade is encouraged. Undoubtedly, the number of container bases will increase as the container trade expands. Study Table 4.7: Shipper's check-list on p. 100.

4.5 Non-containerizable cargo

As we progress through the next decade the development of intermodalism will grow, especially in deep-sea shipping services. This involves the provision of a door-to-door service to the shipper.

An example of tonnage offering such a service is operated by the Atlantic Container Line. It involves the third-generation Ro-Ro container vessels conveying containers, Ro-Ro, trailers cars and non-containerizable cargo. The combined cellular and roll-on/roll-off vessels operate on Europe–North America trade and serve the ports of Bremerhaven, Gothenburg, Le Havre, Liverpool, Rotterdam, Baltimore, New York, Philadelphia, Portsmouth and Halifax (p. 94).

Non-containerizable cargo can be divided into four categories (Table 4.5). These are:

1. Rollable cargo with its own wheels or tracks that can be driven onboard or towed. Road vehicles and agricultural machinery are examples.
2. Cargo that is carried on trailers. This involves 'maafi' and heavy-duty trailers for pier-to-pier movements; flatbed trailers for door-to-door transportation; and trailers for the movement of exceptionally large or heavy loads door-to-door.
3. Special project cargo that requires experience and expertise to find a cost-effective solution. This includes, for example, the conveyance of trains in the Ro-Ro decks by laying rail lines into the ship; developed purpose-built road bogies to carry subway cars door-to-door and special extendable flatbed trailers for the carriage of 22 m (72 ft) long aircraft wings.

TABLE 4.5 Non-containerizable cargo

Rollable	Trailer/'maafi'	Special projects	Neo-bulk
Maximum weight varies according to machine. Items over 60 tonne (132 275 lb) are considered special projects. Please refer to the vessel's cargo specification on weight and dimension	Road Trailers for door-to-door transportation	The shipowner defines special projects as cargo where any one of the following dimensions is exceeded: L 12.19 m (40 ft) × W 3.05 m (10 ft) × H 3.05 m (10 ft), or where the weight exceeds 55 tonne (121 252 lb). Rollable cargo is classed as a special project when the weight exceeds 60 tonne (132 275 lb)	Maximum dimensions for a consignment loaded on a 6.10 m (20 ft) bolster are: L 6.10 m (20 ft) × W 2.43 m (8 ft) × H 2.59 m (8 ft 6 in). Payload maximum is 20 tonne (44 000 lb)
Items may be towed or driven under their own power into the ship	Consignments may be considered 'in gauge' where dimensions do not exceed L 12.19 m (40 ft) × W 2.43 m (8 ft) × H 2.59 m (8 ft 6 in)		Cargo may be loaded on a 6.10 m (20 ft) bolster or on a 12.20 m (40 ft) flatbed trailer. In some cases, the cargo may be blockstowed on the Ro-Ro decks of the ship
Cargo is normally delivered to the port of loading by the shipper or his agent and collected at the port of discharge by the consignee or his agent	Maximum payload without additional charges for 'in gauge' cargo is 18 tonne (39 682 lb). Heavier, indivisible loads can be carried, but prior arrangements and clearance must be obtained	Note that any cargo, regardless of weight which is exceptionally dense will require prior clearance before carriage by shipowner	Equipment may be loaded or discharged at the shipper's or consignee's factory, or at the ACL ocean terminal
The normal ship's securing system using chains, etc. is employed onboard the vessel	Normal available equipment is the 12.20 m (40 ft) flatbed trailer with side-pockets for stanchions	Roll trailers are available for payloads up to 55 tonne and 60 tonne; heavy duty trailers for up to 100 tonne and 180 tonne. Leased trailers, including drop frames, well trailers and extendables are available on a one trip basis from the shipowner	For inland transportation of door-to-door cargo on a 6.10 m (20 ft) bolster or a 12.20 m (40 ft) flatbed trailer, container rules apply
Shipowner does not supply tarpaulins	Equipment may be loaded or discharged at the shipper's or consignee's factory, or at the ACL ocean terminal		Web lashing, signode steel banding, tarpaulins and shrink-wrapping are used to secure the cargo. Tarpaulins are normally supplied by the trucker or shipper
	For inland transportation of 'in gauge' cargo normal container rules apply, but 'out of gauge' cargo requires prior clearance	Roll and heavy duty trailers are for pier-to-pier cargo only but leased trailers may move over the road with permits if required	
	Chains, nylon web lashing and signode banding may be used to secure the cargo	Securing is achieved by chains, steel banding, wire and bottlescrews (turnbuckles) as necessary	
	If required, tarpaulins must be supplied by the shipper or trucker	Shipowner does not supply tarpaulins	
	Shipowner does not supply tarpaulins		
	'Maffi' trailers for pier-to-pier transportation		
	The maximum dimensions of cargo should normally not exceed L 12.19 m (40 ft) × W 3.05 m (10 ft) × H 3.05 m (10 ft)		
	Normal maximum weight is 55 tonne (121 252 lb). Cargo in excess of this is considered a special project		
	Roll trailers are available to carry up to 20 tonne, 30 tonne, 40 tonne, 55 tonne and 60 tonne		

4.   Neo-bulk cargo, a term given to a wide range of staple products that can be efficiently carried in the Ro-Ro decks as unitized break-bulk (e.g. wood-pulp, board, paper, logs and steel). Details of the range of equipment used for non-containerizable cargo are given below and in Table 4.6:

Capacity (tonne)	Length (mm)	Width (mm)	No. of axles	Commentary
Roll trailers				
20	6 096	2438	1	Units with capacities of up to 180 tonne are available for pier-to-pier movements. Operational
30	12 190	2438	2 bogie	advantages include
40	12 190	2438	2 bogie	low timber surfaced cargo
55	12 190	2438	2 bogie	platforms, multi-wheel
60	12 190	2438	2 bogie	bogies for extreme
100	12 190	3048	4 bogie	manoeuvrability, separate
180	12 954	3454	8	lashing points for cargo and trailer, and high degree of stability, even when carrying oversize units.
20	12 190	2438	2	Special house-to-house trailers for through transport of machinery and other outsize and/or high cargo units. These are either owned by the shipper or available on lease. Special heavy-lift trailers for house-to-house movement of extra heavy loads available from shipowner.
Bolsters – flats without hardboards				
20	6 000	2438		This is a unit constructed with a strengthened floor which can be stowed from either the top, sides or ends.

The Ro-Ro container vessels are large and very flexible, with the ability to carry a variety of cargo mixes. The Ro-Ro decks incorporate hoistable car decks which can be raised or lowered according to market demand at the time. Even in the lowered position, the space underneath

TABLE 4.6 Types of cargo

Rollable	Trailer/'maafi'	Special projects	Neo-bulk
Tractors	Boats	Subway cars and rolling stock	Woodpulp
Backhoes	Yachts	Fixed-wing aircraft, Aircraft wings	Linerboard
Trucks	Machinery	Helicopters	Plywood
Cars	Linerboard	Forging machines and presses	Newsprint
Earthmovers	Cotton liner pulp	Crankshafts	Lumber
Mobile cranes	Flowerbulbs	Transformers	Waferboard
Combine harvesters	Mining shields	Boilers	Particle board
Buses	Hay balers	Pipe mills	Press board
Bulldozers	Specialized steel products	Dryers	Iron and steel products
Excavators	Crane parts	Press rolls	Logs
Wheel-loaders	Injection moulds	Steel rolls	
Trackloaders	Compressors	Converters	
Motorgraders	Cranes	Military vehicles	
Air compressors	Alternators	Street cars	
	Rotors	Oilrigs	
	Turbines	Earthmovers over 55 tonne	
	Constructionals	Railway locomotives	
		Ballast cleaners	
		Metal working machinery	
		Large boats and yachts	
		Long and wide loads	

these car decks allows the blockstowing of a wide range of neo-bulk commodities and the stowage of normal Ro-Ro cargo. With the car decks raised, the height permits the carriage of out-of-gauge Ro-Ro cargo, which can be on trailers or wheeled or tracked. Examples include heavy machinery, locomotives, yachts, aircraft, earthmovers, automobiles and caravans. Alternatively, blockstowing in several layers is possible and therefore a high utilization can be achieved in such tonnage.

The vessel is fitted with a 'jumbo angled stern ramp' which permits the simultaneous two-way movement of roll trailers and other Ro-Ro cargo. Loading and discharging of Ro-Ro or blockstowed cargo at the same time as cars is achieved by providing separate ramp systems within the vessel.

TABLE 4.7 Shipper's check-list

1. Name of Shipper	1. Name of Shipper	1. Name of Shipper	1. Name of Shipper
2. Name of Forwarder	2. Name of Forwarder	2. Name of Forwarder	2. Name of consignee
3. Name of Consignee	3. Name of Consignee	3. Name of Consignee	3. Type of commodity
4. Type of Commodity	4. Type of Commodity	4. Type of Commodity	4. Origin of cargo
5. Measurements of cargo	5. Dimensions of cargo	5. Dimensions of cargo	5. Port of loading
6. Weight of cargo	6. Weight of cargo	6. Weight of cargo	6. Final destination
7. Is it self-propelled? Is it wheeled or tracked?	7. Type of packing	7. Final destination	7. Port of discharge
8. Port of loading/ port of discharge	8. Date of shipment	8. Port of loading/ port of discharge	8. Projected volume/ per week/ per month/per year
9. Date of move	9. Origin of cargo	9. Date(s) of shipment	9. Measurement of cargo
10. Is shipowner to be involved on inlands distribution?	10. Port of loading	10. Is a drawing, shipping diagram or sketch plan available?	10. Weight of cargo
11. If wheeled: No. of wheels per axle No. of axles Distance between front axle and rear axle If tracked: Ground contact area of tracks (i.e. length and width actually on ground); internal distance between tracks	11. Final destination	11. Any additional information, for example, config-uration of cargo, configuration of base, accompa-nying cargo such as parts and accessories	11. Present method of transport
	12. Port of discharge		12. Inland arrangements
	13. Is cargo 'in gauge'? i.e. measurements do not exceed L 40 ft × W 8 ft × H 8 ft 6 in		13. Can cargo be double-stacked?
	14. Can shipper/ consignee accept 40 ft trailers at plant?		14. Does shipper/ consignee have clamp truck?
	15. Will cargo be loaded/discharged under cover?		15. Will cargo be loaded/discharged under cover?
			16. If woodpulp (a) are bales unitized? (b) are bales 6 or 8 packed?

4.6 Inland clearance depots

Inland clearance depots (ICDs) are situated at convenient points – usually in industrial and commercial areas outside the limits of any port or air-port. They are operated by a consortium or other approved body and provide facilities for the entry, examination and clearance of goods imported or exported in containers, railway train ferry wagons, unit loads or other approved methods. This facility has been inaugurated in recent years to reduce to a minimum the formalities that have to be observed at ship's side. It enables importers and exporters to gain full advantage of the use of such services as Ro-Ro vessels and containerization cargoes involving the trailer or container travelling under Customs Bond to and from the port. It may be road or rail borne. Overall the ICDs have taken over the traditional role of the conventional port, being served by customs facilities and sheds and accommodation for stuffing and stripping LCLs (less than container loads): shippers/consignees not having sufficient cargo to justify a full container load (FCL) can bring their traffics individually to the ICDs for consolidating, with other traffic into LCL containers for forwarding to/from the goods' ultimate destination/source.

It will be appreciated that the inland clearance depot is essentially a customs term used to identify where customs clearance facilities are provided away from the airport and seaport and for public use. Many are container freight stations dealing with exclusively containerized cargo, and others may be a freight village (p. 95) or dry port (p. 102); the Customs bond is usually TIR (Transport International Routier). They are usually managed by a consortium.

4.7 Dry ports

The development of multi-modalism internationally has seen the emergence of the inland situated dry port. Basically, it is a rail terminal located in an industrial and/or commercial region providing a direct rail link with one or more container ports. It is served by dedicated container trains with the import/export cargo being cleared by customs at the dry port. It handles both LCL/FCL cargoes and overall has all the facilities and logistics provided by the seaport. This includes cargo handling warehousing and open storage; port services documentation and clearance; shipping arrangements, for example freight arrangements; booking of cargo shipping space and through bills of lading; customs brokerage documentation and clearance; insurance; and cargo consolidation.

An example of a dry port is found at Ipoh which serves the ports of Klang (260 km) and Penang (180 km) in Malaysia. The project was developed by the Malayan railway and Port Klang and deals with LCL/FCL container export/import cargoes. The dry port of Ipoh acts as a multi-modal transport operator and provides a comprehensive service. This includes road transport to/from shippers' premises; booking of shipping space and provision of related documentation; road haulage to/from the dry port; and customs brokerage and freight forwarding thus avoiding the need to have agents at the port to handle the shippers' cargo. Daily dedicated container trains operate between Ipoh and the two ports completely integrating with the container shipping schedules and thereby providing a total service.

The dry port occupies an area of 6 ha embracing a container yard for heavy stacking, empty boxes and open storage; additionally, there are import and export sheds. Handling equipment includes fork lifts, cranes and container trailers. Ipoh is managed by the Malayan Railway and Port

Klang, while all the services are contracted out, including handling, freight forwarding, road haulage, customs, security and maintenance. A major factor in the success of the project is the unimpeded flow of containers to/from the two ports thereby speeding up the transit time. The dry port has made a major contribution to the acceleration of the industrial and commercial growth in the region of central Malaysia which it serves.

4.8 Sea transport

During the past 35 years, there has been a radical change in the techniques adopted in the distribution of international trade insofar as maritime transport is concerned. Moreover, the productivity of the world fleet – especially container tonnage – has significantly improved during the past decade. This is due to the economies of scale, larger ships, quicker port turnaround, better ship management and continuous investment in new technology. Overall, efficiency in maritime transport is essential in the continuous expansion of world trade. Basically, some 98 per cent of world trade in volume terms is conveyed by sea transport and the following developments have emerged since the mid-1960s which have aided a more economical distribution thereby encouraging the exploitation of the world resources:

1. Containerization displacing the conventional 'tween deck tonnage has transformed the international distribution of general merchandise introducing a door-to-door service. Moreover, it has substantially improved transit times and raised service quality. Progressively over the next few years the shipping industry will witness the gradual introduction of containerization in the remaining 10 per cent of the general cargo trades.
2. Ro-Ro services conveying road haulage vehicles on international transits again offer a door-to-door service. Likewise, the Ro-Ro service speeds up transits and has raised service standards. This mode of distribution is very popular in the short sea trades especially in the UK/Continental, UK/Irish, Scandinavian and the Mediterranean trades. A number of services have introduced the fast ferry such as found in the Italian and Greek seaboards.
3. Provision of numerous types of purpose-built specialized bulk cargo carriers. These include liquefied natural gas carriers (LNGs), vehicular carriers for shipment of trade cars, cab chassis, lorries, banana carriers, chemical tankers, etc. Moreover, existing long-established vessel types such as oil tankers, ore carriers, timber vessels, LNGs, have been dramatically improved in terms of their design with a particular emphasis on speed of handling, cargo transhipment, ship productivity and quick turn-round time in port.

4. To cater for the need to improve ship turn-round time, versatility of vessel employment, and to contain operating cost, an increasing number of vessels have been introduced, including combi carriers. This vessel is basically a unitized type of cargo carrier combining container and vehicular shipments, including Ro-Ro (p. 94).

5. The development of the multi-modal or combined transport service is very much on the increase (pp. 114–23). It entails the use of more than one mode of transport on a particular journey offered by a single operator acting as principal for the entire journey. The prime advantage is the door-to-door or warehouse-to-warehouse service.

6. Logistics and high technology is now driving container expansion coupled with the growing expansion of the hub and spoke global container network.

Sea transport is basically a capital-intensive method of distribution and involves vast investment sums. Consequently, the life of the ship spans some 15–20 years but, as vessels become more intensely used coupled with the advancement of marine engineering technology, the ship's life is tending to become 10–15 years. The problem facing the shipowner, and to a lesser degree other types of transport, is the degree of inflation inherent in ship replacement and the level of freight rates yield.

It is appropriate to mention that vessels generally in the past decade have tended to become modestly faster; of a much increased capacity; rather more specialized and purpose-built for particular cargoes; much more intensely used with overall rather small crew complements; more shipboard technology; much improved ship productivity; stronger interface in ship design involving shipowner, shipper/port operator and finally, offering a much improved quality of service. Moreover, full advantage is now being taken of computerization in all areas of international trade distribution involving electronic data interchange (EDI). All these factors have aided the development of international trade and in so doing have enabled sea transport to remain competitively priced. An examination of the more important types of vessels follows, but the reader who wishes to know more about these aspects should study Chapters 2, 3 and 4 of *Elements of Shipping* (8th edn.).

1. The oil tanker represents about one third of the world merchant fleet in deadweight capacity terms. In fact, some of the world's larger vessels are tankers, some of which exceed 500 000 dwt. Crude oil is transported from the oil fields to refineries, and petroleum and fuel oil from refineries to distribution centres and bunkering ports, so that there is a worldwide network of tanker routes. Vessels exceeding 200 000 dwt. are called very large crude carriers (VLCC) and those above 300 000 dwt. ultra large crude carriers (ULCC). Currently (2003), the world tanker fleet is going through a period of replacement involving the double hull tanker displacing the single hull vessel to comply with

the new safety ship-construction regulations as prescribed by the IMO. Such investment continues against a background of oil production growth and continuous investment in pipeline networks. However, the ULCC tonnage is in decline, primarily because of economic reasons.

2. Coasters are all-purpose cargo carriers operating around our coast.

3. A container vessel is basically a cellular vessel with crew and machinery situated aft. Each hold of a cellular ship is fitted with a series of vertical angle guides adequately crossbraced to accept the container. The seventh generation of container vessel has a capacity of 8100 TEUs (p. 76) and a speed of 25 knots. Details of major container operators are found in Table 4.1 and each operates through a hub and spoke system. Container ships represent 10 per cent of the world fleet (2004), compared with 8 per cent in 2001. The growth is aided by the post Panamax Container tonnage involving the Trans European Far East trade.

4. LASH. Lighter aboard the ship. This type of vessel enables lighters to be conveyed from one port to another thus combining inland waterway with ocean transportation. This type of vessel is in decline, overtaken by the development of multi-modalism.

5. LNG. The liquefied natural gas carrier fleet is an important part of the world mercantile fleet – and is a growth sector. This product is an important form of world energy. In 2004 the liquefied gas carrier fleet was 3 per cent of world tonnage compared with 2 per cent five years earlier. New ship design has much improved the productivity of LNGs.

6. OBO. Ore/bulk/oil ships are multi-purpose bulk carriers designed for switching between bulk shipments of oil/bulk grain, fertilizer and ore trades. Many such vessels exceed 200 000 dwt. This type of vessel is in decline due to the high maintenance/survey cost and inability of shipowners to find the round trip or triangle schedule of oil/ballast/ bulk dry cargo shipment. Owners prefer single commodity new build bulk cargo tonnage.

7. The single commodity bulk ore carrier represents a third of the world mercantile fleet and remains a growth market.

8. The chemical carrier world mercantile fleet tonnage remains at 1 per cent and is static.

9. Ro-Ro type vessels are designed to carry private cars with passengers, coaches, road haulage vehicles and non-motorist passengers. Such vessels are also termed multi-purpose vehicle ferries and operate in the UK-Continental, the Baltic and Mediterranean trades. The important feature of the Ro-Ro vessel is that the vehicles are driven on or off the ship by means of a ramp at the port/berth thereby permitting an unimpeded transhipment movement. This type of vessel has become very popular in the short sea trades around the world, especially in

the Mediterranean market; a large number of them are designed to convey only freight, involving the accompanied or unaccompanied trailer, containers, 'maafi', and 'out-of-gauge' indivisible loads conveyed on purpose-built trailers.

10. Train ferry vessels carry railway passenger and freight rolling stock. Access to and from the vessel is over a ramp thereby permitting an unimpeded transhipment offering through rail transits.

11. The 'tween deck vessel is a general cargo vessel engaged primarily on deep-sea liner cargo services. This type of vessel has other decks below the main deck called 'tween decks and all run the full length of the vessel. Currently, this type of vessel is being displaced in many trades by the container ship and combi-carrier. The Chinese and Indian fleets have a larger number of such vessels secured on the second-hand market. Currently (2005) the general cargo world mercantile Fleet represents 11 per cent and is declining annually.

12. The combi-carrier is a unitized cargo carrier combining container and vehicle shipment including Ro-Ro. It is tending to displace 'tween deck tonnage and is particularly ideal in Third World country trades where port transshipment facilities are rather inadequate.

13. The introduction of the high speed ferry in 1996 involving the monohull and catamaran is displacing the slower multi-purpose ferries and hovercraft. The latest generation of high speed ferry has a speed of 40 knots and can carry 1500 passengers with cars and trailers. Examples where these services have been introduced include Vancouver Island, Tasmania, Irish Sea, North Sea, Greek–Italian trade and other intra-Mediterranean ferry and Ro-Ro routes.

14. The hydrofoil offering fast passenger ferry services is found in the Greek Islands the Swiss–Italian lakes and other lakes and estuarial areas of the world.

The world mercantile fleet is growing in dead weight tonnage terms at 2/3 per cent per annum. Overall, the world mercantile fleet is becoming more productive through new high-tech modern tonnage and better utilization of the fleet.

The type of merchant vessel employed on a trade route is determined basically by the traffic carried. Broadly there are three main divisions: liners, tramps and specialized vessels such as tankers.

The liner vessel operates on a scheduled service between a group of ports. Such services offer cargo space or passenger accommodation to all shippers and passengers who require them. The ships sail on scheduled dates/times irrespective of whether they are full or not. Container vessels in deep-sea trades and Ro-Ro vessels in the short sea trades feature prominently in this field. The passenger market is found in the high speed and multi-purpose ferries found in the Baltic, Mediterranean, Vancouver Island, Irish Sea, North Sea and Greek–Italian trade. The deep-sea liner services provide regular services serving a group of ports situated in different countries. Examples include the Europe–Asian, Europe–North American and round-the-world services (p. 107). Some services operate under a liner conference system which is highly regulated but in decline (see p. 161). However, the bulk of liner services are deregulated and operate outside the liner conference system. The bill of lading features very prominently as the consignment note used in the liner cargo service, with the exception of the international road haulage shipment which involves the CMR document and rail which involves the CIM consignment note.

The tramp or general trader, as she is often called, does not operate on a fixed sailing schedule, but merely trades in all parts of the world in search of cargo, primarily bulk shipments. Such cargoes include coal, grain, timber, sugar, ores, fertilizers and copra which are carried in complete shiploads. Many of the cargoes are seasonal. Tramp vessels are engaged under a document called a charterparty on a time or voyage basis. Such negotiations usually are conducted by shipbrokers on behalf of their principals. The fixture rate is determined by the economic force of demand and supply insofar as cargoes seeking shipping space and the availability of vessels is concerned. Such vessels are occasionally chartered to supplement existing liner services to meet peak cargo-shipment demands, or by the shipper with a substantial shipment of cargo, that is, trade cars/chassis.

The specialized vessel such as the oil tanker, ore carrier and timber carrier may be under charter or operated by an industrial company, that is, oil company, motor manufacturer, etc. to suit their own individual or market needs. Most oil companies operate chartered tonnage involving oil tankers on long-term charter.

4.9 Pipelines

The basic advantage of a pipeline is the low cost of distribution with virtually no labour content in the distribution network. Costs of installing the pipeline system may be moderately high, but are relatively low insofar as distribution is concerned. A further basic advantage is the 24-hour availability of the pipeline and its low maintenance. Conversely, the pipeline has a fixed capacity which inhibits market growth unless a further pipeline is installed. It has many advantages from an environmental point of view with virtually no noise or fumes. Little disruption is caused to the environment during installation compared with road or rail development. Moreover, it permits more than one type of product to be distributed through it.

Pipelines feature more prominently in the USA where they account for some 8 per cent of the proportion of freight/merchandise distributed. They distribute a wide range of bulk commodities, and a number of the pipelines are so designed to distribute more than one commodity type following completion of the cleansing process. Pipelines feature strongly in oil distribution and it is a growth sector as a low cost distributor. A significant number serve oil maritime terminals, while others form a pipeline network, thereby reducing oil tanker tonnage employment. Oil/gas pipelines are found in Saudi Arabia, Baku, Tblisi and Ceyhan. Also many pipelines pass through Russia, Ukraine, Belarus, Hungary, Slovakia, the Czech Republic and Poland – a major pipeline is the Druzhba. A further example is the Baltic Pipeline which allows Russia to export oil directly from its Baltic Sea Port of Primorsk, rather than shipping through Estonia, Latvia or Lithunia. By 2010, it is expected the global pipeline network will exceed 18 000 km.

4.10 Palletization

Palletization is the process of placing or anchoring the consignment to a pallet or base made of wood or metal. It is a very common technique in air freight where the pallet accompanies the consignment throughout the transit from the factory premises to the retailer. A shrink wrapping technique is frequently used (p. 190). It may be a stillage involving base plates; the box pallets where one side can be dropped; or the skeleton pallet for lightweight cargoes.

Palletization is a growth market in container shipment involving multi-modalism. Accordingly, GE SeaCo have recently introduced the Sea Cell container (see p. 94). Basically, palletization aids cargo handling, reduces packing, facilitates stowage, and mechanizes the technique of cargo handling involving the pallet truck and fork lift truck. To the shipper involved in general merchandise distribution, an enquiry into the possible use of pallets may prove worthwhile. Some shipowners and port operators offer rate concessions on palletized cargo. The pallet is basically a unitized method of transportation and inland waterway operators in Belgium have recognized this relative to their Kempenaar tonnage by providing automatic transhipment with a capacity of 650 pallets (p. 56).

4.11 Seaports

The role and significance of ports has changed dramatically during the past decade and this will accelerate in the twenty-first century. Today they have a higher profile both economically and technically in maritime and international trade. Ports today are not only a link in a transport chain but are also trade and distribution centres. Such changes are being driven by the expanding global container network involving the hub and spoke system and increasing volume of container transhipment (see pp. 76–96).

Logistics is also playing a major role in international trade distribution (see Chapter 6) in a high tech environment together with privatization as governments opt out of state ownership and investment in their ports. Today shippers are looking for dedicated schedules door-to-door with the customs examination being undertaken at the consignor/consignee premises or at a nearby container freight station/dry port/freight village. Hence an increasing volume of business passing through the port will be customs examined outside the port environs thereby reducing the risk of congestion. Other benefits will include a reduction in infrastructure needs in terms of warehousing and a speeding up of transit. Moreover, it will intensify berth utilization and its infrastructure thereby increasing the throughput of the port. With the elimination of customs examination, the dock labour force will be substantially reduced and this will be accentuated by the provision of high-tech computerized cargo handling equipment.

An increasing number of major ports are becoming trade distribution centres, with such developments being concentrated in the port environment. Examples include the ports of Singapore and Rotterdam. The trading areas are called 'Distriparks' or Free Trade Zones and provide industrial companies with a central distribution location with the major benefits of the nearby port infrastructure and prosperous hinterland. Goods are imported and exported through the port and processed through Distripark units involving a warehouse and distribution centre. Companies lease the site and/or warehouse and import the products for assembly, processing, packaging and labelling to serve the nearby markets. This provides enormous cost savings in customs duties, including international cargo distribution; often lower labour and handling costs; the development of customerized products to serve the local market; lower local market distribution costs; an integrated logistics approach to the flow of goods involving 'just-in-time' deliveries; lower inventory costs, due to better control and less inventory; centralized distribution; stuffing and stripping of containerized general cargo; and continuous access to the port infrastructure. The range of products is large, including foodstuffs, garments, machinery, consumer goods, industrial products and so on. Goods leave the Distripark by sea, road, air and canal. An increasing number of exporters are now adopting a policy of purchasing component parts of their products in different parts of the world and undertaking all the assembly work at the Distripark, with each Distripark reflecting the needs of the hinterland it serves. It is very cost effective and will develop especially in regions which have free trade agreements such as the EU, ASEAN, NAFTA and so on.

Three such Distriparks exist in Rotterdam port, and the one at Botlek has a site of 86 ha. The Schenker Integrated Logistics Center became operational in Distripark Botlek at the beginning of the year 2000. Schenker Integrated Logistics has more than a thousand branches worldwide, employs 27 000 people and has an annual turnover of about DM10 billion.

Schenker is one of the world's leading forwarders and logistics service providers. The company also set up a branch in Distripark Botlek in 1998. On its 50 000 m^2 site Schenker can offer its customers a complete package of logistic services. 'From cross-docking to groupage and the despatch of hazardous material, from temporary storage and value added services to highly specialised logistic projects', is how Schenker's Rotterdam manager Ebi van Snek describes the company's services. For Schenker the new premises is an important link in the company's worldwide network. 'We have created a number of junctions worldwide where we can concentrate cargo for our customers', says Ebi van Snek. 'In Asia, that is Singapore. In Europe it is Rotterdam. There are two of these junctions in the United States.' Here Schenker is anticipating the wishes of several of its customers to be active on several continents as companies want to be able to keep their stock on the spot in order to be able to serve the market better. Schenker's investment in the Distripark Botlek project amounts to more than 10 million dollars.

Port Klang plans to open 3300 Distriparks by 2007. Currently (2004) Malaysia has two Distriparks compared to Singapore which has 1200 and Jebel Ali which has 3300.

However, Singapore's port is the market leader in the provision and development of the Distriparks concept. It stems from its being a trading centre and over 500 multinationals and international trading companies use Singapore as their central physical distribution base and logistics centre for the Asia–Pacific region. Distriparks are provided at Alexandra and Pasir Panjang; and a Distribelt embracing a 3700 ha distribution zone runs alongside a 20 km stretch on the southern coast. It embraces the Container Terminal, Keppel Terminal, Pasir Panjang Terminal, cargo consolidation, Alexandra Distripark and Pasir Panjang Distripark. With shipping infrastructure and support, multinational corporations and international freight forwarders operate from this base.

The Pasir Panjang Distripark has ten single-storey centres involving a 162 000 m^2 space with purpose-built ceilings. Additionally, at Pasir Panjang Districentre a three-storey building is provided with 45 000 m^2 including office space of 2000 m^2. It is an ultra-modern warehouse, with each unit able to offer a customerized service in consolidation, repacking, labelling and sorting centres. Round-the-clock security, fire services, fork lift accessibility to every floor, high ceilings, specialized facilities, CCTV security and PA systems are provided. Overall, the Port of Singapore has 14 Districentres within the Distriparks; all have EDI and are fully computerized and automated.

A total of over 750 free trade zones (FTZs) now exist worldwide. The sites are usually situated in the port environs and are free of customs examination and duty until leaving the area. It enables companies to import products and components for assembly, processing, labelling and distribution to neighbouring markets or be despatched to more distant ones. Examples of FTZs are found in the ports of Liverpool, Southampton and Hamburg.

Dubai and Singapore are two major ports which have developed the fast-growing sea/air market to Europe and North America using the nearby airport (p. 111). Singapore port is regarded as the major trading centre of the Far East and more recent facilities include a conference centre.

A new generation of container berths have emerged at the Brani terminal at the Port of Singapore. It has an area of 80 ha and a handling capacity of 3.8 million TEUs. It has 15 000 TEU ground slots and five main berths, together with four feeder berths. Total berth length is 2600 m and the minimum depth alongside the main berth is 15 m and the feeder berth 12 m. It has 1000 power points for reefer containers and 20 single-trolley and four double-trolley quay cranes; some 96 rubber-tyred yard cranes are provided. Overall, 100 prime movers are available, and likewise 100 double-stacked container trailers; it has 14 lanes. Brani terminal, situated on an island just across Tanjong Pagar terminal, is linked to Tanjong Pagar terminal and Keppel Distripark by a four-lane causeway. It is equipped with the Computer Integrated Terminal Operations System (CITOS) which integrates and automates Brani planning, control and documentation procedures.

More recently in 2002 the Port of Rotterdam, to cater for the continuous container growth, installed three new container cranes in the southern side of the Delta Terminal. The cranes are 120 metres high and each weights 1500 tons. They have an outreach of 67.5 metres making them suitable for loading and unloading ships 22 containers wide. The lifting height is 40 metres with a maximum lifting capacity of 77 tons. Overall, 50 per cent of Rotterdam European Combined Terminal is automated and provided with hi-tech equipment. Additionally, in 2004, the Port of Rotterdam confirmed a joint venture between Europe Container Terminals and P&O Nedlloyd to construct a new terminal called Maasvlakte. It will have a quay length of 1800 metres, draught in excess of 19 metres and a surface area of 100 ha. The new terminal will be available by 2008 and enable the port to cope with predicted container growth until 2011.

A relatively new terminal in England called Thamesport reflects modern technology. In 1998 it handled over 500 000 TEUs with 360 staff, of which 150 are traditional dock workers. All operators are regulated by a central computer system. Six post-Panamax ship to shore cranes work the vessels. For the discharge operation, the crane driver inputs the container serial number into the central computer. The computer then informs the tractor driver to which of the nine stacks in the container yard he has to deliver the container. There are 18 rail-mounted gantries which are fully automated without drivers. The rail mounted gantry picks up the container and the central computer informs the crane where to stack it. Lorry drivers coming to pick up imports or drop off exports are given smart cards. These allow the control centre to place drivers in queues and regulate loading and unloading to maximize efficiency. Lorry drivers go to the stack entrances where their containers are taken from or into the stack by the rail mounted gantries. The next stage in the investment programme is the installation of automatic guided vehicles for the transfer operation such as exist on the modern high-tech container berths in the Ports of Rotterdam and Singapore.

Two major port modernization schemes have been completed in the European ports of Le Havre and Barcelona. The Le Havre project, partially funded by the EU, embraced six new container berths, a jetty and new access to the Seine river at a total cost of US$465 million. The Barcelona project of US$290 million embracing two contracts involved the extension of its eastern and western breakwaters to a total of 6.8 kilometres. In the Far East the port of Kwangyang (Republic of Korea) completed four new container berths, one to be operated by Dongbu Co, and the others by HPH, Hanjin Shipping and Hyundai Merchant Marine.

More recently Dubai Port Authority completed phase 1 of the Port of Jebel Ali expansion which raised port capacity from 4 million to 5.7 million TEUs. The investment of US$237 million includes dredging the access channel to a depth of 17 metres, widening it to 325 metres and constructing five additional berths equipped with 14 post-Panamax gantry cranes. Across the Strait of Hormuz, the Islamic Republic of Iran announced an investment of US$313 million in several ports which will upgrade facilities in Bandar Abbas to 2.6 million TEU capacity. The port is already connected by weekly container block trains to Tashkent (Uzbekistan) in Central Asia. The expansion of this port is part of the development of Shahid Rajaee Special Economic Zone for which BOT industrial schemes are contemplated.

The container freight station (CFS) is an inland depôt handling containers. It is usually identified with one or more ports and has all the facilities to handle the container import/export; stuffing/unstuffing; container servicing, cleaning, maintenance and repair; and road/rail served with customs facilities. Such facilities are found in Australia and the Middle East, and in other parts of the world where they are known as container bases/container yards. Details of top container yards are found in Table 4.2.

The development of multimodalism (Chapter 5) in the current decade means that the role of ports will change further, with greater emphasis on trading centres becoming a focal point in terms of resources, infrastructure and professional services for the markets served. It will involve port authorities becoming more closely involved in the markets they serve, embracing both local and international communities. Also, an increasing number will become privatized as governments opt out of state ownership and investment of their ports.

Finally, the shipper in deciding the routing of his cargo must place increasing emphasis on the overall transit time in a logistically driven system. The key to such an evaluation is the overall efficiency of transhipment/intermodal points. The shipper must strive to use a dedicated service with no in-built delays caused by port congestion, customs clearance, poor terminal efficiency, industrial disputes, poor planning, security, inadequate port infrastructure investment and absence of adequate computerized/high-tech resources especially in communication, customs, scheduling and resource planning.

Moreover, the geographical location of the port is a key factor as well as the value added benefit it offers in the distribution network. An example is found in the port of Colombo involving the private container operator SAGT, a subsidiary of P&O Ports, which commissioned 650 metres of new berth equipped with six quay gantry container cranes capable of working containers 18 rows across. The upgrading of this port was completed with the dredging of the basin to 14 metres and the opening of a second entrance with a 10.5 metre draft for feeder services. Moreover, the SAGT and TCT, the public sector container terminal operators in the port have agreed to joint rebates for customers to attract traffic.

The major seaports of the world are not only trading centres as found in Rotterdam, but also hub ports. The leading container ports (p. 79) have an ongoing investment programme both in terms of new technology and expansion.

Analysing the foregoing, the shipper must continuously monitor the global distribution network and keep abreast of new developments. New investments, especially container driven aligned to overland improvements such as the new rail link in the deep sea port of Darwin open up new markets (p. 73).

4.12 Sea/air concept

It is significant that Dubai and Singapore are both the primary trading centres of their regions. Such ports are regarded as 'one-stop ports' as shipowners rely on feeder services to generate cargo. Dubai is strategically placed at the crossroads of Asia, Europe and Africa. Singapore is regarded as the trading hub of the Far East market. Manufacturing and trading companies around the world increasingly recognize that efficient production and marketing must be matched by an equally efficient system for shipping goods from the factory to the customer. Hence, Singapore and Dubai are the distribution hubs of their regions (Table 3.3, p. 61).

The sea/air development/transfer at Dubai and Singapore are both growth markets. A range of established air freight consolidators serve the airports, offering daily services to a range of destinations. Cargo transfer from ship's deck to aircraft take-off takes less than five hours, involving the minimum of customs formalities, with only one custom document for the entire transshipment. Cargo handling facilities and services are provided continuously. The sea/air connection is fast, cost-saving and a reliable mode of transshipment. Repacking services are also provided for goods in transit. Substantial savings can also be made in many subsidiary costs of sea freight, warehouse fees, handling, wharfage, haulage cost and insurance. Overall, transit time of transshipment cargo is guaranteed and insured against delay.

Singapore's port is served by 700 shipping lines and linked to 300 ports worldwide. The airport has 52 airlines serving 110 cities in 54 countries. Dubai's international airport is served by 53 airlines serving over 100 destinations. The new cargo complex is one of the most modern in the world, handling both FCL and LCL TEUs, with the latest technology including computer controlled temperature warehouses and handling 250 000 tonnes annually. The seaport is essentially a transshipment point, with over 60 per cent of import cargo destined for re-export; it handles over 12.9 million TEUs annually. The port is served by over 100 shipping lines.

Recommended reading

Annual report of GE SeaCo.
Annual report of Ports of Rotterdam, Singapore, Le Havre and Dubai.
Annual Review of Maritime Transport published by UNCTAD.
British Airways annual report.
Containerisation International Yearbook.

CHAPTER 5

Multi-modalism

Multi-modalism is the process of providing a door-to-door or warehouse-to-warehouse service to the shipper which embraces two or more forms of transport, and involves the merchandise being conveyed in a unitized form in the same unit throughout transit. It involves a scheduled and/or dedicated service. Forms of multi-modalism are:

1. Containerization – FCL/LCL/road/sea/rail.
2. Land-bridge – trailer/truck – road/sea/road.
3. Land-bridge – pallet/IATA container – road/sea/air/road.
4. Trailer/truck – road/sea/road.
5. Swap-body – road/rail/sea/road.

A development which has emerged in recent years from combined transport operations, multi-modalism is the term used for non-vessel operating carrier (NVOC) operations or non-vessel operating common carrier (NVOCC) operations. Multi-modalism may arise in a container (FCL or LCL) movement or trailer transit. In such a situation, carriers issue bills of lading for the carriage of goods on ships which they neither own nor operate. A freight forwarder will usually issue the FIATA Multi-modal Transport Bill of Lading (see p. 366) for a container or trailer movement or, if the trailer movement is in the UK-Continental trade, a CMR consignment note. For shippers requiring a cargo receipt the freight forwarder will issue a FIATA Forwarders Certificate of Receipt (see p. 376).

An example arises where a freight forwarder offers a groupage service using a nominated shipping line and shipping line equipment. The freight forwarder offers his own tariff for the service but buys from the shipping line at a box rate. NVOCC allows shipping companies to concentrate on ship management and the freight forwarder to utilize his expertise in marketing and consolidating cargo. It is particularly evident in the USA, Far East and Africa trades.

All forms of multi-modalism involve a dedicated service usually under non-vessel operating common carrier (NVOCC) or non-vessel operating carrier (NVOC) arrangements.

5.1 Rationale of development of multi-modalism

Today multi-modalism has become the prime method of distribution in a competitive market. Shippers are looking to the carrier to provide the optimum route for their buyers at a competitive tariff and an acceptable throughout transit time. The development of multi-modalism has arisen due to the following reasons:

1. Development of the 'just-in-time' strategy requiring dedicated and integrated schedules within shippers' warehouse and distribution arrangements.
2. Shippers demanding continuous improvements in the distribution network and a quickening of the supply chain.
3. The documentation involving the carriers' liability and code of practice relative to multi-modalism is now in place through the auspices of the International Chamber of Commerce (ICC) and other international bodies.
4. World markets are changing rapidly from the primary products to the industrialized scene, as found in Malaysia. Value added benefits have become closely involved with the distribution chain.
5. Containerization and its infrastructure through the seaport network continues to expand (pp. 78–82).
6. The development of Distriparks, Districentres and Free Trade Zones (pp. 107–11) continues to grow.
7. Markets are becoming more global and marketeers follow the strategy of manufacturing/processing/packaging in low labour-cost markets and rely on such centres to distribute to nearby growth markets. This is reducing the supply chain timescale and improving the service to the buyers and importers.
8. Operators such as P&O Nedlloyd, Container Line and Atlantic Container Line have customerized logistics departments which counsel their clients to provide the most cost-efficient methods of distribution, packaging and routeing.
9. The development of EDI has greatly facilitated international physical distribution management and control with no boundaries and time zone problems (Chapter 16). This extends to customs clearance.
10. Air/rail/sea/canal/seaport operators are working more closely together to keep pace and facilitate trade development. Examples include the sea/air bridge from Singapore and Dubai (p. 112) and the sea/rail landbridge in North America (pp. 72–3).

11. Governments are taking a keener interest in the development of their nation's economy by encouraging a global trade strategy, and providing the infrastructure to facilitate this objective.

12. The European market, for example, regards the development of a European combined transport network essential to its economic development, and in 1990 the Transport Council adopted a resolution to set up a high-level working group to identify the measures necessary to achieve this objective (p. 541).

Overall, the foregoing factors demonstrate how multi-modalism is leading the growth of worldwide markets.

5.2 Factors driving multi-modalism in the twenty-first century

There is no doubt, in an era of continuing international trade growth varying from 1 to 5 per cent annually, that strategically the role of distribution will become increasingly important. Markets continue to develop globally in line with the efficiency of their infrastructure in an increasingly competitive high tech environment. The pressure to develop multi-modalism is economically driven by industry and politically driven by government. The transport operator as provider of the service has the responsibility of working with other carriers and resource providers to provide a dedicated high-tech multi-modal network at a reasonable tariff. This requires terminal operators – shipping/rail/canal/road/pipeline carriers; international agencies ICC, IMO, IATA, UNCITRAL, WTO – and freight forwarders, agents and transport equipment manufacturers who can provide a uniform global liberalized framework in which to operate on a transparent basis; and finally requires an environment completely deregulated from national prejudice or culture and from any one government's regulations. Innovation and adoption in response to opportunities and threats, both short- and long-term, are key elements in the ongoing development of multi-modalism.

Overall multi-modalism involves a team of providers in a transport chain where all the constituents work closely together in accord with market needs and objectives. It requires each party to the multi-modal operation, including both the provider and user, to take up a strategic position with a view to focusing on the long-term benefits in a fast moving and changing global high-tech infrastructure. Planning is the central key to such strategies if they are to add value to the multi-modal transport chain. This involves improving transit times, reliability, volume throughput, interchangeability – involving swap-body/container transshipments; quality of service and professional management. The development of computerized technology enables management to monitor performance with a view to raising standards.

An examination of the European infrastructure environment in 2004 identified the features driving the intermodal expansion. The enlargement of the EU to 25 Member States will provide a new impetus to a single market logistically driven integrated transport system extolling multi-modalism (p. 541). These included a dissatisfaction with operating conditions and practices; shippers, containership operators and forwarders all confronting a range of problems including over tonnaging, high cost and low rates imposed on the shipping lines by global shippers who in turn were demanding more and more sophisticated services. Solutions to such problem areas include deregulation; the provision of an integrated coherent European network and the development of a service orientated and cost reducing culture.

Accordingly, developments now sought in the European intermodal network include the following:

1. Container lines taking over control of their own inland services, quality and costs.
2. Traditional operators striving to keep or win their share of the market through a more multi-modal focused strategy.
3. Ports and terminals competing through their hinterland links for more multi-modal orientated business.
4. A new international cooperative forum.
5. Formulation of global logistics operators and intermodal marketing companies.
6. The need for a single European infrastructure strategy (see pp. 541–43).
7. The need for a single transport market with harmonization of regulations and competition rules.
8. The identification and elimination of any obstacles to intermodality.
9. The continuous exchange of relevant data among intermodal carriers to facilitate service improvements both on a day-to-day basis and when planning short- and long-term improvements.
10. Complete transparency between all parties in the logistic-driven supply chain crossing international boundaries within the EU.

Europe operates a short distance transport market and has a complex coast line. It has a liberalized trucking industry but the railway network is highly regulated on a national basis. This impedes the development of intermodalization. For example, severe restrictions exist not only for private operators to operate trains over national networks but also to manage and transship swap-bodies and containers at rail served freight terminals. Such operating restrictions which are union influenced are in complete contrast with the United Kingdom network which is fully privatized and operates on a free market access basis with no direct government intervention. A further significant factor is that the European rail network is state funded and accountable, while in the United Kingdom it is in the private sector.

The EU continues to drive forward a coherent integrated transport policy and this challenge will become more demanding with the enlargement to 25 States in 2004. Examples of rail (p. 74) becoming more prominent and inland waterways as a high volume reliable distribution network are coming to fruition. The EU is focusing on more intra-EU transits. Ports are being developed as trading centres on a multi-modal basis with special emphasis on containerization as found in Cherbourg, Antwerp, Rotterdam and Hamburg.

In contrast North America is, like Europe, an industrialized economy which is high-tech and highly developed especially in the USA and Canada. Both are economic blocs as found in NAFTA (see p. 17) and EU (see p. 531). The geographical and political differences are very significant. North America operates in a liberalized free market environment. Overall, the average freight haul is very much longer. The east and west coasts of America have a trade interface with Europe and with Asia and the Far East respectively, in particular the Chinese and Indian growth markets. This opens up enormous intra-trade route opportunities which have been grasped by the ports and railways to provide land-bridge (sea/rail or sea/rail/sea) services (see pp. 73–5). Such developments are strategically wide ranging, involving market partners, investment patterns and strategic operational alliances, based on competition and the volume of business involved. Overall, it reflects a different management culture of deregulation compared with Europe which tends to be a highly regulated market.

We have already mentioned the changing role of seaports globally and the growing trend towards privatization and the movement away from the state controlled Port Authority (see p. 108). At the same time container ship operators are extending their hub and spoke systems (see pp. 76–85). All these port developments are generating more investment in the industry and at the same time provide opportunities to extend multi-modalism to the port hinterland by rail or road. Such developments are global in developed and developing countries, newly industrialized countries (NICs) and less developed countries (LDCs). Each have a different economic profile, but all have the opportunity to develop their economies through such investment. It brings together, through trade, high- and low-cost labour markets of varying skills featuring industrial and agricultural economies.

5.3 Features of multi-modalism

Given below is a broad analysis of multi-modalism:

1. It provides a dedicated service with each operator or carrier committed to the schedule.
2. It operates under NVOCC or NVOC arrangements (p. 114).
3. A strong feature is its provision of a regular, reliable, competitively priced quality door-to-door service with acceptable transit times. Hence

the value added benefit is considerable to the multi-modalism users; and it is usually fully computerized involving EDI, thereby enabling the operator to monitor the package throughout its transit. Overall, it places the multi-modal user in a strongly competitive situation.

4. It develops and coordinates the best features of the transport modes to the advantage of the shipper.

5. It is an ideal environment for EDI and, undoubtedly, as EDI expands on a global scale, the multi-modal network will move with it.

6. The multi-modal network is very extensive and fast growing. The wide range of services it can offer stimulates the development of markets worldwide.

7. It is consumer led and market driven in its development in a logistic environment. Overall, it is bringing markets and the buyer and seller closer together, and especially so in the high-tech and fast-moving consumer markets including foodstuffs.

8. An increasingly large number of operators are providing logistics departments to customize their clients' needs (pp. 115–16).

9. Good asset-utilization of multi-modal infrastructure permits competitive door-to-door or warehouse-to-warehouse through rates to be offered. Thus it exploits the economies of scale and yields a favourable return on transport investment. Basically, it is a high-tech operation.

10. Under the auspices of the ICC and other international bodies a common code of liability and processing of documents is now permitted. This has created confidence in the market and the handling of all the multi-modal documents by banks, carriers, agents, buyers, sellers and port authorities. It has also permitted a through door-to-door or warehouse-to-warehouse rate to be quoted.

11. Operators are strongly committed to multi-modalism, and as time moves on, its extension will gather momentum and the existing networks will be further improved and diversified. It will be market and technology driven, aided by an increasingly discerning shipper.

12. Multi-modalism is giving a new impetus to the role of seaports and airports, especially the former. Port authorities worldwide are developing not only the port enclaves through Districentres and free trade zones, but also initiating and encouraging the infrastructure operators on which they rely, to develop and improve existing multi-modal networks. Examples include the ports of Singapore, Dubai, Klang and Rotterdam. Overall, port authorities are tending to coordinate the activities and develop their strategy on an unprecedented scale. Many are being privatized and have an enhanced role through the development of the hub and spoke system (see pp. 76–85). The port authority of today is only a part of the total product network (pp. 107–12).

13. Associated with item (12), the changing pattern of international distribution is resulting in less port-to-port cargo and the accelerated

growth of multi-modalism. This relieves port congestion and develops ICDs, dry ports, free trade zones and the use of local import control and export control customs arrangements. It encourages the development of a new vision and enthusiasm at all levels of the supply chain to improve the value added benefits which accrue to the exporter and importer in using the network system (see Chapter 5).

14. As indicated earlier, many multi-modal operators have a logistics department to counsel and develop shippers' needs. This is encouraging closer harmony between the shipper and operator and ensures an ongoing market-led commitment from both the user and provider of the multi-modal network.

15. Market research is an essential ingredient to develop the system involving a continuous monitoring of the network.

16. Multi-modalism develops new markets, improves commodity quality, raises loadability and lowers transit times, reduces packing and aids the development of consumer high tech fast-moving markets. Moreover, it brings cultures and the international business world closer together both in their objectives and ideology.

17. The system favours both the large and small shipper by involving the full load or consolidated consignment.

18. Multi-modalism has become computer driven with high-tech communication systems embracing all aspects of the transit including cargo tracking (p. 126). This has resulted in a logistic environment of faster transits and demands high investment in the computer technology and software provision to all those party to the supply chain, especially the exporter and importer.

19. It encourages transparency in the multi-modal supply chain between all parties.

To conclude our analysis, there is no doubt that multi-modalism will contribute significantly to a changing international trade pattern. It will open up countries with low labour-cost skills to the industrialized westernized markets with great buying power. Such industrialized high labour-cost countries are increasingly reliant on the development of their global manufacturing business by producing within the low-cost markets and relying on multi-modalism to distribute the goods in a cost-effective manner to high GDP markets.

5.4 Multi-modalism integration

Multi-modalism is all about integrating transport networks to provide a value added service to the user. It is also linked to logistics and globalization which we will examine in the next chapter. Exporters must constantly scan the market place to identify improvements in the transport networks and how they can benefit from such development.

Detailed below are three cases of cooperation and coordination in Asia involving connecting transport modes and providers.

(a) *New Delhi:* A joint venture between DHL Danzas Air & Ocean and India's Lemuir group commenced in 2003, offering integrated logistics service to a variety of customers. The venture addressed the needs of clients, including small- and medium-sized companies, in sectors such as information technology, automotive, healthcare, electronics, and consumer goods. DHL Danzas Lemuir offer door-to-door integrated services using the breadth of its joint venture partners. The venture effectively positions the DHL global network in a premier position in this very important emerging market. DHL Danzas Air & Ocean, the logistics arm of Deutsech Post, holds 49 per cent equity in DHL Danzas Lemuir Pvt Ltd, while Mumbai-based Lemuir will hold 51 per cent. The company's headquarters is in Mumbai and has a combined workforce of 367 in 15 offices and warehousing facilities covering major cities in India. The venture by Danzas, a unit of Deutsech Post World Net, comes as part of its strategy to consolidate its presence in the Indian sub-continent region. In 2002 it picked Sri Lanka as its new multinational gateway for South Asia.

(b) *Shippers' body eases consolidation:* The Philippine Shippers' Bureau has set up a cargo consolidation network, Carconet, to help provincial shippers move their cargoes more efficiently and to avoid transhipment at Manila. Carconet is now available in Cebu, Davao, Cagayan de Oro, General Santos, Zamboanga, Subic and Baguio. Small- and medium-sized LCL shippers from the regions have difficulty exporting, as many provincial ports are not directly served by international lines, and most shipping lines that do call do not accept LCL cargo. Carconet simplifies the shipment process by the issue of a single transport document as against segmented shipments with multiple service providers. The shippers' bureau, which helped in setting up the network and monitors the performance of the players, accredits freight forwarders and shipping lines to undertake the cargo consolidation.

(c) *Malaysia seaport gets air designation:* In what it claims is a world first, Malaysia's Port of Tanjung Pelepas has been given a dedicated airport code by the International Air Transport Association as part of efforts to spur sea/air intermodal and transhipment business. The IATA code, ZJP, enables airport operators to treat Pelepas as a flight destination like any airport. The service, jointly promoted by the MASkargo arm of Malaysia Airlines System Bhd and the port, promises shippers and forwarders cheaper and faster delivery to North America, Europe, Australasia and East Asia via MASkargo's base at Kuala Lumpur International Airport. It is predicted shippers using this service can expect cost savings of up to 40 per cent. Companies need only to send cargo by sea to Pelepas – among the fastest growing seaports in Southeast Asia – from where it will be trucked to MASkargo's cargo centre at KLIA, then by air to the destination. At the port, cargo will be handled at the special air zone using simplified customs documentation and with fast turnaround.

5.5 Multi-modalism strategy

As we progress through the early stages of the twenty-first century, the multi-modal global network will be further extended. It already exists on a global basis. Continuing seaport and airport investment and the associated hub and spoke system, coupled with the annual growth of containerization in a logistics and high-tech driven environment, will all play very major roles. Consumer and industrial markets will no longer rely on the seaport-to-seaport, or airport-to-airport network, but rather the local clearance procedure (p. 239) on the shippers' premises, or the warehouse-to-warehouse system. This will feature more B2B and B2C inland clearance depots/dry ports – often rail linked to the seaport, which will become more evident in the distribution network. The deep seaport will become a trading port with a hinterland of industry and consumers within a radius of up to several hundred miles as found in Rotterdam/Le Havre/ Dunkerque/Zeebrugge/Seattle seaports.

The strategy to adapt to multi-modalism is essentially market and technology led. It is an ongoing strategy, with market growth providing the cash flow necessary to fund the continuing investment. Moreover, as the system develops, the economies of scale will lower development costs, as has been experienced in computerization. It is an exciting time and one full of opportunity, but it is a strategy which requires complete professionalism and high quality training at all levels. We will briefly consider some of the aspects which require special attention.

1.   Shippers and operators must continuously study trading patterns and trends to identify and develop new opportunities for multi-modalism. Existing systems must be continuously evaluated and improved as the trading pattern changes.
2.   Trading blocs such as ASEAN, NAFTA, EU and EFTA need to review both their internal market and external market multi-modal systems' structure. The closer trading blocs work together, the greater will be the benefit in terms of market growth and distribution improvement. Strategies of empathy must prevail, involving all parties, to the total distribution product.
3.   The Pacific Rim continues to house a number of important markets and will require particular attention in terms of opportunities.
4.   Major shippers, particularly multinationals, are companies with great investment resources and high calibre personnel who are leading the way in the development of multi-modalism in many markets. The

smaller shipper, who may be a subcontractor, is benefiting from such developments.

5. Multi-modalism strongly favours the 'just-in-time' strategy.
6. China and India both have fast expanding markets which shippers must study for new opportunities.
7. Innovation and flexibility remain the keys to develop new markets which emerge as the international multi-modal distribution network changes to accommodate new market opportunities and continuous investment in a changing supply chain network.
8. International entrepreneurs must study continuously the intra-regional trade agreements for new markets which offer preferential and duty free trading opportunities (p. 10) and provide development of logistically driven multi-modalism.

The 'just-in-time' strategy together with the role of Distriparks, Districentres, FTZ, ICD/dry ports, air and land-bridges, Local Clearance Procedure (p. 239), and the industrial plant transplant, will all become established on a global basis. The ramifications of multi-modalism will contribute significantly to raising living standards worldwide.

CHAPTER 6

Logistics and globalization

6.1 Role of logistics

Logistics can be broadly defined as the time-related positioning of resources, ensuring that materials, people, operational capacity and information are in the right place at the right time in the right quantity and at the right quality and cost.

This deceptively simple proposition conceals the complex reality of modern international logistics management. Overall, logistics is a vital component of the economic growth to move goods around the world quickly and cost-efficiently. There are an almost infinite number of circumstances which can prevent any one of the elements of the foregoing definition from being achieved. Human error, transport delays, problems with manufacturing, poor communication, lack of planning and absence of information transparency in the supply chain. Professional logistics management is in essence the application of skills which ensure that every part of the above definition is successfully accomplished. These skills are considerable. In broad terms, logistics comprises international distribution, warehousing, customs and information management. It covers the whole supply chain from manufacturers to consumers. It has become an area of great specialization which calls for high levels of training and professional competence.

Today the world is a single integrated market place in which supply chain efficiency has become a competitive necessity. Manufacturers and retailers have sought cost savings and service improvements to enhance their competitiveness by supplying larger markets with fewer production and distribution centres.

This is also being driven by international entrepreneurs reviewing/ evaluating emerging regional trade agreements which offer duty-free preferential trade terms (p. 10).

The multinational industry or company is now logistically driven and managers must be logistically literate. This has placed new demands on the logistics industry and in order to meet these demands a new industry of global supply chain services is developing. The gains that can be made from inventory reduction due to quick response and just-in-time have been the basis of widespread industry reform.

Logistics is a corporate function and a strategic part of business planning. Many companies now see logistics management as part of the marketing discipline designed to improve customer service and sales. For a logistics operation to be successful on an international scale, two main criteria have to be satisfied: there needs to be an integrated network of professionals throughout all countries concerned to ensure the smooth passage of goods; and secondly there has to be a high level of specialist expertise and knowledge relating to the multitude of laws, conventions and regulations inherent in the conduct of the international trade environment. A further point, transparency of data communication, must be evident at all times between parties in the supply chain. The trend in the past decade has been for international companies to rationalize their business by integrating production, sales and marketing operations across frontiers. Their suppliers have followed suit and in the logistics industry there has been a strong move towards creating international networks either through merger and acquisition, or through confederations of independent professionals. Hence, there is no established pattern of international logistics networks at present. Each logistics company will have its own particular type of network with its own strengths suitable for some types of customers and not others.

Logistics is all about Companies/suppliers becoming competitive in the market place. Under the relentless pressure to compete, companies globally are striving to increase the quality of all their goods or services and at the same time to reduce their costs. Professional logistics management can help with both of these objectives.

The importance of continuously improving the quality of an organization's output has become more and more important in line with the rise in customer expectations. This is a mutually reinforcing process. As expectations rise, so quality and choice go up to match them, generating further rises in expectations.

Logistics can play a key role to improve quality, for example, to reduce the lead times from manufacturer to consumer or by making the goods more freely available in more outlets. First class customer service is regarded by many companies as the most important source of competitive advantage. Strategic planning is an area which sustains every successful logistics operation which yields significant cost savings. Overall, this may be through more cost-efficient management of the supply chain, or through outsourcing of services, which in turn enable the company to free up internal services enabling the company to concentrate on its core business. Companies recognize the importance of logistics management as a strategic part of the business planning to attain the commercial edge globally. Hence, the emergence of logistics expertise at a more senior level in companies – many at Board level. Today, it is a line management activity.

The demand-focused international trade industry does increasingly rely on satellite production, encourage suppliers to have shorter product lifecycles through fashion and technology advancement, and develop in the food industry, through technology, longer shelf life. All these factors help to drive logistics in a shrinking world of global sourcing.

Few service industries have changed more dramatically than international transport in the last decade. The impact of logistics has turned transport on its head. An activity long regarded as a self-defining but unavoidable cost centre is now seen as a means of reducing inventory, cutting costs and improving customer service. Exporters and importers have the tools by which they can become more efficient, more customer focused and more profitable. The many small firms that do not need a customized logistical service can call on the integrators (see p. 58). Led by a handful of mainly US owned multinationals, these companies have been winning market share as their operational ambitions have been extended.

Similarly, information technology systems have equipped transport providers to upgrade their services to improve utilization and yield. Whether it is the transport industry, the port industry, international rail freight or aviation, the current common denominator is to aim for optimal use of capacity and resources, irrespective of whether the equipment is a container gantry crane or a Boeing 747 freighter. To take an example from shipping, major container lines give a shipper or consignee the ability to track his or her container from the start to the finish of its journey. In an ideal world the container would arrive exactly when the consignee wants it and he or she could ignore its journey. But in the real world delays occur. To be able to know 24 hours a day the precise location of the container and maybe altering its estimated time of arrival, is a tremendously powerful tool for adjusting other elements in the business around it. At the other end of the scale, deciding on behalf of a European-wide supermarket chain how many distribution centres it should build and where they should be located to optimize the delivery operation is a complex numerical evaluation aided by computer analysis.

In consequence a growing number of businesses are outsourcing part or all of their logistics management. A number of shipping lines like P&O Nedlloyd (see pp. 115–16), and CSX/Sea Land have logistics subsidiaries to bid for this third party business.

Multinationals are driving the logistics expansion as big companies stipulate quality of service and the medium sized and small firms are simply having to comply. Medium and small companies are changing their organizational structure and what were once standalone shipping departments are becoming part of a larger customer service organization (see pp. 42–5).

Multinationals have built partnerships with their logistics suppliers. Large companies sourcing their materials on a global basis insist on dealing with a logistics company with a worldwide network. Major shippers are looking for cost benefits and the opportunity to add value. Manufacturers are looking to reduce inventory, improve operational performance and enhance customer service.

Logistics generates competitive advantage in the market place and achieves cost reduction. Moreover, it introduces a logistics management culture in a company which in turn raises the quality of service which can be further improved by adding value to the service through a variety of options (see p. 145). The key to it is adaptation and transparency whereby all parties in the supply chain have complete integrity through the continuous exchange of data.

For a logistics operation to be successful on an international scale, two main criteria have to be satisfied.

First, there needs to be an integrated network of professionals throughout all the countries concerned, to ensure the smooth passage of goods. Secondly, there has to be a high level of specialist expertise and knowledge relating to the multitude of laws, conventions and regulations which weave a complex web across international trade. This title contains data on both of these objectives.

The trend over the past decade has been for international companies to rationalize their businesses by integrating production, sales and marketing operations across frontiers. Their suppliers follow suit and in the logistics industry there has been a strong move towards creating international networks, either through merger and acquisition or through confederations of independent professionals.

Consequently, there is no established pattern of international logistics networks at present. Each logistics company will have its own particular type of network with its own strengths, suitable for some types of customer and not others. One crucial part of the special expertise required is knowledge of international laws and codes (Chapter 19). There is a UK framework of laws relating to international trade, but contract law is an extremely complex area as many contracts may be governed by the legal system of other countries where exports and imports are concerned. The Vienna Convention on International Sale of Goods came into force on 1st January 1988 and deals with the rights of buyer and seller, formation of contracts, sharing of risk and so on.

Other areas of expertise are Trade Finance (Chapter 12), EU Legislation (Chapter 18), Customs (Chapter 9), International Transport Conventions (Chapter 19), Documentation (Chapter 14), Product Specification (Chapter 19), Insurance (Chapter 10) and Market Access Options (Chapter 17).

An analysis of the logistic needs for the European focused company is given below.

European companies require a European service from logistics service providers. They do not want:

1. a plethora of service providers when they are consolidating;
2. to manage distribution at a national level when they are operating at the European level;
3. different computer systems throughout Europe when they have introduced European-wide integrated systems;
4. varying reporting methods and measures in different markets.

European companies do not need:

1. a single service provider operating in all markets and geographies;
2. assets owned and managed by the same company in all markets.

They do need:

1. a single management interface for all European operations;
2. a common standard of measures and reports provided centrally by the European logistics service managers;
3. a single systems interface giving visibility of stock movements and locations;
4. a common billing standard;
5. a single agreement.

It is argued that logistics service providers must meet this challenge and must also provide:

1. a consistently high standard in the basic services of transport and warehousing;
2. a visionary approach with new ideas, concepts and approaches;
3. access to best practice from different sectors and national approaches;
4. a clear chain of command with national and locations operations treating all customers as 'ours' and not treating some as 'theirs' and therefore as second-class.

The global and European logistics services market, it is predicted, will undergo 'a significant change' in the next few years. These changes could include:

1. more mergers and acquisitions to reduce excess capacity and increase scope;
2. joint ventures between different types of service providers;
3. joint ventures and operating networks across European and global markets;
4. a move to provide chain management services with 'basics,' such as transport and warehousing outsourced;

5.   joint ventures between logistics and other service providers, including systems houses and consulting groups;
6.   joint ventures between logistics service companies and niche market clients.

A key factor in logistic management internationally is the channel of distribution (see p. 132). The degree to which the channel is simple or complex, will depend on the nature of the goods and the channel strategy. A channel of distribution which involves numerous stages is likely to add considerably to the final price of the goods as each intermediary adds a percentage for profit. Hence, determining the channel of distribution strategy for a logistics operation is one of the most important factors in the whole process. It must reflect the need to maximize sales opportunities, achieve high levels of customer service, minimize cost and ensure accurate information flows. Many companies use a third party logistics specialist.

Warehousing and storage systems play a decisive role in international logistics. It includes the FTZ and Distriparks (see pp. 108–09) as found in seaports and their environs. It epitomizes the role of the seaport today as the trading centre. Effective warehouse management ensures a smooth level of supply to customers. Additionally, it yields the following benefits: economies of scale permitting long production runs and bulk cargo shipments; the ability to build up stocks in anticipation of seasonal or new product demand; improved customer service by, for example, the quick replacement of faulty goods or components; it facilitates break-bulk and other assembly operations as found in Distriparks and FTZ for onward shipment to customers; and finally it provides a secure and good environment to protect goods from damage, deterioration and pilferage internationally. Logistically, focused warehouse management is found in the ports of Singapore, Dubai and Rotterdam where goods are assembled, processed and packaged for distribution to an international market. All the warehouses in these ports are computer controlled.

The foregoing developments are driving many carriers who operate global services to develop a specific logistics product essentially offering a portfolio of integrated services. This applies both to shipowners and airlines.

6.2 P&O Nedlloyd Container Line – Logistics Division

A leading player in the field of global logistics operation is the mega container carrier P&O Nedlloyd Container Line. It has the world's largest number of standing container slots of 224 000; a fleet of 112 vessels including four vessels of 6674 TEU – the latest container tonnage generation; a 540 000 TEU fleet of containers; a genuine global network; a US$4 billion annual turnover; a well-developed EDI system (see pp. 76–81) and in 1997 it carried 2.3 million loaded TEUs. Formed in 1996 with 600 specialist staff working in 44 offices in 19 countries, spanning Europe, the Gulf, the USA, the Far East and the Indian subcontinent, it identifies the following six key areas sought by customers.

1. Strategic solutions to the problems of long-distance product sourcing and movement. This is achieved by matching the client's business needs to the latest techniques and expertise to formulate solutions to the problems of long-distance product sourcing and movement. An example is the European-based departmental stores buying a range of consumer products from the Far East. Key factors are quality control, coping with variations in consumer demand and distributing supplies in a cost-effective manner.
2. Companies which can provide capabilities interfaced across a range of different transport modes including sea, road, rail, canal and air as found in multi-modalism.
3. Improvements in quality of service to end customers. This basically centres on customer asset management – ensuring the goods arrive in a quality condition to a prescribed schedule with zero failure rate.
4. Improvements in profits realized through all the marketing and financial benefits inherent in the global logistic system to the user.
5. Management of 'trade-offs' within the supply chain.
6. A fully outsourced logistics management service.

Users of the service include automotive manufacturers, high-street retailers, wines and spirits producers, footwear, fashion garments, sports goods and electronic manufacturers.

The global logistics operators focus attention on the four key service areas detailed below.

1. *Supply chain management.* This requirement may be illustrated by the leading retail chains sourcing their merchandise from suppliers in Europe, the Far East and the USA. The logistics operator's task is to ensure that goods of a saleable quality are manufactured and transported safely and cost effectively and are delivered on time. This key service covers three aspects:

   (a) vendor management, involving the processing of customers' orders direct to their suppliers and monitoring the production process;
   (b) information, featuring receipt of customers' orders via EDI download (this leads to 24-hour monitoring and reporting of status and cost down to item level);
   (c) communication, permitting customers to receive advance notice of shipments which are off schedule via international e-mail links.

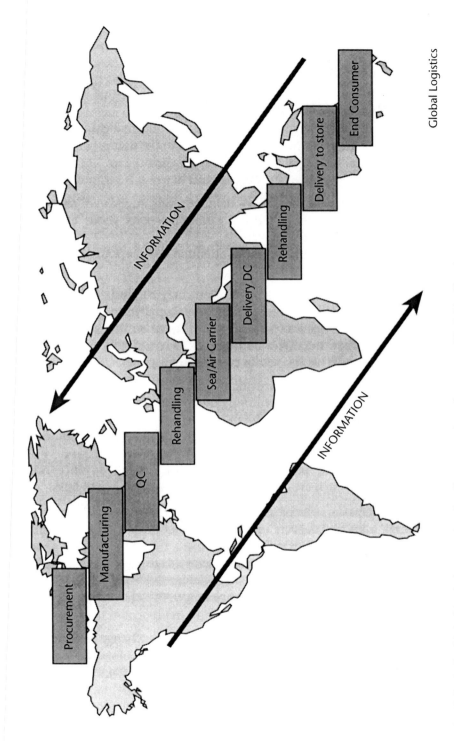

FIGURE 6.1 Global logistics supply pipe line reproduced courtesy P&O Nedlloyd

The key benefits are reduced inventory levels, improved visibility of all costs to item level, improved delivery on time and clearer management responsibility. Study the supply pipe line in Figure 6.1.

2. *Delivery and customs clearance.* An example of this requirement is provided by a leading drinks company with over 50 brands worldwide. The objective is to receive and handle stock and to arrange transport and overseas shipment. The four main features of the service include:

   (a) inventory management, featuring direct data exchange to provide on-line reporting;
   (b) order picking, embracing maximizing deliveries of export shipments direct to the end customer;
   (c) quality control including checking on arrival, arranging, relabelling and repacking as required;
   (d) security, the adoption of sophisticated arrangements suitable for a high-value commodity.

   The key results include delivery only when market demand dictates, secure and cost-effective storage and efficient onward distribution services.

3. *Distribution management.* This is the requirement of a major sportswear company which imports merchandise from suppliers in the Far East. The objective is to improve upstream process controls and maximize direct delivery to high-street stores in Europe. The three main features of the service include:

   (a) quality control, embracing collecting goods from suppliers and ensuring compliance with specified quality standards;
   (b) consolidation and delivery, embracing sorting, labelling and packaging goods according to end-customer order requirements and providing delivery direct to the customer;
   (c) information, embracing full integration via EDI between the customer's purchase order system, their financial and distribution systems and the global supply chain management system.

   The ultimate results were improved supplier quality standards, reduced warehousing and handling costs and shortened order cycle times.

4. *Import logistics and outbound distribution.* This is illustrated by a manufacturer of electronic goods which sources components in the Far East for manufacture in Europe. The objective is to manage the inbound supply of components to exacting production schedules and distribute the finished products across Europe. The three main features of the service include:

   (a) supply chain management, embracing the despatch of orders, the monitoring of production, consolidation and delivery on time to the manufacturing plant;

(b) information, embracing tracking progress in the supply chain so that customers can accommodate changes to the production plan;

(c) consolidation/distribution, featuring maximizing container usage to cut costs and distribution 'on time' to retailers.

The key results are proactive control of delivery schedules and reduced shipment costs from the consolidation and integration of inward and outward distribution.

Overall, the global logistics company concentrates on six core products: supply chain management, warehousing, customs clearance, air freight, consolidation and project cargo. It will improve supply chain visibility by developing tailored processes and tracking systems. This will lead to improved buying processes and decision-making, reduced stock levels and improved reaction times in delivering to end users. Overall, it will reduce supply chain costs, thus cutting lead times, creating fast-flow procedures and introducing upstream controls.

To amplify the foregoing a leading Asian company Li Et Fung operating in the Chinese market, engaged in sourcing, borderless trading and virtual manufacturing and supply chain management identifies seven core principles which underpin the company. These are detailed below:

1. The customer must be at the centre and responsive to market demand.
2. Focus on core competency and outsource new-core activities and develop a position in the supply chain.
3. Develop a low risk and profit sharing relationship with business partners.
4. Design, implement, evaluate and adjust the work flow, physical goods flow and cash flow in the supply chain.
5. Adopt information technology to optimize the operation of the supply chain.
6. Shorten product lead time and delivery cycles.
7. Lower cost in sourcing, warehousing and transportation.

Underpinning its success is globalization which is having the effect of shifting competition between companies away from traditional spheres and more onto the level of efficiency of their supply chains. Moreover, by applying advanced supply chain technologies and global sourcing expertise, it allows clients to focus fully on core competencies, lowers sourcing, warehousing, handling and storage costs, reduces working capital and minimizes capital expenditure on distribution assets. The Company advocates sourcing from several countries for individual products and in so doing is able to form a dialogue with the management and not the ownership supplying the components.

6.3 Factors contributing to the development of logistics

The factors influencing the development of global logistics are numerous. The most salient are detailed below.

1. The development of information technology (IT) has enabled a transformation to take place in communication and data transmission opening up markets and re-focusing strategies in distribution and manufacturing outsourcing and assembly. It has no culture or language barriers, no time zones and is available continuously, bringing together the low and high labour cost nations and their skills for the exchange of goods and services.

2. The globalization of markets with their infrastructure and international trade environment generating business confidence internationally. A major contributor is the WTO (see pp. 27–35).

3. The accelerating development of the global container network has offered a new challenge to the global trader. It has placed a fresh focus on global distribution with an emphasis on added value in the distribution chain. The question posed by the international entrepreneur is how can we further improve and extend the conventional multi-modal container service to the benefit of the shipper and in the interests of efficiency. Shippers are already being offered the option of independent software and systems as an alternative to those available from the carrier. This allows suppliers, carriers, manufacturers and retailers to make optimum routeing decisions and increases the transparency of goods flows. The financial efficiency of the supply chain network is also being examined. This involves developing a product to coordinate the flow of funds more efficiently with the movement of goods thereby allowing the importer and exporter access to cheaper sources of money.

4. The continuous expansion of the integrators TNT and DHL. This has opened up new markets in both the manufacturing and service industries.

5. The decline of the end-to-end/port-to-port liner conference system and the development of the hub and spoke global container network (see p. 77) coupled with the expansion of multi-modalism.

6. The emergence of the mega container operator (see p. 78) which exploits the economies of scale and provides the mega operator the opportunity to provide the 'in-house' global logistics resources such as found in P&O Nedlloyd.

7. The decline of the traditional non logistic focused freight forwarder has emerged as the mega container carriers develop in-house global logistic operations. This has encouraged the trade to entrust the entire distribution arrangement to the logistic shipowner thereby bypassing the freight forwarder (pp. 138–39).

8. The development of the freeport, free trade zones and Distriparks (see pp. 108–09) in the port environs has opened up new opportunities of trade distribution for the international entrepreneur. Such designated areas are immune from customs examination and revenue collection until they enter the domestic market in question. They enable the global trader to outsource the product and focus on such areas as the component assembly point, the packaging and distribution point, and the mixing and blending unit for powdered cargoes such as spices.

9. Value is added to the product through the global logistic network. It may be through better packaging arrangements, more outsourcing of componentized products which offer lower costs and better quality, or through the blending and mixing of food products as found in the Distriparks in the Port of Rotterdam.

10. Companies, particularly multinationals, are being driven by their logistics departments. Moreover, the multinationals now focus on a simultaneous global product launch across all markets to ensure an early cash return on capital expenditure rather than concentrating on a regional launch over a period of time, for example, phase one Europe, phase two North America and phase three the Far East. This favours the logistic operation.

11. Following on from point (10) is the intense competition emerging in the global product market. Hence, to remain competitive the trader must adopt a global logistic strategy.

12. Satellite production demands a logistic network. It is computer driven.

13. Shorter product lifecycle driven by a fashion conscious international market and continuous technical advancement favours logistic efficiency.

14. The ongoing technological developments providing a longer shelf life for many consumer products, especially foodstuffs, needs a logistically based distribution sourcing mechanism.

15. The global logistic facility offers a one-stop operation and the opportunity to deal with one person, the account executive. Hence, both the importer and exporter develop empathy with the global logistics operator on a tailor-made basis, taking full advantage of their professionalism and experience coupled with a competitively priced operation. Traders can therefore concentrate on their core business of marketing, product development, investment and production.

16. The global logistic operation encourages the rationalization of distribution networks. This will accelerate as the hub and spoke system develops through the mega carrier operations.

17. Continuing improvements in the global infrastructure, e.g. port modernization, the development of inland clearance depots and free trade zones, the provision of new and enlarged airports, the development of

road and rail networks serving the ports and airports, all favour the global logistic operation. The development of multi-modalism involving a stronger interface and integration between transport modes and the emergence of dedicated services also favours global logistics.

18. Undoubtedly, the rapid expansion of information technology has been a major driving factor as the global logistic operation is computer driven.

19. Companies today demand responsiveness from the global operator. The discerning international entrepreneur is demanding the 'total logistics product service' (see item 17). When a trader purchases a service, the trader expects the consignment to be delivered or to be informed of delays or challenges encountered. As trade expands and companies move from a regional to a global market basis to exploit the economies of scale, to remain competitive in price and product specification, and to make further market penetration, the quality of the service becomes paramount. Moreover, the global logistics operator, through experience and professionalism, facilitates the trader's expansion from a regional to a global market base. The global operator will be able to help the trader in planning such market expansion and provide data on the culture, the market environment, import restrictions, customs regulations and the best-practice global logistics operation feasible. Today, traders are logistically literate and demand accreditation to product quality control – which includes distribution through global logistics. Moreover, traders demand a quick response to changing and volatile order levels with cycles of peaks and troughs. Again, the mega logistic carrier can best respond to such a challenge.

20. Market research confirms that only 30 per cent of changes in suppliers are motivated by a better or cheaper product. Most changes occur due to a poor service quality or inadequate attention to the individual customer. This also favours the mega logistics global operator.

21. The manufacturer/producer striving to achieve a shorter production cycle realized with the facilitation of many of the ingredients offered by the logistics system.

22. The development of third party logistic contractors such as Wincanton Logistics and Exel Logistics.

23. The continuous improvement in supply chain software. The most important concept underlying management of supply is that of integration. This embraces manufacturing resource planning, inventory management and supply chain design. Goods must be able to flow in a highly organized manner between each stage of the supply chain while at the same time achieving the most desirable balance between sales – stocks – production and customer service – cost – working capital. Every supply chain will have a different set of emphases. For example, a manufacturer of high specification value goods may be

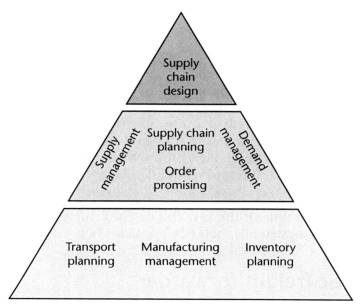

FIGURE 6.2 A focus of the supply chain software
Reproduced by courtesy of Synquest

more interested in speed and security of delivery than achieving the lowest cost. It is essential all parties involved in the supply chain have an agreed set of priorities. Moreover, effective transparent communication and understanding needs to be created of what the supply chain is designed to achieve. Logistic systems are important to be able to send data to where the decisions are taken and to keep all the international business managers and sectors informed about the flow of goods. Figure 6.2 features the supply chain software. Software advances have been accelerated through the rapid globalization of manufacture and distribution.

24. The development of time sharing with the logistics contractor. This involves the contractor being linked to the customer's own IT system – receiving order picking and delivery instructions, implementing them and feeding back the results for processing and evaluation. However, this limits their ability to take a proactive approach to their customer's needs.

25. Economic and trading blocs as found in Europe, North America and the Far East are continuing to develop as Member States realize their benefits. Such blocs favour particularly the global logistic trader who can adopt the strategy of selling a single product in a single market such as the European Union which has no culture or trade barriers and permits the free flow of goods. Supply chain efficiency is here a key factor in sales performance and market penetration.

To conclude our analysis the specific reasons for the increasing interest in supply chain management and global logistics can be summarized as follows:

1. *Concept.* Companies are primarily concerned with reducing delivery times and improving responsiveness to customers, reflecting the shorter product lifecycles they face.
2. *Value.* Equal emphasis is placed upon cost savings (from reduced inventory levels, economies of scale and a reduction in fixed assets) and improved service quality (through reliable delivery, improved stock availability and response times).

To achieve improvements in the management of a supply chain, keeping track of goods at all times is the key. This can be achieved through manual methods or sophisticated EDI tools (see pp. 433–45).

6.4 The logistic freight forwarder

Advances in information technology and the relaxation in Europe of customs barriers have greatly facilitated the emergence of new strategies in trans-European distribution. Gone are the national boundaries as impediments to quick distribution with their attendant customs examination. Today, traders treat the 25 European states as a single market with no trade, distribution, culture or product specification barriers. Consequently, traders are outsourcing their non-core functions and entrusting the pan-European distribution operation to the logistic freight forwarder. This involves the freight forwarder taking over every subsequent function from production line to final delivery and focusing on supply chain management.

A further industrial development is the move to product outsourcing and spreading points of manufacture and distribution throughout a variety of countries. Accordingly, the freight forwarder becomes involved in managing the flow of goods, from warehousing, picking and packing to inventory control and product repairs. A global network and heavy investment in information technology is required. Freight forwarders offer added-value services, logistics management and reliable information to their clients. In short the logistic operation involves the process of order acceptance to the stage of end delivery.

The logistic freight forwarder focuses on intermodal services and endeavours to formulate a cost- and time-effective method of transportation for its customers and a single rate for the through transit. The freight forwarder concentrates on supply chain management and works towards forming partnerships covering parts of the supply chain with its major customers.

Overall, the logistically focused freight forwarder provides value added services including inventory control, sorting, deferred manufacturing, assembly, testing, badging, packaging, labelling and bar-coding. The benefits to the shipper include improved cash flow, lower running costs, reduced capital expenditure, released management time and flexibility.

To conclude, the successful logistic freight forwarder must be prepared to adapt to a changing global logistic scene and invest heavily in EDI and good quality, trained and committed staff. Undoubtedly, this is an opportunity for the mega freight forwarder.

6.5 Greater Columbus – an inland logistic port, USA

Basically, the art of logistics is the ability to get the right product at the right place at the right time. In short it is the planning, organization, control and execution of the flow of goods from purchasing through production and distribution to the final customer in order to satisfy the requirements of the market. In international distribution terms this is the process of warehousing, transporting and distributing goods and cargo and the positioning of containers and/or equipment. It requires, therefore, an integrated and high-quality package of services in which the emphasis is focused on care of the cargo and provision of the most efficient coordination and management of the transport process. It comprises transport forwarding, storage and distribution, all of which are adapted to the specific requirements of the product, the supplier and the buyers: a total package covering all the links in the logistic chain but where the different components can also be offered individually. It combines production, warehousing, distribution and transport for shippers on a global basis.

An interesting inland port featuring a new era in logistics is Greater Columbus situated in the state of Ohio, USA. It was set up in 1992 and is surrounded within a 250-mile radius by major metropolitan areas such as Cleveland, Cincinnati, Pittsburgh and Indianapolis. Columbus enjoys a favourable geographic location and within a 500-mile radius is 58 per cent of the nation's population and disposable income and 50 per cent of the nation's manufacturing capacity. Within 250 miles, over $170 billion of international trade is conducted and over 22 per cent of the nation's GDP generated. Details of Columbus's competitive situation regarding access to the population and transportation time are featured in Table 6.1.

In short, Columbus is situated in the heart of the USA. Hence, strategically it is very favourably situated, a factor enhanced by the development of marketing partnerships with the seaports of New York, New Jersey, Virginia and Los Angeles. Air cargo services are available at Rickenbacker International Airport and partnerships are in place to cater for international air freight with a number of airlines using wide-body aircrafts such as Boeing 747s and DC 10s. Door-to-door transit times to and from the Far East and Northern Europe are shown in Table 6.2.

An outstanding feature of Columbus is its competitiveness with other major US distribution cities such as New York, Chicago, Atlanta and

TABLE 6.1 Competitive situation of Columbus

City	% of population reached in two days	Average time to service US markets
Columbus	53	2.71 days
New York	34	2.83 days
Chicago	41	2.99 days
Atlanta	35	3.21 days
Los Angeles	15	4.16 days

TABLE 6.2 Columbus: transit times

Destination	Air cargo	Ocean expedited service
Far East	21 hours	15–18 days
N. Europe	10 hours	10–12 days

TABLE 6.3 Comparison with other major distribution centres

	Warehouse $/sq.ft[1]	Warehouse $/sq.ft annual increase[2]	Warehouse labour $/hours[3]
Columbus	2.50	0%	11.57
New York	3.50	8%	11.57
Chicago	3.30	8%	23.50
Atlanta	2.75	13%	12.72
Los Angeles	3.90	8%	12.09

[1] Recent estimates of net lease cost for suburban sites.
[2] Represents estimated annual increase in warehouse space costs for the next 12 months.
[3] Represents average wage estimates for material handler/fork truck operator.

Los Angeles. This is demonstrated in Table 6.3 which compares warehousing, labour and redistribution costs.

A major aspect of the successful logistics operation is supply chain management. This involves the integration of all parties involved in the logistics channel. The supply chain may be represented by a series of loops, with each loop representing a member in the channel, from suppliers to the end customer. In the past, channel members often operated independently without sharing information and coordinating material flow. Relationships between channel members were often adversarial. The modern supply chain connects these loops into an integrated chain, with material flow closely coordinated between channel members and facilitated by the sharing of information. Partnerships among channel members replace formerly adversarial relationships, and the result is a more efficient flow of goods and information across the channel. The implementation of information technology has facilitated much of this transformation in the supply chain. Utilizing such tools as POS data acquisition, EDI document transmission, JIT materials management and ECR/QR replenishment, channel members can become more efficient by removing time from the cycle. The result is a streamlined supply chain which delivers enhanced value to the consumer and improves the competitive position of channel members.

To build a high-performance global supply chain through an inland port is a complex operation. As the supply chain increasingly becomes international in scope, the logistical complexities multiply. Columbus is well suited to serve as an inland hub for European shippers trying to reach the US market, as well as for US shippers trying to reach the European market. Columbus boasts excellent air cargo capacity with Rickenbacker International Airport, a former military base now converted primarily to commercial use. Rickenbacker is capable of landing any size of aircraft, and is supported by the services required to efficiently process air cargo. In addition, Columbus possesses the necessary rail infrastructure to allow efficient intermodal connections to coastal port cities. Columbus has established formal partnerships with three of these: New York/New Jersey, Los Angeles and Norfolk. These partnerships provide shippers with enhanced service levels between the port cities and Columbus. Taken together, the logistical benefits of Columbus provide an attractive alternative to moving cargo through the busy and congested ports of larger US cities. In terms of market access, Columbus is within a one-day truck drive of over 50 per cent of the nation's purchasing and manufacturing capacity. In assessing the numerous benefits that Columbus has to offer, it makes sense to include Columbus as a link in a global supply chain.

Thus we can see that Columbus has developed an effective transportation and logistics infrastructure allowing it to become a premier trade centre and modal inland port. It provides a multi-modal transportation system and information system within its region, making it the logical choice of location for companies looking to serve US and Canadian markets from a single distribution, manufacturing or assembly operation.

6.6 Logistic case studies

A wide range of industries now benefits from the international logistics focus. Six examples representing different industries are given below, courtesy of Kay O'Neill Logistics Professionals, Colnbrook, Slough SL3 0AT. www.kayoneill.com

Kuscho and Co: Kuscho makes high quality design-led contract furniture in Germany. In 2001 Kay O'Neill was assigned to re-engineer the supply chain using innovative procedures in the following areas: shorten the delivery cycle by 25 per cent, improve timed delivery performance by 30 per cent, maximize product integrity, provide for future expansion and produce a tailor-made information system to give Kuscho competitive advantage in managing stock and delivering samples. Overall, the results yielded a direct beneficial impact on customer service, sales and financial performance.

Merck Biosciences Ltd: This company specializes in the supply of life science reagents to research institutions. Samples are flown in from the West Coast of America, packed in dry ice and broken down into smaller units prior to distribution. Kay O'Neill was assigned to eradicate the delays inherent in the airport controls. Subsequently Kay O'Neill recommended a change of airport and held meetings with airlines, customs and the regulatory authorities. Ultimately, this strategy yielded a range of benefits including: stock is delivered four times per week; clearance procedures are streamlined; freight is cleared within four hours and delivered to Nottingham at 08.30 hours; and full information on the status of the samples is continuously communicated. Overall, the result yielded an extremely good service and level of reliability which helps Merck to ensure the integrity of the samples. This maintains good customer relations and underpins the excellent commercial performance.

Musto: Musto clothing is much favoured by the yachting fraternity, country-goers and the fashion conscious. With a fast expanding business, Musto assigned Kay O'Neill to take responsibility of the supply chain. The following was introduced: proactive purchase order management, a unique online tracking system and a flexible approach to warehousing and distribution. This strategy enabled Musto's management to concentrate solely on the core business. Furthermore, it enabled Musto to realize its distribution and merchandizing targets, thereby increasing profitability levels.

Bermuda Forwarders: Kay O'Neill through its operating division, Bermuda Forwarders (UK) and its associate company based on the island of Bermuda – Bermuda Forwarders Ltd, is responsible for over 60 per cent of all goods transported from the UK to Bermuda. Bermuda has a resident population of 60 000 and 400 000 tourists each year. The estimated combination of affluent islanders and high spending tourists means that Bermudian shops sell the highest quality merchandise. Companies like Wedgwood, Marks and Spencer, Austin Reed, H J Heinz, Oxford University Press, Portmeirion, Royal Doulton, Waterford Crystal and Pringle, entrust their logistic requirements to Bermuda Forwarders Operation. They provide full FCL/LCL groupage and air freight services all year round on a global basis.

General Motors: When General Motors began to source components from Europe for its Brazilian car and truck plants, Kay O'Neill was assigned to handle the logistics operation in the UK. In partnership with J.H. Bachmann, part of the Krupp organization, they have been responsible for coordinating supplies from 40 components manufacturers and ensuring their safe, on time delivery to Brazil. Technological support includes EDI links with the factories and online shipment data.

The products range from tiny items like door rubbers to whole sub-frames. Part of Kay O'Neill's expertise is employed in devising original packaging solutions to meet these wide ranging requirements. For example, they designed a disposable crate which could be fitted on to the end of the production line.

The volumes are considerable. Kay O'Neill ships over a thousand containers every year and air freights hundreds of thousands of kilos of more urgent parts. The customs regulations are particularly complex.

The relationship between Kay O'Neill and GM has grown closer over the years not only because of the benefits of shared knowledge and experience, but also because they have enabled a major customer to improve the cost-efficiency of their logistics operation and helped to reduce downtime at the plants. This has created more opportunities for the two companies to work together.

Haworth UK: For over eight years Kay O'Neill has provided a full range of logistics services to Haworth UK, the British arm of the fast growing global office furniture company. Each year has seen the challenges grow bigger and bigger as Haworth's activities have expanded in the UK, Ireland and mainland Europe. During this time Kay O'Neill have continued to redesign their services to meet this customer's rapidly changing requirements. For Haworth, Kay O'Neill process around 50 trailers and containers every month.

The products, which comprise systems furniture, seating, storage and desking lines, travel lightly packed, particularly in Europe. This means that extra special care must be taken throughout the physical handling process to protect the valuable merchandise from any kind of damage. This is where their special expertise in handling and protecting high value goods really pays off.

Use is made of the latest communication systems. Kay O'Neill has set up an EDI network with Haworth's manufacturing facilities in America, Canada and Europe. Consequently they have become an integral link in Haworth's international distribution chain to the point where Kay O'Neill can often anticipate problems and provide guidance on difficult decisions.

Readers are urged to study the Supply Chain Order Process Flow diagram – fully computerized Figure 6.3.

6.7 Criteria of logistic supplier selection

As suppliers to the logistics industry have developed their organizations and widened their range of services, the possibility for companies to out-source their logistics operations has increased dramatically.

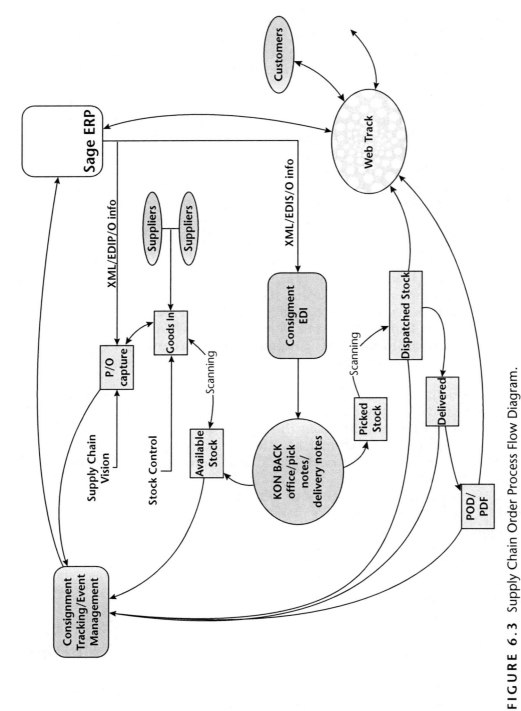

FIGURE 6.3 Supply Chain Order Process Flow Diagram.

Reproduced by kind permission of Kay O' Neill

There are many reasons for outsourcing but the most common include accessing economies of scale, increasing flexibility, refocusing of business on 'core' activities, reducing overheads and simplifying organizations.

The first stage in the selection task is to consider the implications of distribution strategy for the achievement of business plan goals including the effect on cost, quality and flexibility. This will probably involve an in-house evaluation of the activities involved. The next step is to conduct a full costing exercise taking into account the type of service to be provided, the price of the service, the net revenue released by reducing the in-house resource and the cost of switching. The final stage is to identify the number of viable suppliers in the market bearing in mind that no two logistic companies are exactly the same. All have their own areas of specialization. Particular attention should be given to the professional qualifications of the directorate; membership of a trade association; the company's track record; the level of commitment, interest and experience in the area of logistics sought; and their contract terms, resources and client base. Adequate time should be devoted to supplier selection and meaningful discussions conducted with potential candidates.

6.8 Future of logistics

The logistics industry continues to move at an accelerated rate globally. Initially it started with freight companies/freight forwarders who provided collection, distribution, customs, packaging and delivery services. The next generation was the logistic company who responded to customer needs and developed a new level of technological sophistication to the management of supply chains. Today, the industry has entered its current phase which is a closer integration with its customers. This process is driven by three fundamental trends. First, delivery lead times have become shorter in response to higher standards of customer service; secondly, global competition has exerted an inexorable downward pressure on cost leading to more outsourcing; and thirdly, technological advances have resulted in logistic specialists being able to offer services to companies which simply cannot be provided 'in house'.

The philosopher Edmund Burke once said 'You can never plan the future by the past'. Nowhere is this more true than in the world of logistics where entirely new structures are emerging. New types of partnerships are being forged between logistic providers and their customers spurred on by new techniques in handling and transporting goods. Innovation and change will remain pivotal to increasing the efficiency of international trade and improving the competitiveness of individual companies. This will be driven/facilitated by logistics in a global competitive environment.

6.9 Globalization

It is appropriate that logistics and globalization are examined simultaneously, as one feeds off the other in terms of their development.

During the past 20 years, the pattern of international trade has changed dramatically. This is due to a variety of factors, in particular technology, politics, economics, cultural and legal considerations. Trade does not pass unless there is business confidence but the legal framework and infrastructure in which trade is conducted today is very different from two decades ago. The world is opening up with faster travel, common mass media and open communication systems.

There are, of course, numerous other factors which we will examine subsequently but a book of this nature would not be complete without a focus on globalization. To define a global company we could say that it represents the process of the whole organization targeting the selection and development of market opportunities and building up the infrastructure essential for that objective to be realized; such a process being conducted on a global basis.

Globalization has two sources of origin: political and technological. The political source may be attributed to economic liberal forces aimed at enhancing trade and integrating economies. This is realized through political effort manifested by the International Agencies such as WTO, UNCITRAL and WCO and the development of Economic blocs such as NAFTA, MERCOSUR and ASEAN and the emerging regional trade agreements. The technological area embraces a range of items such as E-commerce and high-tech infrastructure supply chains.

Globalization of markets and trade results in the provision of a product or service which can be sold virtually in any market of the world providing the economic infrastructure and culture can support it. The key to it is the design and specification of the product or service and the added value it provides to the user or consumer. The product may be produced on a regional basis such as in Europe, Asia, North America, South America, etc. to serve those markets on a customerized basis but with the same core specification. For example, cars produced for cold climates would have heaters, while those for hot climates would have air conditioning.

An example of a major global logistic market is cars. Major car carriers are Wallenius Wilhelmsen Lines, which have 60 vessels and Eukor Car Carriers with 75 Ro-Ro vessels. The market is rapidly changing. Major flows embrace Asia/Europe and Asia/North America. China has become a net exporter of cars and is forecast to produce 1.5 million yearly by 2010. Moreover, the emergence of South Africa, Mexico, South Korea and Australia is significant. Europe remains a high volume car exporter. Hence car production remains fragmented as the traditional car producers of Japan and some EU countries decline consequent on their outsourcing of car production plants and high regulated labour costs. The car carriers operate on hub port basis and provide extensive facilities. This includes vehicles that are to be cleaned, repaired, modified, customized and put through a pre-delivery inspection prior to despatch to dealerships on a JIT basis. The operation is fully computerized (EDP). New supply chains are emerging driven by demands set by logistic providers rather than shipping companies. An increasing number of car carriers' hub ports are providing transhipment services to spoke ports thereby opening up new supply chains.

6.9.1 Advantages of globalization

In a highly competitive world market environment, driven today by logistics and computer literacy in management and consumer needs, some of the benefits globalization of trade brings to world markets are detailed below.

1. World living standards are raised. This is in the earliest stages of its realization, as globalization of an economy will only benefit those parts of an economy or region which globalization has reached, such as in India and China.
2. Globalization brings cultures closer together through the added value products or services offered to their consumers and users. This may be through films, technology, etc.
3. Overall, globalization develops world resources.
4. Greater integration via economic blocs or customs unions bring countries closer together to exploit their economic well-being. Such cooperation is usually based on the development of those products which have the greatest economic potential in world markets.
5. Globalization encourages investment globally.
6. Emerging from item (5), governments which are stable and subject to the democratic processes are more likely to attract trade and investment.
7. Global trade encourages the development of the infrastructure within a country, as a high standard of infrastructure is an essential ingredient to that country's participation at a global level. This includes airports, seaports, transport multi-modalism, banking systems, information technology, education and training, energy resources and an acceptable legal environment. Examples of such countries are South Korea, Malaysia, Thailand, Southern and North Eastern China, Mumbai/New Delhi in India and so on.
8. Globalization encourages tourism which brings wealth, cultural understanding and economic and social development in many regions of the world.

6.9.2 Factors driving globalization

A wide range of factors are driving globalization and these are detailed below:

1. It reduces trade barriers (see pp. 496–97).
2. It encourages standardization of products as distinct from adopting the product to meet the needs of a particular culture or group of customers.
3. Standardization of products lowers production costs and design expenses, and enables goods to reach the market sooner as the lead time is much reduced.
4. It favours strong brand management such as Ford Motors, NIKE, Chanel, Kodak and Sony.
5. It exploits logistics (see pp. 134–38).
6. Information technology stimulates globalization as it has no time zones, language barriers or culture impediment.
7. Quicker and more efficient distribution is a key factor to develop global markets. (see also item 5) Examples include development of the hub and spoke system (see p. 107), port privatization, development of multi-modalism and continuing expansion of new or modernized airports and seaports.
8. International agencies who provide the framework for international trade and greatly facilitate its globalized development are playing an increasingly important role. Examples include ICC, WTO, UNCTAD, UNCITRAL, OECD, IMF and INMARSAT.
9. It is opening up global financial markets such as Stock Exchanges in Africa.
10. Economic blocs stimulate globalization of their products and services, as found in the EU and NAFTA. Also, the EU constitutes a Single Market and encourages both economic and monetary union as found in the launch of the euro in January 1999 (see pp. 551–54).
11. Companies which wish to compete in global markets must remain competitive and profitable to generate investment. Hence, the need to drive down costs, especially in areas of research and development, a move towards having fewer layers of administration resulting in a flatter organization structure; more regional autonomy structures; a greater focus on the customer; more out-sourcing of components – global sourcing; shorter product lifecycle; satellite production; reduced financing costs; proactive marketing anticipating customer needs; technological developments providing longer shelf life; and a shorter lead time in design and product development aided by technology. All these factors focus on the need for the multinational industries (MNI) to remain competitive and result in buoyant merger and acquisition markets or strategic operating alliances. Such strategies reduce costs,

attract continuing investment, improve profitability and provide a wider market share.

12. The MNI is driving the global market and today accounts for over 60 per cent of world trade.

13. Globalization is developing a wide range of global service industries in mega container operators, airlines such as British Airways, management consultancies, banks and fast foods – McDonalds, Burger King, etc.

14. The youth culture involves the younger generation favouring globalization. This emerges through travel, education, especially higher education, involving studying overseas, the impact of the media and availability of high technology through the Internet, E-commerce, etc.

15. The development of regional trade agreements offering preferential trade terms and duty free (p. 10).

To conclude this analysis one must stress that the MNI must continually review its position in the market place and especially in the area of focusing on customer needs and developing them on a global basis.

6.10 Global village

Emerging from the globalization concept is the global village. This is basically where all the major global brands are available especially in the consumer market. It includes cameras, restaurants, perfumery, clothes, hi fi equipment, radio, televisions, shoes, petrol, cars, white goods, medical needs and so on.

The global village concept may be found at major airports and major cities and tourist and commercial centres worldwide. Annually, the range of global village products is extending and likewise their location.

6.11 Factors obstructing globalization

There is no doubt that market globalization is favouring countries which wish to participate in the economic and social benefits it yields. Conversely, there are many parts of the world where inhabitants resent globalization strongly for a wide variety of reasons which we will briefly examine.

1. It changes the culture and social standards of a country. Cultures and religion are very deep-rooted in many areas of the world and globalization, embracing the global village, represents an intrusion into heritage and deep-seated cultures and beliefs, extending to many generations. Improved education and more travel can help bring change to such situations in the long term.

2. Globalization develops a homogeneous consumer rather than a heterogeneous client. Overall, it restricts choice and can encourage a quasi monopolistic situation which may not always operate in the interests of the consumer. Hence, the need in some countries to provide legislation for more consumer protection.

3. The arrival of the global village, particularly with the franchise concept (see p. 485), involving rigid retail outlet design, may alienate the culture and local architect philosophy. This needs to be handled with care and understanding.

4. The global player, the MNI, has a larger income often in excess of a less developed country. This tends to place the MNI in a strong position when entering a less developed market, which can be exploited if not handled with care and empathy.

5. The globalization of markets can destroy local manufacturers and alienate the populace. Alternatively, the arrival of a large MNI will raise standards, bring new economic prospects to a region and improve a country's trade balance. Such situations require continuous dialogue to ensure both parties benefit from the venture and the social implications are not disregarded. Careful planning and the development of improved living standards must be sought.

6. Distribution plays a major part in the globalization of markets. This does result in many countries not featuring in such globalization. For example, countries which are not on a global container network are seriously disadvantaged in the development of their trade in a multi-modal logistic international trade environment.

7. Brand development. Numerous brands exist in the global market in cosmetics, fashion, white furniture, automobiles, featuring names such as Dyson, Jaeger, Benetton and Burberry.

8. Finally, politics play a major role in the globalization of markets. An example is the G8 group and major economic blocs such as EU, NAFTA and MERCOSUR.

6.12 Developing the global economy

The dynamic ideal based on a new global economy offers the possibility of lifting billions of people into a worldwide middle class. But it also contains within it the seeds of new instabilities, new inequalities and new threats of the global economy. The challenge to the millennial generation, therefore, is to create a world trading system attuned to the pace and scope of the new global economy, one that offers an opportunity for all our people and one that meets the profound environmental challenge we share.

The international agency driving world trade is the World Trade Organisation (see p. 27). Formed in 1995 as a successor to GATT at the Uruguay Round of talks, the WTO has generated, in four years, an increase of 25 per cent in world trade. It has helped to build the infrastructure for the global economy and formulated agreements on information technology, telecommunications and financial services affecting trillions of dollars in global commerce each year.

Discussed briefly below are the essential ingredients to develop globalization in the twenty-first century, many of which were discussed at the 50 year anniversary of GATT/WTO in Geneva in 1998.

1. The development of an ever more open global trading system. Economic freedom and open trade have brought unprecedented prosperity in the twentieth century. It is essential that the circle of opportunity is widened in the twenty-first century. For every country engaged in trade, open markets dramatically widen the base of possible customers for goods and services.

2. Countries must recognize that in the new global economy, the way we conduct our trade affects the lives and livelihoods and the health and safety of families around the world.

3. There is a need to harmonize the goal of increasing trade with the goal of improving the environment and working conditions. Enhanced trade can and should enhance the protection of the environment. Hence, international trade rules must permit sovereign nations to exercise their right to set protective standards for health, safety and the environment and biodiversity. Nations have a right to pursue these protections – even when they are stronger than international norms.

4. The WTO must modernize by opening its doors to the scrutiny and articipation of the public. Thus, the need to take every feasible step to bring openness and accountability to its operations. Hence, the need to conduct all hearings by the WTO in public, and not, as at present when one nation challenges the trade practices of another, behind closed doors.

5. There needs to be a trading system that taps the full potential of the information age. Today, there are no customs duties on telephone calls, fax messages, e-mail or computer links when they cross international borders. Hence, the need to continue liberalization of the electronic global commerce with no trade barriers.

6. The WTO strategy and other international agencies must continue to encourage governments to conduct trade on an open, honest and fair basis extolling the concept of best practice. This embraces government procurement being based on open and fair bidding and not on national prejudices. Another area is the need to adopt the anti-bribery convention developed by the OECD in 1997.

7. There should be provision for an open global trading system that moves as fast as the market place. This embraces quicker ways of eliminating trade barriers, without resorting to meticulous evaluations, which are often inspired by time delaying tactics. Such an area

is agriculture with its subsidies and quota systems. It is a fast growing market with yet greater potential, which could be realized through greater liberalization. Indeed, another fast growing industry area, is the service sector – banking, tourism, transport, insurance, energy, express delivery, audio-visual, consultancy, professional services, etc. It is the area least disciplined by WTO rules.

8. There is a need to spread the benefits of globalization. This embraces the need to help developing countries integrate into the global economy and thereby gain from the benefits of globalization.

9. Trade liberalization should be extended.

10. World trade expansion should be developed but not at any cost. The paramount need is to protect the environment. Governments need to consider the environmental impact of everything they do, including the trade sphere. Trade rules should not be used to impose unfair standards on developing countries, nor to discriminate against their exports.

11. To help cash flow management of the export order an increasing number of sellers are opting for stage payments of the export sale contracts. This involves a 20 per cent down payment on confirmation of the order, followed by four subsequent payments on a timescale agreed between the seller and the buyer. This practice is long established in major contracts but extends to the SME trade finance strategy.

12. The LDC and developing nations of the world must benefit more from the globalization of trade. This means more inwards investment, improvement/development of the infrastructure, joint ventures, more emphasis on training, development of FTZ/ICDs, identity of industries – agricultural/industrial – which could be developed with export potential with modern management and hi-tech resources; logistics development and a stronger interface with empathy between the LDC/developing nations and OECD countries. More regional trading agreements would facilitate the global development of LDCs. Investment, technology and hi-tech professional culture arrangement with a good – infrastructure are key factors (pp. 148–49).

Undoubtedly, the foregoing criteria of ingredients to accelerate globalization of trade will be constrained by political and economic considerations. The reader may wish to monitor the extent to which these proposals are developed.

6.13 Interface between logistics and globalization

The cost and quality of multi-modal transport and logistic services are increasingly relevant for the participation of developing countries in the globalized economy. It is estimated the doubling of transport costs leads to a drop in the economic growth rate of more than half a percentage point and that variables related to transport costs account for more than two thirds of the statistical variation *per capita* income between countries.

For today's requirements, traditional transport services are often insufficient. What is needed today are more complete logistic services involving the use of information and communication technology (ICT) and multi-modal transport operations which have a service provider assuming responsibility for the entire transport chain. This type of service is often not available in developing countries and practically non-existent in LDCs, landlocked countries and most SIDs.

The determinants of inexpensive and high quality transport and logistic services include exogenous factors, such as distance and total trade volumes. They do, however, also include areas where the public sector can make a difference. Such areas where obstacles to multi-modal transport and logistic services exist can be grouped into (a) infra-structure and technologies; (b) security and safety; (c) facilitation; (d) legal aspects; and (e) market access. While necessary action in many cases has to be taken at the national level, there are important areas where the international community can provide assistance through coordination, technical assistance, multilateral agreements and common legal frameworks.

Logistic services include the management and often the provision of packaging, warehousing, information, and transport services within the supply chain. International logistic services are a determining factor of a country's competitiveness as they are crucial for production processes and for delivering exports. In particular, increased trade in unfinished products, i.e. the movement of intermediate goods within production processes requires logistic services of ever higher quality with regard to the reliability, safety, security and frequency of deliveries.

Transport tends to be the main component of logistic services and its share in overall logistic cost has been increasing in recent years. In particular the growth of containerized transport, together with technological developments improving the systems for transferring cargo between different modes, has considerably affected modern transport patterns and practices. Increasingly, goods, particularly manufactured, are carried across the globe by means of multi-modal transport. Moreover, shippers and consignees often prefer to deal with one party (the multi-modal transport operator) who arranges for the transportation of goods from door-to-door and assumes responsibility throughout, irrespective of whether this is also the party that actually carries out the different stages of the transport.

The participation of developing countries in the use and provision of multi-modal transport and logistic services varies widely, with small island, land locked and least developed countries not effectively participating at all. The latter do not usually have companies that provide such services, and nor do international providers usually offer such services in these countries. The foregoing situation is in complete contrast to what is provided in OECD member countries where the multi-modal transport and logistic services are well developed.

International freight costs have an impact on trade equivalent to customs tariffs or the exchange rate. A reduction in the cost of transport directly stimulates exports and imports just as an increase in the exchange rate makes exports more competitive and a reduction in national customs tariffs lowers the cost of imports. Landlocked countries in Africa, for example, on average, pay four times as much for the international transport leg of their imports than do developed economies. Moreover, the price of the vast majority of traded goods is exogenous for developing countries. Econometric estimates suggest that the doubling of an individual country's transport costs leads to a drop in its trade of 80 per cent or even more.

Spending on transport is increasing because of improved quality of service, especially greater dependability on just-in-time delivery. In the case of the USA, for example, it is estimated that during the two decades up to 2002, spending on transport rose by 160 per cent, while spending on inventories grew by only 27 per cent during the same period. While in 1982 inventory spending was still higher than spending on transport, today spending on transport is almost double that of inventory cost.

The freight and insurance costs of international transport also tend to increase as a percentage of GDP. The reason for this is that trade is growing at a faster pace than GDP. In the 1990's the rate of growth of world exports was more than double that of GDP, and although transport costs have fallen as a percentage of the value of trade, trade itself has expanded and with it international freight's share of GDP.

The geographical location of countries is less relevant for today's trade pattern than are transport and logistics. Countries mainly trade with one another depending on their patterns of production, income and whether they belong to economic blocs with the distance between them also having some bearing. There is an assumption of a close link between distance and transport costs, which would explain why countries closer to one another trade more than with countries further away. In practice, however, distance also tends to have a bearing on other characteristics of countries, which lead them to trade more.

Empirical studies have concluded that *'ceteris paribus'* (other things being equal) greater transport costs lead to lower levels of foreign investment, a lower savings ratio, reduced exports of services, reduced access to technology and knowledge and a decline in employment. As indicated earlier, a doubling of transport costs leads to a drop in the rate of economic growth of more than half a percentage point, which lowers growth over the long term of *per capita* income. Hence, variables related to transport costs may account for 70 per cent of the statistical variation in *per capita* income between countries.

When analyzing techniques on how to improve international logistic services, there arises a need to identify a range of different influencing factors and to know which of these factors can be influenced by public policies. Today, improvements in infrastructure and expansion of containerization have confirmed the same price of a tonne of cargo can buy a quicker and more reliable transport service than a decade ago on most trade routes. Additionally, greater commercial demands as regards speed have at the same time given rise to an increase in the global share of air transport as compared with maritime transport. Even when single-mode transport services are compared, large differences in transport costs persist. Transporting a 40 foot container from Douala (Cameroon) to Bangui (Central African Republic) over a distance of 1600 km costs three times as much as moving the same container over a distance of 1885 km from Walvis Bay (Namibia) to Johannesburg (South Africa).

Containerization of general cargo is the main component that has led to the introduction of multi-modal transport and logistics in developed regions. Today, it is recognized that containerization is a necessary condition for an increasing proportion of trade in merchandise and intermediate goods, also in developing countries. Containerized cargo requires fewer but better qualified personnel in ports where reforms are still pending in many developing countries. This embraces port, rail and road infrastructure as well as the corresponding regulations and labour regimes. These inland links are often incomplete and poorly maintained and constitute one of the main practical obstacles to transport providers offering multi-modal transport in many developing countries. A further factor inherent in containerization is the provision of information and communication technology which today has radically changed the way in which international trade and transport are conducted. A successful example of the use of ICT in developing countries is the Advanced Cargo Information System (p. 464).

The legal framework of multi-modal transport of goods is complex and still under discussion and adoption. Market access is another key area and the WTO continues to strive to open up markets and develop the concept of most favoured nation treatment (Chapter 19 and p. 573).

To conclude our analysis, access to logistics and multi-modal transport services is an increasingly important prerequisite for competitiveness in a globalized economy. The requirement that operators must be able to provide adequate logistics and multi-modal services is growing in line with increasing demands for faster more frequent, reliable and secure deliveries. These requirements are related to (a) infrastructure and technology; (b) security and safety; (c) trade facilitation; (d) the legal framework; and (e) market access.

Recommended reading

Freight Management International.
Global Supply Chain Management and International Logistics, 1st edition
    (forthcoming 2007). A.E. Branch, Routledge www.routledge.com
International Freighting Weekly.
Lloyd's Freight Transport Buyer.
WTO Annual Report.

Freight rates

7.1 Theory of freight rates

Freight is the reward payable to the carrier for the carriage of goods in a mercantile or recognized condition ready to be delivered to the merchant.

The pricing of air or sea transport services, usually in combination with land transport services, is dependent on the forces of supply and demand, but the factors affecting both supply and demand are perhaps more complicated than is the case of most other industries and services. The demand for a particular international transport service mode(s) is basically derived from the demand for the commodities carried and is, therefore, affected by the elasticity of demand for these commodities.

The demand for sea or air transport is affected by both direct competition between carriers and, because it is a derived demand, by the competition of substitutes or alternatives for the commodity carried. On any particular route, the shipowner or airline is subject to competition from carriers on the same route, and also from the carriers operating from alternative supply areas. The commodities carried by the latter may be competitive with the commodities from his or her own supply area and, to that extent, may affect the demand for his or her services. On many routes there is also competition from more than one form of transport.

The elasticity of demand for sea or air transport varies from one commodity to another. In normal times, an important factor affecting elasticity of demand for sea or air transport, is the cost of transport in relation to the market price of the goods carried. Although it may be small, the cost of sea or air transport is often a significant element in the final market price of many commodities. It can vary from 3 to 15 per cent depending on the transport mode and the commodity. (See pp. 205–07 *Maritime Economics, Management and Marketing*).

The price eventually fixed for a chartered vessel or aircraft depends largely on the relationship between buyers and sellers. Where both groups are numerous and have equal bargaining power, and where demand is fairly elastic, conditions of relative perfect competition prevail. Under these conditions for chartered tonnage, prices are fixed by the 'haggling of the market' and are known as contract prices. The market for tramp charters operates under such conditions and the contract is drawn up as a agreement known as a charterparty.

Under these conditions, the rate structure for tramps is a very simple product and emerges from the competitive interplay of supply and demand. From the economist's point of view, rates made in this way represent the most efficient method of pricing; for when price is determined under conditions of perfect competition, production is encouraged to follow consumer wishes and price itself does not deviate to any great extent from average total cost. A similar criterion applies to air freight charterers. It must be borne in mind, however, that the air charter market extends both to the very large shipment offering, for example, an indivisible load urgently required such as a ship's propeller, and the smaller split charter involving consignments of 500–2500 kg. Some air freight forwarders have their own charter subsidiaries.

Chartering can also extend to Ro-Ro vehicles in the trades and markets beyond. The shipper/freight forwarder can charter a portion of the vehicle from the road operator either on a regular or spasmodic basis. In general terms the shipper must critically examine, including alternatives, the total freight cost of the transit and reconcile it with the distance. Generally, the shorter the total journey distance, the greater the need to ensure the cost is proportionate to the distance, otherwise it could quickly price the goods out of the overseas market. Generally too, documentation and customs entry cost do not vary greatly. Liner cargo services are now dominated by container tonnage with rates broadly reflecting market conditions whether on an FCL or LCL basis and determined by the shipowner. In contrast, a few container trades are under the aegis of the liner conference (see p. 161).

Air freight rates operative on regular scheduled international services are decided collectively by the airlines through the IATA mechanism which adopts a policy of parity on the level of rates on individual services/routes. The rates reflect market conditions and service cost. A major share of the air freight market is now conveyed under agent sponsorship involving consolidation arrangements and integrators (see p. 58).

Overall, a properly compiled tariff should encourage the movement of all classes of cargo to ensure the best balance between revenue production and the full utilization of the transport unit.

7.2 The constituents of the freight rate

Rate making has changed significantly in recent years as a result of the development of multi-modalism (Chapter 5). No longer is the rate based on one carrier on a port-to-port or airport-to-airport basis; it also involves two or three carriers providing a dedicated door-to-door service featuring one overall composite rate and the sea/land-bridge from the Far East to North America using the gateway ports of Vancouver, Los Angeles, Seattle and double-stack container trains (p. 77). For example, a consignment from Malaysia to industrial Europe via Dubai would embrace three major legs of the transit: (a) the rail journey from the dry port of Ipoh (p. 101) to Port Klang; (b) the maritime trip between ports Klang and Dubai; and (c) the flight from Dubai (p. 61) to Frankfurt (p. 63). Additionally, it would feature the collection and delivery charges which may involve a 40-mile road journey to Ipoh and a 70-mile rail journey to the consignee warehouse from Frankfurt. Furthermore, the transhipment and handling charges at the ports of Klang and Dubai, and Dubai airport will be included. Overall, the rate would feature the following:

1. Consignor premises and collection to Ipoh, based on zonal road rate charge.
2. Processing of cargo/handling/packaging/documentation at Ipoh.
3. Agents' charges including customs formalities.
4. Rail journey Ipoh to Port Klang.
5. Handling charges to Port Klang raised by the port authority to cover transhipment costs.
6. Shipowner's freight costs Port Klang to Port Dubai.
7. Handling and transhipment charges at Port Dubai to convey goods from port to airport; these are raised by the port authority and agent.
8. Handling charges at Dubai Airport, including documentation and the agent; these are raised by the airport authority and agent.
9. Air freight charges from Dubai to Frankfurt raised by the airline.
10. Handling/documentation/customs import duty at Frankfurt Airport. These are raised by the airport authority and the agent.
11. Delivery by rail or road to consignee's warehouse; rail charges raised by the German railways; and road charges raised by road hauliers.

The foregoing use of freight forwarders demonstrates their role as one of coordination and facilitation. The rate from Ipoh to Frankfurt will not feature any import duty as this is a local charge for the importer at Frankfurt. Overall, the above demonstrates the complexity and range of parties involved in developing a multi-modal rate; it excludes cargo insurance and provision made for CAF. The freight rate for the three major legs would be based on the W/M (weight/measurement) criteria (p. 177) and the consignment under notice would be consolidated into an LCL container at Ipoh, which would be unstuffed at Dubai port for transhipment to the nearby airport.

Basically, the tariff raised for a consignment can embrace a number of elements other than the sea, air, plus inland transport tariff and these are listed below.

1. *Tariff cargo rate.* In the case of air freight, this will be between the relevant airports for the airline rate. In the case of the agent's consolidated rate, the charge could be a through tariff from the shipper's

factory to the importer's distribution warehouse. Likewise for maritime transport, it will be the port-to-port container, Ro-Ro vehicle, or general cargo rates. The same criterion applies to a chartered aircraft or ship. The charterparty will determine the extent to which the charterer bears the cargo handling transhipment cost included in the overall fixture rate. It should be noted that there is an increasing tendency to develop the combined transport operation concept with through rates and documentation. This is particularly true of containers and Ro-Ro traffic.

2. *The customs clearance charge* is usually based on the local port authority or airline tariff. Charges vary between import/export, commodity type, quantity, and the degree of ultimate customs physical turn out examination of the consignment. The latter is usually a separate charge. It includes the presentation of the requisite documents/entry to customs. HM Customs have the legal authority to examine all imported consignments originating outside the EU, but, in reality, only random inspections are made at the discretion of the local customs officer. Customs clearance may be undertaken at an inland clearance depôt or the shipper's premises (LCP – Local Clearance Procedure) by prior arrangement, with the goods travelling under bond to and from the seaport. The actual presentation of the goods to customs and their ultimate clearance will be undertaken on behalf of the shipper by the port authority or airline, or the freight forwarder acting on behalf of his client.

3. *Freight forwarder's commission.* Many small exporters engage the services of a freight forwarder to look after the distribution arrangements of the consignment. The role of the freight forwarder is explained on p. 518, and accordingly raises a commission charge with the exporter/importer. This is usually between 2.5 and 5 per cent of the total freight account.

4. *Customs duty* will vary according to commodity specification and applies to imported consignments. It also extends to value added tax or something similar depending on the importing country.

5. *Disbursements.* These embrace a variety of items including freight services, telephone calls, E-commerce messages, currency surcharge, security cost, fuel surcharge, cost of feeding livestock, additional cost to police a valuable consignment, etc. Again it will depend on the nature of the cargo and the particular circumstances obtaining at the airport, seaport, or inland clearance depôt.

6. *Cargo insurance premium.* Usually the premium is lower for air freight than for sea transport but much depends on the latter method of forwarding, namely container, Ro-Ro, or general freight in break-bulk 'tween deck tonnage.

7. *Delivery/collection charge.* The collection and delivery of the cargo is usually undertaken by road transport. The rate is normally assessed

on distance within a zonal rating. This is related to the weight or cubic measurement of the consignment. This task may be undertaken by the exporter and/or importer's own vehicles. In other circumstances, the delivery and/or collection may be included in the through rate.

8. *Transhipment charge*. This arises when cargo is transhipped en route to continue its transit. It may occur at an airport or seaport. Again it could be an inclusive charge within the through rate, but much depends on the circumstances. When the cargo involves special arrangements being made to tranship it, due to its awkward shape, excessive weight or size, or the general nature of the commodity (e.g. livestock), additional charges are normally raised.

9. *Documentation charge*. Circumstances arise when it is necessary to obtain a certificate of origin to accord with the importing country customs' requirement to establish or verify the place of manufacture of the goods. This document, to be obtained by the exporter, is available from the local Chamber of Commerce, or if a consular invoice is required, from the consulate of the importing country. A charge is raised by the consulate office for this service which can be as much as £75 in some cases.

10. *Demurrage*. Cargo detained at an airport, seaport or inland clearance depot beyond a prescribed period attracts a daily demurrage charge. The cargo may be delayed due to wrong presentation of customs clearance documents, non-availability of an export/import licence, pending payment of customs duty, awaiting collection by consignee, etc.

11. *Handling cost*. This embraces cost of handling the cargo at the terminal. It is sometimes included in the through rate. In the case of containers, it is usually based on a tariff per container lift, ship to shore and vice versa. It can vary by container type, empty or loaded. Extra charges are raised for special lifts, i.e. indivisible loads.

12. *Wharfage charge*. This is a charge raised by the port authority for cargo transhipment.

13. *Cargo dues*. Again a cost raised by the port authority for goods passing over the quay.

14. *Rebate*. In the case of sea freight, exporters originating substantial quantities of traffic are granted a rebate provided they adhere to the shipowner/liner conference conditions. It may be an immediate rebate offering 10 per cent on the published tariff or possibly 10.5 per cent on a deferred rebate payable six months after the traffic has passed. Basically, a deferred rebate is a device to ensure that shippers will continue to support a conference or shipping line. Hence the shipper has an inducement to remain loyal to the liner conference or shipping line insofar as he stands to lose the rebate by using a non-conference vessel.

15. *Bunker or fuel surcharge* (bunker adjustment factor, BAF). In an era when fuel costs now represent a substantial proportion of direct voyage cost, shipowners are not prepared to absorb the variation in fuel prices. They take the view that price variation of bunker fuel tends to be unpredictable, bearing in mind that it is usually based on the variable dollar rate of exchange, and that it is difficult to budget for this cost realistically and reflect it adequately in their rate formulation. Moreover, an increase in the bunkering price erodes the shipowners' voyage profitability.

16. *Currency surcharge* (currency adjustment factor, CAF). This arises when the freight rate is related to a floating currency such as sterling. For example, if the rate were based on euros which both operate fixed rates of currency, then the sterling rate of exchange in January would probably be different to the situation the following July. For example, when sterling is depressed, it would probably earn more euros per £1 sterling in January than in the following July. Accordingly, a currency surcharge is imposed to minimize losses that the shipowner would incur, bearing in mind the shipowner obtains less sterling equivalent in euro rated traffic while, at the same time, port expenses in euros would be greater due to the depressed sterling rate of exchange.

An example of a currency surcharge scale is given below, involving the Anglo–euro trade. The freight tariff is sterling based on 1.40 euros to £1, and the rate per tonne is £20 or €28.

When charges are to be paid in euros to £1	Surcharge in euros (per cent)
1.466 to 1.484	5
1.51 to 1.465	4
1.436 to 1.450	3
1.421 to 1.435	2
1.396 to 1.420	1

No surcharge 1.315 to 1.395 (void area) nil (no surcharge)

When charges are to be paid In sterling: euros to £1	Surcharge in sterling (per cent)
1.381 to 1.404	1
1.366 to 1.380	2
1.351 to 1.365	3
1.336 to 1.350	4
1.316 to 1.335	5

The percentage of surcharge will be determined each week by reference to the average rate as published in *Le Monde* and the *Financial Times* on Saturdays (i.e. Friday's closing prices):

(a) Payment in sterling – exchange rate €1.350 to £1   £
    10 tonnes at £20 per tonne   200
    4 per cent surcharge based on exchange rate of €1.350   8

         208

(b) Payment in euros – exchange rate €1.428 to £   €
    10 tonnes at 28 euros per tonne   280
    5 per cent surcharge based on exchange rate of €1.482   14

    Total euros   294

17. Surcharges are usually raised for heavy lifts such as indivisible consignments and on excessive height or length of Ro-Ro rated traffic, together with any other traffic where special facilities are required.

It will be appreciated that special rates exist for particular cargoes. These include indivisible loads such as a transformer; antiques such as furniture of high value; household effects requiring special packaging for international transit; and livestock involving special facilities on the transport unit. The level of rebate is usually negotiated between the shipper and shipowner. Obviously the ultimate rate, mode of transport and route will be much influenced by the export sales contract and the delivery terms contained therein.

7.3 Factors influencing the formulation of freight rates

We will now examine the salient factors which influence the formulation of freight rates.

1. Competition. Keen competition on rates exists among various modes of transport. For example, in the UK-Europe trade, competition exists amongst air freight agents offering consolidated services, Le Shuttle (EuroTunnel), ISO containerization in the Asia/Europe, Asia/North America and Europe/North America trades and international road haulage.
2. The nature of the commodity, its quantity, period of shipment(s) and overall cubic measurements/dimensions/value.
3. The origin and destination of the cargo.
4. The overall transit cost.
5. The nature of packaging and convenience of handling.
6. The susceptibility of the cargo to damage and pilferage.
7. The general loadability of the transport unit.
8. Provision of additional facilities to accommodate the cargo, namely heavy lifts, strong room, livestock facilities, etc.
9. The mode(s) of transport.

10. Actual routeing of cargo consignment. Alternative routes tend to exist, particularly in air freight, with differing rate structures and overall transport costs.
11. Logistics – the supply chain value added benefit (p. 135).

The factor which has come to prominence in recent years in rate assessment is the 'value added benefit' the shipper derives from the mode(s) of distribution used (Chapters 6 and 13). The overall rate may be high, but it enables cost savings to be realized in lower inventory cost; improved service to the importer's clients; much reduced down time on unserviceable machinery undergoing repair; replenishment of stocks to meet consumer demand; assembly of component parts undertaken in low labour-cost markets, and with suppliers sourced worldwide; and the benefits the high-profile quality distribution network gives to the shipper. Reliability, frequency and transit time, and the overall quality of the service which involves the total product concept embracing all the distribution ingredients, are major and decisive factors. An increasing volume of air freight is now consigned under a logistics driven programme (see pp. 141–43).

We will now examine the varying methods of available freight rates by mode of transport.

7.4 Air freight rates

The formulation of air freight rates is controlled by the International Air Transport Association (IATA) insofar as major world airlines are affiliated to it, representing approximately 98 per cent of international air freight services. IATA has no influence on internal – for example, Glasgow–London – domestic flight air freight tariffs or charter flights. The significant aspect of the IATA affiliated airline is that no competition is permitted on air freight rates, that is, parity obtains, and competition is permitted only on service quality, frequency, etc.

Basically there are seven types of air freight rates in existence, each of which is designed to stimulate traffic in various ways. Moreover, it is relevant to say the same individual rates do not necessarily apply in both directions thereby reflecting the differing market situations. For example, a commodity rate for product type A may exist from London to New York but not in the reverse direction. Moreover, routeing of cargo is significant both in terms of transit time and tariff. If two routes are available, the shorter route in distance terms is likely to be the cheapest, but may be the longer in transit time due to the less frequent and slower schedules or connections.

International air cargo is charged by weight, calculated either as actual gross weight or in equivalent volumetric units, whichever is the greater. Thus air cargo is charged by weight except where the volume is more than

366 in^3/kg. In such cases, volumetric charges apply and each unit of 366 in^3 is charged as 1 kg. To calculate this, the maximum dimensions of the piece should be multiplied together to give a volume in cubic inches. This volume must be divided by 366 and the result will be the volumetric weight. If this is more than the actual weight, then the volumetric weight will be the chargeable weight. Where the consignment consists of pieces varying in density, the volumetric calculation will be based on the whole consignment. For metric measurements, 6000 cm$^3 = 1$ kg (see example, p. 177).

Air cargo rates are quoted per kilogram (gross weight or volume equivalent) and apply from airport of departure to airport of destination; they do not include charges for cartage, customs entry and clearance, etc.

A brief examination of each air freight rate classification now follows:

1. *Specific commodity rates.* These reduced rates apply to a wide range of commodities and to qualify the shipper must comply precisely with the commodity specifications as found in the tariff. Likewise, the rate will apply only between specified airports of departure and arrival – it is not possible to send goods at these preferential rates to alternative destinations, even where the alternative airport is on the same route and nearer to the airport of origin. The minimum quantity allowed at each rate is 100, 300, 500 and 1000 kg (shipping above the limit is allowed but not below it). Hence a consignment of 85 kg would be charged at the minimum kilogram rate, that is, 100kg at 95p which equals £95. This type of rate has done much to stimulate air freight development, and by encouraging quantity shipments, has produced cost savings in documentation, handling and packaging. In the event of the merchandise not qualifying for the reduced commodity rate, the shipper is advised to contact the agent or airline who may be able to introduce a special rate when regular and substantial shipments are involved.

2. *Classification rates (surcharges and rebates).* Classification rates apply to the following commodities where no specific commodity rate is available:

    (a) Newspapers, periodicals and books. Consignments of newspapers, periodicals, magazines, books, catalogues, talking books for the blind and Braille-type equipment are carried at reduced rates. Special rates are available on application to the airline.

    (b) Human remains. The regulations governing the carriage of human remains vary from route to route. Prior application is necessary to the airline.

    (c) Valuable cargo. Certain types of gold and platinum, diamonds (including industrial), rubies, emeralds, sapphires and pearls (including cultured pearls), legal bank notes, travellers cheques, securities, shares and share coupons and any article having a declared value for carriage of £450 or more per gross kilogramme are charged at the normal air cargo rate plus a

100 per cent surcharge. The minimum charge for valuable cargo is the normal applicable minimum charge plus a surcharge of 100 per cent, but not less than US$50 (operative rate October 1992). Quantity rates are not applicable.

(d)   Live animals. Collection charges are not normally available for the carriage of live animals except under special circumstances. Prior arrangements must be made for the carriage of animals. Stringent regulations apply regarding documentation and travel facilities and conditions. Special rates are applicable for the conveyance of live animals, usually at normal general cargo rates (i.e. the under 45 kg or under 100 kg rate as applicable); quantity rates are not applicable. The minimum charge for the carriage of live animals is the normal minimum charge increased by 50 per cent. Every consideration will be given to flight conditions such as altitude and temperature, but no responsibility can be accepted by the airline in the event of death or injury to the live animals due to atmospheric or climate conditions or to natural causes. A shipper's certificate for live animals is required.

3.   *Valuation charge.* Where consignments are offered for international carriage, a declaration of value must be made. It is permissible to make the statement 'no value declared'. Where goods have declared a value for carriage per kilogram higher than a certain level, a valuation charge will apply in addition to the freight charges.

4.   *General cargo rates.* These are the basic rates and fall into three categories as below:

(a)   minimum charges;
(b)   normal rate – the '100 kg' rate;
(c)   quantity rate – applicable on the various minimum quantities shipped, called break-points. It is permissible to charge a consignment at a higher weight rate if a lower charge results overall.

5.   *Unit load device (ULD) rates.* This applies to any type of container, with an integral pallet, or aircraft pallet whether or not owned by an IATA member, and whether or not considered to be aircraft equipment.

(a)   Aircraft ULDs. These are units which interface directly with an aircraft loading and restraint system, and meet all restraint requirements without the use of supplementary equipment. Such units are an integral part of the aircraft. Aircraft ULDs can be loaned to shippers and agents for loading purposes provided the shipper or agent can prove that he is equipped to handle them.

(b)   Non-aircraft ULDs. These units do not interface with the aircraft restraint system. They must be registered with IATA and conform to IATA standard specifications. Non-aircraft ULDs, in order to be eligible for rating incentives, must be owned by a shipper or agent.

Rating of ULDs: two rating method exist – 'method A' and 'method B'.

Method A. On certain routes, rating method A charges shall apply at the request of the shipper for consignments carried from airport of departure to airport of destination entirely in ULDs. In order to qualify for bulk unitization rates, the cargo must be carried from origin to destination in the same ULD. The charge for the consignment shall consist of a flat minimum (pivot) charge for a specified pivot weight above which an additional charge (over-pivot rate) per kilo or pound will apply. Charges for airline-owned aircraft ULDs shall be based on the actual gross weight less the actual tare weight of the ULD. Charges for shipper- or agent-owned aircraft ULDs or non-aircraft ULDs shall be based on the actual gross weight less the actual tare weight, but not more than the IATA tare weight allowance for the particular ULD.

Method B. Discounts and tare weight allowances only apply when shipments are delivered to the airline packaged in registered shipper-owned, standard size non-aircraft units. Charges are based on the actual weight of the shipment, less the tare weight allowance, but not less than the minimum chargeable weight for the particular container used. The tare weight allowance is always that which is printed on the actual container. A discount is also granted under this programme, which refers to each type of non-aircraft ULD. The amount of discount can be deducted from the weight charge, but shall not exceed 10 per cent of the charges applicable to the consignment carried in the ULD. In no case shall the charges established under method A be applied cumulatively with the discount authorized under rating method B.

Dangerous goods, live animals, or human remains will not be accepted in a ULD, rated under either method A or method B.

6. *Cabotage.* United Kingdom cabotage is the term used for goods carried when points of origin and destination are both within the sovereignty of the UK, where special non-international rates may apply. The carriage of UK cabotage traffic is reserved for UK airlines, and the airlines of the Colonies, Protectorates, Trust Territories or Protected States listed below. Traffic between the UK and the listed territories, or between any of the territories is 'United Kingdom cabotage', and cannot be carried by foreign airlines without special permission. The listed territories are: Anguilla, Ascension Islands, Bermuda, British Virgin Islands, Caicos Islands, Cayman Islands, Falklands Islands, Gibraltar, Hong Kong, Montserrat, St Christopher, St Helena, St Vincent, Turks Islands.

7.   *Express handling units.* These provide a fast and flexible handling service for cargo shipments and courier traffic. British Airways operates a well-established courier service as described on p. 58.

7.4.1 Charges

1.   *Payment of charges.* Charges can be paid at the time of despatch by cash, cheque or credit card (most major credit cards are accepted). However, regular shippers make use of credit facilities which are usually available from most major airlines. This enables their air freight charges to be billed for settlement on a monthly basis.

2.   *Charges forward.* Goods despatched to most countries may be sent 'charges forward', i.e. cartage, export fees and freightage payable by the consignee. Consignments cannot be sent with carriage and valuation charges partly prepaid and partly forward. Charges forward facilities are not available on domestic routes, when all charges must be prepaid. This service is not normally available for perishable goods or live animals.

3.   *Cash on delivery.* No COD consignments can be accepted on most airline air waybills or services.

4.   *Disbursements.* Most airlines will charge 10 per cent with a basic minimum fee of US$20 (valid, October 1992) for collection from a consignee of any disbursement shown on the air waybill. This charge will be made when collection is on behalf of any shipper or agent. Disbursements will not usually exceed the freight charges shown on the air waybill. When the issuing carrier cannot collect the amount to be collected from the consignee for any reason, the amount will be charged to the shipper or agent.

5.   *Perishable cargo.* Air freight charges for perishable cargo must normally be prepaid. If required, a deposit to cover surface reforwarding charges from the airport of arrival will be collected from the consignor.

6.   *Mixed cargo.* A mixed consignment is one which contains a number of different commodities which do not qualify for the same rate and conditions. Charges for mixed consignments are based on the applicable general cargo rate. Where the shipper declares separately the weight, or volume and contents of each package in the consignment, charges are based on either the appropriate commodity rate or the general cargo rate for each package.

7.   *Packaging of the consignment* will be charged on the basis of the highest rated article in the consignment. Articles which cannot be included in mixed consignment are: live animals, perishable goods, human remains, diplomatic bags, baggage shipped as cargo, and valuable cargo which includes articles with an actual value of US$20 000 (valid October 1999) or equivalent, or more per gross kilo.

8. *Cargo subject to regulations* relating to the carriage of dangerous goods must be offered separately, and clearly indicated in the Shipper's Declaration (pp. 214–24).

All these air freight rates exclude customs clearance charges duty, road or rail collection and distribution, warehousing, demurrage, etc. In addition to the foregoing, for special or large consignments, an aircraft can be chartered. Rates vary according to market conditions and other factors. The shipper conducts his negotiations through an air charter broker found on the Baltic Exchange or directly with an airline or air freight forwarder. As indicated earlier, a certain degree of bargaining can emerge to settle the ultimate charter rate for the larger air freighter. Much depends on whether prospects exist for the aircraft to be chartered on the next flight, otherwise the operator will be faced with an empty aircraft to fly to the next assignment. Little room exists for bargaining for split charters for small consignments varying between 500 kg and three tonnes. The charterer may need to wait a few days in such circumstances to combine with other cargo thereby obtaining a favourable rate based on a full aircraft.

7.4.2 Air freight consolidation

Our study of air freight rates would not be complete without consideration of air freight consolidation.

The ongoing development of air freight consolidation shows no abating as we progress through the early years of the twenty-first century. Growth may, however, be slowed down as the logistics market focuses more on air freight. Air freight consolidation involves the freight forwarder – usually referred to as the agent – who has a contract with an airline on specified flight(s) to provide consolidated cargo for allocated cargo hold space which the agent undertakes to fill. Thus the agency agreement involves the forwarder offering a consolidation (CONSOL) service on specific regular flights. The consolidated consignment is under agent sponsorship and may involve up to 30 consignments including differing consignees and consignors. Each consignment tends to be destined for the same or similar destination, area or region which enables the shipper to take advantage of the favourable competitive rate and convenient regular quality service. The cargoes are mixed subject to their compatibility except that dangerous classified cargo is exempt from such a facility (p. 214). Limitations are imposed on weight and general dimensions of the cargo. The agent is responsible for the overall consolidated consignment of some 30 consignments and sponsors them. The agent prepares a cargo manifest to accompany the master air waybill (MAWB) throughout the flight and issues house air waybills (HAWB) to individual shippers. The MAWB is prepared by the airline who issues it. The HAWB is produced and issued by the agent. The agent's responsibility includes cargo collection and/or delivery, payment of all reasonable costs throughout the transit including collection or delivery charges (usually involving the agent's own vehicles), air freight, airport/airline disbursements, documentation, customs and so on. The agent is able to charge an inclusive rate throughout which is usually much lower when compared with a package or consignment sent as an individual parcel. Usually the agent works in close liaison with a corresponding agent in the destination area or region, and the two agents work on a reciprocal basis, developing the consolidated air freight business in both directions.

Details of the scheme are given below:

1. It is particularly attractive to the exporter/shipper engaged in despatching small consignment(s) which can be conveniently accommodated into a ULD subject to its compatibility with other cargo shipped. If there are any queries on weight or dimension limitations, the shipper should contact the agent.
2. Documentation is simplified and all the documentation needs relative to the transit are usually taken care of by the agent. The agent issues at the time of flight departure a 'house air waybill' (HAWB) which is identified with the master air waybill (MAWB) including number and cargo manifest details.
3. The promotion of the consolidated service is undertaken by the agent who takes care of all the transit needs of the consignment including documentation. This enables the airlines to concentrate on providing a quality air freight flight service and to become less involved in marketing the service involving contact with individual shippers.
4. The rate is calculated on a W/M (weight/measurement) basis (pp. 177–78).
5. The agent promotes the service – a feature of it is the competitive inclusive rate structure compared with an individual package despatched under IATA fare structure arrangements (pp. 165–68).
6. The scheme enables the airlines to obtain the maximum income from the allocated aircraft hold accommodation earmarked for the agents and thereby improves the airline profitability through good capacity utilization.
7. It enables the airline to plan ahead with confidence in the knowledge that air freight consolidated consignments are being developed by the agent and in so doing facilitates the guarantee of traffic to the airline.
8. The agent agreement with the airline usually permits the agent to vary, cancel or reduce his pre-booked cargo hold space up to 36 hours before flight departure time, thereby permitting the airline to use the cargo hold space for other shippers.

9. The air freight consolidation facility does not exist on every air freight service, which tends to restrict the user. However, it is a fast-growing market and the initiative for its expansion in terms of extending the range of flights and services on which it is available rests with the agent in consultation with the airline.

10. The rates structure is inclusive of collection and/or delivery charge, documentation, customs clearance, airline disbursements and so on, which is a good selling point of the service. It permits the shipper to avoid the minimum freight rate regulations found in the airline (IATA) approved rate structure (pp. 165–67).

11. Packing costs are substantially reduced and the risk of cargo loss and/or damage is minimized, thereby lowering insurance premiums.

12. Consolidated consignments tend to result in quicker customs clearance.

13. It encourages the freight forwarder to maximize profitability through an equal spread or mix of high- and low-density cargoes.

14. It encourages the use of ULDs with all the attendant advantages.

15. It enables the agent to offer guaranteed services, thereby aiding quality of service and development of the market.

16. Its general competitiveness and favourable quality of service facilitates the development of international trade.

17. Quicker and reliable transit times are offered which is a good selling point of the service.

18. A major benefit to the industry and shippers is the extensive network of consolidator services worldwide. An increasing number are involved in the sea/air package (p. 61). Such frequency of service and a global network substantially increases the 'value added benefit' to the shipper and develops the just-in-time concept through quicker transit times and more competitive rates.

19. An increasing number of consolidators tend to specialize in certain commodities which encourages the development of overseas markets on a low-cost international distribution basis.

20. Most air freight consolidators operate on a minimum consignment weight basis and, accordingly, regular shippers of the consolidators' service usually build up a collection of consignments over several days to take advantage of the most economical rate rather than despatching daily and being charged a 100 kg rate for a commodity of 15 kg.

21. The airline system is fully computerized (pp. 446–57).

Air freight consolidation services exist worldwide and there is every evidence to suggest that its growth will continue. It is ideal for the smaller exporter and through its competitiveness and quality of service is aiding the development of international trade by air.

7.5 Canal and inland waterways freight rates

The portion of the international transit conveyed by canal will have a tariff based on distance, commodity type, transhipment cost, handling charges and any other miscellaneous charges. For example, if the consignment is an indivisible load, it may involve some special, heavy lifting equipment. Special rates usually exist for containers, palletized cargoes and special contract tariffs are available for regular shipments. The tariffs and range thereof vary by individual country and canal authority. They exclude customs clearance charges. The rates are based on either a weight or measurement assessment.

Distribution of international trade by inland waterway based on the major European ports is very extensive on the Continent for a variety of reasons. Rates are based on weight or cubic measurement and vary by commodity and trade. It is a highly competitive method of distribution for certain commodities and/or trades and one which is likely to continue to expand as the system is modernized and further developed.

The integration of inland waterways with deep-sea services, especially in the field of containerization and bulk commodities, is being developed at many European ports, principally Dunkerque, Antwerp, Rotterdam and Hamburg (pp. 54–57). The rates are usually inclusive under the intermodal combined transport system. For containers, it is based on TEU criteria.

7.6 International road haulage freight rates

The development of the international road haulage market UK/Europe–Asia–Middle East has been outstanding in recent years, particularly for the UK–Continent under CMR conditions. Undoubtedly the fixed links involving Le Shuttle and those in Scandinavia (see pp. 72–73) has facilitated this development.

The rates charged to the international road freight forwarder to convey the vehicle and/or trailer on the vehicular ferry are based on the trailer/vehicle length, and whether it is empty or loaded, accompanied or unaccompanied. Additional charges are raised for excessive width and/or height. Special rates usually exist for declared valuable cargoes. Rebates are given to hauliers and agents who originate substantial quantities of traffic annually to an operator for a particular route or service. These rates are exclusive of customs clearance charges, etc. Keen competition exists among operators particularly on rates and fringe benefits, namely free cabins or meals for drivers, together with free passage for drivers. An increasing number of large-, and indeed medium-sized, exporters now undertake their own international distribution by road. It has many advantages particularly if the cargo flow can be balanced in each direction.

To the shipper using the international road freight forwarders service – much of which is groupage traffic – the actual rate is based on the cubic measurement or weight of the cargo, whichever produces the greater revenue. This is related to the commodity classification, and origin and destination of the cargo. The cargo measurement 3 m^3 (three cubic metres) equals 1 tonne (1000 kg). The calculation is based on the W/M option (p. 177). Rates are very competitive particularly compared with air freight for merchandise destined outside the European Community. To improve vehicle crew utilization in an era of rising cost, an increasing number of the larger road haulage operators despatch their vehicles unaccompanied on the vehicular ferry. This enables the driver to deposit his trailer at the ferry terminal and collect another one waiting. It avoids driver lodging allowance cost being incurred and enables better vehicle control to be achieved with improved reliability and lower cost. Shippers using the road trailer unit network may opt for the EuroTunnel rather than a cross-Channel ferry.

7.7 International rail services rates

Details of the international rail service rates are given below:

1.   Cargo wagons (Table 4.5) containers, and road trailers (Table 4.5), are available for contract hire from one month to several years thereby forming part of a shipper's in-house transport operation throughout the European rail network.

2.   Groupage services offering collection and delivery between UK freight villages and key industrial and commercial centres. Rates are based on the W/M concept and are available from leading rail freight forwarders such as MAT Transport and Danzas. This involves the cargo wagon (Table 4.5) and palletized merchandise.

3.   Purpose-built car transporter wagons in complete train load formation (pp. 70–71). Rates are negotiated direct with suppliers to move the cars between factories and distribution points.

4.   Maritime ISO container trains. Rates are negotiated with the container operators to convey TEUs between seaport and container terminals usually in complete train load formation.

5.   Intermodal services, the UK and the Continent. This involves 1200 intermodal wagons operating between UK-based rail Euro terminals and 15 Continental industrial centres. The wagons are 2.77 m high and 2.5 m wide and refrigerated units are 2.75 m high and 2.6 m wide. They can accommodate swap-bodies (Table 4.5) and containers in the form of tilts, tanks, reefers, flats, dry boxes, etc. Rates are based on a range of options to meet shippers' needs including the chartering of wagon space on a regular or irregular basis, to the chartering of a complete train.

6.   The Le Shuttle rate for the road haulage vehicle travelling between the portals will be based on the vehicle unit. Hauliers who can guarantee a certain volume of business annually will be given a discounted rate.

7.8 Maritime container rates

The general practice is to formulate individual rates by container type, capacity, and the actual origin and destination of the merchandise. The through rate will embrace the inland transportation cost known at the time of despatch, embracing collection and terminal handling expenses, but it will usually exclude customs clearance charges, demurrage, etc. Much of course depends on the trade. This practice applies to full container load (FCL) traffic. Some of the containers are stuffed and unstuffed at the container base, which may be an inland clearance depôt (ICD).

The mega container operator with a fleet in excess of 250 000 TEUs tends to formulate their rate structure on three factors:

1.   the cost of the service;
2.   the value added benefit the service provides to the shipper;
3.   the opportunities in the market place for containerized goods.

The rate structure and level of rates is very flexible. The bulk of the container services globally operates outside the liner conference system constraints. Some large multinational companies own/lease ISO containers. They are usually of a specialized type offering a two-way traffic flow. The tariff for such traffic is usually a specially negotiated contract rate.

A very substantial volume of traffic which is conveyed in containers is less than container load (LCL) traffic involving the NVOCC concept (pp. 114–15). The cargo is assembled and stuffed into a container at a container base or inland clearance depôt with each individual consignment attracting separate rates. Such rates are calculated on a weight or cubic measurement basis whichever produces the greater revenue. They naturally reflect the origin and destination of such merchandise, together with, when practicable, likely disbursement charges, namely handling, customs clearance, etc. The LCL rate is based on W/M. Volume shippers who guarantee a specified tonnage annually are granted discounted rates.

Rates parity is unlikely to exist in each direction between two seaports and the reasons are numerous. Major factors include the imbalance of the traffic flow, and differing types of cargo and the varying specifications of containers used. An imbalance of cargo flow is very common and generates problems for the shipowner. For example, a country may have a severe imbalance of exports compared with imports shipments. It may export primarily industrial manufactured goods, involving covered containers, and import foodstuffs, requiring reefer containers.

An illustration of the consolidator rates strategy under NVOCC is given below:

Shipowner rate

1.	50 individual shipments of 2 tonne at LCL rate of US$60 per tonne charged by the shipping line (US$60 × 100 tonne) <u>US$6000</u>

Consolidator rate

2.	50 individual shipments of 2 tonne at consolidator rate of US$30 per tonne (US$30 × 100 tonne) <u>US$3000</u>

                      Total Rate Difference   <u>US$3000</u>

3.	Rate per tonne charged by consolidator to individual shippers (50 shipments at 2 tonne = US$5000) US$50
4.	Saving per tonne to shippers (i.e. US$60 – US$50) US$10
5.	Margin of profit per tonne to consolidator (i.e. US$50 – US$30) US$20
6.	Saving to shippers (50 shipments at 2 tonne US$6000 shipowner's rate – 50 shipment at 2 tonne US$5000 consolidator rate) US$1000
7.	Profit to consolidator <u>US$2000</u>

The above demonstrates a situation where the shipowner's LCL rate per tonne is US$60, whereas the NVOCC consolidator rate to shippers is US$50, yielding a profit to the consolidator of US$20 per tonne on the basis that the wholesale rate is US$30 per tonne quoted by the shipowner.

For consignments requiring special facilities such as livestock or indivisible loads requiring heavy lifts, additional charges are raised.

Maritime container rates are very competitive and this mode of transport now constitutes a substantial volume of deep-sea worldwide general merchandise cargo.

7.9 Sea freight rates

We will now examine the sea freight tariff formulation relative to liner cargo rates involving break-bulk cargo, LCL container shipments and ship chartering. It should be mentioned that the terms tariff and rate are synonymous inasmuch as various forms of transport use either, according to circumstances.

Liner rates are based partly on cost, and partly on value. Many freight rates are quoted on a basis of weight or measurement at ship's option. This means that the rate quoted will be applied either per ton of 2240 lb (weight) or on 40 ft^3 (cubic measurement) per ton, whichever will produce the greater revenue. The reason for this method of charging is that heavy cargo will bring a vessel to her loadline before her space is full, while light cargo will fill her space without bringing her down to her maximum draught. To produce the highest revenue a vessel must be loaded to her full internal capacity, and immersed to her maximum permitted depth. In most trades, cargo measuring under 40 ft^3/ton weight is charged on a weight basis, while cargo measuring 40 ft^3 or more per ton is charged on a volume measurement basis. With the spread of the metric system, many freight rates are quoted per 1000 kg or m^3 (ICBM – one cubic metre) (p. 177).

Liner tariffs quote rates for many commodities which move regularly. These rates are based on the stowage factor (rate of bulk to weight), on the value of the cargo and on the competitive situation. Many tariffs publish class rates for general cargo not otherwise specified. Some tariffs publish class rates whereby commodities are grouped for charging into several classes. On commodities of very high value, *ad valorem* rates are charged at so much per cent of the declared value. When commodities move in large quantities, and are susceptible to tramp competition, shipowners often employ 'open rates', that is, the rate is left open, so that the shipping line can quote whatever rate it determines. For heavy lifts and extra lengths it is usual to make additional charges in order to cover the special handling of such cargo.

Insofar as chartered vessels are concerned the negotiation is usually undertaken by a shipbroker, who may be on the Baltic Exchange communicating with other shipbrokers having a vessel available to hire. Alternatively, the shipbroker may go direct to the shipowner.

The rates are not pre-determined but are based on economic forces of supply and demand. A voyage charter is a contract for a special voyage, while a time charter is a contract for a period of time which may cover several voyages. Therefore, the voyage charter rate is a short-term rate, while the time charter rate is often a long-term rate. When trade is buoyant and voyage rates are rising, charterers, in anticipation of further rises, tend to charter for longer periods to cover their commitments; when rates are expected to fall, they tend to contract for shorter periods. Therefore, the current time charter rate tends to reflect the expected trend of voyage rates in the future. If rates are expected to rise, it will tend to be above the current voyage rates; if they are expected to fall, it will tend to be below the current voyage rates. Generally speaking, the two rates move in the same direction, but because time charter rates depend on market expectations, they tend to fluctuate more widely than voyage rates. When conditions are improving, long-term rates tend to rise more rapidly than voyage rates; when conditions are deteriorating, voyage rates tend to fall more rapidly.

In more recent years there has been a tendency in an increasing number of liner cargo trades to impose a surcharge on the basic rate. This includes bunkering or fuel surcharge, currency surcharge and finally surcharges raised on heavy lifts such as indivisible consignments or on excessive height or length of Ro-Ro traffic (pp. 162–63).

It is relevant to mention that the bill of lading is the document usually associated with liner cargo and the charterparty with chartered vessels.

7.10 Calculation of freight rates

To illustrate the calculation of the freight rate applicable to all transport modes, an example is given below.

Consider the despatch of the following luxury food items from Birmingham to Milan; all items are packed in tri-wall cartons:

6 cartons 120 × 80 × 80 cm; weight of each carton 50 kg

Freight rates are:

Air £2.50 per chargeable kg
Sea US$150 per tonne W/M (assume $1.8 = £1)
Road £200 per 1000 chargeable kg

Chargeable weight/volume ratios for each mode should be assumed to be:

Air 6 CBM = 1000 kg
Sea 1 CBM = 1000 kg (CBM = cubic metre)
Road 3 CBM = 1000 kg

Air – Volumetric –

$$\text{One carton} = \frac{12 \times 80 \times 80}{6000} \text{ kg}$$

$$\text{Six cartons} = 6 \times \frac{12 \times 80 \times 80}{6000} \text{ kg} = 768 \text{ kg}$$

Air freight rate − £2.50 per kilogram
Total air freight volumetric − 768 kg × £2.50 = £1920

Weight

1 carton 50 kg
6 cartons, 6 × 50 kg = 300 kg
Air freight rate − £2.50 per kilogram
Total air freight − weight = 300 kg × £2.50 = £750
Sea − rate − US$150 per tonne (1000 kg)
Rate sterling US$150 ÷ 1.8 = £83.33 per tonne
Rate sterling per kilogram £83.33 ÷ 1000 = £00.08

Volumetric

$$1 \text{ carton} = \frac{12 \times 80 \times 80}{6000} \text{ kg}$$

$$6 \text{ cartons} = \frac{6 \times 12 \times 80 \times 80}{6000} \text{ kg} = 4608 \text{ kg}$$

Sea freight rate − £00.08 per kilogram
Total sea freight rate volumetric 4608 kg × £00.08 = £368.64

Weight
    One carton = 50 kg
    Six cartons, 6 × 50 kg = 300 kg
    Sea freight rate − £00.08 per kilogram
    Total sea freight rate = 300 kg × £00.08 = £24.00.

In some trades the rate would be based on the nearest tonne, in which case the volumetric rate would rise from 4608 kg to 5000 kg and yield £416.65, and the weight from 300 kg to 1000 kg to produce £83.33.

Road
    Rate £200 per chargeable 1000 kg
    Road rate per kilogram £200 ÷ 1000 = £00.20

Volumetric

$$1 \text{ carton} = \frac{120 \times 80 \times 80}{3000} \text{ kg}$$

$$6 \text{ cartons} = \frac{6 \times 120 \times 80 \times 80}{3000} \text{ kg} = 1536 \text{ kg}$$

Road freight rate £00.20 per kilogram
Total road freight 1536 kg × £00.20 = £307.20

Weight
    1 carton 50 kg
    6 cartons, 6 × 50 kg = 300 kg
    Road freight rate £00.20 per kilogram
Total road freight rate 300 kg × £00.20 = £60.

Most carriers would calculate the road freight when mention is made of 'per 1000 kg' chargeable on the basis of rounding up to the nearest 1000 kg. Hence the volumetric would rise from 1536 kg to 2000 kg yielding £400, and the weight from 300 kg to 1000 kg producing £200.

    The carrier would charge the volumetric or weight rate which will yield the highest income. Accordingly, in the example the answer would be as follows:

Air (volumetric)	£1920	
Sea (volumetric)	£364.64	(£416.65, nearest tonne)
Road (volumetric)	£307.20	(£400, nearest 1000 kg).

    An alphabetical list of salient freight rates is given below:

Ad valorem. This is based on the declared value of the cargo whereby merchandise declared at £1000 with 2.5 per cent *ad valorem* rate would be charged £25.

Antiques. Antiques including art treasures require special packaging by an accredited company and special freight rates apply. Freight forwarders tend to specialize in this business.

Bloodstock. This involves the movement of racehorses. Special arrangements and rates apply by air and Ro-Ro ferry. All must be accompanied by a groom.

Box. A container rate (pp. 174–75).

Commodity. See p. 165.

Commodity box. A container rate.

Consolidated. The rate is for consolidated consignments usually based on W/M option. Also termed the 'groupage rate' (p. 175).

Dangerous cargo. Conveyed under ADR, RID, IMO and IATA regulations, involving a rate about 50 per cent above the general cargo rate (pp. 201–24).

Dead freight. This usually arises when a charterer fails to provide a full cargo for a ship.

Express Air Freight Service. For packages, documents, usually involving couriers (p. 58).

FAK (freight all kinds). This rate applies to all types of cargo irrespective of commodity type.

Fixture. Chartering a vessel (p. 176).

Groupage. See consolidated entry (pp. 169–71).

Household effects. Removal of household furniture. Special packaging and rates apply. Some agents specialize in this business.

Indivisible loads. Such consignments are of excessive weight or dimensions and require special handling equipment and arrangements (p. 172).

Livestock. Special rates and arrangements apply.

Lump sum freight. This is an amount payable for the use of the whole or portion of a ship.

Pallets. Rates applicable to palletized cargo (p. 107).

Postal. There is a wide variety of postal services ideal for documents, small packages and samples (pp. 180–01).

Project forwarding. This involves the coordination through a freight forwarder of all the international transportation arrangements of all products relative to a major capital project such as a new airport terminal, power station, etc.

Rebate. A discount on a published rate attained through negotiation on a guaranteed volume over specified period, etc. (p. 161).

Ro-Ro rates. Applicable to road haulage movement (p. 172).

Trade vehicles. Rates involving the movement of trade cars, lorries, buses, etc.

W/M. Option weight/measurement ship option based on weight or measurement evaluation (pp. 177–78).

7.11 Royal Mail International

Royal Mail International (RMI) operates a strategic business within Royal Mail. Overall, it is the foremost UK based international carrier and has effective links with the world's postal administrations and offers a guaranteed delivery to 225 countries. It offers the following range of services.

The Royal Mail has a worldwide distribution hub network covering 365 500 square metres, handling 58 500 packages per hour. The international hub based in Coventry has a capability to export 2000 parcels per hour. It is at the forefront of innovation and automation. Overhead scanners and volumetric measuring technology provide accuracy and speed, while on-site customs teams and 11 'rapidscan' x-ray machines ensure that international regulations and tight security are maintained at all times. This leading edge technology allows Royal Mail to give customers the advantage of faster processing and later cut-off times. It permits quick and easy online tracking at each stage of the transit by entering the consignment number.

Overall, the Royal Mail has five services for worldwide parcel delivery which we will now briefly examine – www.parcelforce.com

International Datapost.   This provides a guaranteed service to 225 countries and territories worldwide by noon delivery (to selected destinations) and by close of business to many other destinations.

Euro 48.   A guaranteed delivery in two working days to major European cities, and elsewhere in Europe, between three and four working days, depending on the destination. This includes many Eastern European destinations.

Ireland 24.   A guaranteed next working day delivery from Northern Ireland to any destination within the Republic of Ireland.

International Standard.   Worldwide delivery to 240 countries and territories. Europe from three working days and the rest of the world from five working days. Delivery times are not guaranteed and parcels may be held in some countries for collection by the recipient.

International Economy.   Worldwide delivery to 200 countries and territories. Europe from 10 working days and the rest of the world from 20 days. Delivery times are not guaranteed and parcels may be held in some countries for collection by the recipient.

Parcel force worldwide complies with the strict transport regulations. These include the dangerous goods classification as featured in the latest edition of the Civil Aviation Organisation's Technical Instruction which features nine hazard classes (p. 213).

Royal Mail also offers an Echo Pack Service permitting consignments to be conveyed easily and cost effectively between European countries.

Courier packs are also available permitting documents and small items to be despatched by express delivery. Royal Mail also provides a pallet service and international break bulk. It enables multiple businesses or consumers to palletize their goods for delivery in each of the countries covered by the service. Once the pallet arrives, it is broken down into individual items and delivered to each customer's address.

Royal Mail service is subject to the appropriate international trade documentation, HM Customs Notice 143 – www.hmce.gov.uk.

Recommended reading

IATA Annual report.
International Freighting Weekly.

CHAPTER 8

Export cargo packaging, stowage, marking and dangerous cargo shipments

8.1 Factors influencing type of cargo packaging

Packaging techniques today are becoming increasingly sophisticated to meet a market which is seeking continuous improvements in the following areas:

1. Improved standards to reduce risk of damage and pilferage. This in turn encourages competitive cargo insurance premiums and maintains good relations with the importer. Cargo received in a damaged condition seriously impairs the exporter's product overseas market prospects as it loses goodwill with the importer. Moreover, the exporter is ultimately obliged to replace the damaged goods, which can be a costly task.

2. A better utilization of transport capacity to lower distribution cost. This is particularly relevant to ISO container use when suitably sized packaged cargo can be firmly stowed in it with no broken stowage. Full advantage should be taken of high-capacity containers for volume cargoes, and use made of a stowage plan. This reduces the risk of damage, and ensures all container capacity is utilized, subject to the total weight limitations not being exceeded. Moreover, it reduces the need to use dunnage and, by attaining higher utilization/load factor of container capacity, lowers the freight cost of each unit distributed.

3. Improved cargo handling. Cargo packaging in design, namely dimension and configuration, should facilitate the most economical method of handling. This is particularly relevant to awkward shaped cargo. Moreover, it applies from the time the goods are packaged, which may be in the factory, until it reaches the importer's warehouse/distribution centre. Mechanical and computerized and high-tech cargo handling equipment is now in extensive use to reduce labour cost and speed up cargo handling.

4. Packaging costs among various manufacturers are now very competitive. The shipper is very conscious of containing packing costs and

the exporter is well advised to engage a specialist packaging company to obtain professional advice and gain the best results.

5. The European Packaging waste legislation required each Member State by 2001 to have 50–65 per cent of used packaging to be recovered, 25–45 per cent to be recycled and a minimum of 15 per cent of each main type of packing material to be recycled. Hence, manufacturers and retailers in the EU and importers are continually looking for innovative cost effective solutions to their distribution problems.

Two sizes in common use are the Euro-pallet 800 mm × 1200 mm and the industrial pallet of 1000 mm × 1200 mm which has a capacity of two tonnes. Additionally, a wide range of pallet sizes are constructed which are tailor-made to the unit load. It may be white furniture, cartons, etc. The pallets are affixed to the goods using stretch-wrapping techniques.

An increasing number of global transport operators provide a complete range of packing services. Nedlloyd Districentres of the Netherlands provide such a service. It operates in 40 countries and specializes in warehousing, stock control, order processing, assembly, modification, packing, domestic and international distribution and customs documentation. It provides multilingual instructions such as shipment to Italy in Italian; consolidation of a range of small products from a shipper; despatch of promotional material using plastic film; product test; product assembly; shipment of goods on fixed units or pallets or other techniques; and packing in shock-absorbent polyurethane foam or plastic foil on pallets using stretch-wrapping techniques. Packaging specifications vary by transport mode, type of pallet commodity and transit routeing. Each overseas sales contract cargo needs to be individually considered to obtain the best results and sustain/develop overseas markets. Moreover, one must bear in mind that packaging not only protects but also gives the shipper's product added value.

An examination will now be made of the various factors influencing the nature of packaging for an international consignment.

1. *Value of the goods.* In the main the high-value consignment usually attracts more extensive packing than low-value merchandise. Much, of course, depends on the nature of the commodity. If packing is inadequate, bearing in mind transit and declared cargo valuation, problems could be experienced in carriers' liability, acceptance and adequate cargo insurance coverage. Moreover, high-value consignments, such as a valuable painting, require adequate security and likewise attract higher freight rates. Such packing must be done professionally.

2. *Nature of the transit.* The type and length of transit. Is the movement national, European or transglobal? What form of transport will be used during the transit – road, rail, short-sea, deep-sea or air? All have varying characteristics which make varying demands of the packaging of the goods. Moreover, one must consider the method of shipment; it

may be break-bulk, LCL or FCL. The more handling goods must endure, the stouter the packaging required; furthermore, the greater the degree of overstowage that the goods must endure, then the stronger the packaging needed. Certain forms of transport, particularly air and ISO containerization, usually require less extensive packing. This is a strong marketing feature of their service. Air transport particularly encourages palletized consignments with cargo strapped/anchored throughout the transit. Fibreboard cartons for consumer products are very popular with both air and ISO container shipments. For break-bulk shipments involving several transhipments at the ports and other points en route, more elaborate, robust packing is required. Such traffic movement is found in general cargo non-containerized shipments from China and India. Cargo wagon and Ro-Ro consignments have modest packing requirements, but much depends on their collection and delivery arrangements and the degree of robust packing needed. Packing needs for cargoes despatched in purpose-built transport units are usually minimal. This is particularly so with containerization. Packing needs are obviously modest for transport services offering a door-to-door service with no transhipment en route.

3. *Nature of the cargo.* This concerns the characteristics of the goods concerned and their susceptibility to various loss/damage. It is important to bear in mind that packaging offers protection against pilferage as well as damage. This factor together with item (2) are the two major factors which determine the type of packing for an individual consignment. Cargo shipped in bulk requires little or no packing, while general merchandise needs adequate packing. For example, apples can be consigned in cases, boxes, cartons or pallet boxes. Cement on the other hand may be shipped in containers or in bulk. Motor vehicles are usually shipped unpacked to reduce freight, with each vehicle being individually secured and stowed on a vehicular/car deck. Grain, ores and coal are all shipped in bulk.

4. *Compliance with customs or statutory requirements.* This is particularly relevant to dangerous cargo where strict regulations apply both by air and sea concerning the carriers' acceptance, packing, stowage, documentation, marking and carriers' liability. This aspect will be examined later in the chapter. Statutory regulations also apply to the transportation of foodstuffs involving the temperature enforcement of the food. Such regulations are found in the Food Hygiene (Amendment) Regulations 1990. In the EU stringent regulations exist under the European Packaging Waste Legislation of 2001. This embraces a high proportion of packaging to be recovered and recycled after use. It has led to a significant increase in the use of returnable transit packaging (rtp).

   In some countries, straw is an unacceptable form of packing due to the risk of insects being imported. Quarantine regulations are particularly extensive in Australasia where materials such as wood products, rice husks, straw and similar plant material may not be used as packaging material or dunnage. This ensures that all packing materials are free from soil and contamination from animal products which can harbour pests, particularly insects, which are capable of causing wholesale devastation in forests. If the exporter does use wood it is advisable to have it suitably treated, namely by fumigation, kiln drying or impregnation, and to obtain a certificate to this effect for despatch to the importer. If in doubt the exporter is advised to consult his agent.

5. *Resale value, if any, of packaging material in the importer's country.* In some developing countries, large drums, wooden cases, or bags have a modest resale value. This helps to offset the packaging cost.

6. *General fragility of cargo.* In the main, the more fragile the cargo becomes, the greater the degree of packaging required. This is very much related to the mode of transport, particularly air freight which has only limited packaging needs and low value of consignment. A judgement must be made on the most acceptable form of packaging to adopt and if in doubt advice must be sought.

7. *The international consignment delivery terms of sale* (Incoterms 2000, p. 398). Again the actual packing specification may be contained therein and it is important to take into account who will bear the cost. This is usually the exporter.

8. *Variation in temperature* during the course of the transit. Temperature variation can be quite extensive during transit and packaging must take account of this to permit the cargo to breathe and avoid excessive condensation/sweating, see item (4) above. Again advice should be sought when necessary from the airline or shipowner.

9. *Ease of handling and stowage.* Awkwardly shaped cargoes packed in cartons or containers can greatly facilitate stowage, particularly in a container and using mechanical cargo handling equipment. Cargo stowage and obtaining the maximum practicable utilization of available transport unit capacity are areas worthy of study to lower unit distribution cost. Likewise, if awkwardly shaped cargoes are conveniently packed this will speed cargo handling. Moreover, cargoes of an awkward shape can attract additional handling charges and a freight surcharge in some circumstances. Furthermore, such cargoes are more vulnerable to damage and could therefore attract higher cargo insurance premiums.

10. *Insurance acceptance conditions.* Cargo which is particularly fragile or which has a bad record in terms of damage/pilferage may be subject to a prescribed packing specification. Otherwise, the insurance company or underwriter will refuse to cover them at a competitive cargo insurance premium. Insufficiency of packaging is usually an adequate defence in most carriers' contracts of carriage to claims of certain kinds.

11. *The size of the cargo and its weight.* Basically there are three main considerations to be observed when determining the form that a package should take and these include size, shape and strength.

    (a)   The size of the package will be governed by the size of the marketable unit as, for example, a sliced loaf and a packet of 20 cigarettes. Comparison between the sizes of marketable units of various products frequently reveals the phenomena that products of low bulk command relatively higher prices than those of greater bulk. The reasons for this are two-fold. First, a readily saleable unit of an expensive product tends to be small in order to come within the means of the average consumer, for example, ladies' perfume. Secondly, the purchase of a large quantity of a product normally results in an overall reduction in the cost per basic marketable unit. This means that the customer pays less for the product, or alternatively is able to buy a larger quantity for the price he or she is prepared to pay. An example is found in the retail shop when the basic-sized package of a household product may cost €2.50 while the family size containing almost twice the quantity costs €3.15.

    (b)   Shape to a large extent is determined by the shape of the goods to be enclosed within the package. Loose goods, the shape of which is flexible, may be accommodated within a package designed to meet one or more of a range of requirements, for example, the cylindrical shape of the package containing a household bleach cleaner makes it convenient to use with one hand, yet the package is self-balancing upon a flat and stable base. More rigid products, such as a pair of tailor's scissors must be packaged within a container of a more regular shape – in this instance, an oblong package.

    (c)   Associated with size and shape is strength. Some products by their very nature need protection provided by the package, for example eggs, while others lend support to the package material, for example, metal ashtrays. Some products possess a rigid natural shape, but need cushioning by the package to protect a delicate mechanism, for example, a model electric train, while others rely upon the package for protection and retention of shape, for example, tinned fruit.

Finally, one must bear in mind that the final shape, dimension and weight of consignment, will determine level of freight rate.

12. *Marketing considerations.* An overriding consideration, certainly for consumer goods and increasingly so for industrial products, is that the package should fit into the overall marketing concept. On a company strategic level, it must enhance and reinforce the company's image with the customer, while, on a lower level, it must sell positively by

putting across three cardinal points: the nature, the price and the advantages of the product. Moreover, it must endeavour to generate further sales with the same customer by performing satisfactorily while the product is in use. Additionally, one must bear in mind any advertising motif to be accommodated on the packaging.

13. *Facilities available at the terminal;* namely airport, seaport, one-stop and feeder ports, container base, inland clearance depot, warehouse, districtparks, free trade zones, dry ports, container freight stations, freight villages, etc. Lifting equipment at some seaports and particularly airports may be of limited capacity. Accordingly, relative to an indivisible load, the shipper may be compelled to despatch it in two parts instead of one integral unit. Moreover, not all airports have Customs clearance facilities and this could lead to an alternative air terminal being used with differing handling equipment capacity.

14. *Type and size of container* (pp. 85–96), cargo wagon, pallet, Ro-Ro vehicle or aircraft. The configuration of the transport unit together with access thereto will influence the actual ultimate dimension of the packaging, its maximum weight and shape.

15. *Marking of cargo packaging.* Each package must bear a marking code and use a symbol to ease handling (Figure 8.1).

16. *Cost of packaging.* This is becoming an increasingly important aspect in deciding on the type of packaging. In a world where overseas markets are becoming more competitive the exporter is constantly exploring ways and means of reducing distribution cost and improving marketing techniques. Packaging features very much in this evaluation.

Packaging, therefore, is not only designed as a form of protection to reduce the risk of goods being damaged in transit, but also to prevent pilferage and aid marketing. It is, of course, essential to see not only that the right type of packing is provided, but also that the correct quality and form of container is used. There are numerous types of packing and a description of the more important forms follow.

8.2 Types of packaging

Many goods have little or no form of packing and are carried loose. These include iron and steel plates, iron rods, railway rolling stock, and steel rails. Such cargoes are generally weight cargoes with a low stowage factor. Heavy vehicles, locomotives and buses are also carried loose, because of the impracticability and high cost of packing.

Baling is a form of packing consisting of a canvas cover often crosslooped by metal or rope binding. It is most suitable for paper, wool, hay, peat, cotton, carpets and rope. Basically, it is a cheap and effective form of packing which aids handling. It affords limited protection to cargo.

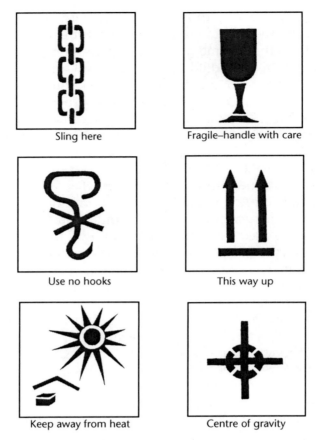

Sling here

Fragile–handle with care

Use no hooks

This way up

Keep away from heat

Centre of gravity

FIGURE 8.1 Recognized international cargo marking symbols

Bags made of jute, cotton, plastic, or paper are a cheap form of container and are ideal for a wide variety of products including cement, fertilizer, flour, oil cakes, animal feeding products, chemicals and many consumer products. Their prime disadvantage is that they are subject to damage by water, sweat, leakages or, in the case of paper bags, breakage. The bags can be stacked on pallets to facilitate handling.

Barrels, hogsheads and drums are used for the conveyance of liquid or greasy cargoes. The main problems associated with this type of packing are the likelihood of leakage if the unit is not properly sealed, and the possibility of the drums becoming rusty during transit. Acids can also be carried in plastic drums and bottles. Such a form of packing, particularly drums, can have a resale value in certain countries overseas, while others are used indefinitely in numerous transits, particularly hogsheads.

Boxes, cases and metal-lined cases are also used extensively particularly in break-bulk and LCL cargoes. It is an expensive form of packing but it has some resale value in certain countries overseas. Overall, this type of packing gives complete protection and lessens the risk of pilferage plus it is an aid to handling. Basically, this form of packing is wooden in construction and varies in size and capacity. Moreover, it may be strengthened by the provision of battens and metal binding. Many of them, such as tea chests, are lined to create airtight packing which helps to overcome the difficulties that arise when passing through zones of variable temperature. This form of packing is particularly prominent in surface transport and is used for much machinery and other items of expensive equipment. However, it is becoming less popular as the cost of timber has risen sharply in recent years and containerization has lessened the need for such elaborate robust packing in certain trades.

Carboys, or glass containers enclosed in metal baskets have a limited use and are primarily employed for the carriage of acids and other dangerous liquids transported in small quantities. Again, it is a packing form found primarily in sea transport.

Cartons are a very common form of packing in all modes of international distribution involving in particular consumer products. They may be constructed of cardboard, strawboard or fibreboard. This form of packing is very much on the increase as it is relatively inexpensive, expandible, aids marketing, handling and stowage. It is particularly ideal for containerization and palletized consignments – the latter featuring prominently in the air freight field with the cartons affixed by metal bands to the pallet. The principal disadvantage is its susceptibility to crushing and pilfering. It is a very flexible form of packing and, therefore, prevents the breakage which may occur if rigid containers are used. Polystyrene now features more and more as a packing aid in cartons.

Crates or skeleton cases are a form of container halfway between a bale and a case. They are of wooden construction. Lightweight goods of larger cubic capacity such as machinery, domestic appliances like refrigerators, cycles and certain foodstuffs, for instance oranges, are suitable for this form of packing. It is used both in air and sea transport, including containerized shipments for skeleton cases.

Aluminium transport and storage containers are globally used. Constructed of aluminium, they are lightweight and can be both stacked and interstacked. A leading supplier is Bott Ltd who manufacture the Bott Ali Container range. They have a tare weight range from 5.6 kg to 26.0 kg spanning seven sizes. Examples are given below:

Length (mm)	Height (mm)	Width (mm)	Tare weight (kg)
600	400	240	5.6
800	400	330	8.0
800	600	400	12.5
800	600	600	12.5
1200	800	500	26.0

All are compatible with the pallet sizes 800 × 1200 mm or 1000 × 1200 mm.

Four new packing techniques have emerged in recent years. The first one is the bulk liquid bag or container. It can store various kinds of liquid cargo. When not in use the bag can be folded to 2 per cent of its volume. Other cargoes can be conveyed in the unit on the return trip. It costs about one-sixth of the price of a steel drum and one-quarter of a tank container. Each bulk liquid bag can carry a volume of liquid cargo equivalent to 210 large-capacity steel drums.

The second development is shrink-wrapping. It is very popular with air freight consignments, and consolidated consignments whether conveyed by air or surface transport. The cost is much less than the wooden case and similar relatively high cost material. The shrink-wrapping is provided by placing the goods to be covered on a base – usually a pallet for ease of handling – and covering it with a film of plastic. This is shrunk to enclose the items by the use of hot-air blowers (thermo-guns). It is a relatively cheap form of packing, particularly in relation to timber and fibre-board cartons. Moreover, it gives rigid protection to the cargo and its configuration follows the outline of the goods.

The third development is flat wrapping. This enables, for example, furniture such as kitchen and dining room wooden chairs to be flat wrapped. This enables the wooden component units to be laid on top of one another and permits the furniture to be assembled in the customer's home. Furniture manufactured in Malaysia is manufactured and despatched globally using high cube containers and retailed by IKEA. Hitherto, the furniture was manufactured as a finished unit which resulted in much broken stowage.

The fourth development is driven by the European Packaging Waste Legislation 2001 whereby a range of innovative and cost effective solutions have emerged relating to the distribution problems arising from the EU Regulations which we will now examine. The Regulations cover one trip packaging but importers must absorb the 'rolled up' obligations of their suppliers. Hence, a retailer – located in an EU state – importing a packed product, incurs all the obligations of the raw material supplier, packaging, manufacturer and packer. In contrast when a returnable or reusable package first enters the system, its tonnage becomes obligated, but there is no obligation on subsequent trips – however long it is in the system. In fact there may be some situations where users of returnable packaging systems may have no recycling or recovery obligations. Hence, because of costs and other requirements in meeting the Regulations relating to packaging waste, many suppliers/exporters conducting trans-EU business are adopting the returnable package in their logistic operations.

Combined with the growing sophistication and speed required in supply chain management, the returnable transit packaging has become an increasingly viable proposition. Plastic manufacturers have been encouraged to develop imaginative new concepts and innovations to meet market needs while corrugated fibre board transit cases and collapsible boxes made from metal or timber are long established. A new generation of plastic containers has been developed to satisfy supply chain requirements. The majority have been heavy duty crates and more recently stackable and nestable boxes which minimize the cost of moving empty packaging. When being used to transport goods from the manufacturer/supplier/exporter, the shipping cube can be fully utilized. For other transits in the supply chain the empty fold-down boxes provide a 140 per cent better utilization of transport space compared with nestable containers. Plastic fold-down transit boxes cater for a wide variety of requirements. Their sizes range from 400 mm by 300 mm up to 1200 mm by 3000 mm. Height variations range from 200 mm to 1300 mm. We will now examine three case studies.

(a) As well as transport cost savings, fold-down boxes also provide protection and easy handling for the products they contain. An example of the benefits of this type of container is provided by Karstadt, the German department store group. Believed to be one of the largest retail enterprises in Europe, Karstadt previously used a 12 cwt wooden pallet and collar – effectively a box without a base – for the distribution of larger items to its stores – smaller goods were transported in plastic fold-down boxes.

Karstadt decided to look for a more flexible distribution system which, as well as providing maximum possible protection, could cope with all the different sizes and shapes of its merchandise. It was also necessary for containers used for the system to utilize transport space fully and to fold flat for return journeys. To meet this need, a standard 800 mm by 600 mm module was developed which would be capable of incorporating a number of different sizes and types of containers. The system comprises four basic units: a dolly – mobile – with two fixed and two swivel wheels for ease of movement and maximum control; a large folding box supplied with or without a security lid; a similar sized collar; and the smaller folding box already in use by Karstadt, which was exactly half the length of the other units.

From this choice of components, Karstadt can make up the ideal distribution system for its requirements. For example, four of the systems make a perfect fit across the floor for its transport vehicles.

(b) Another container now in increasing use by many types of companies is a one-action folding box. Originally designed and developed to meet the exacting specifications of car manufacturer Nissan, the single action enables the box to be folded in seconds, enhancing efficiency on the motor manufacturer's assembly line. The containers are suitable for internal storage and distribution of automotive components and engineered parts and are ideal for RTP systems. The boxes were designed to meet Nissan's requirement for containers which can be folded down quickly to a height of 69 mm, featuring a snap-to lock and unlock mechanism for rapid, failsafe resistant to impact damage. Flat bases enable successful transportation on all types of conveyors and the smaller container will stack on top of the larger one, making both suitable for forming heavy palletized loads. The two sizes of containers are 396 mm × 297 mm × 235 mm and 594 mm × 396 mm × 235 mm, respectively. With a capacity of 21 litres, the smaller container can carry a maximum load of 240 kg when stacked ten high, while the larger 45 litre capacity box carries a load of 240 kg when stacked eight high. The system is enhanced by optional extras which include label holders and security seals. A choice of colour options is available subject to quantity, and a comprehensive range of printing options is on offer for personalizing containers to assist identification of property.

(c) In addition to their advantages with regard to product protection and efficiency in RTP operations, fold-down boxes can provide fast capital pay-back. This is illustrated by the case of SmithKline Beecham Pharmaceuticals, which users almost 5000 folding boxes for distribution of ethical pharmaceuticals, primarily to wholesale chemists. The company felt that it needed a system of returnable storage and distribution boxes to replace one-trip packaging. Prior to selecting fold-down containers, evaluation indicated that a payback period of five years could be achieved. In fact, it was achieved in three years.

Because they fold down when not in use, they offer SB Pharmaceuticals considerable space savings during return trips and when stored. Also, the straight parallel sides of the folding box ensure maximum utilization of the vehicle cube. Constructed from tough, injection-moulded polypropylene, the containers have interlocking lids secured with seals to provide tamper evidence and a deterrent against pilferage. Product picking into the boxes is monitored by a hand-held radio data terminal (RDT) unit. A picking list for a customer is displayed on the RDT, then as a product is picked its bar code is scanned. When each folding box is filled, or the order picking completed, the box is sealed and the RDT is used to scan the container's bar code to generate a despatch note automatically.

Most of SB Pharmaceuticals customers take delivery of their products in folding boxes mounted on pallets. For smaller deliveries, customers are supplied with wheeled dollies to enable easy movement of the containers.

Initial trials showed that the life expectancy of the individual container would average ten years in this particular application.

FIGURE 8.2(a) Cargo handling equipment – fork lift trucks and pallet

Palletization is closely associated with packing and becoming increasingly popular with the sea cell container developed by Seaco (see p. 94). The pallet may be of steel or wooden construction. The pallet, in appearance, is like a platform on which the cargo is placed. An aperture is provided at each side to enable the fork lift truck to mobilize/handle the pallet. Wooden pallets, by which the cargo is anchored, are very common in air freight thereby facilitating cargo handling on a unitized basis. The pallet accompanies the cargo throughout the transit. Wooden pallets are regarded as expendable

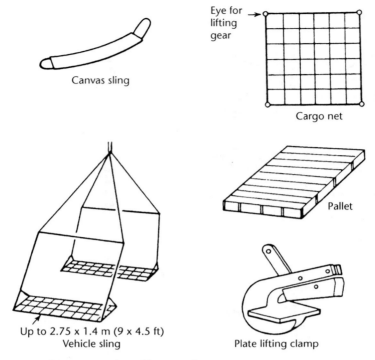

Canvas sling

Eye for lifting gear

Cargo net

Pallet

Up to 2.75 x 1.4 m (9 x 4.5 ft)
Vehicle sling

Plate lifting clamp

FIGURE 8.2(b) Cargo handling equipment

equipment when provided by the shipper who anchors the cargo to it. The pallet is manoeuvred by one of the fork lift trucks described and illustrated in Figure 8.2(a).

Packaging is now universally recognized as a decisive selling point in the realm of household consumer goods and similar products. Mass production, marketing, consumer advertising, display, design, presentation, protection hygiene and self-service retailing have made mechanical wrapping an almost universal necessity for small consumer goods. Modern packaging materials combine with modern handling equipment to make stacking at a greater height possible resulting in saving of floor space. Improvements are constantly becoming possible in the durability and protective quality of the package as technology progresses.

To the UK exporter who is anxious to improve his packaging and distribution technique, it is suggested he or she consults the Packaging Division of the Research Association for the Paper and Board, Printing and Packaging Industries (PIRA) of Leatherhead, Surrey. This organization provides services for which a fee is charged; details are given on p. 608.

Finally, the shipper must continuously review the form of packaging used in the light of the foregoing factors and the need to remain competitive coupled with rising standards.

8.3 Stowage of cargo

To the exporter, it is important he or she is aware of the principle of cargo stowage, particularly in an era where more shippers are stuffing containers or operating their own TIR international road haulage vehicle or intermodal service between the UK and the Continent, and beyond. Overall, the prime consideration is the safety of the transport unit employed which may be a container, vessel, aircraft or road vehicle. It is the overriding factor to be borne in mind throughout the transit that the merchandise does not impair the general safety of the transport unit and likewise is not a danger to others. Moreover, one must bear in mind that stowage standards are rising all the time and the shipper should always seek prior advice if in doubt. This is particularly relevant to containerization where most major container operators provide a free advisory service on the principles of container stowage.

Basically there are four main factors to consider in the stowage of cargo.

1. The best possible use should be made of the available dead weight or cubic capacity. It may be a container, road vehicle, ship or aircraft. Broken stowage, which is space wasted by cargo of irregular-shaped packages or irregularity of cargo spaces, should be kept to a minimum, consistent with the general stability of the transport unit. Generally 10–15 per cent of the total cubic capacity is allowed for broken stowage. A stowage plan detailing the cargo location can greatly facilitate achieving a good utilization of available space compatible with safety standards and is therefore used extensively in shipping, air freight cargo hold distribution, containerization and the large TIR international road haulage vehicle used by freight forwarders. Then, as far as practicable, full use should be made of the cubic capacity of the transport unit. An uneven distribution of cargo can result in an unstable load and encourages cargo movement throughout the transit. In the case of a vessel, uneven distribution of cargo can be compensated by ballasting the portion of the ship empty of cargo.

2. Allied to the previous item is the need to prevent damage to the ship, road vehicle, aircraft or container. Not only must there be a proper distribution of cargo to ensure adequate stability and trim, but it must also be properly secured to prevent shifting. If there is a movement of the cargo during the transit, it will tend to cause the transport unit to become unstable thereby creating a serious hazard. In the case of a vessel, she will tend to list, which is particularly relevant to movement of bulk cargoes such as grain, small coal, flintstone or iron ores. The situation is more serious when dangerous cargoes are involved irrespective of the transport mode. To reduce the risk of cargo movement, dunnage is provided. This takes the form of foam

rubber, polystyrene, timber boards, mats or inflatable bags which are placed between the cargo to prevent movement during transit. The shipper must be careful which type is chosen for some countries, particularly Australasia, where stringent regulations exist prescribing which dunnage material may not be used, for example, timber. Again one cannot stress too strongly the need to have total regard to the safety of the transit which is the prime consideration.

3. Similarly, cargo which is fragile, taints very easily, is liable to leakage, scratches easily, has strong odours, or is liable to sweat requires proper segregation, otherwise the carrier will be faced with heavy claims and possible loss of goodwill among shippers. Obviously a crate of oranges with a penetrating odour cannot be stowed adjacent to a consignment of tea, which taints easily, and machinery cannot be placed on top of chinaware.

4. Finally, a proper segregation of different consignments for various destinations, areas, ports and countries must be made to prevent delay in distribution and avoid double handling. This is a task primarily for the shipowner, airline, container operator or freight forwarder – the latter two being particularly involved in consolidated and groupage consignments. Again the stowage plan has a significant role to play in such a situation.

Our study of cargo stowage would not be complete without an examination of the principles of ISO container stowage, which is an increasingly popular method of international distribution, the container specification is found on pp. 76–94, see also Figure 4.1. Moreover, an increasing number of exporters are using the full container load consignment and undertaking their own stowage. The principles of container stowage are as follows. Again it cannot be stressed too strongly that safe container transport depends primarily on a correct and immovable cargo stow and an even weight distribution.

1. The container must be stowed tightly so that lateral and longitudinal movement of the cargo within is impossible. Tight stowage can be achieved by making the shape and the dimensions of the package an optimum module of the container. Alternatively, if a unit load is being used such as a pallet, the base of it must form a module of the container.

2. As an alternative to item (1), the cargo must be effectively restrained within the container. This is necessary for a variety of reasons including: (a) to prevent collapse of the stow while packing, unpacking, or during transit, for example, rolls of felt on end; (b) to prevent any movement during transit of part-loads or if single heavy items, for example, large pieces of machinery (the heavier the item the more damage it will do if allowed to move); and finally, (c) to prevent the 'face' of the stow collapsing and leaning against the container doors,

that is, to prevent it from falling out when the doors are opened at final destination or for customs inspection.

3.   The consignment must be adequately secured. Details of the various techniques are given below:

(a)   *Shoring* – bars, struts and spars located in cargo voids to keep the cargo pressed against the walls or other cargo.

(b)   *Lashing* – rope, wire, chains, strapping or net secured to proper anchoring points within the container and tensioned against the cargo.

(c)   *Wedging* – wooden distance pieces, pads of synthetic material, inflatable dunnage to fill voids in the cargo and keep it immobile against the container walls.

(d)   *Locking* – cargo built up to give a three-dimensional brick wall effect.

Overall, a container safely transported depends chiefly on a correct and immovable stow and an even weight distribution.

Basically, there is no simple formula to apply when securing cargo in a container and only experience can aid perfection and solution. Each cargo must be treated on its merits – the type of cargo, the way in which it is stowed, the cargo handling equipment available and the permanent fittings in the container. The built-in securing points, dunnage brackets, etc. should be used extensively. Any timber dunnage used must be dry and comply with any quarantine regulations. Any shoring which presses against the container wall should have extra timber laid longitudinally between the wall and point of support to spread the weight over two or more side posts. Useful filler pieces for wedging or preventing chafe include old tyres, polyurethane slabs, macerated paper pads and, for light packages, rolled-up cardboard. Unless an identical stow is anticipated on the return container journey, it is best if the lashing equipment chosen be considered as expendable. Where synthetic strapping material is used, terylene is preferable to nylon for heavy loads as it is less liable to stretch.

To restrain cargo various techniques exist. Again it depends on the commodity involved. Top-heavy articles should be wedged, shored and lashed to prevent toppling. Heavy weights should be secured to stout ring-bolts (sited in the container floor and side walls) and/or be shored with timber. Chain or wire with bottle screws may be used. Wheeled vehicles should be chocked, and lashed with Spanish windlasses, with the chocks chamfered or padded to protect the tyres. If the floor is of extruded aluminium, portable securing devices must be used. Resilient loads can cause lashings to slacken. This may be overcome by introducing elasticity, for example rubber rope, into the lashing pattern. No securing of pallets is necessary, provided the load is properly secured to the pallet, if the distance between pallets and container walls is 100 mm (4 in) or less. Pallets must not be allowed any longitudinal movement. If securing is necessary, stow pallets against container walls and wedge wood blocks between pallets. It may be necessary to insert sheets of board between pallet loads to protect against chafe and prevent bags, cartons, etc. interweaving and jamming the stow.

In many instances there is a space 400–2400 mm (4–9 in) remaining between the face of the cargo and container doors. Cargo must be prevented from collapsing into this space. It can be achieved in a variety of ways detailed as follows:

1. Use of suitably positioned lashing points with wire, rope, strapping, etc. woven across.
2. A simple wooden gate for the wider gaps and heavier cargo.
3. Use of filler pieces, that is macerated paper pads, polystyrene, wood, wool pads, etc. for the narrower gaps and lighter cargoes, for example cartons of biscuits.

Care must be taken to ensure that there is no 'fall out' when the container doors are opened. This is particularly relevant to a container which has been completely packed with cartons or sacks. Although this can sometimes be achieved by interlocking tiers of packages, it is better to make sure by using any fixing points located in the door posts of the container. Nylon strapping, polypropylene or wire threaded through such points forms an effective barrier.

To ensure there is adequate and correct overall distribution of cargo within the covered container, the goods must be secure within their packages. Moreover, the pack itself must be as full as possible so as to resist pressures external to it. Packages must be sufficiently rigid to withstand the weight imposed upon them when stacked, usually to a minimum height of 2.10 m (8 ft). If more than one type of cargo is stowed in the container, it is essential they are all compatible and cannot contaminate or be contaminated. Heavy items and liquids should be placed at the bottom with light and dry ones on the top. Within practical physical limitations of handling, the unit package should be as large as possible since this can reduce costs by up to 20 per cent and increase volumetric efficiency by up to 10 per cent. Consult when practicable the consignee about the proposed method of loading and sequence. This will facilitate discharge at the destination. Where relevant, stowing should be carried out in sequence which will permit rapid checking and stowage operations during and subsequent to unloading. In the event of the consignment being subject to customs pre-entry procedures, it would facilitate customs examination, should this occur and obviate unloading, if such cargo were stowed at the door end of the container. Shippers should avoid having a gap in the stow along the centre line of the container or at the sides as this will generate cargo movement in the transit and possible cargo damage.

Undoubtedly much of the foregoing cargo stowage principles relative to ISO covered containers can likewise be applied in many areas to stowage in other transport modes particularly in cargo wagon and the TIR international road haulage unit conveying consolidated and groupage cargo in a covered enclosed transport unit and inter-modal transits.

It would be appropriate to deal briefly with the equipment used in container stowage and discharge particularly as many exporters/importers have such cargo handling equipment in their factory or warehouse. Basically, the handling method used should be the one which gives the greater efficiency, with economy, and makes full use of any existing facilities and the equipment available.

The most versatile tool for tiering or stacking cargo in a warehouse or container base, etc. and for transporting loads up to a maximum of 2000 kg is the fork lift truck. Its general characteristics such as capacity, height of lift, speed, etc. will depend on overall work factors. The fork lift truck specification required for container work includes: a maximum collapsed mast height of 80 in; a free lift minimum of 48 in; its motive power must be either battery or electric depending on circumstances; the mast tilts must be as large as possible; the gradient capacity laden minimum 1 in 10, cushion tyres, and spot light and wheel loadings in accord with maximum permitted load.

A wide variety of fork lift trucks exist and these include the following which are illustrated in Figure 8.2:

1. *Side shift mechanism.* This moves the forks laterally either side of centre and thus considerably reduces the necessity to manoeuvre the fork lift truck inside the container.
2. *Extension forks.* These are used for handling awkward loads and to obtain extra reach. They are particularly useful, if the fork lift truck is of sufficient capacity, for clearing a space equivalent to the depth of the pallets on each side of a trailer mounted container, thus providing easy operation of the pallet transporters.
3. *Boom.* Ideal for carpets, pipes, etc.
4. *Barrel handler.* In addition to clamping the barrel with two sets of upper and lower arms, it also revolves so that the barrel can be picked up and handled in the roll, or in the upright position.
5. *Crane jib.* This converts the fork lift truck into a mobile crane.
6. *Drum handler.* This permits the fork lift truck to handle one or two drums at a time.
7. *Squeeze-clamps.* This is used for handling unit loads and individual items without the aid of pallets. The design and application of this attachment must be selected carefully since the operation of the clamp arms may be impeded by the container walls.

The foregoing types demonstrate the versatility of the fork lift truck.

8.4 Marking of cargo

Associated with packing is the marking of cargo. Basically, the export shipping mark and number is vital in the correct identification of the shipment irrespective of the transport mode. Moreover, it must be simple, easily identifiable and not masked with irrelevant information or old markings.

When goods are packed, they are marked on the outside in a manner which will remain legible for the whole of the transit. First of all, there is some mark of identification and then immediately underneath this for a maritime consignment, the port mark is shown. For example the merchant may be S. K. Winter Ltd and the goods are being shipped in the *mv Suffolk* to Gothenburg in which case the marks will be as follows:

S. K. W.
O/no. 1725
BORAS
Via GOTHENBURG
Nos 151–157

The consignment is identified, first, by a neutral abbreviation of the consignee's name; this reduces the risk of pilferage as potential criminals or receivers cannot easily relate the contents as they could if the full name of the customer were shown. The second line is the consignee's order number, and by this he or she can identify the consignment without having to open the packages; this is especially useful if he or she buys from a number of suppliers, or in cases where goods may be stored before use. The final delivery point is shown in the third line, while the fourth clearly shows the port of entry, thus helping to reduce the risk of the goods being routed incorrectly. Finally, the package numbers are shown – very useful to a supplier if kept in a strict sequence as it can be seen at a glance where a particular manufacturing run has been allocated, and equally useful to the consignee if this set of numbers is peculiar to one particular supplier.

Marks and numbers are the only common identification factor of any particular consignment after it has been packed for despatch. It is this detail which is shown in invoices, customs documents, bills of lading or air consignment notes, insurance certificates and collection/delivery notes. If the mark is interpreted wrongly on any of these documents, it is possible that mis-delivery or loss of the goods will occur and it follows that the marks or numbers must be shown clearly and indelibly on all the packages by means of stencil or secure tie-on labels. In addition to the mark, all goods should be labelled by the supplier showing the ship-berth, dock and loading brokers and sender's name and address.

In some trades, the practice is to give the dimensions of the package in metres which may be used in assessing the freight. Moreover, it is preferable for the gross and net weights to be likewise shown. Overall, it is desirable that the foregoing markings should be portrayed on three faces of the package – preferably side, end/or ends and top – with all markings clearly shown using large, clear lettering. All of the above criteria of cargo marking apply to other international transportation distribution modes such as air freight, road haulage, cargo wagon, and containerization, but it must be borne in mind they vary by individual trade and circumstance. It is also important to mention that the cargo markings correspond exactly with those on the bill of lading or other consignment note, such as CMR, CIM, air waybill used according to transport mode. In regard to containerized shipments both for FCL and LCL cargoes, especially the latter which are subject to break-bulk movements, all packages should be marked as under:

1. container operator's/shipowner's booking reference number;
2. intended ship or voyage;
3. name of combined transport operator.

In no circumstances should marks be used as advertising as they encourage pilferage.

To facilitate handling and to overcome differing language problems a recognized international marking symbol code is used, such as, 'this way up', 'keep dry', etc. These are printed on the exterior of the packing and a selection of them which have been accepted by the International Standards Organization is given in Figure 8.1.

Finally, it must be mentioned that the consignment must be adequately labelled giving the delivery address details. Nevertheless, it is relevant to note that the export shipping mark forms the principal identification for the movement of the goods.

8.5 Dangerous cargo

Dangerous goods have been defined as those substances so classified in any Acts, rules or by-laws or having any similar properties or hazards. The legislation applicable to all British-registered tonnage or other vessels loading in British ports are contained in the Merchant Shipping (Dangerous Goods and Marine Pollutants) Regulation 1997. Other regulations include Dangerous Substances in Harbour Areas Regulations 1987, the Health and Safety at Work Act 1974, the Environment Protection Act 1990, Carriage of Dangerous Goods (Classification, Packaging and Labelling) Regulations 1996 and Management of Health and Safety at Work Regulations 1992 (as amended). These require that all packaged goods are:

1. Classified and declared by the shipper to the Master.
2. Packaged in a manner to withstand the ordinary risk of handling and transport by sea, having regard to their properties.
3. Marked with proper shipping name and indication of the danger.

4. Properly stowed and effectively segregated from others which may dangerously interact.

5. Listed in a manifest or stowage plan giving stowage details. This must be aboard the ship.

The requirements of the Merchant Shipping (Dangerous Goods and Marine Pollutants) Regulations 1997 reflect the International Maritime Dangerous Goods Code (IMDG), produced by the International Maritime Organization (IMO). The Code has been adopted by 50 countries, representing 85 per cent of world tonnage. A consolidated four-volume 1990 edition produced by IMO incorporates extensive revisions adopted by the IMO Maritime Safety Committee at its 1989 session and effective from 1 January 1991. The latest IMDG Code is the 27th amendment effective from 1 July 1995. A supplement to the Code contains emergency procedures, Medical First Aid Guide, Code of Safe Practice for Solid Bulk Cargoes, Reporting Procedures for Incidents, IMO/ILO Guidelines for Packing Cargo in Freight Containers and recommendations for the safe use of pesticides in ships.

The IMDG code chapter VII of IMO SOLAS convention was developed as a uniform international code for the transport of dangerous goods by sea covering such matters as packing, container traffic and stowage, with particular reference to the segregation of incompatible substances. The latest amendments were adopted in May 2002 and these amendments make the code mandatory. They came into force on 1st January 2004. The code is kept under constant review in a two-yearly time cycle to make necessary amendments in line with development.

It is estimated that more than 50 per cent of the cargoes transported by sea today can be regarded as dangerous, hazardous and/or harmful (marine pollutants) under the IMO classification, designation or identification criteria. Some of them are dangerous or hazardous from a safety point of view, but are also harmful to the marine environment; others are harmful to the marine environment alone. The cargoes concerned include products which are transported in bulk such as solid or liquid chemicals and other materials, gases and products for and of the oil refinery industry. Between 10 per cent and 15 per cent of the cargoes transported in packaged form, including shipborne barges on barge-carrying ships, freight containers, bulk packagings, portable tanks, tank-containers, vehicles, intermediate bulk containers (IBCs), unit loads and other cargo transport units, fall under these criteria.

As the world becomes increasingly industrialized and as industry itself becomes even more complex, so the transport by sea of these cargoes will continue to rise and the lists of products will grow. It is essential, if shipping is to maintain and improve its safety record, that these cargoes are stored, handled and transported with the greatest possible care.

Volume I of the IMDG Code also contains the alphabetical General Index of dangerous substances, materials and articles, and the marine pollutants. This index is followed by the Numerical Index (the table of UN numbers with corresponding IMDG Code page numbers, EmS numbers and MFAG table numbers) and a list of definitions, including commonly used abbreviations.

8.5.1 Revised Annex I to the IMDG Code, containing the packing recommendations

Revised Annex I to the IMDG Code contains recommendations on the packing of dangerous goods, and on the construction and testing of packagings. Annex I was adopted by the Maritime Safety Committee in 1984 and is included in Volume I of the IMDG Code. From 1 January 1991, only tested and marked packagings should be used for the transport of dangerous goods.

The recommendations take into account the mandatory requirements on packing set forth in regulation 3 of Chapter VII of the 1974 SOLAS Convention, as amended. Regulation 3 requires packages containing dangerous goods to be capable of withstanding the ordinary risks of handling and carriage by sea and lays down other specifications.

Annex I closely follows the United Nations Recommendations in respect of the packing of dangerous goods, as contained in Chapter 9 of the Orange Book.

The principle of dividing dangerous goods, other than those covered by classes 1, 2, 6.2 and 7, into three packaging groups according to the degree of danger they present, i.e.

packaging group I: goods presenting great danger;
packaging group II: goods presenting medium danger; and
packaging group III: goods presenting minor danger

is reflected in the recommendations of Annex I and has an impact on the detailed provisions for the construction and performance testing of types of standard receptacles, packagings and packages ready for shipment.

The recommendations of Annex I are intended for manufacturers of dangerous goods and of packagings for these goods, the shippers and carriers as well as competent authorities, and are to be used in conjunction with the IMDG Code.

8.5.2 General Index of the IMDG Code

All substances, materials and articles which appear in the IMDG Code are listed in alphabetical order of the proper shipping name (correct technical name) in the General Index of the IMDG Code, which also gives the product's

UN number, its Emergency Schedule number (EmS No.), Medical First Aid Guide Table Number (MFAG Table No.), the IMDG Code page number of the individual schedule, class, packaging group and subsidiary risk label(s).

A number of dangerous goods are not listed by name in the Code and, therefore, will have to be shipped under a generic name/entry or a Not Otherwise Specified (NOS) entry. These entries have also been included in the General Index. For some goods, secondary names and synonyms also appear.

Following the General Introduction, Annex I and the indices, the IMDG Code then details the nine classes of dangerous goods, divided as follows:

Class 1.1 – Mass Explosion Hazard
Class 1.2 – Projection Hazard
Class 1.3 – Fire Hazard
Class 1.4 – No Significant Hazard
Class 1.5 – Very Insensitive Substances with Mass Explosion Hazard
Class 1.6 – Extremely Insensitive Articles with No Mass Explosion Hazard
Class 2.1 – Flammable Gas
Class 2.2 – Non-Flammable Compressed Gas
Class 2.3 – Poisonous Gases
Class 3.1 – Flammable Liquid – Flash-point below $-18°C$
Class 3.2 – Flammable Liquid – Flash-point between $-18°C$ & $+23°C$
Class 3.3 – Flammable Liquid – Flash-point between $+23°C$ & $+61°C$
Class 4.1 – Flammable Solid
Class 4.2 – Spontaneously Combustible
Class 4.3 – Dangerous When Wet
Class 5.1 – Oxidising Substance
Class 5.2 – Organic Peroxide
Class 6.1 – Toxic Substance
Class 6.2 – Infectious Substance
Class 7   – Radioactive Material
Class 8   – Corrosive Substance
Class 9   – Miscellaneous Dangers Substances and Articles

A complete revision of the IMPG code is undertaken by IMO at ten-year intervals. Amendments to United Nations recommendations are undertaken on a two-year cycle and approximately two years after their adoption. In that way a basic set of requirements applicable to all modes of transport is established and implemented, thus ensuring that difficulties are not encountered at inter-modal interfaces. Amendments to SOLAS chapter VII (Carriage of dangerous Goods) adopted in May 2002 make the IMDG code mandatory from 1st January 2004 and known as amendment

31. However, the provisions of the following parts of the code will remain recommendatory:

> Chapter 1.3 (Training).
> Chapter 2.1 (Explosives, introductory notes 1 to 4 only).
> Chapter 2.3, section 2.3.3 (Determination of flashpoint only).
> Chapter 3.2 (columns 15 and 17 of the dangerous goods list only).
> Chapter 3.5 (transport schedule for class 7 radioactive material only).
> Chapter 5.4 section 5.4.5 (multi-modal dangerous goods form) in so far as layout of the form is concerned.
> Chapter 7.3 (special requirements in the event of an incident and fire precautions involving dangerous goods only).

In practice this means that from the legal point of view, the whole of the IMDG code is made mandatory, but provisions of recommendatory nature are editorially expressed in the code to clarify their status.

8.5.3 Non-classified materials

A list of materials hazardous only in bulk (MHB) is included in section 24 of the General Introduction to the Code. Each class or category of goods is identified by a distinctive mark, label or placard. The marks, labels and placards are shown in Annex 4. Where appropriate, each individual schedule (page) in the Code shows the label or labels (100 mm × 100 mm) and, if applicable, the Marine Pollutant mark to be affixed to a receptacle, package, article, unit load or IBC, or as placards (enlarged labels of 250 mm × 250 mm) to be affixed to portable tanks, freight containers, vehicles or other cargo transport units, as provided for in the IMDG Code. Some consignments of dangerous goods should have the UN number of the goods displayed in the lower half of the placard or on a rectangular orange panel (120 mm × 300 mm) to be placed immediately adjacent to the placard.

All placards, orange panels and Marine Pollutant marks should be removed from cargo transport units or masked as soon as both the dangerous goods or their residues, which led to the application of those placards, orange panels and marine pollutant marks, are discharged.

The individual schedules of the Code follow a similar pattern. The substance's, material's or article's proper shipping name (correct technical name), and any known and commonly used alternative names (synonyms) appear at the top left of the schedule. To the right of this, other relevant information or observations are given, such as the UN identification number (UN No.) assigned to a substance or article by the United Nations Committee of Experts on the Transport of Dangerous Goods, its chemical formula, explosive limits, flash-point and so on. As an example, the schedule for 1,1,1 – Trichloroethane (Methylchloroform) (UN No. 2831), which is given with Trichlorobutene (UN No. 2322) on IMDG Code page 6272, is reproduced in Annex 5. 1,1,1 – Trichloroethane is widely used as typewriter cleaning fluid and thinner, 'Tipp-Ex'.

The other headings used in the individual schedules include properties or descriptions (such as the substance's, material's or article's state and appearance), special observations, packing, stowage and segregation. The schedule also shows the label(s) or placards and, if applicable, the Marine Pollutant mark, as appropriate to the substance, material or article. This is basically one of the marks, labels or placards shown in Annex 4, but a label or placard may also contain additional information. Those used for explosives, for example, also give the substance's or article's division number and compatibility group. Class 3 labels or placards sometimes contain a reference to the flash-point or flash-point group. For class 7 labels or placards additional information on the contents, activity and transport index is required.

Details of the salient points emerging from the IMO regulations, relative sea transport and RID (see p. 224) and ADR (see p. 223) international rail and road regulations are as follows:

1. Dangerous goods to be declared by their correct technical name and their principal hazard to be shown by reference to their dangerous-goods class.
2. Persons responsible for loading vehicles or containers to complete a container or vehicle packaging certificate.
3. Packagings, vehicles, containers, etc. to be marked to indicate the hazard or hazards presented by the contents.
4. The goods to be packed in an adequate manner.
5. The goods to be stowed so that they do not give rise to a hazard.
6. The employer/employee to ensure health and safety as far as possible of those involved in transport of dangerous goods.
7. The ship's Master to have a record of dangerous goods on board and where they are stowed.
8. Regulations apply to all UK ships and other vessels while they are loading or discharging cargo within the UK.
9. Prohibition for certain dangerous goods on passenger ships.
10. On-deck only stowage on passenger vessels when specified in IMDG Code or Department of Trade Blue Book must be strictly applied.
11. Powers described for prosecution for non-compliance with statutory requirements.

The International Maritime Dangerous Goods Code, and Department of Trade Blue Book, are recommendations on how the requirements of the dangerous goods regulations can be satisfied.

In fact the regulations state in a number of places that in the event of an incident, if it can be shown that the recommendations of the Blue Book and IMDG Code have been met then the requirements of the regulations have been complied with. Some elements apply to all dangerous goods and some apply only to certain substances or articles. These include:

1. Class
2. Proper Shipping Name (PSN)
3. UN Number
4. Packaging Group (PG)
5. Subsidiary-Risk (sub-risk)
6. Flash-point (F/P)
7. Marine Pollutant (MP)
8. Control Temperature (C/Temp)
9. Emergency Temperature (E/Temp)
10. Net Explosive Content (NEC)/Net Explosive Quantity (NEQ)
11. Hazard Division
12. Compatibility Group
13a. Radioactive Schedule Number
13b. Radiation Dose Rate
13c. Transport Index (TI)
14. Limited Quantities (LQ)
15. Waste
16. Empty Packagings

The shipowner like the airline will only handle such dangerous cargo by prior written arrangement and on the express condition the shipper provides a very full and adequate description of the cargo. If accepted, a special stowage order – often referred to as a dangerous-goods form – will be issued which will indicate to the Master that the cargo conforms to the prescribed code of acceptance laid down by the shipowner. It cannot be stressed too strongly that shipment will not take place until a special stowage order has been issued by the shipowner, which is the authority for shipment. Moreover, the shipper must fully describe the cargo and ensure it is correctly packed, marked and labelled. This he can do through a freight forwarder, which is often the practice.

Before dangerous goods can be authorized for shipment the following information is required:

1. Name of sender.
2. Correct technical name of dangerous goods (the trade name may not be sufficient to identify the hazard) followed by the words 'Marine Pollutant' (if applicable).
3. Class of dangerous goods.
4. Flash-point (where applicable).
5. UN No. to identify substance.
6. Details of outer packing.
7. Details of inner packing.
8. Quantity to be shipped in individual packages and in total.

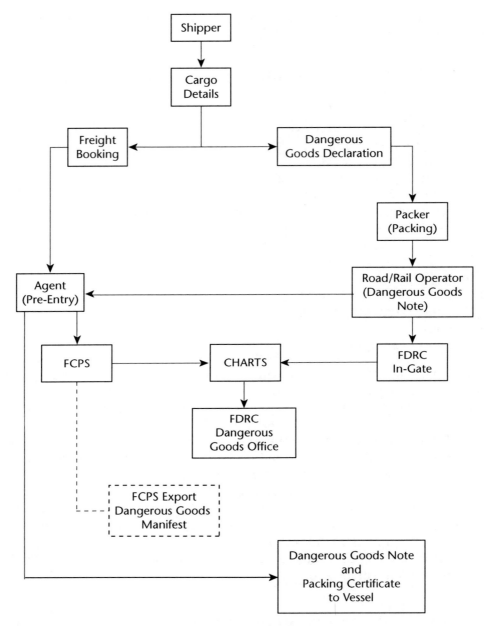

FIGURE 8.3 Export dangerous goods declarations
Reproduced courtesy Felixstowe Dock and Railway Company

9. Additional information for radioactive materials, explosives and consignments in bulk (e.g. tank containers, road tankers, etc.)

A flow chart courtesy of Felixstowe Dock and Railway Company relative 'export dangerous goods' declaration is found in Figure 8.3.

The dangerous-goods authority form will bear a reference number and will show the sailing details including port of departure and destination on which consignment is authorized: the hazard class, UN No., labels, key number (for emergency in event of any incident, spillage, etc), and any special instructions (i.e. special Department of Trade approval or restrictions on stowage, i.e. on deck only (passenger ship), freight vessel only, etc.).

On arrival of the goods at the departure port, the goods and authority to ship are submitted to the Master of the ship for ultimate approval prior to loading and customs clearance.

A further example is found in the deep-sea container shipment. It is the responsibility of the person loading the vehicle or freight container to ensure the packaged goods are correctly stowed, segregated and secured in accordance with the IMDG Code. It is ideal for the shipment of dangerous cargo particularly as it avoids multiple handling, protects the goods from interference by unauthorized persons and eliminates the risk of damage from the use of inappropriate methods of slinging. The following information is required at the time of booking the container:

1. name of vessel;
2. port of loading;
3. port of discharge;
4. number, kind and size of individual packages (including inner packages if valid) and total quantity – i.e. gross and net weight in kilos;
5. correct technical name of substance, as defined in IMDG code;
6. classification of substance (IMO);
7. UN No. of substance;
8. marine pollutant – if applicable;
9. packaging group;
10. flash-point – if any;
11. EmS Number (as listed in IMDG Code);
12. MFAG Table Number (as listed in IMDG Code).

With 'tween deck or bulk cargo shipments the loading of the ship is undertaken by stevedores, but with containerization this is done by container packers who are usually container operators or freight forwarders. Accordingly, with regard to the latter, a 'packing certificate' must be completed which certifies the following:

1. The container was clean, dry and fit to receive the cargo.
2. No cargo known to be incompatible has been stowed therein.
3. All packages have been inspected for damage, and only dry and sound packages loaded.
4. All packages have been properly stowed and secured and suitable materials used.
5. The container and goods have been properly labelled.

6. A dangerous-goods declaration has been received and completed for each dangerous consignment packed in the container.

It is paramount that the packing certificate is duly completed and signed by the shipper as it confirms to the shipping line and the Master that the task of packing the container has been properly carried out. The document accompanies the goods throughout the voyage. In regard to FCL containers, the Dangerous Goods Packing Certificate is incorporated in the IMO Dangerous Goods Note.

To comply with Classification, Packaging and Labelling of Dangerous Substances Regulations 1984, and the Road Traffic (Carriage of Dangerous Substances in Packages, etc.) Regulations 1986, a Transport Emergency Card (Tremcard) or equivalent must be supplied for substances within the following groups:

1. Any quantity of an organic peroxide or self-reactive flammable solid which has a self-accelerating decomposition temperature of 50°C or below, or where it is required to be conveyed below a specified temperature.
2. In receptacles with a capacity of 51 kg or more where the substance is an organic peroxide (not subject to the above paragraph), a flammable or toxic gas, asbestos or asbestos waste, certain other hazardous wastes and any other substance allocated to Packing Group I of CPL/IMO regulations.
3. In receptacles with a capacity of 2001 kg or more where the substance is allocated to Packing Group II of CPL/IMO regulations.
4. In receptacles of 2001 kg or more where substance is allocated to Packing Group III of CPL/IMO regulations.

Basically the code of 'one class–one container' must be observed unless the container operator has expressly agreed to a relaxation. Substances which fall into the same class but are incompatible must also be stowed in different containers, for example, peroxides and permanganates (both oxidizing substances). Dangerous goods may be incompatible with certain non-dangerous substances. Examples are poisons and foodstuffs, or those which react in contact with harmless organic materials, such as nitrates, chlorates, etc.

A container in transit is subjected to acceleration and deceleration factors in a longitudinal and to some degree, a lateral direction when travelling overland, and in a vertical and lateral direction at sea. At all times it is subjected to some degree of vibration. Hence, the contents must be firmly stowed and secured against movement and chafing. Particular care with dangerous cargoes must be taken to ensure that the contents will not fall outwards when the doors are opened. Dangerous cargoes forming only part of the load must be stowed in the door area of the container for ease of access and inspection. In the case of non-dangerous goods, damage arising from poor stowage is usually confined to the container concerned, but in the case of dangerous goods the effects could be widespread.

A dangerous goods note (DGN) (see p. 615) and Container Vehicle Packing Certificate (see p. 211) is required to be completed. This document must always accompany the goods and the Container/Vehicle Packing certificate section must be completed for any Shipper-packed FCL container and must be signed by the Shipper. This is in lieu of an SSW if the goods are of a hazardous nature. For FCL containers, the shipper is responsible and legally liable for attaching four labels of the appropriate class to the container. It is relevant to note that obnoxious/irritant substances are classified as non-hazardous, but must be stowed and treated as dangerous cargo. Hence, any cargo having such substances must be clearly labelled prior to shipment and the carrier notified.

Labels and placards (Figure 8.4) are assigned to each class of dangerous goods in the IMDG Code, and denote the hazards involved by means of colours and symbols. Colours and symbols should be as illustrated, except that symbols, texts and numbers on green, red and blue labels and placards may be white. It is a legal requirement that the labels are affixed to the container.

The class number should appear in the bottom corner of the label or placard. The use of the texts shown on the illustrations and of further descriptive texts is optional. However, for Classes 6.2 and 7 the text should always appear on the labels and the special placard. If texts are used for the other classes, the texts shown on the illustrations are commended for the purpose of uniformity.

Dangerous goods which possess subsidiary dangerous properties must also bear subsidiary risk labels or placards denoting these hazards. Subsidiary risk labels and placards should not bear the class number in the bottom corner.

Labels for packages should not be less than 100 mm × 100 mm, except in the case of packages which, because of their size, can only bear smaller labels. Placards for cargo transport units should not be less than 250 mm × 250 mm; correspond with respect to colour and symbols to the labels; and display the number of the class in digits not less than 25 mm high.

Some consignments of dangerous goods should have the UN number of the goods displayed in black digits not less than 65 mm high, either against a white background in the lower half of the placard or on a rectangular orange panel not less than 120 mm high and 300 mm wide, with a 10 mm black border, to be placed immediately adjacent to the placard.

All labels, placards, orange panels and marine pollutant marks for subsidiary dangerous properties should be removed from cargo transport units or masked as soon as the dangerous goods are unpacked and any residue removed. The detailed requirements regarding marking, labelling and placarding are contained in the IMDG Code.

FIGURE 8.4 IMO dangerous goods labels
Reproduced courtesy IMO

Class 1	**Explosives**	This class is comprised of the divisions: 1.1, 1.2, 1.3, 1.4, 1.5 and 1.6. Explosives also have a compatibility group letter. **Usually, only explosives of Class 1, Division 4, compatibility Group S are acceptable for carriage on passenger aircraft.**
Class 2	**Gases**	This class comprises three divisions: 2.1 Flammable gases, 2.2 Non flammable, Non toxic gases and 2.3 Toxic gases.
Class 3	**Flammable liquids**	Remember that the *flash point* of a Flammable Liquid is the temperature at which a vapour from the liquid could be ignited by a flame or spark. *It is not* the temperature at which it would ignite spontaneously. This has no sub-divisions.
Class 4	**Flammable solids Spontaneously combustible substances Water reactive**	This class comprises three divisions: **4.1** Flammable solids, **4.2** Substances liable to spontaneous combustion, and **4.3** Water reactive substances which in contact with water, either emit flammable gases or become spontaneously combustible. (Also known as 'Dangerous When Wet').
Class 5	**Oxidising substances; Organic peroxides**	This class comprises two divisions: **5.1** 'Oxidising Substances and **5.2** Organic Peroxides'.*
Class 6	**Toxic and infectious substances**	This class comprises two divisions: **6.1** Poisonous substances, and **6.2** Infectious substances.
Class 7	**Radioactive materials**	This class has no divisions, but there are three categories for non-fissile materials which are determined by the radiation level of the complete package. **Fissile materials are not usually acceptable for air carriage without special arrangements.**
Class 8	**Corrosives**	Substances in this class cause damage to the skin and/or metal. This has no sub-divisions.
Class 9	**Miscellaneous dangerous goods** (including magnetized materials)	This class comprises substances whose properties do not match those of any of the other eight classes, but would pose a risk to safety if not properly prepared for carriage. This has no sub-divisions.
NOTE:	**Subsidiary Risk**	Some Dangerous Goods have properties which meet the definition of more than one hazard class or division. The less serious hazard of such substances is described as a subsidiary risk.

FIGURE 8.5 IATA Dangerous goods classifications

Reproduced courtesy British Airways. See Dangerous Goods Regulations 45th Edition published by IATA, pages 73–96: classification; pages 537–60: labels-data subject to continuous review. www.iata.org/dangerousgoods

The universal adoption of the International Maritime Dangerous Goods Code (IMDG) has greatly facilitated the movement of dangerous goods between countries. Accordingly, a dangerous goods labelling code for maritime consignments exists and some codes are given in Figure 8.5.

With regard to the inland transport dangerous cargo movement on the inland transport document and on the transport emergency (TREM) card, which must accompany the goods, the Accord European relation du transport international des merchandise Dangereux par Route (ADR) classification (p. 223) and UN number must be shown, as well as the description of the goods. These cards are prepared by the European Chemical Industry Council (CEFIC) of Brussels according to the regulations of ADR.

With regard to dangerous classified cargo conveyed by air, it is the legal responsibility of every person involved in the shipping of dangerous goods to be aware of and to comply with the ICAO Technical Instructions for the Safe Carriage of Dangerous Goods and the IATA Dangerous Goods Regulations which govern the carriage of these goods. The technical instructions are a set of international regulations governing the carriage of dangerous goods by air. They are published by the International Civil Aviation Organization (ICAO) and are based on the United Nations recommendations for the safe transport of dangerous goods. They contain a dangerous goods list showing which goods may be carried by air and giving details of the requirements for carriage including quantity limits, packing, marketing, labelling and documentation requirements.

The IATA dangerous goods regulations are published by the IATA Dangerous Goods Board pursuant to IATA resolutions 618 and 619, and constitute a manual of industry carrier regulations to be followed by IATA member Airlines. The IATA regulations is based on the requirements of Annex 18 to the Convention of International Civil Aviation (Chicago 1944) and the 2003–2004 Edition of the Associated Technical Instructions for the Safe Transport of Dangerous Goods by Air (Doc9284-AN/905) adopted by the Council of ICAO and published by ICAO. Annex 18 to the Chicago Convention and the Associated Technical Instructions for the Safe Transport of Dangerous Goods by Air are recognized as the sole authentic legal source material in the air transport of dangerous goods. Significant changes and amendment to the 2004 (45th) Edition are found on pages XXI–XXII of the Dangerous Goods Regulations published by IATA.

The air transport regulations for dangerous classified cargo acceptance are more severe than those for maritime transport. Some substances are entirely prohibited, others may only travel in all-cargo aircraft, while some are permitted to be conveyed in passenger aircraft. All those which may travel by air require special packaging, labelling and documentation. Moreover, quantity restrictions are also applied per flight in the interest of safety. Details of the air freight dangerous-cargo classification – formulated by IATA – are given below:

Class 1: Explosives – this class is comprised of the divisions: 1.1, 1.2, 1.3, 1.4, 1.5 and 1.6. Explosives also have a compatibility group letter. Only explosives of Class 1, Division 4, compatibility Group S are acceptable for carriage on passenger aircraft. Division 1.6 embraces extremely insensitive articles which do not have a mass explosion hazard.

Class 2: Gases – this class comprises three divisions: 2.1 flammable gases, 2.2 non-flammable and non-toxic gases and 2.3 toxic gases.

Class 3: Flammable liquids – remember that the flash-point of a flammable liquid is the temperature at which the liquid emits a vapour which would be ignited by a flame or spark. It is not the temperature at which it would ignite spontaneously.

Class 4: Flammable solids – spontaneously combustible substances – water reactive. This class comprises three divisions: 4.1 flammable solids, 4.2 substances liable to spontaneous combustion and 4.3 substances which in contact with water emit flammable gases.

Class 5: Oxidizing materials, organic peroxides – this class is comprised of two divisions: 5.1 – oxidizing materials, and 5.2 – organic peroxides.

Class 6: Toxic, and infectious substances – this class is comprised of two divisions: 6.1 – toxic substances, and 6.2 – infectious substances.

Class 7: Radioactive materials – this class has no divisions, but there are three categories for non-fissile materials which are determined by the radiation level of the complete package. Fissile materials are not usually acceptable for air carriage without special arrangements.

Class 8: Corrosives – substances in this class cause damage to the skin and/or metal.

Class 9: Miscellaneous dangerous goods (including magnetized materials) – this class is comprised of substances whose properties do not match those of any of the other eight classes, but would pose a risk to safety if not properly prepared for carriage.

Classes 7, 8 and 9 have no sub-divisions.

Subsidiary risk – some dangerous goods have properties which meet the definition of more than one hazard class or division. The less serious hazard of such substances is described as a subsidiary risk.

The nature of the flight conditions the package is likely to encounter will vary and falls under three main areas: temperature variations, pressure variations, and vibrations. We will now examine each briefly.

The extremes of temperature which may be encountered in all transportation are in the order of −40°C and +55°C (−40°F and +130°F). Modern pressurized aircraft cabins and cargo holds are pressurized at the equivalent of about 3050 m (10 000 ft) altitude, irrespective of the actual flight level, which might be as high as 13 720 m (45 000 ft). 3050 m (10 000 ft) is equivalent to a pressure of 0.7 bar (10.1 lb/sq. in) and represents a difference of 0.3 bar (4.7 lb/sq. in) between the ground atmospheric pressure and cabin pressure. In certain extreme circumstances, this may rise to a difference of about 0.65 bar (9.4 lb/sq. in). In older-type non-pressurized aircraft, which may still be in use in certain parts of the world for cargo purposes, the differential may also be as high as 0.56 kg/sq. cm (8 lb/sq. in).

Vibrations in commercial aircraft to which packagings may be exposed range from 5 mm amplitude at 7 Hz (corresponding to 1 g acceleration) to 0.05 mm amplitude at 200 Hz (corresponding to 8 g acceleration).

Most packagings for dangerous goods must be subjected to performance tests designed to ensure that the contents of the packaging can be carried safely under normal transport conditions. The approval of packagings is by national authority testing organizations and only packaging identified as meeting the specifications required can be used for the carriage of dangerous goods.

Packaging is the essential component in the safe transport of dangerous goods by air. The IATA Dangerous Goods Regulations provide packing instructions for all dangerous goods acceptable for air transport with a wide range of options for inner, outer and single packagings. The packing instructions normally require the use of UN performance-tested specification packaging. However, these are not required when dangerous goods are shipped in limited quantities under the provision of limited quantity 'Y' packing instructions. The quantity of dangerous goods permitted within these packagings is strictly limited by the Regulations so as to minimize the risk should an accident occur. For the precise requirements for the packagings for dangerous goods always refer to the applicable sections in the dangerous goods regulations.

Given below are some guidelines:

Breakable or puncturable containers.	Glass, earthenware and plastic must be well-cushioned in absorbent material and packed in strong, approved containers.
All packaging must be resistant to its contents.	Make sure that the packaging contains nothing which could be eroded by its contents, or could form a hazardous compound with them. Certain types of plastics are unsuitable for packing some ethers, mineral oils and acids. You will find that most plastic container manufacturers publish compatibility lists.
Absorbent materials must be chosen carefully.	It must not react dangerously with the contents.
Do not exceed the net quantity per package limitations.	Remember that the type of packaging employed may impose additional limitations.
Some different dangerous goods must be packed individually (unless otherwise permitted).	Outside containers must not enclose inside containers of substances which, when mixed, would cause a dangerous evolution of heat or gas, or produce corrosive substances.

Packages must be marked on the outside with:

1. the proper shipping name and corresponding UN or ID number;
2. the full name and address of shipper and consignee;
3. if required, the specification packaging markings.

The correct hazard labels must be attached to each dangerous goods package. If possible, the labels should be placed next to the shipper or consignee's address. 'This Way Up' labels must be used on combination packagings containing liquid dangerous goods, excluding flammable liquids in inner receptacles of 120 ml or less. Where freight is restricted to carriage on cargo aircraft only, the 'Cargo Aircraft Only' label must be affixed to the package.

Most packaging for dangerous goods must be subjected to perform-ance tests designed to ensure that the contents of the packaging can be carried safely under normal transport conditions. The approval of pack-agings is by national authority testing organizations and only packaging identified as meeting the specifications required can be used for the car-riage of dangerous goods. The precise requirements for the packaging for dangerous goods is found in the applicable sections of the IATA dangerous goods regulations.

Documentation relative to restricted air cargo is most important and must be strictly adhered to. The shipper's declaration for dangerous goods must be completed in duplicate by the shipper. Under no circumstances shall it be signed by an IATA cargo agent, consolidator or forwarder. The proper declaration of dangerous goods by the shipper ensures that all in the trans-portation chain know what dangerous goods they are transporting, how to properly load and handle them, and what to do if an incident or accident occurs either in-flight or on the ground. Visit www.iata.org/dangerousgoods to keep up-to-date on any changing dangerous goods regulations.

8.6 The air waybill

The 'Nature and quantity of goods' box of the air waybill should show a general description of the goods and the 'Handling information' box should include the statement 'Dangerous Goods as per attached Shipper's Declaration' or 'Dangerous Goods as per Transport Document for Dangerous Goods.' If the shipment is acceptable only on cargo aircraft, the words 'Cargo Aircraft Only' should be added.

If a Shipper's Declaration is not required for dangerous goods, the 'Nature and quantity' box of the air waybill should show a description of the goods followed by, in sequence, the proper shipping name, class or division number; UN or ID number; subsidiary risk, if any; number of packages; net quantity per package; the packing instruction; and the UN packing group. The words 'Dangerous Goods – Shipper's Declaration Not Required' should be shown in the 'Handling information' box.

The same air waybill may cover other articles, whether dangerous or not, but the dangerous goods must be stated separately by showing them, first, on the air waybill. If the shipper is not sure that the goods are not classified as dangerous but they are described on the documents in a way that might indicate a restriction (e.g. chemicals, toiletries, etc.), add after the description of goods the statement 'Not Restricted'.

Before accepting a consignment containing dangerous goods, the airline requires the shipper to complete an 'Acceptance Check-list' consisting of a set of questions relating to the information given by the shipper on the documents, and to the condition of the packages. In addition to the Shipper's Declaration for dangerous goods form, an Air Waybill must be completed for each consignment of dangerous goods. There are separate lists for non-radioactive materials and radioactive materials.

Dangerous goods acceptance check-list – non-radioactive materials

1. Complete this check-list in duplicate.
2. Answer all questions as appropriate.
3. If goods are acceptable, sign the check-list and attach original copy to the AWB and retain duplicate on station file.
4. If any question is answered 'No', do not accept the shipment but give original to the shipper and pass a copy to the locally designated official.

(A) Shipper's Declaration

1. Are there copies in English and in the IATA format?
2. Has any amendment or alteration been signed by the shipper?
3. If the AWB number and places of destination and departure are not shown, enter them.
4. If the number of pages is not shown, check with the shipper and enter them.
5. Are the names and full addresses of the shipper and consignee shown? – For Division 6.2, is the emergency contact name and telephone number shown?
6. Has the 'non-applicable' aircraft limit and 'Radioactive Shipment' type been deleted?

Is the following information correct for each entry:

7. Proper shipping name, supplemented with technical name(s) when applicable?
8. Class or division number? For Class 1 the compatibility group also?
9. UN or ID number?
10. Subsidiary risk(s) corresponding to the subsidiary risk label(s) applied to the package?
11. Number and type of package(s)?
12. Quantity of each package?
13. If relevant, is the 'Q' value shown?
14. Indication that an 'Overpack Used'?
15. Packing group?
16. Packing instruction number?
17. If applicable, indication that shipment is 'Limited Quantity'?

18. If applicable, the special provision number?
19. If applicable, indication that government authorization is attached? If so, is there a copy in English?
20. If appropriate, is the 'Emergency Response' telephone number(s) shown?
21. Are the name, title, place and date shown?
22. Is the declaration signed?

(B) Air Waybill

Does the 'Handling Information' box show:

23. 'Dangerous Goods as per Attached Shipper's Delcaration?
24. If applicable, the words 'Cargo Aircraft Only'?
25. If no Shipper's Declaration required, is the applicable information shown in the 'Nature and Quantity' box?

(C) Packages

26. Do the number of packages delivered agree with the number shown on the Shipper's Declaration?
27. Does the type of packaging correspond with the type shown on the Shipper's Declaration?
28. Are the package(s) free from damage and leakage and in a proper condition for carriage?
29. Are the specification markings correctly marked?
30. Are the Proper Shipping Name, including technical name where required and the applicable UN or ID numbers, on the package(s)?
31. Are the names and addresses of Shipper and consignee shown on each package?
32. If 'Overpack Used', and specification marks not visible, has the overpack been marked: 'Inner packages Comply with Prescribed Specification'?
33. Are the correct hazard label(s) and when applicable the subsidiary risk label(s) on the package(s) as prescribed?
34. If special markings are required, are they on each package?
35. Is the 'Cargo Aircraft Only' label affixed as required?
36. Are the handling label(s) affixed as required?
37. For liquids in combination packaging, is the package orientation properly indicated on two sides?
38. Have all irrelevant marks or labels been removed or obliterated?

(D) General

39. Have all applicable special provisions been complied with?
40. Have all applicable state and operator variations been complied with?
41. Where necessary, have advance arrangements been made and confirmed?

Comments ....
....
....

Checked by ....

Signature   Time   Date

....

Name (block capitals)   at (station)

Dangerous goods acceptance check-list – radioactive materials

1. Complete this check-list in duplicate.
2. Answer all questions as appropriate.
3. If goods are acceptable, sign the check-list and attach original copy to the AWB and retain duplicate on station file.
4. If any question is answered 'No', do not accept the shipment but give original to the shipper and pass a copy to the locally designated official.

(A) Shipper's Declaration

1. Are there copies in English and in the IATA format?
2. Has any amendment or alteration been signed by the shipper?
3. If the AWB number and places of destination and departure are not shown, enter them.
4. If the number of pages is not shown, check with the Shipper and enter them.
5. Are the names and full addresses of the Shipper and consignee shown?
6. Has the 'Non-applicable' aircraft limit and 'Non-Radioactive Shipment' type been deleted?

Is the following 'Nature and Quantity' information correct for each entry:

7. Proper shipping name, Class 7 and UN number?
8. If applicable, subsidiary risk?
9. The words 'Radioactive Material', if not included in proper shipping name?
10. Name or symbol of radionuclide(s)?
11. Physical and chemical form or, if relevant, special form, if not included in proper shipping name?
12. If relevant, the group for LAS material or SCO using terms 'LSA-I', 'LSA-II', 'LSA- III', 'SCO-I', 'SCO-II', 'SCO-III' as appropriate?
13. Number and type of package(s)?
14. The activity in each package specified and within limits?
15. Indication that an 'Overpack Used'?
16. Category of the package(s)?

– for Category II and III only, the Transport Index and dimensions of each package?

– for fissile material, the words 'Fissile Excepted'?

17. The identification mark for each applicable competent authority certificate and are copies of such certificates attached? If so, is there a copy in English?
18. If appropriate, is the 'Emergency Response' telephone number(s) shown?
19. Is the name and title of the signatory and place and date of signing shown?
20. Is the declaration signed?

(B) Air Waybill

Does the 'Handling Information' box show:

21. 'Dangerous Goods as per Attached Shipper's Declaration'?
22. If applicable, the words 'Cargo Aircraft Only'?
23. If no Shipper's Declaration required, is the applicable information shown in the 'Nature and Quantity' box? (Note: This also includes 'Dry Ice' requirements.)

(C) Packages

24. Do the number of packages delivered agree with the numbers shown on the Shipper's Declaration?
25. Does the type of packaging correspond with the type shown on the Shipper's Declaration?
26. Are the package(s) free from damage and leakage and in a proper condition for carriage with the sealing intact?
27. Are the proper shipping name and UN number shown? Are the proper shipping name, including technical name where required and the applicable UN or ID numbers, on the package(s)?
28. Where applicable, is each package marked either 'Type A' or 'Type B(U)' or 'Type B(M)'? (Note: All 'Type B' packages must be complete with the identification mark, serial number and embossed trefoil symbol.)
29. Are the names and addresses of shipper and consignee shown on each package?
30. If 'Overpack Used', and 'Type A' or 'Type B' markings not visible, has the overpack been marked: 'Inner Packages Comply with Prescribed Specifications'?
31. If gross weight exceeds 50 kg, is it marked on the package?
32. Are all required radioactive materials and subsidiary risk labels correctly affixed?

33. Is each radioactive label marked with:

    (a) the radionuclide symbol (except for 'LSA-I')?
    (b) the 'LSA-I', 'LSA-II', 'LSA-III', 'SCO-I', 'SCO-II' markings as applicable?
    (c) Activity? (or the mass if fissile material).
    (d) For Categories II and III, the transport index?

34. If applicable, the 'Cargo Aircraft Only' label?
35. Have all irrelevant marks or labels been deleted?

(D) General

36. Have all applicable special provisions been complied with?
37. Have all applicable state and operator variations been complied with?
38. Where necessary, have advance arrangements been made and confirmed?

Given below is a list of commodities which are hazardous and need special packaging, labelling and documentation when conveyed by air transport.

Aerosols
Ammunition
Arcton (trade name for compressed non-inflammable gas)
Automobile parts (could indicate batteries, cellulose paints, etc.)
Barometers (may contain mercury)
Batteries (may contain acid)
Bleach
Breathing apparatus (may indicate compressed gas cylinders)
Bull semen (refrigerants such as liquid nitrogen are used)
Butane
Chemicals or 'harmless chemicals' (often found to be hazardous)
Cryogenic liquid (liquid gases used as refrigerants – e.g. liquid nitrogen)
Cylinders (may contain compressed gases)
Dental apparatus (may indicate gas cylinders, alcohols, resins, etc.)
Dry ice (solid carbon dioxide, used as a refrigerant)
Electrical equipment (may contain magnetized material or mercury)
Electrical powered apparatus (may contain batteries)
Electron tubes (may contain mercury)
Engines (may contain fuel)
Freon (trade name for compressed, non-flammable gas)
Frozen food (may be packed in dry ice)
Gas(es) – 'gaseous' (may be a hazardous chemical; check proper name in IATA regulations)
Hair tonic (may be flammable)

Household goods/personal effects (may contain hazardous materials)
'Inhibited' or 'uninhibited' materials (may be hazardous)
Insecticides (may be flammable, poisonous or corrosive)
Laboratory equipment (may contain hazardous chemicals)
Lacquer (may be flammable)
Lighters – cigarette (may contain liquid fuel)
Lightmeters
Machinery (may have compressed gases, flammable liquids, batteries, radioactive materials, etc.)
Magnets, magnetized materials
Manometers (may contain mercury)
Medical supplies
Motorcars or cycles or parts thereof (may contain fuel or indicate batteries or cellulose paints)
Oil drilling equipment (may contain mercury)
Paint, enamel, etc. (may be flammable)
Perfume (may be flammable)
Pesticides (may be flammable, corrosive or poisonous)
Pharmaceuticals (may contain hazardous chemicals)
Polymerizable materials
Rectifiers (may contain mercury)
Refrigerators (may contain compressed gases)
Repair kits (may contain adhesive, cellulose paints, solvents, etc.)
Sample for testing (may contain hazardous materials)
Soda-water makers
'Stabilized' or 'unstabilized' substances (may be hazardous)
Switchgear (may contain mercury)
Toys (especially those made of cellulose)
Vaccines

Finally, in regard to the movement of dangerous goods by road within Europe, the relevant conditions are found in the European Agreement concerning the international carriage of dangerous goods by road (ADR). This came into force on 29 July 1968 in the territories of those countries which had notified or acceded to the Agreement. At present these countries are Austria, Belgium, Croatia, Czech Republic, Denmark, Finland, France, Germany, Hungary, Italy, Luxembourg, the Netherlands, Norway, Poland, Portugal, Slovakia, Spain, Sweden, Switzerland and the UK. The purpose of ADR is to ensure that dangerous goods being conveyed by road are able to cross international frontiers without hindrance, provided such goods are packaged, marked, documented and labelled in accordance with regulations and likewise the vehicles. This includes vehicle marking, equipment, training, tanker requirements and Tremcards. Most countries insist that Tremcards which accompany the goods on their international journey are in the language of the importing country. The dangerous goods classification under the ADR transport regulations is the same as for sea transport in the IMDG code. The nine classifications are listed on p. 212. The packaging, labelling, vehicle, tank vehicle and tank container requirements are thus dependent on the class, item number and properties of the goods to be carried.

An important feature of ADR is that tank vehicles and certain other vehicles carrying explosives are subject to technical inspection and a certification procedure in their country of registration to ensure that they conform with ADR requirements and with the normal safety regulations in force in the country of origin governing brakes, lighting, steering, etc. The competent authority (the Department of Transport in the case of the UK) will issue a certificate of approval for vehicles which pass this inspection. The ADR certificate is therefore acceptable by other contracting parties during its period of validity, which will not be longer than one year. The term 'tank vehicles' in this context means vehicles with fixed tanks intended for the carriage of liquids or gaseous, powdery or granular substances, and does not include demountable tanks, tank containers or fixed tanks intended for the carriage of solids.

Our study of dangerous cargo would not be complete without a mention of the movement of such cargo internationally by rail throughout its transit. The merchandise is primarily bulk cargo and regulations are very stringent. Within Europe they are found in the International regulations concerning the carriage of dangerous goods by rail (RID) 1978 and subsequent amendments. The dangerous goods classification under the RID transport regulations is the same as for sea transport in the IMDG code. The nine classifications are listed on p. 212.

To conclude our study of dangerous cargo one cannot stress too strongly the need to ensure the relevant regulations are complied with at all times and shippers and exporters are advised to contact their freight forwarder or shipowner and/or airline when in doubt. Visit IATA/IMO dangerous goods website as below.

Readers fresh to the subject and keen to understand the wide range of dangerous cargo terms will find it useful to obtain a copy of the Fifth Edition (2005) of my Dictionary of Shipping International Business Trade Terms and Abbreviations, published by Witherbys – e-mail books@witherbys.co.uk which contains 18 000 entries embracing over 1000 dangerous goods terms/definitions.

Recommended reading

(a)   Dangerous Goods Regulations 45th Edition, latest edition (a new edition is published annually) IATA – www.iata.org/dangerousgoods
(b)   IMDG Code – IMO latest edition – amendment 31 – www.imo.org

Export customs practice

9.1 Introduction

This chapter examines the customs procedures adopted in the United Kingdom which are laid down by HM Government. The UK is a member of the European Union (EU) and accordingly goods are in free circulation for those commodities which originate and are manufactured in any of the 25 states forming the single market – see Chapter 18. Goods which are exported or imported from a third country which is outside the single market such as the USA, the Far East, Switzerland, etc. are subject to rigorous customs procedures.

Customs procedures and legislation are subject to government policies and the political climate both nationally and internationally. Countries which are members of an economic bloc or Customs Union such as ASEAN are subject to the customs policies agreed within the membership.

It is appropriate at the commencement of this chapter to focus on customs policy in the early part of the twenty-first century covering the international movement of goods, excluding intra-EU trade. This involves an evaluation of the following major international initiatives and developments in the business world which are driving further changes in the business and customs environment.

1. Growth and globalization of international trade involving the global village and product outsourcing on a logistic basis (see Chapter 6).
2. Exploitation of new markets through new technology and continuing improved international distribution networks through multi-modalism (see Chapter 5).
3. World liberalization of trade realized by the WTO initiatives and strategies (see pp. 27–35).
4. Falling customs duty rates emerging from the GATT Uruguay and WTO agreements.

5. The continuing international simplification/harmonization of customs requirements and procedures.
6. The continuing mergers and overall growth of multinationals. This exploits the economies of scale.
7. The rapid advances in technology and developments in electronic commerce. This involves the development of electronic commerce to produce 'seamless' international trade transactions.
8. The growing influence of the EU and its enlargement coupled with the growth of other economic blocs and Customs Unions globally.
9. The internationalization of criminal activity.
10. The growing demand for environmental restrictions.
11. The measures to combat terrorism.
12. The compatibility with the trade dominance growth of China and India.
13. The development of the inland clearance depot as a vehicle for combined transport interface and driven by logistics.
14. The growth and dominance of containerization linked to the remodelling of the global container network embracing the hub and spoke network and continuous investment in maritime container hi-tech terminal. An increasing number are trading centres.

To facilitate the realization of effective customs strategies within the context outlined, it must be recognized that global competition will intensify – a factor recognized by the WTO. Additionally, other critical success factors of implementation are more customer focused: the appropriate international legal framework, the further development of efficient and effective customs procedures and systems and finally the maintenance of effective frontier admissibility controls.

Undoubtedly, the foregoing developments will be facilitated by the World Customs Organisation (WCO) which is an inter-governmental organization with worldwide membership whose mission is to enhance the effectiveness and efficiency of customs administrations. It is based in Brussels.

One of the important instruments developed by the WCO was the Harmonised System Commodity Description and Coding system known as the Harmonised System or HS (see p. 232). The HS was implemented in 1988 by an International Convention known as the 'International Convention on Harmonised System Commodity Description and Coding system'. It is administered by the WCO – more specifically the Harmonised System Committee: its goods classification system nomenclature is applied by more than 150 countries (including 88 contracting parties to the HS convention) for Customs tariffs and trade statistics, thereby facilitating international trade.

Overall, the main work of the WCO is the revision of the Kyoto Convention – the convention for the simplification and harmonization of customs procedures. A significant development is a change in emphasis from consignment based controls at the frontier to control, inland, using traders' records.

Currently the role of the HM Customs and Excise embraces five areas which are dealt with below: landing and shipping; warehousing; excise; value added tax; and preventive duties.

Landing and shipping officers are the people who directly control the importation and exportation of goods. They are responsible for ensuring that correct documentation is produced to cover the transaction, that all governmental requirements are fulfilled and that all revenues due are collected.

The lodgement of goods into a bonded warehouse is a method by which traders may defer payment of duty, or at times, reclaim duty already paid. The term 'bonded warehouse' indicates accommodation for which the owner has given his or her written promise under bond to comply with certain conditions laid down when the Commissioners approved the premises for 'Customs' business. Bonds maybe given as security for a number of different transactions and will be described fully later in the chapter. The warehouse officer is responsible for the control of all receipts into the warehouse, operations within the warehouse, for example bottling of wines, and deliveries of goods from the warehouse. The warehouse officer is also required to ensure that duty is paid on all goods delivered from warehouse to a dutiable use.

9.1.1 E-commerce – Customs

The UK is the leading industrial nation in the development and operation of E-commerce in the conduct of Export and Import customs declarations/procedures and aligned customs derivatives such as Excise, IPR, OPR, etc. The systems have been developed in close association with the WCO and the EU Member States to promote the freedom of movement of goods under a disciplined environment.

The core of the HM Customs is CHIEF (p. 237) from which there has been developed NES (pp. 236–38), CFSP (pp. 233–34) and NCTS (pp. 249–52). Hence, the manual system has been virtually eliminated and Exporters/Importers/Agents/Seaports/Airports/Carriers operate 'in line' with customs. These developments started with CHIEF in 1992 followed by NES/CFSP/NCTS in 2000/2002. Moreover, the situation is ongoing as technology develops and trade facilitation and globalization expands. An area of concern is the fraud element in E-commerce and effective measures of detection and prohibition.

The trader today must ideally have the adequate computer resources and software to handle customs E-commerce. It cannot be stressed too strongly in the fast changing world of exporting, that companies have an adequate IT software system to maximize the benefits emerging from electronic documentation, not only in customs (NES pp. 236–38, CFSP pp. 233–34 and NCTS pp. 236–38), but also processing export consignment (see pp. 423–25). It also extends to VAT.

There are many factors driving the change in Customs regulations/ control and transmitted into E-commerce, but this is found particularly in logistics. Traders are urged to keep up-to-date with the ongoing changing regulations.

9.2 Value Added Tax

From 1 January 1993, following the completion of the Single Market, there were important changes in the way that VAT is charged and accounted for on goods moving between Member States of the European Community (EC – now EU). For VAT purposes, the terms 'imports' and 'exports' for intra-EU movements of goods disappeared. They were replaced by new arrangements for zero rating intra-EU supplies of goods. VAT on goods traded between EU Member States is not collected at the frontier on importation. Instead, goods supplied between VAT registered traders are zero rated on despatch and any VAT due is payable on acquisition of the goods by the customer. The customer accounts for any VAT due on their normal VAT return at the rate in force in the country of destination of the goods. When VAT registered traders despatch goods to unregistered traders or private individuals in another EU country, the supplier must usually charge VAT at the rate in force in the country of despatch.

There are also special rates for freight transport and associated services. Special rules were introduced from 1 January 1993 for determining the place of supply of freight transport services, ancillary transport services and the services of intermediaries arranging freight transport and ancillary transport services. When the services are supplied to customers registered for VAT in EU Member States, the place of supply is the supplier's Member State when the suppliers belong in the Member State of the customer. The supplier will charge and account for VAT on the supply at the domestic rate. The customer will be able to recover input tax subject to the normal rules. Conversely, when the customer's Member State of the supplier does not belong in the Member State of the customer, the customer gives the supplier a valid VAT registration number. The supplier will not charge VAT on the supply but will still be able to recover any input tax incurred in making the supply subject to the normal rules. The customer must account for VAT under the 'reverse charge' procedure.

If a customer has not given a valid VAT registration number or the supply is to a private individual, the supplier will have to tax the service in the EU Member State in the case of the following: the transport of goods where the transport of the goods originates; ancillary services where they are physically performed; the services of intermediaries arranging freight transport connected with the movement of goods between EU Member States – where the transport of the goods originate; or the services of intermediaries arranging ancillary services connected with the movement of goods between EU Member States – where the ancillary services are physically performed.

VAT goods purchased from other EU countries are immune from any VAT payment at the time of import. However, for most transactions between VAT-registered businesses, VAT will become due on acquisition of the goods by the customer and will be accounted for in the normal VAT return.

When non-VAT-registered businesses or private individuals in the UK purchase goods from a VAT-registered trader in another EU country, they will normally be charged VAT by the supplier at the rate applicable in that country. However, to avoid distortions of tax once the value of goods purchased from other EU countries exceed a certain threshold, the UK customer will, in certain circumstances, be liable to account for tax on the goods in the UK as acquisitions. Such persons will then have to register for VAT in the UK.

For VAT purposes, goods imported from outside the EU are treated as imported into the UK when:

1. they arrive in the UK directly from outside the EU and the trader enters them for home use in the UK or customs duty otherwise becomes payable on them; or
2. they have been placed in another EU country or in the UK under a duty suspension arrangement involving one of the following situations and the trader enters them for removal to home use in the UK, or customs duty otherwise becomes payable on them;

    (a) temporary storage,
    (b) free zones,
    (c) customs warehousing,
    (d) inwards processing relief (duty suspension system),
    (e) temporary importation (including means of transport) with total relief from customs duties,
    (f) external Community Transit (T1) arrangements,
    (g) goods admitted into territorial waters,
    (h) excise, warehousing.

The value for VAT-imported goods will be their customs value, plus the ancillary charges for freight, etc. The customs computerized system for handling import entries (CHIEF) will allow VAT paid on the traders' imports under the government contractor, registered consignee, and bulked entry procedures to be included in VAT certificates. Basically, when Customs duty is due on goods, it coincides with VAT importation payment. Current import VAT arrangements are described in HM Customs Notice 700 and 725 (VAT the Single Market).

With respect to export under VAT terms, it will only take place when goods leave the territory of the EU, either directly or via another EU country. Goods which are despatched or transported to another EU country are not treated as export but are called 'despatches'.

When goods are received from outside the EU which are consigned to another EU country, the trader must put the goods into free circulation in the UK with payment of any customs duty and/or import VAT due, or place the goods under the external Community Transit (TI) arrangements. In this situation, any duty and/or VAT will be payable in the EU country of destination. Unless the traders' goods are warehoused in the UK for excise duty purposes, the trader will have to pay import VAT when the goods are put into free circulation in the EU country where that is done. Hence traders will not normally be able to put goods into free circulation in one EU country and pay import VAT in another. No import VAT will be payable, either in the UK or in the EU country of destination.

Generally speaking, the export transaction is zero-rated for VAT purposes subject to compliance with certain conditions, especially in the area of proof of the export transaction. Hence the goods are VAT zero-rated for goods transferred abroad, used for temporary exhibition or processing and exported on a sale or return basis. Proof of export is essential to qualify for VAT zero rating and consists of valid commercial or official evidence of export. In regard to sea freight, valid proof of export will include bill of lading, sea waybill and certificate of shipment; while for air freight, it embraces the air waybill. For groupage, the house air waybill or house bill of lading is acceptable, subject to it including the cargo description, sailing and/or flight details, seaport or airport of despatch and container or railway wagon number. In all cases such commercial and official evidence should be supported by other commercial documentation.

9.2.1 VAT distance selling arrangements

Distance selling occurs when a taxable person in one Member EU state supplies and delivers goods to another Member EU State who is not registered or liable to be registered for VAT. These persons are known as non-taxable persons and will include private individuals, public bodies, charities and businesses which are not VAT registered because their turnover is below the threshold or whose activities are entirely exempt. The most common examples of distance sales are mail order or goods ordered over the Internet. Each Member State is responsible for setting its own threshold which is set in its own currency. Traders registered for VAT in the UK and making distance sales to customers in another EU Member State, should charge UK VAT until the value of the traders' supplies exceeds the distance selling threshold in that country. Once the value of the trader distance sales exceeds this threshold, the trader is liable to register and account for VAT in that country. Study HM Customs Notice No 725.

9.2.2 VAT EU Sales Lists

Arising from the abolition of the fiscal frontiers between Member States of the EU, UK traders registered for VAT who make supplies of goods to traders registered for VAT in other EU countries are required to send lists of their EU supplies of goods to HM Customs and Excise. The information provided on the EU Sales List (ESLs) is used in the UK and by other Member States to ensure that VAT has been correctly recorded. It is a condition of zero-rating that the trader you supply must have a valid VAT registration number for the EU customer. ESLs maybe submitted monthly or quarterly.

9.2.3 Intrastat

Intrastat is the system for collecting statistics on the trade in goods between Member States. Intrastat replaces customs declarations as a source of trade statistics within the EU. It exists throughout the EU and requirements are similar in all Member States. The supply of services is excluded from Intrastat except where they are related charges such as freight and insurance and form part of the contract to supply goods. The Intrastat trade statistics are compiled from the totals of EU trade declared on VAT returns by businesses below a legally set threshold and from the detailed information given by larger businesses on Supplementary Declarations.

9.2.4 Freight transport and associated services

The cost of transport and insurance forms part of the value of goods for customs purposes. VAT will be due on the receipt or acquisition of the goods by the customer. Hence VAT will be accounted for in the same EU country as the one in which the customer has the right to recover the tax. The transport of goods between EU Member States is taxed either in the Member State where the customer is registered for VAT or if the customer is not a VAT registered person, which includes a private person, in the Member State from which the goods are removed, i.e. the place of departure.

Supplies of ancillary services and the services of intermediaries connected with the movement of goods between Member States are taxed according to the same rules as apply to intra-community transport services. However, when supplied to a customer who is not registered for VAT, ancillary services are taxed in the Member State in which they are physically performed and intermediary services are taxed in the Member State where the service which is being arranged is taxed.

9.2.5 Preventive duties

Though numerically small, the preventive staff or waterguard, as they are often called, are probably the best known members of the Customs and Excise Department. These are the people seen manning the ports and airports, and whose main task is the prevention of smuggling and the apprehension of smugglers. Besides these purely customs tasks, they are involved in the control of imported and exported goods, and are employed both for customs purposes and for local and central government purposes where they have an agency function.

9.3 Customs tariff and classification

All products exported must be identified with the current correct class or commodity code. The rationale of such classification is to ensure the trader pays the correct amount of duty and VAT; receives any export refund due on some agricultural goods, provided all other conditions are satisfied; contributes to the accuracy of import and export trade statistics and ascertains if an import or export licence is required. Traders experiencing difficulty in classifying their goods may seek guidance from a Trade Association or Chamber of Commerce. For some goods such as foodstuffs, independent laboratory analysis may be sought. It follows that the code used by the exporter should be the same as the importer. A full and accurate description of the goods is required.

The basis of the tariff is found in the Integrated Tariff of the United Kingdom which is based on the Combined Nomenclature (CN) of the European Community. It is published annually by the Official Journal of the European Communities. The CN is based on the Harmonised Commodity Description and Coding System used worldwide. The tariff also includes TARIC requirements.

There are six general rules governing the interpretation of the nomenclatures procedure which must be applied to the traders' goods and in sequential order.

The trader having correctly determined the commodity code from the tariff must clarify the following: any licensing requirements; any fiscal measures such as excise or anti-dumping duties; a temporary suspension of duty; a preferential rate of duty; and the rate of duty and import VAT applicable to the goods. The system for collecting intra-EU trade statistics is called 'Intrastat'. Exporters are urged to exercise effective customs planning in the area of tariff classification and the cash flow management. See HM Customs Notice 600.

9.4 Export controls

There are two main reasons for controlling the exportation of goods. These are:

1. revenue interests;
2. trade statistics.

9.4.1 Revenue interests

These interests (and the economy) may suffer if the following types of transaction are not controlled:

1. Transhipment goods – should these goods not be transhipped, there is the possibility of loss of revenue.
2. Goods for re-exportation after temporary importation.
3. Goods exported from a bonded warehouse.
4. Goods exported from an excise factory.
5. Goods exported on drawback.
6. Cars supplied free of VAT to overseas residents.
7. Goods exported for process and subsequent re-importation.

Should these types of transaction not be controlled, there is a strong possibility of loss of revenue through dishonest people claiming that goods had been exported, etc. when in fact they had found their way on to the home market. The insistence on proper documentation of these transactions ensures that the revenue is safeguarded.

9.4.2 Trade statistics

Overseas trade statistics provide important information about the United Kingdom export trade with third countries. Published monthly they are regarded as economic indicators by the Government and are widely used by industry and commerce.

In regard to UK trade within the EU, this is obtained from Intrastat data (see p. 231).

9.4.3 Customs Freight Simplified Procedures (CFSP)

The HM Customs and Excise introduced in November 1992 an exports sub-system called Customs Handling of Import and Export Freight (CHIEF). It is the Government computer customs entry processing system.

The Customs Freight Simplified Procedures (CFSP) eligibility applied to imported third country goods. It has the three main principles as found in its counterpart NES – items (a), (b) and (c) plus audit (see p. 236). In common with NES, traders must submit statistical and fiscal details electronically to CHIEF using the supplementary declaration (see p. 231). Advantages of CFSP maybe summarized as follows:

(a)   Gain accelerated release of the importers' goods from Customs at the (air)port or at an inland clearance depot, subject to anti-smuggling checks.

(b)   Use one or more of the simplified procedures (see p. 238) in combination with normal entry and warehouse procedures to suit the needs of the importers' business.

(c)   Achieve cash flow benefits. For example Local Clearance (see p. 239) allows the importer to store goods for up to 20 days before release to a Customs procedure or use. This means that within this time the trader can choose the release date (and therefore the tax point date) at the most convenient time for the importers' business.

(d)   Carry out UK Transit movements under the Local Clearance Procedure (see p. 239) and apply for a 0 per cent guarantee (waiver), avoiding the need to finance a comprehensive guarantee (except for high risk goods).

(e)   Submit most frontier declarations (including UK Transit) and all Supplementary Declarations (see p. 231) by electronic means resulting in paperless trading and reduced documentation.

(f)   Build a partnership with Customs so that assurance visits are cost effective, selected on the basis of risk, and test the completeness of internal controls.

(g)   Use third party service providers to submit electronic declarations.

See HM Customs Notice No. 760.

9.5 Export documentation and procedures

Goods presented by shippers for or at other places may do so at the following locations in the UK:

  (i) A customs approved port or airport.
 (ii) An inland clearance depot.
(iii) A designated export place (see p. 240).
 (iv) Free zone.
  (v) Traders own premises under local clearance procedure.
 (vi) Inland grain premises approved for CAP purposes.
(vii) An approved depository for retail export scheme.

Traders in the UK do not have to make any export declaration for UK goods despatched to other Member States of the Community. The trade statistics for acquisitions and despatches within the EU are collected via the intra-EU trade statistics system. UK traders are required to make a declaration in the following circumstances:

(a) Goods exported to a non-EU country (including EFTA countries).
(b) Goods sent to one of the special territories of the community.
(c) CAP goods exported to those entitled destinations listed in Regulation (EEC) No 800/99 Article 36 including supplies within the Community for victualling; seagoing vessels; aircraft serving on international routes including intra-Community routes; supplies to international organizations established in the Community; and supplies to the armed forces stationed in the territory of a Member State, but not coming under its flag.

Customs require export declarations for the following reasons:

(a) To ensure that export licensing requirements are met.
(b) To provide accurate details for the Overseas Trade Statistics.
(c) To prevent the unauthorized return of duty free or VAT zero-rated goods to the home market.
(d) To provide information to assist VAT export verifications.
(e) To enable checks on goods subject to specific Customers CAP controls to be carried out.
(f) To check that only valid Community Transit documents are authorized.

Goods are declared electronically and likewise cleared electronically in the UK as explained under the New Export System (p. 236).

All goods for export must be declared completed by the exporter or their representative involving a full pre-shipment declaration. This may be in the form of an electronic declaration to CHIEF under NES (see p. 236) or using a paper entry Single Administrative Document (see p. 252). SAD declarations take longer to clear compared with CHIEF. This will impact on the time of release of any goods declared to Customs manually using the paper SAD. In both cases the goods must be presented to Customs and the declaration lodged before the goods are loaded for export. In the case of controlled goods, the export declaration must be accompanied by any other documents or information required.

By using the CHIEF computer system, the NES allows authorized operators to submit electronic export declarations. CHIEF captures all export declarations. They may be submitted directly or else keyed in by Customs after they have accepted a SAD or other manual declaration that has been lodged with them. Customs will not accept a lodged declaration unless the goods covered by it have been presented to them. Presentation may take place at the office of export or at some other Customs designated place.

At those locations where the port system operator has developed special inventory systems which are linked to CHIEF exports, exporters and their representatives may input the following pre-shipment and post-shipment information to CHIEF electronically: full pre-shipment declaration; low value pre-shipment advice; non-statistical pre-shipment advice; all Simplified Declaration Procedure (SDP) (see p. 238) and all Local Clearance Procedure declarations (see p. 239) – see HM Customs Notice No 275.

9.5.1 New Export System (NES)

The New Export System (NES) was introduced by HM Customs and Excise initially at seaports and airports in the UK. The system was operative nationwide by 2003. Basically it applies to exports to non-EU countries replacing Period Entry, Local Export Control and Simplified Procedures. It does not apply to goods removed to destinations in other Member States as these are categorized as removals or despatches. There are three key messages to be submitted to the Customs CHIEF – Customs Handling of Import and Export Freight – computer as detailed below:

(a) Pre-shipment advice – export declaration.
(b) Goods arrived at port – arrival.
(c) Goods loaded aboard ship – departure.

After each message CHIEF will issue an acknowledgement concerning clearance to proceed to the next stage in the process. When full clearance has been given by CHIEF, after successful completion of the first two stages, the goods can be despatched. To enable the goods to be despatched promptly, the trader must fully comply with all export procedures in terms of both the issuing of correct documentation and the issuing of correct export instructions.

The NES provides for the electronic declaration of goods for export using the following: Simplified Declaration Procedure (SDP); Local Clearance Procedure (LCP); the Full Declaration Procedure; and Low Value and Non-statistical Procedure used with either SDP or LCP.

The NES involves the appointment by Customs of nominated port operators of Community System Providers (CSPs) to operate systems for inputting, storing and processing import and export freight data and sharing this information with the CHIEF computer which is the repository for all declarations.

The largest CSP is based at Southampton port and called Community Network Services (CNS). CNS offers two levels of service for NES. The first option provides access to CHIEF using the CNS portal and the CNS InSite Service. This provides a high functionality, low cost, user-friendly solution giving the user instant access to CHIEF with immediate responses via their browser. The second option, CNS Express provides a fast track into CHIEF and is particularly suitable for high volume users because it is designed to accept either pre-formatted EDI message (such as EDIFACT or TRADA-COMMS) flat files, or XML messages that can be translated and despatched. The system uses secure routes and has capacity to accept bulk entries automatically.

The principle features of using the NES may be summarized as follows. (NES can only be used to destinations outside the EU.)

(a) Authorization. This requires Customs approval to use/operate LCP, SCP and DEP.

(b) Accelerated removal/release. The NES will speed up customs clearance under all available procedures to become almost instantaneous for most consignments declared at either inland or frontier points.

(c) Electronic transmissions. It will capture electronically all export declarations.

(d) Arrival message. Traders are required to submit to Customs for all direct exports an electronic message to CHIEF providing details of the arrival of the goods removed under a 'Permission to Progress' from an approved inland place. For indirect exports, i.e. via other Member States, an arrival message is only required for duty suspended excise goods. For goods not declared at an approved inland place, the act of presentation of goods will fulfil the same function as an arrival message.

(e) Departure message. Exporters are required to give Customs an electronic message only for direct exports from the UK irrespective of where they are declared to the export procedure.

(f) Export consignments eligibility available 24 hours per day throughout the year.

(g) Trader can predict clearance with greater certainty.

(h) The availability of a range of declaration procedures electronically to suit traders needs *(item a)*.

(i) Paperless trading for majority of declarations submitted.

(j) Opportunity to build partnership with Customs around risk-based audit control providing both operator and Customs with a high level of system assurance.

(k) A choice of electronic routes to Customs including via the Internet.

(l) Access to links with other government departments and agencies such as CAP export refund claims.

(m) Improved quality and assurance to obtain official evidence of export for VAT and economic regimes.

(n) Provision of DEP for inventory linked consolidators (p. 240) to clear cargo at their own approved premises. Approved DEP operators can use SDP or full electronic declarations, but not LCP.

(o) Permits ICD's to continue under NES. Goods can be declared to Customs and brought under Customs control using normal and SDP (but not LCP) procedures.

(p) Reducing inventory levels.
(q) Decreasing penalties.
(r) Increased efficiency.
(s) Reducing delays.
(t) Tracking trends and trading partners' performance.
(u) Preventing overpayment duties.
(v) Managing forwarder performance and cost.

For the air cargo community, the procedure is basically the same. Traders operate through transit shed operators at the Airport who operate usually under the SDP declaration. The electronic declaration will feature UCR and WCO recommended number of characters for audit control purposes. In common with sea transport, some documents will be submitted in paper format such as certain transit documents, health certificates, T5's and preference certificates. The central customs computer (CHIEF) requires a CUSDEC, an EDI message which is part of the EDI for administration, commerce and transport (EDIFACT) standard. CHIEF will return a CUSRES.

Details of the accompanying documents/certificates required when processing goods for export are examined in Chapter 14. These embrace B/L, NSSN, DGN, AWB, HAWB, CMR, CIM and SWB.

9.5.2 Standard full pre-shipment declaration

The exporter may submit a standard full pre-shipment declaration electronically at the airport or seaport, inland clearance depot or via a designated place operator (p. 239). The exporter will need prior authorization to have approval for access to CHIEF. Hence, the trader must have their own CHIEF 'role and location' codes from the Customs entry processing control office. Traders who are approved to operate a designated place operator and provide a full pre-shipment declaration procedure are required to make an electronic declaration to CHIEF.

9.5.3 Simplified Declaration Procedure (SCP)

The Simplified Declaration Procedure is a simplified export procedure involving a two-part declaration. The first part requires the exporter to submit to Customs brief details of the export consignment. Once the goods have been presented to Customs, and CHIEF has accepted the declaration and released the goods, they maybe loaded for export shipment. The second part of the declaration must take place within 14 days of the acceptance by CHIEF of the 'goods departed message' or date of export, whichever is earlier. Both parts of the declaration must be submitted to

Customs electronically. To make a pre-shipment declaration the trader must allocate a Unique Consignment Reference based on the WCO standard for each export consignment so that Customs can trace the consignment through the trader's records. Additionally, the exporter must make a simplified electronic pre-shipment declaration to CHIEF either directly or via a Local Clearance Procedure with the requisite information.

9.5.4 Local Clearance Procedure (LCP)

In contrast the Local Clearance Procedure (LCP) is a simplified procedure where goods for export may be declared at the trader's own premises or other nominated inland premises. The facility is also available for imported cargo. However, the LCP may not be used as a designated export place (DEP) (p. 240). For exports of excise goods only, a warehouse keeper maybe approved to operate a LCP. When the goods are presented and ready for export, the exporter or representative submits an electronic notification to CHIEF. Once CHIEF has accepted the declaration, permission is given to move goods to the frontier. Where Community Transit (CT) is required to cover the movement of the goods from the LCP premises, then they must not be removed until the CT documents have been authenticated. LCP operators who need to use CT usually become an Authorised Consignor whereupon the traders are able to authenticate their own CT documents. On arrival at the UK port of export a 'goods arrival message' is entered to CHIEF by the port inventory system, or the loader/carrier at a non-inventory linked location.

The second part of the declaration – the supplementary declaration, must be made within 14 days of the acceptance by CHIEF of the 'goods departed message' or date of export, whichever is earlier. Hence, the trader must specify the date when the 'goods departed message' was made. Both parts of the declaration must be submitted electronically to Customs. If a trader wishes to operate LCP in their name, Customs approval must be sought. To use an LCP the trader must adopt the following:

(a)   Need to allocate UCR in WCO standard for each export consignment.
(b)   Make a simplified (electronic) pre-shipment notification to CHIEF either directly or via a CSP.
(c)   Enter the pre-shipment information on traders' records.
(d)   Move the goods to the UK port of export when approval is given electronically and normally immediately.

When the goods arrive at the UK port of export, CHIEF is notified by the port inventory system, or the loader/carrier at a non-inventory linked location with a 'goods arrival message'. Customs will then normally give immediate clearance for the goods to be exported. When the goods have been exported from the territory of the UK, CHIEF is subsequently notified by the port inventory system, or the loader/carrier at a non-inventory linked location, with a 'goods departed message'. As an authorized LCP trader, the exporter can submit a normal pre-shipment declaration from the trader approved premises.

9.5.5 Designated Export Place (DEP)

The Designated Export Place allows an approved operator such as a consolidator, exporter, forwarder, or airline to present and submit declarations for export to Customs or their Customs approved inland premises. Excise goods, however, cannot be exported from a DEP.

It also permits goods which have been declared to CHIEF under NES by an exporter or third party to be presented to Customs. This would be where the DEP is only presenting and holding the goods pending their release to Customs to move them to the UK frontier for shipment. Hence, a DEP operator does not need to be authorized to operate the Simplified Declaration Procedure. In this situation, if the SCP is to be used for goods held at the DEP, then the declarant (not the DEP operator) needs to be approved to operate SDP.

The trader does not need to be approved to submit an electronic full pre-shipment declaration, but does require permission to access CHIEF. The DEP operator must comply with the following:

(a) Maintain an electronic inventory system for obtaining and recording CHIEF clearance notification messages.
(b) Record all goods for export entering and leaving the facility.
(c) Submit all declarations made in the trader's name to Customs electronically.

The electronic in-house inventory system is formulated by the trader and approved by Customs. It must be a secure system allowing full control and audit of export consignments and include provision of agreed listings and appropriate release documentation. Customs controls at the DEP cover both fiscal (dutiable and restricted goods) and most anti-smuggling checks when a DEP inventory system is linked to the inventory system at the port/airport where the goods exit the UK. All anti-smuggling checks are carried out at the UK frontier.

The procedures which can be used at a DEP embrace full pre-shipment declaration; low value declaration; non-statistical declaration and SDP. All declarations must be made electronically.

9.5.6 Unique Consignment Reference (UCR)

A unique consignment reference is a reference allocated by the authorized trader to each export consignment which can be used by HM Customs during an audit to trace that consignment in the trader's records.

Under the NES the use of Declaration Unique Consignment Reference (DUCR) is mandatory for traders authorized for simplified procedures. Although a DUCR is not mandatory for normal procedures, there are system benefits where one is used. For example, some air and shipping lines use the UCR so that they can check the Customs status of the consignment during the booking process. Under normal procedures CHIEF will derive a Declaration Unique Customs Reference – based upon the entry reference – when none is supplied. Hence, inventory systems and the like may always operate in these terms if they know either the DUCR or the CHIEF entry reference.

Additionally, there exists the Master Unique Consignment Reference (MUCR), which is normally used to associate or link several DUCRs. This could be useful when a container holds a number of consignments from different exporters each of which has a DUCR. Rather than have to quote individual DUCRs for each consignment, consolidators, inventory systems etc., can advise CHIEF that each of the DUCRs in the container are associated with a single MUCR. Subsequently, the trader is required to quote the MUCR rather than every DUCR to refer to all the consignments in the container. MUCRs can be associated with other MUCRs. Moreover, a MUCR can be associated with one or many DUCRs. A DUCR may at any time only belong to one or none MUCR.

There does exist the Bulk Consignment Reference (BUCR). This involves under NES a facility whereby an approved agent or representative can submit one declaration for consignments from up to 99 exporters. The bulk entry facility is similar in concept to that provided under import bulk entry procedures as it allows the submission of one declaration – and therefore only one DUCR – for up to 99 different commodities on behalf of up to 99 separate consignors.

Depending on the circumstances, and the terms of the approval, a list of the TURNs of all the exporters must also be supplied, including a reference number (BUCR) for each TURN. Although this bulk UCR is not supported as a reference by CHIEF, and so does not need to be unique, declarants must be able to use this BUCR to trace consignments back through their records.

9.5.7 Low Value and Non-Statistical Exports

Traders requiring to export low value goods under the NES must use a special Customs procedure code to identify the goods to CHIEF. A simplification of the normal procedure allows an input of reduced information for all goods except those that are dutiable or restricted. No supplementary declaration is required for low value goods exported under the normal procedure. A supplementary declaration is required, however, if the goods are exported under LCP or SDP. A manual declaration involving a paper declaration is permitted for low value goods under the normal procedures. Customs will then key in the declaration into NES.

For non-statistical export goods under the NES the trader must use a special customs procedure code to identify the goods to CHIEF. No supplementary declaration is needed for non-stat exports under any procedure.

9.5.8 Processing Export Consignment as DEP Trader

To be eligible to apply to use the simplified procedures electronically, the DEP trader must meet the following criteria:

(a)   Have a TURN.
(b)   Be a legal entity in the UK, e.g. Sole proprietor, Partnership, Public Limited Company, Private Limited Company.
(c)   Have a good record of compliance with the Customs and other related requirements, e.g. INTRASTAT submissions, VAT returns.
(d)   Regularly declare goods.
(e)   Remove goods from authorized premises.

As part of the authorization, traders using the simplified procedures or operating a DEP must comply with the following as well as those regimes which are authorized to use, e.g. IPR/OPR.

(a)   Allocate a UCR to each export consignment. This must be constructed in accordance with WCO standard of four elements.
(b)   Hold authorizations for other regimes such as IPR and OPR which they wish to use in conjunction with the simplified procedures.
(c)   Declare only eligible goods.
(d)   Submit electronically to Customs directly or via a third party in the specified form and content the pre-shipment declarations for all consignments (p. 238) and complete supplementary declarations within the time limit.
(e)   Notify electronically to customers amendments to consignment details which occur prior to shipment.
(f)   Ensure that any errors and amendments to the pre-shipment and/or supplementary declarations are notified to the designated Customs office.
(g)   For exports via other EU states make available to Customs at the external frontier a certified/authenticated SAD copy 3 or equivalent document generated by the traders system which contains all the information required for control.
(h)   Hold evidence as export to support VAT zero rating.
(i)   Relevant licences.
(j)   Hold and maintain a set of commercial records for the goods declared under these procedures as required under the Customs Traders (Accounts and Records) Regulations 1995.

(k) Maintain a system in support of the records kept which establishes their relationship to the declarations made, and is adequate to enable Customs to undertake effective checks on compliance with any other provisions governing the exportation of goods covered by the authorization.

(l) Ensure that a reference is made in traders records to any pre- or post-shipment consignment changes which take place after entry in the records is made.

(m) Maintain an archive of all declarations made for the required period after the date of their submission and make this available to Customs on request.

(n) Ensure that computerized systems are capable of catering for all authorization requirements and any further requirements laid down by Customs.

(o) Allow Customs to audit their system when requested.

(p) Comply with all the relevant provisions as laid down in EU and UK Customs legislation, and all relevant requirements imposed by Customs & Excise which are set out in official Notices or other official publications.

(q) Notify Customs promptly of any changes of address and legal entity and any other changes which may affect the goods authorization and notify Customs promptly of any changes to hardware or software which bear on the authorization.

(r) To be responsible for the physical security of the goods in transit including ensuring that, when required, a vehicle or container is satisfactorily sealed using approved seals.

(s) Where required, provide a comprehensive CT guarantee or guarantee waiver (certain CAP goods required an individual guarantee for each consignment).

(t) Export goods only from approved premises and for LCP, after notification has been given enter pre-shipment details immediately in their records.

(u) DEP operators to maintain an electronic inventory system which is updated when a message is received from CHIEF that the goods can proceed for export. The inventory can be provided either by a Community System Provider or an equivalent in-house system which provides the required management information and record electronically on the inventory all goods for export entering and leaving the DEP.

There are a number of control documents that are required to be lodged with Customs at the pre-shipment stage. These include Accompanying Administrative Document; Hazardous waste control document issued by the Government; British Government military equipment exports and Government Bill of Lading; Retail exports scheme (RES). Forms VAT 407 and VAT 435; Radioactive goods. United Kingdom Atomic Energy Authority Form C52; TIR carnets; MIB – Merchandise in Baggage; Preference certificates

(EUR1) for authentication and supporting evidence; NF forum; Common/ Community Transit documents; T5s; Export licences (applicable only where the licence is in the form of documents) and Advance Fixing Certificates and Refunds Certificates issued by Other Member States. See HM Customs Notice No 276.

9.6 Customs reliefs

9.6.1 Inward processing relief

A range of duty reliefs are available for goods imported into the UK and their availability is dependent on the goods being re-exported under control of the Customs authorities. An example is found in inward processing relief (IPR). Duty is relieved on imports of non EC goods which are processed in the Community and re-exported provided the trade does not harm the essential interest of Community producers of similar goods. Overall, IPR provides relief from Customs duty, specific Customs duty, anti-dumping duty and countervailing duty. It does not provide relief for excise duty. Import VAT is not due when entered to IPR suspension but is due if entered to IPR drawback. Processing can range from repacking or sorting goods to the most complicated manufacturing. Traders can obtain relief when IPR goods are received from another approved trader in UK or another Member State. If the trader disposes of the finished goods other than by re-export, the trader can still claim relief.

There are two methods of duty relief, suspension or drawback. Customs duties are suspended when the goods are first entered to IPR in the EU. Import VAT is not due unless the goods are released to the Community Market.

Customs duties and import VAT are paid when the goods are entered to IPR. However, the trader can claim duty back if the goods or products are exported, and transfers them to an IPR suspension authorization holder or disposes them in a method approved by Customs. See HM Customs Notice No 221.

9.6.2 Outward processing relief, Standard Exchange System and Returned Goods Relief

Outward Processing Relief (OPR) permits partial or total relief from duty on goods that are exported from EU for processing or repair and subsequently re-imported. OPR provides duty relief on imports from third countries of goods which have been produced from previously exported Community goods. It enables businesses to take advantage of cheaper labour costs outside the EU while encouraging the use of EC produced raw materials to manufacture the finished products. Goods may be also temporarily exported to undergo processes not available within the Community.

The Standard Exchange System permits traders to import replacements for faulty goods which have been exported from the EU if it is not practicable to have them repaired. The replacement goods must be of equivalent commercial condition and value.

If a trader has IPR goods in the EU which are needed to export temporarily for further process or repair, the trader can obtain duty relief on the cost of the process when the goods are re-imported by exporting them under the OPR arrangements. However, to be eligible for OPR, the trader on re-importation of the processed goods must put them back into IPR and they must not be entered for free circulation.

A further form of duty relief is the returned goods relief (RGR). Traders are permitted to re-import goods in the same state as they were exported, or they undergo only unforeseen minor treatment outside the Community, for example to keep them in working order. In such circumstances the goods are returned free of duty and tax.

Finally, if the trader imports goods which are defective or not in accordance with the contract and rejects and returns the goods, the importer can obtain repayment or remission of duty and VAT. See HM Customs Notices Nos 235, 236 and 266.

9.6.3 ATA and CPD carnets

An ATA carnet is an international document that is presented to Customs each time goods enter or leave a country. It permits goods to be temporarily imported without payment of customs charges for up to one year and can cover one or more different types of goods. It can be used in place of normal customs documents to temporarily export certain goods for use outside the EU. It can also be used to temporarily import non-EU goods for use in UK.

The carnet may be valid up to one year and issued by an accredited Chamber of Commerce and Industry who provide a guarantee. Types of eligible goods vary between the 58 participating countries. The benefits of using an ATA carnet are as follows:

(a) Avoids the need to complete national customs declarations or provide fresh security for Customs charges potentially due in each country visited.
(b) Simplifies Customs clearance of goods in each country visited.
(c) Can be used in different countries around the world.
(d) Can help overcome problems that may otherwise result from language barriers and having to complete unfamiliar Customs forms.

Goods covered by ATA carnets are subject to normal export/import prohibitions and restrictions and licensing rules.

The CPD carnet is an international Customs document for temporary importation and exportation of road motor vehicles regulated under the ATA to Istanbul Convention. It is administered by Alliance Internationale de Jourisme (AIT) and Federation Internationale de L'Automobile (FIA) and is not required for use within the EU or other European Countries. It is mainly used in Africa, Asia, the Middle East, Oceania (Pacific) and South America. See HM Customs Notice No 104.

9.6.4 The TIR procedure

The TIR procedure allows goods in road vehicles or containers sealed by customs to cross one or more countries en route to their destination with the minimum of customs interference. TIR carnets are used for this purpose. The arrangements for obtaining them and other conditions of the procedure are explained in HM Customs and Excise Notice 464.

Traders cannot use the TIR procedure for transit movements from the UK which are to be wholly within the EU. CT procedures must be used for these movements. Requirements to provide export declarations on the SAD are unaffected by the TIR provisions.

9.6.5 Customs warehousing and free zones

A customs warehouse is a storage facility. It permits payment of import duties and/or VAT to be suspended or delayed when non-community goods are stored in premises or under an inventory system authorized as a customs warehouse. Advantages of customs warehousing are as follows:

(a) Delay payment in import duty and/or VAT on imported goods.
(b) Trader may wish to delay having a customs treatment applied to imported goods.
(c) Trader may wish to re-export non-community goods (in which case import duty and/or VAT may not be payable).
(d) Importer may experience difficulty at the time of import in meeting particular conditions such as import licensing requirements.
(e) Traders may wish to discharge another customs procedure such as IPR (p. 244) without physically exporting the goods.
(f) Importer may wish to use a customs warehouse for co-storage of goods subject to another customs procedure such as free circulation, IPR and PCC.

Basically, a customs warehouse is a storage place/premises or an inventory system authorized by Customs for storing non-community goods that are chargeable with import duty and/or VAT, or otherwise not in free circulation. It may be the whole of a building, a small compartment in a building, an open site, a silo, or a storage tank.

The customs warehouse may be public or private. There are six different types of warehouse classified as A-F. Types A, C, D and E are available in the UK as detailed below.

Type A – A public warehouse.

Type C – The basic private warehouse.

Type D – Ideal for traders who import goods for free circulation. Any removals to free circulation must be made using the Local Clearance Procedure. The rules of assessment cover the nature, volume and quantity of the goods.

Type E – Another form of private warehouse in which a company and its commercial accounting and stock control systems are authorized. The rules of assessment are the same as type D. Goods permitted to be stored in a warehouse are outlined below:

(a)   Non-community goods liable to customs duties and/or VAT (whether or not eligible for preference).

(b)   Non-community goods for which necessary supporting documents (such as DoTI licence) are not available at the time of import.

(c)   Non-community goods imported to another suspensive regime (such as IPR or TI) warehoused for export from the Community.

(d)   Non-community PCC products.

(e)   Non-community goods that are not subject to a full rate of Customs duty in the tariff, but are liable to import VAT.

(f)   Community produced goods or non-community goods released to free circulation, eligible for CAP refunds on export. These goods should be warehoused in a specially approved warehouse under the CAP pre-financing arrangements.

(g)   Non-community goods in free circulation that are subject to a claim under the Rejected Imports arrangements.

A free zone is a designated area in which non-community goods are treated as outside the customs territory of the Community for the purposes of import duties. Hence, import duties (including agricultural charges) are not due provided the goods are not released for free circulation. Import VAT is also suspended until the goods are removed to the UK market or used or consumed within the Free Zone. There are no special reliefs in free zones from other taxes, excise duties, or local authority rates. See HM Customs Notice No 2002.

9.7 Duty preference and origin

The EU and UK in particular have a range of multilateral and bilateral agreements with economic blocs and trading nations permitting preferential tariff treatment on exports and imports. Many of the tariff preferential agreements emerge from WTO (p. 27) and bilateral agreements by government or economic bloc. The EU in particular has a range of tariff preferences.

The rules of origin and preferential tariff treatment terms are stringent and subject to continuous change. UK exporters/importers are urged to visit the HM Customs and Excise website: www.hmce.gov.uk and overseas readers are urged to do likewise in their country.

The benefits are intrinsically financial and encourage the flow of imports and exports in a large range of goods between countries. Reduced tariff levels or their complete elimination encourages free trade and opens up new markets globally. It is important to acknowledge that duty preference is sometimes associated with the tariff quota constraint. Tariff quotas are an EU system to allow the importation of limited amounts of specific goods (sometimes from specific countries) at a rate of duty lower than would otherwise apply. The amount which may be imported can be expressed in units of quantity, value, volume, or weight and the period during which the Tariff quota is available may be limited. See HM Customs Notices Nos 375, 812, 828 and 829.

9.8 The Common Agricultural Policy (CAP)

The prime aim of the CAP is to provide stability of prices and supplies of agricultural product in the EU. The CAP was set up as a common market for agriculture for two reasons: the dependency of agriculture on natural conditions such as type of soil, weather, disease, pest etc., and social and economic factors which influence the structure of agriculture and consumer demand for its products.

The Treaty of Rome created the European Community. When it was signed the agricultural policies of the six signatory countries were very different. A common policy was needed to stimulate agricultural production under controlled conditions. This policy is called the Common Agricultural Policy.

The five main objectives are: increased agricultural productivity; a fair standard of living for the farming community; stable markets; guaranteed security of supplies and an assurance of reasonable prices to consumers.

The standard way of making export declarations and claims to export refund is to use electronic methods. The electronic document will be both the export declaration and export refund claim. The CAP export can be conducted under the standard export procedure (p. 227) or the Local Clearance Procedure (p. 239). CAP goods may be exported from the UK to special destinations within the EU or to non-community countries. Goods must be declared/exported under a levy; an export refund; a mandatory CAP export licence; or other CAP payment or charges. See HM Customs Notice No 800.

9.9 New Community/Computerized Transit System (NCTS)

The New Community/Computerized Transit System, introduced in 2003, is a European-wide system to allow the electronic processing of customs documentation. It is designed to provide better management controls and lower costs in respect of Community and Common transit. Basically, the Community System is a Customs procedure which allows goods not in free circulation and those few Community goods for which Community Transit (CT) is required to move within the Community. Goods not in free circulation travel under the external transit (T1) procedure; Community goods travel under the internal transit (T2) procedure. The system is extended to the European Free Trade Area and Visegrade countries, by virtue of a separate convention, and this is known as Common transit.

The CT procedure is based on the appointment of a principal who is responsible for the completion of the CT operation. These responsibilities include providing a guarantee and producing the goods intact at the Customs Office of destination within a prescribed time limit. The procedure is finalized on the return of an officially receipted copy of the transit document to discharge the movement and guarantee. The CT procedures must be used for movement of goods in the following situations.

(a) Non-community goods that have not been put into free circulation or another Customs procedure which permits movement within the Community.

(b) Community goods when they are travelling via an EFTA or Visegrade country; goods travelling overland to an EFTA or Visegrade country; travelling to or from one of the 'special territories' of the Community except between UK and Channel Islands; subject to a Community measure involving their export to a third country – CAP; travelling to or from San Marino and Principality of Andorra.

A range of situations exists when the CT procedures must not be used including: movements of Community Goods to other EU countries or territories; movements direct to a non-community country (other than EFTA or Visegrade countries); movements of either Community or non-community goods travelling to or from Andorra; and goods despatched by post, rail or inter-container, under TIR or ATA carnet; under NATO; and using either air or sea simplified CT procedures.

The CT system operates on the basis that the trader/principal undertakes to transport goods from one point in the Community to another, or to an EFTA or Visegrade country, or in certain circumstances to San Marino or Andorra. The trader is responsible for providing a guarantee to cover the duties and taxes which may become due if the movement is not satisfactorily completed and for producing the goods intact to the Customs office of destination within a prescribed time limit. The trader completes a CT declaration on the SAD (p. 252) manually or electronically and presents it together with the goods and any other necessary supporting documents to Customs at the office of departure. Customs at the office of departure undertake any necessary examination and/or control of the goods and documents and register the movement. If satisfied, the CT document is authenticated. Customs retain copy 1 of the SAD and return copies 4, 5 and 7 to the trader. The trader must ensure that copies 4, 5 and 7 travel with the goods.

When goods transit through a non EU country during a CT movement, the trader must complete a Transit Advice Note (TAN) form C1128. A separate TAN must be presented with the goods and transit document at the last and first EU offices when the consignment leaves and re-enters the EU. To complete the movement, the goods and CT documents must be presented at the office of destination within the prescribed time limit. Customs at the office of destination will certify that the goods have arrived safely or provide details of any discrepancies or irregularities and return copy 5 of the CT document to the office of departure or to a central office designated for this purpose.

The movement is discharged when Customs at the office of departure or the central office are satisfied that the movement has been satisfactorily completed or when any charges due for lost goods have been paid in full. The foregoing procedure can be used for goods entering or moving through all EFTA and Visegrade countries. To prove Community Status the goods must be transported between two points of the EU through the territory of a non-EU country; transported by air or sea from an airport or seaport in a non-community country to an airport or port in the community; or transported by sea on other community shipping services. Customs documents featured in the Community System are detailed below:

1. Form T2, used for declaration for goods in free circulation.
2. Form T1, used for declaration for goods originating in non-community countries.
3. Form T2L, used to provide evidence of Community Status.
4. Form T2M, used to certify the Community Status of fish in certain limited circumstances.
5. Form C88EL, an export declaration.
6. Single Administrative Document (SAD) Copies 1, 4 and 5.
7. Accompanying Administrative Document (AAD) is a four part control document that covers the movement of excise goods moving in duty suspension between EU Member States and for exports from the Community. It contains relevant information about the consignment, its origin, and destination and provides confirmation that the consignee has received the goods.
8. ATA carnets – (p. 245).
9. TIR carnets – (p. 246).

Traders who opt to operate under the new community transit system embracing the NES do so electronically. The movement commences at the approved premises of an Authorized Consignor (p. 236). This involves SDP and LCP. The full declaration procedure maybe operated at a customs warehouse and excise warehouse. For goods such as CAP travelling through, or to, an EFTA or Visegrade country, the transit must start at the place where the goods are declared to Customs. Traders operating the NCTS using the LCP facility are likely to be authorized consignor for CT purposes.

The NCTS provides electronic information about transit shipments replacing the paper based SAD; T forms T1/T2/TSF Customs clearance processing earlier described. It gives electronic notification of the arrival, ending and discharge of movements between EU, EFTA and Visegrade countries. All customs offices are linked to the NCTS, but traders may use the old paper-based system if they prefer. Advantages of NCTS are featured below:

(a) Waiting time at customs offices is reduced as the declaration is sent electronically beforehand.
(b) Audit data is held on a client profile further reducing need for manual activity.
(c) Faster and earlier discharge of the transit procedure.
(d) Lengthy and costly paper-based declaration procedures are reduced. Error responses from Customs can be corrected on screen with no need to re-key unaffected data.
(e) Time gained at office of destination because Customs will have decided in advance whether the consignment should be controlled.
(f) Information can be uploaded/downloaded from 'in house' systems thus reducing typing.
(g) Improved communication and co-ordination between Customs administrations.
(h) Electronic load list produced as standard.
(i) No repetition of data entry. Built in pre-lodgement of data.
(j) Replies from Customs are returned direct to the PC screen and not to e-mail address.
(k) Good after sales service.
(l) Useful for cargo tracking purposes.

Traders are required to use EDI procedures set up for communications with HM Customs. The main NCTS requirements are detailed below:

(m) Transit declaration presented in paper or electronic form.
(n) Movement reference number (MRN), a unique registration number (p. 240).
(o) Transit accompanying document (TAD) (p. 250).
(p) Relevant arrival, transit and control results messages.

Additionally, under NCTS there exist the following documents:

(i) Form C1147 – the Community transit comprehensive guarantee. This is a Customs form covering transits identifying duties and other charges arising. In exceptional circumstances form EUR7000 may be used for each transit operation. Form C1147 requires for each transit, the movement date, date of registration, transit declaration/manifest/ SFD entry number, name of office departure/destination, goods description (or at least the six figure HS heading gross weight) and amount of duty and charges due. Each time the trader starts a transit operation, the amount of duty must be offset, and other charges, against the reference amount. The CCTO/authorizing office must be informed if the reference amount falls below a level sufficient to cover the trader transit operations or the trader wishes to take out additional individual guarantee.

(ii) Special loading lists or descriptive lists are required for export/ despatch formalities. Companies using an integrated electronic or automatic data processing system may submit such data electronically. When the transit declaration is registered the loading list must be given the same registration number as the form to which it relates together with the requisite number of copies. See HM Customs Notice No. 750.

9.10 The Single Administrative Document

The Single Administrative Document (SAD) is a multi-copy form which is used throughout the Community, EFTA and Visegrad countries for the control of imports, exports and goods in transit. In the UK it is known as Form C88. It is an eight-part document, although only the following copies are used for CT purposes:

Copy 1 Office of departure;
Copy 3 CT principal/consignor/exporter's copy;
Copy 4 Office of destination, or Community status (T2L) document;
Copy 5 Transit return copy;
Copy 7 Statistical copy for use in the Member State of destination.

Copy 4 can be used as a Community status (T2L) document. Copy 7 is not required for UK Transit movements. The other copies of the SAD are for the following purposes:

Copy 2 Export declaration;
Copy 6 Import declaration;
Copy 8 Consignee's copy.

Customs and Excise provide various combinations of the eight-copy set. For transit purposes, the following sets maybe obtained: Export and transit (C88:Export/transit) comprising Copies 1, 2, 3, 4, 5 and 7; Status only (C88 Status) comprising Copy 4; for UK transit only (C88: UK Transit) comprising Copies 1, 4 and 5.

Alternatively, two sets of four copies, printed mainly for use when computerized declarations are made, can be used. Each copy has a dual function: 1/6, 2/7, 3/8, 4/5. The first set corresponds to copies 1–4, the second to 5–8. In each four-copy set the numbers of the copies used must be shown by deleting numbers of the copies not used.

The continuation sheet is a form used to supplement the transit document when more than one item is being despatched and there is insufficient room for details of all the goods. It may also be used when a consignment contains both T1 and T2 goods. A separate sheet is used for each status of goods, the SAD providing the common information and a summary of the sheets for each different status.

There is no official printout of a loading list for use with transit and status documents and traders have to make their own arrangements for obtaining commercially printed forms. Where a CT document is combined with an export declaration, Form C88 EL must be used. Firms whose records are based on a system of electronic or mechanical data processing which makes it impossible to produce loading lists in the standard layout may be allowed to use lists which do not fulfil all the requirements. However, the lists must include for each item the number, kind and marks of packages, description of goods, gross weight in kilograms, the country of consignment and any special references required by Community Regulations and be otherwise suitable. These must be approved by Customs before being used for transit.

The HM Customs Service has now made available a system authenticated SAD copy 3 in accordance with Commission Regulation 2454/93. The system produced SAD copy 3s are authenticated by the electronic insertion of a number unique to the consignment (p. 240).

Where goods are declared for export in the UK, but leave the Community via another Member State, a Customs endorsed SAD copy 3 must normally accompany the goods to the office of exit. This is evidence that the consignment has been subject to export control in the UK.

Under NES the exporter is permitted to produce a certified SAD copy 3 equivalent from the traders computer system. The document will contain a unique declaration number allocated by CHIEF. Traders who wish to make use of the CHIEF SAD copy 3 version are able to do so through their appropriate software system (p. 237). Under the Direct Trader Input procedures a facsimile stamp will replace the manual Customs stamp on all trader generated SAD copy 3. Hence, there is no need to present the travelling SAD copy 3 to Customs unless other documents are being processed. In these circumstances the copy 3 must be presented to show export formalities have been carried out and to allow Customs' staff to perform any necessary checks against the accompanying documentation. The term trader generated copy 3 includes the CHIEF printout, plain paper, official pre-printed and laser printed SAD versions.

Recommended reading

HM Customs Notices 275, 276 and 725

HM Customs and Excise Internet website – www.hmce.gov.uk – readers are urged to visit the website regularly and study relevant HM Customs Notices.

CHAPTER 10

Cargo insurance

Marine insurance is defined in the Marine Insurance Act 1906 thus; 'a contract of marine insurance is a contract whereby the insurer undertakes to indemnify the assured in a manner and to the extent thereby agreed, against marine losses, that is to say, the losses incidental to marine adventure'. Hence this includes cargo insurance involving the maritime conveyance of merchandise from one country to another.

Cargo insurance is an extensive subject and it would be wrong not to include a chapter on it in a book of this nature. Nevertheless, in so doing the reader must be reconciled to the fact that it is only possible to deal briefly with the salient parts of the subject. For further study the student is recommended to read one of the excellent cargo insurance textbooks available on the market.

This chapter deals with the practical considerations which affect export interest in terms of financial protection of goods in transit to overseas destinations. It is not an in-depth study of marine insurance as such; insurance and exporting can and do exist independently of each other. Furthermore, it is by no means coincidental that the insurance of ships and goods is the oldest form of insurance protection. Moreover, the advantages which accrue from a proper appreciation of the role cargo insurance plays in the transference to others of those risks to which goods consigned by sea and air are exposed, must be thoroughly understood by the exporter and shipper.

In its proper context, cargo insurance must be seen as an indispensable adjunct to overseas trade. Adequate insurance is vital to protect the interests of those with goods in transit. Accordingly, the student of the subject is well advised to obtain a copy of the Marine Insurance Acts of 1906 and 1909. The 1906 Act contains the basis of all cargo insurance affecting export consignments, while the 1909 Act deals with the prohibition of gambling in maritime perils. Apart from the protection aspect, cargo insurance also plays a vital role in the financing of overseas trade by making it possible for banks to lend money against cargo in transit – a proposition they will only consider if the cargo is protected by insurance. It is appropriate to mention that this chapter will not be dealing with credit insurance as this will be found in Chapter 11.

It is important to indicate that in examining cargo insurance one must reconcile it with ship insurance insofar as maritime transits are concerned. The reason being that the voyage is still regarded as 'marine adventure' which involves both ship and cargo being at risk to maritime perils. This joint cargo/ship interest emerges when, for example, a general average contribution arises involving jettison of cargo to preserve the general safety of the marine adventure.

10.1 Cargo insurance market

There are no fixed rates in marine insurance and the actual premium for a particular ship or cargo is assessed on the incidence of losses in that trade and the risks that the ship and other conveyances transporting the cargo are likely to experience. This process of assessing the premium is known as 'underwriting' and the marine insurance contract is embodied in a document called a policy. Marine insurance is underwritten by Lloyd's underwriters and insurance companies.

Lloyd's is a society of underwriters which has its origins in the late seventeenth century when shipowners, merchants and underwriters met at Edward Lloyd's coffee house in the City of London. Edward Lloyd provided the facilities for the clientele of his coffee house to carry on the business of marine insurance. He personally had no involvement in this business and had no responsibility or liability in respect of the risks underwritten. Lloyd's was incorporated by Act of Parliament in 1871. Today the Corporation of Lloyd's performs the same function as that of Edward Lloyd 300 years ago, in so far as it provides the premises and the necessary services for the underwriting members to conduct the business of underwriting. The Corporation itself incurs no liability whatsoever in respect of the business accepted by the underwriting members. In effect, business is placed at Lloyd's and not with Lloyd's. Today the business written includes non-marine, motor and aviation insurance, as well as marine insurance.

For the purposes of transacting business, the underwriting members – or 'names' as they are more frequently known – are grouped into syndicates of varying sizes. While each syndicate is concerned primarily with writing one of the main classes of business (marine, aviation, non-marine or motor) it has become permissible, since the beginning of 1991, for a syndicate to accept risks in any of the other classes.

The monetary strength – or 'capacity' as it is known – of each syndicate is based upon the collective wealth shown by its underwriting members.

The syndicate is managed by an underwriting agent, known as a managing agent, who appoints the active underwriter and supporting staff of the underwriting box of the syndicate in the Underwriting Room at Lloyd's. The underwriter, who is also an underwriting member of the syndicate, sits at the underwriting box of the syndicate and accepts risks on behalf of his members who bear the proportion of their particular share in the syndicate, i.e. each member receives his particular percentage share of all premiums and pays the same percentage of all claims emanating from the risks for which he or she has received premium. Each member has a separate and unlimited liability in respect of the risks written on his or her behalf by the underwriter of the syndicate.

In accordance with the provisions of the Lloyd's Act of 1982, which repealed many of the provisions of the earlier Acts, Lloyd's is now controlled by the Council of Lloyd's. This Council consists of 28 members – 12 elected from the working members and 16 from the external members. (A working member is a person who is primarily occupied with the conduct of business at Lloyd's either by a Lloyd's broker or an underwriting agent; an external member is a person who is not a working member of the Society.) A chairman is elected from the 12 working members who form the Committee of Lloyd's. The Council is responsible for the long-term planning and management of the affairs of the society, while the Committee is responsible for the day-to-day running of the business.

A significant proportion of the business transacted in the London market is placed with insurance companies. Apart from the many British companies operating in the market there are also a large number of overseas companies. The tendency today is for the importer to arrange the insurance cover in their own country for a variety of reasons. However, any re-insurance by the broker could be through the Lloyd's London Market. The basic difference between the Lloyd's underwriter and his company counterpart is that the liability of the former is 'several and unlimited', whereas the latter is a salaried employee of a limited liability company and has no personal liability in respect of the risks which he underwrites on behalf of his employer. Apart from this, generally speaking, the insurance companies transact business in a similar manner to that followed by Lloyd's underwriters. Certainly there is no difference at all as far as the underwriting of a risk is concerned, and it is quite usual for both Lloyd's and insurance company underwriters to participate in the same risk.

The great majority of the business transacted in the London market is handled through the intermediary of an insurance broker. Any individual or body corporate wishing to describe themselves as an 'insurance broker' must be registered with the Insurance Brokers' Registration Council in accordance with the provisions of the Insurance Brokers Registration Act 1977. The public does not have direct access to the underwriters at Lloyd's and business can only be presented to them by a Lloyd's broker.

In addition to meeting the requirements of the Insurance Brokers' Registration Act 1977, the Lloyd's broker must also satisfy the rather more rigorous standards set by the Council of Lloyd's before he or she can operate in the market. The general – or non-Lloyd's broker – may possibly operate in the Lloyd's market via a Lloyd's broker with whom they enter into agreement for the handling of business.

The broker is the agent of the assured, his or her principal, and as such is subject to the common law of agency insofar as, if his or her principal is prejudiced as a result of negligence, then the principal may sue for damages. Effectively, brokers' services are provided without cost to the assured, whose remuneration, brokerage, is paid by the underwriters with whom the principal's business has been placed. While a broking company may be a small organization of less than a dozen people, the large Lloyd's brokers of today are international organizations employing several thousand people worldwide.

The role of the broker is, first, to advise clients as to their insurance needs and, secondly, to comply with clients' subsequent instructions and obtain the cover required at the best possible rate of premium. The salient details of the risk are entered by the broker on a document known as a 'slip', which the broker presents to underwriters inviting them to accept all or a proportion of the risk specified thereon. Unless the risk is a small one (i.e. of low monetary value), it will be placed with a number of underwriters in the market, each accepting a proportion (usually a percentage) of the sum insured. Upon completion of placing the risk, the broker issues a policy embodying the terms and conditions stated on the slip, having previously sent the principal a cover note informing him or her of the terms and conditions on which the risk has been placed and specifying the insurers participating. A further service provided by the broker on behalf of the principal is the negotiation and collection of any claims arising on insurances placed.

10.2 Lloyd's agents

In almost every port in the world will be found a Lloyd's Agent. These agents may be individuals or companies appointed by the Corporation of Lloyd's to serve the maritime community in their area. Like the Corporation which appoints them, they have no underwriting powers. Their main duties are:

1. Protecting the interests of underwriters (Lloyd's or otherwise) according to instructions which may be sent to them, for example by endeavouring to avoid fraudulent claims.
2. Rendering advice and assistance to Masters of shipwrecked vessels.
3. Reporting to Lloyd's information regarding all casualties which may occur in their district and information as to arrivals and departures.

4. Appointing surveyors to inspect damaged vessels and granting certification of seaworthiness when called upon to do so by Masters of vessels which have suffered damage.
5. Notifying London headquarters of all information of relevant interest which may come to their notice.
6. Surveying or appointing surveyors when called upon by consignees of cargo or by underwriters to survey damage and issuing reports stating the cause, nature and extent of all damage. Lloyd's agents will survey and issue reports in connection with damaged goods at the request of any interested party on the payment of a fee, quite apart from any question of insurance. All reports issued by Lloyd's agents are made 'without prejudice' and subject to the terms, conditions and amount of any policy of insurance.

10.3 Fundamental principles of insurance

Marine insurance is governed by the Marine Insurance Act 1906, which came into force on 1 January 1907. This Act did not create any new laws, but codified all the legal decisions which had been made during the preceding 300 years. The basic principles of insurance are specified in the Act. They are insurable interest; utmost good faith; indemnity and subrogation.

10.3.1 Insurable interest

The Marine Insurance Act 1906 provides that a person has an insurable interest in a marine adventure (any ship goods or other moveables exposed to maritime perils) where he or she stands in any legal or equitable relationship to the adventure or insurable property at risk therein in consequence of which he may:

(a) benefit by the safety or due arrival of the insurable property, or
(b) be prejudiced by its loss, or by damage thereto, or by the detention thereof, or
(c) incur liability in respect thereof.

It is important to understand the difference between the subject matter insured and insurable interest. Insurable interest is the financial interest of a person in the subject matter insured. Thus the insurable interest of the cargo owner is not the goods – the subject matter insured – but his financial interest in such goods and, accordingly, he should insure to the extent of that interest.

While ownership of property – the subject matter insured – is the prime example of insurable interest, there are other circumstances in which a person may possess an insurable interest. For instance, persons responsible for goods while in their care, custody and control (e.g. a ware-houseman), have an insurable interest in respect of their legal liability for such goods, even if the owner himself has effected insurance. Where goods are consigned to an agent for sale on commission, the agent has an insurable interest because, if the goods are lost, he will be precluded from earning his commission on their sale. In this instance, his insurable inter-est is his financial interest, i.e. the amount of his anticipated commission. The underwriter who insures goods has an insurable interest insofar as, if they are lost or damaged by one of the perils insured against, he will have to pay the claim made against him under the policy. Accordingly, he may limit his liability in respect of such a claim by insuring part of it with other underwriters. This is known an 'reinsurance'.

A policy effected without insurable interest is void, i.e. it has no legal value and is unenforceable at law. In all classes of insurance there is, there-fore, a legal requirement that insurable interest exists at the time the insurance is effected. An exception to this rule applies in the case of cargo insurance. The Marine Insurance Act 1906 provides that the person enter-ing into a contract of marine insurance must have an insurable interest or an expectation of acquiring one. This effectively covers the case of the buyer under a CIF contract who acquires his interest when the title to the goods purchased is transferred to him sometime after transit has com-menced from the seller's premises.

Proof of insurable interest is not required at the time of effecting an insurance. But when making a claim, it is necessary for the assured to be able to show that he had an insurable interest at the time of loss. Cargo insurance effected in respect of CIF contracts of sale is invariably based on what is known as 'lost or not lost' conditions which means that the assured may recover any loss, even although he may not have acquired his interest until after the actual time of loss.

The most common forms of insurable interest in cargo insurance are:

1. *Ownership of the goods.* The cargo owner has an insurable interest in the goods since he will benefit by their safe arrival or be prejudiced by loss of or damage thereto. Ownership usually involves two parties – seller and buyer, or consignor and consignee. The insurance require-ments of these parties will depend upon the terms of the contract of sale.
2. *Charges of insurance (premium).* The assured has an insurable interest in the premium paid in respect of any insurance he may effect. While in hull insurance the shipowner effects a separate policy to cover the amount expended upon insurance premiums, in cargo insurance the sum insured reflects the cost of the goods plus the cost of insurance.
3. *Freight.* This is the cost of transporting the goods from the con-signor's premises to the consignee's premises and is either pre-paid or

payable at destination. In most cases, it is advanced or pre-paid freight not returnable even if the goods are lost and not delivered. In these instances, therefore, the freight pre-paid is at the risk of the cargo owner and, as in the case of premium, is merged in with the value of the goods. Consequently, the sum insured reflects the cost of the goods plus the cost of insurance (premium) plus the cost of transportation (freight).

Other forms of insurable interest in cargo insurance are:

1. *Defeasible interest.* This term describes an interest which may cease for reasons other than the operation of maritime perils. For example, the insurable interest of the seller of goods ends when the title to the goods passes to the buyer. The seller has a defeasible interest.
2. *Contingent interest.* As the defeasible interest of the seller ceases the interest of the buyer commences. The contract of sale may contain a provision allowing the buyer to reject the goods in certain circumstances, e.g. delayed delivery. Where the buyer exercises this right of rejection, the interest immediately and automatically reverts to the seller. The seller has an insurable interest in respect of this contingency.
3. *Forwarding expenses.* The contract of affreightment will probably include a clause allowing the carrier to discharge the goods at a port other than the one designated where, for some reason, they cannot be delivered or discharged at the destination port. For example, the destination port may be strikebound and the shipowner diverts the ship to another port. This would involve the cargo owner incurring 'forwarding expenses', i.e. the cost of getting his cargo on-carried to its intended destination. These charges are not covered under the standard cargo clauses, and when this situation occurs, it is usually too late for the cargo owner to effect insurance as the risk has already occurred. A prudent cargo owner would cover this interest by effecting an insurance on an annual basis for an amount sufficient to cover his possible expenditure in such circumstances.
4. *Commission.* An agent may act for a cargo owner on a commission basis. The amount he or she anticipates earning will depend upon the arrival of the goods and he or she accordingly has an insurable interest to this extent.

Before leaving the subject of insurable interest, it is important for the reader to appreciate the relationship of this principle to the delivery terms specified in the contract of sale – i.e. where the individual insurable interests of the seller and the buyer attach and terminate – as this governs the extent of the insurance cover required by both. It is not proposed to consider here in any depth this aspect of the various forms of contract of sale as they are the subject of detailed examination elsewhere in this book.

As an example, however, under a Free on Board (FOB) contract the seller is required to arrange transport of the goods to the port and ensure that they are loaded into the vessel. At this point, when the goods pass over the ship's rail, this insurable interest ceases, and that of the buyer commences and continues until arrival of the goods at his or her premises. The seller, therefore, needs insurance cover from the time the goods leave his or her warehouse to FOB ship; the buyer needs insurance cover from FOB ship to arrival at his or her warehouse.

On the other hand, a Cost Insurance and Freight (CIF) contract places responsibility on the seller for arranging the transport of the goods from his or her warehouse to that of the buyer and paying the freight involved. He or she is also responsible for effecting insurance cover from 'warehouse to warehouse' in accordance with the buyer's instructions and paying the premium required. It is essential, therefore, that the insurance is arranged so that, in line with the transfer in title to the goods from the seller to the buyer, the beneficial rights of the insurance may be similarly transferred. This is known as assignment of the policy. Assignment of the insurance is effected by the seller (the assignor) endorsing the policy or certificate of insurance by blank endorsement to the buyer (the assignee). Blank endorsement means that the assignor signs his or her name above the company stamp on the back of the document and passes it to the assignee.

It is important to understand that assignment of the interest does not automatically assign the policy, and an agreement to assign the policy must exist before the seller parts with his or her interest. In practice, under a CIF contract there is an implied agreement that the policy will be assigned before the interest passes. By assigning the policy, the assignor passes to the assignee all the beneficial rights afforded by the insurance, thereby entitling the assignee to claim under the insurance as though he or she had had an insurable interest throughout the duration of the transit. It must be emphasized that the assignee cannot be in a better position than the assignor; his or her interest is derivative, i.e. he or she has exactly the same rights as the assignor. A breach of good faith or warranty on the part of the assignor would prejudice the assignee since the underwriter has exactly the same rights in relation to him or her as he had against the assignor.

10.3.2 Utmost good faith

The Marine Insurance Act 1906 provides that a contract of marine insurance is a contract based upon the 'utmost good faith' (*uberrimae fidei*), and if the utmost good faith be not observed by either party, the other party may avoid the contract.

It would not be practical or, indeed, possible for underwriters to check the accuracy or completeness of information submitted to them in respect of a risk to be insured. They have to rely upon the other party – the proposer or the broker acting on his or her behalf – observing the principle of utmost good faith which means a full disclosure of all material circumstances relating to the risk before the contract is concluded. A material circumstance is one which would influence a prudent underwriter as to the desirability of the risk. Where there is a non-disclosure of a material circumstance, the underwriter may avoid the contract. The underwriter may also avoid the contract if the broker is guilty of misrepresenting the risk during the placing negotiations. It is important to understand that avoidance of the contract does not render the contract void. A void contract is one which has no legal value and is, therefore, inadmissible as evidence in a court of law. If an underwriter avoids the contract, always provided that there is no fraud, the policy remains a valid document and the assured may contest the underwriter's action in a court of law. In practice, this situation usually arises where an underwriter refuses to pay a claim on the grounds that there has been a non-disclosure or misrepresentation at the time of placing the insurance. If the assured does not accept this allegation, they may challenge the underwriter's right to avoid the contract.

10.3.3 Indemnity

The purpose of insurance is to protect the insurable interest of the assured whereby, in the event of loss of or damage to the subject matter insured resulting from an insured peril, he or she is placed in the same position that he or she enjoyed immediately before the loss occurred. This is 'indemnity'. As will be appreciated, this basic principle of indemnity provides, in effect, that after indemnity the assured may not be in a better, or worse, position than they were in before the loss.

While replacement is the means of effecting indemnity in some types of insurance, it would not be practical for marine insurers to replace ships and cargoes. The manner of indemnity is, therefore, a cash settlement. As explained above, the extent of this indemnity is the value of the insured property immediately before the loss occurs. This value is the insurable value and the basis for its calculation is specified in the Marine Insurance Act 1906. In the case of cargo, it is the prime cost of the goods, plus the incidental costs of shipping and insurance upon the whole. Where goods are, say, totally lost, this basis of indemnity would place the exporter of goods in the same position as if the goods had never left the warehouse and, therefore, conforms with the basic principle. Nevertheless, it falls somewhat short of the indemnity they would wish insofar as they would prefer to be in the same position as if the goods had arrived safely at their destination, i.e. realized their profit. The inadequacy of basing the indemnity upon the insurable value is further illustrated in the case of the frequently used CIF sales contract. Here the seller is responsible for arranging the shipment and insurance of the goods and the sales invoice to the buyer will accordingly reflect the freight and premium paid, in addition to the price charged for the goods, which will reflect the prime cost plus his or her percentage of profit.

The wise men who drafted the Marine Insurance Act at the beginning of the last century were obviously very much aware of this problem and they accordingly worded the relevant section to overcome it. The section provides in its preamble to the bases for valuation 'Subject to any express provision or valuation in the policy the insurable value of the subject matter insured must be ascertained as follows'. Thus, the Act permits an agreed valuation, i.e. an insured value, to be declared in the policy, and only in the absence of such a valuation will the formula for arriving at the insurable value be used. The Act provides that a valued policy is one which specifies the agreed value of the subject matter insured and, in the absence of fraud, it is conclusive of the insurable value of the subject matter insured whether the loss be total or partial.

Consequently, cargo is always insured under a valued policy stating an insured value in line with the cargo assured's particular requirements. A valued policy will contain both a value – the insured value – and the sum insured. These may be expressed in different ways, e.g.:

> Sum insured £2 000 000 on
> 2000 cases merchandise, valued at £2 000 000
> or
> Sum insured £2 000 000 on
> 2000 cases merchandise, so valued.

The sum insured is the total of underwriters' subscriptions to the insurance and is, therefore, the maximum amount payable in respect of a claim. The sum insured is also the figure applied to the rate percentage, charged by the underwriter for writing the risk, to arrive at the premium due for the insurance. Effectively it represents the amount of insurance bought and it follows that, in the event of loss, one cannot expect to recover more than one has paid for.

In order for the subject matter insured to be fully insured, the sum insured and insured value must of course be for the same amount. If the sum insured is less than the insured value, this would mean that, for some reason, there is under-insurance or the assured has elected to bear a proportion of the risk himself. For instance, a sum insured of £1 600 000 on an insured value of £2 000 000 would indicate that the assured is bearing 20 per cent of the risk. In other words he will bear 20 per cent of every claim, recovering 80 per cent from his underwriters. In return for this he will save 20 per cent of the premium.

10.3.4 Subrogation

Subrogation is the corollary of indemnity in so far as its application prevents the assured defeating the principle of indemnity by recovering his loss from more than one party. For instance, insured goods may be damaged as a result of faulty stowage by the carrier. Under an 'all risks' insurance the cargo assured would be entitled to indemnity from his or her underwriters. He or she would also have recourse against the carrier. While he or she may lodge claims against both, they may not recover and retain amounts received from both underwriter and carrier as this would defeat the principle of indemnity. In practice the underwriter, upon payment of the claim for the damage, would automatically be subrogated to all rights and remedies the cargo owner had against the carrier and, accordingly, may exercise these rights either in his or her own name or that of the assured for a recovery against the amount paid by him or her under the insurance. Any recovery the underwriter effects in this respect is limited to the amount of the claim paid under the insurance. It is possible, for example, where the insured goods have been undervalued, that the underwriter may recover more than the amount paid by him or her as a claim. In this event, he or she must pass the surplus proceeds to the assured.

The rights of subrogation pass to the underwriter upon payment of any type of claim. However, where the claim is in respect of a total loss, the underwriter is additionally entitled to proprietary rights in respect of whatever may remain of the insured goods and, accordingly, may dispose of these as is seen fit, retaining the whole of any proceeds even though these may exceed the amount of the claim paid.

10.3.5 Effecting Cargo Insurance

In the majority of international trade transactions, the contract will clearly state which party is responsible for arranging insurance for the goods being supplied and, in some cases, the point at which responsibility changes from supplier to buyer. This will be reflected in the Incoterm applied to the contract. Irrespective of the responsibility, it is important that the insurance cover is in force for the entire journey being undertaken, including any loading, unloading and temporary storage. Accordingly, insurance cover for the goods should embrace the following:

1. Transportation of merchandise to the seaport or airport of departure.
2. Period during which the goods are stored awaiting shipment or loading.
3. The time while on board the ship, aircraft or other conveyance such as the international road haulage operation.

4. The 'off loading' and storage on arrival at destination airport, seaport or other specified place.
5. Transportation to the buyer's premises or address.

Where the supplier is responsible for arranging insurance, the insurance certificate or policy will be sent with the shipping documentation as evidence of cover. Insurance cover arranged by the supplier may end when the goods are landed at the port of arrival which can lead to problems such as the following.

1. Cover needing to be arranged for the transit of goods from the port of arrival to the buyer's premises or those of the ultimate purchaser.
2. Goods arriving damaged or incomplete at the port of arrival may lead to disputes between seller and buyer. Unless the goods are inspected immediately upon arrival, it will be difficult to prove where the loss or damage occurred.
3. Settlement of claims may be delayed if insurance is arranged by an overseas insurer.

These problems can be circumvented by several mechanisms including:

1. Extension of the seller's marine insurance cover to the ultimate destination, with the buyer assuming responsibility for the insurance premium relating to the period after arrival at the port of entry.
2. Separate insurance cover being arranged by the buyer covering the final stages of the transit though this may not resolve demarcation disputes.
3. The buyer taking responsibility for insurance from the supplier's premises to the ultimate destination.

10.4 Cargo insurance policy form and clauses

10.4.1 The SG policy form

A form of policy was included in the first schedule of the Marine Insurance Act 1906. This was the SG (Ship Goods) form adopted by Lloyd's on 1 January 1779. The insurance companies which developed in the nineteenth century never actually adopted the SG form of policy as specified in the Marine Insurance Act 1906, but preferred their own versions which, although including some slight variations, followed in general the same wording as the SG form and provided the same cover.

These company forms are now standardized in the form used by the Institute of London Underwriters (ILU) which signs policies on behalf of its member companies in the same way that Lloyd's Policy Signing Office signs policies on behalf of the syndicates at Lloyd's. Most insurance companies writing marine business are members of the ILU.

Subject to certain amendments and the attachment of clauses amplifying the cover to meet modern requirements, the SG form served the marine market for more than 200 years. Its strength and consequent retention for so long a time stemmed from the fact that during this period virtually every word and phrase has been the subject of litigation in the courts and its exact meaning established. Nevertheless, the archaic wording of the form together with the proliferation of clauses attached made it a complicated document, and following pressure from the United Nations Conference on Trade and Development (UNCTAD) for its replacement, a new form, the MAR Form (MAR being Marine), was introduced on 1 January 1982.

10.5 Cargo insurance rating

Premium rates are determined by numerous factors which are detailed below.

1. *The carrying vessel.* The age, classification, flag, ownership, and management of the ship are an important consideration.
2. *Nature of the packing used.* This has to be related to the mode of transport and its adequacy as a form of protection to the cargo. Air freight and maritime container shipments tend to require less packing.
3. *Type of merchandise involved.* Some commodities are more vulnerable to damage than others. Additionally, one must relate this to the cover provided and experience, if any, of conveying such cargo.
4. *Nature of transit and related warehouse accommodation.* Generally, the shorter the transit time, the less vulnerable the cargo is to damage or pilferage. Again the mode(s) of transport involved influence premium determination. Maritime containerization has tended in many trades and cargoes to reduce risk of pilferage, but the cargo still remains susceptible to damage.
5. *Previous experience.* If the cargo involved has been subject to significant damage or pilferage the premiums are likely to be high. In the main, the shipper and broker tend to work well together in devising methods to minimize damage and pilferage and overcome inadequate packing.
6. *The type of cover needed.* This is a critical area and obviously the more extensive the cover required, the higher the premium rate. Again the broker will advise the shipper on the extent of cover required, but much depends on terms of delivery.
7. *The volume of cargo involved.* A substantial quantity shipment of export cargo may obtain a more favourable premium, but much depends on the circumstances, particularly transport mode and type of packing, if any.

Normally, alternative rates are available for different covers. For example, glassware may be insured at a high rate against all risks including breakage, or at a much lower rate excluding breakage, cracking or chipping. The degree of fragility is not the same for all commodities and obviously there cannot be a universal rate for breakage. To the exporter fresh to the business, it is wise to shop around to obtain the most favourable rates or seek advice from the freight forwarder.

10.5.1 The new Marine Policy Form and new Institute Cargo Clauses

On 1 January 1982 a new Marine Policy Form and new Institute Cargo Clauses were introduced in the London marine insurance market. As explained earlier the cargo insurance market is underwritten by Lloyd's underwriters and insurance companies. We will now examine a Companies Marine Policy subscribed to by insurance companies which are members of the Institute of London Underwriters.

The Companies Marine Policy serves as a contract of insurance for cargo and as detailed below there are three main types of policy: single shipment, annual and open.

1. Single shipment or Facultative shipment.

    (a) Optional type of policy in that, having agreed to cover a specific shipment, there is no obligation to cover further shipments.
    (b) Used mainly for importers/exporters with occasional shipments, or can be used as a means of building up experience on a new venture prior to the issuing of a longer term contract.

2. Annual policy

    (a) Issued for a 12-month period subject to payment at inception of a minimum and deposit premium or deposit premium with a minimum retention.
    (b) Adjustable at the end of the period on the total value of sendings made declarable as either (i) an annual figure, or (ii) throughout the period, on an individual or monthly basis.
    (c) Suitable for risks where sendings are regular and low value goods are involved.
    (d) It ensures premium up front for the broker and underwriter.

3. Open policy

    (a) Once issued this policy remains in force until no longer required, i.e. can be cancelled by either the Assured or the Insurer.
    (b) Annually reviewed to ensure that the Assured's requirements continue to be met.
    (c) Premium is normally payable in arrears, being calculated according to the value of shipments in a particular month.

Flexibility to meet each customer's individual requirements and variations in the latter two covers may be negotiated. The type of policy offered will depend on:

1. frequency of shipments;
2. annual value of shipments;
3. ease of operation.

The above policies may be subject to Insurance Premium Tax.

Method of declaration

1. Assured's typed declaration letter

    (a) No documentation issued usually by the assured.
    (b) Used where an annual value of sendings or turnover is required for adjustment purposes.
    (c) Usually utilized in small annual policies.

2. Small declaration

    (a) Issued by assured companies to brokers/agents/assureds.
    (b) Used for declaring individual shipments on an import cover or as a request for a Claims Payable Abroad certificate to be issued on an export cover (where certificates have not been issued to a broker, etc.).

3. Large declaration

    (a) Issued by assured companies to brokers/agents/assureds.
    (b) Used when there are regular multiple shipments involved, usually on an import cover.
    (c) Normally submitted on a monthly basis.

4. Certificate of insurance

    (a) Issued by assured companies to brokers/agents/assureds.
    (b) Normally issued on export covers for individual shipments.
    (c) Usually submitted in monthly batches.

5. Evidence of the contract of insurance

    (a) Freely assignable document.
    (b) Reflects cover of the master policy.
    (c) Indicates details of the claims settling agent to be used.

Scope of cover

Marine insurers use standard wordings known as Institute Clauses. Various clauses are used depending on the nature of the goods being carried. The three basic levels of protection offered are detailed as follows.

(i) Institute Cargo Clauses (A)

This represents the widest form of protection and provides all-risks cover against physical loss of or damage to the goods, including both total and partial losses. Exclusions are:

1.   wilful misconduct of the assured;
2.   ordinary leakage, loss in weight/volume or ordinary wear and tear;
3.   inadequate packing including stowage in a container by the assured;
4.   inherent vice;
5.   delay;
6.   insolvency or financial default of carriers;
7.   war and strikes and nuclear risks.

As well as these exclusions, some cargoes warrant more specific exclusions, e.g.:

1.   Machinery or electrical items – excluding electrical and/or mechanical derangement.
2.   Steel goods (if unprotected) – excluding rust, oxidization or discolouration.
3.   Tinned goods – excluding blowing and/or bursting of tins.
4.   Chocolates – excluding heating and/or sweating.

It is important to note that the only storage cover given is that given while in the ordinary course of transit. If the storage is intentional it is not covered. The equivalent cover is also provided by the Institute Cargo Clauses (Air) for sendings by air.

(ii) Institute Cargo Clauses (B)

These clauses are subject to the same exclusions as per the Institute Cargo Clauses (A). Protection, however, is limited to the major named perils listed below:

1.   Fire and explosion.
2.   Loss following upon a major accident to the ocean-carrying-vessel or over-turning or derailment of the land conveyance.
3.   Discharge of cargo at a port of distress.
4.   Earthquake, volcanic eruption or lightning.
5.   General average sacrifice.
6.   Jettison or washing overboard.
7.   Sea, lake or river water damage (not rain water).
8.   Total loss of any package lost overboard or dropped during loading/unloading.
9.   General average or salvage charges.

Cover can be extended to include theft or non-delivery if necessary. These clauses are used when underwriters are not prepared to give 'A' clauses as in the case of second-hand goods or packaged bulk cargoes.

(iii) Institute Cargo Clauses (C)

These afford the minimum protection available and are really only suitable for goods which are customarily insured against major casualties only or which are shipped in bulk, or where the condition of the goods is not known by the underwriter. The cover is loss or damage arising from any of the major perils listed under the Institute Cargo Clauses (B) except numbers 4, 7 and 8.

(iv) Additional Clauses

Institute War Clauses and Institute Strikes Clauses are usually added and give cover against the risks of war, strikes, riots and civil commotion. It should be noted that terrorism cover is granted by the strikes clauses while the goods are in the ordinary course of transit.

As mentioned previously, the preceding are the basic clauses which are used to cover most cargoes. There are, however, some commodities, goods and situations which are normally dealt with under special market trade clauses, e.g.:

Coal	Institute Coal Clauses
Frozen meat	Institute Frozen Meat Clauses
Cocoa, Coffee, Cotton, Fats and Oils not in bulk, Hides, Skins and Leather, Metals, Oil Seeds, Sugar (raw or refined) and Tea	Institute Commodity Trades Clauses (A)

Other aspects

The Companies Marine Policy is not valid unless it bears the embossment of the Policy Department of the Institute of London Underwriters. It is subject to English law and must contain an identical description of the cargo as found on the bill of lading, air waybill and feature the valuation and transportation details.

Check list, discrepancies (i.e. likely errors) and their consequences

If an insurance document is required check the following:

1. It has been issued and/or signed by an insurance company or underwriter or an agent on their behalf.
2. It is not a broker's certificate or cover note unless the presentation of such has been specifically authorized.
3. If the insurance document indicates it is issued in more than one original, all originals are presented unless otherwise authorized in the credit.

4. It is not dated later than date of shipment, despatch or taking in charge.
5. It is issued in the currency of the creditor. If cover in a different currency is required, that it is presented in that currency.
6. It provides sufficient cover and contains the same details in respect of special risks as stated in the credit terms. Unless otherwise stipulated, cover must be 10 per cent above the CIF or CIP value.
7. It has been enclosed to the order of a specified party, issued in a transferable form, or endorsed by the insured if issued in the latter's name.
8. It shows marks, numbers, weights and quantities and a description of goods that match the Bill of Lading and other documents.
9. It does not show unauthenticated alterations.
10. It shows the method of carriage of the goods, the point of loading on board, despatch or taking in charge, the name of the carrying vessel if appropriate and the port of discharge or place of delivery.
11. It specifically covers transhipment when the transport document shows this will take place.
12. It states a named place where claims are payable when required.
13. It covers 'Loaded on Deck' when this is permitted within the Credit Terms or when despatch is effected in containers which may be loaded on deck – check appropriate jettison clauses.

10.6 Cargo insurance claims

Most insurance company policies require that immediate notice be given to the nearest branch or agency in the event of damage giving rise to a claim under a policy on goods. Lloyd's policies stipulate that a Lloyd's agent shall be called in should damage occur.

When notified of damage, the company's agent or Lloyd's agent proceeds to appoint a suitable surveyor to inspect the goods and to report on the nature and extent of the damage. A common practice is for a report or certificate of loss incorporating the surveyor's findings to be issued to the consignees, the latter paying the fee. This is the usual procedure relative to the Lloyd's agent. This certificate of loss is included with the claim papers and, if the loss is recoverable under the insurance cover, the fee is refunded to the claimants.

In some circumstances, the claim papers are returned to the place where the insurance was effected and subsequently presented to the underwriters. However, especially where goods are sold on CIF terms and the policy is assigned to the consignees, arrangements are made for any claims to be paid at destination. In such cases, the consignees approach the agents named in the policy for payment of their claims. Lloyd's agents undertake this service. The policy must be produced by the claimant when a marine claim is put forward because of the freedom with which the marine policy may be assigned. In circumstances where the policy or certificate of insurance has been lost or destroyed, underwriters are generally willing to settle the claim, provided that the claimant completes a letter of indemnity.

The presentation of claims is by negotiation on documents supporting the assured's case. It is very difficult to state with any degree of legal precision exactly on whom the onus of proof falls in every case, but generally speaking, the assured must be able to prove a loss by a peril against which he or she was insured. Once the assured has presented a *prima facie* case of loss by a peril insured against, the onus is on the insurers to disprove liability.

The following documents are required when making an insurance claim:

1. The export invoice issued to the customer together with shipping specification and/or weight notes.
2. The original bill of lading, charterparty, air waybill, or CMR or CIM consignment note.
3. The original policy or certificate of insurance.
4. The survey report or other documentary evidence detailing the loss or damage occurred.
5. Extended protest or extract from ships logs for salvage loss, particular average in goods, or total loss of goods for maritime consignments.
6. Letters of subrogation for total loss or particular average on goods.
7. Any exchange of correspondence with the carriers and other parties regarding their liability for the loss or damage.
8. Any landing account or weight notes at final destination.
9. Account sale (salvage) or invoice for reconditioning charges.

Having established the documents required to deal with the claim, it is important a code of procedure be devised to process it. Figure 10.1 features the 'cargo claim' and the main elements of it. In Figure 10.2 we have the 'development of the cargo claim' and its constituents from the factory to the buyer (consignee).

Brief details are given below if the claims procedure which involves a bulk shipment.

1. Receiver notifies his agent of damage/loss and allows the ship's agent three days to examine cargo.
2. When extent of damage is ascertained by receiver or shipowner's agent, the shipowner and P & I Club must be told.
3. A large claim may require a P & I Club surveyor or a consultant to examine the cargo. An early examination is essential and the agent must establish from the ship's Master and confirm with the shipowner/P & I Club, the actual name of P & I Club involved.
4. When the cargo claim facts are established, correspondence starts as detailed in Figures 10.1 and 10.2 involving interested parties:

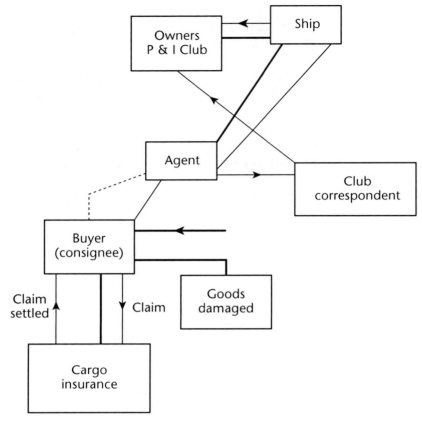

FIGURE 10.1 Cargo claim

shipowner, receiver's agents, P & I Club, cargo receiver, shipowner's agent, cargo insurance company/Lloyd's, lawyers, etc.

5. The receiver's agent's role is decisive in all stages to ensure prompt settlement is obtained and quick action is essential in the early stages.

It will be appreciated circumstances will vary. The claim could emerge at the factory warehouse of the buyer rather than at the destination port as found in the example above.

It is important to bear in mind that clean receipts for imported cargo acceptance should never be given when the goods are in a doubtful condition, but the receipt should be suitably endorsed and witnessed if possible, for example, if one package is missing. Furthermore, if the loss of damage incurred was not readily apparent at the time of taking delivery, written notice must be given to the carriers or other bailees within three days of delivery acceptance.

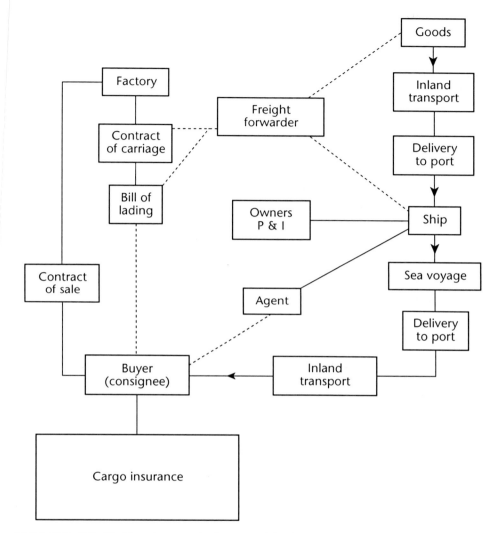

FIGURE 10.2 Development of cargo claim

It is desirable the claim be progressed as quickly as practicable. It is advantageous for the exporter to have a good comprehension of the term general average (GA) which features in any standard maritime policy. It is defined as a 'loss arising in consequences of extraordinary and intentional sacrifices made or expenses incurred, for the common safety of the ship and cargo.' Examples of general average include jettison of cargo, damage to cargo, etc.

In the event of a shipowner declaring a general average loss occurring, each party involved in the voyage must contribute in proportion to their interest in the maritime venture. This, of course, involves shippers who may not have suffered any damage or loss to their cargo. The cargo is only released in such a situation when the shipper/importer has given either a cash deposit or provided a general average guarantee given by the insurers. Overall, this involves signing a general average bond which confirms the importer will pay his general average contribution following the average adjuster's assessment.

10.7 Cargo claims prevention

Claims prevention is the process of devising a system to reduce or eliminate the level of claims emerging from the carriage of goods on an international transit. It is important the exporter gives special attention to claims prevention and thereby maintains a good relationship with the buyer through the goods arriving in an undamaged condition with none missing (Figures 10.1 and 10.2). The circumstances which give rise to a cargo claim vary and the following is a broad summary of the situations:

1. Missing goods.
2. Damaged goods.
3. Stained/mutilated/soiled goods.
4. Non-saleable/marketable goods arising through frustration of the transit such as transit delays causing perishable goods to deteriorate beyond a marketable/saleable product.
5. Failure of the goods to arrive on a specified date resulting in a compensation claim.
6. Poor/inadequate packing.
7. Inadequate/poor stowage.
8. Poor handling/stacking of cargo resulting in damage, crushing, etc.

To minimize the level of cargo claims it is most desirable that adequate measures be taken. The following list should not be regarded as exhaustive but merely as a selection of the more important areas where measures can be taken to reduce claims:

1. A transit test should be employed to determine where the delays, damage or pilferage were encountered and any remedial practical measures necessary should be instituted.
2. Documentation should be continually improved to specify the circumstances of a claim and the reasons for a claim. Comprehensive claims reports permit a realistic analysis of causes and thereby produce a possible pattern of circumstances.
3. Quality control of product, transport service and packaging should be improved. (See also item (4).)
4. Packaging should be analysed for its adequacy, both for handling and stowage and for compatibility with atmospheric conditions, including weather exposure.

5. Pilferage – aim to improve security and properly evaluate alternatives for routeing, packaging, cargo packing, marking identity, etc.
6. Breakage – aim to improve packaging and better handling and stowage techniques and/or transport mode, i.e. break-bulk to containers.
7. An evaluation of the cost of alternative means and/or remedies should be made and their likelihood of success assessed.
8. Staff training should be provided, especially on the handling and stowage of cargo and on measures to lessen such cargo claims; this to include cargo claims report forms and their comprehensiveness and prompt submission.
9. A code of procedure should be devised to report damaged or missing cargo, thereby ensuring that prompt action can be taken to lessen the prospect of further claims and to institute earlier enquiries in order to produce quick remedial measures.
10. Adequate preventative claims staff resources should be provided to lessen such risk.
11. All available modern technology should be used to lessen such claims.
12. Produce a brochure on claims prevention and packaging, stowage and handling techniques.
13. Initiate early discussions with the carrier(s) and other interested parties to devise remedial measures to resolve the difficulties and claims encountered.

It is most important that claims be kept to a minimum and thereby ensure cargo insurance premiums remain competitive and, at the same time, that the buyer is well-satisfied, with goods received in a quality condition. The need to deal with claims promptly and adequately cannot be overstressed. Readers fresh to the subject and keen to understand the wide range of cargo insurance terms will find it useful to obtain a copy of the fifth edition (2005) of my *Dictionary of Shipping International Business Trade and Terms and Abbreviations* published by Witherbys – e-mail: books@witherbys.co.uk – which contains 18 000 entries embracing over 1000 insurance terms/definitions.

CHAPTER 11

Credit insurance

11.1 Export credit insurance

The purpose of export credit insurance is to offer protection to exporters of goods or services who sell their products on credit terms. The exporter is insured against losses arising from a wide range of risks, which may be conveniently categorized into either *commercial risks* or *political risks,* although many private export credit insurers offer cover for commercial risks only. In order to protect the insurers in the private sector against adverse selection, an exporter is usually required to insure its entire book of export orders filled on credit terms, rather than being allowed to seek coverage in respect of countries where the peril is perceived to be the greatest. Credit insurance is primarily focused on short-term exports up to six months. The credit insurers make their own assessment of the credit status (p. 283) of the importer/buyer and will provide a credit limit which will represent the maximum that they will cover on that customer. If the credit insurers refuse to give a credit limit on a customer, the exporters must review their strategy of the prudence of doing business with the buyer/importer involved. The range of services available from credit insurers includes online credit limits and credit assessments of potential customers through to the credit management and debt collection.

Exporters need to focus particularly on the following in their credit insurance strategy:

(a) Continuously manage the credit insurance policies, and attention to detail is absolutely essential.
(b) Companies like Euler Hermes (p. 283) provide help for smaller export companies in the management of their credit insurance portfolio.
(c) Credit insurance claims may take several months to secure settlement.

11.1.1 Commercial risks

Commercial risks would generally include the following:

1. The insolvency of the purchaser.
2. The default on payment by a private purchaser at the end of the credit period or after some specified period following the expiry of the agreed term of credit.
3. Non-acceptance of goods delivered to the purchaser, where such goods comply with any contracts in existence.

11.1.2 Political risks

The scope for losses arising from risks of a political nature is wider than that in respect of commercial risks and would generally encompass all political events which have an impact on any contractual relationships covered by civil law, including the following:

1. Cancellation or non-renewal of an insured's export licence after a contract has been struck.
2. War and other such disturbances in the purchaser's country of domicile which affect the fulfilment of the contract.
3. Foreign currency conversion risks, i.e. difficulties and delays in remitting money from the purchaser's country, including losses arising as a result of a moratorium on external debt issued by that country's government.
4. Transfer risks (also referred to as 'third country transfer risks') where one country can freeze the assets and bank accounts of another country held locally.
5. Any action of a foreign government which in some way hinders the enactment of the contract, including import/export restrictions, the confiscation or expropriation of goods and the nationalization of corporations and industries.
6. Transactions between private exporters and public purchasers, i.e. the default on payment by a public purchaser. Exporters may choose to check out the credit rating from one of the agencies such as Dunn and Bradstreet regarding high political/commercial risk countries.

11.1.3 The rationale behind export credit insurance

In its purest form, export credit insurance provides exporters of goods and services with a significant degree of financial security, thus allowing companies to pursue a bolder export policy, by accepting new purchasers and entering into new overseas markets, but with a smaller impact from the risks of non-payment and political instability. Indirect effects of the purchase of such insurance might include the use of policies as security against bank loans and other financial arrangements. The insurance content of such policies is typically supplemented by the extensive support services which are generally provided by export credit insurers. In particular, such insurers usually have access to extensive information from credit rating agencies and foreign embassies, and are able to provide information to their policyholders regarding the creditworthiness and trading records of potential purchasers of their goods. Such services may be charged for either on a standing charge basis, a per usage fee, or may be built into the premium structure.

Extensions to the basic coverage offered can take many different forms, for example:

1. A manufacturer of specialist goods (which would not necessarily be resaleable elsewhere) might seek additional insurance from the date that the contract is struck to the date of shipment, in order to protect against the risk of the purchaser being subsequently unable to fulfil its contractual obligations prior to completion of the manufacturing process.
2. A policyholder with significant financial exposure arising from one-off products, for example, ship-building, would probably not be covered under the standard terms of its policies as a result of the high monetary values involved. Extensions to coverage in such circumstances might be granted on a discretionary case by case basis.
3. An exporter may often need to offer credit terms which are longer than permitted under the policy's standard conditions, particularly where it is common practice within a specific manufacturing sector to do so.

11.1.4 Limits of indemnity

Generally, cover is provided up to some specified percentage of any loss, typically between 80 per cent and 95 per cent. An excess may also be payable by the insured in respect of certain predetermined types of loss, with the limits of coverage applying to the balance of the claim amount. The element of co-insurance acts, to some extent, as a deterrent to the abuse of the coverage purchased; for example, exporters might simply claim on their policies rather than seek to effect a bad debt collection programme, or find alternative purchasers for goods not taken up by the original buyer.

11.1.5 Recoveries and subrogation

In any event, the export credit insurer will generally seek to effect recoveries on claims paid, either through the courts, via factors; through pressure from British embassies in the purchaser's country of domicile; or via some other form of debt collection in order to offset individual losses.

More typically, the goods concerned would be taken into the insurer's possession where possible, and an alternative buyer sought. If, however, the insurer does not have the necessary administrative or resale capabilities, an arrangement may be entered into with the policyholder such that a specified proportion of any resale revenue is remitted to the insurer. A claim can therefore be settled quickly irrespective of any subsequent recovery prospects, thereby maintaining the insured's cash flow position, but still leaving the insurer free to pursue the possibility of effecting recoveries at a later stage.

11.1.6 Who provides export credit insurance?

Schemes are often operated by the governments of individual countries, as the potential volatility of this form of insurance means that only very large private insurers could weather exceptionally poor claims experience. Furthermore, re-insurance of this form of business is difficult to place in the commercial market owing to the substantial levels of coverage required. State schemes were therefore started up with the original intention of both encouraging and facilitating the export of domestic goods and services abroad. In particular, state-backed schemes have the added attraction of generally being considered to be less likely than private insurance companies to withdraw cover for political risks in respect of specific countries (e.g. in the event of the outbreak of war) and are thus in a position to provide cover for risks which might not be insurable in the commercial market.

There exist, none the less, a number of private insurance companies which can continue to provide coverage in respect of commercial and political risks under such circumstances via the vehicle of re-insurance with the respective governments.

11.1.7 Policy conditions

Typically, private export credit insurers tend to provide short-term cover only, while state organizations additionally insure medium- and long-term risks, as well as offering cover in respect of risks for substantial sums insured and 'national interest' risks. The period over which the insurer is on risk in respect of any one underwriting year depends on the amalgamation of the following.

1. The duration of any pre-shipment coverage, for example during the course of the manufacturing process.
2. The length of the credit terms offered.
3. The period over which the policy is in force.

Typical policy conditions for short-term cover might comprise the following:

1. A policy is generally in effect for 12 months such that all contracts entered into and all goods shipments notified to the insurer within this period are covered.
2. Credit terms from 90 days up to one year from the date of shipment or the date of receipt of goods.
3. Any period between striking a contract and the eventual shipment of completed goods to be limited to 24 months.
4. Premiums levied on the basis of the value of each shipment covered under the policy at terms fixed at the outset for the duration of the policy.
5. Limits on the maximum value of any individual contract or shipment.

11.2 Short-term export credit insurance

As its name suggests, short-term export credit insurance exists to cover exporters against the risks inherent in trading on relatively short (usually up to six months) credit terms with buyers overseas. These types of exports account for the vast majority of exports from the UK and are generally not associated with the longer term 'project' activities looked after by the government's Export Credit Guarantees Department. However, they cannot be entirely divorced from those activities, as much of the project work will also subsequently lead to orders for parts, spares and further services which are then sold on a short-term basis.

The risks for exporters of non-payment by overseas customers can be divided into two separate areas: *commercial* risks and *political* risks. Commercial risk covers straightforward insolvency of the debtor; some credit insurers are also prepared to offer cover for protracted default which, broadly speaking, is where the buyer turns out to have insufficient funds for the goods, and the cost of winding him or her up might be more than the amount of the original debt. On political risk the cover is less straightforward, and can be subdivided into three different areas.

1. *Inconvertibility.* This covers the failure of the buyer's country to transfer foreign exchange as a result of economic, financial or political difficulties. This is the most common cause of political risk claims.
2. *Contract frustration/cancellation.* This covers the failure to pay, where this is due to war (except between the UK and the country of the buyer), any measure of the government of the buyer's country which directly prevents performance of the contract and the cancellation or non-renewal of valid import/export licences.
3. *Public buyer default.* This covers the contractual default of a public buyer which can be the government, a government agency, a

regional or local authority, a nationalized undertaking or a state trade organization.

Notwithstanding the Single European Market and the greater similarity between what have hitherto been divided into 'domestic' and 'export' trades, exporters will still need to consider both the creditworthiness of the buyer (hopefully *before* accepting the order) and the political risks inherent in trading with the country itself. Even for trade with some EU countries, political risk cover is still sought by exporters.

11.2.1 Companies offering credit insurance

Details of companies offering credit insurance are given below. It should be noted that the Export Credit Guarantee Department (ECGD) is a Government Agency embracing a trading fund status from 2005 under the Department of Trade and Industry.

The Export Credits Guarantee Department (ECGD)

The Export Credits Guarantee Department (ECGD) has four operating rules which are subject to continuous review.

1. ECGD underwrites export deals on credit terms longer than two years, both through credit lines and individual packages of cover for specific contracts.
2. ECGD provides reinsurance – for certain high-risk markets, or larger and longer exposures – to private sector credit insurers.
3. ECGD underwrites short-term cover for a small number of national interest markets that are too risky for private sector insurers.
4. ECGD underwrites long and large extended term deals beyond normal short-term insurance parameters.

Euler Hermes

Euler Hermes is a market leader in credit insurance with a 37 per cent market share globally and a presence in 35 countries. It also has a European factoring network through Eurofactor and in 2004 this embraced €1.5 billion of turnover. In the area of credit insurance, more than €600 billion of business transactions were protected worldwide in 2004. It has a rating of A+ (March 2003) by Standard and Poor's. Euler Hermes promotes corporate development whatever the size, sector and nationality of companies. Its primary activity is credit insurance. This extends also to a range of services for the management of companies' trade receivables.

The company's aim is to support the business development of companies in national and international markets, by optimizing and safeguarding the management of their trade receivables.

In the area of credit insurance this includes the prevention of non-payment risk. It arises when the failure of one or more customers occurs (even when a credit insurance policy indemnifies the loss) and is detrimental to a company's commercial development. Through its prevention services and its unrivalled knowledge of risks worldwide, Euler Hermes helps companies base their business development on solvent customers.

Another area is trade debt collection. The Company have specialist teams throughout the world supported by a network of local correspondents. Clients benefit from its negotiation power and knowledge of local payment and collection practices.

Compensation for losses due to buyer insolvency represent losses incurred on unpaid trade receivables. Euler Hermes offer a service of indemnification at a rate agreed between insurer and client. This protects the assets of its insured clients.

The Company also provides a range of services inter-related to credit insurance as follows:

(a) *Financing of trade receivables*. This is basically factoring (p. 313) or by means of securitization transactions.
(b) *Managing trade receivables*. Efficient collection of accounts payable enables companies to significantly reduce the cost of bad debt. Euler Hermes adopts this strategy through a factoring service enabling clients to develop specific products who do not have access to this facility within their credit insurance policy. The Eurofactor is responsible for follow-up invoices, debt collection and accounts management.
(c) *Bonding*. This offers companies/clients a wide range of guarantees and bonding for national contracts and exports therefore maintaining their bank credit potential intact.
(d) *Evaluating trade receivable portfolios*. Euler Hermes has devised a company risk database with its own rating programme. It aims to offer tailor-made rating solutions for diversified receivables portfolios.
(e) *Risk management*. The company have local teams to monitor and evaluate risk within its international network. This helps to avoid the risk of non-payment by enabling them to benefit from its detailed knowledge of buyers. The Company's risk managers at each subsidiary overseas meet regularly to share their experience, assess positions, and adopt common policies for multinational buyers. This is an indispensable tool in assessing risks. The locally based risk experts are in permanent contact with buyers and their financial partners to collect valuable information and feed them into a common database. It has also developed a fully integrated information system embracing information, risk and policy.

(f)   *Securitization.* This is a growth sector and involves a credit insurer in securitization arrangements to help optimize the interest of such deals both in terms of financing and transfer of risks.

Euler Hermes also specializes in the needs of small- and medium-sized export companies. They embrace a range of comprehensive coverage for export risks and include debt collection support (p. 286).

11.2.2 Types of policy available

The vast bulk of policies written are on the so-called 'whole turnover' principle, where the insurer will cover as much of the exporter's book of debts as possible, although this may be restricted to certain markets or the activities of certain divisions, commensurate with there being a suitable spread of risk to offer the insurer. Percentage indemnities will vary with the trade covered, buyer countries and the quality of the customer book, but are generally between 80 per cent and 95 per cent. Premiums are usually expressed as a percentage of turnover, and there will also be a small administration charge. The exporter generally justifies covering him- or herself up to a certain level by reference to an agreed set of criteria, with the insurer agreeing specific credit limits for the larger customers thereafter. Actual amounts of indemnity and first loss will vary according to the level of risk the exporter is prepared to take for himself. However, as with all credit insurance, the value of the service lies just as much in the early warning of a deteriorating situation as it does in the ability to pay claims after the event.

Policies can also be written on a 'catastrophe' basis, where the exporter will accept a very high level of first loss, or excess, him- or herself, with the insurer taking losses thereafter, either to an agreed ceiling level, or to the value of the individual credit limits agreed on the buyers. Still other policies can be written on a 'specific account' basis, although both the exporter and the insurer need to make a careful assessment of the quality and spread of the risk in these cases, and the cost is naturally likely to be higher, given the element of selection against the insurer.

Political risk cover is offered on the basis of the three different types described above and is, of course, contingent on the overall spread of risk being offered to it. Some insurers may insist on all the above types of risk being covered, but individual firms will, of course, vary.

Lastly, some insurers are able to offer policies that combine both domestic and export cover. This can be done on the basis of OECD countries and commercial risk only or else on the wider field of all potential markets, and a degree of political risk.

In the final analysis, the exporter must view all the risks inherent in overseas trade and weigh up the price/risk benefit of taking out an insurance policy to cover him- or herself. While the European Single Market had been heralded almost as the start of a 'Golden Age', it is also true that it signifies the beginning of a period of greater instability both in the UK and the EU as companies start both to look for new markets and to find their own home markets threatened. The quick replacement of cash flow and balance sheet protection offered by credit insurance should be seriously considered. The emergence of the Euro has reduced the currency risk in the EU focused markets.

Recommended reading

Euler Hermes publications. www.eulerhermes.com

CHAPTER 12

Export finance

12.1 Introduction

Trade finance has become a strong bargaining point in the conduct of international trade. Both the seller and buyer are keen to adopt positions in the negotiating strategy which will reduce their financial risk and secure the best deal possible. It involves three areas: currency, credit terms and method of payment.

The seller may opt to use his own currency, thereby ensuring profit margins are maintained and any currency risk variation passes to the buyer. Conversely, the importer may decide only to accept quotations in his own currency such as the Swiss franc and pass any currency risk to the overseas seller based in the United States. Also, the exporter keen to get business may quote in the buyer's currency and thereby enable the buyer to compare quotations with other suppliers based in other countries.

Further options exist with the seller and/or buyer opting for a third currency such as the US dollar, thereby sharing the currency fluctuation risk. The introduction of the Euro currency among the 12 EU states removed any currency risk variation within trading partners operative in the Euro-zone (pp. 551–54).

Whenever buying or selling goods in currencies other than their own, importers and exporters become exposed to currency risk from the fluctuations in the exchange rate in the period between prices being agreed and payment being received. Management of this exposure is essential to minimize the potential risks and to maximize the profit from the underlying transactions. The technique of protecting against future exchange rate movements is usually referred to as 'hedging'. It can be exercised by three methods: spot contracts, forward contracts and currency options (see p. 551).

A further factor is the granting of credit. Whereas at one time the ability to sell goods abroad depended on quality, delivery and price, a new factor has now entered the equation which tends to play an increasingly important part – the ability and willingness to give credit. The granting of credit terms, which are growing longer as buyer pressure increases, means that the exporter is without his or her money for longer periods of time. This automatically reduces cash flow and creates a finance problem for the exporter who, sooner or later, has to seek assistance from his or her bank. The financial aspect of selling goods abroad, which at one time was just a normal step in the export procedure, has now assumed such importance that it has become a problem in its own right. The task of exporting overseas has therefore become a more complex operation, demanding higher professional standards – especially in the area of trade finance. Selling overseas requires a different financial strategy compared with selling in the domestic market. Delivery takes longer, contracts are more complex and payment arrangements more complex. The prime consideration is to ensure that payments are received on schedule and that the exporter safeguards his or her financial interest as much as possible.

The criteria of the method of payment is specified in the contract of sale and is reflected in the export/commercial invoice. Choice of method will involve the following considerations:

1. the range of available financing options;
2. the usual contract terms adopted in the exporters/manufacturer's country;
3. how quickly payment is required (timescale);
4. the political situation in the importer's/buyer's country;
5. the availability and cost of foreign currency to the importer/buyer;
6. the terms of the contract of sale;
7. exchange control regulations, if any;
8. the nature of the relationship between buyer and seller;
9. whether the cost of any credit can be arranged by the supplier (exporter) or buyer (importer);
10. the funding resources of the importer;
11. importer risk – non-payment of invoices, delayed payment of invoices and insolvency of buyer;
12. exporter risk – problems in producing the correct documentation and failure to supply goods in accordance with the sales contract;
13. country risk – political and economic instability, transfer risk, war and import/export regulations;
14. transportation risk – risk associated with the mode of transport, e.g. marine risks and storage facilities in ports;
15. foreign exchange risk – fluctuating exchange rates affect pricing and profit.

Many of the risks can be insured against or mitigated through the payment mechanism. However, reducing the exporter's risk may result in the counter parties having to accept a greater degree of risk and may increase costs, both of which can impact on the exporter's competitiveness. Exporters are urged to study the International Business – Exporting Tree diagram (p. 290).

12.2 E-commerce

The e-environment entered trade finance through the e-supplement to UCP500 (p. 295) in March 2002 and it heralded a new era in International Banking practice. This development will reduce administration costs both in terms of time and fees. Currently a UCP provides a set of rules for the presentation of electronic documents alone, or in combination with paper documents. In the longer term the banking community will adopt as standard digital certificates and signature such as IDENTRUS which will provide an international benchmark based on 'know your customer'. Many Bankers believe in an era of such change and within ten years trade between OECD countries and South East Asian countries will be predominantly electronic.

12.3 Financing the trade cycle

The growth in international trade has greatly increased both the demand for trade finance and the degree of sophistication with which it is delivered. There is now a much greater choice of financial solutions for importers and exporters to consider when developing an international trading strategy. Organizing finance is an important part of any strategy and a key contributor to success in international trade. Indeed, the availability of finance can be a major factor in securing new business as it provides the flexibility to offer competitive terms to overseas trading partners.

The criteria for the chosen payment mechanism has been explained on p. 288 and particularly focuses on customers requirements, your assessment of the risks, the terms of trade and cost. Every company's trade cycle is unique although there will be elements (e.g. purchasing, manufacturing, shipping, credit, etc.) which are common to them all. Each stage in a trade cycle places different demands on a company's finances, but a key component in determining the overall level of working capital required for any business is the time taken between the start of the cycle (i.e. ordering goods or raw materials) and receipt of payment for corresponding sales of finished products.

Many International Trade Banks provide advice to traders to ensure, at each stage of the particular trade cycle, that a structure can be put in place to provide working capital for the different stages in the cycle and in consequence directly relate to the needs of the client business. As the bulk

International Business – Exporting

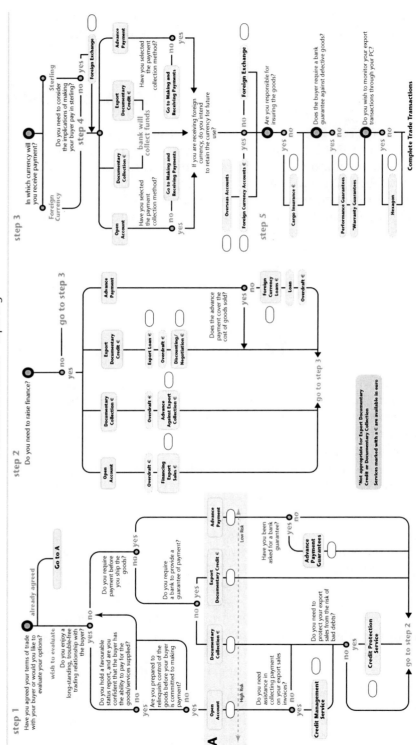

FIGURE 12.1 Exporters Fold out for Decision Tree

Reproduced courtesy of HSBC Bank

of international trade is undertaken on terms of 180 days or less, these facilities are an important consideration for any company involved in importing or exporting. Some exporters take an export loan to fund their working capital to manufacture the goods to fulfil an order. Also, this extends to cover the payment cycle of up to 180 days. The cost of such an export loan would be built into the export price.

12.4 Export and import prices

In the uncertain situation of today, price policy has become much more important but at the same time more difficult. As a matter of policy, the first decision to make as regards pricing is whether to charge in each market 'what it will bear', or whether to charge a price that covers costs and gives a reasonable return on the capital employed. If one does not charge what the market will bear, somebody in that market will add the difference and make an easy profit. The final consumer is not likely to be charged any less. If on the other hand, a price based on cost is more than the market will bear, then orders will be lost.

When considering what policy adjustments to make in the wake of devaluation, it should be borne in mind that a 10 per cent devaluation does not mean a 10 per cent change in the local price. The sterling price is only a part of the final cost to the consumer. Customs duty, import and distribution costs and local mark-ups are expressed in local currency and are not affected. Duty, if *ad valorem,* may vary with the price but the rest of the additions are more or less constant and, in many cases, double the export price by the time the goods are finally sold. So, a 10 per cent devaluation corresponds to about a 5 per cent change in local price.

The whole question of pricing then will revolve around the following factors.

1. How far minimum costs and return on capital can be related to what the market will pay. This will involve a close study of the market, its extent and potential, the strength of competitors and the elasticity of demand for profit.
2. To what extent the fluctuation in exchange rates can be used to advantage.
3. What credit terms are usual in the market and whether the cost of the credit is borne by the buyer.
4. Sources of raw material and possible price changes.

As a basic principle of price policy there is much to recommend selling in the customer's currency and using the forward exchange market. It is a good marketing ploy and a courtesy to the buyer. He or she knows exactly how much the goods will cost in his or her own currency and has no preoccupation with exchange rates. By selling in foreign currency, the exporter has assumed the exchange risk him- or herself but some protection against any exchange rate fluctuations is afforded by selling the currency in the forward exchange market. This is a simple operation through one's bank and means that one is now quoted a rate of exchange at which one's currency will be exchanged when received. Moreover, with currencies such as the Swiss Franc, which are at a premium forward, the forward rate of exchange will be more favourable and more sterling will be received in exchange for the currency received. Alternatively, for those traders resident in the Eurozone and trading within it, there is no currency risk (p. 551).

It is apparent then that export prices must be established in the market place always bearing in mind the cost. There are many instances of goods being sold abroad at prices far below that which the market would be prepared to pay and, on the other hand, many cases of markets lost because the calculation of cost was too high. Marginal selling is not a sound policy; every sale should show some return.

As far as import prices are concerned it is 'what the market will pay' which is all important. Consumer goods have to be retailed at a price which the customer will pay. Raw materials must be at a price which will enable the end product to sell at a profit. Many of the bulk raw materials are sold through specialized commodity markets. Goods purchased at prices expressed in foreign currency will, of course, be subject to exchange rate fluctuations but, as in the case of exports, the exchange risk can be covered in the forward exchange market by buying the currency forward.

12.5 Payments for imports and exports

Credit terms and the method by which payment will be effected are agreed at the time the sales contract is concluded. If the relationship between the buyer and seller is good, then it may have been agreed to trade on 'open account' terms. This means simply that the seller will despatch the goods directly to the buyer, send him or her an invoice and await the remittance of payment from the buyer, as in domestic trading.

There are several methods by which the debtor may remit payment to his supplier.

1. *Debtor's own cheque.* This is not a very satisfactory method from the creditor's point of view. Apart from the usual risk that the cheque may be unpaid, it has to be sent back through banking channels to the buyer's country for collection, thus incurring additional expenses. Cheque clearance cycles vary enormously across the world. Negotiated cheques allow the exporter to obtain the immediate value of the cheque or for a pre-set forward value date in the currency of the cheque. Lock boxes provide a fast and secure method of receiving

cheque payments from overseas. Cheques are not sent to the seller but are paid directly by the buyer into the seller's bank via a PO Box number reducing the clearance cycle.

2. *Banker's draft.* This would be a draft drawn by the buyer's bank on its correspondent bank in the exporter's country. As such it is good payment but there is always the danger that the draft may be lost in the post and a bank draft cannot be 'stopped'. A new draft could only be issued against indemnity.

3. *Mail transfer (MT).* This is the most common method of payment. The debtor instructs his or her bank to request its correspondent bank in the exporter's country to pay the specific amount to the exporter. The whole procedure is done by entries over banking accounts; the buyer's bank debits his account and credits the account of the correspondent bank which, on receipt of the payment instructions, passes a reciprocal entry over its account with the remitting bank and pays the money over to the exporter. The instructions between the banks may be by ordinary mail telex, swift or air mail.

4. *Telegraphic transfer (TT).* The procedure is similar to that of MT except that the instructions are sent by tele-transmission. This means that the payment is effected more quickly.

Where 'open account' terms have not been agreed, then it is for the exporter to arrange for payment to be collected from the buyer. The usual way in which this is done is by the use of bills of exchange. This is the traditional method of claiming that which is due from the debtor, and has been used as a basis for international trade throughout its history.

Instead of merely sending the documents to the debtor with only the covering invoice, the exporter draws a bill of exchange on the debtor for the sum due and attaches the documents to the bill. This is then sent through banking channels for presentation to the buyer. There are several advantages in the employment of bills:

1. The bill of exchange is an instrument long recognized by trade custom and by the law; there is in consequence an established code of practice in relation to bills.

2. The bill is a specific demand on the debtor and, if it is drawn in proper form in respect of debt justly due, the debtor refuses it at his or her peril.

3. The bill is a useful instrument of finance (Chapter 14).

4. The bill provides a useful mechanism for the granting to an overseas buyer of a pre-arranged period of credit. Thus if an exporter has, for some reason, to offer his or her buyer a period of credit, say 90 days, then the bill can be drawn at 90 days' sight. At the same time, the exporter can maintain a degree of control over the shipping documents by authorizing release of the documents on payment, or acceptance of the bill. The bill does provide an instrument on which action can be taken at law.

It should be noted that the drawing of a bill of exchange on the buyer does not guarantee payment and the seller has lost control of the goods to some extent as they are out of his or her country. Moreover, he or she may have to arrange for storage and insurance or even reshipment.

The procedure for the exporter, having obtained the shipping documents, is to draw the bill and lodge it with his or her bank, together with the documents for collection. When lodging the bill, the exporter must give to his or her bank very precise and complete instructions as to what action to take in certain circumstances: whether to forward the bill by air mail, etc., and ask for proceeds to be remitted by telex/fax or air mail; whether the documents are to be released against payment or acceptance of the bill; whether the bill is to be 'protested' if dishonoured; whether the goods should be stored and insured if not taken up by the buyer; whether rebate may be given for early payment; who is the Case of Need to whom the collecting bank may refer in case of dispute (usually the exporter's agent).

The exporter's bank will forward the bill and documents to its correspondent bank in the buyer's country passing on exactly the instructions received from the exporter. The correspondent bank (collecting bank) will present the bill and documents to the buyer, and release the documents to the buyer in accordance with the instructions received. If the arrangement was for payment to be made immediately then the bill of exchange will be drawn at 'sight' and the instructions will be to release documents against payment (D/P). If a period of credit has been agreed, then the bill will be drawn at say '90 days' sight' and the instructions will be for the documents to be released against acceptance by the buyer of the bill (D/A). In this case, the buyer signs his or her acceptance across the face of the bill, which now becomes due for payment in 90 days' time and the buyer obtains the documents of title to the goods. The collecting bank will advise the remitting bank of the date of acceptance, and hold the bill until maturity, when the collecting bank will present it to the buyer for payment. In case of dishonour, and if so instructed, the collecting bank will arrange 'protest' by a notary. This procedure provides legal proof that the bill was presented to the drawee and was dishonoured, and enables action to be taken in the courts without further preliminaries.

The procedures and responsibilities of the banks and other parties are laid down in the 'Uniform Rules for Collection' issued by the International Chamber of Commerce – Publication No 522 – 1995 Revision, in force as of 1st January 1996 and subscribed to by the major banks throughout the world.

The method of collecting payment described above is based on the documentary bill, but in certain circumstances use may be made of a 'clean' bill, that is, a bill to which no documents are attached. Such bills may be drawn for the collection of monies due for services, etc. or for any debt which is not a payment for goods. A 'clean' bill may also be used to

TABLE 12.1 Risk Ladder

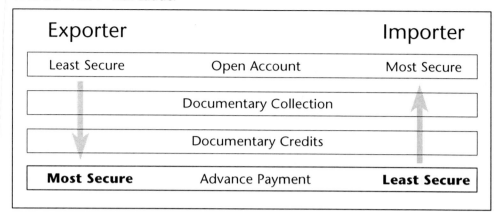

obtain payment for goods sent on 'open account', especially where payment is overdue.

Because they are a traditional and accepted means of obtaining payment in international trade, bills of exchange can be used, with one or two exceptions, throughout the world. In the case of some markets, it would be unwise to operate without the protection a bill can provide. Table 12.1 features the risk ladder for the four main payment mechanisms examined in this chapter. In any trade deal there has to be a balance between making the transaction secure while still making it attractive to the customer or supplier.

12.6 Documentary credits and allied documents

Apart from 'cash with order', the documentary credit provides the most satisfactory method of obtaining payment. It provides reassurance to both the importer and exporter. Overall, the documentary credit is an undertaking issued by a bank on behalf of the buyer (importer/applicant) to the seller (exporter/beneficiary), to pay for goods and/or services, provided that the seller presents documents which comply fully with the terms and conditions of the documentary credit. The documentary credit is often referred to as a DC, LC Letter of Credit or Credit. All documentary credits should be handled according to the International Chamber of Commerce practice known as the 'Uniform Customs and Practice for Documentary Credits'. The current code is defined in the 1993 revision, ICC Publication No 500 and commonly referred to as UCP500. A supplement was issued in 2002 which embraces the evolution from paper to electronic Documentary Credit. It is termed a UCP – electronic presentation – a supplement to UCP500. Overall, it accommodates trade which is either completely electronic or where a mixture of electronic and paper documentation is used.

In 2005 the ICC were formulating a new set of rules governing documentary credits to ease the movement of goods across borders while reflecting the need to tighten security without impeding trade. It will be known as the Uniform Customs and Practice for Documentary Credits UCP600 and displace UCP500 and may be introduced by 2007.

It provides security of payment to the exporter, and enables the buyer to ensure that he or she receives the goods as ordered and delivered in the way he or she requires. It is an arrangement whereby the buyer instructs his or her bank to establish a credit in favour of the seller. The buyer's bank (issuing bank) undertakes, or authorizes its correspondent bank in the exporter's country, to pay the exporter a sum of money (normally the invoice price of the goods) against presentation of shipping documents which are specified in the credit. It is a mandatory contract and completely independent of the sales contract. It is concerned only with documents and not the goods to which the documents refer. Liability for payment now rests with the issuing bank and not the buyer.

The usual form of these credits is the 'irrevocable' credit, which means that it cannot be cancelled or amended without the agreement of the beneficiary (the exporter) and all other parties. Such a credit, opened by a reputable bank in a sound country, means that the exporter can rely on payment being made as soon as he or she has shipped the goods and produced the documents called for in accordance with the terms of the credit. The security provided by an irrevocable credit may be further enhanced if the bank in the exporter's country (advising bank) is requested by the issuing bank to add its 'confirmation'. The exporter then has a 'confirmed irrevocable credit' and he or she need look no further than his or her own local bank for payment. With a credit which is not 'confirmed', however, the point of payment is the issuing bank (abroad), although the advising bank would usually be prepared to negotiate with recourse.

The credit will set out in detail a description of the goods: price per unit and packing; name and address of the beneficiary; the voyage, that is, port of shipment and port of destination; whether the price is FOB, CFR or CIF; and whether part shipments and transhipment are allowed. In some cases, the ship will be nominated. Details of insurance (if CIF) and the risks to be covered will also be shown. The credit will specify a latest date for shipment and an expiry date which is the latest date for presentation of documents.

Exporters are reminded to be extremely cautious about shipping goods on receipt of an unsolicited documentary credit or if a documentary credit is received directly from an issuing bank. From time to time forgeries of documentary credit have arisen and there have been instances where exporters have shipped and presented documents against a completely false instrument. If an exporter suspects a fraudulent transaction, the bank should be informed to check the authenticity of the documentary credit immediately.

Additionally, exporters on receipt of the documentary credit, should not only assess the strength of the issuing bank, but also consider any risks that may arise due to the country in which the issuing bank is based. There have been many instances in recent history where events in a particular country have resulted in an issuing bank being unable to honour its obligation under a documentary credit. Dun and Bradstreet – the credit agency – provide a credit rating on a country basis.

12.6.1 Invoice

The amount must not exceed the credit amount. If terms such as 'about' or *'circa'* are used, a tolerance of 10 per cent is allowed (in respect of quantity the tolerance is 3 per cent). The description of the goods on the invoice and the packing must be exact and agree with the credit. An essential part of the description includes the marks and numbers on the packages. These must appear on the invoice. The invoice should be in the name of the buyer. The commercial invoice represents the sellers claim for payment to the buyer under the terms of the sales contract and outlined in article 37 UCP500.

12.6.2 Bills of lading

This is the document of title to the goods (see pp. 357–74), without which the buyer will not be able to obtain delivery from the shipping company. The credit will call for a full set (they are usually issued in a set of three). They must be clean, that is, bearing no superimposed clauses derogatory to the condition of the goods such as 'inadequate packing', 'used drums', 'on deck', etc. Unless the credit has specifically permitted the circumstances contained in the clause, the negotiating bank will call for an indemnity. The bills of lading must show the goods to be 'on board' – 'received for shipment' bills are not acceptable. They may, however, have a subsequent notation, dated and signed, which states the goods to be 'on board' and they are then acceptable. Under the regulations set out in the 'Uniform Customs and Practice for Documentary Credits' – ICC Publication No 500 – 1993 Revision in force as of 1 January 1994 – articles 23–26, the following bills of lading will be accepted:

1. Through bills issued by shipping companies or their agents even though they cover several modes of transport.

2. Short form bills of lading which indicate some or all of the conditions of carriage by reference to a source or document other than the bill of lading.

3. Bills covering unitized cargoes such as those on pallets or in containers.

Charterparty bills of lading which do not contain the full conditions of carriage but are detailed in a separate charterparty agreement are not acceptable unless specifically allowed in the credit under article 25 of UCP500.

There are many variations for the signing of the Bill of Lading by the carrier, the ship's Master or a named agent signing on their behalf. Any agent issuing a bill of lading must name the carrier on whose behalf they are acting. To constitute naming the carrier, the shipping company name appearing on the bill of lading must be specifically identified 'as carrier'. An extensive list of acceptable variations was published by the ICC in their position paper No 4 dated 1 September 1994.

Unless specifically authorized in the credit, bills of the following type will not be accepted:

1. Bills of lading issued by forwarding agents.
2. Bills which are issued under and are subject to a charterparty.
3. Bills covering shipments by sailing vessels.

The bills must be made out 'to the order of the shipper' and endorsed in blank. If the sales contract is CIF or CFR, then the bills must be marked 'freight paid'. The general description of the goods including marks and numbers must match the invoice. The voyage and ship, if named, must be as stated in the credit. Unless transhipment is expressly prohibited in the credit, bills indicating transhipment will be accepted provided the entire voyage is covered by the same bill. Part shipments are permitted unless the credit states otherwise. Besides stating an expiry date for presentation of documents, credits should also stipulate a specified period of time after the issuance of the bills during which the documents must be presented for payment. If no such period is stipulated in the credit, banks will refuse documents presented to them later than 21 days after the issuance of the bills of lading.

12.6.3 Sea Waybill

This document (see p. 371) has been developed to reduce the problem inherent in short voyage where the documentation (bill of lading) is not available at the time of arrival of the vessel. It is also used increasingly by multinational industries and their subsidiaries (see p. 372). However, it is not a document of title. It is a receipt for goods and evidence of carriage and should be handled in a similar manner to an air waybill.

An original document is not required as delivery is made to the named consignee against proof of identity – usually a delivery order on the consignees headed stationery. The shipper can vary the consignee and delivery instructions at any time prior to delivery. To counteract this problem certain carriers will apply control or waiver clauses to the waybills to meet the requirements of buyers, insurers and financiers. Sea waybills cannot be issued 'to order' or to order of a named party. The non-negotiable sea waybill provisions are found in article 24 of UCP500.

12.6.4 Multi-modal transport document

When goods are carried by more than one mode of transport (usually in containers), a combined (multi-modal) transport document is recommended as the multi-modal transport operator accepts liability for carriage of the goods throughout the entire journey (see p. 366). Where part of the journey is undertaken by sea, some types of multi-modal transport document can convey title to the goods. The multi-modal transport document provisions are found in article 26 of UCP500.

12.6.5 Air waybill or air consignment note

Goods which are transported by air require a waybill to act as a receipt for despatch (see p. 355). It will usually show that the goods are consigned either to the buyer or to the issuing bank and may bear a notified party name and address. Unlike bills of lading, air waybills are not issued in sets and do not convey title to the goods. The copy marked – original[3] (for shipper) should normally be presented under a documentary credit.

The principal requirements for this document under a letter of credit include:

1. the correct shipper and consignee;
2. the airports of departure and destination;
3. the goods description must be consistent with that shown on other documents;
4. any weights, measures or shipping marks must agree with those shown on other documents;
5. it must be signed and dated by the actual carrier or by the named agent of a named carrier – for example EFGH Forwarding Ltd as agents for the carrier Air India (if the credit states that a house air waybill is acceptable, the forwarder's signature alone will suffice);
6. it must state whether freight has been paid or is payable at destination.

If required by the letter of credit, it must also carry a specific notation stating the actual flight date, otherwise the date of despatch will be taken to be the date of issuance of the air waybill. The provisions of the Air Transport document are found in article 27 of UCP500.

12.6.6 Insurance

The document must be as stated in the credit (policy or certificate) and issued by an insurance company or its agent. Cover notes issued by brokers are not acceptable.

The details on the policy must match those on the bills of lading – voyage, ship, marks and numbers, etc. It must also be in the same currency as the credit and endorsed in blank. The amount covered should be at least the invoice amount; credits usually call for invoice value plus 10 per cent. The policy must be dated not later than the date of shipment as evidenced by the bill of lading. The risks covered should be those detailed in the credit. If cover against 'all risks' is called for (which is obtainable) a policy which states that it covers all insurable risks will be acceptable. The provisions for insurance are found in articles 34–36 of UCP500.

According to circumstances, the credit may call for other documents such as a consular certificate; a packing list; a certificate of origin; quality, analysis or health certificate (ensures to buyer that the goods are as ordered); an air waybill; railway (CIM) or road (CMR) consignment notes or Post Office receipt; and pre-shipment inspection documentation including Certificate of Inspection/clean report of findings (see pp. 389–92) and courier receipt (small parcels/packets).

The credit may stipulate a last shipment date and the bill of lading must show shipment by that date. Extension of the shipment date automatically extends the expiry date but not vice versa.

It is very important that exporters, when they receive advice of a credit established in their favour, check the details immediately to see that the goods and terms agree with the sales contract, and they can comply with all the terms and provide all the documents required. If any amendment is required, this can then be taken up with the advising bank in good time for action to be taken before expiry.

Besides the basic irrevocable credit (confirmed or not), there are revocable credits which, as the name implies, can be cancelled or amended at any time without notice to the beneficiary. They do not constitute a legally binding undertaking by the banks concerned. Once transmitted and made available at the advising bank, however, its cancellation or modification is only effective when that bank has received notice thereof and any payment made before the receipt of such notice is reimbursable by the issuing bank. The value of these credits as security for payment is plainly doubtful. They are used mainly for parent companies and subsidiaries, where a continuing series of shipments is concerned or as an indication of good intent.

Where a buyer wishes to provide his or her supplier with the security of payment by documentary credit, but at the same time requires a period of credit, he or she may instruct his or her bank to issue a credit calling for a bill of exchange drawn at so many days after sight instead of the usual sight draft; this would, of course, be an irrevocable credit. In this case, the beneficiary, when presenting the documents, would not receive immediate cash as under a sight credit but his or her term bill would be accepted by the bank. It could then be discounted in the money market at the finest rates. Thus the beneficiary would still receive payment, but the buyer would not be called upon to pay until the bill matured – see the documentary credit flow chart illustrated in Figure 12.2.

12.6.7 Methods of settlement and availability of documentary credits

According to UCP500 (article 10) documentary credit may be made available in one of four ways as detailed below.

1. *Sight payment.* Payment is made to the seller locally upon presentation of conforming documents. A sight draft is usually called for although payment can be made against documents alone. If payment to the seller is made before the account is debited, interest will be charged from the date of payment to the date that the paying bank is reimbursed. If the buyer wishes, he or she can authorize the paying bank to claim payment by tele-transmission and have the seller's account debited upon receipt of the claim.

2. *Deferred payment credit.* This type of credit does not require the presentation of a draft. The nominated bank is authorized to debit the issuing bank's account at a future date against presentation of conforming documents. The date for payment is defined in the documentary credit, usually as a specific number of days after the date of despatch of goods or after the date of presentation of the documents. It has become increasingly popular where the buyer does not wish the credit period to be represented by a bill of exchange as usually, under local law, it attracts stamp duty.

    Consequently, when documents are presented 'in order' by the seller, the bank does not accept a bill of exchange but instead gives a letter of undertaking to the seller advising him or her when he or she will receive his or her money. The main disadvantage is that, should the exporter wish to receive his or her money immediately, he or she does not have a bill of exchange to have discounted. Hence, if the credit is unconfirmed, the undertaking to effect payment on the due date is that of the issuing bank. Payment will only be effected on the due date by the nominated bank after taking account of the same factors involving sight payments. However, if the credit is confirmed, the

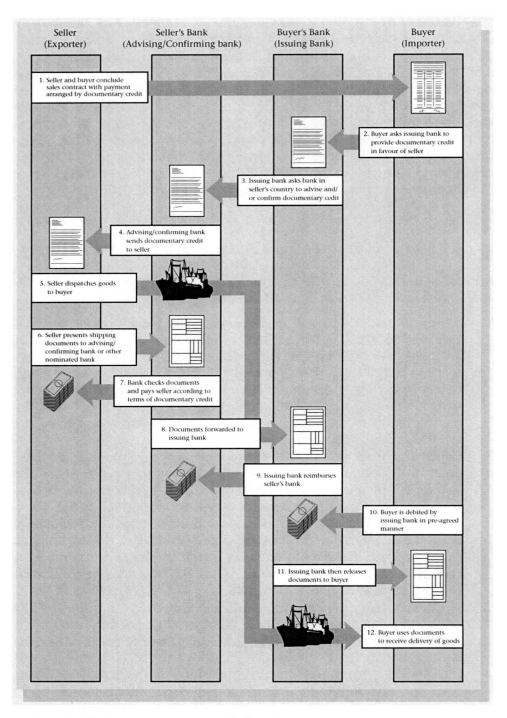

FIGURE 12.2 Documentary credit flowchart
Reproduced courtesy HBSC Midland Bank plc

undertaking to pay is made by the confirming bank. Payment will then be made on the due date by the nominated bank (if any) or by the confirming bank.

3. *Negotiation Sight or usance drafts* may be drawn and negotiated by a bank. The credit may be made freely negotiable with any bank or negotiation may be restricted to a bank nominated by the issuing bank. Under this type of credit, the seller is responsible for any negotiation interest unless the negotiating bank is specially authorized by the buyer to charge interest to his or her account.

4. *Acceptance credits.* This type of credit requires a presentation of a usance draft drawn on the bank nominated as accepting bank. The draft is accepted by the bank, payable at a future date, usually fixed in the documentary credit as a specific number of days from the date of despatch of goods.

Originally this facility was provided by merchant banks. The bank establishes its own credit in favour of the exporter. The credit provides for bills to be drawn by the exporter on the bank which are accepted by the latter and can then be discounted in the money market at the finest rates. It is usual for such credits to run parallel with the bills drawn by the exporter on his or her overseas buyer and which he or she lodges with the bank for collection. The bills under the credit will be drawn on the same terms as those of the buyers and in due course the payment received for the commercial bills will meet the dues to the bank on its acceptances. Exporters who take advantage of finance from their bank under a documentary credit will be charged interest on the amount advanced. The period for which interest is charged will vary for each transaction.

In situations where the buyer has requested an amendment to the documentary credit, it is important that the exporter in varying the payment terms under the documentary credit does not relinquish control of the goods. When an amendment has been received, the following check list must be followed: (a) have all the relevant points been covered; (b) is the exporter in complete agreement with the new terms; (c) has the amendment been made to a confirmed documentary credit, and if so, has the confirming bank chosen to extend its confirmation to cover the amended terms; (d) does the amendment extend the expiry date of the documentary credit, and is this covered by the bank's confirmation; and (e) if the documentary credit is being amended because of the fault of the buyer, can the exporter ensure that all costs related to the amendment are borne by the buyer, including the advising bank's charges.

If the documentary credit is irrevocable, the exporter does not have to accept any amendments, and the exporter has the right to reject any amendment up to and including the presentation of the documents. However, if an amendment has several elements to it, the exporter may either reject or accept all of them.

12.7 Transferable credits

Article 48 of UCP500 covers the provisions of transferable credits, which we will now examine. These arise where the exporter or seller is obtaining the goods from a third party, say the actual manufacturer, and as a middleman, does not have the resources to buy outright and await payment from his or her overseas buyer. Part or all of their rights and obligations under the credit are transferred to the actual supplier of the goods (transferee). The credit is established in favour of the middleman seller (prime beneficiary), and authorizes the advising bank to accept instructions from the prime beneficiary to make the credit available, in whole or in part, to one or more third parties (second beneficiaries). The credit is then advised to the second beneficiary in the terms and conditions of the original, except that the amount and unit price are reduced and the shipment and expiry dates shortened. The original credit is for the price the buyer is paying to the prime beneficiary, but the latter will be obtaining the goods at a lower price and so the credit is transferred for a smaller amount. When the second beneficiary presents shipping documents, he or she obtains payment for his or her invoice price, and the prime beneficiary is called upon to substitute his or her own invoice and receive the difference (i.e. profit). The negotiating bank then has documents in accordance with the original credit.

Where there is more than one second beneficiary, the credit must permit part shipments. If the prime beneficiary does not wish his or her buyer and supplier to be aware of each other, he or she may request that his or her name be substituted for that of the opener on the transfer credit, and that shipping documents be in the name of a third party, blank endorsed.

In the event that the name of the ultimate supplier is known, the buyer can restrict the transfer to that party. Otherwise the buyer could be faced with receiving goods from an unknown supplier without knowledge as to their integrity or ability to provide goods of the required quality. Any subsequent presentation of documents may be made by the transferee rather than the original beneficiary.

12.8 Back-to-back credits

Back-to-back credits arise in circumstances similar to those of the transferable credit and particularly where the supplier as well as the buyer is overseas. In this case, the middleman receives a credit in his or her favour from the buyer and asks his or her bank to establish a credit in favour of his or her supplier against the security of the credit in his or her own favour. Thus, the documentary credit is issued on the back of and against the security of another documentary credit (the Master documentary credit) on the understanding that reimbursement will stem from the documents presented under the Master documentary credit. Both documentary credits cover the shipment of the same goods. There are two separate credits, not one as in the case of a transferable credit, and this can create problems in the matching of documents and credit terms.

Consider the example of a trader who identified that metals readily available in Eastern Europe were urgently required in India. However, in view of the sums involved, the seller insisted that payment by the trader be by means of a Letter of Credit. As the ultimate buyer in India was also willing to issue a Letter of Credit in favour of the trader, the two documents were matched and the deal was successfully concluded to the satisfaction of the East European supplier, Indian buyer and the traders. Back-to-back Letters of Credit are complicated and exporters are advised to contact their international bank for advice.

12.9 Revolving credits

Revolving credits are used where there are shipments in a series at intervals and the parties wish the programme to proceed without interruption. An example would be a structured work flow such as a production run or growth season. A credit is established for a certain sum and quantity of goods with a provision that, when a shipment has been made and documents presented and paid, the credit automatically becomes re-available in its original form and another shipment can be made, and so on.

Such credits can revolve either by time or by amount. In the case of a credit which revolves by time, a stated amount is available in a given period. The full amount is then automatically available when a new period is entered. A credit which revolves by amount is usually expressed as being available up to a fixed amount for anyone drawing.

If the credit revolves automatically the amount drawn immediately becomes available again on the conditions specified in the credit. For credits which do not revolve automatically, each instalment can only be reinstated by way of an amendment to the credit. This option gives the client more control over the operation of the credit.

A further variant is a cumulative revolving credit which, for credits which revolve by time, allows undrawn amounts in a particular time period to be carried forward to a subsequent period. A non-cumulative credit means that any undrawn portion cannot be carried forward in this way.

12.10 Red clause credits

Originally a feature of the Australian wool trade, red clause credits contain a clause (traditionally written in red ink) authorizing the nominated bank to advance a proportion of the value of the credit to the seller before shipping documents are presented. This enables the seller to purchase raw materials or to pay other costs (e.g. transportation) prior to receiving full payment once confirming documents have been presented.

Advances of this nature are entirely at the buyer's risk and are generally made against a simple statement from the seller that they will refund the amount if they do not ship the goods as required. Unless the buyer has made other arrangements, the buyer's account will be debited as soon as an advance has been made.

Advance payments under a credit are more common where they are payable to the seller upon production of a bank guarantee. In this case, the buyer would be able to claim from the guarantor bank if the seller did not repay the advance. If the buyer has any reason to doubt the standing of the guarantor bank, it would be advisable to have such guarantees issued (not simply advised) through the buyer's bank or another major bank well-known to the buyer.

12.11 Bank finance for exports factoring and forfaiting

Theoretically, a company should be able to finance all its operations from the resources available to it, that is, its capital plus whatever it is able to borrow from the bank. Its capital will depend on how much the members of the company are prepared to invest in the enterprise, and its borrowing from the bank will depend on such factors as the balance sheet figures, profit and loss, turnover, etc. or on the security it can offer by way of mortgages, life policies and stocks. Both these sources are subject to strict limitations and, for reasons already mentioned above, they are bound to prove inadequate for a company expanding its export trade. To meet the cash flow problems engendered by long credit terms, extra sources of finance must be tapped over and above the basic sources of capital and bank lending. This finance can best be found through channels relative to the export transactions themselves and, in particular, to the method of payment. Let us examine the various methods by which payment is made and what type of finance it is linked to.

1. *Sales on open account.* Here the exporter is entirely dependent on the goodwill of the buyer to remit payment when due. Admittedly, the outstanding debts will increase the debtor item on the company's balance sheet and may, therefore, enable it to obtain additional overdraft facilities from the bank. The best answer to the problem of finance in this case would be by the use of the services of a factoring company or credit insurance resource (pp. 283–85).
2. *Collection by means of bills of exchange drawn on the buyer.* Extra finance may be obtained by discounting the bills with the bank or

obtaining loan accommodation against the bills outstanding for collection. The bank has some element of security in the documents, covering the goods, which are attached to the bills. The common short form bill of lading has replaced in some trades the traditional shipping company 'long form' bills. It is identical in legal and practical terms to the traditional bills but is simpler and can be used with any shipping line. The possibility of obtaining bank finance in this way is enhanced if the export sale is covered by a credit insurance policy, the rights under the policy being assigned to the bank.

3. *Documentary credits.* Under a confirmed irrevocable letter of credit, the exporter is assured of payment immediately he or she has shipped the goods and presents correct documents to the bank and so his or her need for finance is reduced. With an unconfirmed letter of credit, however, payment is still subject to the risk of non-transfer by the issuing bank, but in these circumstances provision may be available under a basic credit insurance policy. In both cases the exporters may be able to obtain some extra help from his or her bank to produce and ship the goods on the strength of the payment assured under the credit.

As outlined above, export finance is also available from merchant banks by means of an acceptance credit facility.

The services of a confirming house, which acts for the buyer, will provide payment promptly on shipment as the confirming house arranges the credit terms required by the buyer. Exporting through an export merchant will also provide ready cash as the merchant will buy the goods (making it a home sale) and handle the sale to the overseas buyer him- or herself.

12.12 Standby letters of credit

This type of credit differs from other types, in that the buyer and seller hope it will never be drawn upon. A standby letter of credit performs a similar function to a bank guarantee, but is issued in a format corresponding to that of a documentary credit. Standby credit provides a safeguard for the seller, by offering a financial remedy if the buyer does not honour its contractual obligations. Standby letters of credit are often used as security for open account trading where the seller requires some kind of 'back up' in the event of the buyer not paying for the goods. They normally require the issuing bank to make payment to the seller upon presentation of documents evidencing non-payment by the importer. They are also commonly used in some countries as a substitute for a bank guarantee which, due to the regulations in that country are not generally acceptable; a prime example of this method is seen in the USA. Standby credit is not intended to form the payment mechanism for a transaction.

In such instances, standby letters of credit have the advantage of being subject to the Uniform Customs and Practice for Documentary Credits Brochure 400, whereas at the moment there are no internationally agreed regulations for bank guarantees.

12.13 Counter-trade

During the past ten years the volume of world trade conducted under counter-trade terms has much increased. Today it features in the trading techniques of over 100 countries and represents up to 10 per cent of world trade. Basically, counter-trade is an umbrella term for a whole range of commercial mechanisms for reciprocal trade. These mechanisms include barter, counter-purchase, offset, buyback, evidence accounts and switch trading. The common characteristic of counter-trade arrangements is that export sales to a particular market are made conditional upon undertakings to accept imports from that market. For example, an exporter may sell machinery to country X on condition that it accepts agricultural products from country X in payment. Simple barter deals like this are unusual, and most counter-trade deals are much more involved.

Exporters are aware of the potential demands for and the complexities of counter-trade, since it has over recent years become a common feature of trade with more than half the countries in the world. Counter-trade can be a complex, expensive and uncertain mode of trading. It has the potential to distort and disrupt the growth of trade, inasmuch as it replaces the pressures of competition and market forces with reciprocity, protection and price setting. It introduces an unfair bias against small- and medium-sized firms who may be less able to handle the additional costs and staff effort entailed. It increases the risks that subsidized (often low-grade) goods will be dumped in the home market (although most of these in practice go to Third World markets).

Counter-trade is an inherently *ad hoc* activity. The mechanics vary according to local regulations and requirements, the nature of the goods to be exported and the current priorities of the parties involved.

12.13.1 Forms of counter-trade

Counter-purchase

Concurrently with, and as a condition of, securing a sales order, the exporter undertakes to purchase goods and services from the country concerned. There are two parallel but separate contracts, one for the principal order which is paid for on normal cash or credit terms, and another for the counter-purchase. The value of the counter-purchase undertaking may vary between 10 per cent and 100 per cent (or even more) of the original export order. The agreement can vary from a general declaration of intent to a binding contract specifying the goods and services to be supplied, the markets in which they may be sold, the penalties for non-performance and, perhaps, other matters. The goods offered may be quite unrelated to those exported, and the agreement may involve parties unrelated to the sales contract. Counter-purchase is the most common mode of counter-trade, particularly with Eastern Europe and with a number of developing countries, notably Indonesia.

Barter

The direct exchange of goods for goods. The principal exports are paid for with goods (or services) supplied from the importing market. A single contract covers both flows; in the simplest case no cash is involved. In practice, supply of the principal exports is often held up until sufficient revenue has been earned from selling the bartered goods. Though less common than counter-purchase, barter has been sought by some African and Latin American countries with extensive currency restrictions, and by some oil-dependent countries.

Buyback

A form of barter, in which suppliers of capital plant or equipment agree to repayment in the future output of the investment concerned. For example, exporters of equipment for a chemical works may be repaid with part of the resulting output from that work. Most common in connection with exports of process plant, mining equipment and similar orders, buyback arrangements tend to be much longer term and for much larger amounts than counter-purchase or simple barter deals. The CIS favours long-term buyback on policy grounds as a form of industrial cooperation.

Offset

A condition of exporting some products, especially those embodying advanced technology, to some markets is that the exporter incorporates into his final products specified materials, components or sub-assemblies, procured within the importing country. This has long been an established feature of trade in defence systems and aircraft, but it is becoming more common in other sectors, especially where the importing country is seeking to develop its own industrial capabilities. A variant of offset arises in some large contracts, for which the importing country often demands that successful bidders establish local production and other forms of long-term industrial cooperation.

Switch trading (or swap deals)

Imbalances in long-term bilateral trading agreements, usually between East European countries and developing nations, sometimes lead to the accumulation of uncleared credit surpluses in one or other country; for example, Brazil at one time had a large credit surplus with Poland. Such surpluses can sometimes be tapped by third parties, so that (for example) French exports to Brazil might be financed from the sale of Polish goods to France or elsewhere. Such transactions are known as 'switch' or 'swap' deals, because they typically involve switching the documentation (and destination) of goods on the high seas. Switch deals can be very complex, involving a chain of buyers, sellers and brokers in different markets.

Evidence accounts

Companies or traders with a significant level of continuing business in certain markets may be required to arrange counter-purchased exports from those markets at least equivalent to their own imports with the country concerned. For example, a multinational firm with a local manufacturing subsidiary in a developing country may be required to ensure counter-purchased exports of equivalent value to their subsidiary's imports of materials and equipment. Since it is not practical to balance this kind of trade item by item, the firm may maintain an 'evidence account', debiting its own imports and crediting the exports it has arranged over a period. The evidence account must be maintained more or less in balance year by year.

There are many variants to these broad categories, depending on the market, the exports concerned, outside circumstances (e.g. trends in commodity prices) and the expertise of those involved. It is not unusual for a large export deal to involve several counter-trade arrangements (e.g. some long-term buyback, plus some counter-purchase or barter to finance initial down payments). In general terms, counter-trade is sought for one or more of four main reasons.

1. To finance trade which, due to lack of commercial credit or convertible currency, would otherwise be precluded.
2. To exploit a buyers' market to obtain better terms of trade or similar benefits.
3. To protect or stimulate the output of domestic industries (including agriculture and minerals extraction).
4. As a reflection of political and economic policies which seek to plan and balance overseas trade.

The particular consideration applying, and the national counter-trade requirements to which they give rise, vary in every market. An understanding of the particular issues in a given country can often enable an exporter to propose more flexible or cheaper alternatives to onerous counter-trade obligations which none the less satisfy the needs of the importer or his or her principals.

12.13.2 Counter-trade markets

Western industrial markets

Counter-trade remains unusual in trade between the industrialized countries, which transact 75 per cent of their trade between one another. The major exceptions have arisen in defence, aviation and large high technology deals, which often involve an element of direct offset or closely related counter-purchase. In recent years, some European countries (notably Portugal and Greece) have sought counter-purchase for other large export orders, but only on an *ad hoc* basis. Australia and New Zealand, which require offset for public sector purchases, are the only OECD countries with mandatory counter-trade requirements.

East European markets

Counter-trade has been an established feature of trade with the East European markets since 1945, and affects on average something over 25 per cent of their trade with the West.

Developing countries

The main growth in counter-trade demands in recent years has come from the less developed countries (LDCs) of Latin America, Africa and Asia, largely reflecting the effects on their external trade of the international recession. Common factors have been the LDCs' inability to secure or to service trade credit due to accumulated debt problems; loss of currency-earning capabilities because of depressed commodity markets; and a wish to improve their access to Western markets and industrial know-how. Although many LDCs have on occasion sought counter-trade arrangements – usually commodity counter-purchase or barter – the number of deals actually transacted has been constrained by the lack of effective organizational arrangements in the LDCs and by their inability to provide sufficient marketable goods for the counter-purchase. Indonesia was the first LDC to introduce mandatory counter-trade requirements and has since been followed by a number of others; a further group have more or less formal administrative rules with a similar effect. But even in Indonesia, less than 10 per cent of external trade has in practice involved counter-trade.

Oil exporters

In certain oil-producing countries – especially Libya and Iran – exporters bidding for public sector contracts may be asked to accept oil in exchange for goods. There may be several motives for this, the most likely being a desire on the part of the oil producers to secure an assured outlet for their oil at a high rate. By comparison with most other commodities, oil is a relatively serviceable means of exchange, since the size, sophistication and efficiency of the world oil market means that it can be converted into cash fairly easily. Oil barter deals are in essence straightforward transactions; goods are exchanged for oil rather than cash. All the normal considerations which apply to cash deals, notably the need to earn a profit, should be applied to oil barter. The addition, however, of two extra parties to the contract, the oil-producing company and the oil-distributing company, whose interest in the contract do not necessarily coincide with those of the principal participants (i.e. the exporter and the end-buyer), inevitably complicates the issue. The responsibility for overcoming those complications normally rests with the exporter, since he or she is the link between the other three parties.

Counter-trade is a growth market and one for the experienced professional. Approximately one in ten succeed and even the successful transactions can prove more expensive and more difficult than originally foreseen. Major risks include: loss of profits on the principal exports because the costs of counter-trade have not been anticipated; contractual commitments to purchase large quantities of unmarketable goods without any means of disposing of them; and cancellation of export orders because of other parties' failures to meet counter-trade obligations.

A few large exporting firms which regularly encounter counter-trade demands, for example, those regularly trading with East European markets, maintain an in-house capability to handle counter-traded goods on their own account. For the great majority of exporters, however, it is strongly advisable to obtain the assistance of outside specialists. Specialist services of different kinds are offered by trading houses, brokers, consultants and/or agents, bankers and suppliers of market intelligence, usually for a fixed fee or commission.

Additional costs, which exporters should anticipate, will arise from the discount or 'disagio' necessary to dispose of the goods taken in counter-trade. The disagio reflects the marketability of the goods concerned and varies between 2–3 per cent for certain high-grade minerals and commodities to as much as 25–30 per cent for low-quality manufactured goods and machinery. The exporter will be advised to include as far as possible sufficient margin in his or her selling price to cover these costs, but the scope for this can be constrained in competitive bidding.

The simplest method of handling counter-purchase undertakings is to assign the obligation – for a fee – to a third-party trading house or broker, whereafter the exporter need have no further involvement in the counter-trade transaction. Sometimes the third-party trader can be an open signatory to the counter-purchase contract, but often the 'demandeur' country will insist on dealing only with the exporter. Where local counter-trade requirements are not clear-cut or institutionalized, that is in most markets, extended and sensitive negotiations will be necessary, in parallel with those over the exports, before arrangements are settled. The retention of specialized advice during these negotiations will usually pay for itself, if only through the avoidance of costly mistakes. Often the exporter's bankers will be able to advise what support is appropriate and make the necessary arrangements.

12.14 Factoring

The practice of exporters using factoring companies is very much on the increase. Their prime function is to administer the sales ledgers and collect payments once the goods have been shipped. Such factoring companies provide a complete range of services which cover those aspects of exporting, so leaving the manufacturer free to concentrate on export production and sales. For a small service charge of between 0.75 and 3 per cent of turnover, they will provide multi-currency and multi-language sales accounting backed by credit management, which is exercised in the customer's country by the factor's own employees or agents. Also included in this service charge, embracing the administrative and credit cover service, is 100 per cent protection against losses due to the insolvency of the customer and, in some cases, protection against political risk and exchange rate fluctuations. For advances against invoices until they are paid, the factoring company usually charges 1.5 per cent over the base rate. Factoring cannot effectively meet the particular needs of every industry and the most suitable companies are likely to have an expanding turnover in excess of £200 000 and to be selling consumer goods, light industrial products or services on short-term open account credit to buyers in the developed countries of the world. Products include textiles, clothing, food distribution, consumer durables, engineering and electronic equipment. Euler Hermes is a market leader in factoring (see p. 284).

Basically, factoring operates on the principle that an exporter has an agreement with a factoring company to buy all the exporter's receivables in agreed market(s). The factor becomes responsible for collecting customer payments and taking the credit risk, while the factor will pay the exporter 'on account' a proportion (usually up to 85 per cent) of the credit approved sales immediately upon delivery – if the exporter so wishes – with the balance being paid when the customer pays the factor or becomes insolvent. If the buyer does not pay, the factor effects payment of the balance after a set period (typically 120 days) from the date payment fell due, which allows time for any problems to be resolved between the commercial parties. Factoring has five key features: export credit assessment of one's customers; 100 per cent protection against customer failure; efficient collection of outstanding invoices; flexible finance geared to one's volume of sales; and cover against foreign exchange risks.

The advantages to the exporter of using a factoring service are; that it expands sales in overseas markets by offering prospective customers the same terms and conditions as local competitors; offers open account terms, merely invoicing the customer and granting credit terms typical in the customer's market; is fully covered against credit losses; improves cash flow by fast collection and remittance, as well as through savings in administration costs; and it provides a flexible source of working capital linked directly to the growth in export sales.

Export factoring is most suited for short-term debts (typically up to 90 days) involving the sale of products or services which are complete at the point of invoicing and for trade with those parts of the world in which an open account is the accepted method of transacting business. Most factors operate a 'two factor' system whereby a correspondent factor in the buyer's country is used to assess the credit standing of the buyer. Factoring can also provide finance where credit protection is already available to an exporter through a credit insurance policy.

Factoring will also help importers and buyers by expanding their purchasing power without using existing bank credit lines; enabling them to buy goods without incurring the delays and complications of opening lines of credit; generating new sources of product supply; and providing a local point for payment in their own country.

Many factoring companies are members of a worldwide organization called Factors Chain International (FCI), formed in 1968 with 80 member factoring companies located in 30 countries (p. 562). Membership of such an organization provides expertise in each of the 30 countries in the business of managing trade credit and, for the exporter, lessens the problems which can arise through differences in language, law and trade practice thereby facilitating the exporter's development of overseas business.

12.15 Forfaiting

Forfaiting is a method of international trade finance involving the discounting of bank-guaranteed overseas trade bills or notes. It has no recourse to the exporter as he or she surrenders or relinquishes his or her right in return for cash payment from the forfaiter. In such circumstances, the exporter agrees to surrender his or her rights to claims for payment on goods or services which have been delivered to the buyer. Any type of trade debt can be forfaited (i.e. surrendered for cash) but the most common is trade payee; bill of exchange accepted by the buyer; or promissory notes from the buyer. A forfaiter can provide finance for any type and duration of trade transaction but usually credit is provided for the export of capital goods which require finance for periods of between three and ten years.

Forfaiting is a simple form of trade finance involving the purchase of trade receivables from the beneficiary on a totally without recourse basis. It has developed into an alternative method of financing trade and is used throughout the world. It can be applied in the sale of capital goods, small projects, commodities, service contracts and even lease contracts. Traditionally, it is a means of providing medium-term (three to five years) and fixed rate finance, but transactions are now also structured on a floating rate interest bearing basis and for shorter and longer periods of credit (90 days to ten years).

The financial instruments evidencing the obligations of the foreign buyer are predominantly promissory notes or bills of exchange. Such transactions can be structured using deferred payment letters of credit and by assigning the debt in the books of a supplier owed to him under the financial terms and conditions of a supply contract. In addition to such instruments, the 'aval' or irrevocable and unconditional guarantee of the foreign buyer's local bank is required, unless the buyer is of such financial standing and international repute that a guarantee is considered unnecessary.

Although the full sale price can be financed, in a typical forfaiting transaction the supplier receives 10–20 per cent of his or her sale price in cash as a down-payment shortly after signing the supply contract. After manufacture and at the time of delivery of the goods involved, the supplier then receives promissory notes or bills of exchange evidencing the remaining 80–90 per cent due. These promissory notes or bills of exchange usually have incorporated into their face value an element of interest mutually agreed between the supplier and the foreign buyer. A series of promissory notes or bills of exchange is issued evidencing the various repayments during the agreed period of credit (e.g. two-year period of credit – four promissory notes or bills of exchange maturing six, 12, 18 and 24 months after delivery of the goods).

The supplier sells the series of promissory notes or bills of exchange to a forfaiting bank on a without recourse basis. The forfaiting bank deducts interest in the form of a discount at a fixed rate for the entire period of credit involved. The discount rate can be fixed at the time of delivery of the promissory notes or bills of exchange for purchase or up to 12–18 months in advance, thus enabling the supplier to build the discount costs into their sale price. The bank forfaiting may hold the promissory notes or bills of exchange until maturity or may sell them, again on a non-recourse basis, to another forfaiter. The ultimate holder in due course presents them for payment at maturity to the bank at which they are domiciled.

The processing of a forfait transaction is as described below.

1. Commitment letter including fixed discount rate given by forfaiting company to the supplier.
2. Sales contract agreed between the supplier and the foreign buyer.
3. Goods manufactured and delivered.
4. In exchange for title to the goods, a series of promissory notes or bills of exchange is delivered to the supplier.
5. Supplier endorses promissory notes or bills of exchange to the forfaiting company on a without recourse basis.
6. Forfaiting deducts interest at the discount rate agreed at (1) from the face value of the promissory notes or bills of exchange and pays the discounted proceeds to the supplier.
7. At maturity, the forfaiting company presents each promissory note or bill of exchange for payment.
8. Forfaiting company receives payment.

The documentation used in forfaiting is given below.

1. a note or bill purchase agreement executed between the forfaiting company and the supplier (two to three pages);
2. promissory notes or bills of exchange;
3. guarantee or aval;
4. signature confirmations and authentications;
5. copies of necessary governmental approvals.

An 'aval' is an unconditional and irrevocable guarantee written on the face of a promissory note or bill of exchange. As transfer of the guarantee is effected purely by endorsement of the promissory notes or bills of exchange, the aval is the preferred method of guarantee.

The wording of avals is as follows:

(i) Promissory note
Per aval
(name and signature of the guarantor)

(ii) Bill of exchange
Per aval for (name of the drawee/foreign buyer)
(name and signature of the guarantor)

12.16 Guarantee

In some countries the term 'aval' has no legal significance and, in these instances, the guarantee of the guarantor has to be incorporated into a separate document.

Guarantees (and bonds) are used extensively in international trade to secure performance or other obligations. They provide the beneficiary with access to a sum of money should the principal (applicant) fail to fulfil contractual or other obligations in respect of an underlying transaction, contract or order. Such guarantees usually promise payment on demand, i.e. upon presentation by the beneficiary of a simple written demand for payment, or against a written demand accompanied by documentary evidence that the sum is owing. A bank guarantee is, by its nature, a separate transaction from the commercial contract on which it may be based. The bank (the guarantor) is not in any way connected with or bound by this contract, even though it may be referred to in the guarantee.

Unlike documentary credits, guarantees do not, in general, follow any specific format or wording; they tend to be constructed case-by-case. In some countries, guarantees may be subject to local laws and jurisdiction irrespective of what the guarantee might state. For example, some legal systems do not recognize expiry dates on guarantees which can pose problems if release from liability is difficult to obtain from the beneficiary.

The following are the essential requirements of such letters of guarantee: they are irrevocable; unconditional; fully transferable; abstract (the guarantee must not be dependant on performance of the underlying supply contract); and divisible (each individual repayment amount and date must be specified). A summary of the most popular guarantee types is given below:

1. Tender guarantee to support an initial bid or tender for a contract.
2. Advance payment guarantee secures repayment of any monetary advance.
3. Performance guarantee covers a failure to fulfil contractual obligations.
4. VAT/duty deferment bond allows VAT/duty payable on imports to be deferred.
5. Retention monies guarantee secures the release of any monies withheld pending completion of a contract.
6. Carnet or customs guarantee removes the need to pay duty on goods or vehicles imported into countries on a temporary basis (see p. 245).

12.16.1 On Demand Contract Bonds

There are many types of bonds and guarantees, both related and not related to contracts, on demand and conditional. An on-demand bond is sometimes called an independent guarantee. The purpose of the bond is to provide the customer with a degree of security, perhaps in respect of costs he may have incurred or payments that he may have made in advance to the exporter, or for the proper performance of the contract (or of the goods supplied under the contract) by the exporter. It provides a ready redress for the exporter's failure to perform his obligations under the export contract.

Bidder Tender Bond

The bid or tender bond arises when a customer opens a request for tenders for the supply of equipment or the performance of services. In expectation of receiving a number of tender responses, and to accelerate the procedure to select the winning bidder, and avoid the circumstances whereby the exporter refuses to take the contract, the customer insists the bidder provides a bid bond for a small percentage of the price usually up to 3 per cent. A feature of the bid or tender bond is the tendency for customers to specify that the bond could also be called if the successful exporter fails to provide an advance payment bond or a performance bond before providing a bid bond.

Progress Payment Bond

Progress Payment Bond is issued in exchange for a progress payment during the construction of a plant. If work to the value of the payments has been completed, any requirement for a progress payment bond should be resisted.

Performance Bond

The performance bond objective is to permit the customer redress in the event the exporter fails to perform the contract in accordance with its terms. It is usually given at the time the equipment is delivered and will run for either a set period – maybe one year – or until some time after the schedule completion or commissioning date for the project. It is usually for 10 per cent of the contract price. The objective of the bond is to secure the customers' rights against the exporter, akin to liquidation damages. Today, there is a tendency for customers to require the performance bond to be provided at the same time as the advance payment guarantee (as above). Some performance bonds are also used to guarantee the performance of the equipment once it has been installed or commissioned.

Warranty Bond

A warranty bond arises in support of an exporters warranty obligations and its validity is likely to match the warranty period. It may be used in exchange for the expiring performance bond as specified in the bond. It may be possible to combine the performance bond and warranty bond. In such a situation the 10 per cent performance bond reduces to 5 per cent upon completion, and then continues as the warranty bond until the end of the warranty period. This reduces administration costs and eliminates the need to have two bonds outstanding at the same time.

Retention Bond

The retention bond is similar to a warranty bond except that unusually it is a bond that might be volunteered by the exporter. If the payment terms involve a 5 per cent or 10 per cent payment which is retained by the customer for maybe one year after delivery of the equipment the customer will thereby have the security of knowing that they can recover the money in the event of equipment failure.

The Surety Bond

The surety bond is used in the construction and civil engineering industries to guarantee the contractual terms are executed. It provides for financial protection for the beneficiary against loss due to the inability of the principal to discharge damages for breach of contract. Surety bonds are also used to facilitate deferment of duty payable such as petroleum, tobacco and alcohol.

Gw Demand Bonds

Gw demand bonds are issued by banks. These are by institutions. They are willing to issue unconditional undertakings under which they will be required to pay simply if requested to do so, because they will have passed the risk of having to pay back to the exporter by way of an indemnity which the exporter has given to the bank.

FIATA NVOCC Bond

A recent bond adopted by the freight forwarding industry is termed the FIATA NVOCC Bond. It was introduced by FIATA to help those forwarders operating to the USA who are required to post a US$50 000 bond with the Federal Maritime Commission. It took two years to negotiate with Intercargo of the USA following the passage into law of the FIATA sponsored Bonding Amendment Act. The bond is only available to BIFA trading members.

12.17 Less common methods of trade

Consignment trade

Consignment trade describes the situation whereby goods sent are by an exporter to a nominal importer in another country, that nominal importer being, in fact, a nominee or agent of the exporter. The intention is that the merchandise shall come into the physical possession of the agent whose duty it is to sell the merchandise on the exporter's behalf and remit to his principal the proceeds of sale, less all expenses of handling, storing and transport, customs duties and fees and his commission.

Participation

Participation implies a joint venture where a British manufacturer takes a share with a local concern in either marketing the exporter's product, local assembly or local manufacture.

Licensing

Licensing is where a licence is granted to an overseas company to manufacture the products on a royalty basis using either the manufacturer's brand name or the name of the licensee (p. 419).

12.18 International exchange rates

The subject of foreign exchange relates to the exchange of various currencies one for another. On the practical side it concerns the methods of settling foreign debts, the means of payment and the services of banks and brokers. Settlement of debts between parties in the same country is quite simply effected by the payment of money, which the creditor is prepared to accept as it is the legal tender of the country. Where the payer and recipient live in different countries and use different currencies, however, there arises the need for a system of conversion – the foreign exchange market. Unlike the markets in commodities or stocks and shares, the foreign exchange market has no centre but consists merely of telephonic/electronic communications between dealers (at the banks) and brokers.

12.18.1 Rate of exchange

The price of one currency in terms of another is called the rate of exchange; it is the number of units of one currency that will be exchanged for a given number of units of another currency. Hence rates against sterling are the number of foreign currency units to the pound. A glance at the financial press shows that two closing rates are quoted for each currency; the higher is the market's buying rate for that currency and the lower the market's selling rate. Transactions between dealers are conducted at approximately these rates. A banker who is asked to buy or sell foreign currency relies upon the market for cover, and the prices at which he or she can obtain this cover are market rates. Hence in quoting to his or her customer he or she bases his or her rates on those ruling in the market; adjusted to make provision for profit.

The market rates quoted in the press are 'spot' rates, i.e. those applied to transactions for completion immediately or at the latest within two working days from the date of the deal. If the exchange rate has moved in your favour between the signing of a contract and its settlement date, an exceptional benefit over and above that anticipated from the contract terms may be derived. Equally the exchange rate may have moved in the opposite direction, adversely affecting the profitability of the underlying contract. As currency is a commodity like any other, its price will be governed by the interaction of demand and supply and hence by short- and long-term factors influencing buyers and sellers. The short-term factors fall into two categories: commercial and financial.

Commercial operations

Commercial operations relate to trade in goods and services which make up the current account of the balance of payments and give rise to payments and receipts in various currencies, thereby determining supply and demand in the foreign exchange markets. Where a country's total purchases exceed its sales, there will be an excess supply of its currency, which will cause its price to decrease; in other words the rate of exchange will fall. Expectations of future movements in exchange rates give rise to 'leads and lags'; a debtor will pay a foreign currency debt before it is due if he or she expects that currency to appreciate in value (lead) or delay payment if he or she expects it to depreciate (lag).

Financial operations

Financial operations come under a variety of headings.

1. *Stock exchange operations* – the purchase of securities on foreign stock exchanges (bourses) by private or corporate investors in order to yield a return, or in the expectation of a capital appreciation. These are portfolio investments as opposed to 'industrial' investments, which represent capital placed by manufacturers in subsidiary or associated enterprises abroad.
2. *Banking operations* – the transfer of funds by bankers for investment or deposit in foreign centres.
3. *Speculation* – transactions based on the expectation that the exchange rate of a particular currency will change in response to some political or natural event. Whether the operator buys or sells a currency depends on whether he or she anticipates a rise or fall in value.
4. *Interest payments* – interest on loans and dividends from investment.

5. *Loan payments* – the issue of a loan in one country on behalf of a borrower in another gives rise to a payment across the exchanges from the country of the lender to that of the borrower which will have an adverse impact on the exchange rate of the lending country's currency and cause that of the borrowing country to appreciate. This effect would be offset if the proceeds of the loan were used to purchase goods or services from the lending country. Upon repayment of the loan the reverse effect will occur.
6. *Intergovernmental transfers* – governments borrow from, and lend to, each other in the same way as private individuals and trading companies; the payments resulting from such loans have the same effect as that outlined above.
7. *Exchange stabilization* – these are official operations in the foreign exchange market in order to control exchange rate movements by varying the relation between supply and demand. These operations are usually directed at keeping fluctuations to a minimum, although sometimes a government may deliberately seek to raise or lower the exchange rate of its currency.

12.18.2 Forward exchange

In view of the increasing amount of business conducted on credit terms, it is quite likely that a merchant will be liable to pay his or her supplier in the latter's currency at a future date or to receive foreign currency at a future date from a buyer. With exchange rates floating at present, he or she is vulnerable to any changes in currency values that may occur in the interval between conclusion of the contract and the date on which payment is due. It is to provide cover against such exchange risks that the 'forward exchange' market came into existence. The merchant contracts with a bank to purchase or sell one currency in exchange for another at a predetermined rate on an agreed future date. He or she thus knows how much he or she will eventually pay or receive in his or her own currency, and any intervening fluctuations in the exchange rate will not affect him or her.

Forward contracts may be 'fixed' or 'option'. A fixed forward is a contract with a specific performance date. A forward option stipulates a period of time during which performance is to take place, the actual date then being chosen by the customer. It should be clearly understood that the 'option' is not whether the customer deals or not – he or she is fully committed to the transaction – it relates only to the date on which he or she takes or delivers the currency concerned. Basically, the forward contract is one of the simplest hedging techniques allowing the importer or exporter to fix the exchange rate for the sale or purchase of a specific quantity of a currency for delivery at an agreed future date.

As a forward contract is a legally binding contract between the bank and the customer, a bank credit line is required to cover the amount and period of all forward contracts outstanding at any one time. The period of a forward contract can range from one day after spot value up to five years depending on the currencies involved. Maturity of the contract can be arranged either for settlement on a specific date (fixed contract) or on or between two dates (option dated contract) where the precise delivery date is not known.

The key benefit from a forward contract is that the importer or exporter knows in advance the exact value of future transactions in domestic currency terms. As well as eliminating the exchange risk this can aid cash flow management and assist with budgeting, costing and pricing processes. However, one does not have the opportunity to gain from beneficial exchange rate movements during the life of the contract.

12.18.3 Forward rates

The forward exchange rate is linked to the prevailing spot rate and is derived from the interest rate differential between the two currencies over the term of the forward contract. It is not a view of the likely exchange rate movement during that term.

The rates for forward exchange deals are quoted as a premium or discount on the spot rate, i.e. an amount above or below spot; sometimes they are at 'par' with spot. For example, if the forward dollar/sterling rate is quoted at a discount on the spot rate (measured in the conventional way as the number of dollars to a pound) then, in terms of dollars, sterling is cheaper forward than spot. Conversely, if the forward rate is at a premium, sterling is dearer forward than spot. In calculating the rate for a forward deal, a premium is added to the spot rate, whereas a discount is deducted from it. Forward margins (discount or premium) are determined by interest rate differentials and by market expectations of future spot exchange rates. Currencies in which interest rates are relatively low tend to be dearer forward than spot in terms of currencies in which interest rates are relatively high. The press usually quotes forward margins for one, three and six months forward, but by arrangement with the bank it is possible to cover for longer periods, depending on the currency concerned.

A customer who has contracted to buy foreign currency but finds that he or she no longer requires it will still have to take delivery of the currency at the agreed forward rate; he or she can then sell it back to the bank at the ruling spot rate. Similarly, if the customer has not received the foreign currency he or she has contracted to sell, he or she will have to buy the amount required at the ruling spot rate for delivery to the bank. In practice, the bank may merely debit or credit the difference to the customer's account. Where circumstances cause a delay in fulfilment of a contract it may often be extended at an adjusted rate by arrangement with the bank (p. 320).

From the above it will be seen that the forward exchange market enables the ordinary merchant to protect him- or herself against fluctuations in exchange rates. Problems can still arise, however, where expenditure and receipts are expressed in a number of different currencies. One example of this is found in connection with freight charges. For the sake of convenience a shipowner's rates of freight are expressed in a single currency called the 'tariff currency', usually the US dollar. Nevertheless, freight can be paid in another currency, so that agreement has to be reached on the basis for conversion of the sum involved. Where adjustments in relevant currency values have resulted in a reduction in the rates of freight or increases in shipowners' operating costs, it has been the practice of shipowners to increase tariff rates of freight or to introduce or increase a 'currency adjustment factor' (CAF) (pp. 162–63).

A shipowner naturally calculates in terms of his or her own currency and if it depreciates against the tariff unit he or she seeks to impose a surcharge to protect the real value of his or her revenue in relation to his or her expenditure, which may be in a variety of other currencies.

There has been a tendency to regard the CAF as a means of keeping ratios of past rates of exchange fixed for all time. Changes in the terms of trade owing to the different rates of inflation in various countries have not been taken into account when calculating sea freights. Relationships between currencies have, however, changed considerably. When the value of sterling was falling, the system favoured the British exporter in terms of freight rates; when sterling began to appreciate, however, shipowners in other countries applied a currency adjustment. The situation became more complicated when rates of exchange were allowed to float and the dollar was effectively devalued.

12.18.4 Factors influencing level of exchange rates

The level of an exchange rate plays a crucial role in an exporter's strategy. It is a high risk area and exporters continuously study the exchange rate money markets to keep abreast of market trends and the best method available to counter such variations, as discussed earlier (pp. 320–21). Moreover, one must bear in mind that a currency devaluation cheapens exports but increases the cost of imports. This latter point is compounded when a proportion of the exported product contains imported components thereby yielding only a marginal benefit in the export price.

A wide range of factors determine the level of individual country exchange rates. The major ones are detailed below, but it is stressed that the significance of each factor will be determined by local market conditions.

1. The yield on the money markets reflected on the Central Bank interest rate level. This is found in the forward exchange rate which is linked to the prevailing spot rate and is derived from the interest rate differential between the two currencies over the term of the forward contract.
2. The actual central bank interest rate.
3. The Balance of Trade and Balance of Payments performance and constituents. For example, a continuing trade deficit with no evidence of improvement will put pressure on the exchange rate level causing it to decline in value unless remedial measures are taken such as raising interest rates or curbing imports. An example is Japan, with no indigenous sources, relying on imported raw materials and energy for its export base.
4. The indebtedness of the country, such as IMF loans. This applies particularly to LDCs.
5. The short- and long-term market prospects in a country and particularly its composition of agricultural, industrial, commercial and service sectors. Recent trends in many countries have seen an increase in their service sector activities, particularly in tourism, banking and overseas investments. This may occur in a service and manufacturing economy as found in the USA or in primarily agricultural economies involving commodities such as those which exist in many less developed countries in Africa.
6. The economic forecast and range of economic indicators – inflation, interest rates, money supply, employment and production.
7. The government's mandate to manage the economy and the government's competence to actually devise and carry out effective policies to sustain and develop its economy in a competitive global market.
8. Whether the currency is traded on the open market or relies on a third currency such as the US dollar or the euro. Many non-convertible currencies use the US dollar as found in the less developed countries.
9. The general market mood of the currency and its expectation as interpreted by economists, bankers and traders.
10. Any unforeseen situation emerging such as hostilities, earthquake or political developments.
11. The shipping and international trade cycle predictions and trends.
12. Policies adopted by international agencies such as the IMF, the World Bank, WTO and G9.
13. The level of international reserves.
14. The gross and net external debt expressed as a percentage of the gross domestic product.
15. The country's net foreign debt and debt service.
16. The country's net debt service as a percentage of exports of goods and services. This identifies the ability of a country to fund its

indebtedness and the impact it will have on its economy sustainment and growth.

17. Any technological or infrastructure development providing improved prospects for a particular economy such as the provision of a hydro dam, installation of a coal, gas or oil fired energy plant.
18. A country joining a trading bloc such as the European Union.
19. Circumstances which create uncertainty.
20. The monetary policies adopted by a country.
21. The financial market mechanism in a particular country.
22. An analysis of the currency performance and factors determining its variation. Currencies which move from a strong to a weak position usually fall due to a variety of circumstances. The financial markets may decide to sell the weak currency and retain the stronger currency. Such turbulence of currency fluctuation is serious for any major trading currency.
23. A rise in the price of a barrel of crude oil on the world market will undermine the trade balance of some LDCs reliant on oil as an energy resource and may account for more than 25 per cent of their import bill annually.
24. Stock exchange operations, banking operations, interest payments, loan payments, intergovernmental transfers and exchange stabilization (see pp. 321–22 inclusive).

12.18.5 Currency options

In our consideration of exchange rates it is appropriate to consider currency options. A currency option is the right to buy or sell a currency against delivery of a base currency at an agreed exchange rate. The buyer of the option has the right to exercise this option at any date up to and including an agreed date, but he or she has no obligation to do so. The buyer of the option pays a premium for the provision of this right.

Currency options are true options and are different in kind from option date forward contracts which provide an option only as to the date when exchange shall take place, but require exchange at some time within the option period. True options may be regarded as 'whether to exchange' options, as opposed to 'when to exchange' options.

A 'call' option provides the right to buy the currency and sell the base currency at the agreed rate; a 'put' option provides the right to sell the currency and buy the base currency at the agreed rate; Thus, for instance, a treasurer may transact:

Swiss franc call against US dollar (can buy Swiss francs)
Yen call against US dollar (can buy yen)
Canadian dollar put against Swiss Franc (can call Canadian dollar)
Swiss franc against euro (can sell euro)

A currency option is essentially a form of insurance against movements in exchange rates. In this respect, it may be seen as an alternative to forward cover in the foreign exchange market for import and export trade. However, since the holder is not obliged to exercise the option, it is particularly suitable for covering contingent cash flows such as those arising when tendering for a contract.

Advantages of currency options are detailed below:

1. Where cash flow is hedged by a forward contract, the company achieves protection against adverse currency movements – the downside risk is eliminated. Unfortunately, this method also eliminates any upside potential that otherwise would have accrued to the company if exchange rates had moved in its favour.

    By contrast, a principal advantage of an option is that it provides protection against downside risk in the same way as a forward contract, but since there is no obligation to exercise the option, the upside potential is retained.

2. The option buyer knows at the outset what his 'worst case' will be; having paid the premium no further expense is payable. When the main objective is simply to limit downside risk, this is a powerful advantage. In many commercial applications, the option premium can be built in to the pricing process, thus fixing minimum margins.

3. Since there is no obligation to exercise an option, options are ideal for hedging contingent cash flows (which may or may not materialize) such as in tenders.

4. Options may be used as a 'ratchet' to lock up profit to date on a currency position while retaining any remaining upside potential.

The premia for currency options are dependent upon three principal factors:

1. the difference between the exercise price and the current spot price;
2. the time until expiry of the option;
3. the volatility of the exchange rate concerned.

An option premium is normally thought of as consisting of two components, intrinsic value and time value. The intrinsic value is simply the profit difference, if any, between the existing spot price and the exercise price. That is, for a call option where the buyer has the right to buy sterling at a strike price of 1.50 and the current spot price is 1.5275, then the intrinsic value is 2.75 cents. All this means is that a call option at 1.50 exercised today would provide an instant profit of 2.75 cents by selling the option proceeds into today's spot market. So one way to think of intrinsic value is: 'the gain that would result if the option were exercised today'. It is useful when evaluating the relative attractiveness of options at different strike prices to strip out the intrinsic value so that the time value alone can be seen.

Time value is more complicated. It is a measure of the amount the exchange rate might be expected to move in the holder's favour during the balance of the time to run. It is therefore apparent that time value will depend not only on the time to expiry, but also the expected volatility of the exchange rate. The more volatile the exchange rate, the greater is the chance that a given level might be reached during the time left to run. It also follows from this reasoning that the greater the current loss at any time (i.e. the further the price will have to rise in order to profit from exercise of the option), the lower will be the likelihood of this happening so that the time premium will be correspondingly lower to reflect this.

A number of theoretical models have been used in the field of stock options which attempt, with varying degrees of success, to estimate time value depending on time to run and historical volatility. Meanwhile market operators – never people to be overawed by theoreticians of any kind – continue to base their pricing on the ancient and well-tested principle of simply seeing what they are able to sell the option for at the time. Nevertheless, from the above we can establish certain basic conclusions.

1. The option premium may be thought of as the sum of the intrinsic value and the time value.
2. Intrinsic value is the profit that would arise if the option were exercised today.
3. Intrinsic value can never be negative, since at this level the option would not be exercised. (The buyer is under no obligation to exercise at a loss, and therefore presumably will not do so.)
4. Time value can never be negative, although it will fall continuously towards zero as expiration date approaches.
5. At any given time, there will be a choice of exercise prices and expiration dates in the market.
   (a) The more distant maturity dates will have higher premia than the near ones, because the time value will be higher.
   (b) For call options, the higher the exercise price, the lower the premium; intrinsic value will be lower.
   (c) For put options, the lower the exercise price, the lower the premium; intrinsic value will be lower.

The above propositions provide an initial framework for option pricing, but we can take this a few steps further. We have seen how time value varies with time; now we take a look at how it varies with exercise price.

For ease of discussion let us consider a sterling call option. It is readily apparent that if the price is now 1.4980, then a strike price of 1.50 is more likely to be exceeded in the time left to run than is a price of 1.55. It is generally true that the further 'out of the money' the option is, then the less the time value will be, owing to the reducing chance of seeing a profit in the time left to run.

An option at a strike price of 1.50 is really a one-way bet; a downward movement costs little, but an upward movement is pure profit, hence the time value will be high. This is no longer the case for, say, an option at

1.45 because, as time goes by, some of the existing unrealized profit could be lost – there is now a downside risk as well as an upside potential. The time value for 'in the money' options will thus be lower. Deeply in the money options may even have time values very close to zero.

12.18.6 Average rate options

Where an exporter or importer has a series of regular payments or receipts and has budgeted for a particular exchange rate over the period, an average rate option will provide the same protection as a currency option, but because of the averaging process, will be achieved with lower premium cost. Although having the characteristics of a currency option, an average rate option does not involve the physical buying and selling of currency; the underlying transactions are settled independently.

The company selects the rate it wishes to protect – the strike price – and agrees a mechanism by which the bank can calculate the 'average' rate. Average rate options are available in all major currencies for periods up to two years and the basis for deriving the average rate can be daily, weekly, monthly or any other period relevant to the underlying cash flows.

At the end of the period the company is compensated by the bank if the average exchange is worse than the strike price. Compensation is not paid if the average rate is better than the strike price; the company will have benefited from the favourable rate movements when the underlying transactions were settled. However, unless the company deals at the same time as the bank fixes its reference rates, there is likely to be a variation between the bank's average rate and the company's actual dealing average.

12.18.7 Foreign currency accounts

The easy way for the exporter to receive and regularly make payments in another currency, as well as manage international cash flow, cost effectively and conveniently is to have a foreign currency account. International Banks have available foreign currency accounts in all major currencies. It enables the trader to mitigate foreign exchange rate risk and provides a competitive edge by allowing the account holder to buy or sell in the trading partner's local currency. The exporter can open the foreign currency account with his/her local International Bank which is more cost effective than opening an account overseas. Moreover, there is no need to convert the foreign currency into the local currency. Furthermore, the foreign currency can be used when the exporter decides to trade in the foreign currency. Hence, it is cost effective as no currency conversion cost arises. A further benefit is that foreign exchange rate fluctuation risk may be reduced and overall it improves the traders' cash flow management.

The option also exists to open an overseas account in the buyers' country or a third country.

12.18.8 Euro currency

The Euro, operating in 12 countries termed the Euro-zone, embraces 360 million people and is examined in Chapter 18 pp. 551–54.

12.19 Special Drawing Right (SDR)

The Special Drawing Right (SDR) was introduced by the IMF as a reserve currency in 1970. It was intended to replace gold and national currencies in settling international transactions. The IMF uses SDR's for bookkeeping purposes and issues them to member countries. Their value is based on a basket of US dollar (with a weight of 45 per cent) the Japanese Yen (15 per cent) Sterling (11 per cent) and Euro (29 per cent).

Recommended reading

Aon's bonding services www.aon.co.uk

Bankers Almanac www.bankersalmanac.com

BExA guide to Letters of Credit www.bexa.co.uk

BExA guide to On Demand Contract Bonds www.bexa.co.uk

Dictionary of Shipping, International Business Trade Terms and Abbreviations 5th Edition – 18 000 entries of which nearly 1000 are Export/Trade Finance. E-mail: books@witherbys.co.uk www.witherbys.com

Financial Times http://news.ft.com/ft-reports

Hong Kong and Shanghai Banking Corporation Ltd publication *International Trade/Finance* www.hsbc.com

International Chamber of Commerce – URDG (ICC publication No 458) – International Standby Practices (ISP98) (ICC Publication No 590) – www.iccbooks.com

SWIFT www.swift.com

CHAPTER 13

Transport distribution analysis

Transport distribution analysis is featuring increasingly in the exporter's or shipper's evaluation of the technique of processing an export order. Undoubtedly this is due to much increased competition in world markets and the desirability of attaining the best method of distribution considering all the circumstances. Moreover, an increasing number of export companies now have their own shipping department, which is building up an expertise of international distribution techniques designed to secure the best method of distribution for their company products. Many exporters are now scanning the web to determine the range of options available. The result is that these shipping and logistics departments are doing more than earning their keep and are thereby helping to keep their companies' products competitive in very competitive overseas markets. Transport features very much in such an analysis and it is, therefore, appropriate that an examination be made first of the salient points that influence a transport service.

13.1 The relative importance of speed, frequency, reliability, service quality and cost of transport

Basically, there are five factors which influence the nature of a transport service: speed, frequency, reliability, cost and service quality.

Speed is important to the shipper who wants to market his or her goods by an accurate arrival date and to eliminate banking charges for opening credits. This can be achieved by selecting the fastest service available and thereby obtaining the minimum interval between the time the goods are ordered and the date of delivery at their destination. Speed is particularly important to manufacturers of fast-moving consumer goods (fmcg) as it avoids expense and the risk of obsolescence to the retailer carrying large stocks. This is particularly so in the case of ladies clothing which is influenced by fashion, and retails in a very sensitive market.

Reduced stocks result in less warehouse accommodation needs, less working capital by which the company operates, and overall, a better cash flow situation as the turnover is quicker. These factors strongly favour air freight which features very prominently in the distribution of fashionable ladies clothing on certain routes, particularly the North Atlantic.

The development of the wide-body aircraft has enabled airlines to develop new markets through more competitive pricing. An example is the Boeing 747-200C which has a 29-pallet arrangement 96 ×125 in (2.4 m × 3.10 m), a maximum main deck volume of 536 m³ and lower deck volume of 170 m³. The maximum pallet height is 3.05 m with side door loading, and 2.42 m with nose loading. Maximum payload is 100 000 kg, subject to volume and routeing. Such aircraft have facilitated the development of the intermodal sea–air market (p. 61).

Perishable products, computer software, electrical products, livestock – such as day-old chicks, fish and flowers and a range of commodities found in the air freight consolidators' market, require a regular and fast service to ensure successful trading. Air freight is ideal for such products, especially for the longer-distance markets where transit times are critical.

The continuous expansion of the network of global deep-sea container services has been a major stimulant to world trade and has facilitated the development of new markets. It has bridged the gap, in distribution terms, between the wealthy markets of North America and Europe, with the lower GDP markets of the Orient, especially the newly industrialized countries. For example, Kenya has a strong European market for flowers and vegetables. Speed, frequency, reliability and competitive pricing have been the key factors in such trade development.

An area of rapid expansion is the refrigerated cargo market. It may be a trailer, cargo wagon or swap-body, as found in the European and pan North American markets, or in the reefer containers worldwide. A major operator in this field is Sealand, who operate 13 000 all-electric refrigerated containers involving a trio of 12.20 m (40 ft) models. They range from a capacity of 57.20 m³ to 66.80 m³ and tare weight of 4320 kg to 5350 kg. Products carried range from the frozen hardy and sensitive chill to tropicals and flower bulbs.

The development of the reefer container has enabled a growing volume of tropical fruits, Mediterranean citrus fruits, European dairy products and Australian meat products to be distributed in a quality condition on a global basis; the reefer cargoes are shipped at controlled temperatures throughout the transit. Many such cargoes first entered the market using air freight services, for example tropical fruits, but as the volume built up the reefer container took over with a high volume base and lower distribution cost, which was fully integrated into a temperature-controlled network extending to computer-temperature-controlled warehouse distribution points. In drawing such a comparison one must bear in mind that the modern air freighter has a capacity of 100 tonnes compared with

Evergreen's latest generation of vessels conveying 8000 TEUs. Another factor to be borne in mind is that airlines offer more frequent services compared with sea transport.

Improvements will continue to be sought in all areas of physical international distribution. This involves the continuing expansion of multi-modalism (Chapter 5), development of improved technology in the global distribution infrastructure and renewed efforts to improve transit times through dedicated services. Overall, this will yield greatly improved door-to-door services within the total physical distribution concept involving all its ingredients. It will develop further existing markets, identify new ones and expand the global network. The 'just-in-time' concept will be further expanded.

The foregoing demonstrates that regularity and frequency of service are factors in the development of the market, coupled with a competitive transit time at an acceptable freight rate. A balance must be sought between the cost of the service to the shipper, the value added benefit it brings to the goods conveyed, and the frequency and transit times. Modern ship management has substantially reduced voyage time through port rationalization, modern high-tech transhipment methods and a growing reliance on feeder service under the one-stop port operation concept involving the hub and spoke container network (pp. 76–96). This has extended to the infrastructure resources at the ports which are continuously being modernized under multi-modalism. Moreover, the development of Electronic Data Interchange (EDI) has facilitated the unimpeded flow of goods thereby aiding the overall planning of the global distribution of goods from the factory to the warehouse.

Speed is not so important where generally low value cargoes are being carried as in the world tramp trades and where many trades are moving under programmed stockpiled arrangements. In this category are included coal, minerals, ores, etc. and other cargoes which normally move in ship loads and have a low value. These demand a low transport cost.

Frequency of service is most important when goods can only be sold in small quantities at frequent intervals. This is a very strong selling point in favour of the air freight operator, particularly in long-distance markets and is relevant as frequent schedules coupled with fast transits enable stocks to be quickly replenished thereby avoiding excessive stockpiling.

To the tramp charterer, frequency of sailings is not of paramount importance. He must not, of course, allow his stocks to run down too fast, but he will have a margin within which he can safely operate, and will come in to buy and ship when conditions suit him.

Reliability is an essential requirement to the shipper whose goods are sold against expiry dates on letters of credit and import licences. Furthermore, the shipper relies on the operator to deliver his traffic in good condition, which is now becoming an important factor in very competitive overseas markets. To the shipper, therefore, reliability infers that the ship, air freighter, TIR road haulage unit, etc. will depart and arrive at the advertised time; the ship or air freight operator will look after the cargo during pre-shipment, throughout the voyage or flight and after discharge; and finally, the operator can be relied upon to give adequate facilities at the docks or airport and at his offices to enable the appropriate documents and other formalities to be satisfactorily completed. In short, prestige in the liner cargo or air freight trades goes with the reliance that the shipper can place on any particular operator. Reliability infers service quality and, in recent years, this has been a very competitive area among both ship and air operators. The shipper has come to expect the merchandise to arrive in accord with a predetermined schedule and in a good mercantile condition, otherwise the product will be very vulnerable to competition.

Transport costing of individual services is fast becoming an important aspect in transport management today. Transport is a commodity that is difficult to cost, particularly when a multifarious service or joint supply is offered, for example, a vehicular ferry conveying passengers, motorists, cars, lorries and/or trailers, etc. The position is more complex when on one sailing the vessels conveys motorists with their cars, while on another it is simply lorries and trailers with their drivers. The same applies to an aircraft which may be exclusively used for passengers on one flight and for a mixture of passengers and cargo on another.

The operator endeavours to devise a tariff which will maximize revenue and optimize fleet use. This involves market pricing whereby the rate is pitched at the level which will attain high load factors on individual sailings or flights. (Such a philosophy is developed more extensively in Chapter 7.) Therefore, one sees the rate in one direction differing from the rate in the reverse direction, with the sole aim being to attain good capacity utilization.

In very broad terms, the operator will formulate tariffs which will cover all his or her direct or variable costs and make a contribution to indirect or fixed costs. The direct cost represents expenses actually incurred in the service provision including fuel, day-to-day maintenance, dues or tolls, crew cost, etc. Indirect costs embrace administration, depreciation, sinking-fund asset-replacement provision, insurance, annual overhaul and survey costs, etc. The indirect costs are apportioned by flight or voyage relative to the transport user throughout the year. In situations where traffic flows are imbalanced, producing differing tariffs in each direction, an element of cross subsidization takes place to produce a long-term, overall profitable service. Tariffs on scheduled services tend to be rather more rigid compared with chartered vessels or aircraft which are influenced by the economic market forces of supply and demand. (It must be recognized that the foregoing analysis deals only with the freight cost assessment and excludes ancillary expenses, viz. customs clearance, handling costs, collection and delivery, etc.)

The shipper marketing goods of relatively low value must seek the lowest possible transport charge, as the freight percentage of the total value may have a direct bearing on the saleability of the commodity. This involves the tramp vessel which is ideal for this market. The shipper thus has a prime interest in the availability of tramp shipping space at any particular time by reason of the fact that freight and chartering rates will vary, reflecting the economic forces of supply and demand. In a market situation where there are plenty of vessels, the shipper will be able to charter at a rate which will be only marginally above the operating costs of the vessel. In the opposite situation, he or she will be forced to pay more, but there is a limiting factor on the price of the commodity at the point of sale to the rate which the shipowner may receive. In these conditions, the premium returns are earned by the operators of the most efficient ships. In weak market conditions their relative efficiency ensures a small profit while others just break even. Where the market is strong, the proven reliability shown before will ensure that the services of such vessels will be sought out before opportunities are taken up. To conclude, the tramp operator will endeavour to cover his direct costs, and contribute to indirect costs in the overall fixture rate concluded. A similar criterion applies to the chartering of an air freighter.

In the liner trade and scheduled air freight services, the tariffs are more stable and are controlled primarily under the aegis of the liner conference system or IATA. Both the ship and air operator are able to hold their rates at a fair level to show a very modest profit margin based on a fairly high load factor. They must be careful not to hold their rates so high that they price the goods out of the market. At this point, there is need for joint consultation between the shipper and carrier.

However in both the liner trade and air freight market, the freight forwarder or container operator, NVOCC (p. 114), are tending to play a greater role in rate-making due to the fact that they offer not only the trunk haul such as the maritime or flight element, but also the feeder service (collection and delivery) to and from the seaport, ICD CFS or airport in their tariff structure. This trend will continue as both the shipowner and airline prefer to concentrate on providing a quality service and rely on the freight forwarder or container operator to market it.

Moreover, the freight forwarder, container operator and TIR road haulier operator in the liner trades and scheduled air freight markets, offer facilities for consolidated consignments at very competitive rates and transit times. This market is fast expanding particularly in air freight and is ideal for the small exporter.

Quality of service is tied up in all the ingredients which make up the service to the shipper. This includes customer care, reliability, degree of technology, tracking of cargo, level of computerization, quality of equipment, flexibility, competitiveness of tariff and transit time, attitude of staff and, above all, professionalism. Carriers who operate a successful business must be adequately trained and professionally qualified to meet the challenges and opportunities of the market. The closer the carrier gets to the shipper, and empathy develops between them, the more successful the business will become to the mutual benefit of both parties.

As we progress through the early stages of the twenty-first century, the pattern of world trade will change. The Asian markets plus China and India will grow and likewise North America and Europe. The enlargement of the EU will have a long-term growth impact with inter-trade agreements with other trading blocs. It will be driven by logistics and the restructuring of the container global network and the associated overload in infrastructure developments. Overall, high-tech will play a major role with emphasis on value added. Growth will be stimulated as trade is facilitated by a much greater degree of integration between carriers, agents, customs, airport, seaports, railways, road hauliers and shippers to develop multi-modalism. It will feature more prominently the role of free trade zones, Distriparks and trade centres such as Rotterdam and Singapore; development of free trade areas such as the EU and NAFTA; expansion of sea–air networks, expansion of the sea–land bridge such as the trans-Pacific routes serving the west coast ports of Los Angeles, San Francisco and Seattle which are integrated with the double-stack container train transportation distribution to various points in the USA; Electronic Data Interchange in all its areas; and finally, the high-capacity container. The key factor will be flexibility to meet changing market needs and the total commitment to produce a quality service. This will be aided by market research on a continuous basis and good planning. Overall, it will become a global market logistically driven, relying on a very sophisticated and highly efficient shipping and air network. Innovation will play a significant part in the development of new services. Hence the need for the shipper to continuously scan the web for new services, thereby providing new opportunities and new markets.

13.2 Evaluating the suitability of transport modes of an international consignment

Transport distribution analysis to the exporter and shipper involves the process of deciding which is the most ideal mode(s) of transport and route for a particular consignment. Multi-modalism features strongly in this evaluation for fmcg. The ultimate selection can vary seasonally and by quantity. Some services vary considerably from summer to winter due to market demand and climate conditions. Moreover, the despatch of a small quantity, urgently required may be ideal for air freight, but a larger consignment, needed less urgently for later despatch may be suitable for a deep-sea container LCL schedule under consolidation arrangements.

In a world where countries are trying to continuously improve their overall trade balance, an increasing number are insisting on shipment by their own national airline or shipping service irrespective of the commercial or economic advantages there may be in using competitive services. This involves both tariff and non-tariff barriers which impede the free flow of goods and is fully explained in *Maritime Economics Management and Marketing*. This is a difficult situation to combat, but the UK exporter must strive to sell his or her goods under CIF or CIP and buy under EXW or FCA terms to maximize income to the UK balance-of-payments account and thereby exert his or her influence on the transport mode and routeing of the consignment.

Today more and more exporters are setting up their own logistics shipping offices which should be more than self-financing. This means that the cost of running such a department should more than offset the savings realized through international distribution costs. In some companies, such a department has its own TIR road fleet and leases or hires containers. Alternatively, many multinational industries and large departmental stores are entrusting their international distribution arrangements and product outsourcing to a mega container operator such as P&O Nedlloyd, who have specialist logistical departments for such clients.

To conclude, the exporter must continuously review his or her international distribution arrangements and the following are the more important aspects to consider in the evaluation of transport mode and routeing suitability, etc. The exporter must devise a strategy and prioritize the aspects with focus on developing empathy with the buyer and long-term product development. Moreover, emphasis must be given on competitiveness, innovation and the value added benefit.

1. *The customer's choice* is the prime consideration and this is usually found in the export sales contract. It is interrelated with the delivery trade terms. Moreover, there is continuous evidence of the importer insisting on the goods being conveyed on his or her country's national shipping line or airline to save hard currency.

2. *The nature of the commodity*, its dimensions, weight and whether any special facilities are required for it during transit (e.g. livestock requires special facilities, gold requires special security or a strong room, and meat requires refrigerated accommodation). This is a major consideration, and one must establish through research and enquiry whether the actual dimensions are ideal to maximize the use of the available container capacity and lessen the risk of broken stowage. Moreover, one must bear in mind broken stowage usually attracts additional freight payments. The enterprising exporter will constantly review the configuration of the consignment with the shipping department working closely with the production and

design departments. In so doing the consignment may be able to be componentized, thereby enabling it to have a better loadability in the container with reduced freight cost. It may open up other options for distribution such as multi-modalism and the intermodal sea–air services.

3. *The degree of packing and cost thereof.* Packing costs can form a very significant proportion of the overall distribution expense. For example, containerized shipments reduce packing costs and by their configuration protect the cargo throughout its transit. In the case of air freight, packing needs are very much reduced and numerous consignments are conveyed affixed to a pallet with the cargo enveloped in a plastic cover to protect it from scratching, dust, moisture, etc. Likewise, an examination of the type and quality of the packing used can often produce favourable results for the exporter or shipper. One must endeavour to ensure the packing needs are adequate and not over-generous thereby incurring increased packing costs without justification. Numerous specialized packing companies exist and the exporter new to the business is strongly advised to consult them.

4. *The degree to which the consignment as presented aids handling.* For example, palletized cargo facilitates handling by fork lift truck employment, while cartons are ideal for containers, etc. Conversely, the awkwardly shaped cargo may require special facilities and handling arrangements and may be subject to a freight surcharge. Additionally, such consignments encourage broken stowage and tend to be more prone to damage which increases their premium level. In the ideal situation the consignment should be easy to handle from the time it leaves the factory premises until it reaches the retailer. Accordingly, much progress has been made to develop a code of internationally standardized package sizes which will aid distribution and optimize the use of containers and other forms of unit distribution, that is, stillages, pallets, etc (p. 107). A point to bear in mind is the growing tendency to stack cargo to make the best use of warehouse cubic space and accordingly the consignment needs to be adequately robust to survive this situation. This is particularly significant with the growth of Distriparks and warehouse management.

5. *Any statutory obligations imposed relative to the transit.* This is applicable to dangerous cargo and refrigerated foodstuffs. Certain products need special facilities both in the transport mode and terminal. This in itself restricts the choice of route, service and transport mode. For example, the movement of meat, offal, etc. requires special facilities both by the operator who ships it and in terms of inspection facilities at the import terminal. Additionally, most countries have weight and length restrictions on road vehicles. This is particularly relevant to the overall weight of containers. Likewise, there are restrictions on road haulage driver's hours and some EU countries restrict road

haulage movement at weekends. Statutory obligations also influence the type of packaging, for e.g. as found in the Australian trade in the use of straw and wood and the marking of cargo.

6. *Dangerous cargo.* Again regulations are stringent regarding the packaging, stowage and mixture of dangerous cargo with other cargoes during transit. This can restrict service, routeing and schedules. The international distribution of dangerous cargo requires the most careful evaluation, as controls are tending to become more stringent (pp. 201–24).

7. *Suitability of available transport services.* For example, air freighters have limited capacity, weight allowances and dimensions and the cargo may require extensive collection and delivery arrangements. Moreover, it may be necessary to componentize the cargo to enable it to be carried in an air freighter, container, swap-body or trailer within the prescribed weight and dimensions limitations imposed per consignment. Additionally, air freight offers fast transits and reduced packing needs. In contrast, the deep-sea multi-modal container service will have a much slower transit time, probably lower collection and delivery expenses (if it is a consolidated consignment), slightly more packing expense, less frequent service, but a lower freight rate. The Ro-Ro operator will have similar features as the containerized consolidated consignment except that in the UK–Continental trade the transit time is likely to be more competitive with air. Overall, this aspect requires very careful consideration and one must bear in mind that an increasing number of exporters are now using their own vehicles to distribute their products in the UK–Continental trade. In exceptional circumstances, the shipper may resort to chartering an aircraft or vessel if sufficient cargo is available. Remember that some services may be so popular as to have no cargo space available for the next few sailings or flights.

8. *The transit time and related urgency of consignment.* To determine the transit time overall one must take into consideration the periods of collection and delivery of the cargo. The opening of the Euro Tunnel in 1995 has provided new physical distribution opportunities. The multi-modal or intermodal service tends to provide a quicker transit. Similarly a major infrastructure improvement was completed in 2000 and opened up the Scandinavian region for Denmark to become the main route between northern and central Europe. The project involved a suspension bridge – Europe's longest – providing a 14 km permanent road and rail link between Denmark's Jutland peninsula and the island of Sealand via Fünen. Additionally, the scheme involves a 16 km fixed road and rail link between the Danish capital Copenhagen and the Swedish city of Malmö, with three bridges, an immersed tunnel and an artificial island. The project connects with a 1800 km multi-modal project in Sweden and

Finland known as the Nordic triangle. It links Malmö by road and rail with Stockholm and via two routes to the Norwegian frontier. It extends to Finland via the Stockholm–Turku ferry. From Turku the links – by road and rail – proceed via Helsinki to the Russian frontier. Countries which have a poor infrastructure, usually those less developed countries, tend to have poor distribution resources to and from airports and seaports. Moreover, customs clearance, especially at ports, is sluggish and the multi-modal services are still in the process of evaluation and development. Air freight services offer the fastest schedules and are particularly suited to the urgent consignment.

9. *Quantity of cargo and period over which shipment is to be made.* In broad terms, the greater the quantity available for shipment, the lower the overall distribution cost per tonne or kilogram. For example, if the exporter can originate a full container, trailer or cargo wagon load, the overall freight charge will be much cheaper than despatching the cargo under consolidation arrangements. Furthermore, a guaranteed substantial quantity of cargo conveyed over a period of time could attract a concessionary tariff. This is particularly relevant to sea transport. Again, if the circumstances are favourable, it maybe advantageous to charter an aircraft or ship.

10. *Insurance of cargo.* The premium is determined by numerous factors but primarily by the nature of cargo and mode of transport plus type of packaging. Air freight cargo insurance with its quick transits and low risk of damage and pilferage tends to have the most favourable premium rates. Container shipments are also competitive, bearing in mind the longer transit time involved.

11. *Incoterms 2000.* This requires careful evaluation to ensure the correct term is used for the mode of transport (pp. 395–417). Two divisions exist, one for all modes (i.e. combined transport) and one for the conventional port-to-port and sea carriage only. To the exporter wishing to maximize control of the multi-modal transit, CIP, DAF, DDU or DDP should be used. Conversely, for the buyer who wishes to bear the majority of the distribution cost and risk under multi-modal transit, there exist the options of EXW or FCA. The use of FOB and CIF are confined to the conventional seaport-to-seaport operation and remain widely used. Close liaison between the buyer and seller should be maintained to ensure each fully understands their responsibilities – risk and cost – under the Incoterms 2000 used.

12. *Freight and documentation.* In broad terms, the actual cost of sea freight tends to be very much lower than air freight, but it is not practicable to consider such cost in isolation as one must bear in mind the total overall distribution cost to embrace all the elements, viz. packing, insurance, etc. to obtain a fair assessment. Air freight tariffs, compared with road and rail, likewise tend to be high, but the

margin lessens significantly the longer the transit. Documentation costs between various transport modes do not vary a great deal but, with the development of the combined transport concept in recent years involving multi-modalism, it has tended to become simplified on the basis of through rates and consignments notes with no intermediate customs examination in transit countries. The development of the Local Clearance Procedure (p. 239) is on the increase for regular volume shipments. It yields maximum benefits both to the buyer and seller of localized customs control.

13. *Overall distribution costs.* Emerging from the foregoing it is clear that it is necessary to produce an overall distribution cost and evaluation of realistic alternatives in order to arrive at a firm conclusion. The four most decisive factors are terms of export sales contract, commodity specification, freight and overall transit time, including service quality – in short the overall value added benefit obtained by using the transport mode(s) selected. Other factors embrace the cost of packaging – very significant in air freight, the convenience and reliability of the service, charges for insurance, documentation and warehousing. For example a frequent service requires less storage in a warehouse, a reduced risk of product obsolescence, less working capital, the facilitation of smoother production flow and better customer relations that emerge through a regular, reliable service. Moreover, aspects such as a low risk of pilferage or damage and better marketable condition of goods on arrival – the latter becoming of greater importance as competition intensifies – need careful evaluation. A significant factor will be the cargo quantity and, in exceptional circumstances, it may be economic to charter an air freighter or vessel. Alternatively, for the small exporter the consolidated air freight container services, or Ro-Ro services are the more suitable. Overall a plan must be devised and ideally full use should be made of the multi-modal transit where available for fmcg.

14. *Express service.* The development of the air freight express service in recent years has been outstanding. Examples include the Courier Service offered by British Airways (p. 58) and the Post Office Packet (p. 180) services. They are ideal for samples, small parcels and documents.

15. *Planning.* Planning is an essential ingredient in a successful physical international distribution strategy. All parties involved in the transit should feature in the plan which enables adequate coordination, effective use of resources, commitment and continuous monitoring and review to be achieved. Furthermore, coordinating one shipper's distribution strategy with another operating in identical regions or areas could yield substantial freight cost savings and improved service. For example, it may be more economical to despatch a full trailer load, or container once every ten days, rather than use the

daily consolidated service. Customs planning including the tariff, method of shipment embracing the complete unit or CKD, and whether the goods require to be in a Customs warehouse or free zone, need evaluation (pp. 246–47).

16. *Credit insurance.* This needs careful evaluation (pp. 278–86).
17. *Free trade zones.* The development of free trade zones (p. 247) and Distriparks (pp. 108–09) provides the most favourable advantage for the international entrepreneur wishing to set up a distribution point overseas. Such a base would serve markets in the region while assembly and processing would be sourced by imported products from the most cost-effective and competitive countries.
18. *Re-export.* A large volume of goods is re-exported material and shippers should minimize their customs tariffs duties by using IPR and OPR (pp. 244–45).
19. *Logistics.* The shipper transport mode choice is one which is very much logistically driven (see Chapter 6) and which is influenced by the added value the service offers to both exporter and importer.
20. *Cost/benefit analysis.* The need to have a cost/benefit analysis of the options is desirable and this should be done on a regular basis as circumstances and market conditions are subject to continuous change. The value added benefit must be evaluated to determine the intrinsic benefit arising from the transport mode/route choice. It may be speed, cost, convenience in terms of access to exporters and/or importers premises, high-tech, and customer care. A strategic approach is desirable.

13.3 Interface between logistics and transport

The inter-relationship between logistics and transport operation has markedly strengthened in the past decade. Today, logistics is one of the main vehicles driving globalization. It has been greatly facilitated by hi-tech involving the Internet/website development. An increasing number of shippers have online access to their international carrier, whether it be the airline or shipowner. Hence, the shipper can formulate his/her supply chain network and evaluate the options available. Cost is not the prime consideration, but the value added benefit emerging from each option, coupled with developing empathy with the needs of the buyer/importer. Shipowners, Airlines and seaports/airports have a continuous investment programme to develop greater efficiency – often in larger transport units to exploit the economies of scale – and greater high-tech investment. The shipper is driving this investment as more markets across the world are opened up/developed. Examples include India, China and the Far East. The enlarged EU with 25 countries is the largest and wealthiest single market relying more on an advanced infrastructure and logistics input.

The next decade will see a greater integration of logistics and transport especially multi-modalism and featuring containerization. Shippers must review their export strategy to ensure it remains competitive and that they adopt a logistic-driven multi-modal transport supply chain. Moreover, the exporter (seller) must be always conscious that the import (buyer) is continuously reviewing his/her procurement strategy as clients' taste/fashion/technology changes. The exporter must be alert to this situation and be ready to adopt and develop a proactive strategy on product specification and international distribution logistically and consumer-led driven. Again a strategic focus is required.

13.4 Transport distribution analysis

Transport distribution analysis is the technique by which alternative methods of distribution are analyzed and the optimum pattern of transportation selected. It is often called physical distribution management.

In the home market, it is possible to retain overall control of sales outlets and related distribution arrangements. However, where exports are involved, problems of greater complexity arise. Exporting is driven by a market-led approach on a value added basis; this involves a customerized approach. Overall, it involves the fusion of four contracts all of which operate within a disciplined timescale and require continuous monitoring to sustain cost control by all the interested parties. Today shippers are increasingly looking at the total production and value added chain within the just-in-time concept. The one-stop operator will look after all the arrangements regarding the execution of the export sales contract. Distribution involves not one manager, but several in one or more aspects of distribution efficiency. Production planning, components sourcing, effective deployment of company resources, type of documentation, channels of distribution, method of payment, cash flow, level of profitability, loadability of transport mode, cargo routeing, frequency of despatch, customs planning, inventory controls and level of sales, can be substantially improved if the most ideal pattern of physical distribution and Incoterm 2000 is selected. A strategic focus and plan is required with a strong logistic input, and high-tech in all its elements.

We will now identify the various elements involved, as previously discussed on pp. 336–42, and examine case studies of actual international consignments.

1. *Quantity, type of packages and their configuration.* This must specify the quantity of cargo available for despatch and the method of packaging (pp. 331–43).
2. *Total weight of consignment.* This should be quoted on a net or gross weight basis usually in kilograms.

3. *Total volume of shipment.* This should be given on a m^3 or ft^2 basis. Remember that different tariff structures apply to air, road and sea transport. Usually, for certain high-volume commodities, there is an advantage in despatching by air, whereas for sea transport weight and measurement rates (whichever produces the greatest revenue) will apply.

4. *Value of goods ex-works.* This is the value of the goods at the factory awaiting collection for shipment.

5. *Packing cost.* In sea transport, packing cost can represent a formidable percentage of the total distribution cost but, with air freight, it is much reduced and is a strong marketing point in persuading the shipper to use this mode of transport (pp. 59–61).

6. *Inland charges at point of origin.* This incorporates all the costs incurred in transporting the consignments from, for example, the factory production site to the nominated airport or seaport for despatch overseas. This may be as inland clearance depot (p. 100).

7. *Freight.* This embraces the air and sea freight comparisons. Usually, air freight rates are more expensive than sea transport, but each has a differing tariff structure (pp. 177–78).

    The decision over the most profitable method of distribution, however, cannot be based on pure freight cost alone. The related costs and revenues must also be evaluated. Overall, this involves, when applicable, a transhipment cost either at the airport or seaport to another aircraft or vessel to the ultimate airport or seaport destination.

    Basically, the most critical management decision in distribution is the selection of the transport mode. It determines three elements – transport costs, transit time and quality of service. In general, there is an inverse relationship between transit time and transport costs. The quicker the transit, the higher the transport cost. Conversely, the slower the transit, the cheaper the transport cost. With regard to quality of service, an unreliable cheap service is unlikely to obtain strong market support in a situation where arrival times are of paramount importance for the importer (buyer).

8. *Inland charges at destination.* This includes cartage, handling charges, customs clearance, agency expenses and demurrage. Overall, it includes the transportation cost from airport or seaport to ultimate destination. Insofar as shipping is concerned, it could involve transhipment to lighterage. The Port of Rotterdam is a market leader in transhipment cargo through the inland waterway network involving dedicated services (pp. 55–57).

9. *Duty and taxes.* This includes VAT or its equivalent. Likewise it includes import duties. Advantages for air distribution may materialize if duties are based on FOB value (value at the place of exportation). This arises from reduced packing costs and reduced costs to the airport of departure. Duties, for example, are assessed on FOB value in USA,

Canada and South Africa. Conversely, it may be a disadvantage to air freight if the duties are based on CIF value (value at place of importation or destination) as the pure air freight is likewise subject to duty. Similar advantages and disadvantages arise relative to sea transport. Some Customs duties are assessed on the gross weight which is particularly advantageous to air freight, with less packing producing a lower tare weight; Mexico and Switzerland are applying this policy.

10. *Insurance.* Faster transits involving a reduced risk of damage and pilferage on air freight tend to produce more favourable insurance premiums compared with sea transport.

11. *Unpacking/refurbishing.* The inherent advantages of air freight tend to favour such a shipper insofar as unpacking and refurbishing are concerned when compared with maritime transport. Reduced packing tends to make unpacking less expensive. Moreover, any special refurbishing process for the goods before use is not necessary, such as degreasing of machinery and apparatus, ironing of textiles, etc.

12. *Cost of capital tied up with transit.* During the time of transportation from door to door either the exporter or importer has invested money into the merchandise without receiving an equivalent interest, or deriving a profit from it. The longer the transit and the higher the merchandisable value, the greater the capital investment involved. This factor maybe of minor importance for a single shipment, but carry greater significance for all consignments during a specified period. It is of great significance to multinational companies.

13. *Inventory and storage costs.* The costs of keeping stocks at the place of production and consumption involves four basic elements as follows:

   (a) cost of capital tied up in inventories;
   (b) obsolescence, deterioration, insurance, taxes, etc.;
   (c) administration and handling;
   (d) warehousing and accommodation.

   The cost percentage on the average stock value may be as high as 25 per cent per year, but much depends on warehouse location and size, plus type of commodity. The specific advantages of air freight, namely speed, safety, reliability and frequency may result in a reduced lead time for the importer and enable him or her to increase the shipping frequency for the fast-moving items. Instead of shipping quantities covering the demand for several months, it might be more favourable to air freight more frequently, covering only several weeks' demand. This produces a lower working stock, less warehouse accommodation and reduced risk of stock deterioration or obsolescence; it extols the concept of just-in-time. The consignment itself should be of optimum size to contain transportation cost.

   Both the high quality of air freight and the shorter lead-time considerably lower the risk of stockpiling, commodity deterioration or obsolescence to the importer, thereby reducing his or her financial risk. A reduction of working and service stocks results in a reduced average stock level for the importer so that the turnover rate is increased, and the inventory and storage cost decreased. Logistics eliminates inventory and warehouse costs. Shippers, where practicable, must have a strategic objective and thereby become more competetive (p. 145).

14. *Marketing.* With regard to marketing, many export-orientated companies find themselves having great difficulty achieving their marketing objectives because insufficient consideration is given to distribution. Sales and advertising combine to stimulate demand for a product but, unless – by planned distribution – the product is at a point-of-sale when the consumer decides to purchase, a sale is often lost. Even if the sale is not lost, customer service standards fall, in that the customer is forced to delay purchase and, while the demand may be so strong that the delay is suffered, the likelihood of a repeat purchase at a later date is reduced. A similar situation applies to 'after-sales service', a good example being a spare part. The speed with which the customer can obtain a replacement part for a machine strongly influences his opinion of the supplier, and therefore the likelihood of repeat purchase.

    Quick delivery is often vital in providing a high level of customer service which would otherwise only be achieved by holding prohibitively high levels of stock. In fact, situations do exist where the setting-up of a stock-holding could be uneconomic, and dependence is totally upon rapid transit. A good example emerges from test marketing, where a company testing a new product whose success is uncertain will meet demand direct from production without expensive stockpiling.

15. *Speed.* A high-speed transport mode reduces stock levels – both static and transit – and the financial implications are, therefore, apparent. In effect, the average lead time between manufacture and sale is shortened and this must mean a saving in financial resources. In reality, it improves a company's cash flow or liquidity.

16. *Other cost and revenue factors.* In addition to the transportation and distribution costs already mentioned, the specific performance criteria of a transport mode have an influence on other cost and revenue factors in ordering, production and administration. These 'hidden' advantages are often difficult to evaluate but they require consideration by both the exporter and importer to find the most profitable method of distribution.

We will now examine two case studies of transport distribution analysis, which appear in Tables 13.1 and 13.2.

TABLE 13.1 Distribution analysis – example A: textiles from London to Japan. Gross weight for surface transportation: 1024 kg (165.97 ft^3)

	Air transportation cost in UK £s	Surface transportation cost in UK £s
Value ex-works	5500	5500
Transportation cost		
Packing	12	60
Transportation to air/sea port of departure, handling	15	50
Air/sea freight	725	130
Transportation from air/sea port of destination, handling	9	14
Import duties	1020	940
Insurance	14	46
Cost price	£7295	£6740
Cost of capital tied up in transit	7	67
Unpacking/refurbishing/storage	Not evaluated	Not evaluated
Total cost	£7302	£6807
Cost difference	+7%	
Time advantage	38 days	

Cost determinants
(a) Value per kg ex-works   UK £6.00
(b) Freight proportion air/sea   5.5:1
(c) Density   238 in^3/kg

The following points are relevant in the foregoing transport distribution analysis including the two examples given:

1. With the growing development of maritime container services and Ro-Ro services in UK–Continental trade, the advantage differential, particularly in terms of packing cost, reduced transit times and service quality, is being moderately reduced in comparison with air shipment. Conversely, the air freighter is becoming larger with bigger capacity containers thereby reducing unit costs.
2. The differential between air and surface transit, particularly in terms of overall cost, freight rates and packing expenses, tends to be very narrow on relatively short distance transits, as experienced in the UK–Continental trade.

An example of rates strategy is found in a case study regarding the shipment of industrial products in Malaysia. It involved the Selangor Cement

TABLE 13.2 Distribution analysis – example B: electrical appliances from London to South Africa. Gross weight for surface transportation: 173 kg (21.89 ft³)

	Air transportation cost in UK £s	Surface transportation cost in UK £s
Value ex-works	2600	2600
Transportation cost		
Packing	19	53
Transportation to air/sea port of departure, handling	5	20
Air/sea freight	117	12
Transportation from air/sea port of destination, handling	13	43
Import duties	130	134
Insurance	6	7
Cost price	£2890	£2869
Cost of capital tied up in transit	4	34
Unpacking/refurbishing/storage	Not evaluated	Not evaluated
Total cost	£2894	£2903
Cost difference	+0.3%	
Time advantage	41 days	

Cost determinants
(a) Value per kg ex-works   UK £15.00
(b) Freight proportion air/sea   9.9:1
(c) Density   219 in³/kg

Company based in Rowang which had an annual production capacity of 6 million tonnes, but it was seriously under-utilized due to a recession in the late 1980s and the need to develop export markets became urgent in order to avoid closure. Suitable markets for bagged cement were found in Tahiti, Nepal, Sri Lanka, Vietnam, Taiwan and China. At this time, the bulk of Malaysian shipments of clinkers and cement in bags passed through Kampung Acheh in Lumut and Bumirel in Port Dickson. Such ports had low port charges but also poor facilities.

Port Klang, the major port of Malaysia, saw a market potential in such business and negotiated to secure the business. It was able to offer improved port facilities compared with the minor ports used. The shipper recognized such advantage but looked for a competitive price for a guaranteed annual shipment of 100 000–150 000 tonnes. Rowang was also conveniently situated close to Port Klang. A key factor was shipment which was made under F10 terms (p. 377). The cost from Rowang to Lumut or Port Dickson, inclusive of ports cost and inland transport, was

$19.50 per tonne on shipper's account. In comparison the cost of inland transportation between Rowang and Port Klang was $8.00 per tonne and Selangor Cement Company would divert the bulk of the traffic if the total port costs did not exceed $11.50 per tonne, inclusive of port charges, wharfage and stevedorage.

To achieve the $11.50 per tonne objective it would be necessary to provide a dedicated transit shed at Port Klang to enable the shipper, at his expense, to undertake all the processing of the cargo. This would include: off-loading the bags from the lorry or wagon onto the shipper's pallets; palletizing cargo embracing the use of plastic sheets and strapping the cargo into unit loads or pallets; and finally, stacking the unit loads or pallets in the transit shed. Port Klang would not be involved in such activities. However, it would be necessary for industrial relations reasons to hire fork lift trucks and drivers from Port Klang. The transit shed rental was $8.07 per square metre for each 28-day period.

Overall, the deal yielded the following rates per tonne:

	Existing rates as in port authority tariff		Proposed negotiated rates with shipper	
	Palletized	*Non-palletized*	*Palletized*	*Non-palletized*
	$	$	$	$
Port charges	5.50	5.50	3.50	3.50
Wharfage	2.50	2.50	2.50	2.50
Stevedorage	3.50	5.60	3.40	5.60
Total	11.40	13.60	9.40	11.60

Accordingly, the $9.40 rate per tonne was achieved for direct shipment and loading of the palletized cargo. It produced the following financial results for Port Klang and enabled them to enter the cement market:

Proposed consolidated rate inclusive of port charges, wharfage and stevedorage (50 000 tonne at $9.40 and 50 000 tonne at $11.60)	1 050 000
Transit shed rental – 20 weeks	93 750
Hire of forklifts 50 000 tonne – 200 tonne per gang – 250 gangs and $66 per forklift	16 500
Hire of drivers 50 000 tonne – 200 tonne per gang – 250 gangs and $19 per driver	4 750
	$1 165 000

Additional income to the port would accrue from ancillary services such as pilotage, tugboats and berthing. The shippers disbursement costs were calculated as follows:

	Palletized cargo		Non-palletized cargo	
(A) *Fixed cost per tonne*				
Port charge	3.50		3.50	
Wharfage	2.50		2.50	
Stevedorage	3.40		5.60	
		$9.40		$11.60
(B) *Variable cost per tonne*				
Transit shed rental	1.12		0.47	
Hire of fork lift and drivers	0.46	$1.58	0.45	$0.92
		$10.98		$12.52
Less wharfage payable by shipowner		$2.50		$2.50
		$8.48		$10.02

Overall, this case study demonstrates that for guaranteed shipments a rebate can be granted, which in this case was $2.00 per tonne.

To conclude, transport distribution analysis forms an important evaluation today in helping the exporter or importer to decide on the best method of transportation. Airline operators, together with some maritime cargo operators, provide cargo consulting or logistic advisory services which the shipper is well advised to use. Alternatively, the freight forwarder can always help in this regard.

An example of a new development in transport distribution emerged in Switzerland. It concerns Danzas, one of the top five European freight forwarders, which is increasingly moving away from its traditional forwarding, customs brokerage and transportation origins. Danzas sees its role as providing total logistics for large internationally active customers. According to the market, an exporter or importer with a production line in Korea needs not only a European distribution system, but also the pipelines and gateways which feed this distribution system from production sites within and outside Europe. One of Danzas' moves into total logistics was with the world-famous Swiss confectionery firm, Jacobs Suchard Tobler. From the initial negotiations in November 1988, Danzas devised and built an entire temperature-controlled warehousing and distribution system at Schaffhaussen in northern Switzerland. The warehouse was built and completed within nine months and, since the beginning of 1990, the Danzas Logistics Centre at Schaffhaussen has been handling the worldwide distribution of the entire finished goods output of Jacobs Suchard Tobler.

Jacobs Suchard Tobler's annual throughput of mostly branded chocolates and confectionery is around 26 000 tonnes and consists of over 100 000 individual consignments. These consignments have to be distributed throughout the world in carefully controlled conditions. The Danzas Logistics Centre in Schaffhaussen was built to Danzas' specifications with the support of the Technische Universität Berlin. It comprises over 6500 tonnes of steel and concrete and is located on the main road axis of northern Switzerland and is connected to the Swiss railway network (SBB). The maximum dimensions of the building are 100 m long × 17.6 m high × 61 m wide covering an area of 5826 m². It is staffed entirely by Danzas employees – 50 in total.

The Danzas Logistics Centre is divided into five main areas: goods reception; high-rack storage; order processing and consolidation zone; goods despatch; and offices. The goods reception area for Jacobs Suchard Tobler's production has a surface area of 736 m² and a storage capacity of 3311 m³. Palletized goods are received either by road via four ramp height loading bays or by rail at the 48 m SBB-connected loading area. The pallet details are automatically recorded before the pallets move to the storage area. The fully automated high-rack storage area comprises 13 rows with a height of 15 m and three different pallet heights. The rows vary in length between 49 m and 63 m and provide nearly 57 000 m³ of storage space. The storage area is served by three rail-mounted narrow-aisle lift trucks. The total capacity of the storage area is 12 507 pallets weighing up to 750 kg, each with a maximum size of 1300 mm × 900 mm × 2000 mm high.

The order processing zone consists of five order lanes, each 56 m long, which can hold a total of up to 1000 pallets at any time. Orders are individually processed and fed to the goods despatch area. The goods despatch area has six loading bays for trailers, containers and swap-bodies, four loading bays for vans for local deliveries and a 48 m long SBB rail-connected loading bay.

The Centre is controlled by interrelating computer systems with material flow simulations to optimize automatic warehousing operations. The heating (16°C + 1°C/−2°C) and relative humidity (30–60 per cent) in the east and west wings of the high-rack storage area are independently controlled. Heating in the goods reception, goods despatch, order processing and consolidation areas is independently controlled at 18°C (±2°C).

With this dedicated automatic warehouse, Danzas has not only constructed a new building, but has also installed a software package, developed in-house, for the management of all warehousing functions, including the computer link to Jacobs Suchard Tobler, Switzerland.

CHAPTER 14

Export documentation

An important part of export practice and management is a good comprehension of the various documents involved in processing the export consignment. Moreover, the need to understand the role of such documents and their limitations together with likely problems which they may encounter is likewise important. If an exporter has any doubt over the role of, or query over, a particular document the best course to follow is to contact his or her bank or freight forwarder.

In processing an export consignment involving extensive documentation, one must bear in mind there can be up to four contracts to execute. These include: the export sales contract, the contract of carriage, the financial contract and, finally, the contract of cargo insurance. All these have to be reconciled with the processing of the export consignment. The need to have the relevant documentation correctly completed and the checklists found in this and Chapters 12 and 15 closely adhered to, cannot be stressed too strongly. Failure to do so results in delay in payment for goods, loss of goodwill between buyer and seller, late delivery of the merchandise, and so on. Successful international trade is only realized through complete professionalism in the use and execution of documentation with a zero error rate, otherwise delays are encountered when processing the goods through customs, making payments, etc. which are costly to the shipper. Documents presented to customs and banks are frequently incorrect, resulting in delays in customs clearance and extra charges having to be met by the shipper, payment delays occurring and extra bank charges arising.

This chapter, in the main, excludes documentation relating to customs and finance, which is covered in Chapters 9, 10 and 12. A study of the various documents now follows. The subject is comprehensively dealt with in the companion volume *Shipping and Air Freight Documentation for Importers and Exporters* (second edition) Witherbys, 2000 (p. 394).

14.1 E-commerce

Documentation preparation, formulation and transmission is today undertaken in the majority of situations electronically. Hence, exporters are encouraged to have adequate software in the international computer literacy environment which exists today. This extends to Customs documentation (p. 234), Trade Finance documentation (p. 289), Carriers documentation (p. 560), sea/air/road/rail and commercial documentation (p. 425). Moreover, the exporter would have online access to the relevant organization to obtain the booking/tracking/payment, etc, arrangements. The seller/buyer would communicate/negotiate by e-mail. Overall, the electronic age has transformed the international trade environment through quicker and more efficient documentation negotiation and processing procedures.

Bolero (p. 457) has contributed to this change and the accuracy and authenticity of all the documents used in the conduct of international trade is paramount at all times.

An example of electronic transmission is provided by P&O Nedlloyd, who encourage exporters or their agents to submit to them accurate documentation issued promptly after receipt of goods into the system. P&O Nedlloyd like many mega container operators operate a sophisticated computerized system to ensure the facilitation of the fast processing of Bills of Lading, Invoices and Manifests etc. Hence, the need to submit accurate data within an acceptable timescale. Not only does a computer enable large volumes of data to be processed in a fraction of the time of a manual operation, it also ensures the shipowner has a consistency of information throughout the documentary chain. It further allows the production of the Bill of Lading and Invoice immediately goods have been packed with a container, provided the shipowner has in its possession accurate and complete source documentation. Initially when a booking is made, whether FCL or LCL, the Booking Party is allocated a Unique Booking Reference Number. This should be quoted on all source documents to ensure immediate identification of the consignment in question.

14.2 Air waybill

The air waybill is the consignment note used for the carriage of goods by air. It is often called an air consignment note and is not a document of title or a transferable or negotiable instrument. The document travels with the cargo and it is not possible to use it as a negotiable instrument for letter of credit purposes, as the cargo would arrive at the destination airport days or sometimes weeks before the air waybill's arrival via the banking system, thereby allowing the consignee to take delivery of the goods

(p. 417). The air waybill is basically a receipt for the goods for despatch and is *prima facie* evidence of the conditions of carriage. Overall, there are usually 12 copies of each air waybill for the shipper, the sales agent, the issuing carrier (airline operator), the consignee, as a delivery receipt, for the airport of destination, the third carrier (if applicable), the second carrier (if applicable), the first carrier, as an extra copy for the carrier (when required), as an invoice and at the airport of departure. Copies 1, 2 and 3 are the originals. Not every copy is used for all consignments, but merely as circumstances demand. For example, the second carrier's copy would be used only if the consignment was conveyed on another airline to complete the transit – such as British Airways conveying it for the first leg of the journey and Air Canada for the remainder. The conditions of carriage are found on the reverse of the air waybill document and are subject to the Carriage by Air Act 1961. This is based on the Warsaw Rules and a number of other conventions (examined on pp. 575–76).

The standard IATA air waybill (AWB), used worldwide, is the most important feature of the simplified system of documentation for air freight moving internationally. It is the basic airline document covering the movement of shipments on international air freight services. A single air waybill covers carriage over any distance, by as many airlines as may be required to complete the transportation. When goods carried by one airline for part of the journey are transferred to another airline, the original air waybill is sent forward with the consignment from point of original departure to the final destination. When issued by the airline, the air waybill features a unique reference number which commences with the carrier prefix. The air waybill is the key to tracing the flight details of the consignment.

The new 'universal' air waybill (UAWB) was introduced from 1 January 1984 and its use is mandatory. It is compatible with the United Nations (UN) layout key and can be used for both domestic and international transits.

The Warsaw Convention stipulates that the air waybill is mandatory in use and must be completed in at least three parts embracing: (a) the carrier (signed by the consignor), (b) for the consignee (signed by the consignor and carrier) and (c) for the consignor (signed by the carrier). The air waybill must contain the following data:

1. The place and date of its execution.
2. The name and address of the shipper.
3. The names and addresses of the consignor and consignee.
4. Customs data – the AWB is regarded as the skeleton pre-entry document, containing the following information: first carrier (airline); departure and destination airports and any special route to be followed; agents' IATA code (when the shipper is using an agent); value of goods and currency; full technical description of cargo dimensions, commodity code, rate class chargeable weight and freight rate and any shipping marks.

5. Total freight amount prepaid and/or to pay at destination is precisely defined.
6. Details of any ancillary charges payable.
7. Signature of the shipper or agent.
8. Signature of the issuing carrier (airline operator) or agent.
9. Details of booked flight and actual flight.

Efficient service depends on the accuracy and completeness of the air way-bill. Hence shippers themselves must give clear and complete forwarding instructions to the airline or agent. To facilitate this procedure they may use the 'Shipper's Letter of Instruction', a standardized form which may be obtained from any airline, approved IATA Cargo Agent or forwarder. The main functions of the standard air waybill are as follows.

At departure airports it is a contract of carriage, a receipt for goods, provides a unique reference for handling inventory control and documentation reference, includes a description of goods and full rating information, includes special handling requirements, and provides basic details for the aircraft manifest. Post-flight information includes a document source for revenue collection, interlining accounting and proration and cargo statistics. At destination airports the air waybill provides a basic document for notification to the consignee, customs clearance and delivery to the consignee. Additionally it is a source document for clearance and delivery charges accounting.

Where more than one package is involved, the carrier can require the consignor to make out separate air waybills. The air consignment note must be printed in one of the official languages of the country of departure, for example, French, German, etc. Erasures are not admissible, but alterations can be made provided they are authenticated by the consignor's signature or initials. If quantities, weights, or values are altered, they must appear in words as well as figures.

The air freight consolidation market continues to grow (p. 58). This involves the IATA-accredited Air Freight Agency providing a consolidation service and enters into an agency agreement with a forwarder in the country to be served. Usually it is the same company which has a global network. The agent markets the consolidation service and despatches the merchandise as one consignment with the airline. Consolidation usually takes place at the forwarders' premises, usually near or on the airport. Alternatively, it may be at the airline export shed and placed on a pallet or ULD. The documentation involved is the Master Air Waybill (MAWB), which is issued by the airline and identifies the forwarder as the shipper and the consignee as the forwarder in the destination country. Details of all the packages in the consolidation feature in the MAWB including weight, volume and cargo description. Such consignment details are often recorded on a cargo manifest which is attached to the MAWB. The IATA Air Freight Agency issues to each shipper a House Air Waybill (HAWB) which provides a cargo description and records the MAWB number as a cross-reference. The HAWB should contain the information set out under documentary requirements when this need arises.

Under a documentary letter of credit, certain specific information or instructions to be shown on the air waybill may be requested. This usually includes: names and addresses of the exporter, importer and the first carrier or airline, the names of the airports of departure and destination together with details of any special routes, the date of the flight, the declared value of the merchandise for customs purposes, the number of packages with marks, weights, quantity and dimensions, the freight charge per unit of weight or volume, the technical description of the goods and not the commercial description, whether the freight charge has been prepared or will be paid at the destination, the signature of the exporter (or his or her agent); the place and date of issue, and finally the signature of the issuing carrier (or his or her agent).

Today many major world airlines have a fully computerized air freight documentation system permitting online access by major shippers, agents, customs and handling companies. It also extends to the use of bar codes for automatic verifications. This enables cargo handling and sorting to be undertaken electronically. An example of an air waybill is found in *Shipping and Air Freight Documentation for Importers and Exporters*, and p. 618 of this book.

14.3 ATA carnets

ATA carnets may be used to simplify Customs clearance of goods being temporarily exported. They replace normal Customs declarations both at export and re-import. They also replace normal Customs documents and security requirements in many countries worldwide into which goods are being temporarily imported. See HM Customs Notice 104, p. 245.

14.4 Bill of exchange

Under the terms of the Bills of Exchange Act 1882, a bill of exchange has been defined as an unconditional order in writing addressed by one person to another, signed by the person giving it, requiring the person to whom it is addressed to pay, on demand, or at a fixed or determinable future time, a certain sum in money to or to the order of a specified person or bearer. Drafts can be drawn either at sight – payment to be made on demand or on presentation – or at a particular 'tenor' ('usance') – payment to be made at a fixed or determinable future date, usually within 180 days of sight of the bill of exchange by the drawer – or within 180 days of the date of the draft. The general procedure for letters of credit is for drafts to be drawn on a bank, but some credits require them to be drawn on the importer. Drafts can be drawn in pairs called 'first' and 'second' bills of exchange.

The bill of exchange is a popular way of arranging payment. The most normal procedure is for the exporter (seller) to hand the bill of exchange together with the documents to the exporter's (seller's) bank who will send them to a bank overseas for 'collection'. The overseas bank will notify the buyer of the arrival of the documents and will release them to him or her subject to one of two conditions. First, if the bill is drawn at 'sight', the buyer pays the amount of the bill in full, or secondly, if the bill is drawn payable after a certain number of days, the buyer accepts the bill, i.e. he or she signs across the bill his or her agreement to pay the amount in full at the due date.

The salient benefit of this method of payment is that the exporter (seller) can maintain control of the goods until the importer (buyer) has agreed to pay for them. However, there is still no absolute guarantee the importer (buyer) will pay, but legal procedures exist in most countries to recover money owing against bills of exchange.

The bill of exchange contains the following data:

1. the date;
2. a specific sum, which should agree with the amount on the export invoice;
3. the 'tenor', that is, whether payment is to be at sight or at a stated period after sight or at a fixed date;
4. the name of the drawee;
5. the name and signature of the drawer;
6. the name of the payee or order or bearer;
7. the endorsement of the payee where applicable.

Overall, the bill of exchange should be so worded to conform to what is laid down in the credit. The following discrepancies tend to arise in processing bills of exchange and should be avoided:

1. document drawn incorrectly or for a sum different to the credit amount;
2. designation of the signature on the document not specified if required, e.g. director or partner.

14.5 Bill of lading

A bill of lading is a receipt for goods shipped on board a vessel, signed by the person (or his or her agent) who contracts to carry them, and stating the conditions in which the goods were delivered to (and received by) the ship. It is not the actual contract, which is inferred from the action of the shipper or shipowner in delivering or receiving the cargo, but forms excellent evidence of the terms of the contract. It is a document of title to the goods which is the subject of the contract between the buyer (importer) and seller (exporter). It is the most important commercial document in international trade, and is used to control delivery of goods transported by sea (see specimen bills of lading pp. 611–13).

Before examining the salient points, function and types of bills of lading, we will first consider two acts which play an important role in the role and function of this document, namely the Carriage of Goods by Sea Act 1971 which succeeded the Carriage of Goods by Sea Act 1924, and the Carriage of Goods by Sea Act 1992 which repealed the Bills of Lading Act 1855.

The bill of lading starts its life (in almost all cases) containing or evidencing the contract of carriage between the carrier and the shipper, under which the carrier and the shipper promises that the goods will be carried from the port of loading and safely delivered at the port of discharge. During the voyage the ownership of the goods will be normally transferred from the original seller to the ultimate receiver who will take delivery of the goods from the ship. There may in exceptional cases be 100 or more buyers who (or whose banks) will pay for the goods and then receive payment from the next buyer in the chain. During this process the goods are, of course, not in the possession of any of the parties. They are, or should be, safely on board the ship, steadily crossing the ocean. Neither the buyer of an unascertained portion of a bulk nor an indorsee after discharge have rights against the carrier.

The defect at the heart of the Bill of Lading Act 1855 was considered to be the linkage between property in the goods and the right to sue on the bill of lading contract. Under the 1992 Act this is removed.

The 1992 Act provides that any lawful holder of the bill of lading has the right of suit but that *only* he or she has the right (thus preventing more than one claimant for the same breach of contract). If, as can arise, the actual loss has been sustained by someone other than the holder of the bill of lading, the holder must account for the damages to the person who has suffered the actual loss. The Act also recognizes the rights of suit of someone who became holder of the bill of lading after discharge of the cargo, provided that he or she did so under arrangements made before that date (thereby preventing trading in bills relating to goods known to be damaged – in effect, trading in causes of action). Finally, the Act recognizes the rights of parties interested in two forms of shipping documents which are commonly used today but do not appear within the 1855 Act. The consignee under a sea waybill and the holder of a ship's delivery order will both have the right to sue on the contract in question.

This will affect the P & I Clubs who can no longer take unmeritorious defences based on lack of title to sue. Those involved in the bulk commodity trades will gain rights they did not previously have, as will the consignees named in a waybill. Less obvious is the new feature in which the banks who finance international trade will now be able to enforce the bill of lading rights in their own name.

In examining other legislation relative to maritime transport, it is relevant to mention that international conventions set out minimum terms and conditions out of which carriers cannot contract to the detriment of merchants. Carriers can, of course, accept terms more favourable to merchants. Generally speaking, international conventions aim to regulate international carriage and, in most cases, national carriage is allowed freedom of contract, although in most countries there are standard trading conditions which are usually applied.

The Hague Rules were agreed at an international convention in Brussels in 1924 and govern liability for loss or damage to goods carried by sea under a bill of lading. They are officially known as the 'International Convention for the Unification of Certain Rules Relating to Bills of Lading' and were signed in Brussels on 25 August 1924 and given effect in the UK by the Carriage of Goods by Sea Act 1924. The Hague Rules apply to all exports from any nation which ratified the Rules. This is virtually universal wherever they have not been superseded by the Hague–Visby Rules or Hamburg Rules (p. 574), either by the application of law or by contractual incorporation into the terms and conditions of the relevant bill of lading.

The main features of the Hague Rules are as follows:

1. Minimum terms under which a carrier may offer for the carriage of all goods other than live animals, non-commercial goods including personal and household effects, experimental shipments and goods carried on deck where the bill of lading is claused to indicate such carriage.
2. The carrier has to exercise due diligence to provide a seaworthy vessel at the voyage commencement, and this cannot be delegated. Additionally, the goods must be cared for adequately during the transit. Provided the carrier complies with these requirements, if loss or damage still occurs, he or she can rely on a number of stated defences. The majority of these elaborate on the general principle that the carrier is only liable for loss or damage caused by his or her own negligence, or that of his or her servants, agents or subcontractors. However, the carrier remains protected in three situations where the loss or damage has been caused by negligence as detailed below:

    (a) negligence in navigation;
    (b) negligence in the management of the vessel (as opposed to the care of the cargo);
    (c) fire, unless the actual fault or privity of the carrier.

Liability in the UK was £100 per package before the Hague–Visby Rules superseded the Hague Rules. Other nations have set alternative limits: the USA, US$500; Japan ¥100 000; and Greece DR8000. In 1968 at an international conference the Hague Rules were revised primarily in the area of limitation. The amended rules, the Brussels Protocol, were signed on 23 February 1968. They are more popularly known as the Hague–Visby Rules and are reflected in the UK Carriage of Goods by Sea Act 1971.

Limitation was amended to provide a weight or package alternative and originally the limits were set in Poincare Francs – a fictitious currency. This proved unacceptable and, accordingly, the 1979 Special Drawing Rights (SDR) Protocol was adopted in February 1984. Currently there are 33 member countries, primarily European and including the UK. Limitation in terms of SDRs is now the greater of SDR 666.67 per package or unit, or SDR 2 per kilo.

The Brussels Protocol, embracing the Hague–Visby Rules, became operative in 1977 and has 34 contracting Member States and a further six countries who have enacted legislation broadly in line with the Rules. The Visby amendment applies to all bills of lading in the following situations:

1.   the port of shipment is in a ratifying nation; or
2.   the place of issue of the bill of lading is in a ratifying nation; or
3.   the bill of lading applies Hague–Visby Rules contractually.

At their June 1997 Centenary Conference, the CMI who drafted the original Hague Rules and the Visby Protocol, debated the possibility of creating greater uniformity in the law of the carriage of goods by sea. The outcome was inconclusive and the only course of action agreed upon was to cooperate with the UNCITRAL in its wide consideration of the carriage of goods issues. Hence, this eliminates any early action on carriers' liability issues as the problems inherent in overcoming the difficulties in changing from a paper based to an EDI based method of trading and overcoming the Document of Title conundrum seemed to have assumed priority.

In March 1978 an international conference in Hamburg adopted a new set of rules, termed the Hamburg Rules. These radically alter the liability which shipowners have to bear for loss or damage to goods in the courts of those nations where the Rules apply. The main differences between the new Rules and the old Hague–Visby Rules are given below.

1.   The carrier will be liable for loss, damage or delay to the goods occurring while in his or her charge unless he or she proves that he, his servants or agents took all measures that could reasonably be required to avoid the occurrence and its consequences. The detailed list of exceptions set out in the Hague and Hague–Visby Rules is no longer available to the carrier. In particular, the carrier is no longer exonerated from liability arising from errors in navigation, management of the ship or fire.
2.   The carrier is liable for delay in delivery if 'the goods have not been delivered at the port of discharge provided for under the contract of carriage within the time expressly agreed upon or in the absence of such agreement within the time which it could be reasonable to require of a diligent carrier having regard to the circumstances of the case'.

3. The dual system for calculating the limit of liability, either by reference to package or weight as found in the Hague–Visby Rules has been readopted, but the amounts have been increased by 25 per cent to SRS 835 per package and SDR 2.5 per kilo. The liability for delay is limited to an equivalent of two and a half times the freight payable for the goods delayed, but not exceeding the total freight payable for the whole contract under which the goods were shipped. In no situation would the aggregate liability for both loss and/or damage and delay exceed the limit for loss and/or damage.
4. The Hamburg Rules cover all contracts for the carriage by sea other than charterparties, whereas the Hague/Hague–Visby Rules apply only where a bill of lading is issued. The Hamburg Rules are therefore applicable to waybills, consignment notes, etc.
5. The Hamburg Rules cover the shipment of live animals and deck cargo, whereas the Hague/Hague–Visby Rules may not.
6. The Hamburg Rules apply to both imports and exports to and from a signatory nation, whereas the Hague/Hague–Visby Rules apply only to exporters.

The Hamburg Rules became operative in November 1992, involving the requisite minimum 20 nations. In 2003 there were 40 signatory nations with a strong contingent of African nations and 14 European countries. China and South Korea have enacted legislation broadly in line with the LLMC. The adoption of the Hamburg Rules destroys the uniformity which currently exists with the Hague and Hague–Visby Rules, thereby creating a third force in the market.

The liability of the carrier under any of the foregoing sea carriage conventions is subject to the overriding provisions of the relevant Merchant Shipping Acts relating, *inter alia*, to limitation of liability. In the UK this involves the Merchant Shipping Act 1979, which implemented the 1976 International Convention on Limitation of Liability for Maritime Claims (LLMC) which became operative from December 1986. A 1996 Protocol to the 1976 LLMC was agreed on 3 May 1996 as part of the Hazardous and Noxious Substances diplomatic conference in London to up-date the levels of liability introduced on 1 December 1986. The new limits are detailed below. By January 2003 the 1996 protocol had been signed by ten nations – mostly European. In addition, Russia has acceded to, the United Kingdom and Norway have ratified and Finland has accepted the Protocol. The new limits are as follows:

(a) In respect of claims for loss of life or personal injury.

   (i) 1 million SDRs for a vessel with tonnage not exceeding 300 tons;
   (ii) 2 million SDRs for a vessel with tonnage not exceeding 2000 tons; and

       (iii) for a vessel with tonnage in excess thereof, in addition to that mentioned in (ii):
for each ton from 2001 to 30 000 tons, 800 SDRs;
for each ton from 30 001 to 70 000 tons, 600 SDRs;
for each ton in excess of 70 000 tons, 400 SDRs.

  (b) In respect of any other claims;

      (i) 500 000 SDRs for a vessel with tonnage not exceeding 300 tons;

     (ii) 1 million SDRs for a vessel with tonnage not exceeding 2000 tons; and

    (iii) for a vessel with tonnage in excess thereof, in addition to that mentioned in (ii):
for each ton from 2001 to 30 000 tons, 400 SDRs;
for each ton from 30 001 to 70 000 tons, 300 SDRs;
for each ton in excess of 70 000 tons, 200 SDRs.

By article 15 of the Convention, contracting states are allowed to make alternative provisions for vessels under 300 tons. The United Kingdom has availed itself of this concession to provide for increased limits instead of the 166 667 SDRs for loss of life and personal injury, and 83 333 SDRs for other claims limits under the 1976 Convention. These figures are increased to 1 million SDRs and 500 000 SDRs respectively under the 1996 Protocol. Under the Merchant Shipping (Convention Limitation of Liability for Maritime Claims) Amendment Order 1998 the protocol limits will replace the Convention limits when the Protocol enters into force internationally.

    The salient points incorporated in a bill of lading can be conveniently listed as follows:

1. the name of the shipper (usually the exporter);
2. the name of the carrying vessel;
3. a full description of the cargo (provided it is not bulk cargo) including any shipping marks, individual package numbers in the consignment, contents, cubic measurement, gross weight, etc.;
4. the marks and numbers identifying the goods;
5. port of shipment or dry port/CFS;
6. port of discharge or dry port/CFS;
7. full details of freight, including when and where it is to be paid – whether freight paid or payable at destination;
8. name of consignee or, if the shipper is anxious to withhold the consignee's name, shipper's order;
9. the terms of the contract of carriage;
10. the date the goods were received for shipment and/or loaded on the vessel;
11. the name and address of the notified party (the person to be notified on arrival of the shipment, usually the buyer);
12. number of bills of lading signed on behalf of the Master or his or her agent, acknowledging receipt of the goods;
13. the signature of the ship's Master or his or her agent and the date.

There are several types and forms of bills of lading and these include the following.

1. *Shipped bill of lading.* Under the Carriage of Goods by Sea Act 1971 (Hague–Visby Rules), the shipper can demand that the shipowner supplies bills of lading proving that the goods have been actually shipped. For this reason, most bill of lading forms are already printed as shipped bills and commence with the wording: 'Shipped in apparent good order and condition'. It confirms the goods are actually on board the vessel.

    This is the most satisfactory type of receipt and the shipper prefers such a bill as there is no doubt about the goods being on board and, in consequence, dispute on this point will not arise with the bankers or consignee, thereby facilitating the earliest financial settlement of the export sale.

2. *Received bill of lading.* This arises where the word 'shipped' does not appear on the bill of lading. It merely confirms that the goods have been handed over to the shipowner and are in his or her custody. The cargo may be in his or her dock, warehouse or transit shed, or even inland such as at a dry port/CFS/ICD, etc. This bill, therefore, does not have the same meaning as a 'shipped' bill and the buyer under a CIF or CFR contract need not accept such a bill for ultimate financial settlement through the bank unless provision has been made in the contract. Forwarding agents will invariably avoid handling 'received bills' for their clients unless special circumstances obtain.

3. *Through bills of lading.* In many cases it is necessary to employ two or more carriers to get the goods to their final destination. The on-carriage may be either by a second vessel or by a different form of transport (for example, to destinations in the interior of Canada). In such cases it would be very complicated and more expensive if the shipper had to arrange on-carriage him- or herself by employing an agent at the point of transhipment. Shipping companies, therefore, issue bills of lading which cover the whole transit and the shipper deals only with the first carrier. This type of bill enables a through rate to be quoted and is growing in popularity with the development of containerization. Special bills of lading have to be prepared for such through-consigned cargo, see item (17), p. 366.

4. *Stale bills of lading.* It is important that the bill of lading is available at the port of destination before the goods arrive or, failing this, at the same time. Bills presented to the consignee or his bank after the goods are due at the port are said to be stale. A cargo cannot normally be delivered by the ship owner without the bill of lading and the late arrival of this all-important document may have undesirable consequences such as warehouse rent, etc.

5. *Groupage and house bills of lading.* A growth sector of the containerized market is the movement of compatible consignments from individual consignors to various consignees usually situated in the same destination

(country or area) and forwarded as one overall consignment. The goods are consolidated into a full container load and the shipping line issues a groupage bill of lading to the forwarder. This is the ocean bill of lading and shows a number of consignments of groupage of a certain weight and cubic measurement in a cargo manifest form. The forwarder issues subsequent cross referencing to the ocean bill of lading, through the house bill of lading. It is merely a receipt for the cargo and does not have the same status as the bill of lading issued by the shipowner. Shippers choosing to use a house bill of lading should clarify with the bank whether it is acceptable for letter of credit purposes, and ideally ensure it is stipulated as acceptable before the credit is opened. Advantages of groupage include: less packing; lower insurance premiums; quicker transits (usually); less risk of damage and pilferage; and lower rates when compared with such cargo being dispatched as an individual parcel or consignment (p. 159).

6. *Transhipment bill of lading.* This type is usually issued by shipping companies when there is no direct service between two ports, but when the shipowner is prepared to tranship the cargo at an intermediate port at his or her expense.

7. *Clean bills of lading.* Each bill of lading states: 'in apparent good order and condition', which of course refers to the cargo. If this statement is not modified by the shipowner, the bill of lading is regarded as 'clean' or 'unclaused'. By issuing clean bills of lading, the shipowner admits his or her full liability of the cargo described in the bill under the law and his or her contract. This type is much favoured by banks for financial settlement purposes.

8. *Claused bills of lading.* If the shipowner does not agree with any of the statements made in the bill of lading he or she will add a clause to this effect, thereby causing the bill of lading to be termed as 'unclean', 'foul' or 'claused'. There are many recurring types of such clauses including: inadequate packaging; unprotected machinery; second-hand cases; wet or stained cartons; damaged crates; cartons missing, etc. The clause 'shipped on deck at owner's risk' may thus be considered to be claused under this heading. This type of bill of lading is usually unacceptable to a bank.

9. *Negotiable bills of lading.* If the words 'or his or their assigns' are contained in the bill of lading, it is negotiable. There are, however, variations in this terminology, for example, the word 'bearer' may be inserted, or another party stated in the preamble to the phrase. Bills of lading may be negotiable by endorsement or transfer.

10. *Non-negotiable bills of lading.* When the words 'or his or their assigns' are deleted from the bills of lading, the bill is regarded as non-negotiable. The effect of this deletion is that the consignee (or other named party) cannot transfer the property or goods by transfer of the bills. This particular type is seldom found and will normally apply

when goods are shipped on a non-commercial basis, such as household effects.

11. *Container bills of lading.* Containers are now playing a major role in international shipping and container bills of lading are becoming more common in use. They cover the goods from port to port or from inland point of departure to inland point of destination – which can be an inland clearance depot, dry port or container base. Undoubtedly, to the shipper, the most useful type of bill of lading is the clean, negotiable 'through bill', as it enables the goods to be forwarded to the point of destination under one document, although much international trade is based on free carrier (named place) FCA, free-on-board (FOB), cost, insurance, freight (CIF) and carriage and insurance paid to (named point of destination) CIP (pp. 414–15) contracts.

12. *Combined transport bill of lading.* With the development of combined transport operations, an increasing volume of both liner cargo trade and bulk cargo shipments will be carried involving the bill of lading being issued in association with a selected Charterparty. An example is found in the Combined Transport Bill of Lading 1971 – codename 'Combiconbill' issued with selected Charterparties. The combined transport document rules are found in the ICC Rules for a Combined Transport Document (brochure no. 298). They are widely used by major container operators and reflect the earlier Tokyo–Rome Rules, the Tokyo Rules and TCM Convention, see item (16), p. 366.

13. *Straight bill of lading.* A 'straight bill' is one where the consignee is clearly nominated by name without any qualification ('To the order of' or similar). It is the opposite of an 'order bill' which is one where the consignee is shown as being 'To Order' or with a named person qualified by the words 'To the order of' or similar. The straight bill is not negotiable and cannot be used to transfer title by endorsement (or passage of a blank endorsed bill) in the way that an order bill can. In the USA, the Pomerene Act provides that delivery of goods represented by a straight bill can be made to the nominated consignee without surrender of any documentation but merely upon production of proof of identity. Elsewhere in the world the position of the carrier delivering against a straight bill is unclear.

14. *Negotiable FIATA Combined Transport Bill.* This document is becoming increasingly used in the trade and is a FIATA bill of lading (FBL), employed as a combined transport document with negotiable status. It has been developed by the International Federation of Forwarding Agents Associations and is acceptable under the ICC Rules Uniform Customs and Practice for Documentary Credits (ICC publication no. 500) – revision 1993. The FIATA bill of lading should be stipulated in letters of credit where the forwarders' container groupage service is to be utilized and a house bill of lading is to be issued (see also p. 366).

FIATA states that a forwarder issuing a FIATA bill of lading must comply with the following:

(a)   the goods are in apparent good order and condition;

(b)   the forwarder has received the consignment and has sole right of disposal;

(c)   the details set out on the face of the FBL correspond with the instructions the forwarder has received;

(d)   the insurance arrangements have been clarified – the FBL contains a specific delete option box which must be completed;

(e)   the FBL clearly indicates whether one or more originals have been issued.

The FIATA, FBL terms create more shipper obligations in the areas of packing, general average, payment of charges and description of goods. Additional rights are also conferred on the forwarder in the areas of lien, routeing of cargo and storage handling and transport of consignments.

15.   *FIATA Multi-modal Transport Bill of Lading (MTBL).* The FIATA Multi-modal Transport Bill of Lading (MTBL) is recognized worldwide as a negotiable document of title in line with the International Chamber of Commerce Uniform Rules for such documents. It is widely stipulated in Letters of Credit and Shipping Instructions and is recognized by the ICC Banking Commission Group as a carrier's bill and by the British Bankers Association. The FIATA MTBL carries the logo of the ICC in addition to that of FIATA and BIFA. BIFA is the sole UK authority to approve and register applications to use the MTBL. Applicants must be trading members of the Association and must show evidence of sufficient liability insurance over 2 SDRs per kilo. Members are only authorized to issue BIFA supplied or licensed MTBLs in the UK. If overseas agents or branches wish to issue an MTBL they may do so after approval by their local forwarders' association, provided that the association is an Ordinary Member of FIATA, see item (16), p. 366.

16.   *Combined Transport Document/Multi-modal Transport Document.* Two names for the same document. This is a document issued by a Combined/Multi-modal Transport Operator (CTO/MTO) that covers the multi-modal transport on a door to door basis in the one contract of carriage. The CTO/MTO, issued by the CTD/MTD, undertakes to perform, or in his own name, carry out the performance of the Combined/Multi-modal Transport. Hence, a CTD/MTD is a document issued by a carrier who contracts as a principal with the Merchant to effect a Combine/Multi-modal Transport. Therefore, the CTO/MTO issuing the CTD/MTD is primarily liable to the Merchant under the terms of the CTD/MTD throughout carriage.

17.   *Through Transport Document (TTD).* The TTD is a contract of carriage involving more than one Carrier. The Carrier who issues the TTD acts

as a principal only during the carriage of his own vessel(s) and as an Agent only at all other times. Therefore, the liabilities and responsibilities are spread over several Carriers and the Merchant is in contract with different carriers under different (and probably unknown) conditions at different stages of carriage.

Many so called CTDs/MTDs are in fact, by the definitions featured in items (16) and (17), TTDs, so the fact that a Bill of Lading bears the wording 'Combined Transport Document/Bill of Lading' is no guarantee that it is so. A careful examination of the document is needed to reveal its authenticity.

Basically the bill of lading has four functions. Broadly, it is a receipt for the goods shipped, a transferable document to the goods thereby enabling the holder to demand the cargo, evidence of the terms of the contract of affreightment but not the actual contract, and a quasi-negotiable instrument.

Once the shipper or his or her agent becomes aware of the sailing schedules of a particular trade, through the medium of the web or some form of advertisement, he or she communicates with the shipowner with a view to booking cargo space on the vessel or container. Provided satisfactory arrangements have been concluded, the shipper forwards the cargo. At this stage, it is important to note that the shipper always makes the offer by forwarding the consignment, while the shipowner either accepts or refuses it. Furthermore, it is the shipper's duty, or that of his or her agent, to supply details of the consignment. Normally, this is done by completing the shipping company's form of bill of lading and the shipping company then signs the number of copies requested.

When the goods have been received on board the ship, the bill of lading is dated and signed by or on behalf of the carrier, usually by the Master of the ship or his or her agent, and stamped 'freight paid' or 'freight payable at destination' as appropriate. If the cargo is in good condition and everything is in order, no endorsement will be made on the document and it can be termed a 'clean' bill of lading. Conversely, if the goods are damaged or a portion of the consignment is missing, the document will be suitably endorsed by the Master or his or her agent and the bill of lading will be considered 'claused' or 'unclean'. The complete set of bills of lading is then returned to the exporter (seller) for prompt despatch to the importer (buyer). The buyer must have a negotiable bill of lading with which to clear the goods at the port of destination.

Bills of lading are made out in sets and the number varies according to the trade. Generally, it is two or three – one of which will probably be forwarded immediately, and another by a later mail in case the first is lost or delayed, together with a number of non-negotiable copies for office and filing use. In some trades, coloured bills of lading are used, to distinguish the original (signed) bills from the copies which are purely for recording purposes. The reverse of the bill of lading bears the terms and conditions of the contract of carriage. The clauses on most bills of lading are similar in effect if not in wording.

Where the shipper has sold the goods on letter of credit terms established through a bank, or when he or she wishes to obtain payment of his or her invoice before the consignee obtains the goods, he or she will pass the full set of original bills to his or her bank, who will in due course arrange presentation to the consignee against payment. The financial role of the bill of lading is explained in Chapter 12.

The shipowner or his or her agent at the port of destination will require one original bill of lading to be presented to him or her before the goods are handed over. Furthermore, he or she will normally require payment of any freight due, should this not have been paid at the port of shipment. When one of a set of bills of lading has been presented to the shipping company, the other bills in the set lose their value.

In the event of the bill of lading being lost or delayed in transit, the shipping company will allow delivery of the goods to the person claiming to be the consignee, if he or she gives a letter of indemnity. This is normally countersigned by a bank and relieves the shipping company of any liability should another person eventually come along with the actual bill of lading.

Many bills of lading are consigned 'to order' and in such situations are endorsed, normally on the reverse, by the shipper. If the consignee is named, the goods will only be released to him or her, unless he or she transfers his or her right by endorsement subject to the bill of lading providing for this.

The following items are common discrepancies found in bills of lading when being processed and should be avoided.

1. Document not presented in full sets when requested.
2. Alterations not authenticated by an official of the shipping company or their agents.
3. The bill of lading is not clean when presented, such as, when it is endorsed regarding damaged condition of the specified cargo or inadequate packing thereby making it unacceptable to a bank for financial settlement purposes.
4. The document is not endorsed 'on board' when so required.
5. The 'on board' endorsement is not signed or initialled by the carrier or agent and likewise not dated.
6. The bill of lading is not 'blank' endorsed if drawn to order.
7. The document fails to indicate whether 'freight paid' as stipulated in the credit arrangements, viz. CFR or CIF contracts.
8. The bill of lading is not marked 'freight pre-paid' when freight charges are included in the invoice.
9. The bill of lading is made out 'to order', when the letter of credit stipulates 'direct to consignee' or vice versa.

10. The document is dated later than the latest shipping date specified in the credit.
11. The document is not presented within 21 days after date of shipment or such lesser time as prescribed in the letter of credit.
12. The bill of lading details merchandise other than that prescribed.
13. The rate at which freight is calculated, and the total amount, is not shown when credit requires such data to be given.
14. Cargo has been shipped 'on deck' and not placed in the ship's hold. Basically, 'on deck' claused bills of lading are not acceptable when clean onboard bills of lading are required.
15. Shipment has been made from a port or to a destination contrary to that stipulated.
16. Other types of bills of lading have been presented, although not specifically authorized. For example, bills of lading issued under a charterparty, or forwarding agents' bills of lading are not accepted unless specially authorized in the letter of credit.
17. The document has not been issued by a freight forwarder, unless it indicates that such a freight forwarder is acting as the actual carrier or as the agent for a named carrier.
18. If the credit terms stipulate the bill of lading should evidence that the goods are available to the 'order of a named party', it does not evidence that the goods are 'Straight Consigned' to that party. In the case of the former transfer of title it is simply a matter of endorsement; in the latter case, the bill of lading cannot be endorsed in favour of third parties unless it specifically states otherwise.
19. If the credit terms stipulate that the bill of lading is to be issued to your order, it is endorsed by you as required in the credit.
20. The presentation comprises a full set of originals plus (if required in the credit terms) the specified number of non-negotiable copies.
21. The bill of lading does not include any detrimental clauses relating to defective goods or packing.
22. The document does not show shipment of goods other than or in addition to those required.
23. The vessel name and/or port of loading and/or port of discharge are not prefaced with the word 'intended'.
24. It does not bear a clause with reference to 'Part Container Load' which further stipulates that goods will not be released until all bills of lading issued for that container load are presented.
25. The document includes 'Notify Parties' as defined in the credit.
26. If the terms of the credit require the bill of lading to show the freight charges these are shown.

Our study of the bill of lading would not be complete without a consideration of the national standard shipping note (NSSN), the common short-form bill of lading, and the common short-form sea waybill.

The NSSN has replaced the mate's receipt in most UK ports, and comprises a six-part set, copies of which are retained by these parties handling the goods until they are finally onboard, from which a 'shipped' bill of lading is issued. The document is compiled by the supplier of the goods, or the shipper or freight forwarder, giving full details of the goods similar to those found on the bill of lading, against which it is matched before issue. It accompanies the merchandise to the port or terminal. The document is unacceptable for use with shipments of goods classified as dangerous.

The document also harmonizes the information to be shown among shippers and encourages the provision of better-quality information. Furthermore, it provides a multi-port set of documents for use in different areas of the port and in shipping line offices as proof of delivery of goods in the form of a dock terminal receipt featuring haulier details and receiving authority remarks, loading information and is a means of cross-checking information provided for the issue of bills of lading. The NSSN is an approved document as a skeleton customs pre-entry presentation. It is used internationally for the delivery of non-hazardous conventional break-bulk cargo, full container loads (FCL) and less than container loads (LCL) to the ports, container bases and depots. It is also used sometimes in connection with shipments by air.

The document covers shipper and forwarder and provides bills from port to port and through-transport including container bills of lading. It does not cover combined transport bills of lading. A revised SITPRO standard shipping note was introduced on 1 July 1999 (see specimen p. 614) and it is fully aligned to the UN layout key and has 17 boxes.

The common short-form bill of lading is fully negotiable and the normal bill of lading lodgement and presentation procedures remain unchanged. However, instead of the mass of small print on the reverse, there is an approved 'short-form' clause on the face which incorporates carriers' standard conditions with full legal effect. It has the following salient features.

1. The short-form bill of lading is widely used in the trade. It may be used by shippers and freight forwarders and presented for signature to the carrier or his or her authorized agents, after a perusal and acceptance of the carrier's standard terms and conditions to which the incorporation clause in the short-form bill of lading refers.
2. The short-form is suitable for outward shipments from the UK involving 'through' transit, or 'port-to-port' carriage of cargo for both break-bulk and unit loads of all types traditionally covered by 'long-form' bills of lading.
3. The short-form is based upon an internationally accepted layout adopted by the UN. Such widespread acceptance of its format facilitates fast and accurate recording, processing, transmission and receipt of data relating to the movement of cargo.

4. As confirmed by the ICC, it is acceptable within the 'uniform customs and practice for documentary 'credits'. (ICC brochure no. 500 refers.)

5. The short-form bill of lading is a document recommended by the Chamber of Shipping for use with all outward shipments from the UK and particularly by all UK shippers and carriers and their conference associates.

6. The short-form is a document of title under which the contracting carrier undertakes to deliver the subject goods against surrender of an original document.

7. The short-form is a 'received-for-carriage' bill with provision for endorsement evidencing goods shipped onboard when so required.

8. The short-form is suitable for conventional and through-liner services irrespective of whether the vessel is chartered or owned by the contracting carrier. (Use of the form is not currently permissible for goods carried by combined transport operators.)

9. It is described as a 'short-form' document because of the use of an abridged standard clause on the face of the document which incorporates the conditions of carriage of the contracting carrier. The change eliminates the mass of small print on the reverse side of bills of lading without affecting the status of the document or rights and obligations of any interested party.

10. It is a document fully aligned to the SITPRO 'master' document with the opportunity to complete the bill of lading from such a document without any additional typing.

11. The short-form bill of lading is an aid to achieving lower stationary costs through (a) a reduced need to hold a variety of stocks of long-form bills of lading, with individual carriers' names and conditions, plus (b) the elimination of the risk of using obsolescent forms together with the attendant complications.

The use of the negotiable bill of lading which has to be surrendered to the carrier at the destination in order to obtain delivery of the goods is traditional, but not without disadvantages. The document has to follow the goods and often, for commercial or financial reasons, passes through a variety of hands, resulting in the goods being held up at their destination pending arrival of the document – and thus expenses and additional risks are incurred and customer goodwill is probably lost.

This can be resolved through the use of a non-negotiable type of transport document – a sea waybill – in place of the negotiable traditional bill of lading. The basic feature of the sea waybill is that it provides for delivery to the consignee named in it without surrender of the transport document (see specimen sea waybill p. 613). The sea waybill has the following salient features which are similar in many ways to the common short-form bill of lading.

1. It is a common document upon which the shipper adds the name of the contracting carrier to be used.
2. It is a non-negotiable document consigned to a named consignee and not requiring production to obtain possession of the goods at destination.
3. It is a received-for-shipment document, with an option for use as a shipped document.
4. It is an aid to achieve lower stationery costs through: (a) a reduced need to hold stocks of individual carriers' bills with individual carriers' names and conditions plus (b) it eliminates the risk of using obsolescent forms together with attendant complications.
5. It is a document fully aligned to the SITPRO 'master' document with the opportunity to complete the waybill from such a document without any additional typing.
6. It is described as a 'short-form' document because of the use of an abridged standard clause on the face of the document which incorporates the conditions of carriage of the contracting carrier. The change eliminates the need to reprint documents to accommodate changes and conditions.
7. It facilitates the earlier release of the goods – if received for shipment – and thereby reduces delays associated with negotiability. Moreover, it helps the speedier flow of goods to the consignee. One must bear in mind the named consignee is not required to produce the sea waybill to obtain possession of the goods at destination.
8. The sea waybill is widely used in the trade. It may be used by shippers and freight forwarders and presented for signature to the carrier or his or her authorized agents, after a perusal and acceptance of the carrier's standard terms and conditions to which the incorporation clause in the sea waybill refers.
9. It is suitable for outward shipments from the UK involving 'through' transit, or 'port-to-port' carriage of cargo for both break-bulk and unit loads of all types. Moreover, it is suitable for conventional and through-liner services, irrespective of whether the vessel is chartered or owned by the carrier.
10. It is based upon an internationally accepted layout adopted by the UN. Such widespread acceptance of its format facilitates fast and accurate recording, processing, transmission and receipt of data relating to the movement of cargo.
11. A waybill is not a document of title. Accordingly, it is not mandatory subject to the relevant Carriage of Goods by Sea Act, or the Hague or Hague–Visby Rules as obtains for a bill of lading.
12. The popularity of the waybill will intensify as EDI develops (Chapter 15). It is an ideal document for EDI transmission.
13. The waybill is a personal contract between the carrier and shipper to which the consignee never becomes a party. This gives the

shipper the right of stoppage in transit at any time. It also means that the consignee cannot sue the carrier in his or her own name and that the carrier must settle claims with the shipper rather than the consignee.

14. The Carriage of Goods by Sea Act 1992 recognizes the rights of the consignee in the sea waybill and the rights to sue on the contract (see p. 359).

15. The sea waybill cannot be used in documentary credits as it is not a document of title (see p. 295).

The commercial and financial feasibility of using the sea waybill clearly rests with the shipper and consignee and is dependent upon the type of trade transaction involved. The waybill is the natural choice for trading between multinational companies and associated companies, where no documentary transaction is involved and also for open account sales. It can also be used for transactions between companies where a documentary credit transaction is not required. However, it can additionally be used in many cases involving banking transactions.

The point at which waybills are released will depend upon whether the document is 'received for shipment' or 'shipped onboard'. In signing waybills, the carrier or his or her agent is required to insert the carrier's transmission address within the signature or date stamp.

If a received-for-shipment document were issued and the cargo was subsequently short-shipped or a carrier's clause required (e.g., to indicate that damage was sustained while the goods were on the quay) then a qualification report should be issued to the shipper, consignee and those concerned within the carrier's organization; information concerning such reports should also be made available to insurers on request. Use of the 'shipped' option would, however, obviate the need for a qualification report, and, in such circumstances the normal bill of lading procedures would apply.

If a 'shipped onboard' document were issued, then the provision of the 'shipped' option should be in a manner which if the document were to be presented under a documentary credit, will satisfy 'Uniform Customs and Practice for Documentary Credits' 1993, No. 500. This refers to a procedure whereby waybills can be endorsed to specify that the goods mentioned have been loaded onboard a named vessel or shipped on a named vessel, the loading onboard date being specified. Electronic trading is now commonplace and Bolero is dealt with in Chapter 16 and CMI rules for Electronic Bill of Lading (pp. 569–71).

Today the waybill will become more widely used, especially between established consignors and consignees who have been trading for many years and wish to take full advantage of EDI benefits.

To conclude our study of bills of lading, it is relevant to mention that the legislation is not identical in every country, as has been demonstrated in earlier pages (pp. 352–53), through various conventions. Exporters/ importers are reminded the Bill of Lading and Sea Waybill now feature in paperless trading – the electronic transmission of documents – see Bolero pp. 457–63.

14.6 Cargo insurance policy and certificate

It is most important to have insurance cover against loss or damage that may occur during shipment. The export sales contract with the buyer must clearly state who is responsible for arranging the insurance at all stages from the time the merchandise leaves the exporter's premises until the buyer takes possession. This embraces transportation of the goods to the seaport, airport, or inland clearance depot, the period during which the merchandise is stored awaiting shipment or loading, the periods while the goods are on board the ship, aircraft or other conveyance such as the through international road transport, the off-loading and storage on arrival, and finally transportation to the buyer. This involves primarily Incoterms 2000 (pp. 395–417).

The cargo insurance policy is fully explained in Chapter 10 (see specimen p. 619).

Overall, the insurance policy certificate must contain the following:

1.   the name and signature of the insurer;
2.   the name of the assured;
3.   the endorsement of the assured when applicable so that the rights to claim may be transferred;
4.   a description of the risk covered;
5.   a description of the consignment;
6.   the sum or sums to be insured;
7.   the place where claims are payable together with the name of the agent to whom claims may be directed.

Basically, the insurance policy certificate must embrace the following relative to the processing of the international consignment:

1.   cover the risk detailed in the credit arrangements;
2.   be in a completed form;
3.   be in a transferable form;
4.   be dated on or before the date of the document evidencing despatch, for example, bill of lading;
5.   be expressed in the same currency as that of the credit.

The insurance policy certificate must avoid containing the following discrepancies when presented under a letter of credit.

1. The amount of cover is insufficient or does not include the risks mentioned in the credit.
2. The insurance is not issued in the currency of the credit.
3. The insurance policy certificate is not endorsed and/or signed.
4. The certificate or policy bears a date later than date of shipment/despatch.
5. The goods are not correctly described.
6. The alterations on the insurance policy certificate are not authenticated.
7. The insurance policy certificate is not in a transferable form when required.
8. The carrying vessel's name is not recorded.
9. The insurance policy certificate does not cover transhipment when bills of lading indicate it will take place.

When a policy is called for under a letter of credit, a certificate is not acceptable. However, a policy is acceptable when a certificate is requested. Broker's cover notes are not acceptable unless specifically permitted in the credit.

It is important to bear in mind when the shipper, exporter, or agent is preparing the insurance document for presentation to the bank, that it is in the currency of the documentary letter of credit; the insurance is for the value specified in the credit; it covers all risks specified in the credit; the insurance document is dated prior to the despatch of goods or indicates that cover is effective from the shipment date; and finally the insurance policy is presented when the credit so stipulates.

14.7 Certificate of origin

The certificate of origin specifies the nature, quantity and value of the goods, etc. together with their place of manufacture. Such a declaration, stating the country of origin of the goods shipped is required by some countries, often to simplify their customs duties. It is frequently incorporated in the customs invoice. In a minority of cases, the declaration has to be authenticated by a Chamber of Commerce. It could also incorporate the selling price of the goods termed the current domestic value (CDV), in which case it is likely to be embraced in the invoice.

Generally, certification of origin for non-preferential purposes is a trade policy issue with wider connotations than preferential origin. It may be required to identify favoured nation status goods, in order to reduce import duties or, from a negative perspective, to identify commodities originating from certain regions or countries the importation of which may be restricted or prohibited. The declaration may also be made on other commercial documents, such as the packing list or consignment note *(inter alia)*. The documentation for each system varies, but comprises basically of one of the following.

Certificate of Origin

This is a standard document and is required in a number of countries. The certificate must conform to specific conditions, which govern the format and layout of the document as well as specifying the quality of the paper required, for example, it must be printed with a guilloche background. It must be endorsed by an authorized body in the issuing country before it is valid.

Arab Certificate of Origin

This is required for exports to Arab nations – with the exception of Iran, which accepts the EU Certificate. Some countries also require the EU Certificate of Origin, but endorsed by the Arab Chambers. The form is in a prescribed format, with both the language of the issuing country and Arab box titles. Normally it has to be authenticated by both the local Chamber of Commerce and the Arab Chamber of Commerce before it is valid.

14.8 Certificate of shipment

The FIATA Forwarder's Certificate of Receipt (FCR) and Forwarder's Certificate of Transport (FCT) are becoming increasingly accepted in the trade as the recognizable document confirming a receipt of the goods. Alternatively the freight forwarder may issue a letter detailing the goods received by the forwarder, or in a form similar to a Bill of Lading (where the goods have actually been despatched).

The FCR and FCT are usually issued under FCA Free Carrier Incoterms 2000, involving a multi-modal transport operation. Alternatively, they may be used when the supplier sells the goods ex-works or when the goods are being despatched via a forwarder's groupage service and a recognized document is needed to prove that the goods are no longer in the control of the seller. In such situations, the freight forwarder would be acting as principal or as road carrier.

14.9 Charterparty

A charterparty is a contract whereby a shipowner agrees to place his or her ship, or part of it, at the disposal of a merchant or other person (known as the charterer), for the carriage of goods from one port to another port on being paid freight, or to let his or her ship for a specified period, his or her remuneration being known as hire money. The terms, conditions and exceptions under which the goods are carried are set out in the charterparty.

A very large proportion of the world's trade is carried in tramp vessels. It is quite common to find that one cargo will fill a whole ship and, in these circumstances, one cargo owner or one charterer will enter into a special contract with the shipowner for the hire of his or her ship. Such a contract is known as a charterparty. It is not always a full ship, although this is usually the case. There are basically two types of charterparties: demise and non-demise.

A demise or 'bareboat' charterparty arises when the charterer is responsible for providing the cargo and crew, while the shipowner merely provides the vessel. In consequence, the charterer appoints the crew, thus taking over full responsibility for the operation of the vessel, and pays all expenses incurred. A demise charterparty is for a period of time which may vary from a few weeks to several years.

A non-demise charter arises when the shipowner provides the vessel and her crew, while the charterer merely supplies the cargo. It may be a voyage charter for a particular voyage, in which case the shipowner agrees to carry cargo between specified ports for a prearranged freight. The majority of tramp cargo shipments are made on a voyage charter basis. Alternatively, it may be a time charter for a stated period or voyage for a remuneration known as hire money. The shipowner continues to manage his or her own vessel, both under non-demise voyage or time charterparties under the charterer's instructions. With a time charter, it is usual for the charterer to pay port dues and fuel costs, and overtime payments incurred in an endeavour to obtain faster turn-rounds. It is quite common for liner companies to supplement their services by taking tramp ships on time charter, but this practice may lessen as containerization develops.

There are several types of non-demise voyage charter and these are given below. It will be seen that they all deal with the carriage of goods from a certain port or ports to another port or ports and the differences between them arise mainly out of payment for the cost of loading and discharging and port expenses.

1. *Gross form of charter.* This is probably the most common form of charter used by tramp ships today. In this form, the shipowner – in return for a higher freight – meets the cost of employing the stevedores at either the loading port or the port of discharge or both.
2. *Net terms.* Under those terms the cargo is loaded and discharged at no cost to the shipowner. The cost of stevedores at the loading port is borne by the shipper and, at the port of discharge, by the receiver. The term net terms is not in common use but is generally referred to as 'free-in-and-out' (FIO) with exactly the same meaning.
3. *FIO charter.* Under this charter the cargo is loaded and discharged at no cost to the shipowner. The cost of stevedores at the loading port is borne by the shipper and at the port of discharge by the receiver.

4.   *Liner terms.* Under this charter, usually found in the short sea trade, the shipowner is responsible for loading, stowing and discharging the cargo. Usually the shipowner selects and appoints the stevedores, but this can be an area of discussion during the fixture negotiations.
5.   *Lump sum charter.* In this case, the charterer pays a lump sum of money for the use of the ship and the shipowner guarantees that a certain amount of space (that is, bale cubic metres) will be available for cargo, along with the maximum weight of cargo that the vessel will be able to carry. A lump sum charter may be on either a gross basis or an FIO basis. Such a charter is very useful when the charterer wishes to load a mixed cargo – the shipowner guarantees that a certain amount of space and weight will be available and it is up to the charterer to use that space to his or her best advantage.

The above forms of charter are all quite common today and, in each case, the ship owner pays the port charges.

There are, of course, numerous variations that may be made to the above broad divisions and this is a matter for negotiation when the vessel is being 'worked' for future business. For example, the gross and FIO charters may be modified to an FOB charter: free on board meaning that the charterer pays for the cost of loading and the shipowner pays for the cost of discharge, or alternatively the charter may be arranged on the basis of free discharge, that is, the charterer pays for the cost of discharging. The same general terms of contract are found in all the above types of charter.

The Baltic Exchange based in London provides a unique professional market for cargo interests, shipowners, shipbrokers, port operators, agents and all those involved in international freight transport by sea. Overall, it is a market place which is self-regulated with strict business ethics. It deals with cargoes, buying and selling ships, commodities and aircraft chartering. The chartered tonnage may be for a voyage, period of time (time charter), trip time chartering, contract of affreightment, joint ventures, pooling, paralleling or bare-boating.

The shipowner may be a fleet mega-operator or a single operator (family business), or the vessels may be state-owned tonnage, privately owned national registered tonnage, offshore registered privately owned tonnage or bare-boat. The charterer may be a single commodity dealer, a trader, a state enterprise, a ship operator, a liner operator involving NVOCC or parallel tonnage.

The modern Baltic Exchange today relies on electronic communications. Today, there are some 400 chartering and brokerage firms in the Baltic Exchange in London, together with about 150 sales and purchase operations of ships. The London based broking firms handle most of the world's sale and purchase deals. The Agents for the Greek shipowning community in London employ some 3000 brokers, though not all are Baltic Exchange members. Traditionally, the Baltic Exchange membership has been drawn from those based in the City of London, but since 1994 overseas members have been permitted. This latter category, subject to the same business ethics of the Baltic Exchange, is growing quickly.

The services provided by the shipbroker are wide ranging. Nowadays modern communications – E-commerce and the Internet, relying on computers and VDUs – enable brokers to keep abreast of current developments and opportunities, but the tradition of meeting face to face continues but with little trading significance. The Baltic Exchange brokerage clientele is in daily contact with the other major international dry cargo market centres based in Hamburg, Oslo, Piraeus, New York, Tokyo, Hong Kong and Singapore.

It will be appreciated that the terms and conditions of a charterparty will vary according to the wishes of the parties to the contract. Nevertheless, the Chamber of Shipping together with the Baltic and International Maritime Conference have approved a number of charterparties (about 50) for certain commodities in specified trades. These include primarily the tramp trades, namely coal, wheat, timber, ore, etc. The parties to the contract are free to make any amendments to such charterparties to meet their needs and there is no obligation to use any particular charterparty for a particular trade.

The subject of chartering is dealt with extensively in Chapter 15 of *Elements of Shipping* 8th edition, published by Routledge.

14.10 Convention on the Contract for the International Carriage of Goods by Road (CMR)

The International Convention Concerning the Carriage of Goods by Road (CMR) came into force in the UK in October 1965, and is fully explained on pp. 574–75.

The contract of carriage, found in the CMR consignment note, is established when it is completed by the sender and carrier with the appropriate signatures or stamp being recorded thereon. The senders and the carrier are entitled respectively to the first and third copies of the consignment note, and the second copy must accompany the goods. If the goods have to be loaded in different vehicles, or are of different kinds, or are divided into different lots, either party has the right to require a separate consignment note to be made out in respect of each vehicle or each kind or lot of goods. The CMR consignment note is not a negotiable or transferable document or a document of title.

The consignment note must contain the following particulars: the date when and the place where it is made out; the names and addresses of the sender, the carrier and the consignee; the place and date of taking over the goods, and the place designated for delivery; the ordinary description of the nature of the goods and the method of packing and, in the case of dangerous goods, their generally recognized description; the number of packages and their special marks and numbers; the gross weight of the goods or their quantity otherwise expressed; charges relating to the carriage; the requisite instructions for customs and other formalities; and a statement that the carriage is subject, notwithstanding any clause to the contrary, to the provisions of the convention.

Furthermore, the consignment note must contain the following particulars where applicable: a statement that transshipment is not allowed; the charges which the sender undertakes to pay; the amount of 'cash on delivery' charges; a declaration of the value of the goods; a declaration of the amount representing any special interest in delivery; the sender's instructions to the carrier regarding insurance of the goods; the agreed time limit for the carriage; a list of the documents handed to the carrier. Where the carrier has no reasonable means of checking the accuracy of the statements in the consignment note as to the number of packages and their marks and numbers, or as to the apparent condition of the goods and their packaging, he must enter his reservations in the consignment note specifying the grounds on which they are based. Where the sender requires the carrier to check the gross weight of the goods or their quantity otherwise expressed or the contents of the packages, the carrier must enter the results of such checks; and any agreement that open unsheeted vehicles may be used for the carriage of the goods. The parties may enter any other useful particulars in the consignment note.

The sender is liable for all expenses, loss and damage sustained by the carrier by reason of the inaccuracy or inadequacy of certain specified particulars which the consignment note must contain, or by reason of the inaccuracy or inadequacy of any other particulars or instructions given by him or her.

The carrier is liable for all expenses, loss and damage sustained by the person entitled to dispose of the goods as a result of the omission of the statement that the contract is subject to the convention.

For the purposes of the convention, the carrier is responsible for the acts and omissions of his or her agents and servants and any other persons whose services he or she uses for the performance of the carriage as long as those agents, servants or other persons are acting within the scope of their employment.

There is a duty on the carrier to undertake the following:

1. to check the accuracy of the statements in the consignment note as to the number of packages and their marks and numbers, and the apparent condition of the goods and their packaging;
2. if the sender so requires him or her, to check the gross weight of the goods or their quantity otherwise expressed or the contents of the packages;

3. to check that the statement that the contract is subject to the con-
    vention is properly included in the consignment note.

The sender is responsible for the accuracy and adequacy of documents
and information which he or she must either attach to the consignment
note or place at the carrier's disposal for the purposes of customs or other
formalities which have to be completed before delivery of the goods.
   There is a duty on the sender:

1. to ensure that the goods are properly packed;
2. in the case of dangerous goods, to inform the carrier of the exact
    nature of the danger and indicate, if necessary, the precautions to be
    taken (pp. 201–17);
3. to ensure the accuracy and adequacy of certain specified particulars
    which the consignment note must contain and of any other particu-
    lars or instructions given by him to the carrier.

The great majority of international road transport European (EU) consignments are conducted under open account payment terms. A bank will
normally only make an advance against goods conveyed by CMR
International Consignment Note if the goods are consigned to a bank in
the buyer's country and are only to be released under payment by the
buyer. The CMR consignment note must be carried on all hire-and-reward
journeys involving an international transit.

14.11 Courier receipt

This document is used where the goods are despatched by courier service,
usually involving small parcels and packets. Under UCP500 the presentation of a receipt issued by any courier company is allowed unless one is
specified in the letter of credit.

Customs forms CN22 and CN23 (Royal Mail International packages)

Exporters despatching packages by Royal Mail International Services (see
p. 180) are required to complete customs declaration on the green label
for letter mail form CN22 and white label form CN23 for parcel post. It
is attached to the mail item with an SP301 plastic wallet. It features
details of consignor, consignee, senders reference (bar coded label), list
of contents and number of articles, country of origin of goods, net and
gross weights (each item to be shown separately), any supporting documents, whether the contents is a gift or sample and the sender's signature. Goods originating within the EU and being despatched to Member
States do not require a customs declaration, see HM Customs Notices
275 and 143.

14.12 Dock receipt

This may be issued by a Port Authority to confirm receipt of cargo on the quay or warehouse pending shipment. It has no legal role regarding processing financial settlement of international consignments.

14.13 End use Certificate

This is a document completed by the international buyer indicating/ specifying the use to which the product or service will be employed and details of any 'on sale' and likewise the use to which the product will be engaged. Required by many Governments in countries anxious to avoid the illegal/abusive use of arms/defence equipment sold overseas. This document is required by Customs for customs clearance and forms a Government approval of the overseas sale. The document would be certified by a Government department.

14.14 Exchange permit

The exchange permit is found particularly in Middle East trades and is usually associated with the issue of an import licence. They are usually issued by Government departments, Chambers of Commerce, or Chambers of Industry, thereby authorizing import of a specific commodity. It is a means of regulating the flow of specific commodity imports and the funds associated with them.

14.15 Export Cargo Shipping Instruction (ECSI)

At the time of booking a cargo for shipment, exporters or their agents complete the Export Cargo Shipping Instruction and forward it to the shipping company, usually electronically. It provides all the relevant data which the carrier needs to complete the bill of lading and specifies who is responsible for freight charges. This includes packing specifications. Additionally, the ECSI makes provision for supplementary services such as customs entries. It applies to both general, LCL and FCL cargo.

14.16 Export invoicing

Export documents are never static – there is a continual stream of new overseas import regulations along with new developments and a constant issue of new forms, etc. Accordingly, the requisite invoice for a particular market should be checked to ensure the correct one is used otherwise serious delays will be encountered in processing the export order through customs. Moreover, the exporter's invoice should be carefully and accurately completed. Details of the various types of invoices are now examined.

1. *Commercial invoice.* The commercial invoice gives details of the goods and is issued by the seller (exporter). It forms the basis of the transaction between the seller and buyer, and is completed in accord with the number of prescribed copies required. Usually it bears the exporter's own headed invoice form stationery. The invoice gives a description of the goods, stating prices and the relevant Incoterm 2000 exactly as specified in the credit, as well as shipping marks. Overall, it contains the following information:

    (a)   name and address of buyer (importer) and seller (exporter);
    (b)   buyer's reference, that is, order number, indent number, etc.;
    (c)   number and types of packages;
    (d)   weights and measurements of the consignment;
    (e)   place and date of issue;
    (f)   details of actual cost of freight and insurance if so requested;
    (g)   total amount payable, embracing price of goods, freight, insurance and so on;
    (h)   the export and/or import licence number;
    (i)   the contents of individual packages;
    (j)   the method of despatch;
    (k)   shipment terms;
    (l)   letter of credit number and details – if so requested;
    (m)   country of origin of goods;
    (n)   signature of exporter.

    Basically the invoice is a document rendered by one person to another in regard of goods which have been sold. Its primary function is a check for the purchaser against charges and delivery. With regard to insurance claims, and for packing purposes, it is useful evidence to verify the value and nature of the goods and, in certain circumstances, it is evidence of the contract between the two parties, e.g., packing not being up to specification may give underwriters redress against the sellers. The invoice is not necessarily a contract of sale. It may form a contract of sale if it is in writing and contains all the material terms. On the other hand, it may not be a complete memorandum of the contract of sale and, therefore, evidence may be given to vary the contract which is inferred therefrom. In particular circumstances, the commercial invoice can be certified by Chambers of Commerce and/or legalized by the resident consul in the UK.

2. *Consular invoice.* Consular invoices are mandatory when shipping goods to certain ports of the world particularly to those countries

which enforce *ad valorem* import duties. This applies particularly in South America. The invoices are specially printed documents which must be completed exactly in accordance with requirements and certified by the consul of the country to which the goods are consigned. This is done at the nearest convenient consular office to the port, airport or ICD of departure. The invoices are issued at the consular office and a fee is payable on certification, often based on a percentage of the commercial invoice value of the goods. The consul of the importing country retains one copy, returns one copy to the shipper, and forwards further copies to the customs authorities in his or her own country. The consular invoice may be used in some circumstances as a certificate of origin. The forms are available from consuls or possibly through Chambers of Commerce and freight forwarders. In many countries both the consular invoice and the commercial invoice are required.

3. *Customs invoices.* Customs invoices may be required by the authorities of the importing country. An adequate number should be provided for the use of the customs authorities overseas.

4. *Pro-forma invoice.* This type of invoice is prepared by the exporter and may be required in advance for licence or letter of credit purposes. The document includes the date, name of the consignee, quantity and description of the goods, marks and measurements of packages, cost of the goods, packing, carriage, freight, postage, insurance premiums, terms of sale, terms of payment, etc. The pro-forma invoice is despatched to the buyer to facilitate obtaining from the bank the requisite currency to buy the goods and subsequently issue a letter of credit. Additionally, it may be needed for an import licence. In countries with serious hard debt problems delays can be experienced by the buyer when seeking the necessary funds, and exporters, when dealing with such territories, tend not to process the order until receipt of the letter of credit.

The following discrepancies relating to processing invoices under letters of credit do arise and should be avoided:

1. value exceeds credit amount;
2. amount differs from that of bill of exchange;
3. prices of goods not as indicated in credit;
4. omission of the price basis and shipment terms, for example, FCA, CFR, CIF, FOB, CPT, etc.;
5. inclusion of charges not specified in the credit;
6. invoice not certified, notarized or signed as required by credit;
7. buyer's name differs from that mentioned in the credit;
8. invoice not issued by the exporter;
9. invoice does not contain declaration required under the credit;
10. description of goods differs from that in the credit;

11. extra charges and/or commissions are not levied unless authorized within the credit terms;
12. when combined Certificates of Value and Origin (CVO) are required the Certificate of Origin should have been completed and signed.
13. when the transport document (e.g. bill of lading, air waybill, etc.) is required to indicate the amount of freight paid, the invoice does not show an amount in excess of or less than this sum (similarly, when an insurance premium has to be stated, either separately or on the insurance document itself, check the invoice does not reflect an amount in excess of, or less than, this figure);
14. Marks, weights, number of cases/packages, name of vessel, etc. agree with the bill of lading and all other documents.

The following items must be borne in mind when the shipper, exporter or agent prepares the invoice and presents them to the bank under a documentary letter of credit.

1. The invoice description of the goods agrees exactly with the documentary letter of credit.
2. The invoice is addressed to the importer.
3. The invoice includes the exact licence and/or certificate numbers required by the credit.
4. The invoice shows the terms of shipment mentioned in the credit.

14.17 Export licensing

The UK strategic export controls are imposed by an Export of Goods (Control) Order made under the Import, Export and Customs Powers (Defence) Act 1930. They are administered by the Export Control Organization of the Department of Trade and Industry. Three types of licence are provided: open general export licence (OGEL); the Open Individual Export Licence (OIEL); and the individual or bulk licence.

Such exchange controls on goods are imposed for a variety of reasons including; the collective security of the UK and its allies in NATO; foreign policy requirements; international treaty obligations and commitments; the UK non-proliferation policy; and concerns about terrorism or internal repression.

In 1993 the DTI introduced a code of practice on export licensing control compliance. Controlled goods include arms and military equipment; high-technology industrial goods for example chemical and petroleum equipment, electrical and electronic equipment (including computers), scientific apparatus and instruments, atomic energy materials, antiques and scarce materials. These are subject to continuous review – visit the website (p. 605). Under the NES (p. 236) the export licence may be processed electronically or manually.

14.18 Health certificate

A health certificate is issued when agricultural and animal products are being exported to certify they comply with the relevant legislation in the exporter's country. It is issued at the importer's request to comply with the country's health regulations and confirms the product was in a good condition at the time of inspection – prior to shipment – and fit for human consumption. A health certificate issued in the UK confirms that the Food Hygiene Regulations have been complied with.

14.19 Intermodal certification

This document arises from the Intermodal Safe Container Act which became operational in the USA from April 1997. Under this Act it is a requirement that any load with a gross weight exceeding 29 000 lbs must be declared to the trucker by means of an Intermodal Certification in an acceptable form before the load is taken onto the highway.

14.20 International Convention concerning the Carriage of Goods by Rail (CIM)

The International Convention Concerning the Carriage of Goods by Rail (CIM) has existed in some form since 1893 and is described on p. 575. It permits the carriage of goods by rail under one document, a consignment note (not negotiable), under a common code of conditions applicable to 29 countries, mainly situated in Europe and the Mediterranean areas. It embraces the maritime portion of the transit subject to it being conveyed on shipping lines as listed under the Convention. Advantages of using CIM throughout a rail consignment involving a container or cargo wagon include through rates under a common code of conditions, simplified documentation and accountancy, flexibility of freight payment, no intermediate handling (usually), nor customs examination in transit countries, through transits, and minimum customs documentation.

The CIM consignment note is completed by the shipper, agent or originating rail carrier and has six copies. It embraces the original of the consignment note, the invoice, the arrival note, the duplicate of the consignment note, the duplicate of the invoice, and a supplementary copy.

The following information must be recorded in the CIM consignment note:

1. The date and originating rail station of the consignment.
2. The names and addresses of the sender and the consignee.

3. The originating rail station accepting consignment and the station or place designated for delivery.
4. The ordinary description of the nature of the goods and method of packing and, in the case of dangerous goods, their generally recognized description.
5. The gross weight of the goods or their quantity.
6. The charges relating to the carriage.
7. The requisite instructions for customs and other formalities.

The foregoing may also be required under a letter of credit. Such a document is used for cargo wagon, containerized movement, and swap-body, passing through the EuroTunnel or international rail transits. From 1 January 1993 a form known as Consignment Note CIM was introduced. It is also known as a truck waybill.

14.21 Instructions for despatch

International IATA scheduled airlines require shippers to complete an Instructions for Despatch form (IDG) to enable an air waybill to be raised detailing the carriage to be performed. Shipping documents and advices should be attached securely to the freight or posted to the airport of despatch. The IDG will feature all details of the consignment including consignor, consignee payment arrangements and departure and destination airports. Cargo airlines will also accept a letter of instruction as a substitute for the IDG.

14.22 Letters of hypothecation

This is a banker's document outlining conditions under which the international transaction will be executed on the exporter's behalf, the latter of whom will have given certain pledges to his or her banker. It may be by direct loan, acceptance, or negotiations of draft thereto.

14.23 Letters of indemnity

The role of the letter of indemnity is to permit cargo to be released to a consignee without production of the original endorsed bill of lading, or to permit the issue of a duplicate set of documents when the original bills of lading have been lost or mislaid in transit. It is a document of legal and commercial convenience, and should be used with care and caution. The need for this form arises from the risks involved in permitting delivery of cargo without an original bill of lading, or in issuing a duplicate set of bills of lading. It usually requires the counter signature of a reputable bank – but this is not necessary when it is submitted on behalf of a National Government.

14.24 Mate's receipt

A Mate's receipt is sometimes issued in lieu of a bill of lading. It has no legal authority regarding the processing of the financial settlement of international consignments but merely confirms cargo is placed on board a ship pending issue of a bill of lading. In many countries the National Standard Shipping Note has replaced the Mate's receipt.

14.25 Packing list

In recent years the role of the packing list document has intensified and it is becoming a mandatory document required by customs and banks under documentary credit systems. It is very much in evidence in containerized shipments.

The document, sometimes called a packing note, is provided and completed by the shipper at the time the goods are despatched and accompanies the goods and the carrier's documents such as bill of lading, sea waybill, air waybill, CIM and CMR consignment notes throughout the transit. It is placed in the container, trailer, pallet, ULD, etc. The packing list gives details of the invoice, buyer, consignee, country of origin, vessel or flight date, port or airport of loading, port or airport of discharge, place of delivery, shipping marks, container number, weight and/or volume (cubic) of the merchandise and the fullest details of the goods, including packaging information.

14.26 Parcel post receipt

The parcel post receipt is issued by the Post Office for goods sent by parcel post. It is both a receipt and evidence of despatch. It is not a document of title and goods should be consigned to the party specified in the credit. An airmail label should be fixed to a postal receipt in respect of air parcel post despatch; alternatively the Post Office should stamp the receipt 'air parcel'. Goods sent by post should be consigned to the party specified in the documentary credit. See also p. 381, Customs Form CN22 and 23.

14.27 Phytosanitary (plant health) certificate

The importation of all plant material, forest trees and other trees and shrubs, and certain raw fruit and vegetables must be accompanied by a phytosanitary certificate in most countries. In some countries the importation of certain species of plants from certain areas of the world is prohibited. Application for such plant health certificates should be made to the agricultural department of the exporting country.

14.28 Pre-shipment inspection certificate

An increasing number of shippers and various organizations, authorities and governments in countries throughout the world are now insisting on inspection of goods. This embraces their quality, the quantity being exported and the price(s) proposed and market price(s) comparison at the time of shipment. An organization which undertakes such work – which can extend to transhipment *en route* – is the Société Générale de Surveillance (SGS) or ship classification societies such as Bureau Véritas. The SGS representative will examine the goods at the place of manufacture or assembly prior to despatch. This is to ensure they comply with the description found in the export sales contract, bill of lading or export invoice. Subsequently the goods will be examined and checked as they are loaded into the container or onto the ship. In situations where sellers are at variance with SGS opinion, they may present their position to the SGS principals, either directly or through the importer.

If everything is in order, a clean report of findings (CRF) will be issued by SGS to their principals. This is required together with other commercial documents such as the bill of lading, the letter of credit, the invoice in order to obtain payment via the commercial bank and/or customs clearance import. If a non-negotiable report of findings (NNRF) is issued by SGS, the seller (exporter) may opt to discuss the matter with the principal involved, who remains the final arbiter. Such a situation arises where goods are shipped before SGS inspection has taken place. In due course, SGS will issue the pre-shipment inspection certificate to confirm the goods have been supplied in accordance with the contract.

The SGS do not have the right to approve or prevent shipment of the goods. The opinion expressed by SGS is given after all the factors are provided to SGS by the seller. It is made in good faith but without any liability to the seller for any loss, damage or expense arising from the issuance of the report of findings. Currently some 35 countries require that both the letter of credit and contracts relevant to the import of goods contain a condition that a Clean Report of Findings covering quality, quantity and price must be presented together with other documents required to negotiate payment.

The International Federation of Inspection Agencies (IFIA), on behalf of the members administering government-mandated pre-shipment inspection programmes, is promoting the following Code of Practice to be observed by those members.

1. Activities of pre-shipment inspection companies (hereinafter 'PIC') in the country of export may be undertaken on behalf of a foreign government, government agency, central bank or other appropriate governmental authority and may include:

   (a) physical inspection for quantity and quality of goods;
   (b) verification of export prices, including financial terms of the export transaction and currency exchange rates where appropriate;
   (c) support services to the customs authorities of the country of importation.

2. The general procedures for physical inspection of goods and the examination of the price of exports out of any particular country will be the same in all exporting countries and the specific requirements established by the importing country will be administered by the PIC in a consistent and objective manner.

3. The PIC will provide assistance to exporters by furnishing the information and guidelines necessary to enable exporters to comply with the pre-shipment inspection regulations of the importing country. This assistance on the part of the PIC is not intended to relieve exporters from the responsibility of compliance with the import regulations of the importing country.

4. Quantity and quality inspections will be performed in accordance with accepted national and international standards.

5. The conduct of pre-shipment activities should facilitate legitimate foreign trade and assist *bona fide* exporters by providing independent evidence of compliance with the laws and regulations of the importing country.

6. Pre-shipment activities will be conducted and the Clean Report of Findings, or notice of non-issuance thereof, will be sent to the exporter in a timely and convenient manner.

7. Confidential business information will not be shared by the PICs with any third party other than the appropriate government authority for which the inspection in question is being performed.

8. Adequate procedures to safeguard all information submitted by exporters will be maintained by the PIC, together with proper security for any information provided in confidence to them.

9. The PIC will not request from exporters information regarding manufacturing data related to patents (issued or pending) or licensing agreements. Nor will the PIC attempt to identify the cost of manufacture, level of profit or, except in the case of exports made through a buying agent or a confirming house, the terms of contracts between exporters and their suppliers.

10. The PIC will avoid conflicts of interest between the PIC, any related entities of the PIC or entities in which the PIC has a financial interest, and companies whose shipments the PIC is inspecting.

11. The PIC will state in writing the reason for any decision declining issuance of a Clean Report of Findings.

12. If a rejection occurs at the stage of physical inspection, the PIC will, if requested by the exporter, arrange the earliest date for re-inspection.

13. Whenever so requested by the exporter, and provided no contrary instruction has been issued by the government authority, the PIC will undertake a preliminary price verification prior to receipt of the import licence on the basis of the binding contractual documents, pro-forma invoice and application for import approval. An invoice price and/or currency exchange rate that has been accepted by the PIC on the basis of such preliminary price verification will not be withdrawn, provided the goods and the previously submitted documentation conform with the information contained in the import licence. The CRF, however, will not be issued until appropriate final documents have been received by the PIC.

14. Price verification will be undertaken on the basis of the terms of the sales contract and it will take into consideration any generally applicable and allowable adjusting factors pertaining to the transaction.

15. Commissions due to an agent in the country of destination will be treated in confidence by the PIC and will be reported to the appropriate government authority only when so requested.

16. Exporters or importers who are unable to resolve differences with the PIC may appeal in writing, stating facts of the specific transaction and the nature of the complaint, to a designated appeals official of the PIC. Exporters wishing to appeal the results of a pre-shipment inspection may also seek review of the decision of the PIC in the importing country.

In cases where a PIC is considered not to have observed any article of this Code of Practice, this may be reported to the Director-General of IFIA.

The World Trade Organisation's Uruguay round of talks in 1994 established an independent review procedure administered jointly by an organization representing PIC Agencies and an organization representing exporters – to resolve disputes between an exporter and PIC Agency. The obligations placed on PIC user governments include non-discrimination, transparency, protection of confidential business information, avoidance of unreasonable delay, the use of specific guidelines for conducting price verification and the avoidance of conflicts of interest by the PIC Agencies.

The Pre-shipment Inspection System (PIS) has been introduced for the following reasons.

(a) To minimize the loss of foreign exchange through over-invoicing; concealed commission payments and illegal money transfers.
(b) To minimize losses of revenue and duty payments through under-invoicing.
(c) To reduce evasion of import controls and help combat smuggling.
(d) To help control landed prices and therefore control local inflation.
(e) To avoid dumping of cargo through the incidence of shipping merchandise of substandard goods.
(f) To avoid the incidence of loss through shipment of underweight cargo or short shipments.

A specimen of the documents is found on pp. 104–15 of *Shipping and Air Freight Documentation for Importers and Exporters*

14.29 Quality certificate

A quality certificate is issued by the exporter and confirms for the importer that the quality/specification of a particular consignment of goods is in accord with the export sales contract at the time of shipment. It is usually required under letter of credit terms.

14.30 Shipper's letter of instruction

A shipper's letter of instruction is a standardized form prepared by the shipper and submitted to the airline or IATA agent giving clear and complete forwarding instructions. It has no legal content, but the exporter is responsible for the validity of the data relative to the cargo description on the air waybill. Misrepresentation of the facts by the exporter has serious legal implications. The document (in duplicate) is handed to the vehicle driver at the time the goods are collected. The duplicate copy should be signed upon receipt of goods by the airline or its IATA agent as proof of goods for shipment and returned to the shipper (p. 355).

14.31 Ship's delivery order

A delivery order is written authority to deliver goods, etc. to a named party in exchange for the bill of lading, usually at the port of destination. It is issued at the port of destination and is subject to all the terms and conditions of the carrier's bill of lading. It must not contain any reservations or clauses other than those appearing in the bill of lading except where increased obligations or extra cost may be incurred in giving delivery beyond the bill of lading. The document is issued at the port of destination in exchange for an original bill of lading and is legally recognized as a token of an authority to receive possession.

The delivery order should be addressed to the ship's Master, and the need for it arises, for example, when the buyer may not wish to know the identity of the supplier abroad for trade reasons. Hence the delivery order issue may prove a useful document. It is important the document is endorsed by the party to whom it is made out. However, if it is issued in one port for delivery in another and the freight is payable at destination, the order would then be 'consigned' to the carrier's agent to ensure that it would have to be presented and released before collection of the goods is authorized.

14.32 Veterinary and health certificate

A veterinary or health certificate may be required when livestock, domestic animals or agricultural products are being exported. It should be signed by the appropriate health authority in the exporter's country.

14.33 Weight certificate

A weight certificate confirms that the goods accord with the weight specified on the bill of lading, invoice, certificate of insurance or other specified document. In so doing it confirms to the buyer, seller, insurance company or other specified party that the goods were at a specified weight at the time of shipment. It is requested by the importer to confirm the weight of the goods is in accord with the export sales contract at the time of shipment. It is usually required under a letter of credit involving a bulk cargo shipment.

Recommended reading

Shipping and Air Freight Documentation For Importers and Exporters and Associated Terms. (2nd edition – nearly 100 documents.) E-mail: books@ witherbys.co.uk website: www.witherbys.com

Processing the export order

An important activity of export practice is the processing of the export consignment through all its numerous procedures. It is an area which must be fully understood by the exporter. However, before examining the procedures involved, which must be read in conjunction with the following chapter on EDI/E-commerce, we must first consider the contract of affreightment embraced in the terms of delivery.

15.1 Contract of affreightment: terms of delivery: Incoterms 2000

The basis of a price quotation depends on the correct interpretation of the delivery trade terms. The export marketing manager will, through experience, accumulate information which will enable him or her to quote accurately. It is important to bear in mind each delivery trade term quoted embraces three basic elements: the stage at which title to the merchandise passes from the exporter (seller) to the importer (buyer), a clear definition of the charges and expenses to be borne by the exporter and importer, and finally, the stage and location where the goods are to be passed over to the importer.

The international consignment delivery terms embrace many factors including, in particular, insurance, air or sea freight plus surface transport costs, customs duty, port of disbursements, product cost, packing costs, etc. Moreover, the importance of executing the cargo delivery in accordance with the prescribed terms cannot be overstressed and this involves a disciplined process of progressing the export sales contract order dealt with elsewhere in this chapter. In the ideal situation, the sales export contract order, also embracing the delivery terms, should be undertaken on a critical path analysis programme devised by the export marketing manager in consultation with department colleagues within the company, and relevant outside bodies, that is, booking shipping space, processing financial aspects, obtaining export licences, etc.

There must be no ambiguity in the interpretation by either party of the delivery terms quoted, particularly in the area of cost and liabilities. If such problems arise, much goodwill is lost and the exporter could lose the prospect of a repeat order in a competitive market. Moreover, costly litigation could arise. It is essential, therefore, that the exporter (seller) and the importer (buyer) agree on the terms of delivery and their interpretation. Such a situation could be overcome by quoting the provisions of Incoterms 2000 dealt with in the latter part of this section. It must be borne in mind that special provisions in individual export sales contracts will override anything provided in Incoterms 2000. In addition, it should be remembered that breaches of contract, and their consequences, together with the ownership of the goods are outside the influence of Incoterms 2000.

The need for every exporter to have a thorough knowledge of Incoterms 2000 cannot be over-stressed, and likewise the sales and marketing personnel who negotiate the export sales contract terms on behalf of the seller. The booklet Incoterms 2000, No 560 is available from local Chambers of Commerce.

An international trade deal can involve up to four contracts and the exporter (seller) must have a broad understanding of each of them. The four contracts are: the contract of carriage, the export sales contract (usually involving Incoterms 2000), the insurance contract, and the contract of finance. (See ICC booklet No. 500 on Uniform Customs and Practice for Documentary Credits, 1993.) A new edition UCP600 may be published by ICC in 2007. There are three main areas of uncertainty in international trade contracts and their interpretation: the uncertainty as to which country's law will be applicable to their contracts; the difficulty emerging from inadequate and unreliable information; and the serious problem of the diversity of interpretation of the various trade terms. The latter point can involve costly litigation and loss of much goodwill when a dispute over the interpretation of such terms arises. Hence study ICC booklet No 5600.

The role of Incoterms 2000, adopted in 96 countries, is to give the business person a set of international rules for the interpretation of the more commonly used terms such as FOB, CIF and EXW in foreign trade contracts. Such a range of terms enables the business person to decide which is the most suitable for their needs, knowing that the interpretation of such terms will not vary by individual country.

It must be recognized, however, that it is not always possible to give a precise interpretation. In such situations, one must rely on the custom of the trade or port. Business persons are advised to use terms which are subject to varying interpretation as little as possible and to rely on the well-established internationally-accepted terms. To avoid any misunderstandings or disputes the parties to the contract are well advised to keep trading customs of individual countries in mind when negotiating their export sales contract. However, parties to the contract may use Incoterms as the general basis of their contract, but may specify variations of them or additions to them relevant to the particular trade or circumstances. An example is the CIF (cost insurance freight) plus war risk insurance. The seller would base his or her quotation accordingly. Special provisions in the individual contract between the parties will override anything in the Incoterm provisions.

An important point to bear in mind is the need for caution in the variation, for example, of CFR (cost and freight), CIF (cost insurance freight) or DDP (delivered duty paid): the addition of a word or letter could change the contract and its interpretation. It is essential that any such variation be explicitly stated in the contract to ensure each party to the contract is aware of its obligations and acts accordingly.

The seller (exporter) and buyer (importer) parties to the contract must remember that Incoterms only define their relationship in contract terms, and has no bearing directly or indirectly on carriers' obligations to them as found in the contract of carriage. However, the law of carriage will determine how the seller should fulfil his or her obligation to deliver the goods to the carrier on board the vessel as found in FOB, CFR and CIF. A further point to be borne in mind by both seller and buyer is that there is no obligation for the seller to procure an insurance policy for the buyer's benefit. However, in practice many contracts request the buyer or seller to arrange insurance from the point of departure in the country of despatch, to the point of final destination chosen by the buyer. A summary of the 13 terms are given below (see also Figure 15.1, p. 398, Incoterm 2000 group analysis):

Incoterms 2000

Group E	EXW	Ex-works (named place)
Departure from factory – all carriage paid by buyer		
Group F	FCA	Free carrier (named place)
Main carriage unpaid by seller	FAS	Free alongside ship (named port of shipment)
	FOB	Free on board (named port of shipment)
Group C	CPT	Carriage paid to (named place of destination)
Main carriage paid by seller	CIP	Carriage and insurance paid to (named place of destination)
	CFR	Cost and freight (named port of destination)
	CIF	Cost, insurance and freight (named port of destination)
Group D	DAF	Delivered at frontier (named place)

Incoterms 2000 – Group Analysis

Group E

> EXW – Ex Works (. . . named place) – suitable for all modes of transport – buyer collects and responsible for all carriage, the seller to load the goods onto the buyer's collection vehicle

Group F

> FCA Free Carrier (. . . named place) – suitable for all modes of transport – main carriage unpaid
>
> FAS Free Alongside Ship (. . . named port of shipment) – suitable for maritime and inland waterway transport only – main carriage unpaid
>
> FOB Free On Board (. . . named port of shipment) – suitable for maritime and inland waterway transport only – main carriage unpaid

Group C

> CPT Carriage Paid to (. . . named place of destination) – suitable for all modes of transport – main carriage paid, the seller to provide the buyer, upon request, with the necessary information for procuring additional insurance
>
> CIP Carriage and Insurance Paid to (. . . named place of destination) – suitable for all modes of transport – main carriage paid
>
> CFR Cost and Freight (. . . named port of destination) – suitable for maritime and inland waterway transport only – main carriage paid, the seller to provide the buyer, upon request, with the necessary information for procuring additional insurance
>
> CIF Cost Insurance and Freight (. . . named port of destination) – suitable for maritime and inland waterway transport only – main carriage paid

Group D

> DAF Delivered at Frontier (. . . named place) – suitable for all modes of transport – delivered at frontier point
>
> DDU Delivered Duty Unpaid (. . . named place of destination) – suitable for all modes of transport – delivered at named place of destination
>
> DDP Delivered Duty Paid (. . . named place of destination) – suitable for all modes of transport – delivered at named place of destination
>
> DES Delivered Ex Ship (. . . named port of destination) – suitable for maritime and inland waterway transport only – delivered on board the vessel at the named port of destination
>
> DEQ Delivered Ex Quay (. . . named port of destination) – suitable for maritime and inland waterway transport only – delivered on the named quay (wharf) at the specified port of destination, the buyer to pay for costs after discharge

E Term – is the term in which the buyer's obligation is at its maximum.

F Term – requires the seller to deliver the goods for carriage as instructed by the buyer.

C Term – requires the seller to contract for carriage on usual terms at his own expense.

D Term – requires the seller to be responsible for the arrival of the goods at the agreed place or point of destination at the border and within the country of import. The seller must bear all the risk and cost in bringing the goods thereto.

FIGURE 15.1 Incoterm 2000 analysis

Arrival – carriage to delivered paid by the seller	DES	Delivered ex-ship (named port of destination)
	DEQ	Delivered ex-quay (named port of destination)
	DDU	Delivered duty unpaid (named place of destination)
	DDP	Delivered duty paid (named place of destination)

Incoterms 2000 can be divided into recommended usages by modes of transport as under: all modes (i.e. combined transport), EXW, FCA, CPT, CIP, DAF, DDP, DDU; and conventional port-to-port or maritime and inland waterway transport only FAS, FOB, CFR, CIF, DES, DEQ. The seller must ensure the correct terms are used. Consider a containerized contract applying FOB or CFR where the risk transfers from seller to buyer on loading onboard ship. On delivery damage is discovered. It is impossible to show where damage arose, before or after shipment. Under FOB/CFR a dispute would ensue; under FCA/CPT it would be clear that the risk would be with the buyer once the goods are in the hands of the combined transport operator for carriage. Incoterms 2000 reflect the changes and development of international distribution during the past decade, especially the development of combined transportation and associated documentation, together with electronic data interchange. In analysing each term the seller and buyer should identify the following aspects:

Seller

1.   supplying good(s) in conformity with the contract;
2.   licences and authorizations;
3.   place of delivery (not delivery of goods);
4.   carriage of goods contract and insurance;
5.   documentation and notice to buyer;
6.   transfer of risks;
7.   transfer and division of costs;
8.   checking, packages, marking;
9.   other obligations.

Buyer

1.   licences and authorizations;
2.   notices, receipt of documents;
3.   taking delivery;
4.   transfer of risks;
5.   transfer and division of costs;
6.   other obligations.

The use of bills of lading is now becoming less common in the liner trade and is being replaced by non-negotiable documents such as sea waybills, liner waybills, freight receipts and combined or multi-modal transport documents (p. 366). Today the transmission of such documents is electronic (pp. 569 and 572). As we progress into the new millennium with the expectation of more competitive pricing, the buyer/importer will demand a delivered Incoterm 2000 price quotation. This will allow the buyer to compare the quotations on a like-for-like basis from different originating countries, and will enable them to avoid having to calculate the distribution cost as an add-on to the Incoterm 2000.

15.2 Factors determining choice of Incoterms 2000

Personnel involved in negotiating the sales contract have a wide choice in selecting the cargo delivery term most acceptable to the sale. The prime consideration is to ensure that each party to the contract is clearly aware of their obligation to ensure the consignment is despatched without impeding the transit arrangements. The following factors are relevant in the evaluation of the choice of the cargo delivery term.

1. Basically, the buyer is the stronger party in such negotiations, especially as he or she has to fund the carriage charges directly through his payment to the carrier under FCA/FOB or indirectly through CIP/CIF to the seller.
2. The seller has the opportunity of controlling the transit arrangements together with cost when concluding the arrangement, and funds them directly with the carrier. He or she may, through other contracts, be able to get a discount through the volume of business generated to the trade or route.
3. An increasing number of Third World and Eastern European countries now follow a policy of directing all cargoes on to their national shipping line or airline and buy under EXW/FCA/FOB/CIF terms. For example, a government may require all imports to be bought on a FOB basis and all exports sold on CIF. This saves hard currency and develops their shipping and airline companies. It also reflects, in many situations, cargo preference laws enforced by the buyer's government as part of their trading policy.
4. The seller, under CIP/CIF terms, can maximize the national income from such a sale and thereby despatch the consignment on the seller's national shipping line or airline, and likewise obtain insurance cover through brokers.
5. In some circumstances neither the buyer nor the seller has any choice to make. This applies to some commodity trades where there

are standard international contracts of sale which relate to specific Incoterms 2000.

6.   Conversely, with regard to item (2) the buyer may wish to take charge of the transit arrangement and cost when concluding the arrangements and selects the carrier and funds them directly with the transport operator(s). This may include EXW/FCA/FOB terms and thereby facilitate the development of a logistics strategy.

Overall, the most decisive factors in determining the most acceptable Incoterm are experience of the trading market and the development of a good business relationship between seller and buyer on a long-term basis. Every effort should be made to sell under combined transport terms.

Salient Features Emerging From Incoterms 2000

(a) the Incoterms have tended to focus on the tangibles in the contract of sale and not intangibles as found in computer software;

(b) Incoterms embraces the contract of sale and relations between the buyer and seller. It only has an interface with the contracts of insurance, transport and finance and no *prima facie* legal specifications regarding the duties the parties may wish to include in the contract of sale;

(c) Incoterms remain primarily intended for use where goods are sold for delivery across national boundaries;

(d) revision needed to adapt to the terms of contemporary commercial practice;

(e) substantive changes have been made in two areas: customs clearance and payment of duty obligations under FAS and DEQ (see pp. 408–10) and loading and unloading obligations under FCA (see pp. 413–14);

(f) the terms are, wherever possible, the same expressions as those in the 1980 UN Convention on the Contracts for the International Sales of Goods;

(g) the opportunity has been taken in the 'introduction' of ICC booklet No 560 to clarify a number of terms featured in the 13 Incoterms. These include shipper, delivery, usual charges, ports, places, points, premises, ship, vessel, checking, inspection, no obligation, customs clearance, and packaging;

(h) a feature of the 1990 revision of Incoterms identified the clauses dealing with the seller's obligation to provide proof of delivery permitting a replacement of paper documentation by EDI messages provided the parties had agreed to communicate electronically. The 2000 revision has endeavoured to improve upon the drafting and presentation of the Incoterms in order to facilitate their practical implementation.

FIGURE 15.2 Incoterms 2000 – salient features

15.3 Description of Incoterms 2000

EXW (Ex-works) (named place)

This term means maximum involvement by the buyer in arrangements for the conveyance of the consignment to the specified destination. The exporter merely makes the goods available by an agreed date at his or her factory or warehouse. The seller minimizes his or her obligations while the buyer obtains the goods at the lowest possible price, by arranging to use his or her national shipping line or airline and by securing insurance cover in his or her own country. This eliminates the need to fund such provisions using hard currency and thereby improves the importer's trade balance. This practice is on the increase nowadays, particularly in Third World and Eastern European markets. The seller's obligations cease when the buyer accepts the goods at the factory or warehouse. It is usual for the buyer to appoint an agent in the seller's country to look after all the collection, transportation, insurance and documentation arrangements, possibly in consultation with the national shipping line or airline.

The term provides two options: 'Ex-works cleared for export', and 'Ex-works uncleared for export'. The following is based on 'uncleared for export'. The principal obligations of the seller include:

1. supplying the goods in accord with the contract of sale;
2. making available the goods to the buyer at the customary delivery point, or as specified in the contact of sale to enable the goods to be conveyed on the transport unit arranged by the buyer;
3. providing at his or her expense the necessary packing (if any) to enable the buyer to convey the goods on the specified transport;
4. giving the buyer prompt notice when the goods will be available for collection;
5. bearing all risk and expense of the goods until they have been placed at the disposal of the buyer as specified in the contract of sale;
6. rendering the buyer on request every assistance to provide, in the country of delivery or of cargo origin, all the relevant documentation required in the process of exportation.

Obviously the responsibilities of the buyer are more extensive. These include:

1. taking delivery of the cargo and paying for the goods in accord with the contract of sale terms;
2. funding any pre-shipment inspection expense;
3. bearing all the cost and risk of the goods from the time they have been placed at his or her disposal by the seller in accord with sales contract terms;
4. funding any customs duties and taxes arising through exportation;

5.   bearing additional costs incurred and related risks inherent through the failure of the buyer to give instructions about the place of delivery within the prescribed period;
6.   funding all costs in obtaining the documents required for the purpose of importation and exportation and for passing through the countries of transit.

The EXW term should not be used where, according to regulations of the country of export, the buyer cannot directly or indirectly obtain the export licence. In such a situation, the FCA term should be used.

FOB (free on board) (named port of shipment)

Under such terms the goods are placed in the ship by the seller at the specified port of shipment detailed in the sales contract. The risk of loss of, or damage to, the goods is transferred from the seller to the buyer when the goods pass over the ship's rail. Under such terms the seller bears all the cost and the risk of conveyance up to the ship's rail and the buyer accepts the residue of the transit cost, including sea freight and insurance. This term is used frequently in international trade and is to the advantage of the buyer because the cargo can be conveyed on his or her national shipping line, thereby ensuring it is funded by the national currency. Insurance provision can likewise be arranged in his or her own country with similar benefit. It is usual for the buyer to appoint an agent in the seller's country to look after the pre-shipment, documentation, insurance, etc. arrangements in consultation with the shipping company.

The principal seller's obligations found in a FOB sales contract include:

1.   supplying the goods in accord with the contract of sale;
2.   delivering the cargo on the named vessel at the specified port of shipment within the agreed period or on the agreed date and in so doing promptly informing the buyer;
3.   providing at his or her expense any export licence or other governmental authorization necessary for the export of goods;
4.   bearing all costs and risks of the goods until such time as the cargo has effectively passed over the ship's rail at the named port;
5.   providing at his or her expense the customary packing of the goods unless it is the custom of the trade to ship the cargo unpacked;
6.   paying the cost of any cargo scrutiny prior to delivery of the cargo;
7.   supplying at the seller's expense the requisite documentation as proof of delivery of the goods alongside the named vessel;
8.   providing the buyer on request and at the buyer's expense the Certificate of Origin;
9.   supplying the buyer on request and at the buyer's expense every assistance to obtain a bill of lading, sea waybill and other documentation issued in the country of shipment or origin necessary for the

importation process both in transit countries and the destination country.

The buyer's responsibilities are extensive. These include:

1. arranging at his or her own expense and risk the pre-shipment cargo inspection;
2. bearing all cost and risk of the cargo from the time it has passed the ship's rail at port of shipment and paying the price as specified in the sales contract;
3. bearing all the cost and risk emerging from the failure of the shipowner to fulfil the contracted pre-shipment arrangements (such as the cargo being shut out) – this is subject to the seller making the cargo available at the loading berth in accord with the sales contract, and in the event of the buyer failing to give pre-shipment details to the seller within the prescribed period, all additional cost and risk to be borne by the buyer;
4. paying all cost to the seller to obtain bills of lading, certificate of origin, consular documents and any other documentation required to process the cargo through importation both in transit countries and in the country of destination.

The FOB term may only be used for sea or inland waterway transport. When the ship's rail serves no practical purpose, such as Ro-Ro or container traffic, the FCA term should be used.

CFR (cost and freight – named port of destination)

Under this term the seller must pay the costs necessary to bring the goods to the named port of shipment, the risk of loss or damage to the goods, as well as of any additional expenses, is transferred from the seller to the buyer when the goods pass over the ship's rail. This is identical to CIF except that the buyer is responsible for funding and arranging the cargo insurance.

The seller's obligations in CFR include:

1. supplying the goods in accord with the contract of sale terms;
2. arranging and paying for the conveyance of the goods to the specified port of destination by the customary route and funding any unloading charges at the destination port;
3. providing and paying for any export licence or other governmental authorization necessary to export the cargo;
4. arranging and paying for, on a specified date or in a specified period, the cargo loading at the agreed port (if no such loading date or period is quoted, such a task to be undertaken within a reasonable period);
5. bearing all the cargo risk until such time as it passes over the ship's rail at the port of shipment;

6. supplying promptly and paying for the clean shipped negotiable bill of lading for the agreed destination port, together with any invoice of the goods shipped;
7. providing and paying for the customary packing of the goods unless it is the custom of the trade to ship the cargo unpacked;
8. funding any cargo scrutiny prior to loading the cargo;
9. paying any cost of dues and taxes incurred relative to the process of exportation in respect of the cargo prior to shipment;
10. providing the buyer on request and at the buyer's expense a Certificate of Origin and consular invoice;
11. rendering the buyer on request and at the buyer's expense and risk every assistance to obtain any documents required in the country of shipment and transit countries necessary for the conveyance of the cargo to its destination.

A point for the seller to note especially with the CFR term is the need to supply a full set of clean onboard or shipped bills of lading. If the bill of lading contains a reference to the Charterparty, the seller must also provide a copy of the latter. The buyer must ensure these provisions are complied with by the seller.

The factors relevant to the buyer include:

1. acceptance of the documents as tendered by the seller (subject to their conformity with the terms of the contract) and payment of the goods, etc., as specified in the contract of sale;
2. receiving the goods at the port of destination and, with the exception of the sea freight, all the costs and charges incurred during the voyage(s);
3. funding all unloading expenses at the destination port including lighterage, wharfage, etc. unless such costs have been included in the freight or collected by the shipowner at the time freight was paid;
4. funding any pre-shipment cargo inspection arrangements;
5. undertaking all the risk when the cargo has passed the ship's rail at the departure port, in the event of the buyer failing to give instructions (by the specified date or within agreed period) relative to destination port, all additional cost and risk will be borne by the buyer subject to the goods being duly appropriated to the contract;
6. paying all the costs to obtain the Certificate of Origin and consular documents;
7. meeting all charges to provide any other documentation specified relative to processing the consignment in the country of shipment or transit countries;
8. paying all customs duties and other taxes raised at the time of importation;
9. obtaining and paying for any import licence or related documentation required at the time of importation.

In the CFR contract sale the buyer can arrange the cargo insurance in his or her own country thereby saving foreign currency. Many importers are tending to favour this arrangement. The CFR term should be used only for sea and inland water transport. When the ship's rail serves no practical purpose as in the case of Ro-Ro or container traffic, the CPT term should be used.

CIF (cost, insurance, freight) (named port of destination)

This is a popular cargo delivery arrangement. The seller, in addition to CFR obligations, is obliged to procure marine insurance against the risk of loss of, or damage to, the goods in transit. In other words, the seller contracts with the insurer and pays the insurance premium.

The salient features of the contract as far as the seller is concerned include:

1. supplying the goods in accordance with contract of the sale terms;
2. arranging and paying for the carriage of the goods to the specified destination port by the customary route and funding any unloading charges at the destination port;
3. providing and paying for any export licence or other governmental authorization necessary to export the cargo;
4. arranging and paying for, on a specified date or within an agreed period, the cargo loading at the agreed port (if no such loading date or period is quoted such a task to be undertaken within a reasonable period);
5. informing the buyer promptly when loading is completed;
6. arranging and paying for insurance of the cargo in a transferable form against the risk of loss or damage during the transit – such cover shall be Institute Cargo Clauses (Institute of London Underwriter) and embrace the CIF price plus 10 per cent, and the insurance will be in the currency of the contract;
7. bearing all the risk of goods until they have effectively passed the ship's rail at the port of shipment;
8. supplying to the buyer promptly, at the seller's expense, a clean negotiable 'shipped onboard' bill of lading for the agreed port of destination and insurance policy or certificate of insurance;
9. providing and paying for the customary packing of the goods unless it is the custom of the trade to ship the goods unpacked;
10. paying the cost of any cargo scrutiny prior to loading the cargo;
11. bearing any cost of dues and taxes incurred relative to the process of exportation in respect of the cargo prior to shipment;
12. providing the buyer on request and at the buyer's expense a Certificate of Origin and consular invoice;
13. rendering the buyer on request and at the buyer's expense every assistance to obtain any documents required in the country of shipment or

transit countries necessary for the conveyance of the cargo through-out the transit.

A point to bear in mind concerning insurance cover is that the seller has to procure marine insurance against the buyer's risk of loss or damage against minimum coverage and duration to the goods during the carriage.
The responsibilities of the buyer include:

1. acceptance of the documents as tendered by the seller (subject to their conformity with the terms of the contract) and payment of the goods, as specified in the contract of sale;
2. funding any pre-shipment cargo inspection arrangements;
3. receiving the goods at the agreed destination port and bearing, with the exception of the freight and marine insurance, all costs and charges incurred during the voyage(s);
4. funding all unloading expenses at the port of destination, including lighterage and wharfage, unless such costs have been included in the freight or collected by the shipowner at the time freight was paid;
5. undertaking all the risk when the cargo has passed the ship's rail at the departure port;
6. in the event of the buyer failing to give instructions, by the specified date or within an agreed period, relative to the port of destination, all additional cost and risk will be borne by the buyer subject to the goods being duly appropriated to the contract;
7. paying all the costs in obtaining a Certificate of Origin and consular documents;
8. meeting all charges to provide any other documentation specified relative to processing the consignment in the country of shipment or transit countries;
9. paying all customs duties and other taxes raised at the time of importation;
10. obtaining at his or her own expense any import licence or related documentation required at time of importation.

The CIF terms enable the seller to obtain the maximum income from the sales contract with the insurance and freight charges contributing to the invisible exports if the goods are carried on the national shipping line and the insurance is effected in the country of origin. The CIF term should be used only for sea and inland water transport. When the ship's rail serves no practical purpose as in the case of Ro-Ro or container traffic, the CIP term should be used.

DES (delivered ex-ship – named port of destination)

This sales contract terms is not used extensively. It obliges the seller to make the goods available to the buyer on board the vessel at the destination port as specified in the sales contract. The seller has to bear the full cost and risk involved to bring the goods to the destination port before discharging.

The seller's main obligations include:

1. supplying the goods in accord with contract of sale terms;
2. making the goods available to the buyer on board the vessel at the agreed destination point to enable the cargo to be conveniently discharged;
3. bearing all risk and expense of the cargo conveyance to the destination port until promptly collected by the buyer;
4. providing and paying for the customary packing of the goods unless it is the custom of the trade to ship the goods unpacked;
5. paying the cost of any cargo scrutiny prior to collection of the cargo by the buyer;
6. promptly informing the buyer of the expected date of arrival of the vessel and providing the buyer with a bill of lading and any other documents necessary to enable the buyer to take delivery of the consignment;
7. providing the buyer on request and at the buyer's expense the Certificate and consular invoice;
8. rendering the buyer on request and at the buyer's expense every assistance to provide the requisite documentation issued in the country of shipment and/or origin required for importation in the destination country or transit countries.

The obligations of the buyer include:

1. bearing all the risk and expense from the time the cargo has been placed at the disposal of the buyer on board the vessel awaiting discharge at the destination port;
2. bearing all the cost associated with the provision of documentation obtained by the seller necessary for the importation of the goods both in destination and transit countries;
3. obtaining at the buyer's expense all licences or similar documents necessary for the importing process;
4. bearing all customs charges and other duties and taxes incurred at the time of importation.

This term can be used only when the goods are to be delivered by sea or inland waterway or multi-modal transport on a vessel in the port of destination.

DEQ (delivered ex-quay – named port of destination)

Under this term the seller arranges for the goods to be made available to the buyer on the quay or wharf at the destination port detailed in the sales contract. The seller has to bear the full cost and risk involved to bring the goods to the named port of destination and discharge the goods on the quay. But the buyer has to clear the goods for import and to pay for all formalities, duties, taxes, and other charges upon import.

The seller's obligations include:

1. supplying the goods in accord with the contract of sale terms;
2. making the goods available to the buyer at the specified quay or wharf within the period given in the sales contract and bearing all the associated risk and cost: the buyer being responsible for clearing the goods for import and paying for all the formalities;
3. providing and paying for the customary packing of the goods unless it is the custom of the trade to ship the cargo unpacked.

The buyer's task is twofold:

1. to take delivery of the goods as specified in the contract;
2. to bear all the expense and risk of the goods from the time the cargo has been effectively placed at the disposal of the buyer including import Customs clearance.

The cost of the pre-shipment cargo inspection is borne by the buyer unless when mandated by the authorities of the country of export.

This term can be used only when the goods are to be delivered by sea or inland waterway or multi-modal transport on discharging from a vessel onto the quay (wharf) in the port of destination.

FAS (free alongside ship – named port of shipment)

The obligations of the seller are realized when the goods have been placed alongside the ship in the quay or on lighterage at a specified port of shipment. At this stage and thereafter the buyer has to bear all the cost and risk of loss of or damage to the goods excluding export customs clearance.

The salient features of FAS for the seller include:

1. supplying the goods in accord with the contract of sale terms;
2. arranging delivery of the cargo by the date or within the agreed period alongside the specified vessel at the loading berth and port as named by the buyer;
3. to obtain at the sellers expense any export licence and other official authorization and carry out all custom formalities necessary for the export of the goods;
4. bearing all cost and risk of the goods until they have been effectively delivered alongside the specified vessel and cleared through customs;
5. providing and paying for the customary packing of the goods unless it is the custom of the trade to ship the cargo unpacked;
6. rendering to the buyer on request and at the buyer's expense the Certificate of Origin;

7.   assisting the buyer on request and at the buyer's expense to obtain any documents issued in the country of origin or shipment including bill of lading and/or consular documents required for importation of the goods into the destination country and their passage through transit countries.

The buyer's responsibilities include:

1.   giving the seller prompt notice of the name of the vessel, loading berth and delivery dates;
2.   bearing all the expense and risk of the goods from when they have been effectively delivered alongside the vessel as specified which includes the export clearance undertaken by the seller;
3.   funding any additional cost and accepting the risk in the event of the vessel not arriving on time or the shipowner being unable to accept the cargo;
4.   in the event of the buyer failing to notify the seller of the name of the vessel, and port of shipment within the prescribed period, the buyer would bear all consequential cost and risk from the expiry date of the notification period, subject to the goods being duly appropriated by the seller to the contract including export customs clearance;
5.   meeting all cost of obtaining any documents necessary for the importation of the goods, including the bill of lading and consular documents.

The cost of the pre-shipment cargo inspection is borne by the buyer unless when mandated by the authorities of the country of export. This criterion applies to other Incoterms where applicable.

This term can be used only for sea or inland waterway transport.

DAF (delivered at frontier – named port)

Under the 'delivered at frontier' term the seller's obligations are concluded when the goods have arrived at the named frontier point and place or customs examination border. It is usual, to avoid ambiguity, to quote the two countries separated by the frontier. This term is used primarily for rail or road borne traffic but can be used for other transport modes in varying circumstances. Its use could become more common through the development of the combined transport operation for international consignments. The term requires the seller to clear for export.

The seller's main obligations include:

1.   supplying the goods in accord with the contract of sale terms at the seller's risk and expense;
2.   placing the goods at the disposal of the buyer at the specified frontier point within the stipulated period and in so doing providing him or her with the necessary customary documentation including consignment

note, export licence, delivery order, warehouse warrant, etc., to enable the buyer to take delivery of the cargo;

3. funding any customs charges and other expenses incurred up to the time when the goods have been placed at the buyer's disposal, and bearing all the risk throughout this period;

4. obtaining and paying for all documentation necessary for the exportation of the cargo, including transit countries' needs and placing them at the disposal of the buyer as appropriate;

5. funding all transport costs (including incidental charges raised during the transit) up to the nominated frontier point, if no particular frontier point is quoted, the seller may choose the one which is most convenient to him or her provided he or she notifies the buyer promptly and it offers adequate customs and other facilities to enable the contract to be executed satisfactorily by both parties;

6. supplying the buyer on request the through consignment note embracing the origin and destination place in the importing country – such a request to be executed by the seller on the condition he or she incurs the risk, or expense other than it is customary to incur;

7. in the event of the goods being unloaded on arrival at the frontier point, such cost to be borne by the seller, including lighterage and handling charges (this would also apply if the seller used his or her own transport);

8. promptly notifying the buyer that the goods have been despatched;

9. providing and paying for the customary packing of the goods unless it is the custom of the trade to ship the cargo unpacked;

10. funding any cargo scrutiny necessary to transport the goods to the specified frontier point;

11. bearing any additional cost incurred to place the goods at the buyer's disposal;

12. rendering to the buyer on request and at the buyer's expense all reasonable assistance to obtain documents inherent in the importing process in the destination country.

The buyer's obligations include:

1. accepting delivery of the goods at the specified frontier point and to accept all transportation and handling costs therefrom;

2. meeting the risk and customs duties and other costs incurred from the time the goods have been placed at the buyer's disposal relative to the process of importation of the cargo;

3. funding incidental expenses incurred to unload the cargo at the specified frontier point, in the event of the buyer not taking delivery of the cargo duly put at his or her disposal in accord with the sales contract, the buyer will pay all additional cost and bear all the risk resulting therefrom;

4.   obtaining at his or her expense any import licence and other documentation required to process the cargo through importation;
5.   funding any additional expense incurred by the seller to obtain the consignment note for the buyer which could include documentation;
6.   supplying the seller on request with details of the ultimate destination of the goods;
7.   funding any expense incurred by the seller to provide the buyer with any third-party certificate of conformity of the goods stipulated in the contract of sale.

The cost of the pre-shipment cargo inspection is borne by the buyer unless when mandated by the authorities of the country of export. This term may be used irrespective of the mode of transport when goods are to be delivered at a land frontier. When delivery is to take place in the port of destination, on board a vessel or on the quay (wharf), the DES or DEQ terms should be used.

In addition to the foregoing eight cargo delivery terms, which are the most popular, five other terms appear in Incoterms 2000. A brief commentary on them follows:

DDP (delivered duty paid – named place of destination)

It will be recalled that under the term 'ex-works', the seller has the minimum obligation in terms of despatching the cargo. Conversely, the term 'delivered duty paid' places the maximum obligation on the seller regarding the cargo despatch arrangements. Under such terms the seller is responsible for the conveyance of the goods at his or her own risk and expense to the named destination located in the buyer's country in the country of sale. This includes the task of processing the cargo through both exportation and importation including duties and taxes plus customs clearance, loading and unloading, together with the related documentation which the buyer usually obtains as necessary on request but at the seller's expense. The seller may use his or her own transport throughout the conveyance.

The buyer's role is to accept the goods at the named place of destination, and the buyer is responsible for all subsequent movement costs of the goods including handling. Any form of transport can be used. The cost of the pre-shipment cargo inspection is borne by the buyer unless when mandated by the authorities of the country of export.

The DDP term should not be used if the seller is unable to obtain, directly or indirectly, the import licence. If the parties wish that the buyer should clear the goods for import and pay the duty, the DDU term should be used.

Hence the seller fulfils his or her obligation when he or she has delivered the goods, cleared for export, into the charge of the carrier named by the buyer at the named place or point. If no precise point is indicated by the buyer, the seller may choose, within the range stipulated, where the carrier shall take the goods into his or her charge. When, according to commercial practice, the seller's assistance is required in making the contract with the carrier (such as in rail or air transport with fixed freight rates), the seller will act at the buyer's risk and expense. This term may be used for any mode of transport, but when delivery is to take place in the port of destination on board the vessel or on the quay (wharf), the DES or DEQ terms should be used.

DDU (delivered duty unpaid – named place of destination)

The seller fulfils his or her obligations when the goods have arrived at the named point or place in the country of importation, and delivers the goods to the buyer, not cleared for import, and not unloaded from any arriving means of transport at the named place of destination. The seller has to bear the full costs and risks involved in bringing the goods thereto, excluding duties, taxes and other official charges payable upon importation. If the parties wish to include in the seller's obligation some of the cost or official charges payable upon import of the goods (such as value added tax, VAT) this should be made clear by adding words to this effect (e.g., 'delivered duty unpaid, VAT paid'). The term may be used irrespective of transport mode, but when delivery is to take place in the port of destination on board the vessel or on the quay (wharf), the DES or DEQ terms should be used.

FCA (free carrier – named place)

This term is primarily for the combined transport operation such as a container or Ro-Ro operation involving a road trailer and sea ferry. The term is based on the FOB principle except that the seller fulfils his or her obligations when he or she delivers the goods into the custody of the carrier at the named place found in the sales contract or subsequently agreed by the parties. The chosen place of delivery has an impact on the obligation of loading and unloading the goods at that place. If delivery occurs at the sellers premises, the seller is responsible for loading. If the delivery occurs at any other place, the seller is not responsible for unloading. This term is likely to be used by a freight forwarder engaged in the international road haulage business. The risk of loss of or damage to the goods is transferred from the seller to the buyer at the time the nominated carrier accepts them at the prescribed place and not at the ship's rail as with FOB. When the seller has to render to the buyer, or other person prescribed, the bill of lading, waybill or carrier's receipt as evidence of the delivery acceptance of the goods, the seller's contractual obligations are fulfilled.

Hence the seller fulfils his or her obligation when he or she has delivered the goods, cleared for export, into the charge of the carrier named by the buyer at the named place or point. If no precise point is indicated by the buyer, the seller may choose within the range stipulated where the carrier shall take the goods into his or her charge. When, according to commercial practice, the seller's assistance is required in making the contract with the carrier (such as in rail or air transport with fixed freight rates), the seller will act at the buyer's risk and expense. The FCA term may be used for any mode of transport. The buyer must contract at his own expense for the carriage of goods from the named place, except when the contract of carriage is made by the seller at the buyers request, risk and expense.

CPT (carriage paid to – named place of destination)

Under the CPT term the seller pays the freight for the carriage of the goods to the named destination. The seller is responsible for export clearance and associated cost. The buyer's risk commences when the goods have been delivered into the custody of the first carrier. Moreover, at this point the buyer accepts full liability for any additional cost incurred in the conveyance of the goods. On request, the seller may have to provide a bill of lading, waybill or carrier's receipt to the buyer or other person prescribed, at which stage the seller's obligations are fulfilled. In common with the 'free carrier' term, CPT is ideal for the multi-modal transport operation which includes Ro-Ro and container movements.

CIP (Carriage and Insurance Paid to – named point of destination)

Under the CIP term, the seller delivers the goods to the nominated carrier as prescribed by the buyer, but the seller must in addition pay the cost of carriage necessary to bring the goods to the named destination. Hence, the buyer bears all risks and any additional costs occurring after the goods have been so delivered. The seller also has to procure insurance against the buyer's risk of loss of or damage to the goods during the carriage. The seller has to clear the goods for export. This term may be used irrespective of the mode of transport including multi-modal transport. Again it is ideal for the combined transport operation and the seller's liability ceases when the cargo has been accepted by the first carrier at the named place and any requested bill of lading, waybill or carrier's receipt has been handed over.

Exporters should fully comprehend the 13 Incoterms described. A major feature of Incoterms 2000 is that it recognizes the electronic message (EDI). Hence the seller and buyer may communicate the document electronically. The importance of all those involved in negotiating and executing sales contracts understanding the foregoing cargo delivery terms cannot be overstressed. The following checklist may prove helpful to the seller (exporter).

1. Endeavour to do as much planning as possible for each exported consignment. Close liaison with the buyer's agent is essential.
2. Ensure the personnel concluding the export sales contract are fully conversant with the Incoterm used, especially the impact it will have on the total price of the goods at the time of exportation and the workload and responsibility imposed on the seller regarding transportation and documentation. Substantial income may be realizable if the transportation and insurance arrangements are undertaken by the exporter using his or her national airline or shipping line and effecting the insurance in the exporter's country.
3. Exercise great care in selecting a suitable forwarding agent, both in the seller's and buyer's country (pp. 518–23).
4. Monitor closely the stages of the product being exported. It will help to identify any problem areas and, through the adoption of remedial measures, lessen the risk in the future.
5. If the distribution arrangements are unsatisfactory, endeavour to establish what the competitors offer – can any lessons be learned?
6. Study closely the Uniform Customs and Practice for Documentary Credits 1993, ICC brochure No. 500, when dealing with commercial documentary credits together with the eUCP - electronic presentation – a supplement to the UCP500 (p. 295).
7. Review distribution arrangements and cargo delivery terms regularly to ensure that they are the most suitable in the situation obtaining.
8. With the growth of multi-modalism globally, endeavour to use one of the terms outlined in Figures 15.1 – EXW, FCA, CPT, CIP, DAF, DDU and DDP.
9. Exporters are urged to have a good software package to take full advantage of the electronic transmission of documents and take a pragmatic strategy with what Bolero offers to develop export business on open account (pp. 433–45) paperless trading basis.
10. Endeavour to develop a logistics strategy.

The formulation of the export sales contract represents the conclusion of some possibly difficult negotiations and accordingly, particular care should be taken regarding the preparation of its terms. It must be borne in mind that an exporter's primary task is to sell his or her products at a profit and, therefore, the contract should fulfil this objective insofar as his or her obligations are concerned. Above all, they should be capable of being executed under reasonable circumstances and ultimately produce a modest profit. It is, of course, realized that in the initial stages of developing a new market overseas a loss may be incurred, but with a long-term marketing plan objective of increasing market share, the exporter should ultimately gain a favourable profit level. A further point to remember is that the export sales contract also has regard to the cargo delivery terms reflecting the contracts of carriage insurance and finance arrangements.

Details of the typical content of a UK export contract are given below, but it must be stressed that such contracts differ by individual country:

1. The exporter's (seller's) registered name and address.
2. The importer's (buyer's) registered name and address.
3. A short title of each party quoted in items (1) and (2).
4. The purpose of the contract. For example, it should confirm that the specified merchandise is sold by the party detailed in item (1) to the addressee quoted in item (2), and what the latter has bought according to the terms and conditions laid down in the contract.
5. The number and quantity of goods, precisely and fully described to avoid any later misunderstanding or dispute. In particular, the contract must mention details of any batches and reconcile goods descriptions with custom tariff specifications.
6. The price. This may be quoted in sterling depending on its general stability or some other currency which is not likely to vary in value significantly throughout the life of the contract, such as American dollars or euros. Goods sold in the seller's currency ensures the exporter maintains his or her profit margin and any currency exchange risk is experienced by the buyer who is compelled to convert sterling into his or her local currency, which may not be stable. Conversely, the seller quoting in the buyer's currency ensures the importer can compare the quotation with other suppliers and is assured there will be no currency risk. The seller runs the risk of the buyer's currency being unstable and consequently this may erode the seller's profit margin unless adequate provision can be made (pp. 292–330). The euro, currently the national currency in 12 countries within the European Union, eliminates any currency risk between the seller and buyer in export contracts undertaken within the euro-zone states (see p. 551). To counter inflation, particularly in a long-term contract, it is usual to incorporate an escalation clause, and to reduce the risk of sterling fluctuations implications, the tendency is to invoice in foreign currencies.
7. Terms of delivery. It is important that the correct Incoterm 2000 is selected (pp. 395–414).
8. Terms of payment, for example, open account, cash with order, letter of credit, open account or documents against payment or acceptance. Again this requires careful consideration (pp. 292–95).
9. Delivery date and shipment date or period. The exporter should check with his or her production department that the delivery date quoted is realistic and that the shipping or air freight space will be available on the date or period specified. The exporter's obligations regarding the latter will depend on the terms of delivery.
10. Methods of shipment, for example, container, cargo wagon, Ro-Ro or air freight. An increasing volume of trade is now conveyed under combined transport operation arrangements.

11. Method of packing. It is desirable that both parties be fully aware and agree on the packing specification to ensure no dispute arises later regarding packing or any variation to it.
12. Cargo insurance policy or certificate terms (see pp. 268–72).
13. Import or export licence details or other instructions. The period of their validity must be reconciled with the terms of payment and delivery date or shipment date or period.
14. Shipping, freight and documentary requirements and/or instructions. This includes marking of cargo.
15. Contract conditions, for example, sale, delivery, performance (quality) of goods, arbitration, etc. With regard to arbitration, this tends to speed the settlement of any disputes without costly litigation.
16. Signature. Both parties must ensure the contract is signed by a responsible person at director or managerial level, and the date should be recorded.

Obviously the terms of the export sales contract will vary by circumstance but other areas which may feature include agency involvement, after-sales activities such as the availability and supply of spares, product servicing, training, advertising and promotion cost and so on. Additionally, it must be reconciled with any logistics-driven strategy (see pp. 597–98) and outsourcing of components and third country assembly as found in the NIKE case study (see p. 39). Moreover, any risk areas must be evaluated and minimized such as currency fluctuations, liquidation of the buyer and political developments. The contract will also mention whether the documents, item 8., may be electronically transmitted; any performance bond (p. 318); the contract is subject to English law or the National Sovereignty of the buyer/seller country; and an arbitration clause.

A copy of the contract should be retained by each party. It must be recognized that an increasing volume of business is conducted on the basis of the export invoice containing the contractual terms. Again one must stress that such a document must be carefully compiled to reflect the terms of the original quotation to the buyer and the importer's acceptance.

15.4 Receipt of export order

A sound export management strategy is required when processing the export order. Full use should be made of computerization (p. 433) and the tactics adopted to execute the strategy require continuous review in the light of changing market conditions. Six areas need especial attention: cash flow; administration; payment; insurance; risk areas; and total cost.

The timescale for payment of the goods can impose a severe strain on the smaller company with limited cash resources. A range of options exist for earlier payment with much improved cash flow such as providing up to 80 per cent of the value of the export invoice on shipment through factoring (pp. 306–07).

An efficient sales ledger is desirable and companies which do not wish to handle much of the documentation work can entrust it to those companies who prepare all the export documentation and institute credit control on behalf of the exporter.

Payment for the goods needs an effective and professional system. This requires continuous monitoring.

Insurance is an area which is subject to premium variation in the light of market conditions and the risks encountered. Ensure the insurance cover is adequate and check such provision particularly while the goods are in the possession of the exporter including the leg from the seller's premises to the departure airport or seaport or ICD.

Finally, the total cost of the export credit processing must be continuously evaluated. This includes bank charges and the varying cost of the payment options including the timescale and resultant risk. It also should embrace the cost of running a shipping department to handle all the documents compared with entrusting the work to freight forwarders, logistic factoring companies which take over the sales ledgers of their clients accounts.

Before dealing with the export order acceptance, it is essential that a number of check-points be processed as detailed below.

1. *Terms of payment.* A full audit of the buyer's needs to be undertaken to establish creditworthiness. Usually a bank can help in this regard. Additionally, the following points require attention: payment timescale; relations with the buyer, short- and long-term; the political situation regarding the buyer's currency; nature of the order; terms of payment; exchange control – import regulations; currency profile – whether it is a convertible currency and the exporter's ability to offer credit terms; and the cost and risk to the seller embracing timescale, bank charges and insurance. Many exporters use the services of Dun and Bradstreet who monitor country risks. The Company produces a monthly review on international risk and payment covering 31 countries. It features changes in business risk and a country's prospects in the short- to medium-term. Exporters who have regular overseas clients would be able to monitor the buyer payment profile found in the customer's portfolio. However, exporters fresh to the business may use the Standard and Poors of Stockholm company public ratings. This Company provides a credit rating with regard to a particular financial obligation of the buyer. The long-term rating scale is AAA to D with plus and minuses in each grade from AA to CCC. The range of payment options are found on pp. 292–95.
2. *Credit insurance* – arrange credit insurance to safeguard the transaction.
3. *Orders* – retain the customer's official order in writing.
4. *Contract* – advise your customers in writing of the agreed contract terms.

5. *Delivery* – ideally ensure that Incoterms 2000 are used.
6. *Currency* – decide in good time whether there is any exchange rate risk and if the exporter should forward sell.
7. *Despatch* – ensure the seller has proof of despatch as such documentation is likely to be required for any subsequent claim.
8. *Continuously monitor progress* of the goods throughout the transit duration.
9. *Product liability.* Check any product liability implications as, for example, obtain in the USA.

The following points should be checked prior to the order of acceptance:

1. An adequate and clear description of goods indicating tariff or trade code number. This area requires special attention to ensure the correct customs tariff classification is used. Options may exist to present the cargo in a different profile and thereby have a changed tariff which may be more favourable to the buyer in import duty terms (pp. 232–33).
2. Specification – use metric units.
3. Quantity to be supplied with delivery programme details.
4. Price: (a) amount or per unit, (b) currency, (c) delivery terms which may involve part shipments over scheduled period and/or tranship- ments: ensure they are specific, e.g. CIF (New York).
5. Terms of payment including provisions for currency rate variation.
6. Terms of delivery, ex-stock, forward, etc. relevant estimate.
7. Transportation mode(s), that is, container, air freight, sea freight or road haulier – check out the implications if a sea–air or sea–rail land-bridge is involved.
8. Insurance.
9. Packaging and packing.
10. Offer by pro-forma invoice (pp. 384–85).
11. Identity of country of origin of goods and country of shipment together with the requisite customs documentation – this may involve the buyer requesting certificates of origin or inwards or out-wards processing relief (pp. 244–45).

Prior to receipt of the indent or order, a customer may need a pro-forma invoice, essential before a customer can open a bank credit in the sup- plier's favour. On receipt of the indent or order from the overseas client, the export marketing manager will check the specification and price in the order with the quotation, together with its period of validity. Care must be taken to ensure the client is not trying to take advantage of an out-of-date quotation. For example, where the quotation was CIF, the export marketing manager must note whether the customer wishes the supplier to arrange for freight and insurance on his or her behalf. The method of payment will be noted and checked with quotation terms. For example, where payment is to be made under a documentary credit, the documents required by the banks must be carefully noted. The required delivery date in particular must be noted. If the delivery date is given and the client has been obliged to obtain an import licence for the particular consignment, the date of expiry must be noted.

Given below is a receipt of order checklist.

1. Goods:

    (a) quality;
    (b) quantity;
    (c) description.

2. Payment:

    (a) price;
    (b) method, i.e. letter of credit, open account, or documents against payment or acceptance;
    (c) timescale;
    (d) currency variation provision.

3. Shipment:

    (a) mode(s) of transport, route, transshipment;
    (b) any constraints, i.e. packing, weight, dimensions, statutory restrictions;
    (c) timescale;
    (d) any marks, i.e. special marking on cases or cartons to identify them.

4. Additional requirements:

    (a) insurance;
    (b) inspection requirements;
    (c) documentation;
    (d) specific packing – see item 3(b);
    (e) commissions or discount.

5. Comparison with quotation. A pro-forma invoice is a document similar to a sales invoice except that it is headed 'pro-forma'. It is not a record of sales effected, but a representation of a sales invoice issued prior to the sale. As the pro-forma invoice contains all relevant details, for example, full description of goods, packing specifications, price of goods with period of validity, cost of cases and, where relevant, cost of freight and insurance, it is used for quotations to customers and for submission to various authorities. Terms of payment are also always shown but it may not be possible to give shipping marks until a firm order is received. When used as quotation the pro-forma invoice constitutes a binding offer of the goods covered by its price and condition shown.

As soon as the exporter receives the letter of credit, he should check it against his pro-forma invoice to ensure both documents agree with each other. Usually, the contract will be in a more detailed form than the letter of credit, but it is important the exporter should be able to prepare his or her documents complying with both the contract and the credit. For general guidance the following checklist should be adopted by the exporter.

1. The terms of the letter of credit which maybe revocable or irrevocable.
2. The name and address of the exporter (beneficiary).
3. The amount of the credit which maybe in sterling or a foreign currency.
4. The name and address of the importer (accreditor).
5. The name of the party on whom the bills of exchange are to be drawn, and whether they are to be at sight or of a particular tenor.
6. The terms of the contract and shipment (i.e. whether EXW, CFR, CIF, FOB, CIP and so on).
7. A brief description of the goods covered by the credit. Basically too much detail may give rise to errors which can cause delay.
8. Precise instructions as to the documents against which payment is to be made.
9. Details of shipment including whether any transhipments are allowed. Data on the latest shipment date and details of port of departure and destination should be recorded. Advantage is gained to permit shipment 'from any UK port' thereby permitting the shipper a choice in the event of strike action. Similar remarks apply to the port of discharge.
10. Whether the credit is available for one or more shipments.
11. The expiry date.

It is important to check the reverse side of the letter of credit and any attachments thereto, the credit as further terms, and any conditions which form an integral part of the credit. Ideally both the seller (exporter) and the buyer (importer) should endeavour to make the credit terms as simple as practical.

In situations where the seller (exporter) is uncertain of just how much of the credit he or she will draw, arrangements should be made with the buyer (importer) to have the value of the documentary letter of credit prefixed by the word 'about'. This will permit up to a 10 per cent margin over or under the amount specified. The word 'about' preceding the quantity of goods similarly allows a 10 per cent margin in the quantity to be shipped. Alternatively the documentary letter of credit may specify a 'tolerance' – such as '7.5 per cent to 5 per cent more or less' – by which the seller (exporter) should be guided.

Documentation will usually involve the clean onboard bill of lading or, for air freight, the air waybill. For international rail movement it is the CIM consignment note, and for the international road haulage transit the CMR consignment note. Particular attention should be given to pre-booking cargo space on the required sailing or flight, and for container traffic, booking a container suitable for the goods. With regard to items sent by parcel post or air freight, the credit and despatch arrangements may vary slightly insofar as the foregoing is concerned.

Today most exporters have a computer software package which progresses the export sales contract as for example Export Master Systems Ltd (see pp. 433–46).

15.4.1 Functions and procedures of export documentation

We will now consider the processing of export documentation (pp. 423–25) and the various procedures involved. Details of the salient points follow:

10 March	Order received for delivery end-April
(extracts from	All wool tissues (Description of goods –
original folder)	wool and worsted piece goods)
	Order No. B 2
	Market: Lebanon
	Port: Beirut
	Packing type: six cases wood, waterproof
	paper, paper lined cases
	Marketing: LAS Beirut 6

Time scale of deliveries	
15 March	*Pro-forma*
1 April	Payment terms (L/C, etc.) received
2 April	Payment terms checked
5 April	Works store promise
18–22 April	Receiving/closing date of shipment
23 April	Insurance dealt with
25 April	Sailing date
28 April	Letter of credit – shipping date
4 May	Bill of lading required by this date
7 May	Completion of documentation to bank
12 May	Proceeds received
15 May	Letter of credit expiry date

It must be recognized that the number of documents and their type vary by individual consignment, mode of transport, commodity, contract of sale, importing country, customer's country, statutory obligations, financial arrangements, etc.

15.5 Processing the export consignment

The task of processing the export order from the time of the initial enquiry until payment for the goods is received is an important one. Basically, it involves the execution of four contracts each within a certain timescale: the contracts of sale, finance, insurance and carriage. All are interrelated and the order processing sequence of an export order is as follows:

1. manufacturer receives, in export sales office, initial export enquiry;
2. costing department calculates approximate total weight or volume of the finished packed goods;
3. details of weight and measurement of goods are submitted to shipping department to obtain insurance and freight rates to destination delivery point (this involves obtaining quotations from freight forwarders and checking out documentation required such as export licence, certificate of origin, etc.);
4. costing department completes non-transport calculations;
5. credit controller obtains satisfactory status report on potential customer;
6. insurance and freight quotation submitted to costing department to formulate overall quotation;
7. formal quotation prepared including currency, terms of delivery (Incoterms 2000) and required terms of payment;
8. quotation sent to prospective overseas buyer – it includes a validity clause;
9. telex, fax or electronic mail sent asking buyer to expedite reply;
10. purchase order (offer) received;
11. export sales office checks out stock availability, manufacturing lead time and delivery schedules;
12. export sales office re-checks credit status report and notes any change from item 5.;
13. agree to accept order only if customer will pay by confirmed letter of credit;
14. export sales office raises order acknowledgement (acceptance) to establish sales contract;
15. export sales office despatches acknowledgement to buyer (NB: if seller not being paid by letter of credit, pass to item 23.);
16. await receipt of letter of credit if item 13. applies;
17. letter of credit received;
18. export sales office checks out whether all the conditions can be met;
19. export sales office requests amendment or extension to letter of credit;
20. export sales office awaits amendment or extension to letter of credit;
21. export sales office receives amendment or extension to letter of credit and checks out all the conditions have now been met;

22. export sales office confirms all the conditions have now been met and despatches acknowledgment to the buyer;
23. export sales office issues authority for the goods to be manufactured and packed. (The task of monitoring progress of manufacture of goods and packaging is handled by the Shipping Department who maintain close liaison with the Production Department to ensure the despatch date is maintained within the timescale as defined in the letter of credit, export or import licence, and that cargo space is booked on carrier's flight, sailing or trailer);
24. Shipping Department establishes total weight and measurement of packed goods and has the completed order checked out;
25. Shipping Department raises shipping documents and cargo shipping instructions noting any letter of credit conditions including any pre-shipment inspection obligations;
26. Pre-shipment inspection completed (if applicable) and clean report of findings issued. Goods despatched to airport, seaport, inland clearance depot, etc. in accordance with the terms of sale Incoterms 2000 and freight forwarders or buyer's agent instructions (documents to be provided include BL/AWB/CMR consignment note, packing list, export licence, certificate of origin, certificate of insurance, commercial invoice, etc). The range and nature of the documents will vary by commodity, terms of sale or destination country. These will be provided by the seller. The task of processing cargo through customs is likely to be undertaken by the freight forwarder, unless the seller has the goods cleared under the local export control arrangement, in which case the seller handles all the export documentation and customs clearance arrangements);
27. await shipping documents;
28. shipping documents received confirming goods despatched on specified flight, sailing or trailer – buyer informed;
29. documents checked by Shipping Department – errors found, and corrected documents requested;
30. receive corrected documents;
31. Shipping Department collates documents and letter of credit;
32. seller raises bill of exchange signed by a director;
33. Shipping Department checks all documents against letter of credit;
34. Shipping Department presents all documents to the bank within agreed timescale;
35. seller awaits payment or acceptance of the bill of exchange;
36. seller receives funds from the bank (if the funds are not in the seller's currency (i.e. sterling), the exporter should sell at spot or place, against which finance should have been arranged under 15.);
37. legal requirements followed such as VAT.

It will be appreciated the foregoing arrangements will vary by circumstances and many companies computerize their export consignment processing. A critical area of variation is the terms of payment, the method of carriage and the customs arrangements. It is important to bear in mind the seller is responsible for providing the buyer with all the requisite documents to enable the goods to be processed and imported through customs in the destination country. These must be checked out by the seller. The overall factor to bear in mind is to adhere to the timescale to ensure the goods arrive on the agreed date, and all the documents are in order to support the consignment arriving in a quality condition.

15.6 Presentation of documents to the bank: checklist

When preparing his or her documents for presentation to the bank, the exporter should bear in mind the following points which can form a checklist.

1. All the documents are presented within the expiry date.
2. Goods are shipped within the stipulated period.
3. Documents are presented to the bank within 21 days of the date of shipment or despatch or such shorter time as laid down in the letter of credit.
4. The aggregate amount of the drawing is within the credit amount.
5. All documents requiring endorsement are correctly endorsed, for example, bills of lading, bills of exchange, insurance documents.
6. Invoices contain exact credit description.
7. Invoices are addressed to the importer.
8. Invoices contain exact licence numbers and/or certifications required by credit and such certifications are signed, and must be worded exactly as specified in the credit.
9. Invoices show terms of shipment mentioned in the credit.
10. Quantity, weight – both gross and nett – shipping marks, unit price, etc. agree with credit and with all the relative documents.
11. Bills of lading show goods 'onboard' a specified named vessel.
12. Bills of lading show correct name and address of party to notify.
13. Bills of lading are in a full set of signed originals (that is, 2/2, or 3/3) or as called for by the credit.
14. If FOB shipment, ensure bills of lading show freight payable at destination.
15. If CFR or CIF shipment, ensure bills of lading are marked 'freight paid' or 'freight pre-paid'.
16. Insurance document is in currency of credit.
17. Insurance is for correct value (for example, as specified in the credit).

TABLE 15.1 Export documents required

	Bank	Customer	Agent	Customs clearance	Consulate	Total
Commercial invoices	–	3	–	–	–	3
Certified invoices	3	1	2	1	3	10
Certificate of origin	–	–	–	–	–	
Bill of lading	2/2	2 copies	–	–	2	2/4
Certificate of shipment	–	–	–	–	–	
Insurance policy	–	–	–	–	–	
Insurance certificate	–	–	–	–	–	
Weight and contract note	1	1	–	–	1	3
Bank draft statement	1	–	–	–	–	1

18. Insurance covers all the risks as specified in the credit.
19. Original letter of credit accompanies the presentation.
20. The insurance document is dated prior to despatch of the goods or specifically states that cover is effective from shipment date.
21. Insurance certificate is not presented where credit stipulates insurance policy.

The foregoing checklist must not be regarded as exhaustive, it merely deals with the salient points. To the exporter dealing with a documentary letter of credit, the following data must be contained on it relative to a consignment by sea.

1. The name and address of the beneficiary.
2. The type of credit (revocable or irrevocable).
3. The amount of credit in sterling or a foreign currency.
4. Whether the credit is available for one or several drawings or shipments.
5. The expiry date.
6. The name of the party on whom the drafts are to be drawn and whether they are at sight or of a particular tenor.
7. Precise instructions as to the documents against which payment is to be made.
8. A brief description of the goods covered by the credit (too much detail may give rise to errors which can cause delay).
9. Shipping details including whether transshipments are allowed. The names of the ports of shipment and discharge should also be recorded, and the latest date for shipment.
10. The terms of contract and shipment (that is, whether ex-works, FOB or CIF).

Credits should further state that they are subject to the Uniform Customs and Practice for Documentary Credits (1993 UCP) International Chamber of Commerce Publication No. 500. A new edition UCP600 may be published by ICC in 2007.

The following checklist must be rigorously adopted by the exporter when handling the letter of credit.

1. Is it confirmed by a British bank?
2. Is the quantity described correct?
3. Is partial shipment permitted or required?
4. Is the letter of credit irrevocable?
5. Is the name of the exporter and that of the customer complete and spelt correctly?
6. Is shipment permitted from any place in the UK, or only one named point?
7. Does the named destination quoted (port of discharge) agree with the letter of credit?
8. Are the following needed?

    (a) export licence;
    (b) import licence;
    (c) exchange licences.

9. Is the letter of credit amount sufficient to the quotation? The following aspects should be checked:

    (a) cost of goods plus profit element;
    (b) inland transport cost to ship, including wharfage and handling charges at port of loading, or similar charges relative to air freight or air freight charges;
    (c) shipping – sea freight or air freight charges;
    (d) forwarding fees;
    (e) consular fees;
    (f) insurance cost;
    (g) inspection and/or miscellaneous charges.

10. If it is 'on-deck' cargo, does the letter of credit authorize 'on-deck' shipment?
11. Compare the contract of sale with the letter of credit to ensure its compatibility.
12. If a chartered vessel is involved, does the letter of credit state 'charter-party/bill of lading acceptable'?
13. Can the exporter comply with the insurance risk required in the letter of credit and does the credit request a policy or certificate?
14. Does the expiration and shipping date give sufficient time to assure payment?
15. Is the letter of credit irrevocable?
16. Can the exporter obtain the following relevant executed documents to conform with the letter of credit?

    (a)   bill of lading;
    (b)   air waybill;
    (c)   parcel post receipt;
    (d)   invoice packing list;
    (e)   consular invoice;
    (f)   certificate of origin;
    (g)   insurance policy or certificate;
    (h)   certificate of inspection;
    (i)   certificate of quality;
    (j)   certificate of health;
    (k)   pre-shipment inspection – Clean Report of Findings.

Circumstances do arise which make it impossible for the exporter to present documents to the bank exactly as stipulated or within the prescribed time. Moreover, unforeseen circumstances can arise. In such situations, a number of options exist for the exporter after presenting the documents to the bank.

1.   Request the advising bank to fax, telex or e-mail the issuing bank for permission to effect payment despite discrepancies in the documents. The actual fax, telex or e-mail cost would be for the beneficiary's account.

2.   Ask the advising bank to accept a guarantee order that the exporter requests payment against an undertaking to hold the bank harmless for any loss or damage incurred through making payment against presentation of irregular documents.

3.   Instruct the advising bank to send draft and documents to the issuing bank on a collection basis, that is, documents to be delivered to the importer against authority to pay.

In circumstances where the documents can be corrected or amended, the exporter should arrange for this to be done ensuring that the documents are returned to the paying bank as soon as possible but within the expiry date of the credit. The exporter should remember to check the reverse of, and any attachment to, the credit; further terms and conditions may appear and form an integral part of the credit. Basically, the simpler the credit terms between the exporter and the importer, the easier it is for trade to take place and expand between the parties and countries concerned.

    Although it is often desirable for the UK exporter to ensure that the credit is opened in sterling, that is, the currency of his or her country, this may not be possible and a foreign currency may be used. In the EU the euro is adopted for international trade transactions within the euro-zone (see p. 551). To protect him- or herself from any losses due to rate fluctuations in the period between the time he or she ships the goods and receives payment, he or she may wish to sell the foreign currency forward to his or her bank. The bank will quote him or her a special rate and, no matter what happens to the exchange rate in the meantime, the importer knows exactly how much he or she will receive. On the other hand, there may be distinct advantages in invoicing in foreign currencies.

In circumstances where extended credit is granted to the importer, the beneficiary should be contracted to pay interest and will receive an acceptance or usance credit providing for payment at a future date.

At the time of drawing up the contract, the period, rate and method of payment of interest should be agreed with the importer and can be incorporated in the price, or the importer could ask his or her bank to add a clause in the credit stating that the interest is for the importer's account and may be claimed accordingly. Alternatively, the term 'discount charges are for buyer's account' could be incorporated in the credit terms. Interest rates fluctuate, sometimes on a daily basis.

Following presentation of documents in order, the accepted bill can be discounted (that is, sold to a discount house) usually by the bank accepting the bill, or by the beneficiary's own bankers. An interest charge is levied by the discount house which, if for the buyer's account, will be paid by the importer. In effect, the beneficiary then receives settlement as if the bill had been drawn at sight.

If the credit makes no reference to settlement of the discount charge, the bill can still be discounted at any time, but the interest charge levied should be for the beneficiary's account. Unless the credit specifies that drafts are needed in duplicate, a single draft will be acceptable.

Many credits stipulate the name of the port from which shipment is to be made but in some circumstances it may be advantageous to the exporter for shipment to be allowed 'from any UK port', thereby providing a choice. This must be arranged in consultation with the importer and provides a degree of flexibility. It can be extended to include the port of discharge.

There are three features which are basic for export success in terms of documentation: namely quality of management, quality of staff, and effective communication. Exporters are not simply selling a product, they are also selling their – hopefully – efficient service. It is vitally important to examine each problem as it arises, to obtain correct information without delay, to use it effectively and to make correct decisions.

The overseas customer has the same attitude to business detail as the good businessman in the UK. Hence, he or she will be impressed by clarity and accuracy and will be suspicious of the exporter who fails to produce the correct documents in the correct sequence. Export documents must be precise and accurate. Documentation is required for the following reasons:

1.   To provide a complete and specific description of the goods including values and all relevant details so that goods can be correctly assessed for customs purposes.

2. Documents may be needed for exchange control regulations – quantitative or quota restrictions and also for statistical purposes.
3. The buyer requires the relevant documents for his or her own purposes, for example, in order to obtain the goods.

Delays in the delivery or despatch of shipping and other documents has reached serious proportions in recent years and has resulted in excessive delays in despatching goods. These delays have arisen for many reasons which can be summarized as follows.

1. Non-availability at time of despatch of commercial invoices and packing lists.
2. Late submission of bills of lading by manufacturers and/or shippers to shipping companies, etc.
3. Delay in releasing bills of lading by shipping companies.
4. Errors in compilation of bills of lading, insurance certificates, etc.
5. Delays in communication between clerical staff in seaports, airports, ICDs, dry ports and CFS and shippers.
6. Delay in obtaining necessary consular invoices.
7. Inadequate scrutiny at time of receipt of letters of credit.
8. Delay by banks in processing documents due to discrepancies found in them.
9. Delay due to one or more of the following:

    (a) letter of credit expired or withdrawn;
    (b) partial shipment, i.e. only part of consignment sent;
    (c) stale or incorrectly completed bill of lading;
    (d) insurance certificate not enclosed, or dated after shipment, or cover incorrect in terms of value or currency;
    (e) incorrect invoices, consular documents or draft drawn incorrectly.

10. Documents sent by surface post when they could be delivered by air.
11. Documents sent to small local branches of banks when the main or foreign branches deal with shipping documents.
12. Wrongly completed documents including customs invoices, delaying customs clearance. To overcome the foregoing problem, the exporter should do the following:

    (a) employ the professional services of a freight forwarder; and/or
    (b) provide an adequately trained staff of good calibre;
    (c) study the letter of credit carefully so there is time for amendments to be made if necessary and send copy to freight forwarder;
    (d) apply the aligned documentation system (This involves the use of the simplified method of documentation with standard-size forms. By engaging the aligned system and mechanization, and one-run series of production, the complete operation is speeded up);
    (e) maintain a record of documents flow and status reports in order to isolate consistent bottlenecks with a view to correction;

(f)   utilize fully electronic mail and other aids for the rapid transmission of information when appropriate;

(g)   develop a computerized documentation system (pp. 431–45).

Finally, it must be stressed that an increasing number of multinational industries entrust their international trade distribution and product sourcing arrangements to mega-container operators' logistic divisions. Two market leaders in this field are P&O Nedlloyd and Hapag-Lloyd – the latter involving Pracht Forwarding and Logistics. Such developments have arisen through more sophisticated production and distribution systems developed globally – materials sourcing from one country, production and assembly in two or more countries, followed by distribution worldwide.

15.7 Computerized export department

Our study of processing the export consignment would not be complete without examining the increasing role computers play in processing the export consignment. The subject is also examined in a wider context under Electronic Data Interchange – EDI, Chapter 16.

A successful export computerization project requires careful preparation and planning. It yields the following benefits and features.

1.   Word processing eliminates routine administration export correspondence such as shipping instructions.
2.   Exporters tend to have a long list of overseas customers. Electronic mail provides global access to world markets and overseas customers involving the Internet.
3.   Exporters maintain complex and often multiple pricelists for many territories which can be created on a word processor and updated as required.
4.   Computer systems can provide spreadsheets which are ideal for monitoring distribution costs, territory analysis and forecasting.
5.   Similarly, the computer is ideal for maintaining accounts.
6.   Modern computer networks have access through electronic data interchange to shipment information, customs and airline interfaces, tracking and tracing, document preparation, rating and routeing, sailing schedules, port information, accounting and invoicing, estimated time of arrival, cargo reservation and so on.
7.   Computers eliminate laborious and time-consuming aspects of export administration thereby improving staff morale and productivity.
8.   Computerized systems allow a firm to produce accurate delivered prices, and rapid quotations which benefits sales activities.
9.   Establishing an efficient computer system can improve order processing and administration, up-grade general performance and order costing control and thereby increase profitability.

10. Valuable time can be saved by management personnel delegating to less senior staff costings and administrative tasks which hitherto were too complex.
11. Following on from item 10. management and export staff can devote more time to business development and sales-oriented activities and less to administrative and clerical functions.
12. Computerized systems permit high-speed assembly of export orders.
13. Similarly quicker assembly, extension and printing of export quotations are facilitated.
14. Automatic export order processing and production of commercial and internal export documentation can be carried out.
15. Order and shipment progress chasing and status reporting becomes more straightforward.
16. The computer can speed up the production of shipping and customs documentation.
17. Consignment costings can be produced easily, including those for multiple product shipments.
18. A computer allows for the provision of a general export database, including products with costs and packing specifications; customers; territories with commission agents; currency exchange rates; Incoterms 2000; and container and trailer specifications.
19. A modern export department computer unit would need the ability to interface with other computer networks within the company via a specially designed module.

Overall, the installation of a sound computer export package will allow a company to develop a modern image of an export company participating at the global level, with a logistic and computer management culture.

Given below are the specifications for modules found in two areas of the computer network, namely export quotations and order processing.

The *export quotation module* creates a fully documented quotation on screen, rapidly and accurately, and prints the data on the exporter's stationery for despatch to the overseas client. The computer system:

1. uses standard customer, territory and product details from file, or allows one-off entry;
2. takes prices automatically from pricing and costing calculations or from list prices (with optional mark-up or discount) or allows manual entry;
3. prepares quotations in any currency, automatically converting pre-set prices in the currency selected;
4. prints quotations as pro-forma invoices, if required, showing customer and consignee details, shipping marks, sales and payment terms, origin, shipment method and delivery time;
5. handles percentage surcharges or discounts for one item only or for the whole quotation;

6. allows flat-rate surcharges or deductions;
7. permits any rate of VAT on any item;
8. calculates all extensions automatically;
9. shows packing specifications per item or for the whole quotation only;
10. permits the use of invoicing 'clauses';
11. allows the insertion or deletion of items at any point;
12. prints ready-to-use quotations on standard stationery;
13. stores quotations on file for later use or modification, or for conversion into orders.

The *order processing module* comprises the following facilities and would be fully integrated with the pricing and costing quotations and consignment costing modules:

1. high-speed order assembly from standard information on file or manual input;
2. automatic conversion of quotations or pro-forma invoices into orders (with or without alteration);
3. adaptation of past orders for creation of repeat or similar new orders;
4. documentation as required: masters; confirmations; works, stores and purchase orders; marking instructions; credit control applications; shipping instructions; shipment advices; commercial invoices; packing lists; commission credit notes and all relevant shipping, customs, banking, insurance and origin documentation;
5. order status reports;
6. progress chasing;
7. automatic preparation of documents triggered by appropriate status or order.

15.7.1 Export software – Exportmaster Systems Ltd.

Today, international trade conducts its business in an electronic communications network. It has transformed the scale and alacrity of international business. Each year the software package enters a new phase in its development. This is recognized by the ICC trade finance transaction cycle (p. 289), Customs in electronic clearance (p. 227), Bolero (p. 457) and traders/carriers/terminal operators across the world in a logistic driven environment.

Exportmaster is one of the leaders globally in devising the most comprehensive international trade software system. Its adaptability and configurability make it suitable for almost any export or trading situation. It is used in a wide range of industrial and commercial sectors by companies of all sizes. Given below are the salient benefits emerging from the latest software system.

(a) Customer service is much improved through continuous online contact. Overall, the software is not only a processing system, but also the design is geared to help deliver the best service to the customers through speed of response, efficient shipment handling, quality and accuracy of documentation and general efficiency of operations.

(b) Price profitability. The software package enables the trader to devise the most appropriate prices for all the markets targeted by engaging the traders pricing and costing input data in the exporters prescribed strategic manner. It enables distribution and selling costs to be kept under close control. The sophisticated software management reporting system permits the exporter to monitor profitability by territory, customer and product.

(c) Cost reductions are realized through automated documentation and processing compared with the more expensive and longer manual system. Savings are effected on pre-printed stationery via computer-generated forms and on postage via direct faxing and e-mailing of complex documentation.

(d) Sales development. Increased sales can emerge through more prompt response to enquiries in the form of quotation. This helps to improve the conversion rate of quotes to orders. A special analysis module permits the exporter to monitor quotation progress and compare offers with orders received.

Overall, the software adds value to the exporter's service to the customer. Overall, exporter orders are not secured on product specification or price alone, but the overall service provided to the buyer as a total package of which software provisions form a part.

While most export software products have limited their functionality to the area of shipping documentation, the 'Exportmaster Systems Ltd.' package addresses the entire export transaction cycle (Figure 15.3). The exporter can work out delivered prices for different export destinations, incorporating selling expenses and distribution costs through from ex-works to be delivered duty paid. These prices can be used for quotations and pro-formas which are produced, along with personalized letters, during the processing and progress-chasing of sales enquiries. Before issuing a quotation, the exporter is able to check its profitability against known or estimated distribution and selling costs. Date-based deadline reporting ensures that offers are chased up or progressed when necessary.

A summary of Exportmaster key areas are as follows:

(a) *Graphical user interface.* An expandable menu system allows the user to access any part of the program from a single screen. Different modules open simultaneously and the user can click between them. Moreover, one can even configure the system to open up automatically at start-up with the modules the client uses most frequently.

FIGURE 15.3 The Exportmaster Systems Ltd transaction cycle

(b) *Shippers work flow system.* The system permits the exporter to define their own activities and check lists. Procedures can be set up for different customers that determine which activities need to be carried out for them and in what sequence. Totally different sets of activities can apply to different types of areas of business. They can be defined for use in home market and import situations as well as for export operations. The activity lines can be action lines that prompt the shipper to do something, control lines that hold up work flow until they have been satisfied, document lines that produce particular documents or lists of documents, and task lines that trigger automated routines within Exportmaster. Hence, the software is ideal for complex international trade situations.

(c) *Processing the order or shipment.* This is a double click activity and the software will record who did it and feature in the audit trail columns. The system will automatically release dependent activities for action. Likewise a double click document activity will activate printing, faxing or e-mailing of a document or double click a document-list activity to trigger production of a complete individualized list of documents for a customer. Enter a deadline date against an activity to force its inclusion in special deadline reports. On-screen or printed action reports identify what has and has not been done, and which activities need to be done at the moment. Activities can be assigned to individual users so that personal to-do lists can be generated.

(d) *Documentation production.* The documents may be produced automatically as part of a pre-defined procedure for an order, shipment or sale enquiry; on demand at any stage; or items such as faxes, adhesive labels, memos or e-mails. Documents can be output to different printers on a network to fax software and to e-mail systems.

(e) the Exportmaster software package embraces the following additional items:

    (i) document design;
    (ii) master data files;
    (iii) shipping data;
    (iv) packing specification;
    (v) Customs and NES;
    (vi) hazardous cargo;
    (vii) sales enquiries and quotations;
    (viii) costing and pricing module;
    (ix) expense database, and;
    (x) costing models.

(f) Further modules embrace;

    (i) structured pricing;
    (ii) port shipments;
    (iii) consolidations;
    (iv) EU VAT and INTRASTAT;
    (v) integration;
    (vi) product and customer data interface;
    (vii) orders and quotations interface;
    (viii) management information
    (ix) sales analysis, and;
    (x) orders and quotations analysis.

Exporters are urged to study the following Exportmaster diagrams:
Exportmaster Transaction Cycle (Figure 15.3)
Exportmaster Sales Process (Figure 15.4)
Exportmaster Shipping Process (Figure 15.5)
Export operation flow chart (Figure 15.8(a–d))

The forgoing demonstrates the need to have the most advanced software to develop the 21st century export/import business successfully.

The program can convert quotations into orders, and orders can also be prepared from scratch. A user-configurable processing system takes the order through all stages of preparation, producing company internal documents, as well as commercial paperwork such as confirmations, requests for shipping instructions and routine correspondence items. Additional facilities for the export trader permit the sourcing of required items from multiple potential suppliers with automatic production of purchase orders for the suppliers eventually selected.

If export packing is involved, the program holds details both of the outers and of their precise contents, from which packing lists and allocation sheets can be printed. Exportmaster Systems Ltd. can produce a full set of shipping documents for the consignment, printing them on to pre-printed stationery or on to plain paper using images stored in a laser

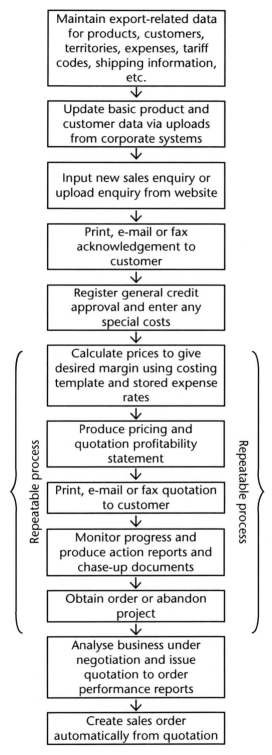

FIGURE 15.4 Exportmaster Sales Process

```
┌─────────────────────────────┐
│  Key in sales order or create it │
│        from quotation           │
└─────────────────────────────┘
              ↓
┌─────────────────────────────┐
│   Produce estimated order       │
│  costing using distribution cost │
│   template and stored rates     │
└─────────────────────────────┘
              ↓
┌─────────────────────────────┐
│   Approve order content and     │
│            credit               │
└─────────────────────────────┘
              ↓
┌─────────────────────────────┐
│     Print, fax or e-mail        │
│   acknowlegement to             │
│          customer               │
└─────────────────────────────┘
              ↓
┌─────────────────────────────┐
│  Progress-chase and produce     │
│       action reports            │
└─────────────────────────────┘
              ↓
┌─────────────────────────────┐
│  If required, split order into   │
│  part-shipments based upon      │
│       goods received            │
└─────────────────────────────┘
              ↓
┌─────────────────────────────┐
│     If required, create         │
│  consolidated shipment from     │
│      multiple orders            │
└─────────────────────────────┘
              ↓
┌─────────────────────────────┐
│   Enter export packing details  │
└─────────────────────────────┘
              ↓
┌─────────────────────────────┐
│  Issue shipping instructions    │
│   and advance documents         │
└─────────────────────────────┘
              ↓
┌─────────────────────────────┐
│  Print, fax or e-mail shipment  │
│            advice               │
└─────────────────────────────┘
              ↓
┌─────────────────────────────┐
│     Produce packing lists       │
└─────────────────────────────┘
              ↓
┌─────────────────────────────┐
│  Produce territory-compliant    │
│     shipping documents          │
└─────────────────────────────┘
              ↓
┌─────────────────────────────┐
│  Produce territory-compliant    │
│       export invoice            │
└─────────────────────────────┘
              ↓
┌─────────────────────────────┐
│  Send or transmit documents     │
│     to customer or bank         │
└─────────────────────────────┘
              ↓
┌─────────────────────────────┐
│  Generate Intrastat and VAT     │
│  reports for European Union     │
│  and general management         │
│          reports                │
└─────────────────────────────┘
```

FIGURE 15.5 Exportmaster Shipping Process

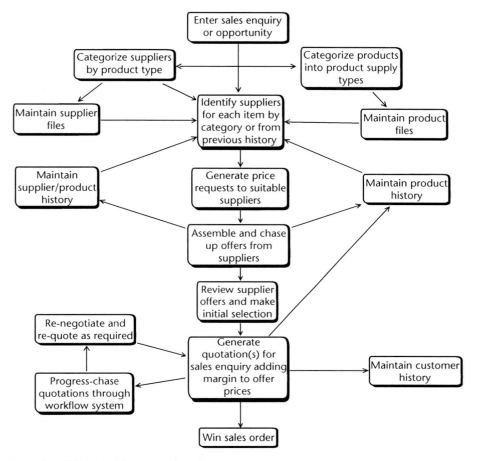

FIGURE 15.6   The Sourcing Process

printer's memory to reproduce the official documents. Customs documents are produced in a similar fashion but the program first sorts and totals the goods by their customs tariff classifications. Facilities exist to transmit documents direct to fax lines without intermediate printing or to have documents printed out at remote locations, for instance, at a despatch department in a factory elsewhere in the country.

After shipment, the program can produce final invoices, bank documents, insurance declarations and other similar items. In particular it can calculate a final shipment costing, showing the net profitability of the consignment once all final selling and distribution costs are known. The finished shipment details can be processed by the sales analysis module to provide management reports and budget monitoring, covering volumes, revenues, costs and profit margins. This information can be used as the basis for the marketing and market-pricing decisions with which the transaction cycle begins.

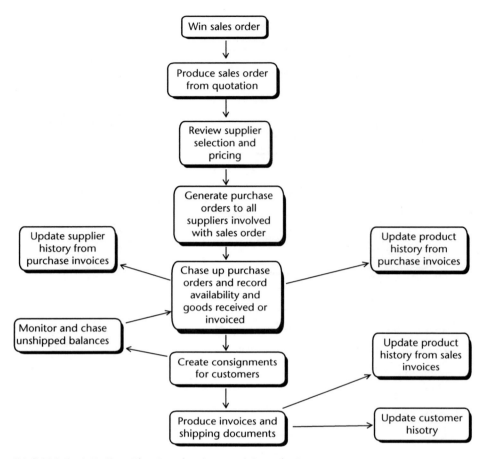

FIGURE 15.7   The Purchasing and Supply Process

Many exporters are involved in product sourcing overseas and the assembly in a third country and subsequently re-exporting. Overall procurement is comprehensively dealt with in my companion title International Purchasing and Management – 1st Edition (2001) published by Cengage Learning. However, Exportmaster have developed a TOPS system – Trading Operations, Purchasing and Supply. It ensures a single entry of data for an enquiry or opportunity and can service all subsequent sourcing, purchasing and selling operations. It is ideal for an export or import merchant, a trader sourcing against sales enquiries and purchasing against sales orders, a commodity trader selling against purchase contracts or opportunities and a manufacturing exporter whose export department handles goods from multiple factories or locations.

The sourcing process (Figure 15.6) demonstrates how TOPS handles the sourcing of products from multiple potential suppliers, controls the process of obtaining price offers from suppliers, facilitates supplier selection

FIGURE 15.8 (a)–(d) Exportmaster Systems Ltd. operations flow chart

and automates the preparation of sales quotations from the supplier offers. These quotations are then chased up and revised as necessary to obtain the sales order.

When a sales order has been received TOPS generates purchase orders (Figure 15.7) to the appropriate suppliers, monitors and chases goods availability, undertakes the picking for shipment process, creates consignments and handles the complete shipping, invoicing and documentation process. In some traders the procedures may be relatively straightforward, with a purchase order, once placed, being executed as a single despatch. Others will be faced with multiple pick up or despatch points, goods being partially available, clients wanting different orders to be incorporated into a single despatch, supplier prices changing during the process and a multitude of similar problems.

Exportmaster uses the latest 32-bit object orientated technology to take full advantage of the Microsoft operating environment. It has been specifically designed to integrate smoothly with other corporate systems.

DATA SOURCES	ACTIVITIES	OUTPUT
Standard costs/prices Customer/territory prices Discount/surcharge tables Export costings	Establish pricing structures	Printed price lists Export costing reports
Customer data Product data Territory data	Log and process sales enquiry	Acknowledgements
Pricing data	Quotations and pro-formas	Quotations Letters Quotation costings
Status system	Progress-chase enquiry	Chase-up letters
Customer data Product data Territory data	Log order or convert quotation to order	
Export sales and distribution cost data	Calculate order profitability	Consignment costing reports
Customer data Product data Territory data Pricing price	Confirm and process order	Confirmations, credit applications, etc.
	Stock allocation, purchase or production	Works requisitions, purchase orders
Packing data	Export packing/marking	Packing lists, packing allocation reports
Packing data	Shipping arrangements and instructions	Shipping instructions, ECSI or EDI message
Shipping and order data	Invoicing and shipping documentation	Invoices, shipping and custom documents, C/O's
	Despatch and stock adjustment	Delivery and consignment notes, stock reports
	Insurance and bank procedures	Insurance & bank docs. or EDI messages
Export sales and distribution cost data	Final costing with freight and shipping figures	Final consignment costing report
Agency commissions data	Commission calculations and processing	Final consignment notes, stock reports
	Transfer to accounts ledgers	Electronic transfer of invoice to accounts
	Analysis to management reporting database	Download of invoice and cost data of statistics
	Final checks and complete procedure	

FIGURE 15.8 (b)

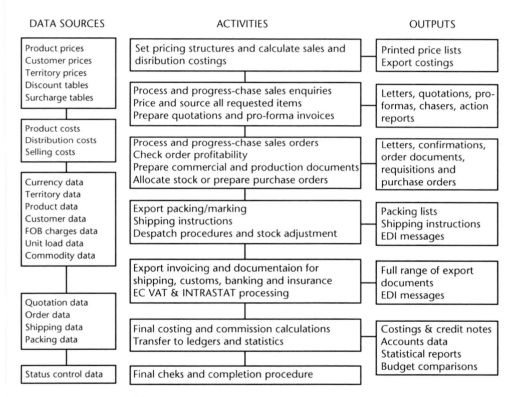

DATA SOURCES

Product prices
Customer prices
Territory prices
Discount tables
Surcharge tables

Product costs
Distribution costs
Selling costs

Currency data
Territory data
Product data
Customer data
FOB charges data
Unit load data
Commodity data

Quotation data
Order data
Shipping data
Packing data

Status control data

ACTIVITIES

Set pricing structures and calculate sales and disribution costings

Process and progress-chase sales enquiries
Price and source all requested items
Prepare quotations and pro-forma invoices

Process and progress-chase sales orders
Check order profitability
Prepare commercial and production documents
Allocate stock or prepare purchase orders

Export packing/marking
Shipping instructions
Despatch procedures and stock adjustment

Export invoicing and documentaion for shipping, customs, banking and insurance
EC VAT & INTRASTAT processing

Final costing and commission calculations
Transfer to ledgers and statistics

Final cheks and completion procedure

OUTPUTS

Printed price lists
Export costings

Letters, quotations, pro-formas, chasers, action reports

Letters, confirmations, order documents, requisitions and purchase orders

Packing lists
Shipping instructions
EDI messages

Full range of export documents
EDI messages

Costings & credit notes
Accounts data
Statistical reports
Budget comparisons

FIGURE 15.8 (c)

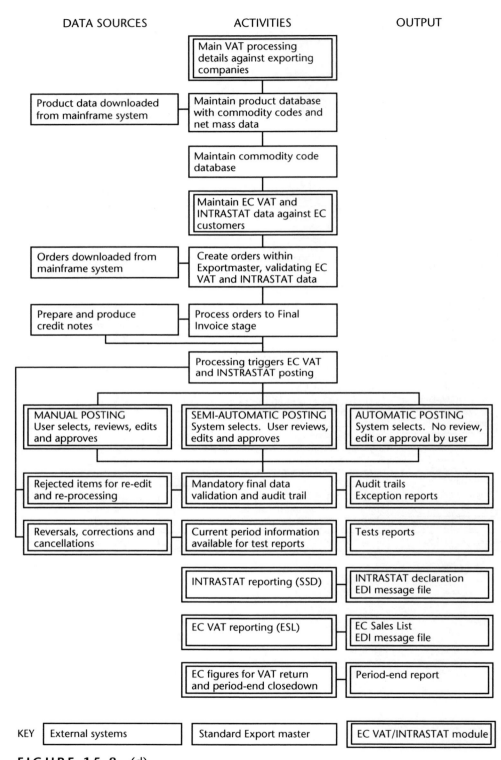

DATA SOURCES   ACTIVITIES   OUTPUT

Main VAT processing details against exporting companies

Product data downloaded from mainframe system | Maintain product database with commodity codes and net mass data

Maintain commodity code database

Maintain EC VAT and INTRASTAT data against EC customers

Orders downloaded from mainframe system | Create orders within Exportmaster, validating EC VAT and INTRASTAT data

Prepare and produce credit notes | Process orders to Final Invoice stage

Processing triggers EC VAT and INSTRASTAT posting

MANUAL POSTING
User selects, reviews, edits and approves | SEMI-AUTOMATIC POSTING
System selects. User reviews, edits and approves | AUTOMATIC POSTING
System selects. No review, edit or approval by user

Rejected items for re-edit and re-processing | Mandatory final data validation and audit trail | Audit trails
Exception reports

Reversals, corrections and cancellations | Current period information available for test reports | Tests reports

INTRASTAT reporting (SSD) | INTRASTAT declaration
EDI message file

EC VAT reporting (ESL) | EC Sales List
EDI message file

EC figures for VAT return and period-end closedown | Period-end report

KEY | External systems | Standard Export master | EC VAT/INTRASTAT module

FIGURE 15.8 (d)

Recommended reading

Dun and Bradstreet website – www.dunandbrad.co.uk

Exportmaster website – www.exportmaster.co.uk

INCO terms 2000 – ICC publication No 560.

The ICC Model International Sale Contract – Manufactured goods intended for resale – ICC publication No 556.

The ICC Model occasional intermediary contract – non circumvention and non disclosure agreement – ICC publication No 619.

CHAPTER 16

Electronic commerce and paperless trading

16.1 Introduction

International Trade today is being conducted in an era of E-commerce embracing paperless trading. Its benefits are intrinsic and wide ranging. It is reducing the trade cycle and opening up new markets. Moreover, it is being greatly facilitated by the International Agencies who have formulated the mechanism under which international trade transactions may be conducted with complete confidence. The benefits apply to all levels of business structure, and logistics (p. 124) is playing a major role in supply chain management and sourcing. Moreover, it is eliminating intermediaries through the development of B2B and B2C. The need, however, for professionalism remains at all levels.

We will now examine various aspects of E-commerce, especially Bolero. This chapter should be read in conjunction with Chapter 15.

16.2 Electronic commerce

Moreover, recent developments in electronic connectivity have dramatically reduced both the price and complexity of EDI system integration. Electronic Data Interchange (EDI) has been defined as the application to application exchange of computer-held information in a structural format via a telecommunications network. It enables the data to pass from an application on one computer into an application on another computer without printing or manual manipulation. Electronic commerce – the ability to conduct business electronically – is transforming the way business is carried out, improving the speed, accuracy and efficiency of business processes and fundamentally changing business relationships. The dramatic rise of the Internet and World Wide Web as business tools underlines the importance of these new ways of working. Organizations cannot afford to ignore the opportunities they present, and departments that develop a good business plan and implement electronic commerce can be in the vanguard for their organizations.

The form is the most important concept of EDI, in that it allows an EDI system to send and receive partially completed information, which it can pass through as well as add to the form without re-entering the original data. The elimination of data re-entry allows for greater efficiency and business process cost savings.

Hitherto, E-commerce trading was identified with the MNI involving a third-party provider or Value Added Network (VAN). The main catalyst for change is the Internet. This has shifted the focus of the communications business away from proprietary networks and towards the cheaper, more open environment of the World Wide Web. Today, unless a company large or small is on the web and trades through E-commerce, it is unlikely to do any international business. Moreover, the fax-based service is in decline in favour of E-commerce while international business communication by air mail has given way to the e-mail communication discipline.

Enter the Internet, which has been undergoing massive expansion just as the need for more accessible EDI has emerged. All the leading VANs have grasped this nettle, and have been developing services which allow Internet links to their existing EDI networks.

Many business and government experts regard electronic commerce as driving wealth creation globally.

To put it simply, electronic commerce can be defined as 'doing business electronically . . . across the extended enterprise'. At a more detailed level the E-centre definition reads: 'Electronic commerce covers any form of business or administrative transaction or information exchange that is executed using any information and communications technology'. This embraces the three main areas of activity, namely: business-to-business; business-to-consumer; and government-to-nation (that includes both businesses and citizens). This definition has been used in the work with the EURIM (European Information Markets) working party on electronic commerce. The leading information exchange tools included in this definition are the Internet and the World Wide Web, intranets, extranets, e-mail and electronic data interchange (EDI). The short definition also embraces the important concept that by trading electronically you reach into your company to share information (via intranets) and reach out from your company to your suppliers and your customers and to the wider global market place by use of extranets or the open world of the Internet.

16.3 Trends and drivers in the development of electronic commerce

16.3.1 Web-based transactions

Use of the Internet as a business tool has increased dramatically particularly with the development of the World Wide Web and its intuitive and user friendly graphical user interface. Worldwide business access to the web has grown dramatically in the past five years, with much of this growth occurring in the Pacific Rim and Europe. Common applications of such information exchange tools include marketing and advertising, publishing, the exchange and dissemination of information on a global scale and, more recently, commercial transactions.

Among the most recent advances is the use of the World Wide Web for business-to-business and business-to-consumer transactions. Much of the recent research has signalled the huge potential of the online transactions market with a number of key developments making the World Wide Web a better place to conduct business-to-business and business-to-consumer transactions. The first of these is security. While the Internet's lack of security has been the most significant operational issue facing organizations considering using the Internet for business, recent surveys indicate a growing confidence that such problems are being overcome. (see p. 450). A range of measures regarding improving security embracing making credit card payments over the Internet have been introduced in recent years, and more are on the way to counter fraud. The ICC, WTO and Banks are very much in the lead through new technology.

16.3.2 Internet and extranets bring electronic commerce to SMEs

The door to the benefits offered by electronic commerce will only stay open to small- and medium-sized enterprises (SMEs) if the Internet becomes more commonly accepted for virtual trading. SMEs must consider the Internet alongside the more traditional VAN-based services that have already developed extensive and sophisticated EDI communities and established the UKs larger businesses as Europe's leading electronic practitioners.

A critical area is the paramount need for any company seeking to synchronize and share data electronically to include Internet communications in its strategy if SMEs are not to be locked out at this stage of the development of electronic commerce.

16.3.3 EDI and the Internet

EDI concerns the regular electronic exchange of commercial information, in a standard format, between established trading partners. In the past EDI has been seen, in particular by the SME community, as an expensive and technical solution mainly of benefit to large organizations. However, there is no doubt that over the last 15 years EDI has driven major improvements and changes in the retail, manufacturing and health care industry sectors, with, for example purchasing in these sectors a key area for implementation.

Among the most recent advances is the use of the World Wide Web for business-to-business and business-to-consumer transactions. Much of the recent research has signalled the huge potential of the online transactions market with a number of key developments making the World Wide Web a better place to conduct business-to-business and business-to-consumer transactions. The first of these is security. While the Internet's lack of security has been the most significant operational issue facing organizations considering using the Internet for business, recent surveys indicate a growing confidence that such problems are being overcome.

Interest in the potential of exchanging EDI messages over the Internet has been aroused largely because of the costs of traditional EDI via dedicated Value Added Networks (VANs). The Internet by comparison is easy to connect to, on a global basis, with relatively low charges, significantly undercutting some of the traditional VANs. The VANs respond to this argument by stressing the high performance levels and secure, controlled nature of their networks compared to the 'open' unregulated Internet. Successful trials include the first successful exchange of digitally-signed EDI data over the Internet in a recent initiative by the US-based Commerce Net organization.

The development of 'simpler' EDI techniques such as web-based EDI forms or 'Lite EDI' is also likely to impact on the purchasing function. These initiatives involve the user accessing the Website of a particular trading partner, selecting products from a catalogue or product and part list and completing an online order form. The information on the completed form is then translated into an EDI standard format and sent to a trading partner who processes the EDI message in the normal way. The essence of this approach is to make EDI more accessible to the SME which may have found it easier, cheaper and less daunting to set up web access than to manage a fully integrated EDI implementation.

The development of extranets in providing a secure trading environment, with the benefits of common TCP/IP communication standards and web browser interfaces, offers great potential to expanding not only electronic commerce transactions over the web, but also the spread of information which is of benefit to customers, suppliers and other interested parties.

EDI is an effective solution for the automatic exchange of large volumes of commercial information on a regular basis between known trading partners and is ideal for some purchasing scenarios. It is clear that those organizations which have already made a significant investment in integrating EDI with their business applications and in the establishment of trading partner communities are unlikely to suddenly stop doing business electronically in this way. EDI, the Internet and web-based solutions each have different advantages over each other and a likely future scenario involves a merging of all three.

16.3.4 Intranets

Intranets – internal company (corporate) controlled networks using Internet communication protocols and web browser technology – have the potential to fundamentally change the way people in large organizations communicate with each other. At the same time, the corporation has full control over who uses the intranet and what information is accessed. Intranet development has shown major growth in recent years, largely because it is seen as a cost-effective and efficient mechanism for making information available to all parts of an organization.

Common applications range from making company-wide information, such as telephone directories, training and human resources information, available to all employees through the provision of sales, support and product data to a network of remote sales offices. Through the use of firewall security solutions, a corporate intranet can also have an external connection to the 'Open Internet'.

16.3.5 Extranets

An extranet can be defined as a private Internet technology-based business network used by a community of trading partners. Extranets are run on a 'community controlled' basis – that is, all the participants in this network know each other and have a common interest, which can even be the exchange of information or actual business transactions performed in a secure environment. An example is a 'hub' purchasing from its 'spoke' suppliers.

The development of extranets in providing a secure trading environment, with the benefits of common TCP/IP communication standards and web browser interfaces, offers great potential to expand not only electronic commerce transactions over the web, but also to spread the information which is of benefit to customers, suppliers and other interested parties.

16.4 E-commerce – B2C best practice

E-commerce as we have already established is transforming the way in which international trade is conducted. The ICC is facilitating this development through the input/encouragement of E-commerce expressed in INCO terms 2000 and the supplement to UCP500 for electronic presentation (eUCP) – the successor to UCP500 – UCP revised edition 600 may be published in 2007 with an electronic communication input.

One area of impediment to business-to-consumer (B2C) electronic commerce is a lack of consumer confidence in doing business 'online'.

Exporters new to E-commerce may be apprehensive of the criteria of best practice to adopt. The organization most concerned with customer satisfaction is the company/the customer to whom they do business with. Moreover, enterprizing businesses recognize intuitively that when a transaction does not go the way a customer wanted or expected, it is an excellent opportunity through empathy and culture development to put things right and create a customer relationship that can last for life. The following has been devised by the ICC to develop best practice for 'online' business and strategies to follow to redress any malaises which arise between B2C.

(a) *Best practices focus on two areas:* (i) the business of how to ensure internal customer redress systems to resolve customer complaints; (ii) and equally what customers expect from a company's internal customer redress system. An ideal solution is to follow a step-by-step analysis through the customer redress process giving practical advice on the most effective ways to deal with customer complaints arising from 'online' business.

(b) *Code of practice to handle customer complaints:* (i) Adopt a redress system to embrace the following: (ii) objective and clear; (iii) credible and supportive to customers; (iv) easily accessible; (v) free for customers; a quick and equitable treatment; (vi) processes should not deprive the customer of any right he/she would otherwise have, and (vii) finally it should be operated with adequate resources.

The customer redress system must be compatible economically with the type and volume of business; an Executive/Director must be responsible with clear lines of responsibility/powers/communication; and there must be full compliance with local laws, regulations and codes of conduct.

Processing the initial customer complaint ideally must embrace the following system:

(a) if a contract is concluded in writing or in a manner including written elements (e-mail, internet, fax, telex), the customer should be informed at the time of conclusion of the contract that if he/she is not satisfied with the fulfilment of the contract, they have the opportunity to complain to the company;

(b) the customer's complaints should be accepted and processed irrespective of their form of communication; on receipt of customers complaint, the complainant should be issued with a confirmation of receipt in the form in which the complaint was lodged – if the confirmation of receipt is in a format such as an e-mail or web page, the customer should be encouraged to print it onto a hard copy for their records and safekeeping;

(c) confirmation of receipt should include an estimate of the time likely to be required for handling the complaint.

Providing guidance and assistance to customers should embrace the following three key areas:

(a)   customers should be encouraged to lodge clear and unambiguous complaints which identify the problem and desired outcome;

(b)   if the complaint is ambiguous/vague, the complainant must be asked to be specific and ideally supported by creditable evidence;

(c)   finally the customer should be encouraged to provide additional documents to support the complaint.

Handling customers' complaints

Six key areas arise as follows:

(a)   a customer's complaint must be treated as an opportunity to resolve a problem and deepen the relationship with the customer, a marketing advantage;

(b)   if it becomes apparent the customer has already lodged a complaint with a supervizing authority, a consumer protection organization or an institution for out-of-court or alternative dispute resolution (ADR) concerning the same matter, or has instituted legal proceedings, the complaint should not be processed any further by the company and the customer should be informed. As the optimal outcome for companies and their customers is for disputes to be settled internally by the company, the company may wish to resume processing the complaint if the customer agrees to withdraw it from where it has been filed elsewhere;

(c)   where possible, a customer's complaint should not be handled by the same staff member whose conduct has been complained about;

(d)   staff members processing complaints should be provided with the necessary powers to take decisions or review decisions of other staff members;

(e)   any staff member handling a complaint should equip himself/herself with all the information pertinent to the case involving obtaining the opinion of all parties concerned;

(f)   finally if the complaint reveals a serious grievance or a risk that the company may face considerable claims, a senior director/manager must be informed without delay.

Resolving complaints

A key area in any business is to preserve/develop a good reputation in the consumer/business market place. This embraces eight areas as follows:

(a)   in examining a complaint the following should be considered: the contract/agreement terms, and other relevant conditions of purchase, aspects of law-statute or non-statute, commercial practice, corporate policy, impact on the public, the prejudicial effect, the effect on any subsequent legal proceedings, any willingness of the complainant to negotiate and avoidance of lengthy/expensive legal proceedings with an uncertain outcome;

(b) the company's final decision to the complaint should be made in an appropriate form;

(c) the company's final decision should clearly show the customer how the company plans to act in relation to the complaint;

(d) any rejection of a complaint should inform the customer of the possibility to submit their request to a competent dispute settlement body such as an ADR or ombudsman;

(e) the entire process from the receipt of the complaint to the termination of its handling should be recorded in a form which makes it possible to reconstruct the process independently even after several years have elapsed;

(f) if the complaint is accepted the company's conduct should be corrected without delay. If this is not possible, the customer should be informed of when their request will be complied with;

(g) if any successful customer's complaint has broad significance for the company, senior personnel must be informed;

(h) if any customer's complaint reveals any shortcomings in the company which do not represent a failure in an individual case, but rather a failure in the company's business practices, the cause should be identified and remedied.

To conclude one must stress that any malaise in the company identified by a customer should be respected and constitute a form of market research. Exporters will experience a varying complaint attitude by individual products and the volume. The exporter must strive for a zero failure rate. The foregoing must be viewed as guidelines and exporters need to adapt according to circumstances. Ideally, the exporter must communicate in the language of the buyer or a mutually acceptable language to both parties.

16.5 Website sales development

In an era of hi-tech it is important exporters are conversant with the essential requirements to manage a successful website on the Internet. Overall, it is recognized that website provision is an essential tool in export marketing strategy for two reasons: to provide a low cost shop window in locations where the exporter does not have a physical presence, and it is open 24 hours daily seven days per week with no culture/trade barriers on communication.

There are three major cost categories when setting up a website: Internet services, promotion, and website designed maintenance fees. Internet services embrace domain name – www.yourname.co.uk – registration, web hosting – process of keeping the website on a specialist company's computer, and Internet connection from the exporters' office personal computer including connection to the website.

Website design and maintenance is a cost area which needs to be carefully controlled and in the first year of operation it may embrace 15–25 days' work from the website designer. The following are the key areas on which to focus on the website management:

(a) The exporter should endeavour to manage the website themself and the designer must be so informed. The site will require a sales database for the exporter's products and a second database for the rest of the content. The site must be so designed to ensure what appears on the information pages is read from the database. The exporter will also need a program on the export office PC for staff to change content in the database directly. When the need arises to change the site content – update descriptions, add new items etc. Someone on the exporter's staff can do so by updating the database without the need to engage and fund a website designer. Overall, this strategy will cost more to set up but only needs the designer for major re-work.

(b) A specification of the website content and objectives is required for the website designer to proceed and focus on the sales and delivery process. Areas can embrace a degree of automation in product selection, and configuration and then ask for person-to-person contact – telephone, fax, e-mail for ordering, payment and delivery. Alternatively, the exporter can simplify some areas – restricted product range – and create more comprehensive user manuals rather than on-site training. The sales data should feature three parts:

(i) *Products:* names, categories, descriptions and availability. Such data may be linked to fact sheets or brochures which customers can download.

(ii) *Customers:* details that customers will provide when they register on the exporters' website.

(iii) *Orders:* with quantities, dates, and prices together with shipment details including relevant Incoterm 2000. Hence, the buyer can compare one quotation with another supplier.

Overall, the experienced exporter will formulate their own details on the web in the light of experience and best practice.

(c) The third criteria is to devise a sequential strategy so that one entry logically follows another, relative to securing the order. An experienced software company such as Exportmaster could give guidance (p. 433). Start with the normal process – sign on, find and select products, place an order, ensure payment, arrange delivery and confirm. Decide when the exporter wishes the customer to register on the website – first enquiry or first order. The range of options available to the buyer are critical in an era of flexibility to secure the export sale. This embraces payment, delivery/transportation, customs and shipping agents. This may embrace lists of accredited Agents for Customs clearance and processing the export order (pp. 395–445). Other areas embrace split orders, samples, dangerous cargoes, and disputes on payment default, damaged or missing cargo. A mechanism needs to be devised for such eventualities. In some situations exporters may limit their sales to particular markets on a direct sales basis and list their Agents in other markets. Automate as much as possible with a question-and-answer list based on the most frequently asked questions by the importer. This will reduce e-mails, faxes and telephone calls.

(d) The website design ideally must be simple and fast to enable customers to follow the process easily. Study the exporter's competitor's website and integrate and empathise with the buyer's interests and needs. Focus on back tracking, cancellation and help line. Manufacturers with a large complex catalogue or complex product specification need to focus on a simple and fast product search and selection process. Multiple purchases into a single transaction also need attention. Again focus on ten special requirements relative to importation in some countries such as import licences, product specification, exchange control and tariff and non-tariff barriers (pp. 496–97). The site must be simple and comprehensible. Navigation from one page to another should be consistent, and 'tabs across the top, menu down the left side' is a popular format. Keep pages small (one or two screens-worth), and avoid lots of pages with single paragraphs. A black text on a white or pale background works well. The 'three click rule' that the buyer can adopt to select the products within three clicks of signing-in is very popular.

A fast site is essential. Regretfully, many exporters have slow or expensive Internet connections. Buyers may not wait for slow page loads. Diagrams, photographs, video clips are useful when presenting products especially when the buyer can download them.

(e) Website identification. Easy access and identification is essential in website promotion – www.export.co.uk or www.tradeuk.com The reference data basis should be listed under industry, profession, trade/profession association, chamber of commerce or product/service. Endeavour to pick up major search engines, i.e. Google, Yahoo and AltaVista. For small suppliers it is usually cost effective to have the 'click ad': the small text ads that appear on the right hand side of search results in Google, and some other search engines. These are 'pay per click' services. The exporter pays a fee for each click – through from your ad to the website. The price is set by companies bidding to have their ads associated with keywords used in searches.

(f) Website Testing. Many websites are inadequate as they do not undergo a testing evaluation whereby potential customers visit the site and provide a critical analysis of all its aspects. This generates suggestions and improves website marketing and customer empathy. Exporters may wish to have the website multilingual and target the language of the buyer.

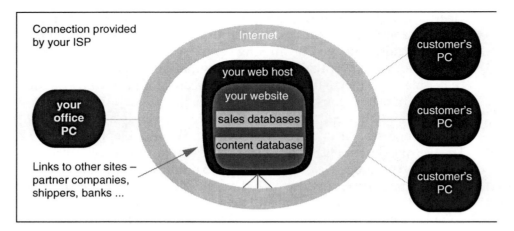

FIGURE 16.1   Website profile
Courtesy of International Trade

(g)   Website review. Study the website user available from the ISP analysis data logs. It will produce a trend of typical user and identify particularly those which generate a sale. Also always have regard to legislation regarding the promotion content on the website.

The successful exporter recognizes the website as a means of promotion. It requires continuous evaluation and ensures enquiries emerging from the web are dealt with promptly. Ideally, many users can place an order directly with the supplier without generating queries. Employ a good website designer and software company. Study Figure 16.1 above – Website profile.

16.6 Export software systems specification and outsourcing

Keeping up with the changing trade regulations and level of paperwork, packaging and labels are just some of the hurdles to overcome in the process of trading overseas. Global trade continues to increase at a rapid rate – in many cases faster than the GNP in most countries of the world. The Internet provides choice to the buyer and in many situations overseas customers are coming to the supplier. Hence the need to have an adequate software package to deal with the complexities of fulfilling international orders which cross international borders.

Export software companies attract many larger trading companies to their services by offering the speed and accuracy so essential to become a successful exporter. The technological solutions now available provide all-inclusive software tools that help users to lower the costs of trade and increase the global market potential of their products. The range of support services available is substantial and includes telemetry systems which allow exporters to measure different levels of inventory in warehouses and thereby reduce the supply chain costs in a logistic driven environment.

Effective export software systems should contain the following:

(a) Global breadth and depth with the ability to adhere to the changing rules and cross border regulations connected with international trade between buyers and sellers around the globe. Exporters must realize that published rules do not necessarily reflect reality which means that the solution provider/export software should have been created with the input of customers' broker and/or trade experts who are adept at interpreting the rules of trade.

(b) Trade specific applications that replace the manual process of documentation within the trading process. This can include customs classification and clearing, bills of lading, regulated materials compliance, electronic filing, duty management and landed cost estimates.

(c) The system must be able to function around the world supporting different measurement systems, providing for currency conversions, and multiple languages for export form filling.

An increasing number of SMEs engage a third-party logistics company to deal with the paperwork rather than operate their own export software facility. Third party resources provide small businesses with a strong export infrastructure such as warehouse tracking systems to back-up their online presence: also to ensure there is a delivery network in place to deliver goods across the world. Small businesses have limited infrastructure resources to effectively fulfil clients' requirements across the globe, but outsourcing delivery to a third party that has the knowledge, resources, and experience of fulfilling orders worldwide, enables the exporter to focus on running their business and still reap the benefits of exporting.

Exporters may wish to contact one of the following to develop their export software: SITPRO: www.sitpro.org.uk – Precision Software, e-mail: leighann.oneill@precisionsoftware.com – Vastera Solutions: www.vastera.com – Formwise, e-mail: stuart@law75.fsnet.co.uk

16.7 Bolero

Bolero is an Internet-based open E-commerce system that facilitates trade through the exchange of all trade documents in an electronic format. It was launched in April 1998. A key issue with Bolero is the framework in which it operates embracing four areas: (a) the rule book – legal framework; (b) digital signatures/certificates of authority; (c) standardized documents; and (d) neutral ownership. To the business involved in international trade, Bolero will allow its users to undertake the following five areas:

(i)   exchange standardized commercial, financial and official documents in a legally binding and secure format;
(ii)   usually standard documentation;
(iii)   integrate back office data systems;
(iv)   improve supply chain efficiency;
(v)   use the open nature of the system to trade in a multi-bank environment.

It is expected that Bolero will become the international standard for Business-to-Business (B2B) E-commerce, as it is supported by the world's largest banks and major logistics companies and is used by a large number of multinational trading businesses.

The development of Bolero has driven the international trade industry to become electronic-literate and in particular exporters/importers should note the mechanism now available for paperless trade. These embrace the CMI Electronic Bills of Lading (p. 569), Incoterms 2000 (p. 395), Uniform Customs & Practice for Documentary Credits – ICC guidelines on E-commerce best practice criteria (p. 289).

We will now examine the salient elements of Bolero.net. International trade has traditionally been fraught with financial logistic and time inefficiencies costing world business hundreds of billions of dollars annually. Created by the world's logistics and banking communities, Bolero.net is eliminating those inefficiencies by moving world trade onto the Internet, allowing documents and data to be exchanged on-line between all parties in the trade chain. Seven of the worlds' top ten banks have now signed up to Bolero.net as well as major trading houses such as Mitsui and Marubeni, and carriers such as Kline, Cosco and Evergreen.

Bolero.net develops transparency and vets every member thereby ensuring full compliance with its structures. The Bolero.net messaging system is operated by SWIFT (p. 293). It utilizes the latest encryption technology, messages are validated and a rigorous registration procedure acts as the gatekeeper for prospective members of the Bolero.net community. Bolero XML is a validated, global, cross industry XML standards solution that allows all parties of a trade chain to seamlessly 'talk' to each other by automating their information exchange (p. 461).

The backbone of the Bolero system is the Core Messaging Platform which enables users to exchange electronic trade documents via the Internet. The system is secure and underpinned by a unique legal structure. It is maintained by a third party. All messages between users are validated, acknowledged and notifications are provided as requested. Additional messages determine whether the recipient accepts or refuses the stated offer. Bolero.net is committed to maintain an open, non-proprietary system working with a range of third party partners who develop specific

'Bolero.net enabled' interface products, and 'Bolero.net qualified' consultancy services, for the community.

The benefits of Bolero.net embrace improved time efficiency; better administrative procedures; improved security systems; improved co-ordination across information systems; improved customer services; better inventory control; consistent legal framework process; and document improvement and fraud reduction. The benefits of Bolero.net extend to all departments – legal, technical, marketing, production and servicing.

Enrolment is the process by which a new user joins the Bolero community and becomes able to use the Bolero System. The Bolero System consists of both legal and technological components woven together, and thus, enrolment has both legal and technological aspects. Because of this dual nature, it is helpful to involve both a legal advisor and a technician, in addition to the person who will sign for the new user.

Legal Aspects of Enrolment: The legal side of the enrolment process consists of the following:

(a) *Confirmed identification of the new user.* One of the benefits of the Bolero System is that all users are identified and listed in a shared registry, so the risk of dealing with an unidentified party or impostor is minimal. To confirm identification of the new user, proof of incorporation, authorization, and authenticity must accompany the application.

(b) *Contract formation.* Another benefit of the Bolero System is that all users are subject to a common set of rules, the Bolero Rulebook, which provides the basic legal support necessary for conducting electronic transactions, including the electronic Bolero Bill of Lading (p. 569). Besides the Bolero Rulebook, each user becomes a member or participant in the Bolero Association through the BAL Service Contract, and each user agrees for operational services with Bolero International.

Bolero International and the Bolero Association are two distinct companies that complement each other and cooperate in providing the Bolero System. In brief, the Bolero Association provides a forum in which all users may participate, progresses development of the Bolero Rulebook, and disciplines users who fail to follow it. For its part, Bolero International operates and engineers the Bolero System and takes the leading role in marketing it.

The identification and contract formation processes occur by means of application forms. One application is for the Bolero Association and includes the Bolero Rulebook and the BAL Service Contract. The other application is for Bolero International and includes the Operational Service Contract. The applications also include blanks for administrative information, such as names, addresses and telephone numbers, to which confidentiality obligations in the contracts apply. To allow time to consider the contracts and fill in the applications, a prospective user downloads and completes the application forms rather than attempting to complete them all in one web session. Copies of the legal documents are available online. See http://www.boleroassociation.org/dow_docs.htm for the Bolero Rulebook and all relevant Bolero Association documents. See www.bolero.net/enrol/dow_docs.php3 for the Operational Service Contract with Bolero International. Several packages of operational services are available to suit the needs of different types of users, and the Operational Service Contract varies accordingly.

The application forms also require information about the technical interface with the Bolero System. The technical side of the enrolment process consists of the following:

(a) *Setting up a user system*, which is the system that a user installs and operates locally to access and use the Bolero System. Bolero International does not supply a user system, but one can be obtained from vendors listed at www.boleroassocation.ord/dow_soft.htm

(b) *Selecting a user identifier*, which identifies the user as a company in the Bolero System. A user can select its own identifier, as long as it is not too similar to another user's identifier.

(c) *Obtaining a digital signature certificate*, which is used to verify the authenticity of messages sent via the Bolero System. To obtain a certificate, a prospective user must request one from Bolero International and provide the public key to be listed in that certificate. To provide the public key, the user must first generate it, and its corresponding private key, by means of the local user system.

Particularly the user system set-up and the certificate request are technical processes that can be rather involved. They are best assigned to a technician to complete and report back to the officer overseeing enrolment.

16.7.1 Process Flow and Completion

When the enrolment applications are complete, the prospective user prints them out and signs them, then sends them by post to the Bolero Association. If Bolero Association accepts the new member or participant, it stores its own application and forwards to Bolero International its application. Bolero International then reviews the proposed Operational Service Contract, processes the certificate request, and, if the proposed Contract is acceptable, issues the requested certificate and sends it to the user for review and acceptance. Study the flow chart (p. 460).

The user's acceptance of the certificate marks the completion of the enrolment process. The new user is then in a position to enable persons within the user's organization to begin using the Bolero System.

The benefits of the Bolero.net for six main areas maybe summarized as follows:

(a) Exporters, suppliers and sales personnel are able to increase customer service through faster, more reliable delivery of merchandise to the buyer. Moreover, cost savings are realized through lower operational

*The applications (one for BIL and one for BAL) each include a contract (plus the Rolebook in the BAL application), a factual statement, a power of attorney and notarial acknowlegment, as well as requests for one or two Certificates. The BAL application also includes a bank reference.

**Bolero International Ltd. may decline to enter into an Operational Service Contract, but rarely declines a proposal in the standard form with selection of options offered to prospective Users via Bolero International's website.

***The User, through its Primary Representative, may decline to accept the Certificate, in which event the certificate remains invalid and unusable. Without a Certificate, the User is practically unable to use the Bolero System.

For more information on enrolment, see the Enrolment Guide, available at www.boleroassociation.org/dow_docs.htm

FIGURE 16.2 Bolero net flow
Reproduced courtesy Bolero Net

cost traditionally associated with order processing, insurance shipping/air freight, and customs clearance. Also opportunities exist to have a faster settlement as a consequence of accelerated re-negotiation of terms and quicker and less error-prone data exchanges.

(b) Importers/buyers/overseas procurement personnel can reduce their working capital through less delays, improved accuracy through eliminating the need for keying and re-keying of order information, improved efficiency of 'just-in-time' logistics programmes and reductions on telephone and courier costs. It offers buyers greater transaction transparency in dealing with suppliers. Overall, it strongly favours a logistic strategy as with item (a).

(c) Carriers – ship/air/road/rail/inland waterways implementing the Bolero.net service can better meet customer demands for speed and accuracy. It gives the carrier the opportunity to improve utilization of both inventory resources such as ships/containers/aircraft, etc. and the associated infrastructure at the port/airport and overland/inland waterway service plus the interface with other transport modes. It strongly favours the logistic strategy and supply chain management and forward planning of resource use. The value to carriers of a single standard window to customers/shippers is also attractive in reducing booking costs. See online booking (p. 460).

(d) Many freight forwarders are today logistic operators exploiting computer technology and Bolero. They offer integrated services with air freight, international road operators, container operators and multi-modalism. Overall, the modern freight forwarder offers online facilities to the shipper.

(e) Financial institutions. The ICC have recognized the benefits of Bolero embracing electronic trading through Incoterms 2000 (p. 395); and the supplement to the Uniform Customs and Practice for Documentary Credits for Electronic Presentation ('e UCP') which supplements the Uniform Customs and Practice for Documentary Credits (1993 Revision ICC Publication 500) ('UCP') in order to accommodate presentation of electronic records alone or in combination with paper documents. It is expected UCP500 will be superseded by UCP600 in 2007 (p. 296). Also the CMI Regulations and Electronic Bills of Lading have enabled the Bill of Lading to be traded electronically. These developments are a major step forward in the electronic financial trade environment and will gather momentum in the next few years, especially B2B and B2C. Overall, trade financial transactions through Bolero.net have enabled such financial transactions to be more efficient, transparent, and with much improved customer satisfaction through value added.

(f) Customs authorities encouraged by the World Customs Organisation have encouraged electronic transmission of customs documentation/message under a National regulatory Customs system (pp. 226–27). It has speeded up Customs procedures, encouraged rationalization of documentation/regulations and facilitated the development of a global logistic network.

To summarize the benefits of Bolero.net one can list a host of features, but the core factor is the system speeds up and maximizes the efficiency of the current international business. It is fast becoming a *de facto* standard for international trade. Moreover, it is reducing the trade cycle as documents and data can be sent instantaneously. This is realized as it enables customers to automate their supply chains more efficiently, both by reducing systems integration costs and time to market. Clients are able to reduce the time required to establish and maintain secure reliable and cost-effective business-to-business linkages.

To develop the role of Bolero XML mentioned earlier, it permits all parties in a trade chain to interact seamlessly with each other by automating their information exchange within a secure environment. Its objective is to enable users of Bolero.net to take full advantage of electronic commerce by providing a set of standard electronic documents that will facilitate inter-operability among the members of the community. Its aim is to eliminate the need for bilateral data interchange agreements that describe the structure and contents of electronic data being exchanged between two parties. This will be achieved by providing a set of common standards that can be applied multilaterally. Inter-operability is a term used to describe the ability of different computer systems to work together, facilitating business transactions across organizations.

The Bolero XML strategy is based on the notion that the existing data interchange standards fail to meet the foregoing criteria. Standards are vital to the exchange of information among parties. When all parties consistently use the same terminology and framework, documents and data flow seamlessly. Bolero.net takes full advantage of electronic commerce by developing a set of simplified electronic documents, known as Bolero XML documents. The Bolero XML documents are based on a common-business model that is technology independent (see www.bolero.net/boleroxml/introduction/). Visit their website to keep up to date.

16.8 Case studies

16.8.1 Trading on the Internet – AMP Connect

http://connect.amp.com
AMO Inc is a global supplier with a large European presence of connection systems and products for the electronics and telecommunications industries. Its 250 000 lines include the plastic seat for the microprocessor in your PC and many connectors used in the consumer electronics and white goods industries. One of AMP's key services is AMP Connect which gives customers the ability to browse, select and order connector products from an online catalogue which features product data specifications. A highlight of the site is its multi-lingual capability which supports AMP's global customer base. This huge electronic catalogue is up-to-date and avoids all the physical problems involved in the updating, production and distribution of large paper-based catalogues. The site is well designed and laid out to meet the needs of buyers, engineers and designers who are encouraged to download the connector specifications and design them into their products – an excellent way to lock in your customer to your products.

16.8.2 H&R Johnson Tiles Ltd

http://www.johnson-tiles.com
This Staffordshire-based wall and floor tile manufacturing company is discovering the benefits of external e-mail, EDI (electronic data interchange) and of using the web for ordering purposes. For example, Johnson's have developed a web-based system which allows their distributors to browse catalogues, check stock levels and then place orders. In addition,

Johnson's are experienced EDI users and are now using this expertise to encourage their smaller trading partners to trade electronically. It is the ability to take orders via the web and via EDI which has demonstrated H&R Johnson's electronic commerce flexibility. The site is very customer friendly and features the ability to locate a tile distributor on a regional basis.

16.8.3 Advance Cargo Information System

An example of a logistics information system has been developed by UNCTAD. It is called Advanced Cargo Information System (ACIS). Overall, it is a logistics information system designed to improve transport efficiency by tracking equipment and cargo on transport modes (rail, road, lake/river) and at interface (ports, internal clearance depots) and by providing information in advance of cargo arrival. ACIS provides both public and private transport operators and ancillaries with reliable, useful and real-time data on transport operations such as the whereabouts of goods and transport equipment, and thus improves day-to-day management and decision-making. It also produces regular statistics and performance indications which enable management to remedy deficiencies and to make full use of the existing infrastructure and equipment capacity.

RailTracker is the railway part of the ACIS. It monitors all the movements of both locomotives and wagons on a railway network; it has proved to be a very useful tool to improve management, and it monitors the movement of a railway client's goods. This feature enables registered customers, from any part of the world, to access the network they are interested in, find out where their cargo is and what has happened to it while in the custody of the railway. RailTracker can also provide the history of the cargo, and some of the RailTracker-equipped railways already offer access via the Internet. To date (2004), RailTracker is installed on the following networks: Bangladesh Railways, Cameroon Railways, Kenya Railways Corporation, Malawi Railways, Régie Nationale de Chemin de Fer du Mali, Société Nationale des Chemins de fer du Congo, Société Nationale des Chemins de Fer du Sénégal, State Railway of Thailand, Sudan Railway, Tanzania Railways Corporation, Tanzania–Zambia Railway, Uganda Railways Corporation and Zambia Railways Limited.

RailTracker has been proved to enhance service reliability and reduce security risks as processes become more transparent and opportunities for pilferage or corruption are being reduced. Its installation requires adequate planning and investment. It may also require the opposition of vested interests that have so far benefited from prevailing inefficiencies to be overcome.

16.8.4 BAT – EDI and logistic case study focus

The fourth case study is found in British American Tobacco (BAT). The strategy intended to make BAT the world's biggest tobacco manufacturer in the next ten years involved folding four of its UK businesses into one. The result was to raise to over 170 the number of markets and territories that the company's UK logistics department has to serve.

The process of restructuring that BAT started in the early 1990s has been followed by a programme of selective expansion. This has been partly by acquisition, as with the recently purchased Mexican tobacco manufacturer; partly by the formation of joint ventures, notably in Russia, Eastern Europe and Central America; and partly by licensing agreements, such as its contracts with the state-owned Turkish and Indian tobacco monopolies. The agreement signed with the Turkish tobacco enterprise took 15 years to bring to fruition.

An underlying benefit has been to enable the company to use its global presence to optimize through the economies of scale, whether in the purchase of wrapping material, tobacco leaf – or transport services. This emerges from a 'best practice' structure that extends across the span of supply chain management, from materials acquisition to final product delivery.

The logistics department has been operating since mid-1993 from BAT's Southampton plant. Staff had previously been based at two sites. This structure has enabled the logistics team to operate as independent coordinators of supply and demand requirements, balancing the needs of production and marketing to optimum effect. Of the 68 members of the department, half are involved in customer service. Their responsibilities are divided along geographical lines in relation to the 450 customers that the UK company serves. Distributors, retailers and duty-free outlets in the Far East account for around 73 per cent of the UK company's exports, Europe for 8 per cent, Africa for 9 per cent and Saudi Arabia and the Gulf states for around 10 per cent. In some countries, supplies are also held in third-party warehouses, as well as in a company-owned UK warehouse, to service duty-free customers.

The Southampton factory's entire output is exported. It comprises such famous brands as Benson and Hedges, State Express 555 and John Player Gold Leaf. The output can exceed 50 billion cigarettes a year. Additionally, the logistics department purchases a further 60 billion cigarettes from other BAT companies and handles their distribution.

Annual departmental costs are put at £10 million, spend on freight at £18 million and warehousing worldwide at £7 million. The logistics department's involvement starts when one of the liner shipping companies with which it works is instructed to load containerized tobacco leaf in the country of origin. The harvested leaf is placed in boxes which are fork lifted into 40 feet containers, each capable of holding 96–99 bales. The containers are filled to optimum capacity. Brazil, the USA, Kenya, Zimbabwe, India, China and Turkey are among the countries from which the company sources tobacco leaf, placing orders two years ahead of the delivery date.

When the containers reach Britain, they are moved to BAT's 375 000 ft^2 tobacco store in Oxfordshire, where the leaf is held at an ambient temperature in strictly hygienic conditions. The leaf is released to the factory in blend sets for immediate introduction to the manufacturing process. Normally, the factory receives between eight and ten loads of leaf a day, amounting to between 800–950 cases. The production department will specify what blends it needs. The leaf is normally on site for no longer than 48 hours before being fed into an automated production process. The only manual involvement occurs when the paletized boxes of banded cigarettes are fork lifted into the 40 ft containers in which they are shipped. No cigarette stocks are held on site and wrapping material is held only to cover production requirements for four to five days.

The logistics department manages the interlocking processes of materials planning and delivery, production planning up to three years in advance, production scheduling, order processing delivery, invoicing and customer service. A commercial team provides back-up covering areas such as risk management and liaison with HM Customs and Excise, together with freight contract negotiations. An in-house insurance service department at its head office arranges cover, spreading risk by placing business with a number of underwriters. The company has experienced few losses from theft despite the spread of its customer base in the expanded European Union. BAT's team of freight buyers, comprising executives from Germany, Brazil, USA and Britain, meets formally four times a year when executives from liner shipping companies are invited to tender for contracts of 12 months' duration. As one of the world's biggest volume shippers, the company sets stringent service criteria while capitalizing on its immense purchasing power. The individual lines' performances are reviewed every quarter.

The outstanding feature of the logistics department has been its investment in EDI systems. Like all such exercises, this entailed an intensive management effort to build systems that would enable the company to communicate electronically with a growing number of its customers and suppliers. The investment was mainly in management time – buying into EDI in terms of hardware and software is small, and it has been a key factor in the ability to absorb the extra work that the department had to undertake as a result of the restructuring.

It estimates that, but for the EDI process, BAT would have been compelled to engage between five and seven additional staff. Self-billing has enabled suppliers to receive payment quickly while reducing documentary errors and queries to near zero. It has strengthened relations with both customers and suppliers with whom the company is now trading electronically. Customers are able to re-stock more quickly, buying smaller quantities and, as a result, tying up less capital in stock. EDI has improved 'visibility' during the supply chain process and enabled BAT to do more, and more complicated, work.

BAT makes one in eight of the cigarettes chosen by the world's one billion tobacco smokers.

16.8.5 Summary – salient points

It is clear that electronic commerce is a reality and in most markets it is already the only way to conduct business. With the rapid development of solutions aimed at making the World Wide Web a more secure business environment this trend can only continue. Electronic commerce techniques are fundamentally changing the way international business is done and traditional ways of working are constantly being reappraised. International business managers need to understand very clearly that the winners will be those who embrace these new opportunities. You only need a very short checklist to guide you.

1. Obtain a senior, budget holding business sponsor to champion your electronic commerce projects.
2. Develop and agree a project plan.
3. Start with a small, simple, realistic project and implement it quickly – thereby hopefully showing some clear business benefits. Set up a project team with your champion, the IT department and a business person who really has hands-on experience of the business process.
4. Talk to your key trading partners and discuss the benefits of electronic commerce with them.
5. Conduct awareness and training sessions. Wherever possible refer to real case studies, ideally from other companies in your sector.
6. Join the e-centre in your country to obtain sane and sensible advice.

The development of an effective integrated global supply chain including all the processes involved in the trade and payment cycle has to be carefully planned, predicted and controlled. Traditional management thinking and past-based procedures are too slow, error prone and inflexible for a global supply chain to operate competitively. This is exemplified when one bears in mind that 11–14 participants are involved in any single export–import process. Overall, the process embraces: banks – exporter – forwarder – customs – port – carrier – port – customs – forwarder – importer – logistics operator.

Planning and coordinating the movement of goods and flow of payment through such a complex system to a predictable level of certainty is virtually impossible without the disciplines which only EDI provides. The use of EDI can provide important cash savings and also enables a company to provide better levels of customer service and gain a competitive edge over its rivals. Thinking further ahead, companies may look to EDI to provide new business opportunities.

The benefits of EDI can be divided into three areas: strategic; operational; and opportunity. They include the overall functioning of the business and affect the very business the company is undertaking. These can include a faster trading cycle, just-in-time manufacturing, terms of trade being dictated by bargaining power and the need to respond to highly competitive market entrants.

Operationally the benefits include reduced costs. These can be split down into paper and postage bills cut dramatically; a reduction in capital tied up in stock; and manual processing costs. There will be improved cash flow, security and error reduction, mainly from the elimination of rekeying or transcribing information from one medium to another and acknowledged receipt.

Overall the benefits E-commerce brings to international trade can be summarized as follows.

1. The standard messages that are being developed are for both national and international trade.
2. Standard procedures being introduced between seller, buyer, trade-related services, customs, etc. to support the implementation of the messages.
3. The hardware, software and network services required are not restricted to national boundaries and should not need to be altered for communication with parties abroad.
4. Language independence is built in through the use of United Nations data elements and international code sets – e.g. terms of payments and deliveries, harmonized coding system for commodities and services, codes for identifying parties and locations, etc.
5. The reduction of the paperwork required in cross-border trade and across the transport chain.

Finally one cannot stress too strongly the E-commerce management culture which has emerged in the last five years and the need for the international entrepreneur to become fully conversant with the skills and opportunities. These are detailed below:

1. it creates a high management and business profile;
2. it provides an easy-to-use system for management data analysis, and data access;
3. it facilitates accuracy, speed and efficiency;
4. it quickens the decision-making process;
5. it raises an organization's international profile and access;
6. it utilizes high technology;
7. there is a value added benefit to the organization;
8. it makes an organization more cost effective.

Failure to become involved in E-commerce will result in businesses or companies no longer being competitive in the market place.

Recommended reading

SITPRO News

CHAPTER 17

Export market entry options strategies and culture

17.1 Introduction – market selection criteria

When a company begins to think about marketing its goods or services overseas (see p. 36) the decision process involves four stages: (a) deciding which market to enter (see p. 473); (b) choosing the market entry option, culture and strategies; (c) formulating a marketing plan; and (d) deciding on a marketing organization (see p. 44). In this chapter we will examine the second phase. A range of market entry options exist and the factors which influence the final selection are now briefly outlined.

1. *The company objectives.* These will be found in the company business plan. They will be determined by company resources and the market forecast and profitability. The Multi-National Industry (MNI) has capital, experience and production capability, while the small- to medium-sized enterprise (SME) may have limited capital, production resources and experience. An MNI is usually better able to take risk and has more negotiating power than an SME.

2. *Legal and political constraints.* This extends to agency agreements, channels of distribution, patent registration, licensing, joint ventures, tariff barriers, franchises, repatriation of funds, taxation employment law and exchange control.

3. *Political and economic stability.* Stable markets favour more commitment by the exporter especially in investment terms. Some countries offer special tax concessions to generate inward investment.

4. *Culture.* The skills, abilities and management culture of the company towards international portfolio development will affect the selection. A number of aspects of the company culture are influential here, including technical and design competences, international logistics capability and computer literacy (p. 470).

5. *The product.* The nature of the product or service and the degree of adaptation and competitiveness it will have in world markets. This will embrace the product life cycle evaluation.

6. The company's experience in the market.
7. Any long-term development in the market.
8. The level of competition, both short- and long-term.
9. Developed or underdeveloped; homogeneous or heterogeneous; near or distant markets.
10. Open or closed markets featuring non-tariff and tariff barriers, (see pp. 496–98 and credit rating – country/company (p. 418)).
11. Market category classification – is it a key market or a cluster market complex?
12. Member of any economic trading bloc or customs union and the accruing benefits.
13. Urgency or speed of entry to the market available, such as a licence (see pp. 491–96) or a franchise (see pp. 485–87).

17.2 E-commerce

The process of conducting business overseas is electronically driven. The web/Internet not only provides a good promotional tool available to procurement companies looking for suppliers, but also for conducting digital trading. Digital trading extends to the digital trade transport network embracing the logistics chain. This includes importers, exporters, freight forwarders and third party logistic providers, terminals, carriers, government departments, banks and financial institutions, insurance companies and inspection agencies – online and paperless trading in as short a time as possible. Hence, from the procurement standpoint it ranges from the issue of purchase orders, insurance and letters of credit to inspections, the insurance of government certificates, trade declarations and payment functions.

Scanning the web to obtain potential overseas buyers and analyzing potential companies and markets is a key area in the exporters' strategy today. It enables both the MNIs and the SMEs to operate in the same environment with similar market penetration strategies crossing international barriers and developing the B2B or B2C contact.

Hence, the exporter, in developing market entry strategies, must have a hi-tech computer resource and software to develop a viable overseas market. Procurement companies are unlikely to do business with suppliers which are not computer focused orientated. A market research strategy must be adopted.

17.2.1 Procurement

The exporter must be a strategist and be able to interpret and understand fully the buyers' needs and aspirations. In particular, to develop synergy with the overseas procurement officer through continuous dialogue.

Areas in which the procurement officer will focus include the following: product requirements/development; payment terms; flexibility of product availability; credit rating of exporter; calibre/professionalism of supplier personnel; commitment to the buyer and overall competitiveness of the product especially in value added benefit terms. Additionally, the exporter must be computer literate, culturally and logistically focused and share the expectations of the role/function of the buyer. A key area for the procurement officer's strategy is quality control, compliance with international/national product standards and non-price areas such as product guarantee, spares availability and maintenance/servicing arrangements. It is important for the exporter to identify why the supplier chose their product and in so doing develop the selection criteria to the benefit of both parties. It may be retailing, assembly industrial plant, re-exporting, FTZs and government procurement. Whatever the reason for the procurement officer's decision to buy the product which may be price, design, availability, durability, non-price areas, etc., the exporter must strive to develop these areas. Overseas clients/markets buy goods for different reasons and place a different emphasis on the product role in the industrial or consumer market environment. For example, the industrial unit may be focused more on production output, durability and spares/maintenance and less on design and price.

To conclude, the exporter and importer/procurement must harmonize their strategies to the benefit of both parties. Ideally, the exporter must develop synergy with the buyer/importer.

17.3 Indirect and direct exporting

Basically, there are two methods of exporting – indirect and direct. *Indirect exporting* is the process of selling goods overseas through a third party, thereby relinquishing control of the selling process of the goods. This has the advantage to the exporter of obviating any need to have an extensive, internationally-focused organization as usually no contact is made with the overseas buyer. Examples of indirect exporting include a local buying office (p. 525), piggy back operations (pp. 496–97), an export house (p. 484) and trading houses (p. 498). This is an attractive mode of entry for an SME as a first step to selling in the international trade market.

Conversely, *direct exporting* is the process whereby the exporter becomes fully involved in and totally committed to the process of exporting on a proactive basis. This generates a proactive situation compared with the indirect exporting which is reactive. Hence, the exporter becomes fully involved in the seven 'Ps' of the marketing mix – product; place; promotion; price; process; people; physical aspects – on an international basis. It does usually involve significant capital commitment and resource allocation of management and production coupled with any adaptation of the product to meet the overseas buyer's needs. Examples of direct exporting include agents (p. 475), distributors (p. 475), joint ventures (p. 490), licensing (pp. 491–92), consortia (p. 484), franchising (p. 485), Free Trade Zones (p. 487), government procurement (p. 488), leasing (p. 489), strategic alliances (p. 497), mergers and acquisitions (p. 482), management contracts (pp. 495–96) and wholly owned subsidiaries (p. 482). Business-to-Business (B2B) (p. 482) and Business-to-Consumer (B2C) (p. 482) feature in this direct exporting category.

17.4 Market environment

Prior to considering the exporter's market entry strategy, we will examine key areas of the overseas market environment on which the exporter must focus. Such research can be undertaken on the web.

(a) Who are the main players in the global market and what are their profiles. An analysis is desirable. In particular focus on market share, financial resources, their position in the market, whether they are a leading player or laggard, future plans and nature of the business in which they operate.

(b) Accessibility to the market and the legal environment. This includes a market stability and infrastructure serving the market, embracing transport, communications, commerce.

(c) Product availability embracing national and international standards coupled with the stage of its development. It may be the first or second generation, low- or high-tech. Also, the added value focus and stage of its development.

(d) Is the market computer and logistically literate and importers/buyers flexible and adaptable.

(e) Exchange rate stability and importation costs such as import duty, sea/airport charges and sales tax. These impact on the product selling price in the overseas market and its competitiveness.

(f) Membership of an economic or trading bloc with favourable import regulations such as the EU single market (p. 533).

(g) Whether the market is fully developed, an underdeveloped LDC or developing. Fully developed markets tend to be high-tech and capital intensive with a fully trained workforce, high labour costs and high GDP as found in USA, Germany and Japan. Conversely, the LDC is agriculturally driven and often a commodity focused economy with low labour cost and low levels of technology. Moreover, LDCs currencies are non-convertible with volatile fluctuations correlated to the seasonal performance of its commodities in the global market place.

(h) Does the market offer inwards investment such as joint ventures, licensing, franchises, merger and acquisition or industrial transplant.

MNIs and SMEs are continuously reviewing the economic and marketing benefits to switch their manufacturing and assembly plants from one country to another based on the strategic criteria of cost infrastructure, labour resources (especially hi-tech trained), access to markets, technology, logistics and general competitiveness. Look at government and local financial environment embracing economic or free trade zone, employment law, taxation and industrial grants.

(i) The perceived benefits of the market. This may include strategic geographical location; national government strategies towards importation; development of FTZs; indigenous resources such as raw materials/commodities; indigenous or multi-ethnic population attitude towards imported products; computer literacy; and the political/economic environment.

Exporters are encouraged to study the country reports available from Banks, International Agencies (OECD) and credit agencies (p. 279).

17.5 Market entry strategy

Companies must have a strategic focus in their decision-making process of selecting and entering a market or a series of markets overseas. This also applies to first time exporters. The following strategic considerations are relevant.

1. To have a customer portfolio which has an international base.
2. To increase production, thereby lowering unit cost and permitting more competitive pricing.
3. To spread the market risk, on the basis that the greater the number of markets served the greater the spread of opportunity and risk.
4. To raise the company profile, thereby raising the capital value of the company and attracting fresh capital into the company to keep pace with new technology and provide funds for research and development, especially in high tech areas.
5. To realize a more volume based and productive utilization of the company infrastructure.
6. To increase market share and dominance.
7. To focus on being a marketing led company rather than one which is product led.
8. To increase the general competitiveness of the company and its product range in all areas of the company profile and on an international scale.
9. To ensure the long-term future of the company.
10. To develop a proactive rather than a reactive company which is globally focused and market research driven, with a continuous focus on the client base and market place environment.

11. To develop an international brand image which permeates through-out the company with a particular focus on the product, personnel and overall commitment of the company to its customers and the overseas markets served.
12. To use all available management techniques in the company opera-tion and management, featuring budgets, marketing plans, logistics, computer literacy, control and audit techniques. It is also vital to have a workforce which is well-trained and well-qualified at all levels, with key personnel being multi-lingual, professionally qualified and capable of working in a high-tech environment.
13. To have the appropriate membership of a trade association and accreditation of management quality BS5750 (see pp. 491–96).
14. To increase the profitability of the company and return on investment.

Research by David Arnold, Assistant Professor at Harvard Business School, into the selection process of entering markets in developing countries embracing the appointment of an independent local distributor, identifies some key points. Many MNIs wish to realize three objectives: desire to control their business at a strategic level; partnering with local distributors at least for the first years to benefit from the local 'expertise'; and mini-mizing cost and risks in these new ventures. Such ideology may be difficult to achieve, especially as changes occur in the later phases of the market entry including a possible switch to directly controlled distribution and the need to redress imbalances which emerged during the initial phases resulting in changes leading to new imbalances.

Overall, managing the life-cycle of the international distributor fea-tures seven key areas:

(a) select the distributors and don't let them select you, such as an approach at a trade fair. An over zealous distributor may prove to be the wrong partner;
(b) look for distributors capable of developing markets rather than those with a few customers. The choice of distributors and the terms of the relationship should serve the multinational long-term goals;
(c) treat the local distributors as long-term partners, not temporary market-entry vehicles. Structure the relationship so that distributors become marketing partners willing to invest in long-term market development;
(d) support market entry by committing money, managers and proven marketing ideas. To retain strategic control, companies must commit adequate resources. This is especially relevant when companies are least certain about their prospects in new countries;
(e) from the start, maintain control over marketing strategy. Independent distributors should be allowed to adapt a company strategy to local conditions. Companies should convene and lead planning sessions

and exercise authority about which products to sell, how to position them and budgeting;

(f) Make sure distributors are provided with detailed market and financial performance data. A company's ability to exploit its competitive advantages in an emerging market depends heavily on the quality of information it obtains from the market. Not having such data can lead to serious problems;

(g) build links among national distributors at the earliest opportunity. Although a company's primary focus after entering a new country is to establish a customer base there, the company should create links among its national distributors quickly.

Finally, in regard to item (f) above, one must stress that financial performance alone is not sufficient to measure a business' total performance – a point stressed by Professor Kaplan, Professor at Harvard Business School in his book *The Balanced Scorecard* – (Kaplan & Norton 1996). It stresses that a company should assess how it performs relative to customers' expectations, examine improvements in internal processes and measure learning and growth alongside financial measures.

We will now consider in more detail the range of market entry options.

17.6 Market entry options

17.6.1 Agents and distributors

The narrow definition of 'agent' in export practice is that he is a party who acts for the exporter, the latter being the principal. The agent does not make a profit but is paid a commission on all orders secured, for which his or her principal obtains eventual payment. It is usual for agents to work for a number of principals, offering a cohesive group of products which are not in direct competition with each other.

There are variations in the type of agency which work on a 'commission only' basis according to what the parties consider suitable to the product and the market. Some examples are given below.

1. *Fee or retainer.* When it is clear from the outset that it will take some time before the product gets established in the market, and thus before the agent can earn a worthwhile commission, it is up to the principal to offer some alternative financial inducement to motivate him or her until a straight commission becomes a viable proposition. Where the agent is selling a range of products for one principal on a commission basis, the agent may be offered a fee to launch a new product which, though within the general range, is an untried newcomer to this market, or some entirely fresh range of products being launched by the principal.

2. *Expenses incurred by the agent.* These may be paid by the principal or shared between the parties on an agreed basis. This introduces a variation from the 'commission only' type of agency. Such expenses may be a 'once only' arrangement such as setting up showroom facilities. Alternatively, they may be continuing, involving the agent being charged with scanning local technical journals and buying them for the principal when appropriate. Additionally there is the cost of E-commerce and fax transmittals. Some special variation of the commission only arrangement can be introduced to cover the agent's outlays or to share them in special circumstances, e.g., an exhibition where it is decided to take a stand, or some exceptional venture in local publicity.

3. *Stockist agencies.* This situation arises where the agent sells on commission but undertakes to buy for his or her own account – or to share in the cost of – stocks of some of the items within the range. This could significantly improve sales turnover where the goods are such that the demand is always for prompt delivery, e.g., components for automobile repair services in a foreign country.

4. *After-sales service.* Many technical products are such that it is necessary to provide a manufacturer's guarantee. This may be undertaken by the agent who sells on commission and may include a repair service outside the maker's guarantee arrangements. Stocks or parts will have to be carried in the market by the agent and, usually, workshop facilities will have to be made available. This involves the provision of an operating manual and a period of training provided by the principal for the workshop personnel. The details of the arrangement between the parties vary widely according to individual circumstances. The principal may supply free spares or stocks, or they may be sent on a consignment basis. Alternatively, the agent may be required to equip a workshop and carry spares at his or her own expense.

5. *Consignment stocks.* The market where sales are made must have goods available for immediate delivery as soon as the commission agent concludes the sale. Such stocks can be entrusted to the agent providing he or she owns or rents suitable warehousing space. Such an agent must be of outstanding integrity and sound financial standing. Moreover, one must ensure the law of the country involved recognizes the continuing legal ownership by the principal of goods physically held by the agent. The alternative is for the stock to be held by an independent warehouseman in the name of the principal, who then sends buyers' delivery orders to enable them to call on the warehouse for release of the goods for which the order was placed through the commission selling agent.

6. *Salaried agent.* In this situation the agent is resident in the country of operation and is paid a salary, with or without expenses and fringe benefits, by his or her principal. This may prove suitable where the

products are capital goods or when the principal is a firm of consultants such as a consortium. Such an agent could keep the principal in touch with conditions in his territory and advise on local opportunities and official tenders over a period of years. For example, he or she could tender on behalf of his or her principal for medical equipment or harbour navigational facilities.

7.   *Distributor/agent.* In some markets, conditions are such that they are dominated by one large firm which dwarfs its competitors, but the market potential cannot be fully exploited unless the smaller concerns are enticed into the sale of the products. The large firm acting as a distributor can also secure orders for shipment direct to the small ones. Such transactions are remunerated on a commission basis. The contract of agency between the principal and such a firm must be drafted with special care, but even so it may prove in practice that the small firms are squeezed out of effective marketing because of the uplift in the price they pay to cover the agent's commission. At best they are somewhat restricted in their activities. This type of agency has proved effective where the big firm comprised members of ethnical or religious majority groups or ruling caste, particularly where the small firms belonged to the minority and monopolized sales to other people in the minority grouping.

8.   *Export management agency.* The function of the export management agent is to act as the manufacturer's export department, either for all markets abroad or for a selected number clearly agreed in advance. He is briefed in regard to the products, both technically and as to future production flows and possible changes in quality and quantity. Price is agreed and a rate of commission fixed, with or without some contribution to the agent's expenses (generally, or for specific purposes such as travel) or a fee plus commission payable on results. It is usual for the export management to be authorized to appoint agents in foreign territories within the agreed sphere of operation. On the other hand, the management does not usually incur any financial risk – he or she would not be expected to put through orders from parties of doubtful standing and would invariably advise the manufacturer about financing; thus the merchants who operate manufacturer's agency departments often take over the goods EXW, FCA or FOB.

Some care must be taken to differentiate between the form of agency explained above and the group sales concept detailed on p. 47. In the latter case, the manufacturers work together as an entity to market their products. However, in an export management agency situation, the agency takes over the export function and decides what shall comprise his or her group of products to be marketed overseas.

9.   Del credere *agent.* Where a commission selling agent, whatever his or her other terms of reference, undertakes that orders passed to the

principal will be paid for in due course by the buyers, he or she is called a *del credere* agent, that is, he or she undertakes a credit risk. Great care is necessary in defining the responsibilities and rights of this special type of agent, and when and how he or she is paid his or her *del credere* commission. Thus, the principal must be certain to instruct the collecting bank when a document is lodged with a *del credere* agent named as 'case of need', that is, if the buyer refuses the bill, the agent is empowered to take possession of the documents and/or the goods.

It must be stressed that there exists a wide variety of different types of agents and the foregoing are only the most common ones. Moreover, one must bear in mind that there are certain similarities in the role of the agents, confirming houses and export houses. The latter two are to be explained later in this chapter.

It is appropriate, however, when examining the role of the agent, to consider the distributor. For example, the manufacturer markets some of his or her products in some territories through commission selling agents, but in other areas through importers, stockists or distributors, who buy the goods for their own account and earn a profit (not a commission) as a basis of their remuneration. The role of the distributor in the overseas market has become increasingly significant and the following are the salient points of difference between the distributor and selling agent.

	Selling agent	*Distributor*
1.	Not financially involved	Buys for own account
2.	Leaves importation to the buyers whose orders he passes to the principal	Imports the products
3.	Is paid a commission at an agreed percentage on orders secured	Marks up the supply price to cover his profit
4.	Any service necessary is rendered by the buyer	Where necessary undertakes responsibility for the service
5.	Carries no stock except for showroom purposes	Normally carries a stock
6.	Unlikely to be involved in publicity except where required to give advice or report on impact	Likely to be involved in local publicity
7.	May be authorized to engage sub-agents	Appoints sub-distributors
8.	No control of resale prices	Controls selling prices in countries where retail price maintenance is possible
9.	Leaves distribution to the buyers	Undertakes distribution in the market

To conclude our study of agents, we now detail the salient clauses usually found in an agency agreement. The clauses may be varied to meet individual circumstances and others may be added as required.

1. *Details of parties to the contract.* For example, names, registered address and short title of each party.
2. *Purpose of contract.* For example, it must state in specific terms that A appoints B as an agent, and that B agrees to act in that capacity in accord with the terms of agreement.
3. *Details of the products involved.* For example, A will supply and B will sell the merchandise prescribed including any brand names.
4. *Territory.* The agreement must outline the geographical area over which the agent is given exclusive sales rights.
5. *Precise duties of the principal* embracing any reference to sales outside the agency, handling direct enquiries, etc.
6. *Precise duties of the agent.* This will incorporate situations such as dealing with other suppliers particularly of a competitive nature. It will provide a description of the goods, the manufacturer, any warranties, and the method of promoting such competitive products.
7. *Exceptions, reservations or restrictions imposed* on either one or both parties to the agency agreement.
8. *Method of quoting prices.* For example, whether FCA or otherwise.
9. *Agent's purchase and resale.* This clause will reflect the type of agency agreement involved as described earlier. For example, if the agent is buying for his or her own account, such as when acting as a distributor, he or she may appoint sub-distributors subject to the manufacturer's approval; fix sale prices and retail list prices; and report back to the manufacturer. This clause requires adequate deliberation and consideration.
10. *Consignments* – in particular terms of delivery. This will embrace under what terms merchandise will be delivered, who pays landing charges, duty, customs clearance, cartage, warehousing, stevedoring, insurance in warehouse or bond and accounting arrangements. Additionally, it should detail property in the goods, arrangements for release to the buyers and disposal of stock on termination of agreement.
11. *Spares for general maintenance and service.* A clause on this item should also outline general arrangements and disposal of the items on termination of the agency agreement.
12. *Cost of airmail, e-mail, faxes and unusual expenses* – not mentioned elsewhere in the agreement – and responsibility for their payment. Most exporters would insist on a fully computerized agents' office/administration unit being available.
13. *Force majeure.* This clause negates responsibility of the principal where *force majeure* prevents delivery from a factory or, in respect of goods ready to leave, prevents despatch or causes diversion of a cargo carrying ship or aircraft.

14. *Permissive clause.* In situations where the products do not meet the competition in design, suitability to market or price, whether or not the agent can handle other goods of the same category. This clause is usually found in a commission agency rather than sole distributorship.

15. *Commission.* The actual commission scale – fixed or sliding rate and how the agent will be credited or remitted. This requires careful deliberation, particularly in an area of floating currencies and devaluation implications.

16. *Accounting.* The agent must maintain reliable audited records of sales and render periodical statements including consignment stocks where applicable. Provision should be made for accounts to be audited or examined by the principal or his or her representative. The data is likely to be computerized.

17. *Overprice.* This usually arises in contracts between merchants and agents in raw materials and semi-finished product trades. It embraces general conditions and the authority of the agent to try to overprice. Moreover, it details the allocation between the two parties to the agreement of the overprice apportionment.

18. *Publicity.* A general agreement regarding sales literature and catalogues, including responsibility for translations, policy in regard to exhibitions, local advertising and special propaganda. It should detail the apportionment of cost between the two parties to the agreement.

19. *Report.* The agent to submit reports at prescribed times and likewise the principal, to keep the agent informed of product development and trade generally. It will extend to production and marketing policy.

20. *General conditions.* Any general conditions not mentioned elsewhere in the agreement and which either party mutually wishes to introduce. For example, to pledge the principal credit or to start legal proceedings without his or her consent.

21. *The duration of the agreement and notice of termination of agreement by either party* – the latter may be one or three months or any other prescribed period.

22. *Breach of contract clause.* This involves a case of breach or default by either party or by the agent without mention of breach of any principle. It also embraces a summary of determination upon liquidation or compensation with conditions or attempts to assign benefits of contract.

23. *Laws and arbitration.* This must indicate which country's law will apply and that disputes will be settled by arbitration in accordance with the terms prescribed in this clause. This will avoid costly litigation and speed up settlement.

24. *Assignment.* Neither party has the right to assign the benefits of the contract without the prior consent of the other. This may be qualified by a merger sub-clause showing what would happen if the original legal entity of party is merged into another legal entity.

The contract document finishes with space for the signature of the parties and an indication of capacity of signatories and witnesses, including formal application of a company's seal where applicable. In a favourable Principal/Agent relationship the Principal would have reciprocal online access to monitor sales and initiate and replenish stock replacement distributions arrangements within an agreed strategy by both parties.

The agent and distributor is employed by small, medium-sized and large companies. It constitutes the intermediary between the seller (exporter) and buyer (importer). Hence, the exporter does not have direct contact with the distributor to determine market research data such as buyer behaviour, buyer profile, product acceptance and selection criteria and size of buyer's account. Further data are not available on market trends and market profiles. Nevertheless, these shortcomings are usually overcome through continuous dialogue between the seller and the buyer involving visiting the market, distributors' or agents' monthly reports, and regular meetings. A similar analysis applies to the agent, but usually the exporter is closer to the buyer (importer) than is the case when a distributor is employed. Overall, there is a need to develop an empathetic strategy between the exporter and the agent or distributor to realize the best results and develop market research-led strategies.

Factors determining the selection of agent or distributor include the following.

1. Membership of the appropriate Trade Association and BS5750 registration – 'Management of quality' accreditation if applicable.
2. Profile of the agent or distributor and nature of business. Ideally one should appoint an exclusive agent – one who does not sell or promote goods or services competitive to the principal business.
3. A value added benefit emerging from employing the agent or distributor.
4. Volume of business the agent or distributor will generate and his or her business record and achievements.
5. The agent's or distributor's resources, including financial, marketing and selling resources, equipment and computerization, nature of the accommodation and training of personnel.
6. Professional qualifications of the Directors and overall quality of the management and resources.
7. Evaluation of the business plan on how the agent or distributor will tackle the principal business.
8. EDI access, (see pp. 448–49)
9. Any association with a legal dispute or fraud.

It is usual to draw up a short list of agents and distributors to evaluate their skills and proposals and their degree of commitment to the task. This involves visiting the market and the agents' and distributors' premises and meeting their staff.

17.6.2 Business-to-Business (B2B) and Business-to-Consumer (B2C) customers

During the past decade and much facilitated by E-commerce internationally we have seen an enormous increase in the Business-to-Business and Business-to-Consumer business. It is, to the exporter, a very efficient way to develop the international portfolio and particularly eliminates the intermediary with significant cost savings and accelerates the decision making process. Moreover, it develops empathy between the two parties and favours strongly a logistic and computer focused approach. It favours both the MNIs and SEMs.

The Business-to-Business E-commerce market is well established. It enables international sales teams to concentrate on selling, which requires face to face interaction, and the back office on E-commerce sales. Moreover, it is a low cost method of exporting and avoids the provision of multiple copies of catalogues. Such B2B emerges when the exporter/importer have a good relationship and complete synergy.

The Business-to-Consumer is distinguished from the B2B by the nature of the customer and how that customer uses the product. In business marketing international customers are organizations such as businesses, government bodies, and institutions such as hospitals. The Business-to-Consumer market is often through E-commerce such as cars and accessories, home appliances and accessories, books, financial services, tourism, transport and food products. It is very popular in the EU single market.

An area of significance with the B2B and B2C is to maintain and develop a good website and have well trained and professional personnel handling enquiries. It should be manned 24 hours per day to handle global enquiries in various time zones. The website must be targeted to focus on individual markets and ideally in the language of the buyer. It is often prudent to feature in distant markets a local contact such as Agent/Distributor/Franchisee who can demonstrate the product to the importer.

It is important to bear in mind that consumer and business markets differ in the nature of markets, market demand, importer behaviour, exporter/importer relationships, buying power, and market environmental influences such as legal, technical, cultural, political, exchange control and economic. Also check the country/company credit rating (p. 418).

17.6.3 Company acquisition

A quick way of entering a market is to buy a locally-based company and develop a strategy of product specification in line with the overseas buyer brand image. This tactic is often termed merger and acquisition. The locally-based company is already established in the market and the foreign buyer may be able to provide much needed capital input, technical specification, management operation and marketing skills in a high-tech computerized manufacturing or service environment. For example, the company's product lifecycle may be in decline and with no financial resources to invest in research and development and a foreign buyer may be able to provide a high-tech state-of-the-art new replacement product to revitalize the company's future prospects.

There are other considerations to be taken into account in the merger and acquisition strategy. On the downside the disadvantages include encountering a culture hostile to foreign investment; the political implications; and the risk of funds being repatriated in the event of nationalization or severe exchange controls; However, the advantages include acquiring an additional market, gaining access to an established distribution network and having an immediate source of revenue in a new market. In addition, the company acquired may be treated as a wholly-owned subsidiary to gain maximum tax advantages. The negotiations are usually undertaken by a merchant bank.

17.6.4 Concessionaires

Concessionaires operate as distributors with a special authority granted by the manufacturer to work in a particular market area, usually on a basis of exclusivity. They tend to be experts in their field and have good contacts in their particular trades. The advantage to a manufacturer or exporter is that regular business is assured, but there is no direct contact with the buyer, and the channels of distribution to that market will be restricted to the activities of the concessionaire.

Thus a manufacturer might make what, at first sight, appeared to be an opportunist sale to a merchant and then receive a repeat tender, coupled with a request for exclusivity for the particular territory in which the merchant is active. This could, in turn, develop into a regular relationship by which the merchant becomes the concessionaire for that market.

17.6.5 Confirming houses

The basic function of a confirming house is to assist the overseas buyer by confirming, as principal, orders already placed so that the exporter may receive payment from the confirming house as and when the goods are shipped. Any credit period the buyer may require is arranged and carried by the confirming house which takes over the credit risk from the supplier. A confirming house, as an export house, is used extensively by the small- or medium-sized supplier involved in the export business.

17.6.6 Consortia

These are groups of organizations which work together as a unit in order to achieve a common purpose. The consortium may operate as a group seller or a group buyer and sometimes will use a nominee in order to preserve anonymity during negotiation of a contract. Consortia tend commonly to be engaged in bidding for large tenders, particularly where the size of the order is feasible only by employing the combined capacity of individual members.

Many consortia of this type have been set up on the initiative of the leading firms of consulting engineers, with the end-products in the foreign country ranging from civil projects such as large dams, irrigation, railway modernization and extension, hospitals, dredging undertakings and harbour installations, to construction works in the electrical field such as power generation, sub-stations and television transmitters.

Since each major undertaking of a consortium is likely to be so different in its nature from any other project put out to tender by foreign governments, municipalities or other principals, it follows that many of these consortia are set up specifically for only that one project and, when this is completed, the consortium is dissolved. Some of the parties may collaborate again on another contract, possibly bringing in new members, but it rarely happens that a second venture is so exactly like the first that the consortium can function unchanged.

From the very nature of these undertakings it follows that the negotiations between the members of the consortium are protracted, difficult and complicated, even before the nominee can submit the tender. This type of operation is always highly technical and, for every tender that is accepted, there will be more than one which is not secured. This involves having to write off the heavy expenses incurred. Such projects are usually associated with ('turn key') cargo delivery terms.

17.6.7 Export houses

Export houses have three main functions as detailed below.

1. An export house can act as an export merchant buying goods outright and selling them on his or her own account. The merchant may buy goods from the exporter against the requirements of an overseas customer. Alternatively, the agent may buy the product and market it overseas. Finally, the agent, by virtue of his or her international trading activities, may indulge in compensation trading, switch deals, etc. (indeed, in any barter type transaction).
2. An export house can act as an agent but retain the role of the principal throughout the transaction. In such circumstances, the export

house will promote the exporter's products overseas; carry the credit risk on the overseas buyer; attend to the physical and clerical work involved; stock goods at home and overseas on the exporter's behalf; follow-up delivery dates or delays; deal with formalities overseas; and occasionally provide an after-sales service. Basically, the degree to which the foregoing work is undertaken by the export house will vary according to individual circumstances and is a matter for negotiation. In the main, the small- or medium-sized export business usually finds it cheaper and more cost effective to engage an export house as their agent rather than employ their own export staff or overseas representative to undertake such work. The payment for these services may be in the form of commission, with the agent quoting the agreed export selling price to customers overseas. Alternatively, there may be some other form of remuneration to the export house negotiated by the exporter. For example, the export house may calculate the export price with the exporter on a 'cost plus profit margin' basis. The profit margin would be for the export house financial controller, who is responsible not only for sales of the product, but also its advertising, marketing, distribution, etc.

3. An export house can act for an overseas buyer in return for which commission is earned. In such circumstances, the export house may find sources of supply or deal with suppliers (exporters) nominated by his or her principal. In either case, the export house will arrange shipment and insurance; progress and despatch of orders; and confirm and finance contracts on the buyer's behalf.

The export house may be a buying agent or merchant. The role of the export house varies: the large ones undertaking virtually all the roles outlined above, and the smaller ones offering a more specialized but less extensive service. Few, if any, export houses are prepared to deal with all goods for all destinations. Most specialize in particular markets, types of goods, or in certain types of products for particular markets. To the exporter who is interested in export house activity, it is suggested he or she contacts the British Export Association whose address is found in Appendix A (p. 603).

17.6.8 Franchising

Franchising is a growth global market. It is focused on both the manufacturing and service sector. Overall, however, franchising has a high service element. It involves the legal right to use branding, products and methods of operation being transferred to a third party. The major examples of franchising found today are in the retailing sector.

Franchising has been defined as a contract between a manufacturer, wholesaler or service company (called the franchiser) and an independent entrepreneur (the franchisee) who purchases the right to own and operate the franchise. The franchiser will receive an initial fee, royalty on sales, lease fees for equipment, profit share or some combination of these four. The three main forms of franchising are manufacturer sponsored retailing, as found in the car industry where a dealer retails automobiles subject to certain conditions imposed by the manufacturer; manufacturer sponsored wholesaling, as found in the soft drinks industry; and, thirdly, service sponsored company retailing, as found in the fast food and car hire businesses. In short, franchising is a facility granted by a principal to a retailer to sell on the principal's behalf a particular product or service using the principal's name, for example McDonald's. In such a situation the retailer must conform precisely to the code of practice stipulated by the Principal.

There are two types of agreement between the franchiser and the franchisee: an area development agreement and a master franchise agreement. Basically, the agreement features identification of rights embracing territory location, extent of rights to use the franchiser's name, payment of fees, franchisee's obligations, sale of the business and termination of the agreement. Royalties may be based on a percentage of sales or a flat management service fee reviewed annually.

An area development agreement will feature the degree of transferability, whether exclusive or non-exclusive rights are to be granted; the number of outlets, exclusive or non-exclusive rights; provision of additional outlets in the event of favourable market conditions; and finally termination arrangements and disposal of outlets.

In contrast, a master franchise agreement includes a specified territory; exclusivity; performance schedule, embracing agreed sales targets; fees – initial and on-going; default clauses, with the arbitration and national law applicable; intellectual property safeguards; training provision; taxation aspects and the rights to be granted.

The franchising market is one of increasing market penetration and is very much in evidence in the global village. It provides to the franchiser speed of entry to an overseas market, and an outlet for the franchiser's goods or services over which he or she has virtually complete control. It does involve capital commitment in terms of premises/retail outlets and facilitating the franchise launch in terms of stock provision, marketing, training and control systems. Overall, it is very much involved in the brand management business on a global scale.

Franchising is a growth market and exporters considering such a strategic focus must carefully research the market. It may be necessary to change the brand name to avoid linguistic embarrassment; the product/service specification may require modification to reflect the local taste; the colour may require changing together with the brand logo and the advertising content. In addition, local employment legislation, repatriation of funds, taxation requirements, intellectual property, environmental demands, packaging, product liability and advertising mode/content need evaluation. Franchising is equally ideal for the MNI and SMEs. It can be extended into licensing. Overall, franchising is a quiet way of entering an overseas market. Examples of Franchises featuring global brands include Coca Cola, KFC, Body Shop, Thorntons, M&S, Boots, Mothercare, Dorothy Perkins, Burberry, Hamleys, MFI, Laura Ashley and Aquascutum.

17.6.9 Free Trade Zones

Free Trade Zones, together with Free Zones, are a growth sector in the development of international business. Over one thousand exist globally and they are available in developed, developing and LDC markets. Governments favour them strongly as they are an excellent option to enter a market through foreign investment and thereby bring to that country an international trade focus of wealth, trade facilitation, industrialization, international management culture skills and global opportunity. Moreover, it provides excellent opportunities to develop its resources economically and not only to add value to such resources, but also to develop new ones which may be derivatives.

A Free Trade Zone is a defined area where trade is based upon the unrestricted international exchange of goods with customs tariffs used only as a source of revenue and not as an impediment to trade development. In contrast a Free Zone is a designated area which has met the Free Zone status. It offers special incentives and privileges to foreign investors including tax concessions, easier repatriation of earnings and more favourable government regulations regarding employment. Many exist in China and are called Special Economic Zones.

A modern Free Zone exists in Hamriyah Shariah, UAE, which we will now examine. It was established in 1995 with the objective of creating an integrated far reaching business driven community. It has 11 state-of-the-art seaports, six airports and satellite links with 230 cities. Overall, the nation is a long established oil producing country, but now the UAE is striving to become a leading industrial development region with its unique geographical location between three continents serving over one billion people. It has modern seaports at Port Khalid on the West coast and Port Khor Fakkan on the East coast. Dubai International Airport is six kilometers from the Sharjah Expo Centre. Sharjah is the only one of seven emirates with ports on the Arabian Gulf's West and East coasts with direct access to the Indian Ocean and an international airport which connects to 230 countries.

Companies opting to invest in the Free Zone have a range of financial benefits: import and export tax exemption; no restrictions on repatriation of capital and profits; leases available for 15 years and renewable for a further 15 years; 100 per cent foreign company ownership; exemption from all commercial levies; no corporate or personal income taxes; no requirements or quotas for personnel recruitment; stable convertible currency; customs privileges for goods destined for the Hamriyah free zone; access to largest cargo hub airport at Sharjah; excellent 14 metre-deep water seaports; quick and simple procedure for approval of licence applications; and access to Internet and e-mail services. Overall, it offers low labour costs, inexpensive energy resources, ability to develop your own land, factory or infrastructure – over 10 million square metres of prime industrial and commercial land with access to deep water berth facilities, pre-built warehouse/factory/office accommodation units for lease and Executive office suites in the International Business Centre for lease.

Overall, the Free Zone provides an excellent opportunity to develop a thriving business in the region with a good strategic location and infrastructure in a growth market of extensive diversity.

17.6.10 Government procurement

Government procurement is a growth business. It not only applies to defence resources/equipment, but also to a whole range of products/ projects. This embraces transport; communication; seaports; airports; infrastructure embracing rail, road, canals and ships; agricultural; hospital hi-tech products especially computerized resources; and hydro schemes. Many of the tenders are conducted on a consortia basis. Moreover, the opportunity exists for the SMEs to bid for the subcontract work which emerges from the consortia project. A significant number also feature turnkey projects. The government procurement invitation to tender may have severe funding constraints and very stringent control mechanisms reflecting the political climate of the country and any restrictions imposed by the donor funding arrangements as may obtain in an LDC.

The following factors are important to consider before bidding for government contracts or state owned companies.

(a) Endeavour to build up partnerships by visiting the market well in advance of any tender issued. Many export orientated companies rely on their Agent to obtain advanced information on possible projects emerging, sometimes embracing a pre-view. Such data is obtained by networking.

(b) Product/service specification is a key area. Good planning and extensive networking may favour an exporter's innovative technology to impress the government entity sufficiently that it designs a tender with the exporter's product or service in mind.

(c) Local participation often strengthens a bid. International companies are sometimes allowed to bid directly for certain contracts. Hence having a local partner can be a bid advantage.

(d) A Supplier's register exists in some countries. Establish if the government entity requires registration of the potential supplier before participating in the bid.

(e) The legal documents must be carefully prepared before submitting the bids. Engage a lawyer familiar with the market. The smallest grammatical error can lead to a disqualification.

(f) Financial documents. Many government entities require a bid bond and a performance bond. Periods and bond amounts must be clearly stated in the bidding guidelines. The bidder will sometimes be asked to provide further information when project financing is required.

(g) Deadlines. Technical clarification, technical proposals and economic meeting dates specified in the tender are important. A missed deadline may seriously jeopardise a bid.

(h) The bidder must review and understand the draft contracts included in the guidelines. Legal advice must be sought well in advance.

(i) Letters of association. When bidding under a consortium or joint venture, the bidder must include documents giving evidence of ties with other companies. The work to be sub-contracted must be clearly identified.

(j) Economic proposal. Some government entities request a thorough breakdown of proposal prices. Any price adjustment will be based on this information. Ideally, the bidder should feature an escalation clause linked to an accredited index to cover inflation.

(k) An arbitration clause and identity if the legal environment recognition is desirable.

(l) Tender evaluation. Government tenders have traditionally been assigned to the company that can give the product/service at the lowest price. However, many governments now focus on the value added benefit. This may embrace a points system for awarding tenders based on value for money, quality of service/products and the bidders track record.

(m) The web is often an excellent resource to obtain data on procurements, published tenders, transparency and future projects.

17.6.11 Leasing

Leasing is a growth market in market entry options. It applies primarily to industrial products where the buyer is unable to fund the product due to the absence of available capital. An example is found in railway rolling stock. The lease provides performance guarantees and a warranty. Rolling stock companies enable their engineering expertise to provide sound asset management skills to manage the fleet throughout its leasing contract. At the end of the operating lease embracing a franchise contract, the residual value risk is with the leasing company alone.

17.6.12 Joint venture

An increasing number of companies are now developing their overseas markets through joint ventures. As a form of market entry, it provides greater cover over sales and distribution; develops local manufacturing packing and assembly; permits technology transfer; provides control over cost and production quality; and enhances market penetration, growth and customer loyalty. A joint venture can bring a new dimension to the business of the new joint company.

Basically, a joint venture is the process of two trading companies from different countries – at least one of them being local – forming an agreement and a new company to market and/or manufacture or produce goods on a joint basis. Both companies must have the same management culture ideology and have jointly competitive features and advantages both wish to exploit. Each company contributes its complementary expertise or resources to the new joint company. Both parties have an investment obligation, the extent of which varies by circumstances. The scale of the shareholding may vary from 10 per cent to 90 per cent but generally is around 25–75 per cent. In many developing countries, governments stipulate a minimum national holding in a joint venture of 60 per cent which constitutes a majority local shareholding. In such circumstances the host country would have the majority of directors on the basis, for example, of four to three in favour of the host country.

The rationale for companies opting for a joint venture include the following.

1. An exporting company can achieve quick access to a market, thereby gaining competitive advantage and an early return on investment.
2. Host countries may impose severe import restrictions making it virtually impossible to enter that market; thereby the joint venture is seen as a profitable option, providing a local manufacturing base.
3. Joint ventures share the risk between the two companies, in proportion to their investment portfolio.
4. Costs are shared, particularly in the area of research and development which can be very substantial in, for example, the pharmaceutical industry. Similar remarks apply to new plant for car manufacturers.
5. Manufacturing within an economic bloc or customs union provides free circulation of goods within the bloc without any trade barriers. This enhances the market share and, additionally, it may offer tax incentives and development grants.
6. Global business today is becoming more competitive with the number of players in the market being reduced through joint ventures and merger acquisitions, a favourite strategy of the multinational industries. The factor driving such strategies is lower unit costs and greater competitiveness. This may be achieved through lower labour and materials cost and lower overheads.

Overall, the joint venture may provide a better capital investment return and facilitates better market research strategies through the new company management structure, and interface with the market and customer.

The procedure to follow prior to embarking on a joint venture would be similar to the points below.

1. Thoroughly research the host company including credit rating (p. 418).
2. Establish how the foreign partner is going to raise capital and under what terms.
3. The degree of host government investment especially in the areas of:

   (a) capital construction;
   (b) land availability;
   (c) labour force deployment, training and redundancy;
   (d) timescale;
   (e) product and plant specification constraints;
   (f) technology;
   (g) expatriate employment terms;
   (h) procurement – raw materials and components sourcing and any constraints;
   (i) marketing, both domestically and internationally;
   (j) quality control;
   (k) the legal environment;
   (l) the attitude to competition domestically and internationally;
   (m) arbitration.

The joint venture is very much a growth market as we progress through the twenty-first century.

17.6.13 Licensing

Licensing is a method of market entry offering a low level of investment and speed of market entry and is ideal for the licensee who is keen to manufacture his or her product in the licensor country. A licence is granted to an overseas company to manufacture products on a royalty basis in accordance with the licensing agreement terms agreed by the licensor and licensee. It confers the right on the licensee to use a combination of the following: technical know-how, patent rights, trade marks rights and copyrights. Both parties to the licence agreement benefit from increased profits. However, it is important to stress that usually it is far better to market products in overseas territories than to licence the patents and/or the production know-how.

The rationale of adopting a licensing strategy by an exporter/licensee incorporates the following features.

1. Licensing involves a limited financial commitment and low level of management resources, together with speed of market entry.

2.   It overcomes any government controls such as import duty tariff and non-tariff barriers, and encourages more competitive pricing in distant markets subject to high freight charges by resorting to local manufacture.

3.   Licensing enables the licensor to market the product as a local manufacture thereby overcoming any national prejudicial effects not favouring imported goods.

4.   The licensee gains access to the licensor's market base and channels of distribution.

5.   Overall, it allows a better return on capital and avoids costly product entry and launch costs in an overseas market with the attendant risks. Moreover, the price is likely to be very competitive.

6.   Licensing allows for speedier entry and access to the market especially in comparison to a joint venture or industrial transplant. This is particularly relevant for fast moving consumer goods (fmcg) and for small- and medium-sized enterprises (SMEs).

7.   Licensing enables the licensee to enter a market with an established customer in place.

Advantages to the importer or licensee include the following.

1.   The acquisition of an internationally recognized brand name thereby enhancing existing sales and reputation.

2.   The extension of the existing product range by acquiring new products which complement existing products.

3.   The development of 'know-how', particularly where high tech products are concerned, thereby avoiding costly research and development. Also new products give additional marketing strength and tangible product advantages over competitors.

4.   It is a low cost venture for the licensee with no research and development costs but simply the expense of setting up the plant to manufacture the goods.

A company may seek to license the production or use of a product; copyright work, process, business format or trade mark which a licensee might accept either has a use or value on its own, or would have if incorporated into another product. Technology, know-how, or a business format may be suitable for licensing, but whatever you wish to license needs to be exclusive to you and not in the public domain, otherwise the foreign party will see no need to buy a licence. If a product or process is protected by a patent, a potential licensee will only feel a need to enter a licensing agreement if he or she cannot readily circumvent the patent. For that reason, some companies prefer not to patent know-how and technology, where it is eligible for patent protection, in the belief that patent registration can aid competitors' research or that, in fact, the new process or product has a finite life span. Hence, the licensee must see a licence as giving him or her tangible benefits as earlier described.

A licensor can sell a licence for a fixed period and for a fixed once-only fee or, more usually, will seek a smaller initial 'disclosure' fee and an ongoing royalty directly related to production or sales value or volume. Alternatively, the rights may be sold without time limit, but this is more likely to be the case if the licensor believes his or her licensed product has only a limited life span before it becomes obsolescent.

Licences can also be granted on an inter-company basis between associated companies and parent corporations. This may be a way of clearly demonstrating ownership rights, or of increasing the level of funds that can be repatriated from foreign markets (although foreign royalties often attract a certain level of tax remittance). Where a product formulation is being licensed a manufacturer may be able to protect his or her formula further by agreeing, as part of the licensing agreement, that a base mix of ingredients will be supplied to the licensee. In such a case the licensor may choose to recover his or her royalties in the form of a mark-up on the price of the base mix, which will generally be used as a fixed proportion of the final product.

The licensor will need to establish that the product or process being licensed can or will comply with all applicable foreign market rules and regulations, such as those relating to labelling, packaging, health and safety, and ingredient usage or composition. All trademarks and patents should be clearly registered in the licensor's name, who can then grant the licences to associated companies or independent licensees.

Overseas licensing can pose many problems and the disadvantages are as detailed below.

1. *Competition from the licensee* – when the licensing agreement finally expires, the licensor may find he or she has established a competitor in the former licensee.
2. *Market exploitation* – the licensee – even if he or she reaches an agreed minimum turnover, may not fully exploit the market, leaving it open to the entry of competitors. He or she may inevitably lose control of the marketing operation.
3. *Revenue* – licence fees are normally a small percentage of turnover and will often compare unfavourably with what might be obtained from the licensee's own manufacturing operation.
4. *Product quality* – quality control of the product is difficult – and the product could be sold under the licensee's own brand name.
5. *Government* – governments often impose conditions on remittances of royalties or on component supply.
6. *Disagreements with licensee* – arguments will arise however carefully the licensing arrangement is drafted. A disaffected licensee can be a serious problem.

Larger companies might create a licensing team, incorporating marketing, legal, financial and technical personnel. Smaller companies with limited resources may only be able to develop through a single individual, but can take advantage of assistance from government departments concerned with promoting trade and investment and also use the services of outside specialist consultants in identifying and developing opportunities.

A licensing agreement is an important step for a company to take and one which should not be taken lightly. The first stage is to formulate a plan with an objective and adhere to it throughout. A competent legal adviser should be employed from the outset: he or she would have the help of the licensing adviser(s) who would be familiar with the legislation of both countries. Great care must be taken not to reveal any detailed information during the preliminary discussions. Details of the points to be covered are as follows.

1. Legality in both countries.
2. The parties and their responsibilities.
3. To retain the products, trade marks, patents and know-how copyrights.
4. Territories and exports to other countries.
5. Finance: royalties, payments and methods of payment, currency.
6. Transfer of information, methods, staff and training.
7. Patents: usage, quality control, infringement, exclusion, patent laws.
8. Cross licences and grant back.
9. Audit and control.
10. Performance based on minimum sales or royalties.
11. Procedures for settling disputes such as an arbitration clause.
12. Applicable laws by which an agreement will be enforced.
13. Investment obligations to plant and machinery.
14. Restriction clause limiting licensee to compete with similar products or markets.
15. Secrecy clause.
16. Product development.
17. Product pricing and supply.
18. Insurance cover.
19. Training.
20. Sub-licensing.
21. Assignment clause.
22. Duration of licence and provision for termination.

The selection of a licensee requires careful evaluation and the following points are relevant.

1. With a specific process for treating a raw material ingredient or waste product, identify producers or users of the ingredient or raw material or generators of the waste item.
2. If a raw material involved is only produced or sold through certain private or government agencies, then enter discussions with

those agencies to establish which of their customers might have applications.

3. For mass markets, seek to identify which companies presently produce similar products, or who distributes them to the end user.
4. If production requires certain ingredients, seek out producers of those ingredients to establish if they have an interest in expanding to supply end-users of the ingredient or raw material.
5. If a product is in a very specific market category, such as an automobile component, consider approaches to the producers of such items who might benefit from a product range extension.
6. If the product must be a component or an integral part of another product, consider who might derive a technical or earnings benefit by incorporating your product.

The criteria for appointing the licensee should have regard to the following.

1. Membership of a Trading Association.
2. Qualifications, calibre and experience of Directors and Senior Managers and company/country credit rating (p. 418).
3. Last three years' annual published accounts.
4. Experience of the type of business in which you are interested.
5. Current product range and product volumes.
6. Outcome and conclusions of any market research exercise undertaken to find suitable licensee.
7. Production and distribution facilities.
8. Market share and marketing capabilities.
9. Any association with a legal dispute or fraud.
10. Date the company was formed and experience and contacts in the market.
11. Degree to which licensee projects a modern outlook and encourages staff training and adoption of modern techniques, e.g. computers, e-mail.
12. Legal constraints in licensee appointment – local conditions.
13. Relationships with other organizations.
14. General competitiveness.
15. Any major shareholdings.
16. Political stability of the licensee country.

To conclude, we can say that licensing, too, is a growth market.

17.6.14 Management contracts

Management contracts is another growth sector of the export business, primarily focusing on the service sector. It broadly involves the provision of management teams to operate a project following its completion. This may be a hospital, power station, railway electrification or signalling system, mass transit system or hydro scheme. An example can be seen in the company Alstom, who supply power turbines to China under a turn key contract and on completion provide management teams to run the plant and maintain it. These are high-tech projects and the management contract provides for training and operation. Ultimately, the management of the plant is handed over to the Chinese.

17.6.15 Piggybacking

Piggybacking arises when two products are promoted one on the back of another, such as greenhouses and garden furniture. This involves two manufacturers: the first manufacturer (greenhouses) carries and promotes the products of the second manufacturer (garden furniture).

The first manufacturer, termed the carrier, is experienced in the market place and has a customer portfolio base. He or she earns commission by acting as an agent or distributor selling garden furniture. Accordingly the carrier adds value to his or her product range and thereby enhances market penetration and sales revenue by jointly offering greenhouses and garden furniture.

17.6.16 The strategic alliance

The strategic alliance – or, as it is called in the maritime industry, the operational alliance – is another growth area in the export market. The impetus to form a strategic alliance comes primarily from marketing, and from the financial, R&D and efficiency considerations of operating in a competitive global market. It involves two like-minded, similarly focused companies forming an alliance which results in the concentration and centralization of the companies' facilities.

The automobile and pharmaceutical industries are globally very competitive. High costs are incurred in the research and development involved in new car models and new drugs. These can be only financed through the large market base and centralized R&D facilities as found in a strategic alliance.

Other examples of strategic alliances embrace cross licensing, the development of the manufacturer–supplier relationship, technology transfer swaps and sharing marketing and distribution arrangements.

17.6.17 Trading companies

Trading companies are long established and are widely used in the market place. They involve numerous contacts with overseas buyers seeking a range of products. The trading company is used especially by SMEs who are seeking markets for their goods. It is a low cost method of entering an overseas market and is unlikely to involve any direct contact between the exporter and buyer as the trading company undertakes all the negotiation and distribution arrangements. Trading companies are also involved in counter trade.

17.6.18 Trade barriers

Trade barriers generate a serious impediment to the free flow of trade between nations. There are two forms of trade barrier: tariff and non-tariff barriers. There are a number of reasons why trade barriers may be put in place.

1. To protect a domestic industry or range of industries from imported goods.
2. To restrict or control the level of imports, thereby managing the trade balance on a bilateral or multilateral country basis.
3. To sustain a nation's currency exchange rate and to protect it from trade market speculators.
4. To ensure imported goods are not priced more competitively than domestic manufacture.
5. To preserve employment levels by restricting imported goods and so protecting home industries.
6. To raise government revenue through import tariffs and higher taxation on overseas companies resident in the country.
7. To maintain product standards and specifications or to develop more onerous measures for importer than for domestically produced goods.
8. To provide an administrative customs entry examination system which is inadequate in terms of resources to cope with the import volume, thereby generating delays and complexity by having all the documentation in the domestic market language.

We now briefly consider examples of tariff barriers.

1. *Import tariff.* An import duty raised on a range of goods. It may be 30 per cent and is often adopted by less developed nations to raise government revenue. It is relatively easy to administer and in some countries the import tariff is raised to protect the indigenous manufacturer in areas of agricultural, automobiles and/or a range of consumer goods.
2. *Ad valorem.* This is based on a percentage of the declared value of the goods.
3. *Temporary import levies.* These are duties raised on a short-term basis to counter an economic crisis in a country. They may be imposed in the aftermath of a devaluation.

4. *Anti-dumping tariff.* A tariff introduced to counter the dumping of specific goods. The effect of the tariff is to bring the goods imported into line with the indigenous manufactured products.
5. *Specific duty.* This applies to a limited range of products selected for economic or political reasons.
6. *Preferential duty.* This is an agreement, on a bilateral or multilateral basis, permitting imported goods to enter the market at a preferential import duty rate. It may be duty free and is practised by the European Union (see pp. 247–48).
7. *Countervailing duty.* Such duties are imposed on imports to counter the effects of export subsidies used by an exporting country.
8. *Discriminatory duties.* This tariff is raised on goods originating from a specific country and is imposed to counter a trade imbalance or for political reasons.
9. *Compensatory levy.* This links the goods the country wishes to import to the types of goods it wishes to export, thereby endeavouring to strike a balance between the level of imports and exports. Accordingly, a payment may be undertaken on exportation to qualify for a concessionary import duty in the destination country.

The range of non-tariff barriers are likewise extensive.

1. *Import licence.* This controls and restricts the quantity and value of specific imported products.
2. *Quota system of both imports and exports.* This again regulates the quantity and/or value of goods imported and/or exported. An example arises on a ceiling of 100 000 cars permitted to be imported to the UK from Japan.
3. *Financial controls.* This includes exchange controls: prior import deposits based on import value; credit restrictions; repatriation of profits from foreign companies; multi-exchange rates involving discriminatory exchange rate policies favouring the indigenous manufacturer.
4. *Restrictive customs procedures* resulting in onerous and lengthy import procedures. This includes product valuation, inspection, documentation, health and safety regulations, permits, licences, etc.
5. *Discriminatory* government and private procurement strategies usually favouring the local national source of supply.
6. *Restrictive* administrative and technical regulations which prolong the importing process.
7. *Product requirements* featuring standards, packaging, labelling, marking, product testing, product specifications, etc.
8. *Government participation.* This embraces subsidies, administrative instructions and government procurement and state trading favouring indigenous resources.

Finally, one of the largest impediments to trade can be the culture of the people, national and governmental, which we will now examine. A number of nations have a nationalistic culture strongly favouring their own products and services. Other nations particularly the USA and UK have a strong open market culture exhibited in the way the populace buys quality high-tech products at competitive prices without recourse to the place of manufacture.

17.7 Culture

Culture has been defined as the configuration of learned behaviour and results of behaviour whose component elements are shared and transmitted by members of a particular society. It embraces demographics, religion, language, education, values and attitude, aesthetic values, wealth, etc. Overall, it features in all areas of international trade embracing both service and industrial sectors. The cultural environment of international business extends to protocol, law and politics, social/economic factors, technology, material culture and social organization. Overall, culture is an area frequently underestimated by first time exporters entering an overseas market.

Culture is driving a fast changing market in many countries and regions of the world and exporters must monitor such changes to identify market entry opportunities. This is evidenced through education, youth culture and immigration.

We will now examine some aspects of culture which pose a real challenge to the exporter in the conduct of international business and its sustainment. This will be followed by a culture analysis and economic focus of key countries. The EU States are examined in Chapter 18.

(a) *Material culture:* this includes all artefacts, i.e. all physical objects which are made, such as pottery, paintings, houses, roads, dams and airports. Material culture is a useful guide to a society's standard of living. The term 'standard of living' must not be confused with 'quality of life' – indeed the two are often in opposition to each other.

(b) *Education:* a highly educated population is easier to communicate with and usually quite sophisticated and more demanding in terms of product quality/ durability/technology/performance, etc. Educated populations are more likely to have a higher standard of consumption and be more discerning on product choice development together with knowledge of the product service often through consumer associations. Moreover, the work force is likely to be well trained with high literacy standards. Market research data will be extensive and reliable.

(c) *Cultural differences:* the 'in one, in all' principle can be applied to cultural as well as economic groups. 'Culture' is usually taken to imply such adornments of a civilization as music, art and language, but in reality culture embraces many other factors. Society's culture is about everything which human beings conform, resulting in a distinctive way of life for its people.

(d)   *Religion:* characteristic attitudes and taboos often result from religion, which extends to food and people's attitudes to a whole range of products from deodorants to alcoholic drinks. It embraces philosophical systems, beliefs, and norms. Rifts within societies are often along religious lines and must be respected in conducting business overseas. There are also implications for business practice: Muslims regard Fridays as their Sabbath, for example, other religions so regard Saturday or Sunday. Additionally, colour has different meanings in different countries – white for mourning in China and orange has political significance in Northern Ireland. This must be borne in mind in advertising material and when presenting gifts.

(e)   *Special organizations, customs and roles:* the social fabric and structure are changing in many countries through the influence of education, investment, travel, communication, migration, immigration, the Internet, inwards investment and technology. The change is driven by the younger generation. In particular by education by the indigenous population and persons who are educated overseas and return to their country to impart and develop economic/technical/ social skills of wealth creation and improved living standards. Social organization represents the way in which society organizes itself and in particular how that society thinks about kinship, social institutions, interest groups and status groups, such as clubs.

Overall, a new era of networking and a changing business environment is emerging. In developed and developing countries 'career wives' are a common feature with an increasing number occupying professions. This is resulting in smaller families or childless couples who opt to develop their careers and not raise a family. Moreover, from families where there have been none before is university graduates likewise changing the social fabric of society as such personnel aspire to greater expectations than their forefathers.

'Convenience goods' is the 'marketeers' watchword here, since the traditional household caterer now no longer has the time or the inclination for such tasks. Takeaway foods – especially precooked meals as found in super/hypermarkets/restaurants, microwave ovens, and many other products owe much of their success to the increase of working wives and the first generation in their profession, also in some countries to an ageing population who favour the precooked meal. Overall, a new life-style is generated for the professional family who consequently have different expectations. For example home ownership rather than living in rented accommodation, and hi-tech modern white furniture in the kitchen.

Social groupings occur around activities such as sailing, music, business clubs, horse riding, Shipping Councils, Trade Associations, Chambers of Commerce, rambling, tourism or embroidery – each offering its own networking opportunities. In less developed societies, these groupings are not so common as they are in the West. Moreover, many families live in agricultural communities, are on lower incomes and have lower living standards.

(f) *Language:* While English is becoming the international business language of the world, and is spoken by a quarter of the world's population as a first or second language, there are also some 2700 other languages, not including dialects. Language can either be a great cultural pitfall or an opportunity in international marketing. The overseas buyer can communicate in the buyer's language, or a third language acceptable to both the buyer or seller. This affects not only normal business negotiations and communications, but also 'marketing communication'. The problem becomes acute where legal documents and the exporters advertising material have to be translated for international purchasing use. In many cases, not only the words, but also the underlying concepts have to be translated, and this can only be done effectively by the indigenous population. There are many examples of brand name 'howlers', resulting from insufficient research into the meanings they might convey in a foreign language. The marketeer communicating in the buyer's language generates confidence, integrity and commitment to the buyer which augurs well for business opportunities and development and also for protocol. Exporters are urged to learn a few basic words of the buyers' language which develops good relationships between seller and buyer.

(g) *Aesthetics:* the term refers to beauty and good taste in art, music, architecture and so forth, and products and product support material should have designs which appeal to local tastes. Some Chinese advertising, for example, for medical products would be found too explicit for the UK, and the standard of public taste exhibited on Japanese television causes Westerners to blanch, in spite of the refinement found in other aspects of Japanese culture. This is not to say that one country's aesthetics are inferior to another's – but the differences must be taken into account. Local aesthetics have a strong appeal to the local populace but can be unacceptable or have less cogency for an overseas culture. It is important the aesthetics of a country, region, or religion are respected.

(h) *Ethics and more:* ethics is all about perception – the customer's expectation and experiences of the product/service are identified in the brand image of the company. Companies with a strong brand usually retain the brand when the merger or acquisition takes place. The buyers' expectation of the brand and therefore of the social and business ethics associated with it, vary considerably around the world. One aspect of business ethics that needs to be mastered is the expectation in many countries that business incentives such as bribes will be issued as a matter of course: they may be essential in some cultures to secure an order. Mores relates to moral matters and generally derives from religion. They may restrict or prohibit the use of particular products; for example, the marketing of contraceptives to the unmarried – this latter constraint is now being eliminated as the World Health Organisation advocates birth control and raising health standards in less developed and emerging markets.

(i) *Political systems:* these are unique to particular societies, trading/economic blocs, and have many implications for exporters. In particular market access, taxation, negotiations, legal environment, repatriation of funds, exchange control and protectionism. It also extends to human rights, company law/structure, and recognition of International Conventions. The exporter must keep in touch with the ideology of governments particularly in situations where there is a change in political allegiance. An increasing number of developing and developed countries are privatizing former state industries and developing mixed economies with limited state control or ownership and more in the private sector as found in China. Widespread privatization is having considerable social and economic implications and is encouraging more inwards investment, strategic alliances, joint ventures, franchise, counter trade/buy back, thereby raising the competitiveness of particular industries or service sectors through modernization and capital investment.

Exporters in high labour cost countries are relocating their manufacturing base to lower labour cost economies where the work force is technically trained, access to materials/components is more competitively priced and the market penetration/access is close by. An example is Dyson, manufacturer of consumer products – vacuum cleaners/washing machines – who switched production from the United Kingdom to Malaysia with financial and market access advantage. Such an export strategy needs very careful evaluation in the setting up of revenue – earning assets overseas. Local attitudes regarding the employment of nationals of the host country, levels of taxation, ownership of equity and repatriation of profits may be particularly contentious and may differ according to local political factions. Also, there is the prospect of nationalization. The prevailing orthodoxy will be reflected in current legislation, but there may be a strong minority who would change this if they were elected. In extreme cases an asset might even be expropriated. The formulation of trading blocs is tending to open up markets and encourage trade on a low risk basis on a multilateral or bilateral trade agreement (p. 10). Political stability favours trade development. International banks such as Barclays, NatWest and HSCB, the OECD and the Economist journal (EIS) provide regular updated country reports for up to 100 countries which feature both the economic and political environment.

(j) *Protocol:* basically protocol concerns how one presents oneself. A topic often underestimated by the exporter visiting a particular

overseas market for the first time, especially having regard that protocol generates first impressions when the parties meet. It extends to
dress code, mannerisms, language, body language, propriety, discretion, non verbal messages, codes of behaviour when conducting
negotiations and the decision-making process. An important aspect
is to respect national protocol and never discuss trade and politics
together. Contrasting protocols exist in European and Asian countries, particularly Japan and China. A culture briefing is desirable
prior to the inexperienced exporter visiting the importer's country to
conduct negotiations and secure a contract.

(k) *Economic systems:* these are usually the outcome of political stances of
one kind or another and may create problems in internal dealings. A
major complication in negotiating deals in controlled economies, for
example, is that orders are placed with the state organization and the
export team are not free to negotiate a deal with the visiting overseas
buyer.

(l) *Legal systems:* these tend to reflect the broad political aims of the country or economic bloc as found in the EU legislation. Legal systems feature trade barriers, market access, multilateral and bilateral trade
agreements, economic customs and trade blocs and the commercial
legal environment. It extends to membership of any International
Convention.

(m) *Management culture:* this embraces the manner and protocol in which
the company conducts its business overseas and also the company
structure, in particular the decision makers and the influencers and
the overall decision-making process including the chain of command. It also reflects the company business-plan objectives and constraints in dealing with any particular country, company or product
overseas. Overall, management culture is a key area the exporter
must research to understand fully how the business is conducted relative to the overseas seller striving to obtain a contract.

(n) *Immigration and migration:* this embraces movements within the population strata which can change the culture, taste, protocol and a
whole range of areas within society. Culture is an area which
demands special attention by the exporter to develop and plan an
appropriate market entry strategy prior to entering the market. It is
probably one of the biggest challenges in international marketing.
Culture is made up of beliefs, values and customs. For example, in
Western Europe the decision of whether or not to buy may be taken
without reference to the wider family network, whereas in Asia buying decisions may involve the extended family. In some extreme
cases, a lack of awareness of cross-cultural differences can be devas-
tating and lead to business failure. For example, the white face of
Ronald McDonald caused offence in Japan where white is the colour
of death. Another example is Walmart, severely ridiculed when it

introduced its US Style 'have a nice day' greetings in its German stores. Social and cultural factors can be one of the biggest barriers to success across borders, so marketeers need to understand their significance in order to achieve profitability. In some situations, the nationality of the exporters' product can actually have a bearing on success. An Italian pasta brand has a more favourable market penetration impact than one from Brazil. Similarly, hi-tech expensive machinery from Germany has a stronger market appeal to the discerning buyer than one sourced from Guatemala.

Finally, the exporter must be aware of the role culture plays in advertising and developing the product or service in the market place. These will be further evaluated in the culture country analysis (p. 505), but the following general points are significant.

Negotiations and personal selling vary enormously and these are influenced by management culture, education, ethical issues and the decision making process. Market research, consumer behaviour and advertising must be focused on individual market segments by social class, language, attitudes, living standards, education and religion. The advertising message must not be cross-culturally focused, but be sensitive to individual tastes and needs. Product specification will depend on national legislation and consumer/industrial tastes and expectations. In many markets, especially consumer, it is standardization versus adaptation. Product evaluation acceptance may be prolonged where keen competition exists, consensus prevails and national prejudice exists. It is a cost benefit analysis. In many markets the importer will purchase the standard product and customize it to meet local market needs. Pricing policy will reflect local conditions and local competition. Price negotiation may be prolonged and tedious in some markets where consensus strategies prevail. Channels of distribution and their efficiency will vary by infrastructure development. In developed and developing markets logistics play a decisive role. Finally, one must stress each market must be treated individually to develop empathy with the culture and adopt a continuous proactive strategy to develop the product/service to the value added benefit of the importer. There is no substitute for regular visits and continuous personal contact by telephone or the Internet.

17.8 Cultural analysis by country/region and economic focus

Culture is closely interwoven in ways which affect the seller and buyer. Problems of cultural adaptation will be highlighted when personal contacts are made especially when the exporter experiences his first visit to the importer/buyer's market. Such a visit enables the exporter to identify the ambience of the market environment under which negotiations are conducted. This will be felt most acutely by expatriate staff. The discerning exporter, to understand better the country to be visited, will obtain a copy of a book featuring its history and the current political thinking.

American culture/economic analysis

The USA has a large and diversified economy with a broad base of natural and human resources and a well developed physical and technical infrastructure logistically driven. Buoyed by a steady flow of immigrant labour, and a large domestic market, it remains a global leader in technological innovation and product dissemination. US multinationals dominate many industries and US trends, particularly in financial services, have a profound impact on virtually all the economies of the world.

The USA has a material culture and Protestantism is the dominant religion. It has a pluralistic society with room for many individual aspirations and high individualism.

The negotiations can be on either an individual or group decision basis. The focus is to realize the desired result and discussions follow an ordered process where each point is evaluated in sequence. The negotiations can be aggressive or confrontational. The buyer has focus on product quality, hi-tech logistically driven, good after sales, competitive pricing and priority of treatment in delivery and development. Overall, a very competitive market with a low risk. Exporters are urged to visit the market once their own market research and pre-planning is completed. The American market is logistically driven and very hi-tech with computer literacy evident across the industrial and consumer spectrum in 50 States. Its population totals 286 million and a GDP per head of US$35 200.

Canada in contrast has a population of 31 million and GDP per head of US$22 390. It is an industrial country of mining and industry and the culture is similar in many areas to the US. Negotiations are positive, polite and focused to realize the objective. A hard sell is unlikely to succeed. Again, decision making can be on either an individual or group basis. Negotiations are an ordered process where each point is discussed in sequence.

Latin America is a diverse continent which includes Chile, Bolivia, Brazil, Argentina, Venezuela, Ecuador, Uruguay and Colombia. The GDP per head in Brazil is US$2910, Argentina US$7170, Venezuela US$5070 and Chile US$4310. Negotiations are conducted in a positive manner and a hospitable climate. The personal one to one relationship is important to establish. Relationship building is secured through socialization which will precede negotiations. Decisions are made by a high level individual.

Chinese culture and economic analysis

What immediately stands out about China is its huge size in terms of its population (1285 million), its land area (9 560 900 km^2) and its economic resources, and its GDP per head of US$900. China's population is equivalent to a fifth of the world's population, and the economic and political logistics of feeding, clothing, housing, educating and providing jobs and medical care for so many people are complex and demanding and exert a considerable strain on China's budgetary resources.

The country is made up of many cultures, religions, languages and groups. There are 56 ethnic groups in China – 53 of which use spoken languages of their own and 23 also have their own written language. Religions include Taoism, Buddhism, Islam, Catholicism and Protestantism.

China has a considerable surplus of cheap labour which provides an advantage in production for labour intensive industries. Moreover the emphasis latterly placed on education and training has boosted productivity levels and encourages a faster application of modern industrial technologies.

China is endowed with significant reserves of energy, minerals, and agricultural resources, access to which facilitates industrial growth. The result is a massive growth in world trade and the impetus still continues (p. 12) as a leading trading nation. Hence, the opportunities to export to China are enormous and ongoing. Currently, it is experiencing a growing liberalization and moving towards a free market economy, as the following will demonstrate.

Following the open door policy initiated in the 1970s, the economy has undergone some major structural changes as a direct result of a series of pragmatic and well co-ordinated economic and financial reforms. The reforms have been prioritized and staggered with efforts concentrated first on restructuring the agricultural sector, then progressing to the town and village enterprises, manufacturing industries and subsequently to foreign trade and foreign investment. China's industrial strategy has focused on the rapid development of the Special Economic Zones in the coastal regions, with foreign finance, foreign technologies, and foreign management playing a key role. Joint ventures feature strongly both for MNIs and SMEs.

Attention is now focused on reforming the state-owned enterprises, banking systems and the stock and foreign exchange markets. China recognizes the need to continue to speed up the reform of the legal, fiscal and accounting institutional framework in order to establish a greater degree of transparency, consistency, predictability and a level playing field, hence membership of the WTO (p. 27).

The role of economic growth and improvements in general living standards (p. 11) have been outstanding during the past decade. However, China remains a poor country with 50 per cent of the population engaged in agriculture, 23 per cent in industry and 27 per cent in the service sector. In terms of the origins of GDP, industry totalled 51 per cent services 32 per cent and agriculture 16 per cent. Overall, 45 per cent of the households have a TV, 13 per cent a telephone and Internet 0.1 per cent. Adult literacy is 84 per cent. There are wide income inequalities between the inefficient state owned enterprises and the town and village enterprises and foreign joint ventures and the special Economic Zones.

The opening up of China as a trading destination has been accompanied by an increase in distribution services from major shipping lines, airlines, express carriers, and freight forwarders. Additionally, the country is investing in its transport infrastructure. With so many major destinations along China's seaboard, many of the shipping services call at ports such as Shanghai or Hong Kong. Feeder services are then used to reach each other and smaller ports around China. Air transport and airports have developed similarly.

China is developing a system of inland waterways, ports and intermodal rail facilities to serve its rapidly growing domestic market needs. With the completion of the Three Gorges Dam in 2003 and the dredging of the Yangtze River, larger barges are now operative on the 1626 miles of navigable waters below the dam. Moreover, intermodal double-stack trains are being developed to serve 18 planned modern intermodal terminals capable of handling 500 000 TEUs per year.

Finally, potential exporters realize China has a massive domestic market and many MNIs and SAEs are following an extensive period of market research including several visits prior to establishing a joint venture. This embraces preparing required documents, and going through an approval and registration process prior to establishing their business in China. Overall, there are five major stages as follows:

(a) The first is for UK investors who want to establish a joint venture (p. 490) in China with a local partner. The letter of intent (LOI) and memo of understanding (MOU) documents provide a basic description of the intended project, the planned equity distribution and the amount of planned capitalization. They should expressly state that provisions concerning exclusivity and confidentiality are legally binding on both parties.

(b) For joint ventures, the next stage is to submit a project proposal to the local or provincial departments in charge of planning or, in some instances, the Ministry of Commerce or its regional body. This is prepared by the Chinese partner and will include the LOI/MOU as an attachment. For wholly-owned foreign enterprises (WOFEs), this is the first step. The investor would prepare and submit the proposal, but many wish to hire a Chinese agent to liaise with local authorities. The planning commission or Ministry of Commerce offices will generally preliminarily approve within 20–30 days of the proposal submission and issue an approval document.

(c) When preliminary approval is obtained, a feasibility study should be prepared by the WOFE investor or by the two joint venture partners. This should be a more detailed version of the project proposal and must include the following: a general description of the project and the parties involved; production plans and a simple marketing study; project location and reasons for selection; explanation of purposes of equipment and technology to be used; organizational structure; environmental protection plans, labour arrangements and construction timetable; sourcing and calculation of capital and attachments such as certificates of incorporation and legal representation, business licence and financial reports.

(d) For joint ventures, the next step is completion of the contract. This incorporates all the understandings and terms from the preliminary agreement, project proposal and feasibility study, though there may be some modifications by mutual agreement between the parties. The feasibility study and preliminary project approval documents are included as attachments when the contract, written in Chinese, is submitted for formal approval. Wholly-owned foreign enterprises do not require a contract, but will have to provide a list of board members and legal representatives and evidence of credit standing.

For both joint ventures and WOFEs, articles of association, also in Chinese, must be drawn up and submitted as part of the formal application process. They should contain basic information about the enterprise such as name, address, scope of business, total capital and organizational framework.

According to Chinese regulations, the Ministry of Commerce or its regional body will approve the formal application within 90 days. Approval will be in the form of a certificate.

(e) Both wholly-owned foreign enterprises and joint ventures should submit their business licence application within one month of obtaining their formal approval certificate via the State Administration for Industry and Commerce (SAIC) or its local delegate. After the payment of a nominal fee, the licence will normally be issued within two to four weeks. The enterprise will be considered to have come into existence on the licence's date of issue.

Investors are advised to obtain a lawyer who is experienced in the Joint Venture Chinese Market. By 2002 there were 424 000 foreign invested projects in China with leading investors emerging from US, Taiwan, Singapore and South Korea with the UK the leading EU investor. China is a signatory to all international laws on trademarks, designs, copyrights and patents.

India cultural and economic focus

Population 1025 million, GDP US$477.3 billion, GDP per head US$470, currency Indian rupee. Official language English.

India is the sixth largest economy in the world and one of the fastest growing. During the 1990s the per capita income of India's one billion population grew by 4 per cent annually, but this growth is not evenly distributed throughout the country. In terms of economic development, the states of Uttar Pradesh and Bihar lag behind the relatively prosperous states such as Gujarat, Rajasthan and Maharashta. Five hundred million of its population exist on the equivalent of one US dollar a day, while the middle class segment of 200 million have increasing buying power for consumer goods, including cars and household electrical goods. Economists predict that the car component industry will double from US$1 billion in 2005 to over US$2 billion in 2010.

India has a well educated work force and economist's predict there will be a rapid growth in trade bilaterally. India and China observers indicate that if China is the factory of the world, then India is its office. Moreover, while China is looking for inward investment, India is focusing on other countries for technical transfers. Areas of opportunity for exporters include automotive, agri-business, financial services, healthcare, education and training, environment technology, ICT, leisure and tourism. Additionally, priority areas of development include bio-technology, e-science, nanotechnology and alternative energy sources.

India's population continues to grow. It is an economy of great contrast between the poor and middle class segment. Some 24 per cent of the GDP comes from agriculture, 27 per cent from industry and 48 per cent from services. In terms of employment structure, 67 per cent are engaged in agriculture, 12 per cent in industry and 21 per cent in services.

India is an emerging leading trading nation and exporters are advised to visit the country on a trade mission following extensive research. Study India's heritage and the religious segments.

Japan cultural and economic focus

Population 127.3 million, GDP US$4141 billion, GDP per head US$32 520, currency Yen. Official language Japanese.

Japan is a leading trading nation (p. 12) and offers excellent opportunities for potential exporters. It is becoming more westernized, especially with the younger generation and enjoys high living standards. Overall, it has a complex culture and exporters must fully understand it before entering this very competitive market. Japanese consumers are only interested in top quality products and are very discerning and protracted in their deliberations and choice. However, when the favourable decision has been made, the Japanese importer requires priority of service. Successful exporters can expect a long-term business relationship providing they develop a culture of synergy and complete commitment with continuous dialogue. Additionally, it is important to bear in mind that 3 per cent of the land area is occupied by 97 per cent of the population which contributes to a tightly knit society.

The key to understanding the Japanese culture and protocol is through the concept of a group which is tightly knit and pervades every aspect of life. Confucian principles of social order mean that an emphasis on hierarchy according to status and age and rigid codes of behaviour exist in Japan. Ethnically, the population is extremely homogeneous and very nationalistic, having one language. Buddhism and Shintoism are the main religions. Family and traditional values permeate the culture. Family size is almost invariably one or two children. Japanese society is very chauvinistic; company and family are the two most important groups and loyalty is very strong.

Overall, company ranks above family – but this is changing with the younger generation – above individuals and the emphasis is on long-term development. Japanese businessmen are very honest but decision making is a long drawn-out collective process – and once a decision is made it is not rescinded.

Japanese etiquette is one of the most elaborate and complex in the world. One to one meetings are rare: usually four persons is the norm. Punctuality is essential and a fairly smart, stylish and conservative dress is expected. A prompt, courteous, professional service should be maintained. There is a strict code of propriety as regards business cards which are seen as being as important as the person themself and must be accorded the same respect. Place your card in your pocket and you could lose the deal. The Japanese traditionally put their family name first but the name of the company must be introduced before your own. If you can do a formal bow it helps, but many Japanese expect foreigners to shake hands and follow this practice themselves. Visitors should be welcomed upon arrival and thanked for their custom upon departure. Seating etiquette demands the guest sits furthest from the door. Meetings will always start off with pleasantries, no matter what the time constraints. In conversation an interest in Japanese culture is appreciated, the Second World War is a taboo subject.

Key points in negotiation embrace understanding the need for flexibility; leaving room for manoeuvre; preparing ahead of time by knowing as much as possible about the other party; expecting the negotiations to take time and avoiding tough appearances which often jeopardizes the reputation of the company and future business.

The Japanese have a deep sense of propriety and discretion. They pay a lot of attention to non-verbal message. Be tentative about gestures, as even blowing your nose loudly in front of others is considered rude. Try not to slouch – the line of the back is an indication of the Japanese character. A Japanese smile in business meetings is often from a reluctance to say 'no' and avoiding eye contact is seen as polite. The full force of eyes is seen as a 'knife in one's hand'.

Gift giving is part of social communication in Japan. It is very rude to refuse a gift, but they are given in the spirit of reciprocity. The number of items given is significant – four of anything means death and for auspicious occasions odd numbered items should be given, but nine suggests suffering.

If you go to a restaurant, you will be expected to take your shoes off and leave them pointing towards the door. Do not help yourself to food or drink in Japan and do not stick your chopsticks into the rice like flagpoles – this is done when the Japanese symbolically offer a bowl of rice to the dead. Conversation is not at a premium during meals and if offered sake from your hosts glass, accept it graciously – it is an honour.

The Japanese seem to be most honest and open when drinking, which you will experience if doing business there. For a nation so self-disciplined, it may come as a surprise that people do not give a second thought about getting roaring drunk and being quite loud and bawdy.

Today, Japan is largely an open economy compared with the 1980s and 1990s, when trade restrictions were rampant and bilateral and multilateral trade negotiations reflected a strategy of procrastination. Nevertheless, despite this relaxation of market access, the culture remains very strongly in favour of the indigenous manufactured product, but less so with the younger generation who are more Westernized in their needs.

Japan has an homogeneous market which is very nationalistic about its own manufactured market. Distribution networks are based on very tight relationships between customers and suppliers. Its major imports are machinery and equipment, food, raw material and a wide range of consumer goods. It is an ideal market for both the small and large exports. A starting point is to visit the country on a Trade Mission following your market research of potential products/buyers.

Malaysia culture and economic focus

Population 22.6 million, GDP US$88 billion, GDP per head US$3890, currency dollar/ringgit (M$). Official language English.

Malaysia has been transformed from a commodity and agricultural country to a newly industrialized market under a series of rolling national economic plans. Nevertheless, it is still abundant in natural resources including palm oil, rubber, timber, pepper, and oil and gas. The economy is primarily based on manufacturing. Malaysia's principal imports include capital goods and transport equipment, manufactured goods, chemicals, machinery instrumentation and food products. In the service sector it features consultancy, banking, education and legal services. Overall, it is largely an open economy.

Malaysia, due to its strategic geographical position, is a natural hub for regional business interests. It has a continuing improving infrastructure involving seaports and airports and motorway and rail links to important industrial and commercial regions. Consequently, many companies have joint ventures and acquisitions in Malaysia. An example is Dyson which manufactures electrical consumer goods such as vacuum cleaners and washing machines (p. 502).

Malaysia is not an Islamic state, the government is secular, but Islam is the official religion of the country. Overall, it is a multi-cultural population. About half of the population are Malays, with a further 35 per cent

Chinese and 15 per cent Indian. These three different races have different religions, languages, customs, taboos and aesthetics. Malaysia is, therefore, better treated as three markets with different complications and opportunities. Malaysia is a federation of 13 states, a constitutional monarchy and a government elected every five years. It is envisaged Malaysia will become a fully developed nation by 2020.

South Korea cultural and economic focus

Population 47.1 million, GDP US$422.2 billion, foreign currency Won.

South Korea is the world's twelfth largest economy. It has the world's third largest seaport, Busan, the largest shipyard, Ulsan, the world's largest car plant, it is the sixth largest steel producer, the world's largest shipbuilder, the fifth largest car builder, and third largest electronics producer. Its economy is much closer to mature OECD economies than those of South-East Asia. All the foregoing industries rely on imported components.

Additionally, South Korea has a strong hi-tech industry together with a wide range of consumer electrical goods. More recent developments feature moves forward in the railway network and environmental biotechnology. Insurance and financial services also are available in a deregulated market.

The industrialized country is a major market in the Asia–Pacific region and a logistic and financial hub for North East Asia. South Korea offers excellent export opportunities which can be extended to include joint ventures, acquisitions, direct investment and strategic alliances.

Russian culture and economic focus

Area 1 707 5400 km^2, population 145 million, per capita GDP US$310 bn, GDP per head $2140, currency Rouble.

The Russian culture has emerged since the millennium from a system of federal communism with state objectives uppermost to an open market economy. Religion is predominantly orthodox. The social organization is primarily monolithic with limited possibilities for exploiting individual life-styles in marketing. Consumers yearn for technical products but demand is limited as no buying power exists. Moreover, the consumer product range is limited due to mismanagement of the economy. Aesthetics is frowned upon and it is creating numerous difficulties in marketing communications. Advertising is only found in major cities. TV ownership and the number of students attending universities compares very unfavourably with the developed markets of USA and France. Russia is not a materialistic, throw away, fashion conscious society like the USA and the economic environment and purchasing power are limited.

Russia is rich in energy resources with major deposits of petroleum, coal, peat and natural gas. It also has significant deposits of aluminium, copper, iron ore, lead, phosphate rock, nickel, magnesium, gold and diamonds. Exports are dominated by raw materials, with petroleum, petroleum products, natural gas, minerals, and metals accounting for about 60 per cent of the total. Hence, Russia is highly susceptible to world price movements in primary products. Principal imports include machinery and equipment, food products, chemicals, metals and a range of consumer products.

Russia has achieved a great deal in the period following the dissolution of the USSR in 1991 when it adopted policies to enable it to become a market economy, up until the sudden dismissal of the Kiriyenko Government in 1998. There followed a period of economic and financial turmoil.

But as we progress through the twenty-first century, Russia has entered a new era of economic and social development under President Vladimir Putin. It has economic stability following the later years of President Boris Yeltsin's Government's economic mismanagement and misuse of constitutional power. Today, the economy in line with forecast continues to grow in industrial production amid relatively tight monetary policy. A financial aid package from the IMF has been rescheduled which will accelerate economic growth and continuous restructuring of the economy moving from a state controlled market to a market-driven free economy. Foreign investment continues to develop the Russian economy including joint ventures and the development of the infrastructure of road, rail, pipelines, seaports and airports.

Russia remains a market of great potential for companies willing to take a long-term view; research the market thoroughly and proceed with caution. An excellent method of entering the market is through a trade mission.

West African markets – culture and economic analysis

During the next decade the Central and West African markets will change as a new business culture emerges driven by national governments and more focus on trade development. The markets are more open to foreign investment and the economies are moving away from an agricultural focus to one of industrialization and service sectors. Poverty and poor infrastructure remain a key factor in the Region, but airports and the transport infrastructure is gradually being improved. The seaports and access to them from key industrial and agricultural sectors is improving with government programmes and foreign aid. It is a market for the experienced exporter who is looking to expand in an interesting region. Companies need to do their market research and develop a strong export strategy. It must be stressed the culture of the market is best understood by researching the history and politics and the route each country has followed to the present day situation. English is spoken widely in the business environment and national customs and protocol prevail. Research the country/company credit rating (p. 418). We will now examine a number of countries in the region.

Ghana: Population 19.2 million, GDP US$4.5 billion, currency Cedi, trading currency US dollar preferred or sterling; official language English.

Business opportunities: road and agricultural vehicles; agri-processing equipment; industrial and electrical equipment; office machines; consumer durables; manufactured goods; clothing/footwear; and packaging. A stable economy with good overall macro-economic performance and strong private sector favouring foreign investors. The world's largest gold mining company, the US Newmount Mining Corporation has substantial investment in the country. Ghana is the gold coast of the world attracting US$1.5 billion in the gold mining industry. A major road-building programme is underway linking the capital city Accra with major cities. The international airport Kotoka has been modernized. Agricultural products are growing internationally, especially organic.

Nigeria: Population 126.9 million, GDP US$41.1 billion, GDP per head US$350, currency Naira; official language English.

Business opportunities: oil, gas, healthcare, power, telecommunications, water, ports, education/training and ICT sectors.

Nigeria is a nation in the van of change following the successful transition from one civilian administration to another in 2003, and moving towards privatization and deregulation making the country more business friendly. It is the world's sixth largest oil producer with a 50 per cent growth forecast in the next few years. It is the ninth largest gas producer in the world and has developed the West African Gas Pipeline project completed in 2004. It is the tenth most populated country in the world with a large number of very wealthy individuals. Serious attempts are being made to tackle financial crime and security. Business is conducted by letter of credit or even cash up front.

The infrastructure is being improved with plans to develop a new deep sea container port outside Lagos, and FTZs, ICD, in key industrial/agricultural regions. Inwards investment is encouraged to modernize existing industries with a new management culture and international focus. The rail and road networks on key routes are being developed. Long-term, Nigeria has the potential to be a formidable multilateral trading nation embracing not only oil and gas, but many industrial and agricultural products and driven by foreign investment and management.

Equatorial Guinea: Population 457 999, GDP US$0.7 million, currency CFS Franc; official languages Spanish, French and some English.

Business opportunities: oil and gas sector, civil engineering (roads, Free Trade Zones, ports) banking services, consumer goods and tourism.

Equatorial Guinea is experiencing an oil and gas boom and is the third largest oil producing country in sub-Saharan Africa after Nigeria and Angola. The currency is aligned to the Euro and since 1997 it is a fast growing economy with a stable government driven by oil and gas revenues.

Sierra Leone: Population 5 million; GDP US$0.64 billion, currency the Leone; official language English.

Business opportunities: construction equipment, power, roads, water, tourism, telecommunications, agri-business, mining/mineral sectors and education.

Overall, a relatively stable economy, with inwards investment opportunities in ports and railways.

Cameroon: Population 15 million; GDP US$8.7 billion, currency CFS franc; official languages French and English.

Business opportunities: mechanical and electrical equipment, transport equipment, agri-business and industrial food products.

Cameroon offers opportunities in the fields of agriculture and construction equipment.

17.9 Visiting the overseas market

A critical aspect of conducting overseas business is the continuous need to visit that overseas market to keep in touch with existing clients and identify or develop new ones. Importantly, such visits display a company's total commitment to the market and the customer base, but they also provide an opportunity to keep in touch with market potential and risk, while evaluating the legal, political and competitive environment. In short visiting the overseas market is a form of market research and intelligence gathering. The rationale for the overseas visit may arise due to any of the following reasons.

1. To see existing clients and identify or develop new ones.
2. To attend or participate in a trade exhibition.
3. To appoint an agent or distributor.
4. To attend or run a sales conference or seminar.
5. To evaluate market opportunities prior to entering a market.
6. To negotiate a contract.
7. To formulate or develop a licence agreement or joint venture.
8. To visit the market prior to making a tender for the contract.
9. To conduct a training session and/or briefing meeting with agents, distributors, importers or franchisers prior to the launch of a new product.
10. To discuss export potential with representatives of governments or other agencies.

The key to any overseas visit is pre-planning and adequate research of the market, its culture and protocol. Ideally, personnel visiting the market for the first time should have a culture briefing. Additionally, the personnel should have a good appraisal of the market and the competitors together with the areas of opportunities and risk. Furthermore, the Executive must be multi-lingual and competent in the language of the buyer or clientele. Personnel able to converse freely in the buyer's language are in a strong position for conducting business. Speaking the local language presents a favourable image in negotiations as it displays a commitment to the country visited and smooths the way in opening business opportunities. It develops the culture and business synergy essential in competitive global business.

The following points are relevant to the planning of an overseas visit.

1. Formulate an itinerary and involve the agents, distributors and clients in the schedule. Take advice on the timescale of the visit and allow time for flight delays and prolonged negotiations. Focus particularly on entertainment.

2. Conduct in-house meetings prior to and following the overseas trip. Identify the objective of the visit and obtain data on customer portfolios, recent orders received and executed, problem areas, summaries of any previous visits, and details of company structure and senior management. It is very important that appointments are made with the decision makers in the company and not the influencers.

3. At an early stage, book flights and other travel arrangements with some degree of flexibility. Also, check the passport, visa and medical requirements.

4. Any samples, videos, brochures in the language of the buyer, training manuals, etc. should be up-to-date and should present the company in a favourable image. Check whether an ATA Carnet may be required (see p. 245).

5. Ensure that details of next of kin and the itinerary plan are deposited with key personnel in the company.

6. Hotels should be four or five star with adequate secretarial and conference facilities. Many exporters have contractual arrangements with International Hotel chains thereby obtaining discount rates and priority reservations. Make full use of your laptop computer.

7. It is common practice to take a gift as a token of goodwill. Advice should be sought if in doubt what to take.

8. Entertainment is a critical part of an overseas visit. Again advice should be sought. Local restaurants may be favoured in preference to the resident hotel.

9. The dress code should be appropriate for both business engagements and entertainment and leisure. Leisure engagements should be free of any business dialogue.

10. Business cards, which should be double sided reflecting both the exporter's and importer's language, should be presented.

11. The travelling executive must be fully briefed on the visit. In particular, he or she should have details of product specifications, competitive advantages, the benefits of the product to the importer, value added concept, price details, terms of delivery and timescale, non-price areas warranty training, spares, manuals, etc.

12. The executive must be in continuous contact with his or her parent office to resolve any local problems. Ideally, after each company or client visit, a report should be produced and any problem areas resolved, preferably before the executive returns home. The key to the success of any overseas visit is adaptability and endeavouring to meet the needs and specifications of the buyer. A spirit of empathy between the seller and buyer should be developed at all times.

13. A provisional negotiating plan should be devised prior to each client visit. Check the company/country credit rating (p. 418).

14. Market research, as indicated earlier, is a key aspect of a successful overseas trip. In particular, research the competition and the pros and cons of the exporter's product in relation to other products on the market. In addition, identify the product areas which most interest the buyer and how they can be improved on. Bear in mind the environment in which the product will be used or consumed.

15. A company culture which embraces logistics and computer technology is vital to any negotiations.

16. The executive must be fully aware of any local technical, health and safety, packaging or consumer liability legislation. Also, he or she should be conversant with the relevant export contract terms embracing Incoterms 2000, UCP500, and supplement to UCP500 for electronic presentation (eUCP) transportation, exchange control, import tariffs, documentation and so on. Particular attention must be given to funding the export contract and any financial package with attendant currency risk.

Unfortunately we live in an era of excessive security at airports, seaports and key industrial/commercial areas to counter terrorism. It is a global problem and exporters are urged to take advice from several sources prior to concluding their travel arrangements. This involves Government sources, travel agencies and the Internet. The next of kin should be given fullest details of the trip and contact numbers.

A further area of developing synergy with the overseas buyer is to obtain information on the heritage of the country and its policies over a period of time. A country report from the Economist Intelligence Unit will focus on a range of relevant political and economic factors.

Some companies, to reduce export-executive foreign travel, adopt teleconferencing. This has proved popular in some markets, but there is no substitute for face to face discussions and negotiations. However, there remains a role for teleconferencing on a secondary basis and especially B2B and B2C.

An area which cannot be over-emphasized is the need to research the culture of the market and avoid any mistakes. The culture briefing will focus on these areas and eliminate such pitfalls as can be found in other cultures (pp. 499–515).

The list on pp. 516 and 517 must not be regarded as exhaustive as each visit will vary, but the key to a successful trip is adequate preparation before the visit and developing empathy with the client during the visit. On return to the parent company the executive must produce a report and circulate it to the relevant personnel and departments and conduct a debriefing meeting. An action plan should then be prepared – and controlled to ensure adequate execution.

17.10 Chartered shipbrokers

The basic function of the shipbroker is to bring together the two parties concerned: the shipowner and the cargo owner. In following negotiations between them, a charterparty is ultimately concluded. The broker's income is derived from the commission payable by the shipowner on completion and fulfilment of the contract.

A further role of the shipbroker, other than fixing vessels, is acting as agent for the shipowner. As such, he or she is responsible for everything which may concern the vessel while she is in port. This includes customs formalities, matters concerning the crew, loading and discharging of vessels, bunkering and victualling, and so on. The duties of the shipbroker can be summarized as follows.

1. As a chartering agent whereby he or she acts for the cargo merchant seeking a suitable vessel in which to carry the merchandise.
2. As a sale and purchase broker acting on behalf of the buyer or seller of ships, and bringing the two parties together.
3. As an owner's broker whereby he or she acts for the actual shipowner in finding cargo for the vessel.
4. As a tanker broker dealing with oil tanker tonnage.
5. As a coasting broker involving vessels operating around the British coast and/or in the short-sea trade, e.g. UK–Continent. Additionally, at the same time, he or she can act for the cargo merchant in this trade should circumstances so dictate. The deep-sea broker, however, will act for the shipowner or cargo merchant, but not both at the same time.

There is no doubt the shipbroker is a person of many parts. In reality, he or she fulfils an intermediary role today he is website logistically marketing focused.

17.11 Freight forwarder

Basically a freight forwarder is a person or company which is involved in the processing and/or movement of goods across international boundaries on behalf of another company or person. The freight forwarder provides services in two main fields: the movement of goods out of a country on behalf of exporters or shippers – in which case the forwarder would be termed an export freight agent; and bringing goods into the country on behalf of importers – in which case the forwarder is called an import freight agent, customs clearance agent or customs broker.

The freight forwarder has four prime activities:

1. to provide a range of independent services such as packing, warehousing, port agency, customs clearance;
2. to provide a range of advice on all the areas relative to the international consignment distribution as found in transport distribution analysis (pp. 331–51);
3. to act as shipper agent processing transport and/or shipping space on behalf of his or her principal or shipper and executing his or her instructions;
4. as a principal, usually as a multi-modal transport operator, conveying the goods from A to B, crossing international frontiers and usually involving several carriers, often as an NVOCC.

The freight forwarder provides some or all of the services considered below, depending on the trade in which the company operates and the resources available. Today many freight forwarders are logistic operators (pp. 138–39).

17.11.1 Export

1. *Transport distribution analysis* – an examination of the options available to the shipper to distribute the goods (pp. 331–51).
2. *Transportation arrangements* – a major function involving the booking and despatch of the goods between the consignor and consignee premises or other specified points.
3. *Documentation* – provision of all the prescribed documentation for the goods having regard to all the statutory requirements and terms of the export sales contract.
4. *Customs* – all the customs clearance arrangements including documentation and entry requirements at the time of exportation and importation.
5. *Payment of freight and other charges* – payment of freight to the prescribed carrier including any handling charges raised by the airport, seaport or elsewhere during the transit.
6. *Packing and warehousing* – packing of goods for transit and warehousing provision.
7. *Cargo insurance* – insuring goods during transit.
8. *Consolidation, groupage and special services* – many forwarders specialize in consolidation offering major benefits to the shipper (pp. 169–71).

17.11.2 Import

1. *Notification of arrival* – the process of informing the importer of the date and location of the goods' arrival and the requisite documents required for customs clearance. It is likely the exporter and importer will have different agents and the two agents will liaise to ensure the smooth flow of the goods through customs, keeping their principals fully informed. Full use will be made of the EDI system.
2. *Customs clearance* – presentation and clearance of the cargo through customs. This involves paying close attention to all the requisite documents. Many major seaports and airports now operate a computerized customs clearance system thereby speeding up the process and eliminating the risk of errors (pp. 239–41).
3. *Payment of VAT duty freight and other charges* – the forwarder will co-ordinate and effect payment of all such payments on behalf of his principal at the time of importation. This avoids delay in the despatch of the goods to the importer.
4. *Delivery to the importer* – the process of delivering the goods to the importer's premises following customs clearance.
5. *Breaking bulk and distribution* – the agent may be an umbrella agent whereby he or she consolidates not only his or her own client's merchandise, but also those of other agents with whom he or she has a contractual arrangement. On arrival of the goods in the destination country, the cargo is handed over to the respective agents to process through customs and to distribute.

The freight forwarder will despatch cargo by air or surface transport modes. Air transportation will involve scheduled passenger aircraft; combi – the modern generation of jets permitting a flexible use of space combining freight and passengers according to market demands; chartered aircraft; and scheduled freighters. For surface distribution the forwarder will deal with containers, usually involving multi-modalism; international road transport and trucking, embracing the Ro-Ro ferry; international rail movement, involving the through train or wagon via the train ferry or the Channel Tunnel; and finally the specialized movement involving project forwarding, consolidators, bloodstock, 'out of gauge' loads, household effects, refrigerated goods or bulk liquids. An increasing number of freight forwarders provide services as an NVOCC or an NVOC (p. 114).

The freight forwarder is very closely involved in the customs clearance and processing arrangements, at the time of both exportation and importation. Today an increasing number of the major forwarders have the facility to undertake, on their own premises, the clearance of cargo at the time of exportation and/or importation. This speeds up the operation and avoids delays at sea- and airports. It is an important feature of multi-modalism. At the export stage, this process is known as Forwarders Local

Export Control (FLEC), and at importation, Forwarders Local Import Control (FLIC). Under FLIC the examination of cargo takes place at the forwarder's premises, while the actual entry can be lodged at the seaport or other entry processing unit (EPU) convenient to the forwarder.

The British International Freight Association (BIFA) represents the freight forwarding industry and incorporates the Institute of Freight Forwarders. Both organizations are committed to developing the industry and the attainment of quality control through the application of the British Standards in Quality Systems, BS5750 (p. 521). BIFA has established a Quality Assurance Manual, and also lays down trading conditions, and companies engaged in the business of moving freight for a period of not less than three years can apply for Registered Trading Membership, provided they meet the criteria laid down by the Association. Affiliated Trading Membership is also available to other firms not directly involved in the freight moving industry yet having a working relationship with the forwarder.

Circumstances giving rise to the employment of a freight forwarder by an exporter or importer include:

1. firms dealing in an unfamiliar overseas market;
2. companies endeavouring to sell under DDP terms;
3. complex shipping or customs arrangements;
4. the workload of the exporter being subject to significant peaks and troughs;
5. the exporter being a small firm which needs to concentrate on the core activity of marketing the product overseas;
6. a freight forwarder can obtain more favourable freight rates especially for groupage shipments;
7. a freight forwarder can access priority booking of cargo space on transport modes, and can provide specialist services or resources including groupage, antiques handling, perishable cargo, livestock, 'out of gauge' consignments, third party logistic operators, etc.

The exporter examining the merits of having an in-house shipping department in preference to employing a freight forwarder must consider the capital and revenue expenditure in office space and equipment; the volume of overseas business; the number of markets and their degree of similarity; the availability of suitably qualified staff; the pattern of the business and degree of seasonal variation; and the nature of the business including the degree of specialism. A detailed financial appraisal is required to make this decision.

Monitoring the performance of a freight forwarder enables the exporter to ensure the situation remains competitive. The exporter should monitor the budget against actual results in terms of price, transit time, etc.; seeking buyer and consignee opinion; undertaking test transits; and assessing the overall quality and reliability of the service and the competence and calibre of the management. Shippers, in their freight forwarder choice evaluation, should check out the viability of the forwarding company; any legal disputes; the trading conditions; the calibre of the management and their qualifications; experience of other customers; degree of technology utilized; quality of overall service; competitiveness of the tariffs; nature of the business and suitability of the equipment and resources; the company position in the market; the liability insurance maintained by the firm; and so on.

Project forwarding is a growth area of freight forwarding. It is often allied to 'turn key' projects. Project forwarding involves the despatch and conveyance arrangements which stem from a contract award. For example, a company in country A has a contract with a consortia in country B to build a factory which involves the importation of substantial quantities of merchandise, especially technical equipment. Thus a great deal of coordination, involving buyers and sellers in terms of despatch arrangements and the site construction programme, is required. These tasks can be undertaken by a forwarder who is contracted specifically for the freight movements associated with this project.

To conclude, shippers wishing to use a freight forwarder must consider in their selection and economic criteria the following:

1. membership of BIFA is highly desirable as is a BS5750 registration;
2. profile of the freight forwarder and nature of his or her business;
3. value added benefit emerging from employing the freight forwarder operations especially logistics operation;
4. alternative cost of the shipper doing the work and the requisite organization structure;
5. volume of business and any seasonal variation;
6. terms of export sales contract.

An increasing number of shippers entrust part of their business to the freight forwarder, especially spasmodic shipments to new markets, while the core of the business is undertaken in-house through their own shipping department directly with a carrier. Smaller companies with limited experience and resources tend to use a freight forwarder. Finally, the role and image of the freight forwarder is changing. An increasing number operate as an NVOCC and thereby form part of the multi-modal logistic network, especially through the European trucking system and global container network. The future of freight forwarding rests with the fast growing development as a third party logistics provider.

17.12 Management of quality: BS5750

As we progress through the millennium the dominance of 'Management of Quality' will become paramount and companies which do not have the appropriate achievement of registration, as found in BS5750, are unlikely to survive in a competitive environment. Moreover, such companies are unlikely to be successful in competitive tendering as a prerequisite will be that the successful tender has BS5750 registration.

Basically, BS5750 is a set of guidelines for the professional management of any commercial venture. It is particularly geared towards manufacturing industries; but it does encompass service industries including transport and freight forwarding; the BIFA fully endorses BS5750. Overall, BS5750 focuses attention on aspects of the organization, and its management systems and procedures, rather than the specific technicalities of the product or service. The strategy is simple: reliable and consistent assurance of quality emerging from a well-structured, professionally run company.

BS5750 is in three parts, and Part II is given below because of its relevance to the freight forwarding industry.

1. Clear policies and strategies for quality with well-defined operational and service standards.
2. Structured and effective management organization with specific allocation of responsibility for all aspects of quality management.
3. A documented quality system and operational procedures.
4. Specified methods of understanding and recording customers' service requirements and verification that the needs have been met.
5. Timely and precise control of all documentation including procedures, standard forms, paperwork systems and software. This to include the relevant communication of all revisions and amendments.
6. Knowledge of the quality abilities of suppliers and evidence that this is taken into account in purchasing decisions.
7. Establishing routines for work planning and the execution of the basic administrative and legislative systems of the business.
8. Management controls and performance measurement and corrective action.
9. Clear plans and procedures for identification and rectification of mistakes, deficiencies and causes of customer complaints.
10. A code of conduct to cover product handling, packaging, transportation and storage whenever these activities are performed within the company.
11. Pre-planned and structured senior management reviews of the major aspects of the quality system supported by formal routine auditing of all operational practices and procedures.
12. Appropriately experienced and trained personnel.
13. Records to demonstrate consistent compliance with all the foregoing issues.

Organizations in the UK which conduct the assessment and registration include the British Standards Institution (BSI), Lloyd's Register Quality Assurance Ltd (LRQA) and Bureau Veritas Quality International (BVQI). Companies, on achievement of registration, will be subject to routine annual surveillance and periodic reassessment to confirm the continued effective operation of the quality system. BS5750 also complies with International Standard ISO9000 and European Standard EN29000.

17.13 Institute of Export

The Institute of Export is a professional body founded in 1924 as the British Export Society and incorporated as the Institute of Export in 1935. The Institute's principal objective is to maintain a continuous supply of export executive staff to British industry and commerce by means of its educational activities.

Membership consists mainly of professional exporters employed in manufacturing companies, export merchant houses and other export organizations. It also extends to certain categories of brokers, civil servants, insurance officials, lawyers, shipowners, and other occupations concerned with export trade.

The objects of the Institute are detailed below:

1. To promote industry and commerce and particularly international trade in goods and services of all kinds.
2. To examine, research and analyse problems connected with industry and commerce, particularly international trade in goods and services of all kinds; to publish the results of such work together with recommendations and advice; and to make the same available to all persons, firms or companies whether or not members of the Institute.
3. To further public education with regard to commerce and industry, and particularly the need for exports and the methods of realizing the same; and further, to educate those who are or may become involved or interested in international trade in all aspects of the same.

The Institute of Export assists both its individual and company members through the medium of its employment bureau, which is officially licensed. It aims to provide candidates for job specifications in the export field.

The Institute issues an educational handbook and interested readers are advised to obtain a copy. The Institute of Export address is found in Appendix A.

17.14 International credit clubs

A number of finance houses can arrange finance through associated companies in other countries, for imports and exports between their respective countries. Credit can be arranged for all classes of durable goods for periods normally of up to two years, but for longer in special cases. Credit can also be provided to enable foreign buyers to take into stock goods imported from the UK and to hold them pending their sale.

International credit clubs, which are reciprocal agreements between leading finance houses in Europe, have also been formed to help exporters of substantial items of capital equipment so that foreign customers can obtain instalment credit finance quickly and cheaply. Similar facilities also exist in both customer and industrial hire purchase. Most of these organizations offer a number of ancillary services such as market research, shipping and forwarding advice on all matters relating to export credit.

17.15 Local buying offices

Many marketing organizations in foreign countries buy so much from UK sources that they find it financially advantageous to maintain buying offices in the UK, particularly in London. In some instances, this office may be part of a chain of buying offices covering Europe. It is usual for the buying office to look after affreightment, insurance and finance.

The advantages of a UK manufacturer dealing with a local buying office is that he or she gets a prompt acceptance of orders; saves time and costs in visiting the markets; avoids outlay on publicity; and avoids excessive correspondence with foreign markets. Against all this must be reconciled the fact that buyers 'shop around' so keenly that their prices are highly competitive, leaving little or no margin of profit for the manufacturer, while there is seldom much prospect of repeat orders. The Export Buying Offices Association address is found in Appendix A (p. 603).

17.16 Case study on developing customer relations

It is appropriate that we conclude this chapter with a case study courtesy of Alstom, the leading Anglo-French global manufacturer in engineering, on how the manufacturer is adapting to the changing needs of their customers in a global environment. This case study emphasizes the reduced product lifecycle cost, improved efficiency and greater equipment availability. Above all, it extols professionalism in the conduct and development of international trade together with the need to adapt to customer needs in the spirit of empathism.

With the growing level of privatization in power and rail utilities and the increasing level of private investment in infrastructure projects, the role of the manufacturer is changing. In addition to supplying equipment, the manufacturer must also be able to provide sophisticated services that enable customers to concentrate on their core activities. There has been an enormous change in the customer–supplier relationship. The traditional concept of carrying out corrective maintenance and unscheduled repairs has been expanded to include preventive inspections, maintenance partnerships, plant upgrading, training and joint product development.

The scale of the change is demonstrated by the fact that customer services accounted for more than 20 per cent of Alstom's turnover in 1996 and this is set to increase in the years to come. That 'entrepreneurial' customers are drawing on the full range of the Company's abilities is proving to be mutually beneficial to all concerned. By making available advances in technology and experience of the operation of similar equipment worldwide, Alstom is able to reduce the customer's operating costs.

17.16.1 Improving performance

Work carried out for Tractebel, in Belgium, at the Tihange and Doel nuclear power stations, which entered service in 1975 and 1982 respectively, was undertaken to improve the plant's competitiveness. The project involved replacing the turbine rotors with rotors built using the latest technology – not only are they more efficient but the modern rotors require maintenance at less frequent intervals. The work was carried out in just 33 days. The success of the project led to similar retrofit orders in the USA and France.

In the rail transport sector, Alstom refurbished 350 passenger cars operated by the Kowloon Canton Railway Corporation. The work included fitting extra doors to enable passengers to enter and leave more quickly. As a result, the trains will need to spend less time in each station and the service will be able to carry more passengers.

In Canada, a number of freight locomotives have been refurbished to enable them to haul passenger trains. The locomotives are being extended and auxiliary electrical generators fitted.

Environmental issues are also driving the demand for plant upgrading. At EdF's 250 MW Blénod coal-fired power plant in France, work carried out by Alstom Stein Industrie on the boiler-firing system reduced NOx emissions and increased operating efficiency.

17.16.2 Sharing experience

That operators may benefit from the experience of others is the philosophy behind the setting up of user groups such as that in China for the operators of Alstom supplied power stations and those set up by European Gas Turbines (EGT) for gas turbine operators. EGT's customers are also able to participate in product development. User group member Alex Fraser, CHP engineer at Arjo Wiggins Buckland Paper Mill in the UK says: 'I am impressed with EGT's desire to involve customers. We would like to play whatever part we can to improve and sustain the service from EGT and get our machines running to the 99 per cent target envisaged. With this in mind, I would like to encourage the trialling of mutually beneficial ideas and modifications'.

Another initiative, ECCLIDE, was developed to improve the operation of hydrogenerators but is equally applicable to other types of electrical machines. By collecting and analysing operational data, advice is provided to operators on preventive maintenance, spare parts management and technical issues.

17.16.3 Reducing costs

In the North Sea, EGT has underwritten the operation of gas turbines on five of BP's production platforms. Their 'risk and reward' contract for the Andrew platform places a percentage of the contract value at risk against agreed performance targets. The reward element is a share in the platform's profits.

Cost reduction is also one of the aims of EGT's three-year maintenance contract for the four Frame 9FA gas turbines at PowerGen's Connah's Quay power plant in the UK, one of the world's largest combined-cycle power plants.

To meet the need for a local presence, EGT set up service centres in Singapore, Argentina, Australia and the UK. Together with the use of remote diagnostics systems, the centres are able to provide the level of service customers need. Condition monitoring through the use of datalinks and remote sensing equipment is becoming commonplace and helps to reduce the risks involved with plant operation by providing an early warning should things start to go wrong and the planning of a 'fast track' for service or repair work.

It is probably in rail transport that the outsourcing of maintenance is most commonplace. According to Michel Olivier, deputy managing director of Alstom Transport Division: 'The Division's success has been brought about by its ability to carry out work at a lower cost than train service operators.' When Alstom received the order from RENFE (Spanish National Railways) for the AVE high-speed train, a maintenance unit was set up in Madrid. Alstom is paid a royalty on the basis of the number of kilometres the trains cover in service. The royalty is subject to strict reliability and availability commitments which Alstom has always met. The Madrid unit uses a computer-based system to assess the status of any vehicle or component and to provide lifecycle cost evaluations. The data obtained also contributes to product development.

Since the Madrid unit was set up, its activities have been extended to suburban trainsets and rolling stock rehabilitation. According to Juan Gasol, head of the unit: 'It is essential to work with our customers, be close to them, possess a profound knowledge of their needs and even be capable of putting ourselves in their shoes. We use the same language and have the same objectives: availability, reliability and quality. We must anticipate our customers' needs as well as those of our customers' customers.'

The need to reduce lifecycle costs has led to the development of some novel types of contracts. In the UK, the outsourcing of maintenance has largely been brought about by the privatization of British Rail and the Government's Private Finance Initiative. The demand covers both routine maintenance and overhaul and refurbishment to bring rolling stock up to standard every 10–15 years. The contract to supply London Underground with 106 trainsets for the Northern Line includes a 20-year guarantee that trains will be available for service. Alstom is also responsible for much of the trackside equipment and has taken over the line's maintenance depots. The depots have since become the most efficient on the London Underground network and this has helped Alstom to win a maintenance contract for the Jubilee Line rolling stock. But it is not only for its own products that Alstom is able to provide such services. In 1994, for example, a 10-year maintenance contract was won in Mexico for 300 diesel locomotives and 24 electric locomotives built by other manufacturers.

17.16.4 Fast response

To offer an efficient service, a supplier must be close to the customer and be able to respond quickly. Alstom New Zealand maintains a major share of the high-voltage transmission grid operated by Trans Power New Zealand. Their three-year contract is designed to encourage innovation and continuous improvement and to minimize supply disruption. The grid comprises 13 000 km of HVAC and HVDC lines, 183 sub-stations, two control centres and a telecommunications network.

Through more than 120 operating units in 40 countries, Alstom's T&D Division provides a local service based on products designed to local standards. Typical of these units is Jakarta-based PT Alstom T&D Indonesia, which specializes in the maintenance of high-voltage gas-insulated sub-stations. By keeping a safety stock of replacement parts, the Division is able to complete repairs in the shortest possible time. Customer visits play a key part in this service and provide a check on how equipment is being used, its condition and the maintenance already carried out. They enable customer satisfaction to be assessed and future maintenance needs to be defined.

The Division also offers comprehensive assistance contracts, such as that with SEP in the Netherlands covering a 400 kV sub-station. The contract not only guarantees the availability of replacement parts but, in the event of a serious fault, the despatch of a senior engineer.

Similarly, in the rail transport sector, through its GT Railway Maintenance subsidiary, Alstom maintains the signalling and electrification equipment in the Midlands, eastern England, mid-Wales and on the West Coast main line between London and Carlisle.

17.16.5 Long-standing relationship

The development of customer–supplier partnerships is not a new idea. The involvement of Alstom Engineering Systems (ESL) with the Joint European Torus (JET) project dates back to the 1970s. The project aims to prove the feasibility of nuclear fusion as a power source. Initially engaged to study and develop construction methods and procedures for the Torus and its ancillary systems, ESL now carries out routine maintenance and systems installation. The company has also provided services and equipment for most of the UK's nuclear power stations going back over the past 30 years. At Sizewell B, the UK's first PWR nuclear power station, ESL is carrying out maintenance work on the nuclear and turbine fluid systems equipment.

An illustration of the breadth of the Company's expertise is its contract with British Airport Authorities at Terminal 1 of London's busy Heathrow Airport. This covers the operation and maintenance of the airside baggage handling system and involves being on call round the clock, allocating and re-allocating flight make-up chutes, identifying baggage, monitoring the system and liaising with airlines, Heathrow's duty management and Customs and Excise.

17.16.6 Meeting objectives

The commissioning of equipment in very short timescales, either to enable production to start ahead of schedule or for emergency needs, is another aspect of customer service. Installation of three Tornado gas turbines on BP's Andrew platform in the North Sea helped production to start six months ahead of schedule and below budget. 'The way in which EGT met the challenge to provide products at minimum cost, without compromising safety or quality, in a spirit of trust and co-operation, has been quite remarkable,' says John Martin, BP's project manager. 'Andrew stands as a tribute to what can be achieved by the sheer enthusiasm and commitment of the whole team.'

In Chile, the speedy installation of four 150 MW Frame 6B gas turbines within three months of the letter of intent enabled the customer to meet 'emergency' power requirements. There are many other similar examples worldwide.

17.16.7 Training needs

Training is also an essential part of customer service. The philosophy is that well-trained engineers are able to respond to faults much faster and much better. At the T&D Division's Villeurbanne training centre in France, for example, over 70 different courses provide customers with the technological expertise needed to design sub-stations, install, operate and maintain equipment and to diagnose faults. The courses ensure that the latest technical and operational experience is readily available. More and more trainees are using the centre each year, demonstrating the confidence placed in Alstom by some of the world's largest utilities.

The evidence is clear, Alstom is no longer just an equipment supplier; it is a company dedicated to serving the customer, providing services across the full range of its activities. In the words of Juan Gasol of the Company's Transport Division: 'without our spirit of collaboration, we would be unable to achieve the success we are currently reaping.'

Recommended reading

British Chambers of Commerce, www.britishchambers.org.uk

Clarkson Research Studies, www.clarksonresearch.com

Containerisation International, www.ci-online.co.uk

Dictionary of Multi-lingual Commercial/International Trade/Shipping Terms in English/French/German/Spanish (over 10 000 entries) – e-mail books@witherbys.co.uk

EIS – country reports – 117 countries, www.store.eiu.com

Financial Times – country reports, http://news.ft.com/ftreports

Hamriyah Free Zone, www.hamriyafz.com

International Freighting weekly – country reports

International Trade, www.internationaltrade.co.uk

Japan Spotlight – bi-monthly journal, www.jef.or.jp/journal/index.html

OECD – country reports

Overseas trade, www.tradepartners.gov.uk

SITPRO, www.sitpro.org.uk

The Export Guide, www.theexportguide.co.uk

CHAPTER 18

The European Union

18.1 Introduction

When the Berlin Wall collapsed on 9th November 1989, Europe was faced with the challenge of healing the divide created by events in the first half of the Twentieth century. The European Union supported the new democracies that came into being in central and Eastern Europe and offered them the prospect of EU membership.

The enlargement of 2004 was the fifth in the history of the European Union. It was the largest ever undertaken and presented many challenges. Today, the 25 Member States have a population of over 500 million. Its citizens enjoy fundamental rights and social policies, freedom of movement and employment and share a respect for cultural and political diversity. The European Union has shown solidarity with its least prosperous regions and has developed co-operation in the areas of justice, as well as foreign, security and defence policies. The EU's principal task is to create an area of peace, freedom, and prosperity by pooling resources in those areas of public policy where concerted action is best. It has never seen itself as an exclusive rich man's club. The expansion policy since its foundation has often incorporated countries less prosperous than the original Member States, as demonstrated in 2004.

18.2 European Union strategies

The objective of creating a single 'common' market in the Former European Community dates back to the European Economic Community (EEC) Treaty (the Treaty of Rome) which established the Community in 1957. In 1985, European Community (EC) Heads of Government committed themselves to completing the Single Market progressively by 31 December 1992. Today it embraces 25 Member States and 500 million consumers.

The Single European Act came into operation on 1 July 1987 and committed the EU to the aim of progressively establishing a Single Market over a period expiring on 31 December 1992. It defines the Single Market as 'an area' without internal frontiers in which the free movement of goods, persons, services and capital is ensured in accordance with this 'Treaty'. The Single Market means a process of liberalization which allows market forces to work throughout the 25 Member States.

18.3 Organization of the European Union

There are four main Union institutions: the Commission, the Council, the Parliament and Court of Justice.

The Commission has its headquarters in Brussels and Luxembourg, and has the following functions:

1.   It proposes EU policy and legislation. It is then for the Council to discuss and, if appropriate, adopt or amend the proposals.
2.   It executes the decisions taken by the Council of Ministers, and supervises the day-to-day running of EU policies.
3.   It is the guardian of the Treaties, and can initiate action against any Member States which do not comply with EU rules.

The Commission has 25 members with one Commissioner nominated by each Member State and the portfolios being allocated by the President. The President is selected by the Member States and in common with the MEP has a five-year tenure in common with the unelected 25 commissioners – five of which are ex-vice-presidents. Each Commissioner is in charge of an area of Community policy, which embrace: competition; transport; science; research and development; justice, freedom and security; tax and customs; Agriculture and Common Agriculture Policy; regional policy; communications strategy; industry and enterprise; internal market; mergers; ante-trust and state subsidies; and trade financial institutions and company law; energy. Each Commissioner formulates proposals within his or her area of responsibility, aimed at implementing the Treaties and reflecting the President's strategies. The current President José Manuel Durâo Baraso – former Prime Minister of Portugal – plans to focus on economic reform, the free market to generate a more competitive EU and counter euro-scepticism. It is expected there will be a decline in the Franco-German influence of earlier years.

The Council is the Community's decision-making body. It agrees and adopts legislation on the basis of proposals from the Commission, and has its headquarters in Brussels. The term Council not only embraces Ministerial Meetings (the Council of Ministers), but also working groups (Council Working Groups) of officials from the Member States and the Committee of Permanent Representatives of the Member States in Brussels.

The European Parliament is a directly elected body of 738 members. Under the EU Treaties, its formal opinion is required on many proposals before they can be adopted by the Council. Members are elected for a period of five years. The secretariat of the Parliament is in Luxembourg.

The European Court of justice rules on the interpretation and application of Community laws. It has 13 judges and judgments of the Court are binding on each member country.

18.4 Single Market constituents

The creation of the Single Market involved radical changes in nine areas summarized below:

1. European standards involving the development of the 'Euro-brand' product acceptable in all 25 States.
2. Liberalization of public purchasing, with contracts being awarded on merit and not on nationalistic prejudice.
3. Liberalization of open markets in information technology and telecommunications.
4. Liberalization of financial services embracing insurance, banking and investment, securities, etc., thereby permitting freedom of capital transfer through the Community.
5. Liberalization of transport services, involving deregulation of shipping, air transport and road haulage.
6. Acceptance of professional qualifications gained in one state and recognized in the remaining States, thereby permitting freedom of labour mobility amongst the professions.
7. Abolition of state subsidies, unfair competition and restrictive agreements and abuses among companies within the market.
8. Adoption of one trade patent throughout the EU.
9. Elimination of physical barriers to trade, thereby permitting freedom of movement of goods and people across frontier points for inter-EU transits.

A commentary on each of the areas now follows.

18.5 European standards

The provision of a Euro-brand product specification acceptable in all 25 States.
Previously Member States had their own standards and laws which are important in setting quality and safety requirements for goods sold in their national home market. The standards were drawn up by national standards bodies such as the BSI. National standards have been a serious barrier to trade when different standards apply in Member States, or a bigger obstacle

when Member States do not recognize each other's arrangements for testing and certifying products to ensure that they meet national or European standards. These 'technical' barriers fragmented the market, and they add to costs by forcing producers to modify their products, or by subjecting them to different national testing and certification procedures if they wish to sell them in other Member States.

The Single Market entity permits any product which can be sold in the Member State in which it is produced to be freely marketable in all other parts of the EU, unimpeded by different national standards and testing and certification practices. It incorporates the following guidelines relative to individual products:

1. Adopt a unified level of quality and safety which products must meet within the EU.
2. Adopt common standards and specifications.
3. Accept other Member States' tests and certificates relative to products manufactured within the EU.

The Euro-brand product particularly affects the following range:

1. Machinery, personal protective equipment, construction products and toys.
2. High technology products.
3. Medicinal products.
4. Food, covering labelling, additives, foods for special dietary uses and materials, and articles in contact with food.

The implication of the Euro-brand product can be summarized as follows:

1. It enables the manufacturer to produce a product in one State and sell it throughout the remaining States without any mandatory modification. It is likely that some products will be modified to meet consumer needs or to reflect cultural tastes and territorial or climatic needs.
2. The opportunity to manufacture a product of one specification for a market of 500 million people enables the entrepreneur to exploit the economies of scale in production, distribution and servicing the market.
3. Economies of scale realized through high production and sales volume lowers unit costs, which allows flexibility in pricing strategy to aid market penetration. Companies which fail to extend their product sales to other States are likely to be less competitive in their home market than imported goods from other States at lower prices.
4. It facilitates efficiency in loadability through improved stowage conveying standardized Euro-brand products.

18.6 Public purchasing

The second area is the liberalization of public purchasing by governments and other public bodies.

In 1992 purchases by governments and other public bodies accounted for some 15 per cent of the EU's gross domestic product. The single market has resulted in public bodies buying on the basis of fair competition, not national identity, and will have particular regard to the following:

1.   Procedures are now more open: for example, through clear requirements to give information on future contracts, to stop using specifications which keep out foreign suppliers and to publish details of contracts awarded.
2.   Enforcement of procedures have been strengthened so that complaints about discrimination can be pursued effectively and action taken against those who violate the rules.

Exporters, both large and small, have good opportunities to enter such markets. It is likely that the competition will be keen but the market profile benefit will be high. Moreover, the financial risks are low and successful tenders or executed contracts can lead to offers of contracts in other states and markets outside the EU. A close monitoring service should be devised to ensure the potential exporter is able to tender. Details of such contracts are available in the trade journals and international press. Further details are available from the trade associations, Chambers of Commerce and Department of Trade and Industry www.europarl.eu.int/enlargement

18.7 Open markets in information technology telecommunications

The next area is the liberalization of the information technology and telecommunication markets.

The markets for many information technology products and services are global. The absence of a European Single Market has resulted in manufacturers having a small home base in a fragmented European market. Achieving a single competitive information and technology market in the EU gives users a wider choice, and manufacturers a large home base from which to tackle world markets.

Hitherto, each major information technology manufacturer makes equipment which operates in a particular way. No two systems are alike. The result is that users are locked into the system of a particular manufacturer from whom they must buy extra equipment to ensure that it is compatible with existing equipment and software. Moreover, in the past, Member States have tended to favour a particular national information technology supplier. This has perpetuated a multiplicity of standards in the public sector so that, in practice, most national public sector markets are far from open. Additionally, users need to know that the equipment which they are buying conforms to agreed standards. This requires recognized testing and certification procedures.

Likewise, information technology is of increasing importance in the modern economy, and the EU market for information services is one of the fastest-growing sectors. An example is the EDI system (p. 544) and its application in International Physical Distribution systems. Crucial to this is the technology which allows information to be stored in electronic form, enabling it to be accessed easily and speedily, and the existence of a modern telecommunications network which allows information to be transmitted swiftly and accurately, thus doing away with traditional paper-based systems. These new services will enable suppliers and customers to exchange orders and process documentation directly and automatically via their computers; it will allow businesses to provide new services direct to consumers through telephone links in areas such as information services, cargo reservations, cargo tracking and schedules.

The foregoing areas are subject to a liberalization of attitudes and criteria, with a view to creating a Single Market in services and equipment. It will strive to adopt common equipment standards developed in a competitive environment. Users of information technology need to choose the most efficient system. Systems must be able to work properly and be compatible with other equipment. These two targets will be met through the development of open systems and interconnection standards for computers and communication, and open purchasing with public sector purchases conforming to BSI standards.

The objectives of the Single Market entity are contained in the Commission Green Paper on telecommunications services and equipment, which includes: full liberalization of the market for terminal equipment; accelerated work on common standards; complete separation of PTT's regulatory and operational functions; full application of the competition provisions of the EU Treaty to telecommunications; a greater emphasis on the development of Europe-wide services; and a liberalized environment for point-to-point satellite telecommunications. It will bring a new era through EDI for international distribution in the EU.

18.8 Financial services

The liberalization of financial services is an important area in the realization of a single market concept.

The creation of a Single Market, however, goes beyond rights or establishment and assumes the right to do business throughout the EU across national frontiers, without the necessity of physically locating in all Member States. Developments in new technology and systems of electronic transfer has increased the opportunities of doing business in this way, and the concern is that national restrictions should not prevent companies from taking advantage of them. This involves the liberalization of capital movements and the creation of a European financial area as follows.

1.   The liberalization of all capital movements, subject to a safeguard clause permitting temporary controls to be reimposed in certain specified circumstances.
2.   A requirement that monetary authorities in Member States be permitted to put certain controls into operation immediately, without enabling measures.
3.   The establishment of a single facility providing medium-term financial support for any Member State's balance of payments.

In the area of securities, common requirements have been established for the authorization of collective investment schemes such as unit trusts. With regard to insurance, EU insurers are able to cover the risk of potential policyholders in any Member State irrespective of where the insurer is established. It provides a more liberal regime for large commercial and industrial risk, including all marine, aviation and transport business.

To conclude, freedom to transfer capital throughout the EU is essential for a Single Market in financial services. The objective was to remove restrictions on the movement of capital. It will result in no restrictions on raising finance in other countries or on the cross-border transfer of funds.

18.9 Transport services

The deregulation of shipping, road and air transport has much potential to improve transport utilization and, in so doing, reduce cost to the user.

Hitherto some Member States required hauliers to have permits which limited the total number of journeys they could operate in a year; such restrictions have been lifted.

In the area of shipping, liberalization operates on competition and unfair pricing practices, phasing out unilateral cargo reservation and deregulates coastal services.

The completion of the Channel Tunnel provides opportunities, through quicker travel by rail, to open up extensive tourist and trade markets. Overland rail freight services will provide quick, cheap and reliable services between the UK and major industrial and commercial centres in Europe.

Civil aviation also benefits from liberalization, which in this instance embraces the following:

1.   The potential for a cheaper and less restrictive fares structure in off-peak periods.
2.   Potential of a more competitive economy and business fares which may run counter to other airlines on the route.

3. Permission for airlines to offer increased route capacity to meet market needs.
4. All major air routes have been opened up to direct competition between airlines.
5. Traffic rights have been made available on as many as 60 new routes out of the UK.
6. The opportunity to have a more economic operation by combining two or more routes into a single multi-stop service.
7. To establish a mechanism for scrutinizing potentially inter-competitive interline agreements.

The liberalization of the EU transport system will facilitate a cheaper and more extensive transport infrastructure to meet consumer demand (p. 541). This is essential to wealth creation. Exporters, as they develop their business throughout the EU, must review: their distribution systems; location of warehouse and distribution centres; the ideal location for manufacturing centres; and plan for the most effective distribution system compatible with market needs in a very competitive environment. It will encourage the Districentre concept (pp. 108–09) and permit a shorter and quicker supply chain concept, also involving just-in-time (JIT) working. Also the direct supplier/buyer relationship development eliminates the intermediaries.

18.10 The professions

The freedom of establishment for the professions is established in the EU Treaty. It recognizes the freedom of movement for people to work throughout the EU.
   The adoption is intended of a system of mutual recognition of 'higher education diplomas' – i.e. professional qualifications so that everyone is able to practise their profession throughout the Community.
   The outcome of such recognition of professional qualification throughout the EU will stimulate labour mobility, especially among people in the 20–35 age bracket and with good linguistic ability. Moreover, it will facilitate the development of multinational workforces throughout the community in all the professions.

18.11 Competition and state subsidies

The abolition of state subsidies, unfair competition and restrictive practices and abuses.
   The EU competition policy has been designed to ensure that trade between Member States takes place on the basis of free and fair competition. It is one of the basic principles in the EU Treaty that the EU provides a system ensuring that competition in the common market is not distorted.

Powers and procedures enabling the Commission to enforce these rules in all areas except transport were laid down in 1962. These were extended to cover inland transport in 1968, to maritime transport in 1986, and to intra-EU air services in 1987.

18.12 Intellectual property

The laws governing intellectual property (patents, industrial designs, trademarks and copyright) are in one sense a derogation from the operation of the free market, intended to stimulate innovation. Firms can recoup their investment in technical or design improvements by having the right, for a limited time, to prevent imitation by others who have made no such investment. Firms can also protect the reputation and goodwill which they have built up by registering their trade or service marks, so obtaining the right to prevent others from using them.

While the EU Treaty prohibits restrictions on imports and exports between Member States, restrictions are allowable where they are justified 'for the protection of industrial or commercial property'. For example, the proprietor of a UK patent can use the rights which it gives him to prevent goods produced elsewhere in the EU from being imported or sold in the UK.

None of this, however, allows the owners of intellectual property rights to use them to divide up the market. Once the goods have been put on the market in the EU by the owner, or with his consent, he cannot prevent them from being reimported or resold. In other words, intellectual property rights cannot be used to reinforce a policy of differential pricing within the EU.

18.13 Physical barriers to trade

Physical barriers to trade involve the imposition of cross-frontier controls relative to persons and goods undertaken by immigration and customs.

Many steps have been taken to make trade easier across EU frontiers. The elimination of customs duties between Member States has been one of the foundations of the Common Market. Less obvious, but nevertheless important, has been the continuing process of administrative harmonization and simplification which is bringing Member States' arrangements gradually into line.

Many of these steps are technical in nature and deal with matters of detail. Individually their effect can therefore be small, but over time their cumulative impact has been substantial.

An EU Customs Code is another important step in providing a comprehensive framework for EU customs law, and promoting procedural harmonization (pp. 249–52). This area is fully dealt with in Chapter 9.

18.14 Conclusion

To conclude our review of the Single Market entity the exporter must consider the following aspects:

1. Examine current physical distribution, channels of distribution and market strategy and develop policies which will increase volume sales and thereby lower unit costs, improve market dominance and aid profitability.
2. Analyse closely the market throughout the Member States, identify major competitors and endeavour to determine their overall strategy in the Single Market. Use the web extensively (pp. 453–56).
3. Undertake a SWOT (strengths, weaknesses, opportunities and threats) analysis of the exporter's company (product(s), physical distribution and service(s)).
4. Review the option of a merger and acquisition policy. Enter negotiations with a merchant bank who can give guidance in this area. Merger and acquisition will increase a company's size and market dominance, increase cash flow and competitiveness, lower unit cost, develop market penetration, enlarge customer portfolio, increase skills, develop volume-oriented physical distribution networks and so on. The option may exist to merge with, or acquire a company with, an identical product or service, or something complementary, and of the same market profile. This may be, for example, a greenhouse manufacturer merging with a garden furniture company, or developing a working collaborative relationship.
5. Critically review personnel resources, logistics, EDI and their adequacy. This may involve retraining, recruitment, etc.
6. Review the distribution arrangements with a logistic focus. This should be geared to a five-year marketing plan.
7. Critically review the product mix and its adequacy in the market. Ensure it features modern technology and adequately research the market to ensure the product is consumer-led.
8. Formulate an action plan and identify one person at least in the company to coordinate and develop the Single Market strategy today embracing 25 States. Such a position should be at senior level.

Additional impacts of the 1992 Single Market entity include increased competition (with lower unit cost), higher standards, greater labour mobility, greater job opportunities, new markets through previously closed procurement areas, more technology and cheaper distribution.

A key area for the future will be physical distribution and devising strategies to achieve improved cost-effectiveness per product/tonne distributed. It will also be important to improve the supply chain timescale and set up distribution centres in key industrial areas. The concepts of just-in-time (pp. 124–46), EDI technology (pp. 446–53), multi-modalism (pp. 114–23) and Districentres (pp. 108–09) will all play a very decisive part.

To the great majority of companies the change will be very radical and profound. Personnel entrusted to lead, develop and execute such changes must be of high calibre and professionally qualified with good linguistic skills and an understanding, and experience, of the differing cultures of each of the 25 countries. Infrastructure will play a major role in the development of the Single Market and the residue countries emerging from the EEA. It will require an ongoing analysis and good market research and control skills to ensure the distribution networks are further improved and developed.

To conclude, the combined EU/EFTA reflected in the EEA will present a new era of opportunity both for its Member States and the global markets. It will provide new opportunities for the company and entrepreneur, both within the EEA and outside it, to develop their exporting skills and take advantage of the Single Market with enormous wealth and the Euro-brand single specification supported by a good infrastructure.

18.15 Customs policy of the EU

The Customs Union is an essential element of the European Union single market of 25 Member States. It has four basic freedoms: the free circulation of goods, persons, services and capital. Its aims are to foster world trade; to promote fair trade; to increase the attractiveness of the EU as a location for industry/trade and create new jobs; to promote development elsewhere; to assist candidates for accession in their future role; to 'ring fence' the single market securing maximum benefit from it for everybody; to collect essential statistics on trade; to ensure protection for the Community's Citizens and business in all areas involving imports or exports; and to collect revenue, customs duties, VAT and excise duties.

The mechanism/documentation/regulation of EU Customs is examined in Chapter 9 (pp. 249–52). A high priority is paperless trading with adequate safeguards.

18.16 European Union transport policy

The enlarged European Union is very conscious of the need to develop and sustain an integrated transport network compatible with the challenges of the twenty-first century. It emerges from the Treaty of Rome in 1957 which committed all Member States to a common transport policy. Regretfully, little has been achieved and a white paper on European transport policy for 2010 was published in 2001.

It outlines a programme of over 60 measures. These embraced revitalizing the railways, promoting transport by sea and inland waterways, developing intermodality, building a trans-European transport network and introducing the concept of 'sea motorways', developing airport capacity and linking the outlying regions on the European continent more effectively and connecting the networks of the ten new Member States.

An interesting development is the launch of the Galileo programme which involves an array of 30 satellites covering the entire planet with local ground transmitters to provide universal services available to all users in any location including sheltered areas (tunnels, underground car parks, etc). The Galileo programme has four phases: study phase 2001; development/test phase for first satellites 2001–05; development phase of 30 satellites 2006–07; and operational phase from 2008 onwards. It is being managed by the European Space Agency. Hence, by 2008 it will provide the EU with a system of global cover over which it will have full control and which will meet its accuracy, reliability and security requirements. It will thus have at its disposal a tool essential to its transport development policy. For example, it will be possible using Galileo instantly to trace goods carried on the railway network, facilitating the development of just-in-time policy. Galileo will permit highly accurate positioning of ships carrying dangerous cargoes and give the maritime authorities the means to ensure safe navigation, particularly in areas of high traffic density such as the Ushant TSS. Galileo could revolutionize transport facilitating logistic development and professional management.

The outcome of the programme will develop/accelerate EU economic development with a greater global focus.

18.17 Inter-governmental organizations

It is paradoxical that the EU which is the world's leading commercial power and conducts a large part of its trade outside its own borders, is excluded from most intergovernmental organizations where it has no more than observer status. The EU has built up a considerable body of law during the past decade, especially in air and sea transport. It has adopted specific regulations which do not always coincide with the recommendations and agreements made in international organizations. In late 2001, the EU embarked on a strategy to exert influence in the international organizations which deal with shipping and civil aviation. Hence, negotiations commenced for the EU to become full members of the International Civil Aviation Organization (ICAO) and International Maritime Organisation (IMO). This can be extended to include the Rhine Navigation Commission, the Danube Commission and Euro-control. Currently, most EU Member States are members of IMO and ICAO representing their Government's political/economic strategies. An example of the EU higher profile in global transport is the Galileo programme in the field of satellite radio navigation.

18.18 EU market access strategy

The EU market access strategy has become one of the pillars of European Trade policy. Through a continuous three-way exchange of information between EU institutions, Member States and the European business, the EU has been able to pursue a proactive dialogue with all its major trading partners in the appropriate bilateral and multilateral form in order to reduce the many obstacles facing European exporters of goods and services.

The composition of trade is changing. Trade in services continues to expand in importance relative to the traditional exchanges of goods. Nevertheless, obstacles to trade remain and assume a new character as domestic regulation changes its focus. Issues such as third countries restrictions on investment and repatriation of profits, or inadequate protection of intellectual property rights, or differing national health, safety, environment and consumer protection standards in third country markets have become important to the wellbeing of the European economy.

The EU market access strategy can help exporters in the following four areas:

(a)   Provide basic information to business on conditions for exporting to and investing in key third country markets via the Market Access Database available via the Internet.
(b)   Follow up complaints received from businesses about barriers to third countries whether in the WTO (p. 577–79) or in bilateral consultations with the countries concerned.
(c)   Ensure EU trading partners effectively comply with their international commitments.
(d)   Contribute to the creation of a suitable framework for international trade.

The EU Market Access Database has the following three functions:

(a)   To list all trade barriers affecting European exports by sector and by country and to ensure systematic follow-up and action for every single barrier identified.
(b)   To provide basic information of interest to European exporters: the rate of duty for individual products, validity of patents in specified countries, import licence obligation and any special customs clearance formalities.
(c)   Interactive means of communication between business and the European Authorities allowing an exchange of information online.

The Market Access Database contains the following main sections: sectoral and trade barriers, applied tariffs, exporters guide to import formalities, services, WTO, and WTO bound tariffs.

The services covered include general trading conditions, economical and political developments, aircraft, automotive, ceramics and glass-chemicals, pharmaceuticals, electronics, mining, iron, steel and non-ferrous metals, machinery, wood, paper and pulp, shipbuilding, telecommunications equipment, textiles and leather, agriculture and fisheries, other industries, intellectual property and service including business, communications, construction, distribution, financial, tourism and travel, transport and others.

The service embraces over 100 countries and is available free on http://www.mkaccdb.eu.int

18.19 EU membership conditions

Before a country can contemplate the possibility of joining the EU, it must demonstrate that it satisfies the three basic membership criteria laid down at the Copenhagen Summit in June 1993. These are as follows:

(a) The existence of stable institutions guaranteeing democracy, the rule of law, human rights and respect for and protection of minorities.
(b) The existence of a functioning market economy as well as the capacity to cope with competitive pressure and market forces within the Union.
(c) The ability to take on the obligations of membership, including adherence to the aims of political, economic and monetary union.

New members have to accept and apply the EU body of law known as *'acquis communautaire'*: respect for human rights, democracy and rule of law are at least as important as economic cohesion.

Bulgaria and Romania are leading contenders to joint the EU in 2007 followed by Croatia in 2008.

18.19.1 EU enlargement

On 1st May 2004, ten new Member States joined the EU: Cyprus, the Czech Republic, Estonia; Hungary, Latvia, Lithuania, Malta, Poland, Slovakia and Slovenia. Eight of them are former Central and Eastern European markets that bring 74 million new consumers into the EU. The 25 Member States have a population of approximately 500 million and have become the largest single market for trade and investment in the world, bigger than USA and Japan combined. It is expected the economies of the new Member States will grow faster than the EU average for several years after accession. New members in the early years of membership may experience accession restrictions (p. 557).

18.20 European Member States

A brief analysis of the 25 Member States is given below:

Austria: Population 8.1 million, GDP US$189 billion, EU member 1995.

Austria annual growth rate in period 1991–2001 was 2.2 per cent. It has a mixed economy and its major trading partners are Germany, Italy, USA and France. The service sector contributed 68 per cent to the GDP, compared with industry 30 per cent and agriculture 3 per cent. Main imports were machinery and transport equipment, consumer goods, chemicals and raw materials. It is a member of the euro-zone.

Belgium: Population 10.3 million, GDP US$230 billion, EU member 1951.

A founding member of the EU, Belgium has had a significant influence on its development during the past 50 years. It has a mixed stable economy with 74 per cent of its GDP originating from the service sector, compared with 24 per cent from industry and 1 per cent from agriculture. It has a good infrastructure and high population density per square kilometre. It has strong trading ties with its neighbouring countries including UK. Main imports to Belgium include machinery and transport, manufactures and chemicals. Some 70 per cent of its trade is within the EU.

Cyprus: Population 642 000, GDP CY£6.2 billion, EU member 2004.

Cyprus is classified among the high income countries. These achievements appear all the more striking bearing in mind the severe economic and social dislocation created by the Turkish intervention of 1974 and their continuing occupation of the North of Cyprus. Since 1974 there has been a de facto partition of the island with the Turkish Cypriot community in the north and the Greek Cypriots in the south. Imports to Cyprus include electrical machinery, apparatus, appliances and parts, office machinery, computers and data processing equipment, and specialist industrial machinery, equipment and parts.

Czech Republic: Population 10.4 million, GDP US$69.5 billion, EU member 2004.

The Czech Republic is the most Westernized and most affluent of the former Warsaw Pact countries of Central Europe. The country came into being following the dissolution of the Czechoslovak Federation in 1993. It has a Western-style democracy, a well-educated populace and a skilled work force. The country's social and economic system has changed dramatically since 1993. Privatization has transformed the country from a centrally-planned into a free market economy. Over 15 per cent of the population has access to the Internet. Imports to Czech Republic include electrical machinery, apparatus, appliances and parts, office machinery, computers and data processing equipment, industrial machinery, equipment and parts and road vehicles. Some 65 per cent of its trade is within the EU.

Denmark: Population 5.3 million, GDP US$161.5 billion, EU member 1973.

Denmark's economy has been focused in trade terms on neighbouring countries Germany, Sweden and Norway, plus the United Kingdom. The culture is renowned globally for its design skills reflected in its products. Its annual growth rate during period 1991–2001 was 2.2 per cent. The mixed economy is strong and supports a strong national currency (Danish Krone). The service industry is 77 per cent of GDP, compared with industry 26 per cent and agriculture 2 per cent. The agricultural sector is intensive like the Netherlands, and it has a strong global and EU market for its food brands. Major imports include intermediate goods, consumer goods and capital goods. Some 65 per cent of its trade is within the EU.

Estonia: Population 1.36 million, GDP US$6.0 billion, EU member 2004.

It is more than ten years since Estonia regained its independence since when the country has made remarkable progress towards a full market economy. Inflation remains low and the economic outlook is favourable. The country has been built on a liberal foreign trade regime, liberalization of prices, fast privatization and effective bankruptcy legislation. Foreign investment is high. Major imports to Estonia include electrical machinery, specialized machinery and textile yarn and fabrics.

Finland: Population 5.2 million, GDP US$120.9 billion, EU member 1995.

The Finnish economy is focused on services – 70 per cent of GDP, compared with 30 per cent industry and 4 per cent agriculture. Inflation is low at 1.8 per cent and it is a stable economy. Imports to Finland embrace raw materials, consumer goods and capital goods.

France: Population 59.9 million, GDP US$1310 billion, EU member 1951.

In common with Germany, a leading trading nation both globally and with the EU. An excellent infrastructure and mixed economy in industry and services. Some 71 per cent of the economy of its GDP is focused on services, 25 per cent on industry, and agriculture 3 per cent. An economy with a strong nationalistic culture. French food products are world renowned – wine, cheese etc. Exporters to France are expected to be fluent in French to develop market penetration/acceptance. The Franco-German influence in the development of the EU since 1951 has been formidable, but this may be less so following the new president in 2004 – José Manuel Durâ Baroso and the enlargement to 25 States. Imports to France feature intermediate goods, capital goods, consumer goods and motor vehicles. Some 60 per cent of its trade is within the EU.

Germany: Population 82 million, GDP US$1846 billion, EU member 1951 (and 1990).

Germany is one of the leading nations of the EU and globally. A founder member in 1951 and much enlarged with the reunification of

Germany in 1990. The economy has 68 per cent of its GDP from services, compared with 30 per cent industry and 1 per cent agriculture. It has a strong economy though unemployment is relatively high at 8–10 per cent. Living standards are high. It has a good infrastructure and German manufactured goods are regarded as high quality and hi-tech. Principal imports to Germany include chemicals, road vehicles, machinery and telecoms technology.

Great Britain: Population 59 million, GDP US$1424 billion, EU member 1973.

Great Britain is a leading trade country globally and within the EU and has a mixed economy supporting its stable national currency, sterling, a leading worldwide currency in strong competition with the US$, Yen and Euro. It has low unemployment and a strong service sector. Overall, services contributed 71 per cent to GDP, compared with industry 27 per cent and agriculture 1 per cent. The country is computer literate and has an industrial base of many global brands. Annual growth in period 1991–2001 was 2.7 per cent, well above other leading EU States. It has strong trading ties with the Commonwealth, USA and EU Member States, especially Germany, France and Netherlands. Main imports include finished manufactured goods, semi-manufactured goods and food, beverages and tobacco. Overall, 55 per cent of its trade is within the EU.

Greece: Population 10.6 million, GDP US$117.2 billion, EU member 1981.

The Greek economy is service focused – 67 per cent of its GDP compared with 8 per cent in agriculture and 24 per cent in industry. It is a maritime nation and has a strong tourist industry. Inflation is at 3.8 per cent and it is a member of the euro-zone. Imports to Greece include machinery, transport equipment and chemicals. Some 55 per cent of its trade is within the EU.

Hungary: Population 10 million, GDP US$65.8 billion, EU member 2004.

During the past decade Hungary has made the transition from one party state and largely command economy to multi-party democracy and market economy. After two years of low economic growth and falling domestic consumption in 1995 and 1996, the Hungarian economy has staged an impressive foreign investment-led recovery with a 5.2 per cent GDP growth in 2000. This is likely to continue. Manufacturing output and productivity has improved since 1998. Many industries have received considerable foreign investment from a growing number of multinationals which see the country as a stable base for a wide range of activities. Successive Hungarian Governments have pursued a policy of privatization and deep reconstruction of traditional industries with the result that over 80 per cent of the economy is now privately owned. Imports to Hungary feature machinery and transport equipment, food and beverages, power generating equipment, road vehicles and medical and pharmaceutical products.

Italy: Population 57.5 million, GDP US$1089 billion, EU member 1951.

A founding member of the EU, Italy has a strong mixed economy and is a leading global trading and EU nation. It is renowned for its global and EU brand products with focus on design and food products. It has a strong tourist industry in all regions, like France. It has relatively high unemployment (10 per cent) and an annual growth of 1.5 per cent. Northern Italy remains industrial and central Italy commercial. The service sector totals 67 per cent of GDP, compared with 30 per cent industry and 5 per cent agriculture. Imports to Italy are engineering products, transport equipment, chemicals and textiles and clothing. Some 55 per cent of its trade is within the EU.

Latvia: Population 2.37 million, GDP US$8.4 billion, EU member 2004.

Substantial changes have taken place in the economy of Latvia since the regaining of independence in 1991. Private property dominates the ownership structure. Foreign trade and prices are almost fully liberalized and the majority of institutions needed for functioning of the market economy have been established. Imports to Latvia include tobacco and tobacco manufacture, telecommunications and sound equipment, textile yarn, fabrics, made-up articles and specialized industrial machinery.

Lithuania: Population 3.5 million, GDP US$12.7 billion, EU member 2004.

Lithuania has the fastest growing economy among all three Baltic States – the growth rate is expected to remain at 6.5 per cent in the coming years. The restructuring and privatization of the energy sector remains the major task. Gas privatization is underway, but issues over oil and gas and nuclear power have yet to be resolved. Imports to Lithuania include textile yarn, fabrics, made-up articles, telecommunications and sound recording, articles of apparel and clothing accessories, and road vehicles.

Luxembourg: Population 435 000, EU member 1957.

One of the smallest EU Member States and one of the six original members formed from the European Coal and Steel Community in 1951. It has a stable economy and much of its trade is with its neighbouring countries.

Malta: Population 397 000, GDP US$3.9 billion, EU member 2004.

Malta has a small agricultural sector, few natural resources and a small fishing industry. The island is developing its economy through tourism and export-dedicated manufacture. Imports to Malta embrace transport equipment, electrical machinery, general industrial machinery, medicinal and pharmaceutical products, paper, paperboard and other articles of paper pulp.

Netherlands: Population 15.9 million, GDP US$380.1 billion, EU member 1951.

A founder member of the EU it has had a significant impact on the development of the EU spanning 50 years. The country has benefited from the strategic geographic location of the Port of Rotterdam regarded by many as the gateway to Europe. It has an excellent infrastructure and a high population density of 383 per square kilometre. The mixed economy is strong with an annual growth rate of 2.7 per cent in 1991–2001. The service sector totals 71 per cent of GDP, compared with 25 per cent for industry and 3 per cent agriculture – much of which is under intensive horticultural farming techniques. Major imports include machinery and transport equipment, chemicals and fuels. Over 60 per cent of its trade is within the EU.

Poland: Population 38.63 million, GDP US$189.3 billion, EU member 2004.

The early 1990s brought essential changes in the geographical structure of Polish foreign trade following the collapse of COMECON in 1989. Economic and political reforms in recent years have significantly transformed the country. Since 1989 a market economy has been introduced which has produced some of the best rates of GDP growth in Europe in the middle 1990s. In 2002, EU countries' share in Polish exports amounted to 70 per cent. Sectors which attracted the most foreign capital in 2002 were manufacturing, financial services, trade and repairs. Imports to Poland feature road vehicles, electrical machinery apparatus and appliances/parts, medicinal and pharmaceutical products, office machinery, telecoms and sound recording and reproducing apparatus.

Portugal: Population 10 million, GDP US$109.9 billion, EU member 1986.

Portugal is less economically developed than Spain, but has grown in economic development through EU membership. It has a mixed economy with 52 per cent of GDP representing services, compared with 35 per cent industrial and 13 per cent agriculture. Its major trading partners are Spain, Germany, France, Italy and the UK. Major imports include capital goods, raw materials and semi-manufactured and consumer goods.

Republic of Ireland: Population 3.8 million, GDP US$103.3 billion, EU member 1973.

Ireland has been a major beneficiary of EU grants to develop its infrastructure and facilitate the change from an agricultural-focused economy to one of industrial and service sectors. The GDP comes 49 per cent from the service sector compared with 29 per cent from industry and 7 per cent from agriculture. The annual growth rate 1995–2001 was 8 per cent and employment opportunities much improved. The country retains much of its culture and charm and has strong trading links with USA and UK. Main imports to Ireland include machinery, transport equipment, chemicals and manufactured materials. Some 60 per cent of its trade is within the EU.

Slovakia: Population 5.37 million, GDP US$23.7 billion, EU member 2004.

In 1993 Czech and Slovakia became two independent states. The Czech Republic is still Slovakia's major foreign trade partner and a customs union between the two states remains in force. Politically and economically the Slovak Republic has had an uneasy childhood and the country has had to introduce a central administration, central banking, monetary and tax system. The government had pegged economic recovery on foreign direct investment. Imports to Slovakia include electrical machinery, apparatus/appliances and parts, office machines and automatic data processing equipment, textile yarn, fabrics, made-up articles and products, and medical and pharmaceutical products. Over 50 per cent of its trade is within the EU.

Slovenia: Population 2 million, GDP US$18.8 billion, EU member 2004.

Slovenia is one of Central Europe's most economically advanced countries with a long industrial tradition and a steady economic growth. In 1998 its GDP was more than twice that of any other country in the region. GDP annual growth is 4 per cent. Slovenia exports are mainly manufactured goods. Imports are raw materials, food and semi-finished products. It has good management and technological/technical expertise and skilled labour force. Its long industrial tradition with technological capacities facilitates fast implementation of foreign technology and know-how. Slovenia has an investor-friendly legal framework whereby overseas companies taking capital participation have the same rights and obligations as other Slovenian companies. Imports to Slovenia include machinery and transport equipment, manufactures, chemicals and mineral fuels. Over 60 per cent of its trade is within the EU.

Spain: Population 39.9 million, GDP US$581.8 billion, EU member 1986.

Spain joined the EU in 1986 together with Portugal. Benefiting from the era of a democratic state and EU membership it has transformed the economy to one of stability and growth. It is a Euro-zone member and has a mixed economy. The service sector – primarily tourism – represents 66 per cent of GDP compared with 30 per cent industrial and 4 per cent agriculture. Like Italy, it has a buoyant agricultural industry. Major imports are raw materials and intermediate products, consumer goods and capital goods. Overall, some 65 per cent of its trade is within the EU.

Sweden: Population 8.8 million, GDP US$209.9 billion, EU member 1995.

Sweden joined the EU in 1995 with Finland and Austria. It has a strong mixed economy and like Denmark sustains its natural currency, the Swedish Krone. Annual growth of 1.7 per cent during period 1991–2001 has been modest. The GDP service contribution is 69 per cent compared with 29 per cent industry and 2 per cent agriculture. Major imports are machinery and transport, manufactured goods, chemicals and miscellaneous manufactures. Its major trading partners are identical to Denmark. Some 60 per cent of its trade is within the EU.

18.21 Euro currency

On 1 January 1999 a single European currency – the euro – was introduced in 12 European Union countries together with the formation of an economic and monetary union. The 12 countries in the euro-zone include Austria, Belgium, Finland, France, Germany, Greece, Ireland, Italy, Luxembourg, the Netherlands, Portugal and Spain. It has resulted in a real change to the business environment throughout Europe. The 12 countries also share a single interest rate set by the European Central Bank and a single foreign exchange rate policy. The European Central Bank, based in Frankfurt, is responsible for the monetary policy for these euro-zone countries involving a total population of 300 million. Monetary policy decisions are taken by the ECBs Governing Council which consists of six Executive Board members plus the presidents of the national central banks of the 12 Member States.

The Euro has produced the following benefits and features:

(a) Cheaper transaction costs – countries in the euro-zone do not have to change currencies when doing business.

(b) Stability of exchange rates resulting in countries in the euro-zone no longer being affected by currency fluctuations when trading with each other.

(c) Transparent price differences – it has become more obvious when different euro-zone countries charge different prices for the same goods and services.

(d) Companies operating in Europe have simplified their accounts and finances by trading in the euro not only in the euro-zone of 12 States, but also in other countries outside the euro-zone embracing the 13 other States in the European Union and also other European non-EU member countries. This extends to budgetary financial management and has resulted in much tighter and more realistic financial controls and disciplines following the removal of cross-border currency risk fluctuations.

(e) Companies situated outside the euro-zone but part of the European Union trade in the euro both as importer and exporter. This produces a competitive advantage in securing business as product price comparisons will be in the euro, leading to intensified competition.

(f) Importers and exporters throughout Europe gain from using the euro as bank charges have fallen and payments have been speeded up.

(g) Businesses have experienced fewer legal problems with the euro in price agreements – this was more prevalent in the national currencies.

(h) Cross-border competition has increased, placing companies outside the euro-zone in a less favourable position against competitors within the zone who share the same currency within a single market environment.

(i) The euro has created an impetus for cross-border mergers and other joint ventures. This is particularly evident with companies in the euro-zone who share the same currency thereby making the merger and joint ventures rather easier.

(j) Distribution and procurement within the euro-zone has become simpler and cheaper because companies do not undergo any exchange rate risk when trading.

(k) Raising finance has become easier and more attractive in the euro-bond and euro-equity share market. Hitherto, the national currencies embraced one country whereas the euro extends to 12 countries thereby spreading the risk under the management of an economic and monetary union through the European Central Bank which controls the interest rate level.

(l) Companies have found it necessary to re-focus their marketing and product sourcing strategies to combat opportunities and threats emerging from the transparency of euro pricing with no exchange risk implication and greater price stability compared with the national currency.

(m) Companies worldwide who export into the euro-zone tend to trade in the euro. This enables the buyer to draw price comparisons from other sources both within the Eurozone and outside it. Moreover, any currency risk fluctuation would arise with the seller based outside the euro-zone.

(n) The development of computerized technology provides a further aid to stimulate the economic growth of the euro-zone, particularly trade within the zone. It has reduced any culture or management cross-border barriers and provides market and business confidence, with the euro and the European Central Bank influenced by determining a common interest rate throughout the euro-zone.

(o) It has strongly favoured a logistic strategy as geographical borders are broken down.

(p) The impact on domestic businesses has been immense and through computer technology: more B2B and B2C is being conducted.

(q) Overall, the euro is encouraging an integrated single market through reduced currency transaction costs, new price differentials and greater transparency.

(r) It is driving a more integrated transport system as state run transport networks, especially rail and air, come to terms with a trans-european transport network strategy (p. 541).

(s) Companies are viewing the euro-zone as a single sourcing zone to build and develop their business with no currency risk within the euro-zone, complete transparency, currency stability and fast developing logistic network. A computer literate euro-zone is facilitating these developments.

(t)   Traders recognize the stringent financial budgetary disciplines and monitoring systems in place within the euro-zone and supervized by the ECB directorate in consultation with the presidents of the national central banks of the 12 member euro-zone states.

Emerging from the benefits and features of the Euro, a number of practical issues arise for the trader which we will now examine.

(a)   *Competitor analysis.* Cross border competition brought about by transparency of pricing, common product specification throughout EU, and removal of transaction costs, not only means significant market penetration opportunities to traders, but also threats from European companies expanding into new markets. Accurate comparison of the price of goods and services means that many businesses are now finding they are no longer able to compete on price alone. Equally, businesses that choose to source their supplies from the euro-zone may find they can significantly reduce their own input costs.

(b)   *Market research and product development.* Undertaking proper research into the relevant market sectors will identify whether a potential opportunity can be exploited. Equally, products and services offered may need to be developed or adapted in order to appeal to potential new buyers.

(c)   *Pricing and profitability.* Traders may need to examine whether or not they can sustain their customer base against prices being offered by competitors in the euro-zone over the long-term. For example, price pointing, the level at which goods and services are offered, can have a significant impact on sales. Research confirms the need to quote in euros in the zone and not in a country's national currency such as sterling, US$ or yen when exporting to the euro market. An important factor in business planning.

(d)   *Fixed assets.* The euro may have a significant impact on the book value of certain fixed assets.

(e)   *Conversion and rounding rules.* Rounding rules for euro conversion dictate the decimal points at which businesses round sterling up or down. They may have a significant impact on profitability, particularly when clients are importing or exporting in large quantities.

(f)   *Data pollution and dual display.* Ensure the appropriate systems and training are in place to ensure that staff avoid data pollution between domestic currencies and the euro.

(g)   *Multi-currency software.* Ensure the software is multi-currency thereby eradicating any manual conversion to the euro.

(h)   *New software packages.* Ensure new software packages have a euro focus and are compatible with other organizations.

Today, the euro is a major world currency competing with the US$, yen and sterling. Annually, the dominance of the euro-zone grows in the global environment. The enlargement of the EU as a single market will enhance its growth and dominance/influence in the politics and strategies of globalization logistics will play a significant part.

18.22 Strategic analysis of the Single Market

Today the Single Market has 25 members and came into effect from 1 January 1993. The 25 members have a total population of 500 million.

The successful international entrepreneur today is very conscious of targeting and sourcing markets which are competitively focused with low risk, ease of access and which are logistically and computer literate. This is particularly relevant in fast moving consumer goods (fmcg) with a limited product lifecycle and high development cost, which must be recouped in high volume sales with realistic profit margins to meet the return on the investment.

The single market has a range of features in its trade structure: these include common core product specification and limited local customized needs in terms of packaging, size of product to meet social and technical requirements, advertising reflecting the local protocol and value added benefit of the product or service to the user and consumer and the environment in which the product or service will be used. It favours strongly a logistics-driven computer-focused strategy.

It will be recalled that to achieve the maximum benefits of the Single Market the goods must be manufactured and produced in the Member States to enable the goods to be transported in free circulation without any customs import duty. However, many Multi-National Enterprises (MNEs) set up assembly or distribution centres in the EU and conduct their EU business from this focal point through online computer access. The goods may be raw materials or products in a partially or completely finished condition enabling the MNE or SME to add value to it, thereby customizing the product. This focal point is called a Free Trade Zone which is free of any custom duty until the goods leave the zone to the retailer or consumer.

Such an area is found in the Distriparks of Rotterdam (see pp. 108–09) whereby, for example, the warehouses accommodate various spices from countries in the Far East such as Thailand. The spice is received in bulk in containers and stored in the warehouses. Each warehouse has online computer access to major distributors and clients throughout the single market. Orders are received daily and executed in accordance with the clients needs, involving packaging and quantity and quality control in accordance with retailers' and consumers' language regulations, the relevant mix of the spices and all relevant documentation. Such Far East Trading Houses and Companies are able to import the goods in bulk and on payment of the import duty are permitted to distribute the goods in free circulation throughout the 25 States of the EU, thereby exploiting economies of scale in the production and supply chain analysis.

Some companies have more than one free trade zone independently operated and strategically geographically located, for example one in the Iberian Peninsula, one in the Dunkerque/Lille region, another one in northern Italy and one in northern Germany serving the North East European and Scandinavian region. A similar strategy exists with component parts where strategically located assembly points are focused on local market needs undoubtedly others will follow arising from the enlargement of 2004. Overall, the strategy is logistically focused and companies formulate their plans based on market demand and conditions, cost, infrastructure resources and the company business plan. Indeed, as more and more companies develop joint ventures (see p. 490), operating alliances (see p. 497) or undertake mergers and acquisitions (see p. 482), the distribution logistics plan changes and responds to maximize profitability, increase market share, develop market penetration and generate higher profits to facilitate greater investment in research, new technology and company expansion.

We now offer a broad strategic analysis of exporting within the 25 Member States of the European Union.

1. It is the wealthiest single market in the world with 500 million people of high literacy standards with a good standard of living. Overall, it has a Westernised–Mediterranean–Scandinavian market profile with high expectation of long–term growth in a stable environment of low inflation.

2. The market has strong buying power with a rising living standard. Overall, it is highly consumer focused with the populace of the 25 States primarily exercising a non-nationalistic prejudice in consumer choice, based on the value added concept and personal taste and preference. The younger age segment especially favours a wide product source range based on their particular needs.

3. One patent office exists to serve the 25 States. Hence, once a product is patented, goods can be sold throughout the market with no market entry impediment.

4. Emerging from item (3), speed of entry into the market is vitally important to gaining maximum market share, volume sales, competitive advantage and profitability. This is particularly advantageous for products with a short product lifecycle which would not be as profitable in a market where entry can be delayed by bureaucratic complexities including patent registration and acceptance certificates to confirm compliance with health and safety requirements.

Such time delays enable existing players in the market place to capitalize on the situation by generating further promotion and product awareness strategies.

5. There exists ease of access to the market for companies producing and manufacturing within the market. Hence, products produced in France – cheese, wine, cars and perfume – have free access to all the other 24 States with no trade barriers or customs duties. Hence, a new perfume or brand of cheese can be retailed, on launch, in all the 25 States.

6. A unified integrated transport system exists with no impediment to freedom of movement at frontier points. Moreover, carriers' documentation and liability are common throughout the market. An increasing number of rail freight services are now operating Trans European services on dedicated schedules. This has been identified as a high priority in both freight and passenger services with the new EU President priorities of 2004. Furthermore in regard to freight rail movement more emphasis is to be given to develop inter-modalism throughout the EU (pp. 541–42). Professional standards are high and the major European seaports are advanced in computer technology, logistics and multi-modalism, offering competitive rates and transits to inland industrial and commercial centres and to industrial and free trade zones. An increasing number of MNEs and SMEs are operating the Local Clearance Systems (see p. 239) for goods originating from or destined for outside the EU territories.

7. The EU is a very low risk market generally. Financial risks are minimal with many companies conducting business on the open account basis. The provision of the euro, which operates in some 12 States (see pp. 551–52), eliminates currency risk fluctuations throughout businesses trading in the euro-zone and generates price stability. The euro is further evidence of an integrated financial European Union.

8. The market encourages businesses to expand as competition drives down prices and, to reduce costs in all sectors of their business, companies adopt a policy of reviewing their position in the market place in sourcing, production, distribution and profitability, adopting strategies such as merger and acquisition to improve their financial performance and market position. This involves rationalizing production, outsourcing components and centralizing R&D and control and administration. Moreover, freedom of capital movement is permitted throughout the EU which encourages such strategies.

9. The market is high tech in all areas including production and communication, embracing the latest computer technology, EDI – paperless trading (see pp. 446–68). This encourages supply chain management

with hub centres performing the assembly and distribution, and spoke centres supplying the componetized units.

10. The single market is well served with market research data which the discerning exporter may use to evolve strategies of market entry and development. Much of the data is on Internet and, in addition, the EU and major trading associations produce a wide range of market reports and analysis. Specialist agencies also exist in all the Member States. Study the market access database (pp. 543–44).

11. Mobility of labour is a key factor of the EU where personnel are able to take up employment in any of the 25 States. However, tax systems and the social structure do vary by State and it is unlikely that these areas will be unified in the short term.

12 The Single European Market is essentially an open market permitting freedom of access with no exchange controls. It is a member of the WTO (see pp. 27–35) and champions their ideology and strategies.

13. Low inflation is one of the key factors aligned to the convergence of EU economies. Such economic stability encourages investment, particularly inwards investment which generates growth.

14. A common product specification exists with unified standards especially in health and safety areas. Having one specification reduces overall design and production costs, thereby allowing lower prices to be charged and hence stimulating market growth. Goods can, nevertheless, be customized to respond to individual EU States' needs in language, packaging, size, local operating needs, colour and capacity.

15. The market is easy to serve and visit with a common ideology of doing business in an environment of stability, high standards, growth and increasing use of technology.

16. It is important to record that the ten new members of the EU may experience on a discretionary basis and on a bilateral or multilateral basis accession restrictions of certain areas within the single market in the early years of membership (p. 544). This may be imposed by Member States on an individual or collective basis focused on the new ten members. Consult the EU website: www.europart.eu.int/ enlargement/ www.europa.eu.int/comm/enlargement

Overall, the single market is one of opportunity and exporters must focus on it seriously if they are to develop their business. Companies must feature the EU in their business plans, which in turn must be integrated into an international marketing plan. Personnel must be encouraged to be 'Europe focused' in order to identify and develop opportunities within the Single Market. Adaptability, total commitment, complete professionalism and, above all, determination, operating within the buyer's culture are some of the essential ingredients required to succeed. Creative thinking, empathy and well thought out strategies and planning all contribute to becoming a successful European entrepreneur, but, above all, his or her approach must be market research driven. Full use should be made of E-commerce and the Internet.

Recommended reading

EU Market Access Strategy, http://mkaccdb.eu.int
The Export Guide, www.theexportguide.co.uk
White paper – European transport policy for 2010, http://www.europa.eu.int

CHAPTER 19

International trade law

19.1 Introduction

International trade law/regulations is at the core of conducting business overseas. It embraces all the ingredients of negotiating, formulating, executing and after sales of the export sales contract. This includes transport, finance, insurance, product specification, intellectual property, product liability, arbitration and advertising. Many of these regulations are found in Conventions and Economic bloc legislation as in the European Union. International agencies formulating trade law/regulations include the World Trade Organisation, International Maritime Organisation, International Air Transport Association, United Nations Conference on Trade and Development, United Nations Commission on International Trade and Law, International Chamber of Commerce and World Customs Organisation.

Exporters are strongly advised to engage a lawyer in the buyer's country when formulating any agreement regarding agents, joint ventures or outsourcing of production, to ensure adequate safeguards and compliance with local conditions. This embraces a whole range of areas such as employment law, repatriation of funds and trade regulations. Clearly a visit to the market is paramount.

As has been demonstrated elsewhere in this book, the documentation of international trade reflects the identities of the parties involved with those different contracts and which rules or laws apply to which of those contracts. The following identifies the situation embracing the execution of four contracts:

Contracts	Parties involved	Applicable Law/Rules
Sale (invoice)	Seller (Shipper) and Buyer (Consignee)	Incoterms 2000
Finance (Letter of Credit)	Bank and Buyer transferring to the seller	UCP500 (UCP600 from 2006) and where applicable eUCP
Carriage (Bill of Lading or Waybill)	Carrier and Seller transferring to Buyer	Hague/Hague – Visby Rules or Hamburg Rules
Indemnity (Insurance Certificate)	Insurer(s) and seller and/or Buyer	Marine Insurance Act 1906

The sale contract is separate from – although allied to – the contract of finance. The contract of carriage incorporates terms of recourse as an incentive to the carrier, but it is not a contract of indemnity, which requires a totally different criteria. Incoterms 2000 are relevant only to the sale contract and have absolutely nothing to do with the contract of carriage. Similarly, only someone who is party to one of the contracts can have responsibilities under that contract so, for example, the carrier has no responsibilities under the contract of finance to comply with UCP500, that is a matter between the bank and buyer/seller, nor under the sale contract to comply with Incoterms 2000 which are solely a matter between seller and buyer.

19.2 International conventions

International conventions set out minimum terms and conditions for the international carriage of goods, below which carriers cannot contract-out to the detriment of merchants. Carriers can offer terms more favourable to merchants. Generally speaking international conventions aim to regulate international carriage, and in most cases, national carriage is allowed freedom of contract, although in most countries there are standard trading conditions which are usually applied.

These international conventions are drafted by various committees under the auspices of the United Nations and are given effect by countries adopting them into their national legislations. It is thus through these national laws that international conventions become mandatorily applicable within the jurisdictions of the countries concerned to carriage in certain defined circumstances.

We will first examine the legal environment/regulatory system in which the actual product/service is sold across international borders. This embraces various conventions – a feature common throughout the international trade environment. UNCITRAL is very much involved in the formulation and introduction of conventions. Our next areas to review are

employment law and the legal framework for information and communication technology. Finally, we will consider international transport law.
Much of this area features multi-modalism which has been examined elsewhere in the book and will be identified in the text.

19.2.1 Vienna Convention

The Vienna Convention is a 1980 United Nations convention on contracts for the International Sale of goods which came into force on 1st
January 1988. It was sponsored by UNCITRAL and makes certain provisions for the sale of goods between parties whose places of business are in
two different States. Significantly it acknowledges that international trade
usages which the contracted parties know about or ought to be aware of,
apply to their contracts. The special trade terms are designed primarily to
define the method of delivery of the goods sold, but also used to indicate
the calculation of the purchase price and this includes the incidental
charges included therein.

The Vienna Convention was founded on the Hague Uniform Laws.
The Vienna Convention consists of four parts:

  (i) sphere of application and general provisions;
 (ii) formation of the contract;
(iii) sale of goods;
(iv) final provisions.

The second part is especially important to exporters as it embraces the offer
and acceptance and the conclusion of the contract and is founded on the
1964 Uniform Law on Formation. Part (iii), however, is formulated on the
1964 Uniform Law on International Sales and embraces five chapters:

  (i) general provisions;
 (ii) obligations of the seller;
(iii) obligations of the buyer;
(iv) passing of the risk;
 (v) provisions common to the obligations of the seller and the buyer.

The fifth chapter of Part (iii) contains provisions on anticipatory breach,
avoidance of contract and damages and exemptions. Overall, the
Convention provides that a contracting State – a country/State that has
signed up to the Convention – by declaration on accession, may adopt
only Part (ii) (on formation of contract) or Part (iii) (on sale of goods).
Overall, the Vienna Convention has greatly simplified the regulation contained in the Uniform Laws and has made it more flexible.

The Vienna International Sales Convention objective is to be the cen-
trepiece of international harmonization of trade law. A number of other
associated conventions are linked to each dealing with a specific area and

being self-contained, but reflecting the provisions of the International Sales Convention. These include the UN Limitation Period Convention of 1974; the Hague Convention on the law applicable to contracts for the International Sale of Goods of 1986. The Geneva Convention on Agency in the International Sale of Goods in 1983; the Ottawa Conventions on International Factoring and the International Financial Leasing of 1988.

It is important exporters are aware the Convention deals with the fundamental and non-fundamental breach of the sales contract which has been defined as follows: 'A breach of contract committed by one of the parties is fundamental if it results in such detriment to the other party as substantially to deprive him of what he is entitled to expect under the contract, unless the party in breach did not foresee and a reasonable person of the same kind in the same circumstances would not have foreseen such a result.'

It is also paramount the exporter is aware the Convention under Article 46 detailed below entitles the importer/buyer to demand specific performance, delivery of substitute goods for non-conforming goods and repair of such goods:

(a) The buyer may require performance by the seller of his obligations unless the buyer has resorted to a remedy which is inconsistent with this requirement.
(b) If the goods do not conform with the contract, the buyer may require delivery of substitute goods only if the lack of conformity constitutes a fundamental breach of contract and a request for substitute goods is made either in conjunction with notice given under Article 39 or within a reasonable time thereafter.
(c) If the goods do not conform with the contract, the buyer may require the seller to remedy the lack of conformity by repair, unless this is unreasonable having regard to all circumstances. A request for repair must be made either in conjunction with notice given under Article 39 or within a reasonable time thereafter.

Exporters are advised to contact a lawyer if in doubt about their export sales contract terms.

19.3 Product liability

Product liability is the liability of the producer of a product which, owing to a defect, causes injury, damage or loss to the ultimate user. The defect may arise due to inadequate quality of the product for its use, insufficient instructions for its use, and failure to give adequate warning of a dangerous propensity of the product. The United States has led the world in imposing liability on suppliers for defective goods and this has influenced the Product Liability Directive applicable throughout the 25 EU Member

States. The EU directive is reviewed every five years. All products sold throughout the EU, must bear the CE symbol. It is the manufacturers' declaration that the product complies with the essential requirements of the relevant European health, safety and environmental protection legislations. Overall, they are termed product directives. Agreements on mutual recognition of conformity assessment exist between the EU and other countries such as the USA, Japan, Canada, Australia, New Zealand and Israel. Due to the unitary character of the EU Community trade mark it has equal status throughout the community. Consequently it can only be registered, transferred surrendered with respect to the entire community. Hence, a single ground for refusal in a Member State is sufficient to prevent a registration.

The claim for damages caused by a defective product may be based on contract, tort, a statutory right, or a combination of these. There are three types of liability:

 (i) *Strict liability* whereby the claimant has to prove the causation. Hence, to demonstrate the damage was caused by the defect of the product.

 (ii) *Qualified liability* arises where the claimant demonstrates the causation, but the producer has the defence available that in view of the state of scientific or technical knowledge existing at the time the product was put into circulation, he could not have been expected to have discovered the defect. It is termed development risk.

(iii) *Fault liability* arises in addition to causation and requires the claimant to prove the producer was at fault, such as being negligent in the manufacture of the product.

In all three cases the claimant has to prove the product was defective and he has suffered damage in consequence.

The EU Directive for liability for defective products is complex and found in Directive 1999/34/EC of the European Parliament and of the Council of 10th May 1999 amending Council Directive 85/374/EEC on the approximation of the laws, regulations and administrative provisions of the Member States concerning liability for defective products.

19.4 Intellectual property

Intellectual Property rights embrace patents, registered designs and the design right, registered trade marks and copyright. These rights make new inventions, designs, brand names and other creations, a form of property. As a result they give the property owners the right to decide who can use their property. So they create a system through which innovators can benefit from their work – whether it be an electronic timer, designing a fashion shoe, marketing chocolate bars under a new brand name, or creating a new musical. Intellectual property and their rights can protect investment in new ventures and encourage new ideas and creativity. The creations and material they protect can be developed and exploited on a global scale.

Exporters when considering protection abroad should look closely at potential markets in foreign countries. If an exporter does not plan to market actively in another country and does not know of anyone who could sell or licence the intellectual property rights to do so, it may be better not to bother to get protection in that country. However, the exporter may prevent the import of goods made legally in another country because he has no rights there if he has rights in the exporter's country.

Most countries have laws which protect the forms of intellectual property. The principles of protecting intellectual property are recognized almost everywhere, although the details may vary considerably. International agreements mean that countries have to open their intellectual property systems to nationals of other countries in the agreement. The WTO is very much in the lead in developing intellectual property rights and their protection (pp. 27–35).

19.4.1 Patents

A patent embraces virtually all machines, products and processes (and the individual parts of them) across industry subject to three conditions:

(i) it is new;
(ii) it is inventive;
(iii) it is capable of industrial application.

Patents are not confined to major technological advances. They cover a wide range of subjects such as agriculture, medicines, paints, electronics and photography – anything from a small detail in an electric switch to a new form of transport like the monorail.

One of the most important rights arising from international agreements is that all the countries involved recognize 'priority dates'. A priority date is the date on which a patent application is first filed with a national patent office. Further application for the same invention can be made in other countries within 12 months of the priority date, and each of those applications will then be given the same priority date. This means that the person applying ends up with a 'family' of patents of the same invention in different countries, all with the same priority date.

Currently there is no world patent, so to get protection overseas, three choices exist:

(i) you can make separate application for each country;

(ii) for EU Member States, an application can be made to the European Patent Office in Munich to get protection in one or more European countries;

(iii) a single application can be made through the UK Patent Office for protection in more than one of the Member States of the Patent Co-operation Treaty.

19.4.2 Designs

There are two forms of design protection detailed as follows:

(i) A registered design protects the appearance of a product if the product is novel and has its own character. You cannot register a design that is purely functional.

(ii) Design right protects the original design of the shape or configuration of items. This includes purely functional items. However, it does not include two-dimensional designs.

There is some overlap between what you protect with registered designs and design right. There is also some overlap between what you can protect with registered designs and copyright. Additionally, there are international agreements and priority dates for registered design protection, but the exporter has only six months in which to make further applications. If the design is registered in the UK, this gives automatic protection in some other countries. Hence, the exporter gets automatic protection equivalent to design right in some other countries. Some countries give protection like design right under copyright law.

19.4.3 Copyright

Copyright gives rights to the creators of original literary, dramatic, musical and artistic works, published editions of works, sound recordings, films (including videos), broadcasts, cable programmes and computer programs. They cover copying, adapting, publishing, renting, performing and broadcasting.

There is no registration for copyright in the United Kingdom. It comes into operation automatically as soon as there is a record of the copyright material. There are international copyright agreements such as conventions and treaties which mean that material created by UK nationals or residents or first published in the UK is protected in each country which is a member of the conventions. This protection is automatic in the UK, but you may need to mark the copyright material with the international © mark, your name and year of publication to get protection in some countries. The protection available in other countries is set out in the national law of that country.

19.4.4 Trade marks

Trade marks are signs which distinguish goods and services of one trader from those of others. For example, the contents of a washing powder sold under a particular registered trade mark may change many times over the years, but the trade mark means that only the company or its licences can sell a washing powder under that sign. Hence, trade marks provide protection for the 'good will' and reputation of a firm in its products and services.

Trade marks are often the single most valuable marketing tool a company will have – whatever its size. They need not be registered. If a mark has built up enough of a trading reputation and goodwill, there is some protection in common law against those who try to pass off their goods and services as those of the person entitled to the reputation from the mark. But getting a registered trade mark will give the trader much stronger protection.

If the mark is not registered and there is a need to take action against someone, the trader has to demonstrate that the mark has an established reputation, and grounds exist that the trade mark is being used to confuse or deceive the public. Hence, the need to demonstrate confusion and prove reputation. Registration of the trade mark provides an immediate right to stop someone using the same or a similar mark on the same or similar goods and service.

As mentioned (p. 563) the CE is the symbol all products sold throughout the EU must bear. It is the EU Community Trade Mark to protect intellectual property throughout the entire EU single market. Hence, a separate registration is not required for each EU State.

The Protocol to the Madrid agreement is a system for the international registration of trade marks. Its pro-centralized register of trade marks is held by the World Intellectual Property Organisation in Geneva and allows all applied for or registered through the National trade mark system to be extended to and protected in the States. The United Kingdom is a signatory to the Madrid Protocol and its provisions were implemented by way of the Trade Marks (International Registration) Order 1996 as amended Trade Marks (International Registration) (Amendment) Order 2000. The main changes are simplified application form provision for the recording of supplementary information, such as disclaimers and licences on the international register.

Effectively, the Madrid Protocol provides a means of obtaining trade mark registrations in a large number of countries at less cost and inconvenience than if the trade mark applications were filed in each country separately. The advantages of the proposed amendments is a clearer set of rules surrounding the international trade mark system and the ability to record additional information on the international register. Benefits will accrue to the international trade mark system through simpler and less bureaucratic procedures. Cost savings are difficult to quantify in monetary terms. The simplified procedures should assist those intellectual property professional clients.

The EU Community trade mark legal basis is set by the Council Registration 40/94 of 20th December 1993 of the EU Community Trade mark, the Commission (EC) No 2868/95 of 13th December 1995 concerning the enforcement of the Regulation (EC) No 40/94 as well as Commission Regulation (EC) of 28th December 1995 on the Schedule of Fees of the Office for Harmonisation in the Market (trade marks and designs).

To conclude our focus on Intellectual Property it is important exporters take legal advice on the areas examined. Furthermore, it is important to note that the WTO in 1997 undertook as part of the Doha Development Agenda (pp. 27–35) to create/negotiate a multilateral system of notification and registration of geographical indications for wine. In 1999 the WTO undertook a review of certain exceptions to patentability and protection of plant varieties. In 2000 the WTO Intellectual property undertook the first of two-yearly reviews of the implementation of the agreement. Visit the WTO website to keep up to date, www.wto.org

19.5 Employment law

Employment law covers both criminal and civil laws. Moreover, it embraces a wide area including contract of employment; employment relationships; discrimination to recruitment, selection, training and promotion; termination of employment; disciplinary and grievance procedure; health and safety at work, taxation – company, employer; co-operation; trade unions and their relations with employers and members; works council; employment tribunal; redundancy; and intellectual property – employee rights. Additionally, there exist a number of institutions/agencies relevant to employment law. This includes the European Union embracing Treaties, Regulations, Directives, Decisions, the supremacy of Community Law over National Law and European Court of Human Rights. The EU may be regarded as a highly regulated employment market but regulations do differ marginally in Member States.

Employment law differs widely. A contrasting situation exists in France which is based on social welfare while in the USA the commercial climate prevails, but varies by individual state. Employment law differs widely globally with the developed countries having a more regulated employment system.

The International Labour Organisation is a United Nations Agency and the basis of the most important source of international standards in employment. One of its major policies is to guarantee freedom of association – a matter of great importance to trade unions. A similar guaranteed freedom in this situation is found in the European Court of Human Rights. Governments globally are free to adopt the ILO standards and many do not recognize it, such as the USA.

Employment law is very relevant to companies embarking on a joint venture, operating alliance, merger and acquisition, and setting up a company in another country. A local lawyer should be engaged to ensure an adequate comprehension is sought of all the local employment law aspects relative to the project. This should be financially evaluated to determine the economics of the project including the company liabilities/obligations in the overseas territory.

19.6 Legal framework for information and communication technology

Information technology is radically changing the way in which international trade and transport are conducted. Electronic means of communication are used to exchange information, enter into contracts, trade goods during transit and conduct negotiations/market research. To reap the benefits of modern technology, a supportive legal framework is required and one which recognizes the legal effect and validity of electronic data messages and thus adequately facilitates their use.

Important steps towards the removal of legal barriers to the use of electronic means of communication in international trade have been taken by the adoption of the UNCITRAL model law on Electronic Commerce (1996) and Model Law on Electronic Signatures (2001). These Model Laws provide Governments with internationally acceptable rules and principles for adaptation of national laws and regulations and the creation of a favourable legal environment for electronic commerce. An important challenge, however, remains the question of the replacement of negotiable transport documents (e.g. marine bills of lading and multimodal transport) with electronic alternatives. In the absence of an appropriate legal framework, contractual solutions have been developed in order to replicate the functions of the negotiable bill of lading by means of electronic messages.

The CMI Comite Maritime International's, (domiciled in Belgium), prime aim is the promotion of international uniformity in the law governing maritime matters. They meet every four years and were responsible for the CMI Rules for Electronic Bill of Lading (pp. 569–72). An important feature is that when not in conflict with the CMI Rules, the Uniform Rules of Conduct for Interchange of Trade Data by Teletransmission 1987 (UNCID) shall govern the conduct between the parties.

The ICC International Chamber of Commerce are also very much in the lead regarding the electronic trade regulatory framework. They have issued a supplement for electronic presentation to be used in conjunction with the ICC Uniform Customs and Practice for Documentary Credits (UCP500) (p. 296). Also, the Incoterms 2000 reflects electronic trading (pp. 395–417). In 2007 a new set of Uniform Customs and Practice for Documentary Credits, to be known as UCP600, may be introduced (p. 396). It will be used by banks across the world reflecting new rules over trade finance. It will displace UCP500 (p. 295). ICC have devised a range of codes of practice and model contracts. This includes the International Court of Arbitration based in Paris, established in 1923, and has dealt with over 13 000 international arbitration cases involving parties and arbitrators from 170 countries and territories.

Bolero has also been very much involved the development of electronic trading and a regulatory framework (pp. 457–63).

The draft instrument is under review within UNCITRAL. It aims at further removing legal barriers by allowing for the use of both 'electronic records' and 'paper transport documents' and giving them legal status. If adopted, a new transport convention will effectively address the use of electronic equivalents to traditional transport documents, an important step in facilitating international trade and transport.

19.7 CMI rules of Electronic Bills of Lading

Electronic trading as demonstrated by Bolero is a major growth area (pp. 457–63). We will now examine the CMI Rules of Electronic Bills of Lading trading.

(a) *Rules of procedure.* The Uniform Rules of Conduct for Interchange of Trade Data by Teletransmission 1987 (UNCID) shall govern the conduct between parties. The EDI under these rules will conform with the relevant UN/EDIFACT standards. However, the parties may use any other method of trade data interchange acceptable to all of the users. Unless otherwise agreed, the document format for the contract of carriage shall conform to the UN layout key or compatible national standard for bills of lading. A recipient of a Transmission is not authorized to act on a Transmission unless he/she has sent confirmation. In any dispute arising between the parties as to the data actually transmitted, an Electronic Monitoring System maybe used to verify the data received. Data concerning other transactions not related to the data in dispute are to be considered as trade secrets and thus not available for examination. If such data are unavoidably revealed as part of the examination of the Electronic Monitoring System, they must be treated as confidential and not released to any outside party or used for any other purpose. Any transfer of rights to the goods shall be considered to be private information and shall not be released to any outside party not connected to the transport or clearance of the goods.

(b) *Form and content of the receipt message.* The carrier upon receiving the goods from the shipper, shall give notice of the receipt of the goods to the shipper by a message at the electronic address specified by the shipper. It will include shipper's name, description of the goods in the same tenor as if a paper bill of lading was issued, date and place of receipt of goods, reference to the carriers terms and conditions of carriage, date and place of shipment and Private Key to be used in subsequent transmissions. The Private Key means any technically appropriate form, such as a combination of numbers and/or letters which the parties may agree for securing the authenticity and integrity of a Transmission. The shipper must confirm the receipt message to the carrier upon which confirmation the shipper shall be the Holder. Upon demand of the holder, the receipt message shall be updated with the date and place of shipment as soon as the goods have been loaded on board.

(c) *Terms and conditions of the contract of carriage.* It is agreed whenever the carrier makes a reference to its terms and conditions of carriage, they shall form part of the Contract of Carriage. Such terms/conditions must be readily available to the parties to the contract. In the event of any conflict or inconsistency between such terms and conditions and these Rules, the CMI rules will prevail.

(d) *Applicable law.* The contract of carriage shall be subject to any international convention or national law which would have been mandatorily applicable if a paper bill of lading had been issued.

(e) *Right of control and transfer.* The holder is the only party who may, as against the carrier, claim delivery of the goods, nominate the consignee or substitute a nominated consignee for any other party, including itself; transfer the right of control and transfer to another party; instruct the carrier on any other subject concerning the goods, as if he were the holder of a paper bill of lading. A transfer of the Right of Control and Transfer shall be effected by Notification of the current holder to the carrier of its intention to transfer its Right of Control to a proposed new holder; confirmation by the carrier of such notification message whereupon the carrier shall transmit the data to the new holder. The new holder will advise the carrier of its acceptance whereby the carrier will cancel the current Private Key and issue a new Private Key to the new holder.

(f) *Private key.* The Private Key is unique to each successive holder. It is not transferable. The carrier and holder are responsible for Private Key Security. The carrier must send an electronic message to confirm to the last holder to whom it is issued a Private Key when such

Holder secures the Transmission containing such electronic message by the use of the Private Key. The Private Key must be separate and distinct from any means used to identify the Contract of Carriage and any security password or identification used to access the computer network.

(g) *Delivery.* The carrier must notify the Holder of the place and date of intended delivery of the goods whereupon the Holder must nominate a consignee to give delivery instructions to the carrier with verification by the Private Key. In the absence of such nomination, the Holder will be deemed to be the consignee. The carrier shall deliver the goods to the consignee upon production of the proper identification in accordance with the delivery instructions, as detailed above and such delivery shall automatically cancel the Private Key. The carrier is under no liability for misdelivery if it can be proved that it exercised reasonable care to ascertain that the party who claimed to be consignee was in fact that party.

(h) *Option to receive a paper document.* The Holder has the option at any time prior to delivery of the goods to demand from the carrier a paper bill of lading. Such document shall be made available at a location to be determined by the Holder, provided that no carrier shall be obliged to make such document available at a place where it has no facilities and in such instance the carrier shall only be obliged to make the document available at the facility nearest to the location determined by the Holder. The carrier shall not be responsible for delays in delivering the goods resulting from the Holder exercising the above option. The carrier has the option at any time prior to delivery of the goods to issue to the Holder a paper bill of lading unless the exercise of such option should result in undue delay or disrupts the delivery of the goods. A Bill of Lading issued under the foregoing shall include the data set out in the receipt message specified in item (b), and a statement to the effect that the bill of lading has been issued upon termination of the procedures for EDI under the CMI rules for Electronic Bills of Lading. The aforementioned bill of lading shall be issued at the option of the Holder either to the order of the Holder whose name, for this purpose, shall then be inserted in the Bill of Lading or 'to bearer'. The insurance of a paper bill of lading under the aforementioned rule shall cancel the Private Key and terminate the procedures for EDI under these Rules. Termination of these procedures by the Holder or the carrier will not relieve any of the parties to the Contract of Carriage of their rights, obligations or liabilities while performing under the present Rules, nor of their rights, obligations or liabilities under the Contract of Carriage. The Holder may demand at any time the issuance of a printout of the receipt message, referred to in item (b) (except for the Private Key) marked as 'non-negotiable copy'. The issuance of such a

printout shall not cancel the Private Key nor terminate the procedures for EDI.

(i) *Electronic Data is Equivalent to Writing.* The carrier and the shipper
and all subsequent parties utilizing these procedures, agree that any
national or local law, custom or practice requiring the Contract of
Carriage to be evidenced in writing and signed, is satisfied by the
transmitted and confirmed electronic data residing on computer data
storage media displayable in human language on a video screen or as
printed out by a computer. In agreeing to these Rules, the parties
shall be taken to have agreed not to raise the defence that this contract is not in writing.

The Exporters/Importers are urged to familiarize themselves with these
Rules when conducting trade using Electronic Bills of Lading.

19.8 International transport law

International transport law embraces all modes, multi-modal, rail, sea, air,
inland waterways and road. A further category is container transport, usually involved in combined transport operation.

A summary of the main areas are also examined in depth elsewhere
in the book (pp. 559–61).

19.8.1 Legal framework for multi-modal transport

While much of international trade is now carried out on a door-to-door
basis, under one contract and with one party bearing contractual responsibility, the current legal framework governing multi-modal transport fails
to reflect these developments. No international uniform regime is in force
to regulate liability for loss, damage or delay arising from multi-modal
transport. Instead the present legal framework governing multi-modal
transport consists of a complex array of international conventions
designed to regulate uni-modal carriage, diverse regional/sub-regional
agreements, national laws and standard term contracts. As a consequence,
both the applicable liability rules and the degree of extent of a carriers' liability vary greatly from case to case and are unpredictable (see www.
unctad.org).

Over the years several attempts have been made at drafting a set of
rules to regulate liability arising from international multi-modal transportation, but none of these has brought about international uniformity.
In view of the absence of international uniform regulation of liability,
there has been a proliferation of diverse national, regional and sub-
regional laws and regulations on multi-modal transport. The lack of global
uniform regime has obliged developing countries to resort to solutions at

the regional and/or sub-regional level, such as the laws and regulations prepared by the ADEAN Community, the Latin American Integration Association (ALADI), and the Southern Common Market (MERCOSUR) and the Association of South-East Asia Nations (ASEAN). While these laws and regulations are often based on the 1980 MT Convention and/or the UNCTAD/ICC Rules, significant differences on key issues among the different sets of rules create a trend of further disunification at the international level (p. 559). A fragmented and complex legal framework creates uncertainty which in turn increases transaction costs as it gives rise to legal and evidentiary enquiries, costly litigation and increasing insurance costs. Without a predictable legal framework, equitable access to markets and participation in international trade are much harder for small or medium players.

A survey was conducted in November 2001 by the UNCTAD secretariat and in consequence a draft instrument (on transport law) was formulated by UNCITRAL. Although primarily designed to cover contracts for the carriage of goods by sea, it has a broad scope of application and as currently drafted, would cover all contracts for international multi-modal transport involving a sea-leg. UNCITRAL – United Nations Commission of International Trade Law – is the United Nations Agency responsible for the formulation/development of global international trade law embracing international transport. Exporters are encouraged to keep up to date by visiting the UNCITRAL website, www.uncitral.org

19.8.2 Combined transport

We will now examine the salient areas of combined/multi-modal transport carriage legislation with particular focus where the aspect has not been examined elsewhere in this publication.

(a) *ICC Rules for a Combined Transport document.* These have found wide acceptance among Combined Transport Operators and are found in ICC Brochure No 298. They represent a combination of the rejected Tokyo–Rome Rules, Tokyo Rules and TCM Convention (pp. 357–74).

(b) *UNCTAD MMO Convention.* This was adopted at an International Conference in Geneva in May 1980 as the United Nations Convention on International Multi-modal Transport of Goods or UNCTADMMO Convention. To date, only nine countries have ratified it, Burundi, Chile, Georgia, Malawi, Mexico, Morocco, Rwanda, Senegal and Zambia. It is unlikely that it will ever come into force as 30 countries must ratify it.

(c) *UNCTAD/ICC Rules for Multi-Modal transport documents.* UNCTAD sought the co-operation of the ICC to review and update the ICC rules for Combined Transport Document (item a). However, deliberations took place with UNCTAD/ICC in the lead on the basis of the

Hague-Visby rules. However, the outcome was the UNCTAD/ICC has not found favour beyond a few NVOCCs.

Subsequently, in 1999 the ICC launched a discussion paper under the leading assessment of 'contentious' text of the MT Convention, but this is likely to be overtaken by the CMI draft Instrument on Transport Law submitted to the UNCITRAL secretariat on 11th December 2001. In April 2002 a meeting in New York raised several objections to the new document, notably whether or not the instrument should apply Port-to-Port, or Door-to-Door. The matter remains under discussion, but if adopted it would have a major impact on door-to-door transport (p. 572).

(d) *European Union – International Liability.* In July 1998 the EU issued a report on Intermodal Liability. It sought to open the debate on Intermodal Transportation and Carrier Liability with a view to producing Model Rules which would be optional, but which would apply automatically unless the carrier contracted out. The situation in Europe and not applicable elsewhere in the world, is that there are uni-modal conventions in Europe governing road and rail transport. Hence, the only way in which a set of rules could be produced which did not conflict with any uni-modal convention would be to make the limit under the rules higher than any uni-modal convention.

(e) *CSC Convention.* The 1972 Convention for Safe Containers introduced a requirement for regular inspection of containers by qualified personnel, a record of which is made by punching details on a metal plate at the door end of the container so that a cursory inspection can verify that a container is 'in time' (pp. 76–96).

To conclude our examination of combined transport law, overseas readers may find it prudent to check out the legislation in their country. However, as law is national, but trade is international, it is useful to check out any unusual features of local laws that affect the contracts for the carriage of goods. Countries of significance include Australia, Austria, Canada, Chile, China, Croatia, Czech Republic, Egypt, Georgia, Germany, Greece, India, Japan, Korea, Lebanon, Mexico, New Zealand, Romania, Russia, Saudi Arabia, Scandinavia, Slovakia, South Africa, UAE and Ukraine.

19.8.3 International Road Transport CMR

The CMR Convention governing the International Carriage of Goods by Road was signed at Geneva in 1956 and enacted into the law of the UK by the Carriage of Goods by Road Act 1965. The Convention only appears to have been adopted by European Nations and applied to contracts for the international carriage of goods by road in vehicles over the territories of two different countries of which at least one is a contracting party to the

CMR. Under this convention the carrier is liable for loss or damage from the time he takes over the goods until the time he delivers them to the consignee, unless he can prove that the loss or damage occurred because of one of a list of excepted perils. The defences available to the carrier are limited and very difficult to establish so that the premise is almost one of strict liability, because the limited exceptions impose such an onerous burden of proof (pp. 79–81).

19.8.4 International Rail Transport COTIF/CIM

The COTIF Convention Concerning International Carriage by Rail was signed in Berne in May 1980. It was given legal effect in the UK by the International Transport Conventions Act 1983 and became operative in May 1985. COTIF abrogated the existing CIM Convention which did not have the force of law in the UK and an amended draft of CIM was attached to COTIF as Appendix B to govern the carriage of goods. Overall COTIF has a wider application and covers passengers, etc., as well as goods. CIM applies if either the place of loading or the destination of the goods is a COTIF Member State. Like CIM, COTIF/CIM applies only to international carriage and is not applicable to domestic traffic. The terms and conditions are similar to CMR but limitation is substantially higher at SDR 17 per kilo (pp. 386–87).

19.8.5 International Air Carriage – Warsaw Convention

The International air carriage of goods is subject to either the Warsaw Convention 1929 or the Amended Warsaw Convention 1955. Which of these Conventions depends on which Convention the countries of departure and arrival have ratified. For one of the Conventions to apply, both of the countries must have ratified the same Convention; if both have ratified the Amended Warsaw Convention then, irrespective of whether they have both also ratified the earlier Convention, the Amended Warsaw Convention applies. Contractual Carriers (such as Freight Forwarders acting as Principals) are also subject to the Conventions. Unlike other transport Conventions, both Warsaw Conventions require that certain information is stated on the Air Waybill, the absence of which will prevent the Carrier from relying on both the exclusions and limitations of liability in the Convention and in the case of the amended Warsaw Convention, will not entitle the Carrier to rely on the limitations of liability.

Montreal Protocol No 4 came into effect in June 1998. The scope of application of this Protocol is presently (2004) unclear – other than it will not apply to carriage by air to the USA. However, where it is applied there will be some important changes as detailed below:

(a) It will no longer be necessary for an Air Waybill to be issued in order for the Convention to be applicable. This is clearly designed to remove the need for tangible documentation to facilitate electronic documentation.

(b) The all necessary measure style defence is replaced by a menu of specific defences.

(c) The possibility of breaching the limitation in Article 22 is removed and this limit is now unbreakable.

On the 28th May 1999 in Montreal a new Convention was adopted and signed by 53 nations. It is intended to replace the Warsaw Convention and its six protocols. While the new Convention is designed to unify the current private airline rules with respect to passenger injury and death claims, it will adopt all the cargo related matters under Montreal Protocol No 4. The liability section of the Convention hopes to reduce costly legal argument on which local limitation of damage law might apply to cargo mishap during any particular part of an intermodal international air conveyance.

This is realised by providing that the carriage is subject to one law and one limitation of SDR 17 per kilo. Additionally, where the contract of carriage reflects intended movement by air and does not mention road or ocean links, the Convention will apply, even though part of the carriage is, in fact, performed by another transport mode of carriage. Hence, if the booking was made to transport goods from Moscow to Glasgow and an Air Waybill was issued which showed that movement, any sea or road links which might be involved in that transport are deemed to be part of the air carriage, since the Air Waybill manifests the goods from Moscow to Glasgow. Countries who have ratified, accepted or acceded to the new Montreal Convention (2003) include Bahrain, Belize, Czech Republic, Japan, Macedonia, Mexico, Slovakia and UAE.

19.8.6 Sea Carriage

The despatch of goods by sea generally involves a Bill of Lading as the evidence of the contract and features the various international regulations. These are examined in depth in Chapter 14 pp. 357–74, but key areas are reproduced below.

(a) *Hague Rules.* International Convention in Brussels in 1974 which govern liability for loss or damage to goods carried under Bill of Lading.

(b) *Hague–Visby Rules.* In 1988 a further international conference adopted some revisions to the Hague Rules principally affecting limitation. The amended rules are officially known as the 'Brussels Protocol' signed on the 23rd February 1968, but are popularly known as the Hague-Visby Rules, and are given effect in the United Kingdom by Carriage of Goods by Sea Act 1971.

(c) *Hamburg Rules.* In March 1978 an UNCTAD instigated international conference in Hamburg adopted a new set of rules (the Hamburg Rules) which radically alter the liability which shipowners have to bear for loss or damage to goods in the courts of those nations where the rules apply. Also applicable to Sea Waybills.

(d) *Limitation of Liability for Maritime Claims (LLMC) – The London Convention.* The liability of the Carrier under any of the above sea carriage conventions is always subject to the overriding application of the provisions of the LLMC or equivalent convention *inter alia* to limitation of liability. The current UK Act is the Merchant Shipping Act 1995 which implements the 1976 International Convention on Limitation of Liability for Maritime Claims (LLMC). This new convention applies a virtually unbreakable right to limit with increased levels of limitation.

19.9 WTO settlement procedure

An important area of conducting trade law involving WTO member nations is full compliance with WTO trade regulations. Disputes do arise and a code of procedure exists relative to their evaluation which we will now examine.

Dispute settlement is the central pillar of the multilateral trading system and the WTO's unique contribution to the stability of the global economy. Without a means of settling disputes, the rules-based system would be less effective because the rules could not be enforced.

Disputes in the WTO are essentially about broken promises. WTO members have agreed that if they believe fellow members are violating trade rules, they will use the multilateral system of settling disputes instead of taking action unilaterally. That means abiding by the agreed procedures and respecting judgements.

A dispute arises when one country adopts a trade policy measure or takes some action that one or more fellow WTO members considers to be breaking the WTO agreements or to be a failure to live up to obligations. A third group of countries can declare that they have an interest in the case and enjoy some rights.

Settling disputes is the responsibility of the Dispute Settlement Body which consists of all WTO members. It has the sole authority to establish 'panels' of experts to consider the case, and to accept or reject the panels' findings or the results of an appeal. It monitors the implementation of the rulings and recommendations, and has the power to authorize retaliation when a country does not comply with a ruling.

The first stage of consultation takes up to 60 days with the second stage up to 45 days plus six days for the panel to conclude. The main stages are as follows:

(a) Before the first hearing each side in the dispute presents its case in writing to the panel;

(b) *First hearing:* the complaining country and defence, the complaining country (or countries), the responding country and those that have announced they have an interest in the dispute make their case at the first hearing;

(c) *Rebuttals:* the countries involved submit written rebuttals and present oral arguments at the panel's second meeting;

(d) *Experts:* if one side raises scientific or other technical matters, the panel may consult experts or appoint an expert review group to prepare an advisory report;

(e) *First draft:* the panel submits the descriptive (factual and argument) sections of its report to the two sides giving them two weeks to comment. This report does not include findings and conclusions;

(f) *Interim report:* the panel then submits an interim report, including its findings and conclusions, to the two sides, giving them one week to ask for a review;

(g) *Review:* the period of review must not exceed two weeks. During that time the panel may hold additional meetings with the two sides;

(h) *Final report:* a final report is submitted to the two sides and three weeks later it is circulated to all WTO members. If the panel decides that the disputed trade measure does break a WTO agreement or an obligation, it recommends that the measure be made to conform with WTO rules. The panel may suggest how this could be done;

(i) *The report becomes a ruling:* The report becomes the Dispute Settlement Body's ruling or recommendation within 60 days unless a consensus rejects it. Both sides can appeal against the report;

(j) *Appeals:* Either side can appeal against a panel's ruling. Sometimes both sides do so. Appeals have to be based on points of law such as legal interpretation – they cannot re-examine existing evidence or examine new issues. Each appeal is heard by three members of a permanent seven member Appellate Body set up by the Dispute Settlement Body and broadly representing the range of WTO membership. The appeal can uphold, modify or reverse the panel's legal findings and conclusions. Normally, appeals should not last more than 60 days, with an absolute maximum of 90 days. The Dispute Settlement Body has to accept or reject the appeals report within 30 days and rejection is only possible by consensus. Overall, the settlement procedure takes one year with a further three months if an appeal is involved.

This chapter must not be regarded as an exhaustive treatment of trade law, but merely an excursion into it, supplemented by other areas of the text where it has been examined. Readers may be persuaded to obtain some of the publications listed under recommended reading.

Recommended reading

Dictionary of Shipping International Business Trade Terms and Abbreviations 5th Edition (2005). Witherbys 18 000 entries (contains over 1000 International Trade Law terms. www.books@witherbys.co.uk

Employment Law Beryl Grant, Thomson Learning

ICC International Court of Arbitration, www.iccarbitration.org

ICC Uniform Customs and Practice for Documentary Credits – UCP 600

Law of International Trade, JCT Chuah, Sweet & Maxwell

The Law and Practice of International Trade, Leo D'Arcy, Carole Murray and Barbara Cleave, Sweet & Maxwell

What is Intellectual Property, Patent Office Cardiff, www.enquires@patent.gov.uk

WTO annual report, www.publications@wto.org

International physical distribution/logistics strategy and management

20.1 Introduction

Exporting is all about professionalism, logistics and profit motivation and closely involves international distribution strategy and management. This embraces the decision-making process of evolving the most suitable and acceptable method of distributing goods to international markets. It is market driven as the international distribution network continues to expand and develop into a high tech operation involving multi-modalism. Moreover, distribution is a fast-moving area, subject to continuous change, and it is market led. Hence the shipper needs to monitor continuously such changes, and feature in them, to remain competitive.

Distribution is also an area which is attracting senior management's attention on an increasing scale as world markets become more competitive and increasing emphasis is being placed on the 'total product concept': the value added benefit the importer obtains from the purchase of the goods. This benefit embraces not only the product and the related benefits associated with trading with the supplier in terms of product specification and non-price areas – after-sales, brand image, position of the company in the market place – but also the method of distribution adopted to enable the goods to reach the buyer. Factors which feature prominently in the choices made include efficiency and quality of service, together with total cost. Close liaison must be maintained between the exporter and the importer to ensure the correct decision is taken. An increasing number of carriers and distributors are obtaining BS5750 or ISO9000 quality standard registration to enhance their market profile (pp. 522–23).

Today the exporter must be computer and logistically focused. Full use must be made of Electronic Data Interchange (EDI) resources and all the ingredients of the logistic elements including supply chain management, computerized warehouse operation and management, customer asset management, barcode systems for inventory control and just-in-time technology. Planning, tracking and adequate control systems with the ability to be flexible to meet changing market needs are essential in the logistic environment.

To devise the correct strategy the company must examine a number of factors which are detailed below.

1. *Company objectives.* These will be found in the company's business plan spanning three to five years. The business plan will be reviewed regularly in the light of changing market conditions. Moreover, it will be market driven and feature company resource use and profitability annually. International distribution will feature in channels of distribution which will vary by overseas territory and product.

2. *Company resources.* Large companies have substantial cash flow and human resources to develop specialism within the company, including the area of logistics (pp. 124–45). Moreover, the high volume of overseas business enables economies of scale to be achieved through lower unit cost. For example, discounted freight rates can be negotiated with carriers on volume-guaranteed contracts. Furthermore, larger companies tend to rely less on intermediaries in the management and execution of the distribution network, thereby realizing significant cost savings and exercising closer and more direct control over the total logistics operation. Also large companies tend to have experienced and high-calibre personnel, although the decision-making process can be slower compared with the smaller company.

   In contrast, the smaller company has limited financial, production and personnel resources. Such companies do not have the high market profile of the larger company and financial resources to accept prolonged payment terms. Many rely on consolidated distribution networks, with its lower unit cost, rather than on full-load volume movements.

   The extent to which both large and small companies have specialist personnel engaged in shipping and warehouse distribution activities depends on the markets, products, international distribution networks they serve, complexity of the operation and the volume of business involved. Companies which have dedicated personnel engaged in the distribution process have complete control over cost and complete performance monitoring of the services they use. Moreover, such companies can obtain competitive rates through volume and loyalty contracts and in so doing can introduce a mark-up on their quotation when trading in CFR, CIF, CPT and CIP terms. This mark-up contributes to the distribution management team cost.

3. *The company's position in the market place.* The higher the company's profile, the more likely is the company to be a market leader and to play a dominant role in the distribution arrangements.

4. *Legal and political constraints.* A number of governments insist that imported goods are conveyed on their national airlines or shipping services and buy FCA or EXW.

5. *The sales forecast and market stability.* Companies may be reluctant to set up an extensive shipping and logistics department to cater for irregular shipments to an unstable market.

6. *Level and nature of competition.* As overseas markets develop, the volume of trade and range of commodities and products sold increases. This stimulates the expansion of the infrastructure, which improves the quality of service provided by the carrier and the degree of high technology. Overall, the distribution network becomes more integrated, quickening transit times, and thereby intensifying competition among carriers and suppliers or shippers to the market. Accordingly, the method by which the goods reach the buyer becomes extremely competitive as the options increase and the value added benefit becomes more closely analysed by the buyer in the selection process of the supplier. Hence the need for the exporter to choose the most advantageous and competitive distribution network to obtain and retain overseas business.

7. *Cost.* In total, there are 30 cost elements in an international distribution network. These include: handling, freight, packing, customs clearance, insurance, import duty, exchange rates, agent's commission, interest on capital in transit, warehouse and so on (p. 416). Exporters should constantly monitor these costs and ensure they remain competitive in the market in which they operate and especially in terms of value added benefit.

8. *Value added benefit.* The choice of distribution network should be evaluated on the perceived benefits it brings to the buyer and the resulting value added benefit. It may be integrated into a just-in-time system or Distripark involving processing, packaging and distribution or transit times which enable the goods to be commissioned on arrival, such as computers or foodstuffs distributed to retail outlets in a quality condition at an attractive price. Shippers are constantly looking for improved efficiency in the distribution network which they can transform into improved profitability and competitiveness derived from the imported product.

9. *Flexibility of service.* A flexible distribution network enables the shipper to exploit market opportunities. Flexibility arises in the range of facilities offered by the carrier and route options such as can be offered by a truck operator in the European market.

10. *Frequency of service,* transit time and services reliability are all major factors. Low frequency services involve a longer lead time to despatch the goods and generates higher stockpiling which does not favour a just-in-time strategy. Low-cost services port-to-port often result in sluggish transits and transhipments. Moreover, the cargo receives a low priority in the handling process. Sluggish transit times are usually unacceptable for consumer cargoes as it deprives the importer of the earlier arrival of the goods which may be disadvantageous to the

buyer in a variety of ways. Basically competitive transit times and frequent, reliable services at a competitive rate are the best ingredients to facilitate overseas market development and enable the buyer to maximize his or her profits from the imported products. Moreover, in such situations, stocks can remain at an optimum low level and can be replenished as they are consumed.

11. *Logistics*. As stressed earlier, the company must be computer and logistic literate and focused on these elements. Hence the need for inventory management. This requires substantial investment in resources, including a trained workforce committed to this ideology. Many smaller companies find it difficult to fund such investment but there is the alternative of having an operating alliance with another company, thereby sharing the cost and adding value to the company services, leading to enhanced competitiveness.

12. *Maximization*. The company business must strive to maximize business volume through flexible pricing strategies. This places particular emphasis on the need to generate high business volume to support the company infrastructure and the resources available to the shipper.

13. *Culture*. The company must fully understand the market culture in which they are dealing and this embraces the importers company management culture, in particular the management decision making process. Overall, the exporter must endeavour to empathize with the importer in a pragmatic professional manner.

To conclude our analysis, it is important to view the exporter's international distribution strategy through the eyes of the buyer. The imported product is part of the buyer's business and it is essential that both work closely together to the mutual and profitable benefit of both parties. A constant dialogue must be maintained with the carriers and all parties involved in the distribution network. Moreover, shipping/exports/logistics managers should regularly visit the markets they serve, attend management courses and keep up to date on infrastructure developments.

In our examination of the tactics of applying the strategy, one must remember that the options are numerous and international distribution operates in an extremely fast-moving market. Hence the partnership and dialogue between the exporter and importer must be vigorous and decisive, to ensure the distribution network chosen is the most competitive for the products conveyed in that market. Market research techniques must be used.

International companies today tend to focus on a global outlook. They constantly search for new sustainable markets. Moreover, they choose to manufacture in low labour-cost markets with technical skills responsive to adequate technical training and with sustainable neighbouring markets to buy their products. This involves transfer pricing and technology; inwards and indigenous capital investment; an indigenous labour force and transfer of management skills. In some situations, an industrial transplant takes place with the supplier/exporter providing some 51 per cent of the inwards investment. Such strategies and the terms of the industrial transplant depend on the buyer's government regulations.

We will now examine the options available for applying the international distribution strategy, but stress that the international company would use a mixture of these options, depending on company resources, infrastructure, products, culture, markets, competition and cost efficiency factors.

1. Near and distant markets. Near markets are easier to serve, manage and control than distant markets. In addition, regular business and control systems are easier to set up; the freight cost is lower and transit time quicker. The distant market may be Malaysia despatching goods to the USA or the EU compared with the near market of Singapore or Hong Kong. Generally exporters tend to have a better comprehension of the near market, especially in the areas of its infrastructure, culture, risk and 'ongoing' developments. Many small companies target the near market in preference, as the distant market may prove costly to serve and will absorb a high proportion of their resources, including slower payments. The distant market is more difficult to control and manage without placing a permanent representative in the overseas territory.

2. Destination seaports play an important part in the decision-making process, reflecting especially the buyer's needs. Countries which are not on the international container network, with modern container berth ports offering a good infrastructure, and served by rail, are seriously disadvantaged. There is no doubt that shippers using the multi-modal container service providing a door-to-door or warehouse-to-warehouse service involving dedicated road or rail services from the port to the inland clearance depot, dry port, etc., are well placed competitively. Many such services involve a feeder service from a hub port. Containerization is a rapidly growing market with larger ships, more container berths, with continuous investment in new technology and port infrastructure – road/rail/inland waterways. Alternatively, the route may be by combi carrier or Ro-Ro ferry – the latter being particularly popular in Mediterranean and cross-channel UK–Continental markets. International trucking is a competitive method of distribution providing a door-to-door or warehouse-to-warehouse service.

    Factors influencing the choice of destination or feeder seaports include: overall efficiency, infrastructure, level of tariffs, overall transit time, degree of technology, general competitiveness, quality of management, range of facilities, proximity of port to the buyer's address, the number of shipping lines using the port and the range of ports served.

3. The criteria for the selection of a destination airport are similar to those for the seaport. Airports are usually located closer to the buyer's premises than the seaport. Moreover, the flight frequency is much

higher compared with the sailing programme and offers much quicker transits.

4. Sea–land bridge and sea–air bridge. As we progress through the next millennium the development of the sea–land and sea–air bridge concepts will continue. Examples of sea–air bridges exist in Singapore and Dubai (p. 61). Such competitively priced services offer quick transit times and provide numerous benefits to the shipper. This transport mode opens up new markets, especially for perishable goods and products selling in fast-moving territories. It also enables good inventory management, invaluable for production which relys on just-in-time and needs stocks to be replenished by quick transits. Exporters in the Far East have benefited enormously from such developments, especially products exported to the wealth-targeted markets of the EU and the USA.

5. Distriparks, found in the major ports of the world such as Rotterdam and Singapore (p. 84), provide a new dimension to international physical distribution. The supplier, shipper or exporter can lease warehouse accommodation in the port environs and assemble, process and label his or her products there with substantial cost savings. The componentized items involved in the assembly process can be sourced from the cheapest markets, and only attract import duty when they enter their market of sale. This is a growth market, especially for consumer goods and foodstuffs.

6. Free trade zones. Similar to the Distriparks, the FTZ (p. 246) enables the user to lease land and accommodation from the port authority and undertake the manufacture and/or componentized assembly process. Again favourable cost savings are realized, including reduced local taxes and rates in the earlier years. Many are called 'industrial zones' and operate in countries which are keen to develop an industrial base. Alternatively, as practised by the Japanese, these zones can be used as an industrial transplant or assembly plant to vitiate the high freight costs, obtain more favourable import tariffs through componentized assembly, overcome the high Japanese labour cost and, finally, as a means to enter markets which are restrictive by using local labour in the manufacturing and assembly process.

7. Customs planning (pp. 598–601). This involves a wide variety of customs activities, including tariff costing outwards, duty preference and origin, freight procurement, VAT, outward processing relief, standard exchange relief, temporarily imported goods, customs warehousing, free zones, carnets, export licensing, export valuation and local export control. Too few exporters or importers examine closely the customs implications of international distribution and fail to check out whether any alternative exists in the customs import tariff payment and the relief options. Outward processing relief and inward processing relief are two examples. Moreover, many shippers

HOW IT USUALLY IS

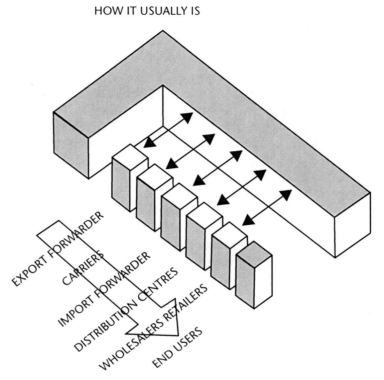

FIGURE 20.1 (a) Localized in-house order processing department of manufacturing company

do not comprehend the reduced import tariff yield when goods are shipped in a componentized or CKD condition rather than as the finished product. Furthermore, the level of import tariff varies by country and such concessions are often inherent in the adoption of Distriparks as assembly or processing plants or FTZs. Overall, customs planning is a complex area. Study Figure 20.2 on p. 588 on computerized customs clearance system.

8. Districentre. An increasing number of the high-profile internationally based transport operators are offering the Districentre concept with an associated range of services. An example is P&O Nedlloyd who operate a complete logistic system as illustrated in Figures 20.1.

    The P&O Nedlloyd Flowmaster system provides a total transportation service package geared to individual manufacturers and their customers' needs. It involves the manufacturer despatching all his products to a strategically located Districentre which is virtually a warehouse. At this stage, P&O Nedlloyd take over all the multiple contacts and customer's orders direct from and supplied by P&O Nedlloyd. The benefits include customerized services designed and

HOW IT COULD BE

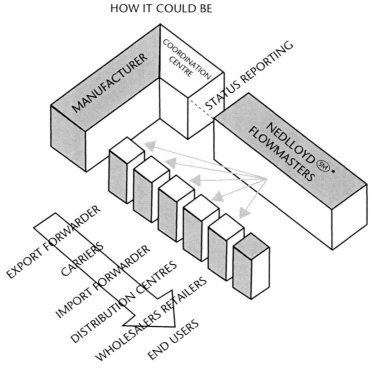

FIGURE 20.1 (b) Nedlloyd Flowmaster diagram

delivered for each client's individual needs; fully integrated services capable of co-ordinating distribution logistics with procurement and production logistics; one-stop shopping for logistic services with most or all services coordinated at one Districentre; improved reliability to enhance clients' ability to keep promises made to their customers; broader market research for clients using an established distribution system; shorter lead rimes for clients seeking to streamline their reaction times in the market place; increased flexibility so clients' market opportunities are not limited by distribution constraints; lower logistic cost with economies of scale; higher satisfaction profile for both manufacturer and their clients; and finally, the value added benefits derived from such services. Overall, it is the process of the manufacturer, supplier and exporter contracting out of distribution and transport: P&O Nedlloyd undertake the complete management of the flow of goods and information and the provision of additional services such as invoicing, packing, sorting and stock control on their behalf. The concept emerges from four major trends which can be distinguished worldwide. In the first place, manufacturers are increasingly concentrating on their core activities: production

CARGO SYSTEMS INTEGRATION

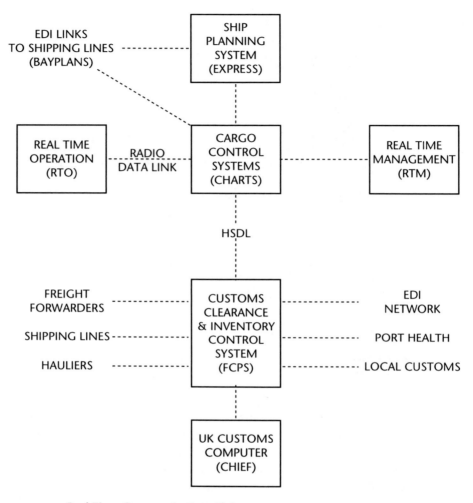

FIGURE 20.2 Computerized Customs Clearance system
Courtesy Felixstowe Dock and Railway Company.

and sales. Secondly, there is a tendency for manufacturers to organize their production decentrally and internationally. Thirdly, the lifecycles of products are becoming shorter so that fast, flexible distribution is increasingly essential. Finally, logistics and EDI are becoming essential in international distribution. Study Figure 20.3 on p. 589 on real time data systems at the Port of Felixstowe.

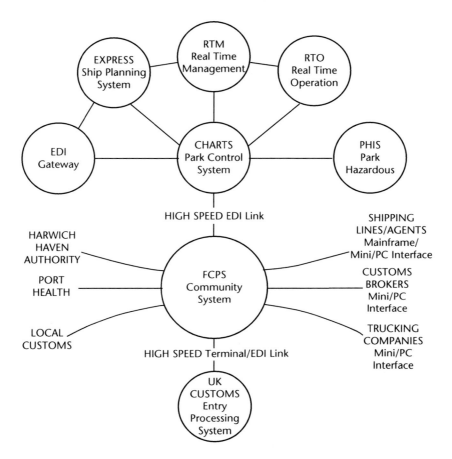

Key systems components include:

CHARTS A management control and planning system for container and Ro-Ro terminals, providing information relating to location, status and availability of cargo.

EXPRESS A twin screen colour graphics shipplanning system with EDI links to shipping lines.

FCPS The community system which processes customs entries and provides inventory control for all imports, exports and hazardous cargoes.

PHIS A park hazardous information system which holds an inventory of all hazardous cargo stores in the terminal.

RTM A real time graphical management system which constantly monitors cargo operations and updates system parameters to meet demands.

RTO A real time operational system, which schedules work to cargo handling equipment using radio data transmission and records the physical location of containers placed in the park.

Felixstowe operates an integrated set of computer systems 24 hours per day, 7 days per week, to support the physical operation and ensure cargo moves through the port in the shortest possible timescale.

Through extensive use of EDI and a dedicated network, shipping lines, agents, customs brokers and trucking companies carry out the majority of their business transactions electronically in real-time. This results in information becoming immediately available to those who need it and eliminates unnecessary, and time consuming, paperwork.

FIGURE 20.3 Real time data systems at the Port of Felixstowe
Courtesy of Felixstowe Dock and Railway Company

9. The benefits of serving a Single Market as found in the EU are outstanding (see pp. 533–40). It offers a high volume of business, potentially good profitability, good infrastructure, very low risk, single product specification, good distribution logistically and computer focused, ease of market entry, free circulation within the market, single currency – the euro, labour mobility within the market and free capital movement. Overall, the euro-zone provides a unique opportunity to the international entrepreneur. Moreover, there are no exchange controls involving repatriation of funds and generally a very stable and low inflation market. It provides opportunities to have regional distribution centres. Furthermore, the enlargement to 25 Member States has further enhanced its trading opportunities.

10. Companies situated in economic blocs and customs unions should strive to export within the bloc or union. This offers the potential to develop volume business and take full advantage of the liberalization of trade within the bloc and the union. It provides an opportunity to develop logistically driven systems with its competitive advantages. Companies should also explore the growing number of regional trade agreement opportunities (pp. 10–11) which can complement the multilateral trading system, helping to build and strengthen it.

11. Routeing. The routeing of the consignment requires critical examination. The ultimate choice will influence transit time, transhipment resources, handling and any constraints on weight, length, etc., customs examination resources, total overall cost, reliability, frequency, mode of transport, value added benefit and insurance. Study the growing number of hub-and-spoke containerized networks with an 'in-built' logistics system.

12. Consolidation. The consolidation of cargo is a growth market by air, truck and container. It is economical and a network of services exists worldwide (pp. 76–82).

13. Packaging. Basically, packing is a form of protection and an aid to handling, identity and stowage. Excessive packing increases the volumetric size of the goods and can thereby increase freight cost on high volume products.

14. Loadability and stowage. Aligned to packing is the general loadability and stowage of the cargo. Shippers with full-load truck and FCL containers should devise a stowage plan to ensure they make the best use of the cubic and weight capacity of the truck or container. Close consultation should take place with the production department to ensure the optimum size packing is devised to maximize loadability. Professional help should be enlisted from the road haulier or container operator and the situation should be continuously reviewed. A 10 per cent improvement in loadability will lower the distribution cost of the product and result in more competitive pricing.

Good loadability and economical distribution can be achieved through the correct use of the mode of transport and type of transport unit. It arises in containerization where the range of container types continues to increase and the shipper must take full advantage of the situation to remain competitive. An example is the high-capacity covered or reefer container of 49 ft or 51 ft long. It may result in the shipper changing the existing distribution pattern and adopting transshipment arrangements to feed into this high-capacity container network.

15. Distribution centres. Associated with the Distriparks, Districentres and free trade zones is the distribution centre. This concept exists whereby the exporter will centralize all his products on one distribution centre which will feed into the neighbouring market. Overall, it could be described as the cluster market distribution centre concept, and instead of the exporter sending goods under consolidated arrangements by truck or container, the merchandise can be despatched as a full truck or FCL container. This provides lower distribution cost and improves the service to the importer. In reality, it is very similar to the just-in-time or Districentre concept.

16. Piggyback and trade associations. A number of exporters selling in common overseas territories have joined forces and operate common distribution channels apportioning the cost. In some situations, the product may be complimentary in the selling process such as two companies working together marketing furniture and furnishings. Such fusing of distribution arrangements lowers the cost significantly as the FCL is used rather than the LCL container movement. Potential exporters often join up with existing exporters in selling their merchandise such as the established overseas exporter selling garden furniture linking up with the company manufacturing greenhouses fresh to the export scene. Such a system is called a 'piggyback' where the inexperienced exporter works on the back of the established overseas exporter. The companies may be situated in neighbouring countries. Another example is a trade association working on behalf of its members through a marketing board promoting and distributing its products overseas; this is particularly evident in foodstuffs.

17. Third countries. An increasing volume of business is now conducted on a third-country basis. For example, an order placed with a Japanese company can be supplied to the EU from a manufacturing plant in Taiwan. This may involve a different distribution network.

18. Buyer's or importer's portfolio and empathy. The wishes of the buyer must be carefully considered and respected. Good relationships and lasting business developments emerge from the strategy of empathy whereby the exporter and importer share each other's views and objectives in the conduct of international trade. Special

attention should be given to the infrastructure obtaining in the buyer's country and the most acceptable, efficient method of distribution.

19. Currency. The freight rate may involve the exporter's or importer's currency or a third currency. Overall, the currency used requires careful evaluation and unstable and non-convertible currencies should be eliminated.

20. Incoterms 2000. Some 13 Incoterms 2000 exist and the one selected should favour both the exporter and importer. An increasing use is now made of multi-modalism and combined transport operation and the appropriate terms used.

21. Audit of carrier or freight forwarder. The selection of the most suitable freight forwarder and carrier requires careful evaluation (pp. 522–23). To test the feasibility of both, test transits should be undertaken. Moreover, a system should be devised to monitor transits to ensure quality is maintained and areas of weakness identified with a view to an early remedy.

22. Direct or indirect marketing. Companies may sell directly to the end-user and thereby follow a strategy of direct marketing. In such situations, the exporter usually has complete influence over the distribution in consultation with the importer. Alternatively, the exporter may sell through an intermediary and have less influence over the distribution arrangements.

23. Transport distribution analysis. This is fully explained on pp. 332–50 and shippers are well advised to use these criteria when the opportunity arises.

24. EDI – Electronic Data Interchange is fully explained in Chapter 16. It is likely that the range of management information relative to international distribution will increase and also the efficiency of processing the cargo internationally.

25. International distribution can be developed more efficiently when operating in an economic bloc or customs union, especially when free circulation obtains with no customs barriers at frontier points.

26. The accelerating development of the LCP (see p. 239) as predicted by the WCO (see p. 227) will facilitate greater efficiency in international distribution. It removes customs barriers at the port, seaport or frontier point of entry or departure and speeds up transit times.

27. Shippers councils exist in many countries and provide a useful contact point to advise on local distribution resources; infrastructure; problem areas and possible solutions; and availability of freight forwarders/logistic operators/customs regulations.

The foregoing list is comprehensive and requires careful evaluation. It points to the fact that international distribution has become highly sophisticated in the past decade and involves many elements each with cost, marketing and efficiency implications. Different products and different markets require different distribution networks. Overall, it is a fast-moving market and a strategy of creating empathy between the buyer and seller is paramount to ensure successful market development. A key factor is the channel of distribution chosen and related distribution network.

20.2 Decision-making process

The process of making the decision relative to the selection of the most acceptable channel of distribution will vary by circumstances. It will involve in particular cost, efficiency ratios, volume of business, transport mode options, nature of cargo, transit times, timescale of cargo shipments, value of cargo, loadability, infrastructure in the seller's and buyer's markets, level of competition and the long-term future of the market. It requires continuous market research and planning to coordinate resources to achieve objectives. Regular visits to the market enable the shipper to evaluate the best distribution network and encourages dialogue with the carrier.

The following checklist has been compiled as a guide to the relevant evaluation criteria.

1. An evaluation of the international physical distribution of an export market in the following areas:

    (a) Potential for sales and growth in the short- and medium-term.
    (b) Market stability reflecting economic, political and social considerations.
    (c) Short- and medium-term profitability.
    (d) Whether it is a near or distant market.
    (e) The infrastructure, both existing and planned, and its compatibility with the home market (focus especially on the sea and airports and road, rail and canal networks on which they rely).
    (f) The routeing and distribution from the seaport or airport to the buyer's premises (including seaport and airport handling charges).
    (g) The import regulations extending to licensing, tariffs and import duty documentation. This can include legislation confirming all insurance cover taken out in the buyer's country.
    (h) The airlines, shipping companies serving the market and their schedules, rates, frequency, transit times, reliability and overall quality of service – consider whether the buyer's government practises flag discrimination, routeing cargoes on their national airline or shipping company.
    (i) Availability and experience of company resources in terms of personnel, finance and overall logistics identifying cost factors both in the short- and medium-term. Companies today focus on logistics and EDI to develop efficient supply chains. Many rely on the logistical resources of a mega-container operator such as P&O Nedlloyd (see pp. 585–87).

(j)   Availability or development of information technology, especially in the areas of management information control and monitoring systems, market feedback, data documentation processing and analysis of the various channels of distribution options.

(k)   The risk areas in terms of exchange risk, political risk and restrictions in the market. For example, is it an open market with no tariff barriers to encourage imports and free trade?

(l)   A profile of the importer and the airlines and shipping companies serving the country, both directly and through transhipment hub routes.

The exporter should produce a grid or comprehensive tabulation relative to the foregoing points as a first stage in the evaluation. The market forecast under item 1(a) will enable the volume of business to be identified on a monthly, weekly or daily basis and thereby reconcile it with the appropriate transport mode options and their loadability. This can be reconciled with the importer's access to any large storage capacity which can receive higher-capacity shipments such as the FCL rather than the LCL container which, in turn, lowers unit distribution costs. Modern warehouses are now computer controlled.

2.   The next stage is to summarize the data of (1) with a view to reconciling them with the export company's international physical distribution strategy. In so doing, carriers which look feasible may require further evaluation and discussions initiated between the shipping manager and carrier.

At this stage, the shipping or international logistics manager will probably have up to three options in response to earlier enquiries. A major factor is the total product cost of each option and the value added benefit each brings, both to the exporter and importer. Many shippers use transport distribution analysis (pp. 331–50) to aid their decision-making. It is possible that shippers will tend to patronize carriers with whom they have existing contracts on other routes, or earlier favourable experience; but when serving new markets, a fresh approach may be desirable to retain competitiveness.

3.   The next stage is to carry out some test transits. In so doing each stage of the transit should be monitored in order to identify any problem areas. Full liaison must be maintained with all parties involved in the transit. A significant factor in the distribution network adopted is the loadability of the transport unit. This is determined by the configuration of the packing and its stowage effectiveness, with broken stowage at a minimum. This involves close liaison between the shipping manager, the production department and the carrier to ensure, for example, that the most suitable truck or container is provided. Loadability can be improved by breaking down the consignment.

4. The next stage is to evaluate the test transit(s), and following consultation with interested parties including the importer, decide on the most appropriate distribution network and firm up the total cost of the product.

5. The final stage is to devise an action plan to execute the decision. Overall, it must be controlled by the shipping manager and be monitored through the budgetary control methods. Good planning is the essential ingredient to an efficient international distribution network, plus total commitment from all parties – production manager, importer, carrier, agent, port, etc. essential in supply chain management.

20.3 Problem areas and possible solutions

International physical distribution is becoming a high-tech and extremely competitive operation. Innovation and the striving for greater efficiency are very much in evidence as we move through the twenty-first century. Generally, it is becoming more logistically and EDI driven. Areas of particular significance are the swap-body, the sea–land bridge, the sea–air bridge, high-capacity containers of 49 ft or 51 ft long and 9 ft 6 in high integrators (p. 58) and finally, the Euro Tunnel. Seaports are playing an increasingly decisive role in the development of trade and are market driven in their strategies and investment. However, one must acknowledge that problem areas do arise in the distribution network which the shipper must resolve. Given below are a number of problems together with possible solutions.

1. Industrial disputes, or a build-up of traffic at a seaport, can seriously disrupt a service and result in the goods arriving late and beyond the expiry date of the import licence and letter of credit. Alternative routes should be explored at the earliest possible time to include transferring to air freight. Such situations usually build up over a period of a few days and a contingency plan should be devised at this stage and put in place.

2. The range of truck and container types tends to increase, but it does generate an imbalance of their use. This is especially true in the container business. An example can also be seen in a market where liquid imports predominate and perishable foodstuffs and machinery are exported thereby requiring two different types of containers. It is primarily a problem for the carriers, but it can result in shortages of specific container types at peak times.

3. Dangerous goods and indivisible loads, such as transformers or engineering plant with a weight of up to 250 tonnes, require special arrangements. Dangerous goods are described on pp. 201–17, but a key factor is to initiate the pre-shipment booking arrangements as early as possible. As for indivisible loads, these products require special

arrangements and the freight forwarder specializing in such work usually has a project forwarding department to handle such transits. The following points are relevant in the international movement of indivisible loads.

(a)   The ports of departure, destination and any transhipment areas need to be checked out to ensure they can handle such a shipment, checking especially for the availability of heavy lifting equipment.

(b)   The shipowner will have to have a plan and specification of the shipment to evaluate the stowage and handling arrangements; and also to identify the weight distribution.

(c)   The transportation of an indivisible load to and from the ports requires pre-planning particularly regarding route and timescale. Usually such goods may only move at night under police escort and subject to the police and/or transport department's permission.

(d)   The rates for transporting indivisible loads are usually assessed on a cost plus profit basis. The cost can be very extensive as it incorporates any heavy lifting equipment and special arrangements to transport the goods overland to and from the ports. Freight forwarders tend to work closely with the correspondent agent in the destination country. Transhipment costs can be much reduced if a 'Mafi'-type six-axle trailer is used as in the Ro-Ro tonnage.

The advantages of the indivisible load shipment to the shipper, buyer or importer include lower overall transportation cost; quicker transit; much reduced site assembly cost; less risk of damage in transit; lower insurance premium; less technical aid and staff resources required by the buyer as there is no extensive site assembly work; equipment is tested and fully operational in the factory before despatch; no costly site assembly work; less risk of malfunctioning equipment; and earlier commissioning of the equipment which, in turn, results in the quicker productive use of the equipment with profitable benefits to the buyer overall.

4.   Companies need to monitor closely all transits and any irregularities, initiating early remedial measures with the parties concerned. If it is difficult to establish the cause of the problems, such as late arrival, damaged cargo, missing merchandise, etc., test transits should be undertaken. Computerization of the shipping logistics office enables much of the routine work to be done much quicker and more accurately, especially documentation processing, thereby releasing staff for more managerial activities within the department (pp. 431–49).

5.   International physical distribution tends in some companies to have a low profile in the management structure, especially at the more

senior level. This is now changing as companies become more globally focused in their market and acknowledge that to remain competitive they must have a professionally qualified team managing their international physical distribution as it is a budget driven element of the business.

6. Exchange risk still remains evident in many markets. Advice should be sought from professional sources, especially the national bank of the importer's country.

7. Cargo insurance features in Incoterms 2000. Exporters should check that the importer has insured the goods as specified in its contract and take contingency measures when in doubt.

8. Documentary credits should be thoroughly checked on arrival to ensure they represent the terms already agreed and the exporter can comply with the distribution arrangements.

9. Faulty documents are a frequent cause of late payment and late delivery of goods (pp. 295–96). Professionally qualified personnel handling such documents can reduce the risk, and attendance at training courses and seminars enables staff to keep up-to-date.

10. Full use should be made of EDI resources and techniques.

11. Finally, a logistics distribution plan should be devised and monitored using EDI resources.

Logistics embracing the supply chain management features complete transparency throughout the transit thereby permitting dialogue among all the parties forming the transit. This provides opportunity to identify problems and resolve them on a preplanning basis.

20.4 Logistics strategy

Shippers are today increasingly looking at the total production and value added chain; in consequence, shippers are looking more closely at the logistics part of their business. Basically, the art of logistics is the ability to get the right product to the right place at the right time. As a result, the shipper is no longer interested in the point-to-point operator, such as airport-to-airport or seaport-to-seaport, but the total product involving the value added chain. This new approach is linked to the just-in-time concept in management techniques. In consequence, this has stimulated the expansion of express air services (p. 58) and integrated operators such as UPS, TNT, DHL and logistic containers/truck operators.

Integrated operators offer a complete package for the air cargo shipper, embracing not only collection and airport-to-airport flight, but delivery to the importer's address with a guaranteed arrival time. The integrator undertakes all the customs documentation and clearance. Products ideally suited to this market are the high-tech and pharmaceutical industries, but it is less appropriate in the traditional engineering and manufacturing sectors.

However, it is likely to grow quickly in the EU. Many of the integrators have logistics departments whose tasks are to identify customers' needs, tailor solutions to their specific problems and provide them with a value added service. Other areas covered by the integrators include provision of waybills, invoices and management reports, availability of a bonded warehouse, stock control and so on. Overall, the aim is to combine production, ware-housing distribution and transport for shippers on a global basis.

Undoubtedly, the mega-container operators such as P&O Nedlloyd are driving the logistic global expansion (see Chapter 6). Many mega-container operators have their own logistics divisions thereby encouraging shippers to place their international distribution arrangements with the shipowners. This embraces all elements of the distribution network including warehousing, supplier selection, packaging, customs clearance and associated documentation.

With an increasingly competitive market, logistics operations are under close scrutiny to minimize the cost while maximizing the customer service. This involves supply chain modelling; warehouse and plant location; warehouse and transport operational modelling; stock optimization; warehouse design and equipment; systems and operations specification; and the implementation of change. Logistics strategies are particularly relevant in trading blocs, and this applies especially to the EU, ASEAN and LAFTA. Also, it is especially relevant to fast-moving products where competition is fierce and service quality is paramount to the customer. Costs must be kept at a minimum if the integrator is to remain competitive.

To conclude our brief analysis, it is likely the logistics strategy will feature more strongly in manufacturers' and suppliers' globalization of their markets and carriers will respond more to the challenge of change and opportunity as we move on through the millennium. Again planning features strongly in the formulation and execution of this strategy. It is market led, and market research plays an essential and continuous role.

20.5 Customs planning

For many years a large number of companies engaged in international trade regarded payment of customs duties and the cost of compliance with customs law and regulations as unavoidable expenses with little or no scope for planning. Today with ever-increasing competition in the market place, companies have to be more competitive in the product they sell. Moreover, with the EU Single Market entity, customs law has become more complex.

Customs planning produces savings not only to the exporter and importer, but also to the ordinary business. If a company uses imported components or manufacturers for export, savings can be realized by the judicious use of the reliefs and facilities available. Most manufacturers' products contain items 'bought in', many of them from sources outside the EU. Hence many of the customs planning considerations apply both to goods sourced from outside the EU and to the sale and export of finished and semi-finished products.

Customs planning involves arranging a company's affairs to ensure that it suffers minimum possible exposure to taxation within the law. The taxes involved are import duties, Common Agricultural Policy levies, excise duties and VAT. Savings can be realized in the cost of complying with customs requirements. Customs and Excise offer a variety of simplified procedures to ease both their own administrative burden and traders' costs of compliance. Effective customs planning offers the following benefits:

1. minimizes the trader's exposure to customs duties;
2. maximizes the trader's use of facilities and reliefs;
3. minimizes the trader's cost of compliance;
4. improves the trader's profitability and cash flow;
5. avoids the risk of seizure and penalties.

Given below are the main areas of customs planning.

1. The tariff is the centre of customs planning. It determines the rate of duty on imported goods according to their description and specification listed against a numerical commodity code. Situations can arise when the goods are wrongly described and attract a higher rate of duty than necessary.

    Customs planning is desirable at the design stage of a new product, whether it is to be imported as a finished article for onward sale or to be used by the importer in a further manufacturing process. Furthermore, if imported items are to be used in the manufacturing process, one must evaluate the financial merits of importing components rather than sub-assembly from individual components. For the business operating in more than one country, there is a further aspect to be considered. Over 50 countries now use the Harmonized System of Tariff Classification and Commodity Coding (HS). Hence the same item will be appropriate to the same commodity code in each of these states, although of course there are likely to be considerable differences in the rates of duty. Thus entrepreneurs must consider the impact in all countries into which they import to ensure that the advantage gained in one is not more than offset by advantages lost in others. Ideally it is worthwhile agreeing the appropriate commodity codes with suppliers when importing and with customers when exporting, well in advance of the consignment crossing international frontiers.

2. More than two-thirds of the world trade governing customs valuation falls within an international code negotiated under WTO. Countries which are signatories to the code have the option of using cost, insurance and freight (CIF) or free on board (FOB). They can

also choose whether to convert foreign to national currencies using the rate of exchange at the time of importation or exportation. Some countries, such as the EU Member States, use a CIF value, while others, such as the USA, accept FOB. An exporter should be aware of which of these variations his customer needs to apply to ensure that both gain maximum results.

3.   The customs value of the vast majority of the consignments is based on the price actually paid or payable for the goods by the importer. Adjustments upwards or downwards frequently need to be made to invoiced prices. These include commission, discounts, transport, insurance and price review clauses. These aspects are of a particular concern when applied to transactions between related parties such as trading between companies in a multinational group.

4.   Customs warehousing is among the most useful of the various reliefs available. It permits goods liable to import duty to be stored in Customs and Excise warehouses without duty or VAT being accounted for until the goods are removed from the warehouse. A limited range of minor handling operations may be carried out on the goods while they are in the warehouse, where they remain for up to five years. When required to be moved, they must be entered for export or removed to another similar warehouse or transferred to another regime such as Inward Processing Relief.

5.   The origin of imported goods and the route they follow to the EU has considerable influence on their liability to duty. If they are imported from a country with a preference agreement with the EU, then the rate is reduced or even zero. If not, inevitably the question arises as to whether the source can be changed or whether the specification can be varied to include less offshore elements of value.

    Suspension of the full rate of duty may be available from specified countries at certain times in particular goods. Similarly, a quota may be in force which allows predetermined quantities of goods meeting certain tariff descriptions to be imported at a lower than full rate of duty. Hence the benefits of preferential rates of duty can be used to reduce manufacturing cost. They are also available to buyers of UK goods, provided that they are imported into a country that has entered into a trading agreement with the EU. Similar rules of origin and consignment apply albeit in reverse. The exporter who plans to ensure that his or her goods originate in the EU and can therefore provide a certificate of origin should find that his or her prices to many overseas customers are more competitive.

6.   Outward processing relief arises when the goods are exported for a manufacturing process and then returned to the EU. Prior authorization by customs is required before the relief is allowed. The duty payable on the goods returned is reduced by the nominal duty that would have been charged on the exported elements (pp. 244–45).

7. Inward processing relief is available to traders who are importing goods from countries that are not members of the EU. The imported goods may be used for virtually any manufacturing process and are relieved from import duty, provided that the products are re-exported beyond the frontiers of the EU. The trader has to seek prior authorization from customs to suspend the import duty (the 'suspension' method) or to recover it once the products have been exported ('draw back' method) (p. 244).

This should not be regarded as an exhaustive list and other items would include free trade zones, processing for free circulation and anti-dumping duties. Customs planning forms an important element in the physical distribution strategy and requires continuous monitoring of the customs duties and regulations.

20.6 The future

As we progress through the twenty-first century it is likely that the pace of change in the conduct and execution of international trade will accelerate. Such change will place more emphasis on management techniques and strategy in the computer literate, logistically focused globalization of international trade.

An increasing number of companies will have the majority of their business overseas with the home domestic market accounting for a diminishing proportion of their sales. MNEs and SMEs will engage in mergers and acquisitions, joint ventures and operating alliances in their endeavours to reduce cost, become more competitive, increase international business market share and rationalize production, research and development. Overall, this will result in such companies being able to expand their business further internationally, generating adequate profit to invest in high-tech and logistic systems which will be so important in the future.

To match company expansion and the growth of world trade, physical distribution will play a larger part. For example, we can already see the development of the hub and spoke system in container networks, the continuing merger and operating alliances of the mega-containers, the increasing importance of ports and their infrastructure, the growing development of customs clearance at the trader's premises and the continuing expansion of multi-modalism. Air freight will continue to expand particularly on the long haul flights with larger capacity aircraft. More airports will be open in the Far East and globally existing ones modernized, especially their air freight facilities. The concept of sea–air bridges will expand further.

The political influence on trade will gain momentum. Governments will stimulate the enlargement of economic blocs and customs unions.

This will result in such economies becoming more economic, productive and competitive, resulting in more investment and trade expansion. The WTO will facilitate such expansion.

The era of change is gaining momentum especially with E-commerce. It has opened up new markets and produced a new generation of international entrepreneurs. This is being transmitted in trade finance transactions, logistics management, negotiation, Internet advertising, research, documentation transmission and many other areas. It has become a very fast-moving international trade market which has become more transparent and more competitive. Globalization is driving political change and cultures are becoming more integrated. Living standards are rising in many communities in many countries as trade brings more wealth opportunities. China, India and Brazil are becoming major players in the trade markets. This is all possible because confidence exists in the global market, through the existence of the mechanism under which trade, distribution and finance is conducted. This is realized through international conventions/regulations and the consensus realized among trading nations. Moreover, the infrastructure is changing through seaport and airport modernization, coupled with the unprecedented level of shipbuilding – containerization, dry and wet bulk cargo, and a range of specialized vessels. Such investment generates confidence in the global marketplace and enables industrial and consumer goods to be distributed in an efficient, productive, reliable, competitive and safe manner across the world.

This title is now 27 years old and the market leader in export management. The fifth edition has a complete focus on present and future practices and strategies. It reflects major changes in the industry especially in the field of E-commerce. A new chapter has been included to feature International Trade Law, and additional material on culture, European Union, Marketing, country analysis, and market entry strategies. More case studies have been included and an increased input from a larger number of organizations and companies. It is hoped the latest edition will help both students and undergraduates and international entrepreneurs in their endeavours to develop and execute a successful international trade strategy.

Addresses of national and international organizations involved in facilitating international trade development

Name and address of organization	Role of organization
Advertising Association 15 Wilton Road LONDON SW1V 1NJ	The professional body representing advertising focused companies
Association of International Courier and Express Services PO Box 10 Leatherhead Surrey KT22 0HT	The professional body representing Couriers and Express Services Companies
Baltic and International Maritime Council (BIMCO) 161 Bagsvaerdvej 2880 Bagsvaerd Denmark www.bimco.dk	An international organization of shipowners, shipbrokers, ship agents and associations of shipowners
Baltic Exchange St Mary Axe London EC3A 8BH www.balticexchange.com	An international shipping market/place where ship chartering is conducted involving both the shipowner and merchant through a shipbroker
British Chambers of Commerce www.britishchambers.org.uk	Organization representing and co-ordinating their activities.
British Exporters Association 16 Dartmouth Street London SW1H 9BL www.bexa.co.uk	A UK organization of some 200 companies which are specialists in all aspects of international trade.

Name and address of organization	*Role of organization*
Food From Britain 4th Floor Manning House 22 Carlisle Place London SW1P 1JA www.foodfrombritain.com	Responsible for developing and facilitating UK food products overseas
British Importers Association Suite 8 Castle House 25 Castlereagh Street London W1H 5YR	A UK organization whose aim is to facilitate the importation of goods into the UK
British International Freight Association Redfern House Browells Lane Feltham, Middlesex DW13 7EP www.bita.org	The professional body representing Freight Forwarding Companies
British Maritime Equipment Council 4th Floor 30 Great Guildford Street London SE1 0HS	Marine standards, marketing, and marketing intelligence, finding an agent and exporting
British Shippers Council (BSC) Hermes House 157 St Johns Road Tunbridge Wells Kent TN4 9UZ www.fta.co.uk	Organization representing British Shippers at both National and International level in all matters concerning the overseas transport of their goods whether by sea or air embracing the interest of both importers and exporters in Great Britain. Part of the FTA
British Standards Institution (BSI) 389 Chiswick High Road London W4 4AL www.bsi-global.com.export	UK organization involved in formulation and management of British Standards for UK products
Chamber of Shipping (UK) Carthusian Court 12 Carthusian Street London EC1M 6EB www.british-shipping.org	Trade organization representing UK shipowners
Chartered Institute of Logistics and Transport Centre PO Box 5787 Corby, Northants, NN17 4XQ www.iolt.org.uk	The professional institute for those personnel involved in logistics and transport
Chartered Institute of Marketing Moor Hall Cookham Maidenhead Berkshire www.cim.co.uk	The professional institute for those personnel involved in marketing

Name and address of organization	*Role of organization*
Confederation of British Industries (CBI) Centre Point 103 New Oxford Street London WC1A 1DU www.cbi.org.uk	Organization which represents British industry
Cotecna International Ltd Hounslow House 730 London Road Hounslow, Middlesex	Organization responsible globally for processing pre-shipment inspection arrangements
UK Trade and Investment Export Control Organization Kingsgate House 66-74 Victoria Street London SW1E 6SW www.dti.gov.uk/exportcontrol/ index.htm	UK government department organization responsible for controlling/issuing export licences
UK Trade and Investment Import Licensing Branch Queensway House West Precinct Billingham Cleveland TS23 2NF e-mail enquiries: www.ilbaimlb. dti.gov.uk	UK government department organization responsible for controlling/issuing export licences
UK Trade and Investment Kingsgate House 66-74 Victoria Street London SW1H 6SW www.tradeinvest.gov.uk/information- centre/home/welcome/index.shtml	UK Government department providing market research data/country profile in countries globally
European Union (EU) European Parliament 97-113 Rue Belliard 1047 Brussels Belgium www.europarl.eu.int	Headquarters of EU involving 25 countries
Exportmaster Systems Ltd 33 St Peter's Street South Croydon CR2 7DG www.exportmaster.co.uk	Company specializing in export software
Freight Transport Association (FTA) Hermes House 157 St Johns Road Tunbridge Wells Kent TN4 9UZ www.fta.co.uk	Organization representing British shippers at both national and international level in all matters concerning the overseas transport of their goods whether by sea or air embracing the interest of both importers and exporters in Great Britain

Name and address of organization	*Role of organization*
Fruit Importers Association (FIA) D 114-115 Fruit and Vegetable Market New Covent Garden London	A national organization specializing in the facilitation of fruit importation into the UK
HM Customs and Excise UK Deferment Section Statistical Office Room 1204 Portcullis House 27 Victoria Avenue Southend on Sea Essex SS2 6AL www.hmce.gov.uk	Customs organization dealing with VAT
Institute of Chartered Shipbrokers 85 Grace Church Street London EC2V OAA www.ics.org.uk	The professional institute for all those personnel involved in shipbrokerage
Institute of Export Export House Minerva Business Park Lynch Wood Peterborough PE2 OFT www.export.org.uk	The professional institute for all those personnel involved in exporting and importing
Institute of Translation and Interpreting www.iti.org.uk	The professional institute for those personnel involved in translation and interpreting work
International Air Transport Association (IATA) www.iata.org/dangerousgoods	A non-governmental organization of 55 member airlines responsible for international rates and fare levels. It also deals with documentation, cargo handling, legal matters, financial and technical aspects with a view to the facilitating and developing of international airline traffic by scheduled IATA services globally
International Association of Ports and Harbours (IAPH) Kotohira Kaikan Building 1-2-8 Taranomon Minato - Ku Tokyo 105 Japan	A non-governmental organization representing seaports internationally
International Chamber of Commerce (ICC) 38 Cours Albert 1 75008 Paris France www.iccwbo.org	A federation of National Chambers of Commerce – embracing some 101 member countries – whose aim is to promote an expansion in international trade and investment by encouraging national economic growth

Name and address of organization	*Role of organization*
International Chamber of Commerce United Kingdom 14/15 Belgrave Square London WS1X 8PS	UK organization which is affiliated to the International Chamber of Commerce
International Maritime Organisation (IMO) 4 Albert Embankment London SE1 7SR www.imo.org	Global organization responsible for developing ship safety, maritime pollution, maritime dangerous cargo and ship construction and survey
International Maritime Satellite Organisation (INMARSAT) 99 City Road London EC1 www.inmarsat.com	Internationally owned cooperative which provides mobile satellite communication worldwide in the areas of commercial, distress and safety applications at sea, in the air and on land
International Monetary Fund (IMF) Washington DC 20431 USA	An international organization – embracing some 141 member countries – which encourages monetary co-operation, exchange policy, promotes stable exchange rates among member nations and makes short term advances and 'standby credits' to members in temporary payment difficulties
London Chamber of Commerce and Industry 33 Queen Street London EC4R 1AP	Organization which represents the industrial and service sectors in London UK
Maersk Sealand UK 1 Canada Square Canary Wharf London E14 5DP www.maersksealand.com	A mega-container operator and ship owner
Organisation for Economic Co-operation and Development (OECD) 2 Rue Andre Pascal 75775 Paris Cedex 16 France www.oecdforum.org	International organization of 25 member countries whose aim is to promote economic and social welfare throughout the OECD area by assisting member countries in the formulation and coordination of policies designed to this end and to stimulate and harmonize members' efforts in favour of developing countries
P&O Nedlloyd Ltd Capital Gate 320 New North Road Hainault Essex IG6 3ES www.poul.com	A mega-container operator and shipowner

Name and address of organization	*Role of organization*
Pira International Rawdalls Road Leatherhead Surrey KT27 7RU	UK research association for paper and board, printing, publishing and packaging industries
SGS United Kingdom Ltd SGS House 217-221 London Road Camberley Surrey GU15 3EY www.sgsgroup.co.uk	Organization responsible globally for processing pre-shipment inspection arrangements
Simpler Trade Procedures Board (SITPRO) Oxford House 8th Floor 76 Oxford Street London W1D 1BS www.sitpro.org.uk	UK organization whose aim is to encourage the rationalization of international trade procedures and information flows associated with them
Technical Help for Exporters (THE) British Standards Institution 389 Chiswick High Road London W4 4AL www.bsi-global.com.export	UK organization providing a versatile service identifying and supplying documents with translations where applicable with a view to giving assistance to UK manufacturers on foreign technical requirements
United Nations Commission International Trade Law (UNCITRAL) Vienna International Centre PO Box 500 A-1400 Vienna Austria	An international organization whose aim is to further the progressive harmonization and unification of the law of international trade
United Nations Conference on Trade and Development (UNCTAD) Palais des Nations CH-1211 Geneve 10 Switzerland www.transport.section@unctad.org	An international organization with 157 member countries whose aim is to help modify the traditional patterns of international trade so that developing countries would be able to play their part in world commerce
World Trade Organisation (WTO) Centre William Rappard Rue de Lausanne 154 CH-1211 Geneve 21 Switzerland www.wto.org	United Nations organization providing the legal and institutional foundation of the multilateral trading system. It provides the principal contractual obligations determining how governments frame and implement domestic trade legislation and regulations

Publications for the international entrepreneur

ABC – Air Cargo Guide
Business Monitor International
Container Journal International
The Economist
Economic Intelligence Unit (EIU) country reports
Exporting World
Export Times
Financial Times – Country Analysis
Freight Management (International)
Freight News
Handy Shipping Guide
Incoterms 2000 – ICC publication
International Chamber of Commerce (reports/publications)
International Freighting Weekly
International Trade
Kellys Export Services
Lloyd's List and Shipping Gazette
Merchant's Guide (P&O Nedlloyd)
Overseas Trade (DTI)
SITPRO Annual Report
UCP500 – ICC publication

Various publications and handbooks on export and import practice and trade finance are available (usually free) from the major international banks, situated worldwide. Also leading national and international newspapers and journals frequently publish, as a supplement, a country report analysis or overview of a particular industry with a global focus.

Export documents

Readers may wish to study documentation in greater depth, in which case they are recommended to read the companion volume *Shipping and Air Freight Documentation for Importers and Exporters and Associate Terms* – published by Witherby & Co., London (2nd Edition 2000). e-mail: www.books@witherbys.co.uk

FIGURE C1 Bill of lading combined transport shipment or port to port shipment
Courtesy of P&O Nedlloyd

Carrier: Hapag-Lloyd Container Linie GmbH, Hamburg   **Bill of Lading**   Multimodal Transport or Port to Port Shipment

Shipper:

Hapag-Lloyd

Carrier's Reference: | B/L-No.: | Page:

Consignee or Order:

Export References:

Forwarding Agent:

Notify Address (Carrier not responsible for failure to notify; see clause 20 (1) hereof):

Consignee's Reference:

Place of Receipt:

Precarrying Vessel: Voyage-No.:

Ocean Vessel(s):   Voyage-No.:

Place of Delivery:

Port of Loading:

Port of Discharge:

Container Nos.. Seal Nos.; Marks and Nos. | Number and Kind of Packages, Description of Goods | Gross Weight: | Measurement:

Shipper's declared Value (see clause 7(1) and 7(2))

Above Particulars as declared by Shipper. Without responsibility or warranty as to correctness by Carrier (see clause 11(1) and (2))

Total No. of Containers received by the Carrier: | Packages received by the Carrier:

RECEIVED by the Carrier from the Shipper in apparent good order and condition (unless otherwise noted herein) the total number or quantity of Containers or other packages or units indicated in the box opposite entitled "Total No. of Containers/Packages received by the Carrier" for Carriage subject to all the terms and conditions hereof (INCLUDING THE TERMS AND CONDITIONS ON THE REVERSE HEREOF AND THE TERMS AND CONDITIONS OF THE CARRIER'S APPLICABLE TARIFF) from the Place of Receipt or the Port of Loading, whichever is applicable, to the Port of Discharge or the Place of Delivery, whichever is applicable. One original Bill of Lading, duly endorsed, must be surrendered by the Merchant to the Carrier in exchange for the Goods or a delivery order. In accepting this Bill of Lading the Merchant expressly accepts and agrees to all its terms and conditions whether printed, stamped or written, or otherwise incorporated, notwithstanding the non-signing of this Bill of Lading by the Merchant.

IN WITNESS WHEREOF the number of original Bills of Lading stated below all of this tenor and date has been signed, one of which being accomplished the others to stand void.

Movement: | Currency:

Charge | Rate | Basis | Wt/Vol/Val | P/C | Amount

Place and date of issue:

Freight payable at: | Number of original Bs/L:

Total Freight Prepaid | Total Freight Collect | Total Freight

90119247

FIGURE C1 *continued* Bill of Lading Multi-modal Transport or Port to Port Shipment
Courtesy of Hapag-Lloyd

FIGURE C2 Non-negotiable waybill for combined transport shipment or port to port shipment
Courtesy of P&O Nedlloyd

FIGURE C3 Standard shipping note – for non-dangerous goods only
Courtesy of SITPRO

FIGURE C4 Dangerous Goods Note
Courtesy of SITPRO

FIGURE C5 Integrate Export Document-Customs Document
Courtesy of Port Klang

1. Company name/logo (print or stamp)

THE BALTIC AND INTERNATIONAL MARITIME CONFERENCE
UNIFORM TIME CHARTER PARTY FOR VESSELS CARRYING
CHEMICALS IN BULK
CODE NAME: "BIMCHEMTIME"   PART I

2. Place and date

3. Owners/full style and address

4. Charterers/full style and address

5. Vessel's name
6. Vessel's flag

7. Warranted average speed in knots on a daily bunker consumption of (also state grade(s) of bunker oil) (Cl. 4(b))

8. Vessel's d.w. all told on summer freeboard

Vessel's tank capacity (state number of stainless steel tanks and coated tanks and total capacity of each category of tanks (100%) in cubic metres) (Cl. 4(a))

9. Vessel's cargo pumps (state number of pumps and designed capacity (cbm./w./h.)) (Cl. 4(a))

10. Status of cargo tanks on delivery (Cl. 4(c))

11. Status of cargo tanks on re-delivery (Cl. 13(b))

12. Maximum heating temperature (state if max. heating temperature is the same for centre- and wing tanks) (Cl.14)

13. Maximum number of types of cargo with complete segregation (Cl. 25)

14. Details of products to be carried (Cl. 4(a))

15. Period of hire (Cl. 1)

16. Port or place of delivery (if applicable, also state time for declaration of port of delivery) (Cl.2)

17. Earliest time for delivery (Cl. 2)

18. Cancelling date (Cl. 3)

19. Port or place of re-delivery (Cl. 12)

20. Number of days' notice of port and place of re-delivery (Cl. 12)

21. Trading limits and exclusions (Cl. 5)

22. Bunkers on delivery (Cl. 9)

23. Bunkers on re-delivery (Cl. 9)

24. Charter hire (also state lump sum for overtime and extras) (Cl. 10 & Cl. 16)

per

Lump sum for overtime and extras specified in Cl. 16

25. Hire payment (state currency, mode and place of payment; also beneficiary and bank account) (Cl. 10)

26. Drydocking (state period between periodical drydockings and also when vessel last drydocked) (Cl. 20)

27. Overhaul and maintenance (indicate no. of hours agreed) (Cl. 21)

28. Compliance with regulations (Cl. 22)

29. War (state value of vessel acc. to sub-cl.(b) and names of countries acc. to sub-cl. (e)) (Cl. 32)

Indicate whether sub-clause (c) agreed or not (state "yes" or "no")

30. General average to be settled in (only to be filled in if place other than London agreed) (Cl. 34)

31. Applicable law (if not filled in, English law shall apply) (Cl. 42)

32. Place of arbitration/arbitration court (if not filled in, arbitration in London shall apply) (Cl. 43)

33. Numbers of additional clauses covering special provisions, if agreed

It is mutually agreed that this Contract shall be performed subject to the conditions contained in the Charter Party consisting of Part I including additional clauses, if any agreed and stated in Box 33, and Part II including the specification as per the TECHNICAL FORM as well as the Tank Coating and/or Stainless Steel Resistance List referred to in Part II, Clause 4(a) and Clause 7, respectively. In the event of a conflict of conditions, the provisions of Part I shall prevail over those of Part II to the extent of such conflict but no further.

Signature (Owners)

Signature (Charterers)

Printed and sold by Fr. G. Knudtzons Bogtrykkeri A/S, 55 Toldbodgade, Copenhagen by authority of The Baltic and International Maritime Conference (BIMCO), Copenhagen.

*(Left margin vertical text:)*
Adopted by the Documentary Committee of the General Council of British Shipping, London

Adopted by the Documentary Committee of INTERTANKO, Oslo

FIGURE C6 Charterparty
Courtesy of the Baltic International Maritime Council

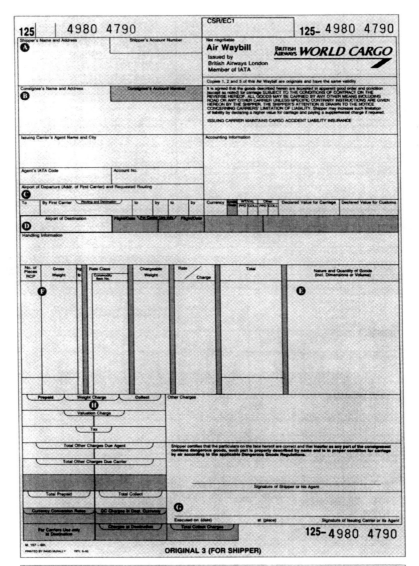

FIGURE C7 Air waybill
Courtesy of British Airways

FIGURE C8 Certificate of Insurance
Courtesy of Guardian Insurance

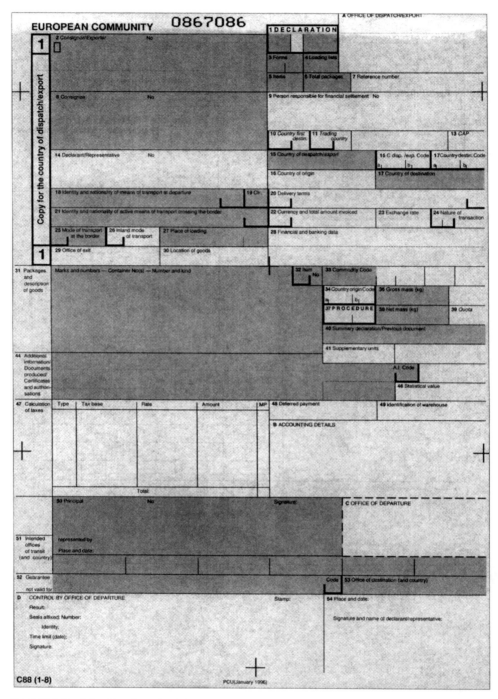

FIGURE C9 Single Administrative Document – Page 1 of 8-page Customs Document-Form C88

Courtesy of H.M. Customs and Excise

Glossary of shipping and international trade terms and abbreviations

AAA	Association of Average Adjusters
About	When referring to the amount or the quantity of items or the unit price of the goods, 'about' means plus or minus 10 per cent. See Article 39 of UCP500.
A/C	Account current.
Acceptance	A written undertaking on the face of a bill of exchange to pay the bill amount on the due date. An alternative name for an accepted bill of exchange.
Accepting Bank	The bank which accepts a draft drawn under a documentary credit.
Accepting house	Financial house, often a merchant banker, specializing in financing foreign trade.
Act of God	Any fortuitous act which could not have been prevented by any amount of human care and forethought.
Action plan	A plan to identify each participant in a coordinated activity.
ADR	European agreement on the international carriage of dangerous goods by road.
Ad valorem freight	Freight rate based on percentage value of goods shipped.
AES (US)	Automated Export System
Affreightment	A contract for the carriage of goods by sea for shipment expressed in charterparty or bill of lading.
Agent	One who represents a principal, or buys or sells for another.
Air waybill	Air freight consignment note.

Aligned Export Documentation System	Method whereby as much information as possible is entered in a 'master document' so that all or part of this information can be reproduced mechanically into individual forms of a similar design.
Amendment	An alteration to the terms and conditions of the credit, issued at the request of the applicant.
AMT	Air mail transfer – a remittance purchased by the debtor from his banker in international trade.
ANF	Arrival notification form – advice to consignee of goods coming forward.
Arbitration	Methods of settling disputes which is usually binding on the parties concerned.
ATA carnet	Admission temporaire. International Customs document to cover the temporary export of certain goods (commercial samples and exhibits for international trade fairs abroad and professional equipment) to countries which are parties to the ATA Convention. Also covers the reimportation of such goods.
Athens Convention	International convention governing carrier's liability for passengers and their baggage by air.
Average bond	Bond in which cargo owners agree to pay their share in the general average losses, each contribution being determined by the average adjuster.
Average deposit	Cash security deposited by the consignee pending assessment of general average contribution.
Back freight	Freight (additional) incurred through cargo being returned from destination port, usually because its acceptance was refused.
BAF	Bunker adjustment factor. Freight adjustment factor to reflect current cost of bunkers.
Balance of trade	Financial statement of balance of a country's visible trade export and imports.
BIFA	British International Freight Association. Trade association of British Freight Forwarders.
Bilateralism	Trade between two countries.

Bill of exchange	Written request from a creditor to a debtor ordering the debtor to pay a specified sum to a specified person or bearer at a certain date. It is usually referred to as a draft.
Bill of lading	Receipt for goods shipped on board a ship signed by the person (or his agent) who contracts to carry them, and stating the terms on which the goods are carried.
Bill of sight	Customs import form, used when importer cannot make customs entry complete owing to insufficient information from the shipper.
BIMCO	Baltic and International Maritime Council. A Danish based organization to which many shipowners belong that represents their interests and assists by preparing standard charterparties and other shipping documents and providing other advisory services including data on seaport and market reports.
B/L ton	Bill of lading ton. The greater weight or measurement of goods where 1 ton is either 1000 kilos or 1 cubic metre. Also called Freight ton.
Bolero	An electronic Bill of Lading System.
Bond	Guarantee to customs of specified amount of duty to be paid.
Box	Colloquial name for a container.
Boxtime	A standard BIMCO time charter for containerships.
B/P	Bills payable.
Break-bulk cargo	Goods shipped loose in the vessel's hold and not in a container.
Broken stowage	Space wasted in a ship's hold or container by stowage of uneven cargo, that is, irregularly shaped consignments.
Bulk licence	Licence issued to manufacturers and exporters to cover their requirements for certain bulk quantity or period.
Bulk unitization	Means to consolidate multiple packages or items into a single-load-device.
CABAF	Currency and bunker adjustment factor – a combination of CAF and BAF
CAD	Cash against documents.

CAF	Currency adjustment factor – freight adjustment factor to reflect currency exchange fluctuations.
CAP	Common Agricultural Policy of the European Union.
Cargo manifest	Inventory of cargo shipped.
Carr fwd	Carriage forward.
CB	Container base.
CCC	Customs clearance certificate.
CCLN	Consignment note control label number.
C & D	Collected and delivered.
CFR	Cost and freight (at named port of destination). Incoterm 2000.
CFS	Container freight station. Place for packing and unpacking LCL consignments.
CFSP	Customs Freight Simplified Procedures.
CHIEF	Customs Handling of Import and Export Freight. The customs entry processing computer system.
CI	Consular invoice.
CIF	Cost, insurance and freight (at named port of destination) Incoterm 2000. This term applies to sea or inland waterway transport only.
CIM	Convention international concernant le transport des marchandise par chemin de fer. International Convention on carriage of goods by rail.
CIP	Carriage and insurance paid (to named place of destination). Incoterm 2000. This term applies to all modes of transport.
CISG	Convention on the International Sale of Goods 1980 (Vienna Convention).
Clean bill of lading	A bill of lading which has no superimposed clause(s) expressly declaring a defective condition of the packaging or goods.
Closing date	Latest date cargo accepted for shipment by (liner) shipowner for specified sailing.
CMI	Comité Maritime International – an international committee of maritime lawyers.
CMR	Convention relative au contrat de transport international des marchandise par route. International Convention on carriage of goods by road.
C/N	Consignment note.

C/O	Certificate of origin or cash with order.
COGSA	Carriage of Goods by Sea Act. In the UK the 1924 version (Hague Rules) now superseded by 1971 version of the Hague–Visby Rules.
COI	Central Office of Information.
Collector's office	Customs accommodation where declaration(s) (entries) are scrutinized and amounts payable collected.
Conference	Organization whereby number of shipowners often of different nationality offer their services on a given sea route on conditions agreed by members.
Confirming Bank	A bank which adds it own undertaking to that of the issuing bank. The confirming bank is usually the advising bank.
Consignee	Name of agent, company or person receiving consignment.
Consignor	Name of agent, company or person sending consignment (the shipper).
Consul	Commercial representative of one country residing officially in another whose duties are to facilitate business and represent the merchants of his or her nation.
Convergence criteria	Established under the Treaty and relates both to performance with regard to price stability, government financial positions, exchange rates and long-term interest rates, and to the compatibility of national legislation, including the statutes of national central banks, with the Treaty and the Statute of the ECB.
COT	Customer's own transport. Customer collects from or delivers to CFS/CY or other specified point.
COU	Clip on unit portable refrigeration units, or Central operating unit – body set up to coordinate consortium operations in a trade.
C/P	Charterparty.
CPC	Customs Procedure Code.
CPT	Carriage paid to (to a named place of destination). Incoterm 2000.
CSC	Container Safety Convention.
CSI (US)	Container Security Initiative.

CT	Combined transport. Carriage by more than one mode of transport against one contract of carriage.
CTD	Combined transport document.
CTL	Constructive total loss.
CTO	Combined transport operator. A carrier who contracts as a principal to perform a CT operation.
Culture	The social economic and artistic resources in a country embodied in its institutions and other hybrid factions such as a museum. Overall culture is the environment and/or manner in which people live together in a society influenced by religion, education, family and reference groups, together with the forces of legal, economic, political and technological aspects. Basically it influences behavioural patterns.
CUSDEC	Customs declaration message (to CHIEF).
CUSRES	Customs response message (from CHIEF).
Customs clearance	Process of clearing import/export cargo through customs examination.
CWE	Cleared without examination. Cleared customs without inspection.
D/A	Deposit account.
DAF	Delivery at frontier (at named place). Incoterm 2000. This term applies to all transport modes but primarily road and rail.
Data logger	Electronic temperature recording device for refrigerated containers.
DDP	Delivered duty paid (at named place of destination). Incoterm 2000. This term applies to all modes of transport.
DDU	Delivered duty unpaid (at named place of destination). Incoterm 2000. This term applies to all modes of transport.
Dead freight	Space booked by shipper or charterer on a vessel but not used.
Deferment account	An account underwritten by a bank or insurance company to which import duties are posted.
Deferred rebate	System whereby shippers are granted a rebate on freight for consistent exclusive patronage over a given period.

Del credere	Agent/broker guarantee to principal for solvency of person to whom he sells goods.
Delivery order	A document authorizing delivery to a nominated party of goods in the care of a third party. It can be issued by a carrier on surrender of a bill of lading and then used by merchant to transfer title by endorsement.
Demurrage	Charge raised for detaining cargo, FCL container, trailer or ship for a longer period than prescribed.
DEQ	Delivered ex-quay (duty paid at named port of destination). Incoterm 2000. This term applies to sea or inland waterway transport only.
DES	Delivered ex-ship (at named port of destination). Incoterm 2000. This term applies to sea or inland waterway transport only.
Detention	Charge raised for detaining container/trailer at customer's premises for longer period than prescribed in the tariff.
DGN	Dangerous goods note.
Dis	Discount.
Discount market	Process of selling and buying bills of exchange and Treasury bills and providing a market for short-bonds.
D/N	Debit note.
D/O	Delivery order.
Doc credit	Documentary credit. The basis of international trade by means of which payment is made against surrender of specified documents.
D/P	Documents against payment.
DPO	Documentary Proof of Origin – customs term.
Drawback	Repayment of duty on re-exportation of goods previously imported.
Drawee	The party to whom a draft is addressed and who is expected to accept and/or pay it upon presentation.
Drawer	The party who issues a draft. Usually the beneficiary of the credit.
Drawing	A presentation of documents under a credit.
DUCR	Declaration Unique Consignment Reference – customs term.
Due date	The date on which a usance draft or a deferred payment becomes due for payment.

Dunnage	Wood, mats, etc. used to facilitate stowage of cargo.
Dutiable cargo	Cargo which attracts some form of duty, that is, Customs and Excise, or VAT.
DWT	Dead-weight tonnage.
ECB	European Central Bank. It has legal responsibility and ensures that the tasks conferred upon the Euro system and the ECB are implemented either by its own activities pursuant to its statute or through the national central banks.
ECSA	European Community Shipowners Association.
ECSI	Export Cargo Shipping Instruction – shipping instructions from shipper to carrier.
EDCS	Electronic Data Capture System – customs term.
EDI	Electronic data interchange. The transfer of structured data from one computer system to another.
EDIFACT	EDI for Administration, Commerce and Transport. Organization responsible to UNECE for the development of standard EDI messages for administration, commerce and transport.
EDP	Electronic data processing.
EEA	European Economic Area. Combination of EC/EFTA.
EFTA	European Free Trade Area. Member countries are Iceland, Norway, Switzerland and Leichtenstein.
EHA	Equipment handover agreement. Agreement acknowledging condition signed when taking over carriers' equipment and returning it, which incorporates terms of contract under which equipment is taken over.
EIC	Excise and International Trade.
Entry	Entry held on CHIEF. It consists of the declaration and central information (e.g. status route).
Endorsement	Signing of a document, (e.g. draft, insurance document or bill of lading) usually on the reverse to transfer title to another party. Documents are often endorsed in blank to permit any future holder to gain title.

EPCO	Entry Processing Central Operations – customs term.
EPU	Entry Processing Unit. Customs office that processes customs entries.
ERN	Export Reference Number.
ERTS	Enhanced remote transit sheds – customs term.
ESCB	European System of Central Banks. It is governed by the Governing Council and Executive Board of the ECB.
ETA	Estimated time of arrival.
ETD	Estimated time of departure.
e UCP	Supplement to the Uniform Customs and Practice for Documentary Credits for Electronic Presentation. See UCP500 entry.
European Commission	The institution of the European Community which ensures the application of the Treaty, takes initiatives for Community policies, proposes Community legislation and exercises powers in specific areas. In the area of economic policy the Commission recommends broad guidelines for economic policies in the Community and reports to the EU Council on economic developments and policies. It monitors public finances in the framework of multilateral surveillance and submits reports to the Council. It consists of 25 members.
European Council	Provides the European Union with the necessary impetus for its development and defines the general political guidelines thereof. It brings together the Head of State or Government of the Member States and the President of the European Commission.
European Parliament	It consists of 738 representatives of the citizens of the Member States.
European Union	A single market embracing 25 Member States.
Euro-zone	The area encompassing those Member States in which the euro has been adopted as a single currency in accordance with the Treaty and in which a single monetary policy is conducted under the responsibility of

	the relevant decisionmaking bodies of the ECB. The euro area or euro-zone or euroland comprises Belgium, Germany, Greece, Spain, France, Ireland, Italy, Luxembourg, Holland, Austria, Portugal and Finland.
Exchange rate	Price of one currency in terms of another.
Export house	An export merchant responsible for buying goods outright and selling them on their own account; acting as an export department or agent on behalf of a client; or acting for an overseas buyer.
Export licence	Government-issued document authorizing export of restricted goods.
Exporter's acceptance	Credit opened by an exporter with his own bank credit which entitles the exporter to draw bills on his own banker.
EXW	Ex Works (at named place). Incoterm 2000. This term applies to all transport modes.
Factoring	Company which administers the sales ledger and collects payments on behalf of an exporter once the goods have been shipped.
FAK	Freight all kinds. Term used to show that the freight rate charged is not based on the individual commodity, but freight all kinds.
FAS	Free alongside ship (at named port of shipment). Incoterm 2000. This applies to sea or inland transport only.
FCA	Free carrier (at named place). Incoterm 2000. This term applies to all modes of transport.
FCL	Full container load.
Feeder vessel	A short sea vessel used to fetch and carry goods and containers to and from deep-sea vessels operating on basis of hub and spoke concept.
FEU	Forty-Foot Equivalent Unit – container term.
FFI	For further instructions.
FIATA	International Federation of Freight Forwarders.
FILO	Free in Liner out – Freight includes cost of discharge but not loading.
FIO	Free in and out. Cargo is loaded and discharged at no cost to the shipowner.

FIO & stowed	Free in and out. Cargo is loaded as a charge to the shipper including stowage, and discharging expense borne by the receiver.
Fixture	Conclusion of shipbroker's negotiations to charter a ship.
Flat rack	A container consisting of a base and two ends but no sides or roof.
Flexi tank	Polythene bag to allow bulk liquids and powders to be carried in GPs.
Floating exchange rates	Currency rate which varies according to world trade distortions and not subject to exchange control.
Floating policy	Cargo policy which underwrites series of consignments declared.
FOB	Free on board (at named port of shipment). Incoterm 2000. This term applies to sea or inland waterway transport only.
Force Majeure	Circumstances beyond the control of either party to a contract – legal term.
Forwarder's bill of lading	A bill of lading issued by a freight forwarder.
Forwarder's certificate of shipment	A document issued by a freight forwarder certifying that the goods have been shipped on a named vessel or service.
Forwarder's delivery order	A document issued by a freight forwarder authorizing the entitled party to deliver the goods to a party other than the consignee shown on the consignment note.
Forwarder's receipt	A document issued by a freight forwarder which provides evidence of receipt of the goods.
FPA	Free of particular average – insurers not responsible for partial loss claims with certain exceptions.
Freight	Amount payable for the carriage of goods or a description of the goods conveyed.
Freight ton	Tonnage on which freight is charged.
FSD	Find supplementary declaration.
G/A	General average.
@global trade	An internet based electronic trading system.
Go(US)	General order. Issued by US Customs as notice of intention to seize goods.
Grand Alliance	A multi-trade consortium in which P&O Nedlloyd operates.

Groupage	Consolidation of several consignments into one overall consignment by air, road or sea usually under freight forwarder's sponsorship.
Groupage agent	One who consolidates, e.g. LCL consignments to offer a carrier as an FCL. Also applicable to air and road transport.
GV	Grande vitesse – fast rail merchandise service.
Harter Act	US national legislation covering carriers liabilities for the carriage of goods by sea.
Heterogeneous cargo	Variety of cargoes.
High stowage factor	Cargo which has a high bulk to low weight relationship, e.g. hay.
H/L	Heavy lift.
Hague Rules	1924 International Convention of Carriage of Goods by Sea.
Hague–Visby Rules	1968 Revision of Hague Rules.
Hamburg Rules	1978 UNCTAD Revision of Hague Rules.
HMC	Her Majesty's Customs.
HMC&E	Her Majesty's Customs and Excise.
HNS Hazardous and Noxious Substances	An international convention which was agreed at a diplomatic conference in 1996.
IATA	International Air Transport Association.
IBAP	Intervention Board Agricultural Produce.
ICAO	International Civil Aviation Organisation.
ICB	International Container Bureau.
ICC Institute Cargo Clauses	IUA standard clauses for cargo insurance.
ICC International Chamber of Commerce	Based in Paris France.
ICC Interstate Commerce Commission	US governmental body to regulate interstate trade;
ICD	Inland clearance depot.
IMDG	Code International Maritime Dangerous Goods Code. The IMO recommendation for the carriage of dangerous goods by sea.
IMO	International Maritime Organisation.
Incoterms 2000	International Rules for the interpretation of trade terms and applicable from 2000. A list of 13 standard trade terms for foreign trade contracts compiled by ICC.
Indemnity	Compensation for loss/damage or injury.
Individual licence	Licence issued for one particular import or export consignment.
Inherent vice	A defect or inherent quality of the goods or their packing which of itself may contribute

	to their deterioration, injury, wastage and final destruction, without any negligence or other contributing causes.
Inland clearance depot	Customs cargo clearance depot situated inland which may be in close proximity to a seaport, airport or inland depot serving an industrial/commercial area.
Invisible exports	Income from exports embracing tourism, net shipping and air receipts, foreign investments, banking and insurance.
IPR	Inward Processing Relief.
IRU	International Road Transport Union. Based in Geneva, its role is to develop national and international transport.
ISO	International Standards Organisation. International organization of national standards bodies responsible, *inter alia*, for setting standards for container construction.
IUA International Underwriting Association	London Marine Underwriters governing body.
Jus disponendi	(Latin) Law of disposal.
Latent defect	A defect not obvious from cursory inspection.
L/C	Letter of credit – document in which the terms of a documentary credit transaction is set out.
LCL	Less than container load – a parcel of goods too small to fill a container which is grouped by the carrier at the CFS with other compatible goods for the same destination.
LEC	Local export control – a system of clearing goods, containers and trucks at an exporter's premises.
Letter of hypothecation	Banker's document outlining conditions under which international transactions will be executed on an exporter's behalf, the latter having given certain pledges to his banker.
Letter of indemnity	A document indemnifying the shipowner or agent from any consequences, risk or claims which may arise through 'clean' bills of lading being irregularly issued.
Lien	A right to retain goods and documents against payment of charges etc. due, but unpaid.

LIFO Liner in Free Out	Freight includes the cost of loading, but not discharging.
Liner	Vessel plying a regular trade/defined route against a published sailing schedule.
Liner terms	Freight includes the cost of loading into and discharging from the vessel.
LLMC	International Convention on Limitation of Liability for Maritime Claims – a 1976 limitation convention enacted in the UK by the Merchant Shipping Act 1979.
LNG	Liquefied natural gas – type of vessel.
Loading broker	Person who acts on behalf of liner company at a port.
Local Clearance Procedure.	A simplified procedure involving pre-shipment notification to CHIEF, entry in commercial records and subsequent submission of a supplementary declaration to CHIEF within a specified period.
LOF '95 Lloyd's Open Form 2000	A standard form of salvage agreement.
LO-LO	Lift on-lift off. A container ship onto which and from which containers are lifted by crane.
Low stowage factor	Cargo which has low bulk to high weight relationship, e.g. steel rails.
Lump sum freight	Remuneration paid to shipowner for charter of a ship, or portion of it, irrespective of quantity of cargo loaded.
Manifest	List of goods/passengers on a vessel/aircraft/truck.
Market rate	Rate charged by brokers, discount houses, joint stock banks and other market members for discounting first-class bills.
Mate's receipt	Document issued to the shipper for ship's cargo loaded from lighterage and later exchanged for bill of lading.
MCD	Miscellaneous cash deposit.
M'dise	Merchandise.
Measurement ton	A cubic metre.
MMO	Multi-modal operator.
MT	Mail transfer – a remittance purchased by the debtor from his banker in international trade.
NCTS	New Community Transit System – customs term.

Negotiable bill of lading	One capable of being negotiated by transfer or endorsement.
Negotiation	The giving of value for a draft or documents which, under the credit terms, the issuing bank has undertaken to pay.
Negotiating Bank	The (nominated) bank which negotiates a presentation under a documentary credit. Usually located in the country of the seller.
NES	New Export System.
Nominated Bank	The bank nominated in the documentary credit to pay, accept, negotiate or incur a deferred payment undertaking.
Notify Party	Party to whom arrival notification form is sent.
NSSN	National Standard Shipping Note.
NVOC	Non-vessel-owning/operator carrier.
NVOCC	Non-vessel-owning/operating common carrier. A carrier issuing bills of lading for carriage of goods on vessels which he neither owns nor operates.
OBO	Oil bulk ore carriers – multi-purpose bulk carriers.
O/C	Overcharge.
OECD	Organisation for European Co-operation and Development.
O/H	Overheight. A container or trailer with goods protruding above the unit profile.
OPA 90	Oil Pollution Act 1990. A US Act with very onerous provisions covering all vessels trading to/from USA.
Open cover	A cargo insurance agreement covering all shipments of the assured for a period of time, subject to a cancellation clause and a limit to the amount insured in any one ship. Other conditions include a classification clause.
OOG	Out of gauge. Goods whose dimensions exceed those of the truck or container in which they are stowed.
OPR	Outward Processing Relief.
O/T Open Top	A container with tarpaulin covered open roof.
Overvalued currency	Currency whose rate of exchange is persistently below the parity rate.
O/W	Overwidth. A container or truck with goods protruding beyond the sides of truck,

	container or flat rack onto which they are stowed.
Part low chart	Paper disc recording charge for refrigeration temperatures on certain refrigerated containers.
Paying bank	The bank which is to effect payment under the documentary credit. It can be the issuing bank itself or a nominated bank, usually the advising or confirming bank.
P & I Club	Protection and Indemnity Association. Carrier's mutual liability insurer.
PCC	Processing under Customs Control.
Per pro	On behalf of.
PHA	Port Health Authority.
PIRA (International)	Research Association for the Paper and Board, Printing and Packaging Industries.
P/L	Partial loss.
POA	Place of acceptance – where the goods are received for transit and carrier's liability commences.
POD	Place of delivery where the goods are delivered and carrier's liability ceases, or proof of delivery – a signed receipt acknowledging delivery.
POR	Place of receipt – where the goods are received for transit and carrier's liability commences.
Pre-entered	Process of lodging with customs appropriate documentation for scrutiny prior to cargo customs clearance and shipment.
Principal carrier	The carrier issuing a combined transport document regardless of whether or not goods are carried on his or her own, a third party's or a consortium member's vessel.
PSA	Pre-shipment advice.
P to P	Port to port.
Rebate	An allowance made as discount on an account/rate.
Receiving date	Date from which cargo is accepted for shipment for specified sailing.
Reefer	Refrigerated.
Reimbursing bank	Normally a third party bank chosen by the issuing bank to honour claims made by the paying/negotiating bank under a letter of credit.

Removal note	Confirms goods clear of customs.
RN	Release note – receipt signed by customer acknowledging delivery of goods.
Ro-Ro	Roll-on/roll-off – a vehicular ferry service.
Rtp	Returnable transit packaging.
SAD	Single administrative document.
SCP	Simplified clearance procedure, under which exporters of goods not requiring special control may submit an abbreviated customs pre-entry or an approved commercial document at the time of export and provide the full statistical information after the goods are exported.
Settlement	Payment, deferred payment, acceptance or negotiation under a documentary credit.
Shipper	The person tendering the goods for carriage.
Shipping invoice	Document giving details of merchandise shipped.
Shut out	Cargo refused shipment because it arrived after closing date.
Sight 'On demand'	If a credit provides for payment or negotiation 'at sight', the issuing or confirming bank is obliged to pay or negotiate upon presentation of conforming documents.
Sine die	(Latin) Indefinitely – without a day being appointed.
SITC	Standard International Trade Classification – method of classifying all types of goods used in tariff.
SITPRO	Simpler Trade Procedures Board.
Slot	Space on board a vessel occupied by a container.
SOB	Shipped on board – endorsement on bill of lading confirming loading of goods on vessel.
SR & CC	Risks of wars, strikes, riots and civil commotions. A clause found in marine insurance.
SSN	Standard Shipping Note.
Stale bill of lading	In banking practice, a bill of lading presented so late that consignee could be involved in difficulties.
Straight bill of lading	An American term for a non-negotiable bill of lading, i.e waybill governed by the US Pomerene Act.
Stuffing/stripping	The action of packing or unpacking a container.

Subrogation	Process of substituting one person for another in marine insurance matters in which the latter inherits the former's rights and liabilities.
Supplementary declaration	An electronic message sent to CHIEF used to declare the fiscal, statistical and control information for all consignments imported under CFSP.
SWIFT	Society for Worldwide Inter-bank Financial Telecommunications – the secure computer network used to transmit documentary credits and other forms of international messages between banks.
TAN	Transit advice note.
Tariff terms	Conditions and scale of charges.
TCM	Draft convention on combined transport.
Tenor	The period of times for which a draft is drawn. The tenor may be at sight or usance.
TEU	Twenty ft equivalent unit – container measurement, i.e. 1 × 40 ft = 2 TEU; 1 × 20 ft = 1 TEU.
THE	Technical Help to Exporters – service of the British Standards Institution.
TIR	Transport International Routier. Bond conditions under which containerized and vehicular merchandise is conveyed internationally under the Convention.
T/L	Total loss.
Tramp	Vessel engaged in bulk cargo or time chartering business, i.e. not a liner vessel.
Transferable credit	One which may be transferred by the first beneficiary.
Transhipment entry	Customs entry for cargo imported for immediate re-exportation.
Trem Card	Road transport emergencies card.
Trucker (US)	A road transport operator.
Trucking	Movement of containers, trucks between terminals and CFSs/CYs.
TT	Telegraphic transfer. A remittance purchased by the debtor from his banker in international trade.
TTD	Through transport document.
TTO	Through transport operator. A carrier who contracts to carry goods (only part of which carriage he undertakes himself) on the basis

	that he is a principal while the goods are in his or her personal care, and as agent only while they are not.
TURN	Trade Unique Reference Number.
UCP500	The Uniform Customs and Practice for Documentary Credits, ICC Publication No.500.
ULCC	Ultra large crude carrier.
ULD	Unit load device.
UN	United Nations.
UNCITRAL	United Nations Commission on International Trade and Law.
UNCON	Uncontainerable goods. Cargo which because of their dimensions cannot be containerized and which are therefore carried other than in a container.
UNCTAD	United Nations Conference on Trade and Development.
UNCTAD MMO	UNCTAD Multi-modal Transport Convention.
Undervalued currency	Currency whose rate of exchange is persistently above the parity.
Unit loads	Containerized or palletized traffic.
Usance	The credit period granted by the exporter to the importer and reflected in the documentary credit terms, e.g. 30 days after bill of lading date, 60 days sight, 90 days after shipment date.
Validity	The period, from the date of issue until the date of expiry, for which the credit is valid.
Vienna Convention	A 1980 United Nations Convention on contracts for the International Sale of Goods which came into force on 1 January 1988.
VLCC	Very large crude carrier.
WA	With average.
Warranty	An implied condition, express guarantee or negotiation contained in marine insurance policy.
Waybill	A receipt for the goods and evidence of the contract of carriage but not a document of title.
WPA	With particular average.
York Antwerp	Rules relating to the adjustment of general average.

NB: Readers are also urged to study the *Dictionary of Shipping International Business Trade Terms and Abbreviations* 5th Edition 2005 (18 000 entries) by Alan Branch published by Witherbys, www.witherbys.com

Further reading

Dictionary of English-Arabic Shipping/International Trade/Commercial Terms and Abbreviations, 1st edition (1988) A.E. Branch, Witherby & Co Ltd.

Dictionary of Shipping International Business Trade Terms and Abbreviations, 5th edition (2005) A.E. Branch, Witherby & Co Ltd (18 000 entries).

Elements of Port Operation and Management, 1st edition (1986) A.E. Branch, Chapman & Hall/Kluwer Academic Publishers.

Elements of Shipping, 8th edition (2007) A.E. Branch, Routledge Ltd.

Global Business Strategy, 1st edition (1997) R. John, G Letto-Gillies, H. Cox and N. Grimwade, Thomson Learning Business Press.

International Purchasing and Management, 1st edition (2001) A.E. Branch, Thomson Learning Business Press.

Introduction to Marine Insurance, 2nd edition (1994) R.H. Brown, Witherby & Co Ltd.

Maritime Economics Management Marketing, 3rd edition (1998) A.E. Branch, Routledge Ltd.

Multi-lingual Dictionary of Commercial International Trade and Shipping Terms: English-French-Spanish-German, 1st edition (1990) A.E. Branch, Witherby & Co Ltd.

Schmitthoff's Export Trade, 9th edition (1990) C. M. Schmitthoff, Sweet and Maxwell.

Shipping and Air Freight Documentation for Importers and Exporters and Associated Terms, 2nd edition (2000) A.E. Branch, Witherby & Co Ltd.

Index